Fifteenth Edition

T5-BYJ-290

ESSENTIALS OF ORGANIZATIONAL BEHAVIOR

Stephen P. Robbins
San Diego State University

Timothy A. Judge
The Ohio State University

Please contact https://support.pearson.com/getsupport/s/with any queries on this content.

Cover Image by David Merron Photography/Moment/Getty Images.

Library of Congress Cataloging-in-Publication Data
Names: Robbins, Stephen P., author. | Judge, Tim, author.
Title: Essentials of organizational behavior / Stephen P Robbins, Timothy A. Judge.
Description: 15 edition. | Hoboken, NJ : Pearson [2021] | Includes bibliographical references and index. | Summary: "This book was created as an alternative to the 600- or 700-page comprehensive text in organizational behavior (OB). It attempts to provide balanced coverage of all the key elements comprising the discipline of OB in a style that readers will find both informative and interesting. We're pleased to say that this text has achieved a wide following in short courses and executive programs as well as in traditional courses as a companion volume to experiential, skill development, case, and reading books. It is currently used at more than 500 colleges and universities in the United States, Canada, Latin America, Europe, Australia, and Asia. It's also been translated into Spanish, Portuguese, Japanese, Chinese, Dutch, Polish, Turkish, Danish, and Bahasa Indonesian."—Provided by publisher.
Identifiers: LCCN 2019020719 (print) | LCCN 2019981062 (ebook) | ISBN 9780135468890 | ISBN 0135468892 | ISBN 9780135468920 (ebook)
Subjects: LCSH: Organizational behavior.
Classification: LCC HD58.7 .R6 2021 (print) | LCC HD58.7 (ebook) | DDC 658.3—dc23
LC record available at https://lccn.loc.gov/2019020719
LC ebook record available at https://lccn.loc.gov/2019981062

4 2021

Pearson

ISBN-10:   0-13546889-2
ISBN-13: 978-0-13546889-0

This book is dedicated to our friends and colleagues in
The Management & Organizational Behavior Teaching Society,
who, through their commitment to enhancing the quality of learning
through education and research, have significantly improved the ability
of students to understand and apply OB concepts.

BRIEF CONTENTS

CONTENTS

PREFACE

This brief text was created as an alternative to the 600- or 700-page comprehensive text-book in organizational behavior (OB). *Essentials of Organizational Behavior* attempts to provide balanced coverage of all the key elements comprising the discipline of OB in a style that readers will find both informative and interesting. We're pleased to say that this text has achieved a wide following in short courses and executive programs, as well as in traditional courses as a companion volume to experiential, skill development, case, and reading resources. It is currently used at hundreds of colleges and universities in the United States, Canada, Latin America, Europe, Australia, and Asia. It has also been translated into Spanish, Portuguese, Japanese, Chinese, Dutch, Polish, Turkish, Danish, and Bahasa Indonesian.

SOLVING LEARNING AND TEACHING CHALLENGES

Students and instructors alike have expressed a need for a text on organizational behavior that is concise, clear, and focused on what matters: *the Essentials*. Since its first publication in 1984, we have tried diligently to keep this book in the range of 325 to 450 pages to meet this need.

Essentials of Organizational Behavior provides a brief overview of the core concepts and theories within the field of OB. Our current text users rave about this approach because it gives them flexibility to include other kinds of learning experiences and content in their OB courses. As a result, this text is currently used in a wide variety of courses and programs—ranging from community colleges to graduate schools, and in both in-person and online courses.

Part of the reason we have been able to keep this book short in length is that it does not include review questions, cases, exercises, or other components. It continues to provide the basic core of OB knowledge, allowing instructors the maximum flexibility in designing and shaping their courses.

In addition, *Essentials of Organizational Behavior* focuses on translating state-of-the art theory and research on OB into actionable practices that can be directly applied by students in the world of work. (See the Implications for Managers section at the end of each chapter.) By focusing on *why* OB matters in the workplace, students can apply what they learn to their own working experiences, regardless of their field of study. In the next section, we describe another facet of the practicality of this book: employability skills.

EMPLOYABILITY SKILLS

As a new feature in this edition, we spotlight five specific skills that research studies have identified as critical competencies that employers look for in job applicants. The competencies have been grouped together to form a broad set of "employability skills." These skills include **critical thinking, communication, collaboration, knowledge**

application/analysis, and social responsibility. We have included a new section in Chapter 1 that introduces employability skills, along with a matrix that identifies which employability skills are targeted by each part of the book. Explicit examples of how OB is relevant for business functions (e.g., marketing, sales) and outcomes are also highlighted in each subsequent chapter.

NEW TO THIS EDITION

State-of-the-Art Research and Examples

In total, nearly 1,000 new examples, research studies, and other forms of content were added to this edition. Content coverage was expanded to include updated research, discussion, and examples of current issues related to all aspects of organizational behavior. Overall, 538 contemporary examples were added to this edition.

OB in Times of Crisis

Given the unprecedented effect of the global COVID-19 pandemic on organizational behavior, new sections were added on OB topics in times of crisis. Four new "crisis" sections were added to the chapters on Decision Making, Teams, Communication, and Leadership. A discussion of COVID-19 and its effects on telecommuting was also included in the Motivation (Application) chapter.

Business Ethics

Events such as the BP Deepwater Horizon Oil spill, the Wells Fargo account fraud scandal, and the now infamous Enron scandal have cemented business ethics as an incredibly important topic area relevant to the study of OB. In this new edition, we have broadly increased our coverage of business ethics topics, including a new standalone section on organizational justice in the Motivation Concepts chapter, as well as new content on (un)ethical behavior (e.g., deviance) in the sections on organizations, behavioral ethics, corporate social responsibility, counterproductive work behaviors, moral emotions, the Dark Triad personality traits, (un)ethical leadership (e.g., abusive supervision), prejudice and discrimination, as well as ethical cultures and climate.

Artificial Intelligence and Machine Learning

Artificial intelligence (AI) and its applications, such as machine learning, have completely revolutionized the field of OB. Given the prevalence of AI applications in organizations and its status as a cutting-edge method in OB, we have included new examples of AI research and application throughout the text. In total, 40 applications of artificial intelligence and machine learning were incorporated across the chapters.

Increased Coverage on Diversity and Globalization

Diversity and globalization topics continue to be hot topics within the study of OB. Increased integration of contemporary globalization and diversity issues were added into topic discussions. Ninety-seven examples relevant to global issues, cross-cultural differences, and globalization were added as well as 129 examples of how OB affects diversity in organizations.

CHAPTER-BY-CHAPTER CHANGES

Chapter 1: What Is Organizational Behavior?
- **New content:** New Trends and Limitations in "Building on Big Data With Artificial Intelligence," Employability Skills
- **Newly revised sections:** *Learning Objectives,* What Is Organizational Behavior?, Management and Organizational Behavior, Complementing Intuition With Systematic Study, *Implications for Managers*
- **New research incorporated in the following areas:** *Introduction*, Complementing Intuition With Systematic Study, Building on Big Data With Artificial Intelligence, Globalization, Workforce Diversity, Social Media, Productivity, Employability Skills

Chapter 2: Diversity in Organizations
- **New content:** Stereotype Threat, Diversity in Groups, Diversity Programs, Gender (the Glass Ceiling and Glass Cliff), Cultural Intelligence, Bias Against Mothers, Work-Life Balance Issues Tied to Diversity
- **Newly revised sections:** Diversity, Discrimination and Stereotyping, Biographical Characteristics, Other Differentiating Characteristics, Implementing Diversity Management Strategies, *Summary, Implications for Managers*
- **New research incorporated in the following areas:** Demographic Characteristics, Age, Gender, Race and Ethnicity, Hidden Disabilities, Religion, Sexual Orientation and Gender Identity, Cultural Identity, Intellectual Abilities, Physical Abilities, Diversity in Groups, Diversity Programs

Chapter 3: Attitudes and Job Satisfaction
- **New content:** Employee Engagement, updated Global Job Satisfaction Exhibits
- **Newly revised sections:** Attitudes, Attitudes and Behavior, Job Attitudes, Job Satisfaction, What Causes Job Satisfaction?
- **New research incorporated in the following areas:** Attitudes, Attitudes and Behavior, Job Attitudes, Employee Engagement, How Satisfied Are People in Their Jobs?, Job Conditions, Turnover, The Impact of Job Dissatisfaction, Managers Often "Don't Get It"

Chapter 4: Emotions and Moods
- **New content:** Positive and Negative Affect, Moral Emotions, Emotional Intelligence
- **Newly revised sections:** What Are Emotions and Moods?, Sources of Emotions and Moods, Emotional Labor, Emotional Intelligence, Emotion Regulation Techniques
- **New research incorporated in the following areas:** The Basic Emotions, Experiencing Moods and Emotions, The Function of Emotions, Personality, Weather, Sleep, Sex, Controlling Emotional Displays, Affective Events Theory, Emotional Intelligence, Emotion Regulation, Emotion Regulation Techniques, Selection and Leadership, OB Applications of Emotions and Moods

Chapter 5: Personality and Values

- **New content:** Other Frameworks includes research on the HEXACO model, Cultural Values, New Exhibit (5.5), Comparison of Hofstede's Framework and the GLOBE Framework
- **Newly revised sections:** Linking Individuals to the Workplace (moved to introductory section), Personality, Agreeableness at Work, Other Personality Attributes Relevant to OB, Personality and Situations, Values, Cultural Values, *Summary, Implications for Managers*
- **New research incorporated in the following areas:** What Is Personality?, Person–Job Fit, Person–Organization Fit, The Myers–Briggs Type Indicator, How Do the Big Five Traits Predict Behavior at Work?, The Dark Triad, Other Frameworks, Core Self-Evaluation, Self-Monitoring, Proactive Personality, Personality and Situations, Situation Strength Theory, Trait Activation Theory, Values, Terminal Versus Instrumental Values, Generational Values, Hofstede's Framework

Chapter 6: Perception and Individual Decision Making

- **New content:** The Threat of Technological Unemployment, Decision Making in Times of Crisis, Deonance Theory
- **Newly revised sections:** What Is Perception?, Person Perception: Making Judgments About Others, Common Shortcuts in Judging Others, Decision Making in Organizations, Influences on Decision Making, Choosing Between Criteria, Causes of Creative Behavior, *Summary, Implications for Managers*
- **New research incorporated in the following areas:** Factors That Influence Perception, Attribution Theory, Stereotyping, The Link Between Perception and Individual Decision Making, Intuition, Overconfidence Bias, Confirmation Bias, Availability Bias, Risk Aversion, Hindsight Bias, Personality, Gender, Reward Systems, Behavioral Ethics, Lying, Causes of Creative Behavior

Chapter 7: Motivation Concepts

- **New content:** Basic Psychological Needs in Self-Determination Theory, Expectancy Theory, Organizational Justice
- **Newly revised sections:** *Learning Objectives*, Motivation, Early Theories of Motivation, Contemporary Theories of Motivation, Other Contemporary Theories of Motivation, Job Engagement, *Summary, Implications for Managers*
- **New research incorporated in the following areas:** Motivation; Two-Factor Theory; McClelland's Theory of Needs; Cognitive Evaluation Theory; Self-Concordance; Basic Psychological Needs; Goal Commitment, Task Characteristics, and National Culture; Goal Setting and Ethics; Individual and Promotion Foci; Equity Theory; Distributive Justice; Interpersonal Justice; Justice Outcomes; Job Engagement; Integrating Contemporary Theories of Motivation

Chapter 8: Motivation: From Concepts to Applications

- **New content:** Job Enrichment
- **Newly revised sections:** *Learning Objectives*, Motivating by Job Design, Job Redesign, Alternative Work Arrangements, Telecommuting, Employee Involve-

ment, Using Extrinsic Rewards to Motivate Employees, Using Intrinsic Rewards to Motivate Employees

- **New research incorporated in the following areas:** Motivating by Job Design, Efficacy of the JCM, Job Redesign, Job Rotation, Relational Job Design, Telecommuting, Employee Involvement and Participation, Participative Management, Using Extrinsic Rewards to Motivate Employees, What to Pay: Establishing a Pay Structure, How to Pay: Rewarding Individual Employees Through Variable-Pay Programs, Piece-Rate Pay, Merit-Based Pay, Employee Stock Ownership Plan, Employee Recognition Programs

Chapter 9: Foundations of Group Behavior

- **New content:** Groupshift, Research on Hidden Profiles and Information Sharing
- **Newly revised sections:** Defining and Classifying Groups, Stages of Group Development, Group Roles, Group Norms, Group Size and Dynamics, Group Cohesiveness, Group Diversity
- **New research incorporated in the following areas:** Social Identity, Ingroups and Outgroups, Role Perception, Role Expectations, Role Conflict, Norms and Emotions, Norms and Conformity, Positive Norms and Group Outcomes, Negative Norms and Group Outcomes, Norms and Culture, Status and Group Interaction, Status Inequity, Status and Stigmatization, Group Size and Dynamics, Types of Group Diversity, Challenges of Group Diversity, Strengths and Weaknesses of Group Decision Making, Effectiveness and Efficiency, Groupthink

Chapter 10: Understanding Work Teams

- **New content:** Crises and Extreme Contexts, Team Trust, Teaming
- **Newly revised sections:** *Learning Objectives, Introduction*, Differences Between Groups and Teams, Updated Exhibit 10-3, Team Context, Team Processes and States (Motivation and Mental Models), Creating Effective Teams, Turning Individuals Into Team Players
- **New research incorporated in the following areas:** Self-Managed Work Teams, Virtual Teams, Multiteam Systems, Creating Effective Teams, Team Context (including resources, leadership, structure, culture, climate, performance evaluation, and reward systems), Team Composition (member abilities, personality, and team size), Team Processes and States (including a common plan, motivation, team identity, team cohesion, and mental models), Turning Individuals Into Team Players

Chapter 11: Communication

- **New content:** Communicating in Times of Crisis
- **Newly revised sections:** *Introduction*, Direction of Communication, Functions of Communication, Modes of Communication, Persuasive Communication, Barriers to Effective Communication, Cultural Factors, *Summary*
- **New research incorporated in the following areas:** The Communication Process, Feedback, Downward and Upward Communication, Lateral Communication, The Grapevine, Written and Nonverbal Communication, Choosing Communication Methods, Information Security, Persuasive Communication (Automatic

and Controlled Processing, Importance/Interest Level, Message Characteristics), Barriers to Effective Communication (such as Emotions, Language, and Silence), Cultural Barriers

Chapter 12: Leadership

- **New content:** Leading in Times of Crisis, Gender and Leadership
- **Newly revised sections:** Trait Theories of Leadership, Contingency Theories, Contemporary Theories of Leadership, Trust, Substitutes for and Neutralizers of Leadership
- **New research incorporated in the following areas:** Personality Traits and Leadership (such as the Big Five Traits and Dark Triad Traits); Emotional Intelligence (EI) and Leadership; Leader Consideration Behaviors,;Cultural Differences; Path–Goal Theory; Leader–Member Exchange (LMX) Theory; Charismatic, Transformational, and Transactional Leadership Styles; Charismatic Leadership's Situational Contingencies; Transactional and Transformational Leadership; Full Range of Leadership Model; (Un)ethical Leadership; Servant Leadership; Trust (including Trust Propensity, The Role of Time, and Regaining Trust); Mentoring; Leadership as an Attribution

Chapter 13: Power and Politics

- **New content:** How Power Affects People and What We Can Do About It, Sexual Harassment: Unequal Power in the Workplace
- **Newly revised sections:** Power and Leadership, Which Bases of Power Are Most Effective?, Social Network Analysis: A Tool for Assessing Resources, Influence Tactics, updated Exhibit 13-2, How Power Affects People, *Implications for Managers*
- **New research incorporated in the following areas:** Power and Leadership, Which Bases of Power Are Most Effective?, Nonsubstitutability, Social Network Analysis: A Tool for Assessing Resources, Using and Applying Influence Tactics, How Power Affects People, How Power Affects People and What We Can Do About It, Sexual Harassment: Unequal Power in the Workplace, The Reality of Politics, Organizational Factors, How Do People Respond to Organizational Politics?, Impression Management

Chapter 14: Conflict and Negotiation

- **New content:** Complicating Conflict
- **Newly revised sections:** A Definition of Conflict, Cognition and Personalization, Managing Conflict, Negotiation, Individual Differences in Negotiation Effectiveness
- **New research incorporated in the following areas:** Types of Conflict (including Relationship, Task, Process, and Complicating Conflict); Potential Opposition or Incompatibility (such as Structure and Personal Variables); Cognition and Personalization; Intentions (Competing and Collaborating); Managing Conflict; Functional Outcomes; Distributive and Integrative Bargaining; Preparation and Planning (for a negotiation); Clarification and Justification (during a negotiation); Personality, Moods/Emotions, Culture and Race, and Gender in Negotiations; Third-Party Negotiations

Chapter 15: Foundations of Organization Structure

- **Newly revised sections:** What Is Organizational Structure?, Common Organizational Frameworks and Structures, Alternate Design Options, The Leaner Organization: Downsizing, Why Do Structures Differ?, *Implications for Managers*
- **New research incorporated in the following areas:** Organizational Structure, Departmentalization, Chain of Command, Centralization and Decentralization, Formalization, The Bureaucracy, The Virtual Structure, The Team Structure, The Leaner Organization: Downsizing, Mechanistic and Organic Models, Volatility

Chapter 16: Organizational Culture

- **New content:** A Definition of Organizational Culture, New Exhibit (16-2) on the effect of culture on organizational outcomes, updated Exhibit 16-6, Culture Creates Climate
- **Newly revised sections:** *Learning Objectives,* What Is Organizational Culture?, Reorganized chapter so that "How Employees Learn Culture" and "Creating and Sustaining Culture" are covered earlier, What Do Cultures Do?, *Summary, Implication for Managers*
- **New research incorporated in the following areas:** Do Organizations Have Uniform Cultures?, Strong Versus Weak Cultures, Rituals, Language, Keeping a Culture Alive (Selection and Top Management's Role), Encounter Stage (of Socialization), Hangover Phases in Socialization, The Functions of Culture, Culture Creates Climate, The Ethical Dimension of Culture, Culture and Sustainability, Culture and Innovation, Culture as an Asset, Barriers to (cultural) Diversity, Toxicity and Dysfunctions, Barriers to Acquisitions and Mergers, Developing an Ethical Culture, Criticism of Spirituality

Chapter 17: Organizational Change and Stress Management

- **New content:** Criticisms of Lewin's Three-Step Model
- **Newly revised sections:** *Learning Objectives*, Change, Creating a Culture for Change, Stress at Work, *Summary*
- **New research incorporated in the following areas:** Forces for Change, Resistance to Change, Overcoming Resistance to Change (including Communication, Participation, Building Support, and Developing Positive Relationships), Action Research, Process Consultation, Managing Paradox, Sources of Innovation, Context and Innovation, Idea Champions and Innovation, Organizational Change and Stress, What Is Stress?, Stressors, Potential Sources of Stress at Work (including Environmental, Organizational, and Personal Factors), Stressors Are Additive, Perception (of Stress), Workaholism, Physiological and Behavioral Symptoms (of Stress), Individual Approaches (to Managing Stress) (including Time-Management Techniques, Relaxation Techniques, and Social Support Networks), Goal-Setting (to Reduce Stress), Employee Sabbaticals, Wellness Programs

ACKNOWLEDGMENTS

We owe a debt of gratitude to all those at Pearson who have supported this text over the past 25 years and who have worked so hard on the development of this latest edition. We want to thank Senior Content Analyst Beth Kaufman, Content Strategy Manager Lynn Huddon, Product Manager Olutosin Aje-Adegbite, Product Marketer Nayke Heine, Managing Producer Melissa Feimer, and Content Producer Yasmita Hota. On the production side, we want to thank Gina Linko, project manager at Integra Software Services. The authors are grateful to David Glerum for his assistance in manuscript editing and preparation. Finally, we would like to thank the marketing team for promoting the book and the sales staff who have been selling this book over its many editions. We appreciate the attention you have given this book.

We would also like to thank the many reviewers who helped make this new edition as strong and solid as possible:

Eli Awtrey, University of Cincinnati
Gerard Beenen, California State University, Fullerton
Jon P. Briscoe, Northern Illinois University
Jeff W. Bruns, Piedmont College
Maryalice Citera, State University of New York at New Paltz
Jeremy Couch, Palm Beach Atlantic University
R Wayne Downing, Northwood University
Rita Fields, University of Michigan–Flint
Kurt H. Gering, Marquette University
Elissa D. Giffords, Long Island University
Jerry W. Gladwell, Marshall University
Matthew D. Griffith, University of Texas at El Paso
Otha C. Hawkins, Alamance Community College
Larry Hodges, Fresno Pacific University
David S. Jalajas, Long Island University
Ralph Katerberg, University of Cincinnati
Amy Kyhos, Loyola University Chicago
Jamie Leddin, Vanderbilt University
Ronald Lesniak, Santa Clara University
Jennifer Moss Breen, Creighton University
Jennifer Murnane-Rainey, Creighton University
Michael Pierce, Fresno Pacific University
Rudy Roberts, Fresno Pacific University
Diane Roman Treuthart, Loyola University Chicago
Pamela K. Sigafoose, Palm Beach Atlantic University
Darren C. Treadway, Daemen College
Jim Westerman, Appalachian State University

ABOUT THE AUTHORS

Stephen P. Robbins
Ph.D., University of Arizona

Stephen P. Robbins previously worked for the Shell Oil Company and Reynolds Metals Company and has taught at the University of Nebraska at Omaha, Concordia University in Montreal, the University of Baltimore, Southern Illinois University at Edwardsville, and San Diego State University. He is currently professor emeritus in management at San Diego State. A full bio is available at stephenprobbins.com. Dr. Robbins's research interests have focused on conflict, power, and politics in organizations; behavioral decision making; and the development of effective interpersonal skills. His articles on these and other topics have appeared in such journals as *Business Horizons,* the *California Management Review, Business and Economic Perspectives, International Management, Management Review, Canadian Personnel and Industrial Relations,* and *The Journal of Management Education.* Dr. Robbins is the world's best-selling textbook author in the areas of management and organizational behavior. His books have sold more than 12 million copies and have been translated into 20 languages. His books are currently used at more than 1,500 U.S. colleges and universities, as well as hundreds of schools throughout Canada, Latin America, Australia, New Zealand, Asia, Europe, and the Arab World. Dr. Robbins also participates in masters' track competition. Since turning 50 in 1993, he's won 23 national sprint championships and 14 world sprint titles. He was inducted into the U.S. Masters Track & Field Hall of Fame in 2005.

Timothy A. Judge
Ph.D., University of Illinois at Urbana-Champaign

Timothy A. Judge is the Joseph A. Alutto Chair in Leadership Effectiveness, and Executive Director of the Fisher Leadership Initiative, Fisher College of Business, The Ohio State University. In the past, Dr. Judge has been a Fellow of the Cambridge Judge Business School, University of Cambridge, and Visiting Professor, Division of Psychology & Language Sciences, University College London. He has held academic positions at the University of Notre Dame, University of Florida, University of Iowa, Cornell University, and Charles University in the Czech Republic. Dr. Judge's primary research interests are in (1) personality, moods, and emotions; (2) job attitudes; (3) leadership; and (4) careers. Dr. Judge has published more than 155 articles in these and other major topics in refereed journals. He is a fellow of several professional societies, including the American Psychological Association, the Academy of Management, and the International Association of Applied Psychology. Among the many professional acknowledgments of his work, Dr. Judge has received the Heneman Career Achievement Award, the Mahoney Doctoral Mentoring Award, and the Scholarly Achievement Award, all from the Human Resources Division of the Academy of Management. In addition, a 2017 study identified him as the most cited out of more than 8,000 scholars in applied psychology. Dr. Judge is a co-author of *Organizational Behavior* with Stephen P. Robbins and *Staffing Organizations* with John Kammeyer-Mueller. Judge's primary nonwork passion revolves around rock climbing and mountaineering. He has climbed the three highest peaks in the United Kingdom and nearly half of the highest peaks in the lower forty-eight states. He and his wife Jill are the parents of three children.

1
What Is Organizational Behavior?

LEARNING OBJECTIVES

After studying this chapter, you should be able to:

1.1 Define **organizational behavior** (referred to as **OB** throughout the text).

1.2 Show the value of systematic study to OB.

1.3 Identify the major behavioral science disciplines that contribute to OB.

1.4 Demonstrate why few absolutes apply to OB.

1.5 Identify managers' challenges and opportunities in applying OB concepts.

1.6 Compare the three levels of analysis in this text's OB model.

1.7 Describe the key employability skills gained from studying OB that are applicable to other majors or future careers.

Right now, you might be wondering, "What is organizational behavior and why does it matter to me?" We will define organizational behavior (OB) very shortly, but first let us begin with the end in mind—why OB matters, and what the study of OB offers you.

Historically, business school coursework on human behavior in organizations has received relatively little attention. This might be surprising to you, because you might be thinking, but "the people make the place";[1] organizations are only as effective as the people who comprise them. Should we not try to understand people in the workplace, as well as how we make decisions, communicate, and interact with one another? Over the last several decades, business schools and organizations have realized the significant role interpersonal skills play in determining a manager's effectiveness. Understanding OB is important to you now, more than ever. We are in the midst of an OB revolution, of sorts, that is gaining traction year by year. As noted in the 2016 Deloitte Global Business Trends report, organizations have figured out that they need to understand "what makes people join, perform well in, and stay with an organization; who will likely be successful; who will make the best leaders; and what is required to deliver the highest-quality customer service and innovation."[2]

A knowledge of OB and interpersonal skills is critical for your success and advancement in the modern workplace. According to Jeff Weiner, chief executive officer (CEO) of LinkedIn, "communications is the No. 1 skills gap across. . . major cities in the

United States."[3] It is also relevant to nearly every job: One study by Monster (a global employment company) mined nearly one million market-wide job postings to determine the most frequently desired skills in applicants.[4] Communication skills was at the top of the list, followed by other OB-relevant skills, including problem-solving and influence skills. Furthermore, these skills are also necessary for your career advancement. A survey of over 2,100 chief financial officers across twenty industries indicated that a lack of interpersonal skills is the top reason why some employees fail to advance.[5] Ultimately, OB can equip you with tools that are critical to success and advancement in the workplace. In this text, we pay special attention to how the knowledge and practice of OB can help you (1) think analytically and critically, (2) make better decisions, (3) communicate and collaborate more effectively with others, and (4) act with a sense of social responsibility in the workplace. Research has demonstrated that these types of "employability skills" are highly valued and desired by employers, and a lack of these skills can lead to problems in the workplace.[6]

From the organizational standpoint, incorporating OB principles can help transform a workplace from good to great, with a positive impact on the bottom line. Companies known as good places to work—such as Lululemon, LinkedIn, Zoom Video, Southwest Airlines, Bain & Company, Google, the Boston Consulting Group, and Facebook[7]—have been found to generate superior financial performance as a result of their attention to OB.[8] Second, developing managers' interpersonal skills helps organizations attract and keep high-performing employees, which is important because outstanding employees are always in short supply and costly to replace. Third, the quality of workplace relationships is strongly linked with employee job satisfaction, stress, and turnover. One study of hundreds of workplaces and more than 200,000 respondents showed that positive social relationships among coworkers and supervisors were strongly related to overall job satisfaction, lower stress at work, and lower intentions to quit.[9] Positive work relationships help employees to flourish, leading to improvements in job and life satisfaction, positive emotions at work, and perceptions that one's work has meaning.[10] Fourth, an emphasis on OB in organizations can foster awareness of social responsibility. Universities have started to incorporate social entrepreneurship education into their curriculum in order to train future leaders in addressing social issues within their organizations.[11] This is especially important because there is a growing need for understanding the means and outcomes of corporate social responsibility (CSR).[12]

In today's competitive and demanding workplace, employees and managers alike cannot succeed by virtue of their technical skills alone. They also must exhibit good people skills. This text has been written to help people in organizations develop those skills along with the knowledge that understanding human behavior provides. In so doing, we believe you will obtain lasting skills and insight about yourself and others.

MANAGEMENT AND ORGANIZATIONAL BEHAVIOR

More than ever, individuals are placed into management positions without sufficient management training or informed experience. According to the US Bureau of Labor Statistics, employers with 100–500 employees provide less than one hour of management training per six-month period, on average.[13] Furthermore, according to a large-scale survey, more than 58 percent of managers reported they had not received any training and 25 percent admitted they were not ready to lead others when they were given the role.[14] Added to that challenge, the demands of the job have increased: The average manager has seven direct reports (five was once the norm) and spends less time supervising them than managers of the past.[15] Considering that a Gallup poll found organizations chose the wrong candidate for management positions 82 percent of the time,[16] we conclude that the more you can learn about people and how to manage them, the better prepared you will be to *be* that right candidate. OB will help you get there.

Effective Versus Successful Managerial Activities

What makes one manager more effective than another? To answer this question, Fred Luthans, a prominent OB researcher, and associates looked at what managers do from a unique perspective.[17] They asked, "Do managers who move up most quickly in an organization do the same activities and with the same emphasis as managers who do the best job?" You might think the answer is yes, but that is not always the case.

Luthans and associates studied more than 450 managers. All engaged in four managerial activities:

1. **Traditional management.** Decision making, planning, and controlling.
2. **Communication.** Exchanging routine information and processing paperwork.
3. **Human resources (HR) management.** Motivating, disciplining, managing conflict, staffing, and training.
4. **Networking.** Socializing, politicking, and interacting with outsiders.

The "average" manager spent 32 percent of their time in traditional management activities, 29 percent communicating, 20 percent in HR management activities, and 19 percent networking. However, the time and effort different *individual* managers spent on those activities varied a great deal. Among managers who were *successful* (defined in terms of speed of promotion within their organizations), networking made the largest relative contribution to success and HR management activities made the least relative contribution. Indeed, other studies in Australia, Israel, Italy, Japan, and the United States confirm the link between networking, social relationships, and success within an organization.[18] However, Luthans and associates found that among *effective* managers (defined in terms of quantity and quality of their performance and the satisfaction and commitment of their employees), communication made the largest relative contribution and networking the least. The connection between communication and effective managers is also clear. Managers who explain their decisions and seek information from colleagues and employees—even if the information turns out to be negative—are the most effective.[19]

Organizational Behavior (OB) Defined

Now that we have established what managers do and why this is important for OB, we turn our focus more broadly toward how people behave in organizations.

Organizational behavior (OB) is a field of study that investigates the impact that individuals, groups, and structure have on behavior within organizations for the purpose

Organizational behavior
A field of study that investigates the impact that individuals, groups, and structure have on behavior within organizations, for the purpose of applying such knowledge toward improving an organization's effectiveness.

of applying such knowledge toward improving an organization's effectiveness. That is a mouthful, so let us break it down.

OB is a field of study, meaning that it is a distinct area of expertise with a common body of knowledge. It focuses on three determinants of behavior in organizations: individuals, groups, and structure. In addition, OB applies the knowledge gained about individuals, groups, and the effect of structure on behavior in order to make organizations work more effectively.

To sum up our definition, OB is the study of what people do in an organization and the way their behavior affects the organization's performance. Because OB is concerned specifically with employment-related situations, it examines behavior in the context of job satisfaction, absenteeism, employment turnover, productivity, human performance, and management. Although debate exists about the relative importance of each, OB includes these core topics:[20]

- Motivation
- Leader behavior and power
- Interpersonal communication
- Group structure and processes
- Attitude development and perception
- Change processes
- Conflict and negotiation
- Work design

COMPLEMENTING INTUITION WITH SYSTEMATIC STUDY

Whether you have explicitly thought about it before or not, you have been "reading" people almost all your life by watching their actions and interpreting what you see, or by trying to predict what people might do under different conditions. The casual approach to reading others can often lead to erroneous predictions, but using a systematic approach can improve your accuracy.

Underlying the systematic approach is the belief that behavior is not random. Rather, we can identify consistencies underlying people's behavior and modify them to reflect individual differences.

Systematic study
Looking at relationships, attempting to attribute causes and effects, and drawing conclusions based on scientific evidence.

These fundamental consistencies are very important. Why? Because they allow predictability. Behavior is generally predictable, and the **systematic study** of behavior is a way to make reasonably accurate predictions. When we use the term *systematic study*, we mean looking at relationships, attempting to attribute causes and effects, and basing our conclusions on scientific evidence—that is, on data gathered under controlled conditions and measured, and interpreted, in a rigorous manner.

Evidence-based management (EBM)
The basing of managerial decisions on the best available scientific evidence.

Evidence-based management (EBM) complements systematic study by basing managerial decisions on the best available scientific evidence. For example, we want doctors to make decisions about patient care based on the latest available evidence, and EBM argues that managers should do the same, thinking more scientifically about management problems. You might wonder what manager would not base decisions on evidence, but most management decisions are still made "on the fly," with little to no systematic study of available evidence.[21]

Intuition
An instinctive feeling not necessarily supported by research.

Systematic study and EBM add to **intuition**, or those "gut feelings" about what makes others (and ourselves) "tick." Of course, the things you have come to believe in an unsystematic way are not necessarily incorrect; one review of hundreds of studies suggest that data-driven judgments (based on algorithms) were about 10 percent more accurate than human's intuitive judgments.[22] Another study found that, contrary to conventional wisdom, laypeople may actually *prefer* data-driven judgments to judgments made by others (e.g., experts) and even to judgments made by themselves.[23] Jack Welch (former CEO of General Electric) noted, "The trick, of course, is to know when to go with your gut."[24] But if we make *all* decisions with intuition or gut instinct, we are likely working with incomplete information—like making an investment decision with only half the data about the potential for risk and reward.

Building on Big Data with Artificial Intelligence

Data has been used to evaluate behavior since at least 1749, when the word *statistic* was coined to mean a "description of the state."[25] Statistics back then were used for purposes of governance, but since the data collection methods were clumsy and simplistic, so were the conclusions. Big data—the extensive use of statistical compilation and analysis—did not become possible until computers were sophisticated enough to both store and manipulate large amounts of information.[26] Let us look at the current use of the application of big data for business, which originated in the marketing department of online retailers.

CURRENT USAGE No matter how many terabytes of data firms collect or from how many sources, the reasons for data analytics include *predicting* events, from a book purchase to a spacesuit malfunction; detecting how much *risk* is incurred at any time, from the risk of a fire to that of a loan default; and *preventing* catastrophes large and small, from a plane crash to the overstocking of a product.[27] With big data, U.S. defense contractor BAE Systems protects itself from cyberattacks, San Francisco's Bank of the West uses customer data to create tiered pricing systems, and London's Graze.com analyzes customers' preferences to select snack samples to send with their orders.[28] Organizations are also beginning to focus more on fast data, drawing on a consistent influx of actionable data that can be used to guide business decisions in real time.[29]

NEW TRENDS The use of big data for understanding, helping, and managing people is relatively new but holds promise. It is good news for the future of business that researchers, the media, and company leaders have identified the potential of data-driven management and decision making. A manager who uses data to define objectives, develop theories of causality, and test those theories can determine which employee activities are relevant to accomplishing those objectives.[30] Increasingly, big data is applied toward making effective decisions (which we discuss in the chapter on perception and individual decision making) and managing organizational change (discussed in the chapter on organizational change and stress management). Big data has enabled organizations to acquire and manage large amounts of data and information. Even more recent advancements have shifted toward how to process and analyze all this information.[31] One way organizations have been able to adapt to the massive amounts of and sheer speed at which data is acquired is through artificial intelligence (i.e., machines programmed to think, work, and react like humans).[32] When you think of artificial intelligence, your mind may wander to robots, regardless of your status as a Star Trek or Star Wars fan. We are certainly seeing robotics becoming used in the workplace (for example, robots can help hospital night staff remotely assist their patients during night rounds).[33] However, much of the modern focus has been on machine learning (i.e., a subset of AI in which software is trained to perform a task, while at the same time "learning" and "improving" from incoming data and feedback).[34] Indeed, 60 percent of the billions of dollars invested in AI has been allocated toward machine learning.[35] Machine learning has contributed immensely to the success of a number of organizations, especially those in the e-commerce industry; one estimate suggests that over a third of Amazon transactions stem from AI-facilitated product recommendations.[36] In the coming chapters, we discuss how and in what ways artificial intelligence approaches, including robotics and machine learning, have contributed to the study and practice of OB.

LIMITATIONS As technological capabilities for handling big data and artificial intelligence have increased, so have issues of privacy and appropriate application.[37] This is particularly true when data collection includes surveillance instruments. For instance, an experiment in Brooklyn, New York, has been designed to improve the quality of life for residents, but the researchers will collect potentially intrusive data from infrared cameras, sensors, and smartphone Wi-Fi signals.[38] Bread Winners Café in Dallas, Texas, constantly monitors all employees in the restaurant through surveillance and uses that data to promote or discipline its servers.[39] These big data tactics and others might yield results—and research indicates that surveillance may increase task performance and citizenship behavior (helping behaviors toward others), at least in the short term.[40] But critics point out that after Frederick Taylor introduced surveillance analytics in 1911 to increase productivity, these techniques were surpassed by Alfred Sloan's greater success, achieved by providing meaningful work to employees.[41]

The use of artificial intelligence also has its own issues of privacy and appropriate application.[42] Despite traditional concerns regarding the safety and job security threats robots and automation bring to mind,[43] perhaps the simplest limitation here is that machines can often fail to capture the obvious "big picture" and may ignore their own limits.[44] For example, an algorithm may inadvertently include pizza topping preferences in predicting which employees are more likely to steal at work (you have to watch out for those pineapple pizza lovers!). As such, it is important for machine learning to be supervised to avoid atheoretical predictions and decision making. AI may also be used to engage in unethical behaviors at work. For example, Facebook banned a large UK car insurance company from mining users' social media information, learning their personality traits, and charging them different premiums based on their personality traits (and predictions for how safely they would drive).[45]

Overall, we are not advising you to throw your intuition out the window. We are also not advising you to base all your decisions on a machine learning algorithm. In dealing with people, leaders often rely on hunches, and sometimes the outcomes are excellent. At other times, human tendencies get in the way. What we are advising is to use evidence as much as possible to inform your intuition and experience. The prudent use of big data and artificial intelligence, along with an understanding of human behavioral tendencies, can contribute to sound decision making and ease natural biases. What we are advising is to use evidence as much as possible to inform your intuition and experience. That is the promise of OB.

DISCIPLINES THAT CONTRIBUTE TO THE OB FIELD

OB is an applied behavioral science built on contributions from several behavioral disciplines, mainly psychology and social psychology, sociology, and anthropology. Psychology's contributions have been principally at the individual or micro-level of analysis, while the other disciplines have contributed to our understanding of macro concepts such as group processes and organization. Exhibit 1-1 is an overview of the major contributions to the study of OB.

Psychology

Psychology seeks to measure, explain, and sometimes change the behavior of humans and other animals. Contributors to the knowledge of OB are learning theorists; personality theorists; counseling psychologists; and, most important, industrial and organizational psychologists.

Early industrial and organizational psychologists studied the problems of fatigue, boredom, and other working conditions that could impede efficient work performance. More recently, their contributions have expanded to include learning, perception, personality, emotions, training, leadership effectiveness, needs and motivational forces, job

Psychology
The science that seeks to measure, explain, and sometimes change the behavior of humans and other animals.

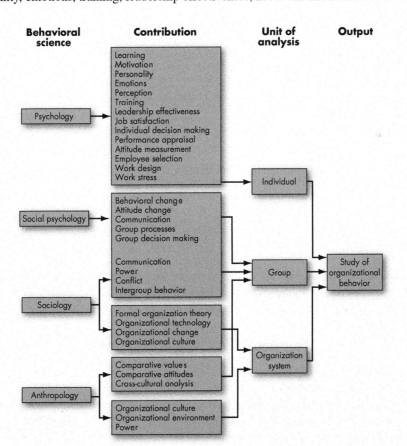

EXHIBIT 1-1
Toward an OB Discipline

satisfaction, decision-making processes, performance appraisal, attitude measurement, employee-selection techniques, work design, and job stress.

Social Psychology

Social psychology
An area of psychology that blends concepts from psychology and sociology to focus on the influence of people on one another.

Social psychology, generally considered a branch of psychology, blends concepts from both psychology and sociology to focus on people's influence on one another. One major study area is *change*—how to implement it and how to reduce barriers to its acceptance. Social psychologists also contribute to measuring, understanding, and changing attitudes; identifying communication patterns; and building trust. Finally, they have made important contributions to our study of group behavior, power, and conflict.

Sociology

Sociology
The study of people in relation to their social environment or culture.

While psychology focuses on the individual, **sociology** studies people in relation to their social environment or culture. Sociologists have contributed to OB through their study of group behaviors in organizations, particularly formal and complex organizations. Perhaps most importantly, sociologists have studied organizational culture, formal organization theory and structure, organizational technology, communications, power, and conflict.

Anthropology

Anthropology
The study of societies to learn about human beings and their activities.

Anthropology is the study of societies in order to learn about human beings and their activities. Anthropologists' work on cultures and environments has helped us understand differences in fundamental values, attitudes, and behavior among people in different countries and within different organizations. Much of our current understanding of organizational culture, organizational climate, and differences among national cultures is a result of the work of anthropologists or those using their methods.

THERE ARE FEW ABSOLUTES IN OB

Laws in the physical sciences—chemistry, astronomy, physics—are consistent and apply in a wide range of situations. They allow scientists to generalize about the pull of gravity or to be confident about sending astronauts into space to repair satellites. Human beings are complex, and few, if any, simple principles explain human behavior. Because we are not alike, our ability to make generalizations about ourselves is limited. Two people often act very differently in the same situation, and the same person's behavior changes in different situations. For example, not everyone is motivated by money, and you may behave much more differently during a job interview than you would hanging out with your friends on a Saturday morning.

Contingency variables
Situational factors or variables that moderate the relationship between two or more variables.

This does not mean, of course, that we cannot offer reasonably accurate explanations of human behavior. It does mean that OB concepts must reflect situational, or contingency, conditions. We can say *x* leads to *y*, but only under conditions specified in *z*—the **contingency variables**.

OB was developed by applying general concepts to a particular situation, person, or group. For example, OB practitioners would avoid stating that everyone likes complex and challenging work (a generalization). Why? Because not everyone wants a challenging job. Some people prefer routine over varied work, or simple over complex tasks.

A job attractive to one person may be unattractive to another; its appeal is contingent on the person who holds it. Often, we will find both general effects (money does have some ability to motivate most of us) and contingencies (some of us are more motivated by money than others, and some situations are more about money than others). We will best understand OB when we realize how both (general effects and the contingencies that affect them) often guide behavior.

CHALLENGES AND OPPORTUNITIES FOR OB

Understanding organizational behavior has never been more important for managers. Take a quick look at the dramatic changes in organizations. The workforce is becoming increasingly diverse; and global competition requires employees to become more flexible and cope with rapid change.

As a result of these changes and others, employment options have adapted to include new opportunities for workers. Exhibit 1-2 details some of the types of options individuals may find offered to them by organizations or for which they would like to negotiate. Under each heading in the exhibit, you will find a grouping of options from which to choose—or combine. For instance, at one point in your career you may find yourself employed full

EXHIBIT 1-2
Employment Options

Sources: J. R. Anderson Jr., et al., "Action Items: 42 Trends Affecting Benefits, Compensation, Training, Staffing and Technology," *HR Magazine* (January 2013) p. 33; M. Dewhurst, B. Hancock, and D. Ellsworth, "Redesigning Knowledge Work," *Harvard Business Review* (January–February 2013), 58–64; E. Frauenheim, "Creating a New Contingent Culture,"*Workforce Management* (August 2012), 34–9; N. Koeppen, "State Job Aid Takes Pressure off Germany," *The Wall Street Journal* (February 1, 2013), p. A8; M. A. Shaffer, M. L. Kraimer, Y.-P. Chen, and M.C. Bolino, "Choices, Challenges, and Career Consequences of Global Work Experiences: A Review and Future Agenda," *Journal of Management* (July 2012), 1282–327.

Categories of Employment	Types of Employment	Places of Employment	Conditions of Employment	Compensation for Employment
Employed	Full-time	Anchored (office/cubicle)	Local	Salary
Underemployed/ underutilized	Part-time	Floating (shared space)	Expatriate	Hourly
Re-employed	Flextime	Virtual	Short-term assignee	Overtime
Unemployed/jobless	Job share	Flexible	Flexpatriate	Bonus
Entrepreneur	Contingent	Work from home	International business traveler	Contract
Retired	Independent contractor		Visa employee	Time off
Job seeking	Temporary		Union/nonunion employee	Benefits
Furloughed	Reduced hours			
Laid off	Intern			

time in an office in a localized, nonunion setting with a salary and bonus compensation package, while at another point you may wish to negotiate for a flextime, virtual position and choose to work from overseas for a combination of salary and extra paid time off.

In short, today's challenges bring opportunities for managers to use OB concepts. In this section, we review some—but not nearly all—of the critical developing issues confronting managers and employees for which OB offers solutions or, at least, meaningful insights toward solutions.

Globalization

Globalization
The process in which worldwide integration and interdependence is promoted across national borders.

Globalization has led organizations, leaders, and employees to become increasingly connected across the globe, now more than ever.[46] Samsung, the largest South Korean business conglomerate, sells most of its products to organizations in other countries; Burger King is owned by a Brazilian firm; and McDonald's sells hamburgers in 101 countries on six continents. Although globalization united the international community following the second World War, the slow recovery from the global financial crisis has caused much of the world's population to be embittered by globalization.[47] In modern times, the world is at a tension point in which societies are choosing between sectioning off their economies versus remaining open to the world, given how globalization can change the employment landscape rapidly for many communities, sometimes resulting in poverty and economic inequality.[48] Meanwhile, we are on the brink of a new Industrial Revolution that has disrupted many industries and left many without jobs.[49] One of the new challenges of this tide of globalization is to forge cooperation between the public and its constituents, and between organizations and their employees across the globe, to pursue the public good with social responsibility in mind.

Furthermore, as a result of globalization, the manager's job has changed. To be effective in the workplace, you should try to anticipate and adapt your approach to the global issues we discuss next.

WORKING WITH PEOPLE FROM DIFFERENT CULTURES In your own country or on foreign assignment, you will find yourself working with bosses, peers, and other employees born and raised in different cultures. What motivates you may not motivate them. Or your communication style may be straightforward and open, which others may find uncomfortable and threatening. To work effectively with people from different cultures, you need to understand how their culture and background have shaped them and how to adapt your management style to accommodate these differences.

ADAPTING TO DIFFERING CULTURAL AND REGULATORY NORMS To be effective, managers need to know the cultural norms of the workforce in each country where they do business. For instance, in some countries a large percentage of the workforce enjoys long holidays. There are national and local regulations to consider, too. Managers of subsidiaries abroad need to be aware of the unique financial and legal regulations applying to "guest companies" or else risk violating them. Violations can have implications for their operations in that country and for political relations between countries. Managers also need to be cognizant of differences in regulations for competitors in that country; many times, understanding the laws can lead to success or failure. For example, knowing local banking laws allowed one multinational firm—the Bank of China—to seize control of a storied (and very valuable) London building, Grosvenor House Hotel, from the owner, the Indian hotel group Sahara. Management at Sahara contended that the loan default that led to the seizure was a misunderstanding regarding one of their other properties in New York.[50] Globalization can get complicated.

Workforce Demographics

The workforce has always adapted to variations in the economy, longevity, birth rates, socioeconomic conditions, and other changes that have a widespread impact. People adapt to survive, and OB studies the way those adaptations affect individuals' behavior. For instance, even though the 2008 global recession ended many years ago, some trends from those years are continuing: many people who have been long unemployed have left the workforce,[51] while others have cobbled together several part-time jobs[52] or settled for on-demand work.[53] Further options that have been particularly popular for younger educated workers have included obtaining specialized industry training after college,[54] accepting full-time jobs that are lower level,[55] and starting their own companies.[56]

Longevity and birth rates have also changed the dynamics in organizations. Global longevity rates have increased by about six years in a short time (since 2000—the fastest increase since the 1960s),[57] while birth rates are decreasing for many developed countries, trends that together indicate a lasting shift toward an older workforce. OB research can help explain what this means for employee attitudes, organizational culture, leadership, structure, and communication. Finally, socioeconomic shifts have a profound effect on workforce demographics. For example, equal access to work and education, regardless of gender identity or sexual orientation, has been deemed a human rights issue by the United Nations.[58] Despite increasing representation in the workforce, people of various demographic backgrounds (e.g., gender identities and sexual orientations) continue to experience inequality, under-representation as managers, prejudice, and even violence.[59] OB researchers study how people from diverse backgrounds fare in the workplace and the unique challenges and benefits they experience as well as how their conditions can be improved. This is just one illustration of how cultural and socioeconomic changes affect the workplace, but it is one of many. We discuss how OB can provide understanding and insight on workforce issues throughout this text.

Workforce Diversity

One of the most important challenges for organizations is in managing increasing **workforce diversity**, a trend by which organizations are becoming more heterogeneous in terms of employees' gender, age, race, ethnicity, sexual orientation, and other characteristics. Though we have more to say about it in the next chapter, diversity presents great opportunities and poses challenging questions for managers and employees. How can we recognize the strengths in our diversity? Should we treat all employees alike, or adapt to accommodate each other's differences? What are the legal requirements in each country that protect workplaces from prejudice, discrimination, and inequality? Does workforce diversity lead to positive outcomes for employees and organizations? It is important to address the spoken and unspoken concerns of organizations today.

Workforce diversity
The concept that organizations are becoming more heterogeneous in terms of gender, age, race, ethnicity, sexual orientation, and other characteristics.

Social Media

As we discuss in the chapter on communication, social media in the business world is here to stay. Despite its pervasiveness, many organizations continue to struggle with employees' use of social media in the workplace. For instance, in February 2015, a Texas pizzeria fired an employee before the first day of work because of an unflattering tweet about the job. In December 2014, Nordstrom fired an Oregon employee who had posted a personal Facebook comment seeming to advocate violence against police officers.[60] These examples show that social media is a difficult issue for today's managers, presenting both a challenge and an opportunity for OB. For instance, how much should HR investigate a candidate's social media presence? Should a hiring manager read the candidate's Twitter feeds, or just do a quick perusal of their Facebook profile? How can managers attract applicants and customers through their *own* social media presence?[61] Managers need to adopt evidence-based policies designed to protect employees and their organizations with balance and understanding.

Once employees are on the job, many organizations have policies about accessing social media at work—when, where, and for what purposes. But what about the impact of social media on employee well-being? One recent study found that subjects who woke up in a positive mood and then accessed Facebook frequently found their mood worsened during the day. Moreover, subjects who checked Facebook frequently over a two-week period reported a decreased level of satisfaction with their lives.[62] Managers—and OB—are trying to increase employee satisfaction and therefore improve and enhance positive organizational outcomes. We will discuss these issues further in the chapters on attitudes and job satisfaction and emotions and moods.

Employee Well-Being at Work

One of the biggest challenges to maintaining employee well-being is the reality that many workers never get away from the virtual workplace. While communication technology allows many technical and professional employees to do their work at home, in their cars, or on the beach in Tahiti, it also means many feel like they are not part of a team. "The sense of belonging is very challenging for virtual workers, who seem to be all alone out in cyberland," said Ellen Raineri of Kaplan University.[63] Another challenge is that organizations are asking employees to put in longer hours. According to one recent study, one in four employees shows signs of burnout, and two in three report high stress levels and fatigue.[64] This may be an underestimate because workers report maintaining "always on" access for their managers through e-mail and texting. Finally, employee well-being is challenged by heavy outside commitments. Millions of single-parent employees and employees with dependent parents face significant challenges in balancing work and family responsibilities, for instance.

As you will see in later chapters, the field of OB offers several suggestions to guide managers in designing workplaces and jobs that can help employees deal with work–life conflicts. Furthermore, there are several suggestions for managing stress and preventing burnout that you can apply, both in school and in the workplace.

Positive Work Environment

Positive organizational scholarship
An area of OB research that concerns how organizations develop human strengths, foster vitality and resilience, and unlock potential.

A growing area in OB research is **positive organizational scholarship** (POS; also called *positive organizational behavior*), which studies how organizations develop human strengths, foster vitality and resilience, and unlock potential. Researchers in this area say too much of OB research and management practice has been targeted toward identifying what is wrong with organizations and their employees. In response, they try to study what is *good* about them.[65] Some key subjects in positive OB research are engagement, hope, optimism, and resilience in the face of strain.

Although positive organizational scholarship does not deny the value of the negative (such as critical feedback), it does challenge us to look at OB through a new lens, pushing organizations to make use of employees' strengths rather than dwell on their limitations. One aspect of a positive work environment is the organization's culture, the topic of the chapter on organizational culture. Organizational culture influences employee behavior so strongly that organizations have employed "culture officers" to shape and preserve the company's personality.[66]

Ethical Behavior

In an organizational world characterized by cutbacks, expectations of increasing productivity, and tough competition; it is not surprising many employees feel pressured to cut corners, break rules, and engage in other questionable practices. Increasingly they face **ethical dilemmas and ethical choices** in which they are required to identify right and wrong conduct. Should they "blow the whistle" if they uncover illegal activities in their companies? Do they follow orders with which they do not personally agree? Should they "play politics" to advance their careers?

> **Ethical dilemmas and ethical choices**
> Situations in which individuals are required to define right and wrong conduct.

What constitutes good ethical behavior has never been clearly defined, and the line differentiating right from wrong is blurry. We see people all around us engaging in unethical practices: Elected officials pad expense accounts or take bribes; corporate executives inflate profits to cash in lucrative stock options; and university administrators look the other way when winning coaches encourage scholarship athletes to take easy courses or even, in the recent case at the University of North Carolina–Chapel Hill, sham courses with fake grades.[67] When caught, we see people give excuses such as "Everyone does it" or "You have to seize every advantage."

Today's manager must create an ethically healthy climate for employees in which they can do their work productively with minimal ambiguity about right and wrong behaviors. Companies that promote a strong ethical mission, encourage employees to behave with integrity, and provide strong leadership can influence employee decisions to behave ethically.[68] Classroom training sessions in ethics have also proven helpful in maintaining a higher level of awareness of the implications of employee choices as long as the training sessions are given on an ongoing basis.[69] In upcoming chapters, we discuss the actions managers can take to create an ethically healthy climate and help employees sort through ambiguous situations.

COMING ATTRACTIONS: DEVELOPING AN OB MODEL

We conclude this chapter by presenting a general model that defines the field of OB and stakes out its parameters, concepts, and relationships. By studying the model, you will have a good picture of how the topics in this text can inform your approach to management issues and opportunities.

EXHIBIT 1-3
A Basic OB Model

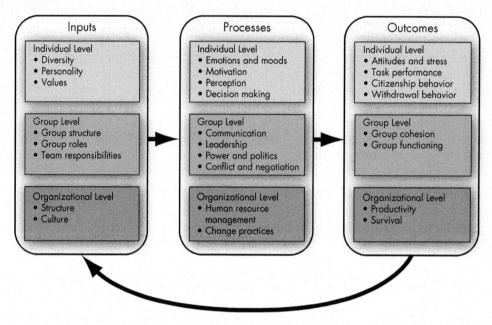

An Overview

Model
An abstraction of reality, a simplified representation of some real-world phenomenon.

A **model** is an abstraction of reality, a simplified representation of some real-world phenomenon. Exhibit 1-3 presents the skeleton of our OB model. It proposes three types of variables (inputs, processes, and outcomes) at three levels of analysis (individual, group, and organizational). In the chapters to follow, we proceed from the individual level (Chapters 2 through 8) to group behavior (Chapters 9 through 14) to the organizational system (Chapters 15 through 17). The model illustrates that inputs lead to processes, which lead to outcomes; we discuss interrelationships at each level of analysis. Notice that the model also shows that outcomes can influence inputs in the future, which highlights the broad-reaching effect OB initiatives can have on an organization's future.

Inputs

Inputs
Variables like personality, group structure, and organizational culture that lead to processes.

Inputs are variables like personality, group structure, and organizational culture that lead to processes. These variables set the stage for what will occur in an organization later. Many are determined in advance of the employment relationship. For example, individual diversity characteristics, personality, and values are shaped by a combination of an individual's genetic inheritance and childhood environment. Group structure, roles, and team responsibilities are typically assigned immediately before or after a group is formed. Organizational structure and culture are usually the result of years of development and change as the organization adapts to its environment and builds up customs and norms.

Processes

If inputs are like the nouns in OB, processes are like verbs. **Processes** are actions that individuals, groups, and organizations engage in as a result of inputs and that lead to certain outcomes. At the individual level, processes include emotions and moods, motivation, perception, and decision making. At the group level, they include communication, leadership, power and politics, and conflict and negotiation. Finally, at the organizational level, processes include HR management and change practices.

Processes
Actions that individuals, groups, and organizations engage in as a result of inputs and that lead to certain outcomes.

Outcomes

Outcomes are the key variables that you want to explain or predict, and that are affected by other variables. What are the primary outcomes in OB? Scholars have emphasized individual-level outcomes, such as attitudes and stress, task performance, citizenship behavior, and withdrawal behavior. At the group level, cohesion and functioning are the dependent variables. At the organizational level, we look at overall productivity and survival. Because these outcomes are covered in all the chapters, we briefly discuss each so you can understand the goal of OB.

Outcomes
Key factors that are affected by some other variables.

ATTITUDES AND STRESS Employee **attitudes** are the evaluations that employees make, ranging from positive to negative, about objects, people, or events. For example, the statement "I really think my job is great" is a positive job attitude, while "My job is boring and tedious" is a negative job attitude. **Stress** is a psychological process that occurs in response to environmental pressures.

Some people might think influencing employee attitudes and stress is purely soft stuff, but as you will learn, attitudes often have behavioral consequences that directly relate to how well you do your job. Ample evidence shows that employees who are more satisfied and treated fairly are more willing to engage in the above-and-beyond citizenship behavior that is so vital in the contemporary business environment.

Attitudes
Evaluative statements or judgments concerning objects, people, or events.

Stress
A psychological process in which an individual is confronted with an opportunity, demand, or resource related to what the individual desires and for which the outcome is perceived to be both uncertain and important (e.g., stressors).

TASK PERFORMANCE The combination of effectiveness and efficiency at doing your core job tasks is a reflection of your level of **task performance**. If we think about the job of a factory worker, task performance could be measured by the number and quality of products produced in an hour. The task performance measurement of a teacher would be the level of education that students obtain. The task performance measurement of consultants might be the timeliness and quality of the presentations they offer to the client. All these types of performance relate to the core duties and responsibilities of a job and are often directly related to the functions listed on a formal job description.

Task performance
The combination of effectiveness and efficiency at doing core job tasks.

ORGANIZATIONAL CITIZENSHIP BEHAVIOR (OCB) The discretionary behavior that is not part of an employee's formal job requirements, and that contributes to the psychological and social environment of the workplace, is called **organizational citizenship behavior (OCB)**, or simply citizenship behavior. Successful organizations have employees who do more than their usual job duties—who provide performance *beyond* expectations. Organizations want and need employees who make positive contributions that are not in any job description, and evidence indicates organizations

Organizational citizenship behavior (OCB)
Discretionary behavior that contributes to the psychological and social environment of the workplace.

that have such employees outperform those that do not. As a result, OB is concerned with citizenship behavior as an outcome variable.

WITHDRAWAL BEHAVIOR We have already mentioned behavior that goes above and beyond task requirements, but what about behavior that in some way is below task requirements? **Withdrawal behavior** is the set of actions that employees take to separate themselves from the organization. There are many forms of withdrawal, ranging from showing up late or failing to attend meetings to absenteeism and turnover. Employee withdrawal can have a very negative effect on an organization.

Withdrawal behavior
The set of actions employees take to separate themselves from the organization.

GROUP COHESION Although many outcomes in our model can be conceptualized as individual-level phenomena, some relate to the way groups operate. **Group cohesion** is the extent to which members of a group support and validate one another at work. In other words, a cohesive group is one that sticks together. When employees trust one another, seek common goals, and work together to achieve these common ends, the group is cohesive; when employees are divided among themselves in terms of what they want to achieve and have little loyalty to one another, the group is not cohesive.

Group cohesion
The extent to which members of a group support and validate one another while at work.

GROUP FUNCTIONING In the same way that positive job attitudes can be associated with higher levels of task performance, group cohesion should lead to positive group functioning. **Group functioning** refers to the quantity and quality of a group's work output. Similar to how the performance of a sports team is more than the sum of each individual player's performance, group functioning in work organizations is more than the sum of individual task performances.

Group functioning
The quantity and quality of a group's work output.

PRODUCTIVITY The highest level of analysis in OB is the organization as a whole. An organization is productive if it achieves its goals by transforming inputs into outputs at the lowest cost. Thus, **productivity** requires both **effectiveness** and **efficiency**.

A business firm is *effective* when it attains its sales or market share goals, but its productivity also depends on achieving those goals *efficiently*. Popular measures of organizational efficiency include return on investment, profit per dollar of sales, and output per hour of labor.

Organizations in the service industry must include customer needs and requirements in assessing their effectiveness. Why? Because a clear chain of cause and effect runs from employee behavior to customer attitudes and profitability. For example, a recent study of over 50,000 online TripAdvisor reviews and nearly 8,000 managerial responses suggests that when managers personally respond to online reviews, financial performance (e.g., revenue per available room) increases.[70]

Productivity
The combination of the effectiveness and efficiency of an organization.

Effectiveness
The degree to which an organization meets the needs of its clientele or customers.

Efficiency
The degree to which an organization can achieve its ends at a low cost.

Organizational survival
The degree to which an organization is able to exist and grow over the long term.

SURVIVAL The final outcome we consider is **organizational survival**, which is simply evidence that the organization is able to exist and grow over the long term. The survival of an organization depends not just on how productive the organization is, but also on how well it fits with its environment. A company that is very productive in making goods and services of little value to the market is unlikely to survive for long, so survival also relies on perceiving the market successfully, making good decisions about how and when to pursue opportunities, and successfully managing change to adapt to new business conditions.

EMPLOYABILITY SKILLS

Challenges relevant to OB can be found in just about every function of business, from finance and accounting to management and marketing. Without a doubt, at some point in your career, you will come across an issue that hinges to a large degree on the behavior of people in organizations. A review of the great challenges that most businesses face reveals that OB is an essential piece of the puzzle in solving many problems that involve managing integrity/social responsibility, managing resources, competing among businesses, bolstering customer and employee loyalty, reducing uncertainty, complying with government regulation, managing risks, and finding the right staff—all while growing revenue and increasing profit.[71]

But OB is not relevant to business majors only; it is important for all students, no matter what their majors are. At first glance, for example, it might not seem as if a university student with a microbiology degree would have any need to take an OB class. But what happens after that student graduates? Wouldn't knowledge of OB principles and concepts help them apply to and be successful at a job as a biology technician with Battelle? What about a graduate with a nursing degree working at the Mayo Clinic? A computer science graduate who is about to begin work with Cisco? OB principles matter for students of all majors and can help increase employability as well as interpersonal skills in the workplace. These skills can even help you to become successful in your classes as you interact with other students and your professors! Clearly, the knowledge of OB concepts such as stress management, change, attitudes, emotions, and motivation, among others, can help you navigate your interactions with your classmates as you continue to learn.

People, along with their behaviors, differences, attitudes, emotions, moods, personalities, values, intentions, thoughts, and motivations, are inextricably linked to life in the workplace. As stated earlier in the chapter, "The people make the place."[72] Employees interact and communicate with one another within and across work groups, departments, teams, and organizations to help accomplish the organization's goals. Leaders within these organizations (along with the employees themselves) seek to effect change, establish an organizational culture, and set policies and procedures—processes that inevitably involve leadership, politicking, conflict, and negotiation. Given the pervasiveness of OB in organizational life, entry-level employees and working professionals would therefore benefit from having solid foundational skills in OB, such as communication, collaboration, critical thinking, problem solving, social responsibility, and knowledge application and analysis.

In this section, we explore the career employability skills that a course in OB can help expand for those who select *any* major—from English, to engineering, to political science.

Employability Skills That Apply Across Majors

Throughout this text, you will learn and practice many skills that hiring managers identify as important to success in a variety of business settings, including small and large firms, nonprofit organizations, and public service. These skills will also be useful if you plan to start your own business, for example:

> *Critical thinking* involves purposeful and goal-directed thinking used to define and solve problems and to make decisions or form judgments related to a situation or

set of circumstances. It involves cognitive, metacognitive, and dispositional components that may be applied differently in specific contexts.

Communication is defined as the effective use of oral, written, and nonverbal communication skills for multiple purposes (e.g., to inform, instruct, motivate, persuade, and share ideas); effective listening; the use of technology to communicate; and the ability to evaluate the effectiveness of communication efforts—all within diverse contexts.

Collaboration is a skill in which individuals can actively work together on a task, constructing meaning and knowledge as a group through dialogue and negotiation that results in a final product reflective of their joint, interdependent actions.

Knowledge application and analysis is defined as the ability to learn a concept and then apply that knowledge appropriately in another setting to achieve a higher level of understanding.

Social responsibility includes skills related to both business ethics and corporate social responsibility. Business ethics includes sets of guiding principles that influence the way individuals and organizations behave within the society that they operate. Corporate social responsibility is a form of ethical behavior that requires that organizations understand, identify, and eliminate unethical economic, environmental, and social behaviors.

The employability skills matrix (ESM) links the five employability skills that were just defined with sections in each chapter. Within these sections, you will be primed to think critically and apply your knowledge to consider special cases and concepts. You will also learn how to improve your collaboration and communication skills by learning what you might do or say in these given situations to navigate the work world positively and

Employability Skills Matrix (ESM)					
	Part 1	Part 2	Part 3	Part 4	Part 5
Critical Thinking				✓	✓
Communication	✓	✓	✓		✓
Collaboration	✓	✓			✓
Knowledge Application and Analysis		✓		✓	✓
Social Responsibility			✓		✓

effectively. You will be confronted with ethical dilemmas in which you will consider the ethics of behaviors in the workplace. We recommend that you review and consider the ESM in advance of reading the chapter so that you have a better idea of the skills you will be developing from each section. All five of these skills are critical to success in careers that are relevant to OB and other majors alike. In the chapters to come, you will engage in a variety of activities and become exposed to several cases in which you will be developing these skills.

SUMMARY

Employees and managers alike need to develop their interpersonal, or people, skills to be effective in their jobs. OB investigates the impact that individuals, groups, and structure have on behavior within an organization, and then applies that knowledge to help employees, managers, and organizations work more effectively.

IMPLICATIONS FOR MANAGERS

- Resist the inclination to rely on generalizations; some provide valid insights into human behavior, but many are erroneous. Get to know the person and understand the context.
- Use metrics rather than hunches to explain cause-and-effect relationships.
- Work on your interpersonal skills to increase your leadership potential.
- Improve your technical skills and conceptual skills through training and staying current with OB trends like big data, fast data, and machine learning.
- OB can improve employees' work quality and productivity by showing you how to empower your employees, design and implement change programs, improve customer service, and help your employees balance work–life conflicts.

2
Diversity in Organizations

LEARNING OBJECTIVES

After studying this chapter, you should be able to:

2.1 Demonstrate how workplace discrimination undermines organizational effectiveness.

2.2 Explain how stereotypes function in organizational settings.

2.3 Describe how key biographical characteristics are relevant to OB.

2.4 Explain how other differentiating characteristics factor into OB.

2.5 Demonstrate the relevance of intellectual and physical abilities to OB.

2.6 Describe how organizations manage diversity effectively.

DIVERSITY

Our world is getting smaller and smaller every day. With the tide of globalization discussed in the previous chapter, it is clearer more than ever that each of us is a mosaic—made up of many tiles that make us unique.[1] Our uniqueness is obvious enough, but employees and managers alike sometimes forget they need to recognize, appreciate, and manage individual differences to forge productive workplaces. Consider Mughal Emperor Shah Jahan, who employed 22,000 artisans from around the world to construct and design the Taj Mahal—today, this "crown of palaces" represents myriad influences, including Islamic, Persian, Ottoman, and Indian, among others.[2] In this chapter, you will learn how individual characteristics like age, gender, race, identity, sexual orientation, ethnicity, and abilities can influence interactions and performance in the workplace. You will also see how managers can develop awareness about these characteristics and manage a diverse workforce effectively. But first, let us take an overview perspective of the changing workforce.

Demographic Characteristics

The predominantly white, male managerial workforce of the past has given way to a gender-balanced, multiethnic workforce. For instance, in 1950, only 29.6 percent of the U.S. workforce was female,[3] but by 2016, women comprised 46.8 percent of the workforce.[4] Both in the United States and internationally, women today are much more likely than before to be employed full time, and women's labor force representation should continue to grow, along with the diversity of the labor force.[5] In addition, the earnings gap between whites and other racial and ethnic groups in the United States has decreased significantly, partially due to the rising number of minorities in the workforce. Hispanics will grow from 13 percent of the workforce in 2014 to 25.1 percent in 2044; blacks will increase from 12 to 12.7 percent, and Asians from 5 to 7.9 percent.[6] Workers over the age of 55 are an increasingly large portion of the workforce as well, both in the United States and globally. In the United States, the 55-and-older age group will increase from 21.7 percent of the labor force in 2014 to 25 percent by 2024, a growth rate three times larger than the overall labor force.[7] These changes are increasingly reflected in the makeup of managerial and professional jobs. They also indicate organizations must make diversity management a central component of their policies and practices.

Levels of Diversity

Although much has been said about diversity in age, race, gender, ethnicity, religion, and disability status, experts now recognize that these demographic characteristics are just the tip of the diversity iceberg.[8] Demographics mostly reflect **surface-level diversity**, and not thoughts and feelings. Surface-level diversity can lead employees to make stereotypes and assumptions about others from certain demographic backgrounds. However, evidence has shown that people are less concerned about demographic differences if they see themselves as sharing more important characteristics, such as personality and values, that represent **deep-level diversity**.[9]

To understand the difference between surface- and deep-level diversity, consider an example. Some of you may have worked in a professional kitchen or as a member of the wait staff at a restaurant. You would certainly agree that these environments are often stressful: during busy periods, things can get hectic both in the kitchen and out on the floor.[10] To top it all off, there are so many people you have to interact with to ensure the customer has an excellent experience: the hosting staff, management, kitchen, runners, bussers—not to mention, the most important people: the customers!

All these people bring their own set of unique characteristics "to the table." One of the kitchen staff members, Bellamy, is a young, transgender person from a black family who grew up in Austin and is working toward an accounting degree. On the other hand, Hector is an older cisgender man who immigrated from Honduras earlier in life, converted to Islam in his late twenties, grew up in Seattle, and is now the general manager of the restaurant. At first, these coworkers may notice their surface-level differences in education, ethnicity, regional background, and gender identity. However, as they get to know one another, they may find they share a common way of thinking about work problems and have similar perspectives on time management. These deep-level similarities can overshadow the more superficial differences between them, and research suggests that sharing similarities (especially similar work styles) will help them work well together.[11] For example, if Bellamy and Hector have similar time management styles (both get to work on time and do prep work well in advance), they will be more likely to get along together and experience less conflict.

Throughout this text, you will encounter differences between deep- and surface-level diversity in various contexts. Diversity is an important concept in OB since individual differences shape preferences for rewards, communication styles, reactions to leaders, negotiation styles, and many other aspects of behavior in organizations. Unfortunately, increased diversity may give way to discriminatory practices, which we discuss next.

Surface-level diversity
Differences in easily perceived characteristics such as gender, race, ethnicity, age, or disability, that do not necessarily reflect the ways people think or feel but that may activate certain stereotypes.

Deep-level diversity
Differences in values, personality, and work preferences that become progressively more important for determining similarity as people get to know one another better.

DISCRIMINATION AND STEREOTYPING

Discrimination
Noting a difference between things; often we refer to unfair discrimination, which means making judgments about individuals based on stereotypes regarding their demographic group.

Although diversity presents many opportunities for organizations, diversity management includes working to eliminate unfair **discrimination**. To discriminate is to note a difference between things, which is not necessarily bad. Noticing one employee is more qualified is necessary for making good hiring decisions. Usually when we talk about discrimination, though, we mean allowing our behavior to be influenced by stereotypes about *groups* of people. **Stereotyping** is judging someone based on our perception of the group to which that person belongs. For example, in the 2018 U.S. Open Finals, professional tennis grand champion Serena Williams was penalized several times in an escalating argument with the umpire.[12] Serena, along with many other experts and officials, believed that her penalties were unduly harsh, when compared with penalties that have been historically levied toward men.[13] As Wharton organizational psychologist Adam Grant notes, "When a man argues with an umpire, it's passion. When a woman does it, it's a meltdown. When a black woman does it, it's a penalty."[14]

Stereotyping
Judging someone based on one's perception of the group to which that person belongs.

Stereotype Threat

Let us say you are sitting in a restaurant (perhaps the one where Hector and Bellamy work!), waiting to meet with recruiters from an organization you want to work at for an informal interview. How did you describe yourself to the recruiters so that they could find you? What identifiable characteristics would you mention so that they know a bit more about you and so that they can recognize you in the restaurant?

Chances are good that you would mention something about what you are wearing or your hairstyle. You might also mention how tall you are if you are remarkably tall or short. Overall, you would give cues to the recruiters about characteristics that are *distinctive*, or that stand out about you. However, with these characteristics follows the fear of being judged or treated negatively based on these superficial characteristics.

Stereotype threat
The degree to which we are concerned with being judged by or treated negatively based on a certain stereotype.

Stereotype threat describes the degree to which we are concerned with being judged by or treated negatively based on a certain stereotype.[15] For instance, older workers applying for a job in a predominately millennial-age workforce may assume the interviewer thinks they are out of touch with current trends. What creates stereotype threat is not whether these workers are or are not up to date with trends but whether they believe the interviewer will judge them based on this stereotype.

Stereotype threat has serious implications for the workplace. Stereotype threat can occur during preemployment tests and assessments, performance evaluations, and everyday workplace exchanges. It can lead to underperformance on tests, performance evaluations, training exercises, negotiations, and everyday interactions with others as well as to disengagement, poor job attitudes, a reluctance to seek feedback, and poor performance in the employees experiencing the threat.[16] Although the occurrence of stereotype threat is not inevitable and occurs infrequently in testing environments, we can combat it in the workplace by treating each other as individuals and not highlighting group differences.[17] The following organizational changes can be successful in reducing stereotype threat: increasing awareness of how stereotypes may be perpetuated (especially when developing policies and practices), reducing differential and preferential treatment through objective assessments, confronting microaggressions against minority groups, and adopting transparent practices that signal the value of all employees.[18]

Discrimination in the Workplace

To review, unfair discrimination assumes that everyone in a group is the same rather than looking at the characteristics of individuals within the group. This discrimination is often very harmful for employees, as we have just discussed, and for organizations.

Exhibit 2-1 provides definitions and examples of some forms of discrimination in organizations. Although many are prohibited by law and therefore are not a part of organizations' official policies, the practices persist. Tens of thousands of cases of employment discrimination are documented every year, and many more go unreported. Since discrimination has increasingly come under both legal scrutiny and social disapproval, overt forms have tended to give way to more covert forms like incivility or exclusion, which can be just as perilous.[19]

As you can see, discrimination can occur in many ways, and its effects can vary depending on organizational context and the personal biases of employees. Like stereotype threat, actual discrimination can lead to increased negative consequences for employers, including reduced productivity and organizational citizenship behavior (OCB; see Chapter 1: What Is Organizational Behavior?), more conflict, increased turnover, and even increased risk-taking behavior.[20] Unfair discrimination also leaves qualified job candidates out of initial hiring and promotions. Thus, even if an employment discrimination lawsuit is never filed, a strong business case can be made for aggressively working to eliminate unfair discrimination.

Whether it is overt or covert, intentional or unintentional, discrimination is one of the primary factors that prevents diversity. On the other hand, recognizing diversity opportunities can lead to an effective diversity management program and ultimately to a better organization. *Diversity* is a broad term, and the phrase *workplace diversity* can refer to any characteristic that makes people different from one another. The following section covers some important surface-level characteristics that differentiate members of the workforce.

Biographical characteristics Personal characteristics—such as age, gender, race, and length of tenure—that are objective and easily obtained from personnel records. These characteristics are representative of surface-level diversity.

BIOGRAPHICAL CHARACTERISTICS

Biographical characteristics, such as age, gender, race, ethnicity, and disability, are some of the most obvious ways employees differ. Let us begin by looking at factors that are easily definable and readily available—data that can be obtained, for the most part, from an employee's human resources (HR) file. These, and several other characteristics, are what comprise surface-level diversity. Variations in these surface-level characteristics may be the basis for discrimination against classes of employees.

Age

Age in the workforce is likely to be an issue of increasing importance during the next decade for many reasons. For one, the workforce is aging worldwide in most developed countries.[21] In the United States, the proportion of the workforce aged 55 and older is projected to be nearly 24.8 percent by 2024.[22] Legislation has, for all intents and purposes, outlawed mandatory retirement. Moreover, reflecting global trends, over forty countries spanning all continents, have laws directly against age discrimination.[23] Most workers today no longer have to retire at age 70, and 53 percent of workers over the age of 60 plan to delay retirement, likely due to the strong financial benefits of delaying retirement.[24] However, one study of Dutch taxi drivers suggests that perceptions of

EXHIBIT 2-1

Forms of Discrimination in Organizations

Sources: J. Levitz and P. Shishkin, "More Workers Cite Age Bias after Layoffs," *The Wall Street Journal,* March 11, 2009, D1–D2; W. M. Bulkeley, "A Data-storage Titan Confronts Bias Claims," *The Wall Street Journal*, September 12, 2007, A1, A16; D. Walker, "Incident with Noose Stirs Old Memories," *McClatchy-Tribune Business News*, June 29, 2008; D. Solis, "Racial Horror Stories Keep EEOC Busy," *Knight-Ridder Tribune Business News*, July 30, 2005, 1; H. Ibish and A. Stewart, *Report on Hate Crimes and Discrimination against Arab Americans: The Post-September 11 Backlash, September 11, 2001–October 11, 2001* (Washington, DC: American-Arab Anti-Discrimination Committee, 2003); A. Raghavan, "Wall Street's Disappearing Women," *Forbes,* March 16, 2009, 72–78; L. M. Cortina, "Unseen Injustice: Incivility as Modern Discrimination in Organizations," *Academy of Management Review* 33, no. 1 (2008): 55–75.

Type of Discrimination	Definition	Examples from Organizations
Discriminatory policies or practices	Actions taken by representatives of the organization that deny equal opportunity to perform or unequal rewards for performance.	Older workers may be targeted for layoffs because they are highly paid and have lucrative benefits.
Sexual harassment	Unwanted sexual advances and other verbal or physical conduct of a sexual nature that create a hostile or offensive work environment.	Salespeople at one company went on company-paid visits to strip clubs, brought strippers into the office to celebrate promotions, and fostered pervasive sexual rumors.
Intimidation	Overt threats or bullying directed at members of specific groups of employees.	African American employees at some companies have found nooses hanging over their workstations.
Mockery and insults	Jokes or negative stereotypes; sometimes the result of jokes taken too far.	Arab Americans have been asked at work whether they were carrying bombs or were members of terrorist organizations.
Exclusion	Exclusion of certain people from job opportunities, social events, discussions, or informal mentoring; can occur unintentionally.	Many women in finance claim they are assigned to marginal job roles or are given light workloads that do not lead to promotion.
Incivility	Disrespectful treatment, including behaving in an aggressive manner, interrupting the person, or ignoring varying opinions.	Female lawyers note that male attorneys frequently cut them off or do not adequately address their comments.

stereotype threat, or that colleagues/customers feel negatively about older taxi drivers in this instance, leads to higher retirement intentions.[25]

Stereotypes of older workers as being behind the times, grumpy, and inflexible are changing. Managers often see a number of positive qualities that older workers bring to their jobs, such as experience, judgment, a strong work ethic, and a commitment to quality. For example, the Public Utilities Board, the water agency of Singapore, reports that 27 percent of its workforce is over age 55 and the older workers provide workforce stability.[26] Industries like health care, education, government, and nonprofit service often welcome older workers.[27] But older workers are still perceived as less adaptable and less motivated to learn new technology.[28] When organizations seek individuals who are open to change and training, the perceived negatives associated with age clearly hinder the initial hiring of older workers and increase the likelihood they will be let go during cutbacks.

Now let us look at the evidence. What effect does age have on two of our most important outcomes, job performance and job satisfaction?

AGE AND JOB PERFORMANCE   The majority of studies have shown "virtually no relationship between age and job performance," according to Director Harvey Sterns of the Institute for Life-Span Development and Gerontology.[29] Indeed, some studies indicate that older adults perform better. In Munich, a four-year study of 3,800 Mercedes-Benz workers found that "the older workers seemed to know better how to avoid severe errors," said Matthias Weiss, the academic coordinator of the study.[30] Related to performance, there is a conception that creativity lessens as people age. Researcher David Galenson, who studied the ages of peak creativity, found that people who create through experimentation do "their greatest work in their 40s, 50s, and 60s. These artists rely on wisdom, which increases with age."[31] Finally, there is evidence that age-diverse teams and organizations perform better than those with similar ages, primarily because both older and younger workers bring a complementary, diverse set of knowledge, skills, and abilities to their teams.[32]

AGE AND JOB SATISFACTION   Regarding job satisfaction, an important topic in the chapter on attitudes and job satisfaction, a review of more than 800 studies found that older workers tend to be more satisfied with their work and report better relationships with coworkers.[33] However, one study drawing on over 20,000 participants spanning forty years suggests that people are becoming less satisfied with their jobs the longer they stay at any given organization—despite this finding, as people age, their job satisfaction tends to increase, most likely because their pay and benefits increase.[34] So as you get older, you should expect to like your work more and more!

Gender

The best place to begin to consider this topic is with the recognition that few, if any, differences between genders affect job performance.[35] Reviews of hundreds of studies on job performance and performance appraisals suggest that there are virtually no differences between genders when it comes to performing well; however, differences in pay, benefits, and rewards are strong and substantial, up to fourteen times the size of performance differences.[36]

Yet biases and stereotypes persist. In the hiring realm, managers are influenced by gender bias when selecting candidates for certain positions.[37] For instance, men are preferred in hiring decisions for male-dominated occupations, particularly when men are doing the hiring.[38] Once on the job, men and women may be offered a similar number of developmental experiences, but females are less likely to be assigned challenging positions by men, assignments that could help them achieve higher organizational positions.[39] Moreover, men are more likely to be chosen for leadership roles even though men and women are equally effective leaders, a phenomenon that has been referred to as the "glass ceiling" (and applies to any underrepresented group that faces obstacles to advancement).[40] In fact, as of April 2020, women hold only 6 percent of CEO positions in S&P 500 companies.[41] Furthermore, a study of twenty organizations in Spain suggested that women are generally selected for leadership roles that require handling organizational crises—positions in which they are usually set up to fail, a phenomenon commonly referred to as the glass cliff.[42] According to Naomi Sutherland, senior partner in diversity at recruiter Korn Ferry, "Consciously or subconsciously, companies are still hesitant to take the risk on someone who looks different from their standard leadership profile."[43]

In other words, these "glass ceiling" and "glass cliff" phenomena may be due to stereotypes which depict white males as ideal leaders, as they are perceived as more agentic and dominating than woman.[44] Furthermore, there is a stereotype that women default to a caregiving or relational role, and they are "penalized" for experiencing work-family conflict.[45] As a result, women may be more likely to experience a "motherhood" bias that prevents them from advancing in their careers, affects their performance evaluations, and their salaries. The perception of this bias can even lead pregnant women on leave from their organizations to be more likely to quit.[46]

These stereotypes counter the evidence that suggests that females are effective leaders in organizations: research from hundreds of studies suggests not only that women are rated as effective leaders in organizations but that women's representation in leadership positions is actually predictive of financial performance in hundreds of thousands of organizations.[47] We have seen that there are many misconceptions and contradictions about male and female workers. Thankfully, many countries, including Australia, the United Kingdom, and the United States, have laws against sex discrimination. Other countries, such as Belgium, France, Norway, and Spain, are seeking gender diversity through laws to increase the percentage of women on boards of directors.[48] Gender biases and gender discrimination are serious issues, but there are indications that the situation is improving.

Race and Ethnicity

In his "Address to the Nations of the World," given in London in 1900, W. E. B. Du Bois noted that the problem of the 20th century was that of "the color-line, the question as to how far differences of race—which show themselves chiefly in the color of the skin ... will hereafter be made the basis of denying to over half the world the right of sharing to their utmost ability the opportunities and privileges of modern civilization."[49] Although problems with discrimination and prejudice, identified earlier in this chapter, are still major societal issues, laws against race and ethnic discrimination are in effect in many countries, including Australia, the United Kingdom, and the United States.[50]

We define *race* as the heritage people use to identify themselves; *ethnicity* is the additional set of cultural characteristics that often overlaps with race. Typically, we associate race with biology and ethnicity with culture, but there is a history of self-identifying for both classifications. Some industries have remained less racially diverse than others. For instance, U.S. advertising and media organizations suffer from a lack of racial diversity in their management ranks, even though their client base is increasingly ethnically diverse.[51] Race and ethnicity have been studied as they relate to employment outcomes such as hiring decisions, performance evaluations, pay, and workplace discrimination.[52]

Members of racial and ethnic minorities report higher levels of discrimination in the workplace.[53] Black people generally fare worse than white people in employment decisions (a finding that may not apply outside the United States). Black people receive lower ratings in employment interviews, lower job performance ratings, less pay, and fewer promotions.[54] Lastly, black people are discriminated against even in controlled experiments. For example, one study of low-wage jobs found that black applicants with no criminal history received fewer job offers than did white applicants with criminal records.[55] Even applicants with black-sounding names were 50 percent less likely than those with white-sounding names to receive interview callbacks in one large randomized experiment.[56]

Disabilities

Workplace policies, both official and circumstantial, regarding individuals with physical or mental disabilities vary from country to country. Countries such as Australia, the United States, the United Kingdom, and Japan have specific laws to protect individuals with disabilities.[57] These laws have resulted in greater acceptance and accommodation of people with physical or mental impairments. In the United States, for instance, the representation of individuals with disabilities in the workforce rapidly increased with the passage of the Americans with Disabilities Act (ADA) in 1990.[58] According to the ADA, employers are required to make reasonable accommodations so their workplaces will be accessible to individuals with physical or mental disabilities.

SCOPE OF DISABILITIES The U.S. Equal Employment Opportunity Commission (EEOC), the federal agency responsible for enforcing employment discrimination laws, classifies a person who has any physical or mental impairment that substantially limits one or more major life activities as *disabled*. One of the most controversial aspects of the ADA is the provision that requires employers to make reasonable accommodations (e.g., comfort and assistance animals) for people with psychiatric disabilities.[59] Examples of recognized disabilities include missing limbs, seizure disorder, Down syndrome, deafness, schizophrenia, alcoholism, diabetes, depression, and chronic back pain. These conditions share almost no common features, so there is no specific definition about how each condition is related to employment.

DISABILITIES AND OUTCOMES The impact of disabilities on employment outcomes has been explored from a variety of perspectives. On the one hand, when disability status was randomly manipulated among hypothetical candidates in a study, individuals with disabilities were rated as having superior personal qualities like dependability.[60] However, according to a review of a number of studies, individuals with disabilities tend to encounter lower performance expectations and are less likely to be hired.[61] Furthermore, managers or supervisors with disabilities tend to experience lower quality relationships with their subordinates, unless policies and procedures are in place that make their workplace more inclusive.[62] Mental disabilities may impair performance more than physical disabilities: Individuals with such common mental health issues as depression and anxiety are significantly more likely to be absent from work.[63]

The elimination of discrimination against the disabled workforce has been a rocky road. In Europe, for instance, policies to motivate employers have failed to boost the workforce participation rate for workers with disabilities, and outright quota systems in Germany, France, and Poland have backfired, although employment discrimination laws in California has met with some success.[64] However, the recognition of the talents and abilities of individuals with disabilities has made a positive impact. In addition, technology and workplace advancements have greatly increased the scope of available jobs for those with all types of disabilities. Managers need to be attuned to the true requirements of each job and match the skills of the individual to them, providing accommodations when needed. But what happens when employees do not disclose their disabilities? Let's discuss this next.

Hidden Disabilities

As we mentioned earlier, disabilities include observable characteristics like missing limbs, illnesses that require a person to use a wheelchair, and blindness. Other disabilities may not be obvious, at least at first. Unless an individual decides to disclose a disability that is not easily observable, it can remain hidden at the discretion of the employee. These are called *hidden disabilities* (or invisible disabilities). Hidden disabilities generally fall under the categories of sensory disabilities (for example, impaired hearing), autoimmune disorders (like rheumatoid arthritis), chronic illness or pain (like carpal tunnel syndrome), cognitive or learning impairments (like attention-deficit/hyperactivity disorder), sleep disorders (like insomnia), and psychological challenges (like posttraumatic stress disorder).[65]

As a result of recent changes to the Americans with Disabilities Act Amendments Act (ADAAA) of 2008, U.S. organizations must accommodate employees with a very broad range of impairments. However, employees must disclose their conditions to their employers in order to be eligible for workplace accommodations and employment protection. Many employees do not want to disclose their invisible disabilities, so they are prevented from getting the workplace accommodations they need in order to thrive in their jobs. Research indicates that individuals with hidden disabilities are afraid of being stigmatized or ostracized if they disclose their disabilities to others in the workplace, and they believe that their managers will think they are less capable of strong job performance.[66] Add this to the challenge of receiving a diagnosis for a condition that one did not previously have and these fears are compounded even more so than if the diagnosis was made for employees when they were younger.[67]

In some ways, a hidden disability is not truly invisible. For example, a person with undisclosed autism will still exhibit the behaviors characteristic of the condition, such as difficulties with verbal communication and adaptability.[68] You may observe behaviors that lead you to suspect an individual has a hidden disability. Unfortunately, you may attribute the behavior to other causes—for instance, you may incorrectly ascribe the slow, slurred speech of a coworker to an alcohol problem rather than to the long-term effects of a stroke.

Research suggests that disclosure helps all—the individual, others, and organizations. Disclosure may increase the job satisfaction and well-being of the individual, help others understand and assist the individual to succeed in the workplace, and allow the organization to accommodate the situation to achieve top performance.[69]

OTHER DIFFERENTIATING CHARACTERISTICS

The last set of characteristics we will look at includes religion, sexual orientation, gender identity, and cultural identity. These characteristics illustrate deep-level differences that provide opportunities for workplace diversity, as long as discrimination can be overcome.

Religion

Religious and nonreligious people question each other's belief systems, and people of different religious faiths often experience conflict with one another. Furthermore, faith can be an employment issue wherever religious beliefs prohibit or encourage certain behaviors. There are few—if any—countries in which religion is a nonissue in the workplace. For this reason, employers are prohibited by law from discriminating against employees based on religion in many countries, including Australia, the United Kingdom, and the United States.[70] Reasonable accommodation, like that stipulated in the ADA, is also required for religious exemptions in the U.S. For example, one jury awarded millions of dollars to Marie Pierre, a dishwasher at a Miami hotel, who was not accommodated (allowed to swap shifts) for needing to request Sundays off for religious reasons.[71]

Religious discrimination has been a growing source of discrimination claims in the United States, partially because the issues are complex. Recently, Samantha Elauf, who was turned down for employment because she wears a hijab—a head scarf—sued for religious discrimination. "I learned I was not hired by Abercrombie because I wear a head scarf, which is a symbol of modesty in my Muslim faith," she said.[72] Discrimination cases like this have also been observed in research; for example, one study found that job applicants in Muslim-identified religious attire who applied for hypothetical retail jobs had shorter, more interpersonally negative interviews than applicants who did not wear Muslim-identified attire.[73]

Sexual Orientation and Gender Identity

While much has changed, the full acceptance and accommodation of lesbian, gay, bisexual, transgender, and other gender identifications (LGBT+) employees remains a work in progress.[74] In the United States, a Harvard University study sent fictitious but realistic résumés to 1,700 actual entry-level job openings. The applications were identical with one exception: Half mentioned involvement in gay organizations during college, and the other half did not. The applications without the mention received 60 percent more callbacks than the ones with it.[75]

Perhaps as a result of perceived discrimination, many LGBT+ employees do not disclose their status. For example, Beck Bailey, a former employee at Stouffers in the late '80s (now deputy director of the Human Rights Campaign Workplace Equality Program), recalled what it was like identifying as a woman and a lesbian in the workplace, where it was difficult to be oneself, as well as the need to keep a picture of a "fake boyfriend" at the desk for fear of being discovered.[76] However, research suggests that disclosing sexual orientation is good for reducing work-family conflict and improving partner satisfaction, physical and mental well-being, and job satisfaction.[77]

SEXUAL ORIENTATION LAWS   As of December 2019, 145 countries have laws providing some form of employment protection for sexual orientation and gender identity—over twice the number of countries that criminalize sexual orientations and gender identities.[78] In the U.S., the federal government has prohibited discrimination based on sexual orientation and gender identity against employees. In a historic ruling during June 2020, the Supreme Court ruled that discrimination against individuals based on their sexual orientation and gender identity represents gender discrimination enforceable under Title VII of the Civil Rights Act of 1964.[79] The picture is also more localized at the state and municipality level: thirty-four states and hundreds of municipalities offer some form of protection for sexual orientation and/ or gender identity in the public/private sector. Across the globe, countries such as Australia and the United Kingdom have passed similar laws against discriminating on the basis of sexual preference, sexual orientation, and gender identity.[80]

ORGANIZATIONAL POLICIES ON SEXUAL ORIENTATION Organizations and managers are beginning to understand, little by little, that there are both ethical and financial reasons to be more inclusive; for instance, the LGBT+ consumer base accounts for almost one trillion dollars in buying power.[81] Companies like Apple are at the forefront of the corporate world in establishing policies that are sexual orientation and gender identity friendly. Apple, which boasts a 100 percent score on the 2020 Corporate Equality Index, has offered health insurance benefits to same-sex domestic partners (and has been doing so for decades) as well as six weeks of parental leave for new parents, including same-sex partners.[82]

Even in the absence of federal legislation, many organizations have implemented policies and procedures that cover sexual orientation. Surveys indicate that more than 90 percent of the *Fortune* 500 have policies that cover sexual orientation (more than 90 percent have policies covering gender identity). In 2001, only eight companies in the *Fortune* 500 had policies on gender identity. Some companies claim they do not need to provide LGBT+ benefits for religious reasons. Moreover, some organizations that claim to be inclusive do not live up to the claim.[83] For example, a recent study of five social cooperatives in Italy indicated that these so-called inclusive organizations expect individuals to remain quiet about their status.[84] Thus, while times have certainly changed, sexual orientation and gender identity remain individual differences that organizations must address in eliminating discrimination and promoting diversity.

Cultural Identity

We have seen that people sometimes define themselves in terms of race and ethnicity. Many people carry a strong *cultural identity* as well, a link with the culture of family ancestry that lasts a lifetime, no matter where the individual may live in the world. Cultural norms influence the workplace, sometimes resulting in clashes, or fostering alienation among cultural minorities. For example, in the best-selling novel, *Native Speaker,* Henry Park is a Korean American industrial spy who must cope with competing cultural identities—his job requires him to interact with multiple people and he struggles with whether to act "more Korean" or "more American," depending upon whom he is assigned to.[85]

Thanks to global integration, today's organizations (and the managers and employees that comprise them) do well to understand, respect, and adapt to the cultural identities of their employees, both as groups and as individuals.[86] A U.S. company looking to do business in, say, Latin America, needs to understand that employees in those cultures expect long summer holidays. A company that requires employees to work during this culturally established break will meet strong resistance. An organization seeking to be sensitive to the cultural identities of its employees should look beyond accommodating its majority groups and instead create as much of an individualized approach to practices and norms as possible. Often, managers can provide the bridge of workplace flexibility to meet both organizational goals and individual needs. Furthermore, employees and managers alike can do well to develop their own *cultural intelligence* (CQ), or ability to function with people of various cultural backgrounds, which can enable employees to work more effectively with one another in organizations.[87]

ABILITY

Regardless of how motivated you are, you may not be able to act as well as Sarah Paulson, play basketball as well as LeBron James, or write as well as J. K. Rowling. Of course, all of us have strengths and weaknesses that make us relatively superior or inferior to others in performing certain tasks or activities. From management's standpoint, the challenge is to understand the differences to increase the likelihood that a given employee will perform their job well. Applicants and employees, then, should market their abilities and develop skills to be successful in the jobs they want.

What does *ability* mean? As we use the term, **ability** is an individual's current capacity to perform the various tasks of a job. Overall abilities are essentially made up of two sets of factors: intellectual and physical.

Ability
An individual's capacity to perform the various tasks in a job.

Intellectual Abilities

Intellectual abilities are abilities needed to perform mental activities—thinking, reasoning, and problem solving. Most societies place a high value on intelligence, and for good reason. Smart people are generally better performers, earn more money, are promoted more often, and attain higher level jobs.[88] However, assessing and measuring intellectual ability are not always simple, partially because people are not consistently capable of correctly assessing their own cognitive ability.[89] IQ tests are designed to ascertain a person's general intellectual abilities, but the origins, influence factors, and testing of intelligence quotient (IQ) are controversial.[90] So, too, are popular college admission tests, such as the SAT and ACT, and graduate admission tests in business (GMAT), law (LSAT), and medicine (MCAT). The firms that produce these tests do not claim they assess intelligence, but experts confirm they do.[91] Many organizations use intelligence tests in hiring decisions: for example, if you want to be a professional football player in the NFL, you will have to take an intellectual abilities test![92]

Intellectual abilities
The capacity to do mental activities—thinking, reasoning, and problem solving.

DIMENSIONS OF INTELLECTUAL ABILITY   The seven most frequently cited dimensions making up intellectual abilities are number aptitude, verbal comprehension, perceptual speed, inductive reasoning, deductive reasoning, spatial visualization, and memory.[93] Exhibit 2-2 describes these dimensions. These dimensions are positively correlated, so if you score high on verbal comprehension, for example, you are more likely to also score high on spatial visualization. The correlations are high enough that researchers also recognize a general factor of intelligence, **general mental ability (GMA)**. Evidence supports the idea that the structures and measures of intellectual abilities can be generalized across cultures: GMA was found in 73.2 percent of countries in one study of over 50,000 individuals.[94] Someone in Venezuela or Sudan, for instance, does not have a different set of mental abilities than an American or Czech individual. There is some evidence that IQ scores vary to some degree across cultures, but this gap is decreasing year by year, and those differences become much smaller when we consider educational and economic differences.[95]

General mental ability (GMA)
An overall factor of intelligence, as suggested by the positive correlations among specific intellectual ability dimensions.

THE WONDERLIC ABILITY TEST   It might surprise you that the intelligence test most widely used in hiring decisions, the Wonderlic Ability Test, takes only twelve minutes to

EXHIBIT 2-2
Dimensions of Intellectual Ability

Dimension	Description	Job Example
Number aptitude	Ability to do speedy and accurate arithmetic.	Accountant: Computing the sales tax on a set of items.
Verbal comprehension	Ability to understand what is read or heard and the relationship of words to each other.	Plant manager: Following corporate policies on hiring.
Perceptual speed	Ability to identify visual similarities and differences quickly and accurately.	Fire investigator: Identifying clues to support a charge of arson.
Inductive reasoning	Ability to identify a logical sequence in a problem and then solve the problem.	Market researcher: Forecasting demand for a product in the next time period.
Deductive reasoning	Ability to use logic and assess the implications of an argument.	Supervisor: Choosing between two different suggestions offered by employees.
Spatial visualization	Ability to imagine how an object would look if its position in space were changed.	Interior decorator: Redecorating an office.
Memory	Ability to retain and recall past experiences.	Salesperson: Remembering the names of customers.

complete. There are different forms of the test, but each has fifty questions. Here are two questions to try:

1. When rope is selling at $0.10 a foot, how many feet can you buy for $0.60?
2. Assume the first two statements are true. Is the final one:

   a. True.
   b. False.
   c. Not certain.

"The boy plays baseball. All baseball players wear hats. The boy wears a hat." The Wonderlic measures both speed (almost nobody has time to answer every question) and power (the questions get harder as you go along), so the average score is quite low—about twenty-one of fifty. Because the Wonderlic can provide valid information cheaply, many organizations use it in hiring decisions, including Publix supermarkets, Manpower staffing systems, BP, and Dish satellite systems.[96] Most of these companies do not eliminate other hiring tools, such as application forms or interviews. Rather, they add the Wonderlic for its ability to provide valid data on applicants' intelligence levels.

INTELLECTUAL ABILITY AND JOB SATISFACTION   While intelligence is a big help in performing a job well, it does not make people happier or more satisfied with their jobs.[97] In fact, research suggests that those with higher cognitive ability and who are high performers in the workplace might be victimized, bullied, and mistreated by their peers due to envy and social comparison.[98]

Physical Abilities

Though the changing nature of work suggests intellectual abilities are increasingly important for many jobs, **physical abilities** have been and will remain valuable. Research on hundreds of jobs has identified nine basic abilities needed in the performance of physical tasks.[99] These are described in Exhibit 2-3. High employee performance is likely to be achieved when the extent to which a job requires each of the nine abilities matches the abilities of employees in that job.[100] For example, certain occupations might require more strength than others (e.g., firefighting); as such, measures of physical ability predict long-term firefighter performance in these occupations.[101] Problems with discrimination can occur, however, when using physical abilities tests, as males tend to score substantially better than females on these tests. To some degree, one can improve the extent to which females meet minimum qualifications through physical fitness training.[102] Therefore, if a job you are seeking employment in requires strength, flexibility, or other physical requirements, it might be best to train to ensure you are sufficiently prepared.

> **Physical abilities**
> The capacity to do tasks that demand stamina, dexterity, strength, and similar characteristics.

In sum, organizations are increasingly aware that an optimally productive workforce includes all types of people and does not automatically exclude anyone based on broad categories of abilities. For example, a pilot program of software company SAP in Germany, India, and Ireland has found that employees with autism perform excellently in precision-oriented tasks like debugging software.[103] The potential benefits of diversity are enormous for forward-thinking managers. Of course, integrating diverse people into an optimally productive workforce takes skill. We discuss how to bring the talents of a diverse workforce together in the next section.

Strength Factors	
1. Dynamic strength	Ability to exert muscular force repeatedly or continuously over time.
2. Trunk strength	Ability to exert muscular strength using the trunk (particularly abdominal) muscles.
3. Static strength	Ability to exert force against external objects.
4. Explosive strength	Ability to expend a maximum of energy in one or a series of explosive acts.
Flexibility Factors	
5. Extent flexibility	Ability to move the trunk and back muscles as far as possible.
6. Dynamic flexibility	Ability to make rapid, repeated flexing movements.
Other Factors	
7. Body coordination	Ability to coordinate the simultaneous actions of different parts of the body.
8. Balance	Ability to maintain equilibrium despite forces pulling off balance.
9. Stamina	Ability to continue maximum effort requiring prolonged effort over time.

EXHIBIT 2-3
Types of Physical Abilities

IMPLEMENTING DIVERSITY MANAGEMENT STRATEGIES

Diversity management
The process and programs by which managers make everyone more aware of and sensitive to the needs and differences of others.

Having discussed a variety of ways in which people differ, we now look at how organizations can and should manage these differences. **Diversity management** makes everyone more aware of and sensitive to the needs and differences of others.[104] This definition highlights the fact that diversity programs include and are meant for everyone. Diversity is much more likely to be successful when we see it as everyone's business than when we believe it helps only certain groups of employees.

Attracting and Selecting Diverse Employees

One method of enhancing workforce diversity is to target recruitment messages to specific demographic groups that are underrepresented in the workforce. This means placing advertisements in publications geared toward those groups; pairing with colleges, universities, and other institutions with significant numbers of underrepresented minorities, as Microsoft is doing to encourage women to pursue technology studies;[105] and forming partnerships with associations like the Society of Women Engineers or the National Minority Supplier Development Council.

Research has shown that women and minorities have greater interest in employers that make special efforts to highlight a commitment to diversity in their recruiting materials. Diversity advertisements that fail to show women and minorities in positions of organizational leadership send a negative message about the diversity climate at an organization.[106]

The selection process is one of the most important places to apply diversity efforts. Hiring managers need to value fairness and objectivity in selecting employees and focus on the productive potential of new recruits. When managers use a well-defined protocol for assessing applicant talent and the organization clearly prioritizes nondiscrimination policies, qualifications become far more important factors than demographic characteristics in determining who gets hired.[107]

Diversity in Groups

As noted earlier in the chapter, working often involves interacting with a number of very diverse people. Like the staff in a restaurant, team members need to establish a common way of looking at and accomplishing major tasks, and they need to communicate with one another often. If they feel little sense of membership and cohesion in their groups, the performance of the team, and the restaurant, will likely suffer.

In some cases, diversity in various traits can hurt team performance, whereas in other cases it can facilitate performance.[108] Whether diverse or homogeneous teams are more effective depends on the characteristic of interest. Demographic diversity (in gender, race, and ethnicity) does not appear to help or hurt team performance in general, although racial diversity in management groups may increase organizational performance in the right conditions.[109] On the other hand, teams of individuals who are highly intelligent, conscientious, and interested in working in team settings are more effective.[110] Thus, diversity in these variables is likely to be a bad thing—it makes little sense to try to form teams that mix in members who are lower in intelligence or conscientiousness, or who are uninterested in teamwork. In other cases, diversity can be a strength. Groups of individuals with different types of expertise and education are more effective than homogeneous groups.[111]

Regardless of the composition of the group, differences can be leveraged to achieve superior team performance. Employees and team leaders should look out for **faultlines**, or divisive differences that may split a group into separate groups based on these characteristics, that can occur especially when the team is under threat or pressure.[112] These effects can be ameliorated by emphasizing similarities among members, capitalizing on complementary differences, and sharing a common goal or vision.[113] For example, if the restaurant staff is diverse with regard to both surface-level and deep-level characteristics, by emphasizing the similarities in shared values, goals, and other characteristics the team can develop a sense of unity and cohesion. Research on seven United Nations peace-building teams in Liberia and Haiti suggests that as teams grow and develop, they begin to forge a collective shared identity.[114] Despite differences, the longer teams are together, the more of a shared identity they begin to form.

Faultlines
The perceived divisions that split groups into two or more subgroups based on individual differences such as sex, race, age, work experience, language, and education.

The conversation of diversity in groups does not just revolve around *who* makes up the team—how diversity affects interpersonal interactions is of the utmost importance.[115] Ultimately, diversity in groups matters because it, in the case of deep-level characteristics, promotes access to diverse information and experiences while "filling the gaps" for the skills the team needs.[116] Restaurant staff with different skills and experiences (e.g., customer service, bartending skills, creativity) can improve team performance by helping other team members learn as well as by filling in "skills gaps." By being both similar "where it counts" (e.g., goals and values) and different "where it counts" (e.g., complementary skills, experiences), employees build trust, learn to effectively communicate with one another, develop a sense of identity, and perform strategically.[117]

Diversity Programs

Organizations use a variety of diversity programs in recruitment and selection policies, as well as in training and development practices. Overall, diversity management programs work; reviews of hundreds of studies suggest that they are effective at improving diversity knowledge and representation.[118] Effective, comprehensive workforce programs encouraging diversity have three distinct components. First, they teach managers about the legal framework for equal employment opportunity and encourage fair treatment of all people regardless of their demographic characteristics. Second, they teach managers how a diverse workforce will be better able to serve a diverse market of customers and clients. Third, they foster personal development practices that bring out the skills and abilities of all workers, acknowledging how differences in perspective can be a valuable way to improve performance for everyone.[119]

Most negative reactions to employment discrimination are based on the idea that discriminatory treatment is unfair. Regardless of race or gender, people are generally in favor of diversity-oriented programs to increase the representation of minority groups and ensure everyone a fair opportunity to show their skills and abilities. Furthermore, research on 155 Canadian firms suggests that, when incorporated as a core component of business strategy, diversity-oriented programs can increase representation of minority groups and positively affect an organization's return on investment (ROI).[120]

Organizational leaders should examine their workforces to determine whether target groups have been underutilized. If groups of employees are not proportionally represented in top management, managers should look for any hidden barriers to advancement. Managers can often improve recruiting practices, make selection systems more transparent, and provide training for those employees who have not had adequate exposure to diversity material in the past. The organization should also clearly communicate its policies to employees so they can understand how and why certain practices are followed. Communications should focus as much as possible on qualifications and job performance; emphasizing certain groups as needing more assistance could backfire. Employees should also confront prejudice as it happens and report instances to HR according to company policies—it is also useful to recognize that others have the capacity to change after confronting prejudice as this can lead to a better outlook, increased job satisfaction, and post-confrontation relations with the person committing the prejudicial act.[121]

Finally, research indicates a tailored approach will be needed in most organizations, with an analysis of the needs of participants along with frequent feedback.[122] Multinational organizations should also tailor their approach to the countries and cultures in which they operate. For instance, a case study of the multinational Finnish company TRANSCO found it was possible to develop a consistent global philosophy for diversity management. However, differences in legal and cultural factors across nations forced the company to develop unique policies to match the cultural and legal frameworks of each country in which it operated.[123]

SUMMARY

This chapter examined diversity from many perspectives, with a primary focus on surface-level vs. deep-level characteristics. Individual differences can lead to discrimination through activating stereotypes, which can lead to unfair working conditions and treatment, and possible legal ramifications for organizations and managers. In this chapter, we reviewed biographical characteristics and abilities and their relationship to workplace functions and outcomes. Finally, we discussed how organizations, managers, and employees can manage diversity. Overall, diversity management must be an ongoing commitment that crosses all levels of the organization, and can be effective at improving minority representation, enhancing diversity, and helping improve employee knowledge about diversity strengths.

IMPLICATIONS FOR MANAGERS

- Increase awareness of stereotypes, how they are perpetuated, and how covert discrimination can manifest in organizations.
- Assess and challenge your own stereotypical beliefs to increase your objectivity.
- Fully evaluate what accommodations a person with disabilities will need and then fine-tune the job to that person's abilities.
- Seek to understand and respect the unique biographical characteristics of each individual; a fair but individualistic approach yields the best performance.
- Understand your organization's antidiscrimination policies thoroughly and share them with all employees.
- Look beyond readily observable biographical characteristics and consider the individual's capabilities before making management decisions; remain open and encouraging for individuals to disclose any hidden disabilities.
- Strive to promote diversity in recruitment and selection practices.
- Develop a comprehensive diversity management program that weaves diversity considerations into the organization's operations.

3

Attitudes and Job Satisfaction

After studying this chapter, you should be able to:

3.1 Contrast the three components of an attitude.

3.2 Summarize the relationship between attitudes and behavior.

3.3 Compare the major job attitudes.

3.4 Identify the two approaches for measuring job satisfaction.

3.5 Summarize the main causes of job satisfaction.

3.6 Identify three outcomes of job satisfaction.

3.7 Identify four employee responses to job dissatisfaction.

ATTITUDES

Attitudes are evaluative statements—either favorable or unfavorable—about objects, people, or events. They reflect how we feel about something. When you say, "I like my job," you are expressing your attitude about your work.

Attitudes are complex. Let us say that you are interested in becoming an accountant. If you were to ask accountants and auditors their attitudes toward their job, you may get simple responses (e.g., "No, I hate my work," "Being an accountant is fantastic!" etc.), but the underlying reasons are likely more complicated. For example, accountants who perceive that their jobs have challenges, great benefits, and supportive management are much more likely to be happier with their jobs.[1] As we will see in this chapter, how satisfied you are with what you do, how committed you are to your employer, and other attitudes are major considerations in the workplace. If you like your job, you are more willing to stay, do your work well, and even go above-and-beyond to make sure the work gets done. To fully understand attitudes, we must consider their fundamental properties or components.

Typically, researchers assume attitudes have three components: cognition, affect, and behavior.[2] The statement "My pay is low" is a **cognitive component** of an attitude—an opinion or belief about the attitude target (e.g., your supervisor). It sets the stage for the more critical part of an attitude—its **affective component**. Affect is the emotional or feeling segment of an attitude reflected in the statement "I am angry over how little I'm

Attitudes
Evaluative statements or judgments concerning objects, people, or events.

Cognitive component
The opinion or belief segment of an attitude.

Affective component
The emotional or feeling segment of an attitude.

EXHIBIT 3-1

**The Components
of an Attitude**

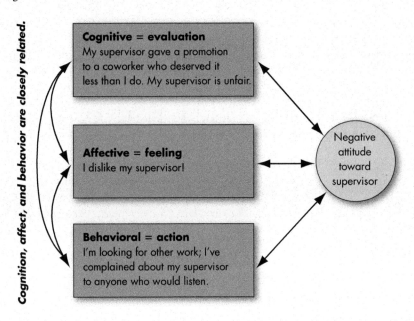

Cognition, affect, and behavior are closely related.

Cognitive = evaluation
My supervisor gave a promotion to a coworker who deserved it less than I do. My supervisor is unfair.

Affective = feeling
I dislike my supervisor!

Behavioral = action
I'm looking for other work; I've complained about my supervisor to anyone who would listen.

Negative attitude toward supervisor

Behavioral component
An intention to behave in a certain way toward someone or something.

paid." Affect can lead to behavioral outcomes. The **behavioral component** of an attitude describes an intention to behave a certain way toward someone or something—as in, "I'm going to look for another job that pays better."

Viewing attitudes in this way helps us understand their complexity and the potential relationship between attitudes and behavior. Exhibit 3-1 illustrates how the three components of an attitude are related. Let us imagine that you did not get a promotion you thought you deserved. Your attitude toward your supervisor is illustrated as follows: You thought you deserved the promotion (cognition); you strongly dislike your supervisor (affect); and you have complained and taken action, or otherwise intend to (behavior).

In organizations, attitudes are important for their behavioral component. If an accountant believes, for example, that they have no attachment to their firm and could get better opportunities with other firms, this belief could lead to whether they stay or leave their jobs. Understanding how this commitment is formed and how it might be changed is important to managers who want to reduce turnover. Interestingly, some research from the Netherlands suggests that the cognitive component is most important for predicting who will become committed to the organization (e.g., newcomers in an onboarding program) or uncommitted (e.g., unattached accountants considering leaving for better positions).[3]

ATTITUDES AND BEHAVIOR

Perhaps it is easy to think of how attitudes can cause people to behave in certain ways. Using our prior examples, accountants who are not satisfied with their jobs or committed to their organizations may start looking for work elsewhere. Research, in general, supports the idea that attitudes predict future behavior.[4]

Several powerful characteristics change the nature of the attitudes–behavior relationship: the *importance* of the attitude, its *correspondence to behavior*, its *accessibility*, the presence of *social pressures*, and whether a person has *direct experience* with the attitude.[5] Important attitudes reflect our fundamental values, self-interest, or identification with individuals or groups we value. These attitudes tend to show a strong relationship to our behavior. However, discrepancies between attitudes and behaviors tend to occur when social pressures to behave in certain ways hold exceptional power, as in most organizations. You are more likely to remember attitudes you frequently express, and attitudes that our memories can easily access are more likely to predict our behavior. The attitude–behavior relationship is also likely to be much stronger if an attitude refers to something with which we have direct personal experience.

Advancements in machine learning (see Chapter 1: What Is Organizational Behavior?) have enabled researchers to understand the attitude–behavior relationship even further. For example, using a machine learning algorithm enabled researchers in one study of hospital nurses to determine that their job attitudes were related to performance in certain conditions, such as when their job responsibilities were clearly defined.[6]

However, there are some instances in which behavior might predict future attitudes. Did you ever notice how people change what they say so that it does not contradict what they do? For example, when women come forward to call out sexual harassment in their jobs, even with clear evidence that the behavior occurred, management and harassers alike will often trivialize, minimize, ignore, or even aggressively justify their behavior.[7] Cases of attitude following behavior illustrate the effects of **cognitive dissonance**,[8] contradictions individuals might perceive between their attitudes and their behavior.

Cognitive dissonance
Any incompatibility between two or more attitudes or between behavior and attitudes.

People seek consistency among their attitudes, and between their attitudes and their behavior.[9] Any form of inconsistency is uncomfortable, and individuals will therefore attempt to reduce it. When there is dissonance, people will alter either their attitudes or their behaviors, or they will develop a rationalization for the discrepancy. For example, university faculty members who were on strike found it difficult to accept their union's recommendation to accept the university's offer and return to work; instead, they sought out additional information to justify their belief that the offer was unfair, instead of accepting the offer outright.[10]

No individual can avoid dissonance. You know texting or talking on the phone while driving is unsafe (there is research to prove it, do not try to justify your attitude or reduce your dissonance to get you out of this one!),[11] but you do it anyway and hope nothing bad happens. The desire to reduce dissonance depends on three factors, including the *importance* of the elements creating dissonance and the degree of *influence* we believe we have over those elements.[12] Individuals are more motivated to reduce dissonance when the attitudes are important or when they believe the dissonance is due to something they can control. The third factor is the *rewards* of dissonance; high rewards accompanying dissonance tend to reduce tension inherent in the dissonance (e.g., dissonance is less distressing if accompanied by something good, such as a higher pay raise than expected).[13]

JOB ATTITUDES

We have thousands of attitudes, but organizational behavior (OB) focuses on a very limited number that form positive or negative evaluations employees hold about their

Organizational identification
The extent to which employees define themselves by the same characteristics that define one's organization, forming the basis for which attitudes are engendered.

work. Research suggests that across all job attitudes, **organizational identification**, or the extent to which employees define themselves by the same characteristics that define one's organization, forms a basis for which attitudes and behaviors are engendered.[14] A review of hundreds of job attitude–behavior studies found that organizational identification strongly predicted job attitude formation across all types.[15] Furthermore, drawing on artificial intelligence theory, some researchers have proposed that humans form attitudes similarly to machines in order to make predictions based on continuously incoming data. For example, employees may experience event (e.g., reduced pay), after event (e.g., downsizing), after event (e.g., cancelled bonuses)—from such events, employees begin to "learn" that the organization may not value paying its employees well, begin to form negative attitudes toward the organization, and begin to dis-identify.[16]

Much of the research has looked at three attitudes: job satisfaction, job involvement, and organizational commitment.[17] Other important attitudes include perceived organizational support and employee engagement.[18] In the following section, we will describe these attitudes.

Job Satisfaction and Job Involvement

Job satisfaction
A positive feeling about one's job resulting from an evaluation of its characteristics.

When people speak of employee attitudes, they usually mean **job satisfaction**, a positive feeling about a job resulting from an evaluation of its characteristics. A person with high job satisfaction holds positive feelings about the work, while a person with low satisfaction holds negative feelings. Because job satisfaction is one of the most important attitudes, we will review this attitude in detail later.

Job involvement
The degree to which a person identifies with a job, actively participates in it, and considers performance important to their self-worth.

Related to job satisfaction is **job involvement**, the degree to which people psychologically identify with their jobs and consider their perceived performance levels important to their self-worth.[19] Employees with high job involvement strongly identify with and care about the kind of work they do; as such, they tend to be more satisfied with their jobs.[20]

Psychological empowerment
Employees' belief in the degree to which they affect their work environment, their competence, the meaningfulness of their job, and their perceived autonomy in their work.

Another closely related concept is **psychological empowerment**, or employees' beliefs regarding the degree to which they influence their work environment, their competencies, the meaningfulness of their job, and their perceived autonomy.[21] The more "empowered" employees are, the more likely they are to perform well, engage in organizational citizenship behaviors (see Chapter 1: What Is Organizational Behavior?), be creative, and the less likely they are to intend to leave the organization.[22]

Organizational Commitment

Organizational commitment
The degree to which an employee identifies with a particular organization and its goals and wishes to maintain membership in the organization.

An employee with strong **organizational commitment** identifies with their organization and its goals and wishes to remain a member. Emotional attachment to an organization and belief in its values is the gold standard for employee commitment.[23]

Employees who are committed will be less likely to engage in work withdrawal, even if they are dissatisfied, because they have a sense of organizational loyalty or attachment, they may not have other options, or it may be difficult for them to leave.[24] Even if employees are not currently happy with their work, they may decide to continue with the organization if they are committed enough.

Perceived Organizational Support

Perceived organizational support (POS) is the degree to which employees believe the organization values their contributions and cares about their well-being. People perceive their organizations as supportive when rewards are deemed fair, when employees have a voice in decisions, and when they see their supervisors as supportive.[25]

POS is a predictor of employment outcomes, but there are some cultural influences.[26] POS is important in countries where the **power distance**, the degree to which people in a country accept that power in institutions and organizations is distributed unequally, is lower. In low power-distance countries like the United States, people are more likely to view work as an exchange than as a moral obligation, so employees look for reasons to feel supported by their organizations. In high power-distance countries like China, employee POS perceptions are not as deeply based on employer demonstrations of fairness, support, and encouragement.

The picture is even more complicated considering how multinational corporations often send people to work for extended periods of time at locations far away from home. In these instances, corporations can extend much-needed support to avoid failed international assignments, which can be costly; they can provide logistical support (e.g., find housing, secure transportation), cultural support (e.g., provide training with how to communicate effectively in the new country), or relationship support (e.g., programs to help these employees make friends and build a social support system).[27]

Employee Engagement

Employee engagement is the degree of enthusiasm an employee feels for the job.[28] Employee engagement, in many ways, represents a combination of attitudes (e.g., satisfaction and commitment) but exceeds these, representing something like "devotion" or giving your "heart and soul" to your work.[29] Highly engaged employees have a passion for their work and feel a deep connection to their companies; disengaged employees have essentially checked out, putting time but not energy or attention into their work. Engagement becomes a real concern for most organizations because disengaged employees cost organizations money—one study suggests that organizations can lose up to $550 billion annually in lost productivity.[30] Employee engagement is related to job engagement, which we discuss in detail in the chapter on motivation concepts.

Engagement levels affect many organizational outcomes. Reviews of the research on employee engagement suggest that employee engagement is moderately related to employee and organizational performance. A study of nearly 8,000 business units in thirty-six companies found that units whose employees reported high-average levels of engagement achieved higher levels of customer satisfaction, were more productive, brought in higher profits, and experienced lower levels of turnover and accidents than at other business units.[31] Molson Coors, for example, found engaged employees were five times less likely to have safety incidents, and when an accident did occur, it was much less serious and less costly for an engaged employee than for a disengaged one ($63 per incident versus $392). Caterpillar set out to increase employee engagement and recorded a resulting 80 percent drop in grievances and a 34 percent increase in highly satisfied customers.[32]

There is some distinctiveness among attitudes, but they overlap greatly for various reasons, including the employee's personality. Generally, if you know someone's level of job

Perceived organizational support (POS)
The degree to which employees believe an organization values their contribution and cares about their well-being.

Power distance
A national culture attribute that describes the extent to which a society accepts that power in institutions and organizations is distributed unequally.

Employee engagement
The degree of enthusiasm an employee feels for the job.

satisfaction, you know most of what you need to know about how that person sees the organization. Next, we will consider the implications of job satisfaction and then job dissatisfaction.

JOB SATISFACTION

We have already discussed job satisfaction briefly. We know that it is one of the most important job attitudes, and that it predicts several important business outcomes. Now let us dissect the concept more carefully. If I am a manager and I want to get a better idea of how satisfied the people in my organization are, how do I measure job satisfaction? How satisfied are people with their jobs, in general? You may be surprised with some of the answers to these questions below.

How Do I Measure Job Satisfaction?

Two approaches are popular. The single global rating is a response to one question, such as "All things considered, how satisfied are you with your job?" Respondents circle a number between one and five on a scale from "highly satisfied" to "highly dissatisfied." The second method, the summation of job facets, is more sophisticated. It identifies key elements in a job, such as the type of work, skills needed, supervision, present pay, promotion opportunities, culture, and relationships with coworkers. Respondents rate each of these on a standardized scale (e.g., from one to five, dissatisfied to satisfied), and these ratings are added to create an overall job satisfaction score.

Is one of these approaches superior? Intuitively, summing up responses to several job factors seems likely to achieve a more accurate evaluation of job satisfaction. Research, however, does not entirely support the intuition.[33] This is one of those rare instances in which simplicity seems to work as well as complexity, making one method essentially as valid as the other. Both methods can be helpful. The single global rating method is not very time consuming, while the summation of job facets helps managers zero in on problems and deal with them faster and more accurately.

How Satisfied Are People in Their Jobs?

Are most people satisfied with their jobs? In the 2017 World Happiness Report, people in 160 countries worldwide (and representing 98 percent of the world's population) were surveyed; the majority of employees in 92.5 percent of those countries were satisfied with their jobs.[34] Job satisfaction levels can remain quite consistent over time. For instance, average job satisfaction levels in the United States were consistently high from 1972 to 2006.[35] However, economic conditions tend to influence job satisfaction rates. In late 2007, the economic contraction precipitated a drop-off in job satisfaction; the lowest point was in 2010, when only 42.6 percent of U.S. workers reported satisfaction with their jobs.[36] Approximately 51 percent of U.S. workers reported satisfaction with their jobs in 2017,[37] but the rebound was still far off the 1987 level of 61.1 percent.[38]

The facets of job satisfaction levels can vary widely. As shown in Exhibit 3-2, people have typically been more satisfied with their jobs overall, the work itself, and their supervisors and coworkers than they have been with their pay and promotion opportunities.

Furthermore, one review of dozens of studies with more than 750,000 participants suggests that there are slight racial differences: White employees tend to be slightly more satisfied

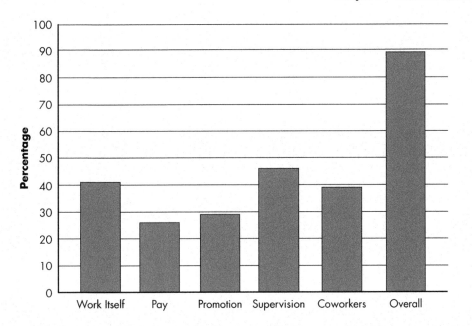

EXHIBIT 3-2

Average Job Satisfaction Levels by Facet

Source: Society for Human Resource Management, "2017 Employee Job Satisfaction and Engagement: The Doors of Opportunity are Open," April 24, 2017, https://www.shrm.org/hr-today/trends-and-forecasting/research-and-surveys/pages/2017-job-satisfaction-and-engagement-doors-of-opportunity-are-open.aspx

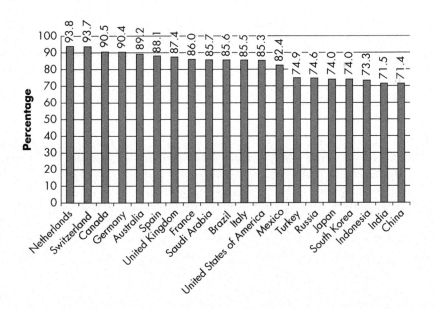

EXHIBIT 3-3

Average Levels of Employee Job Satisfaction by Country

Source: J-E. De Neve and G. Ward, "Happiness at Work," in J. Helliwell, R. Layard, and J. Sachs (Eds.), *World Happiness Report* (World Happiness Report APPENDIX, 2017).

than black employees in general, especially in more complex jobs.[39] Regarding global differences in job satisfaction, Exhibit 3-3 provides results from the 2017 World Happiness Report and, more specifically, from the twenty countries with the largest economies in the world. In these countries, over 70 percent of employees are satisfied with their jobs. It is difficult to discern all the factors influencing job satisfaction worldwide but exploring how businesses consider and address job satisfaction worldwide may provide an answer.

WHAT CAUSES JOB SATISFACTION?

Think about the best job you have ever had. What made it great? The reasons can differ greatly. Let us consider some characteristics that likely influence job satisfaction, starting with job conditions.

Job Conditions

Generally, interesting jobs that provide training, variety, independence, and control satisfy most employees. Interdependence, feedback, social support, and positive interactions with coworkers and even customers are also strongly related to job satisfaction, even after accounting for characteristics of the work itself.[40] It goes without saying that toxic workplace environments lead to dissatisfied employees. For example, if you experience workplace racial discrimination, you are likely to become dissatisfied (and some research suggests, might even experience a decline in physical and psychological health).[41]

As you may have guessed, managers also play a big role in employees' job satisfaction. One review of nearly 70,000 employees from twenty-three countries found that the quality of exchange between the leaders and their employees is more strongly related to job satisfaction in more individualistic (e.g., Western) cultures than it is in more collectivistic (e.g., Asian) cultures.[42] Furthermore, "fitting in" matters for job attitudes, worldwide. Another review of over one hundred studies in East Asia, Europe, and North America suggests that fitting in with your organization and job matters more in North America, whereas fitting in with your team or supervisor matters more in East Asia.[43]

Thus, job conditions—especially the intrinsic nature of the work itself, social interactions, and supervision—are important predictors of job satisfaction.[44] Managers would do well to make sure the job conditions are satisfying enough to make employees happy. For example, Bain & Company is listed as the number one best place to work in 2019, according to Glassdoor; one employee re-emphasizes the value of social support, noting that "at a local level, my colleagues are at once my mentors, confidantes, and closest friends."[45]

Personality

Core self-evaluation (CSE)
Believing in one's inner worth and basic competence.

As important as job conditions are to job satisfaction, personality also plays an important role.[46] People who have positive **core self-evaluations** (CSEs; see the chapter on personality and values for further discussion)—who believe in their inner worth and basic competence—are more satisfied with their jobs than people with negative CSEs. For those in collectivist cultures, those with high CSEs may realize particularly high job satisfaction.[47]

Pay

You have probably noticed that pay comes up often when people discuss job satisfaction. Pay does correlate with job satisfaction and overall happiness for many people, but the effect can be smaller once an individual reaches a standard level of comfortable living.[48] As a corollary, money does *motivate* people, as we discover in the chapter on motivation applications. But what motivates us is not necessarily the same as what makes us happy.

Corporate Social Responsibility (CSR)

Would you be as happy to work for an organization with a stated social welfare mission as you would for an organization without one? An organization's commitment to

corporate social responsibility (CSR), or its self-regulated actions to benefit society or the environment beyond what is required by law, increasingly affects employee job satisfaction. Organizations practice CSR through environmental sustainability initiatives, nonprofit work, and charitable giving.

> Corporate social responsibility (CSR) An organization's self-regulated actions to benefit society or the environment beyond what is required by law.

CSR is good for the planet and good for people. Employees whose personal values fit with the organization's CSR mission are often more satisfied. In fact, of fifty-nine large and small organizations recently surveyed, 86 percent reported they have happier employees as a result of their CSR programs.[49]

"The next generation of employees is seeking out employers that are focused on the triple bottom line: people, planet, and revenue," said Susan Cooney, founder of philanthropy firm Givelocity.[50] CSR allows workers to serve a higher purpose or contribute to a mission. People who view their work as part of a higher purpose often realize higher job satisfaction.[51] However, an organization's CSR efforts must be well governed, and its initiatives must be sustainable for long-term job satisfaction benefits.[52]

In sum, CSR is a needed, positive trend of accountability and serving. It can also contribute significantly to increased employee job satisfaction when managed well.

OUTCOMES OF JOB SATISFACTION

Having discussed some of the causes of job satisfaction, we now turn to some specific outcomes.

Job Performance

As several studies have concluded, happy workers are more likely to be productive workers. Some researchers used to believe the relationship between job satisfaction and job performance was a myth, but a review of 300 studies suggested the correlation is quite robust.[53] Individuals with higher job satisfaction perform better, and organizations with more satisfied employees tend to be more effective than those with fewer.

Organizational Citizenship Behavior (OCB)

It seems logical that job satisfaction should be a major determinant of an employee's organizational citizenship behavior (known as OCB or citizenship behavior; see Chapter 1: What Is Organizational Behavior?).[54] Evidence suggests job satisfaction *is* moderately correlated with OCB; people who are more satisfied with their jobs are more likely to engage in citizenship behavior.[55] Why does job satisfaction lead to OCB? One reason is trust. Research in eighteen countries suggests that managers reciprocate employees' OCBs with trusting behaviors of their own.[56] Individuals who feel their coworkers support them are also more likely to engage in helpful behaviors than those who have antagonistic coworker relationships.[57]

Customer Satisfaction

Because service organization managers should be concerned with pleasing customers, it is reasonable to ask whether employee satisfaction is related to positive customer outcomes. For employees who have regular customer contact, the answer appears to be yes. Satisfied employees appear to increase customer satisfaction and loyalty.[58]

Several companies are acting on this evidence. Online shoe retailer Zappos is so committed to finding customer service employees who are satisfied with the job that it offers a $2,000 bribe to quit the company after training, figuring the least satisfied will take the cash and go.[59] Zappos employees are empowered to "create fun and a little weirdness" to ensure that customers are satisfied, and it works: Of the company's more than twenty-four million customers, 75 percent are repeat buyers. For Zappos, employee satisfaction has a direct effect on customer satisfaction.

Life Satisfaction

Until now, we have treated job satisfaction as if it were separate from life satisfaction, but they may be more related than you think, with evidence suggesting that they mutually influence one another.[60] Furthermore, life satisfaction decreases when people become unemployed, according to research in Germany, and not just because of the loss of income.[61] For most individuals, work is an important part of life, and therefore it makes sense that our overall happiness depends in no small part on our happiness in our work (our job satisfaction).

THE IMPACT OF JOB DISSATISFACTION

What happens when employees dislike their jobs? One theoretical model—the exit–voice–loyalty–neglect framework—is helpful for understanding the consequences of dissatisfaction. The framework's four responses differ along two dimensions: constructive/destructive and active/passive. The responses are as follows:[62]

Exit
Dissatisfaction expressed through behavior directed toward leaving the organization.

Voice
Dissatisfaction expressed through active and constructive attempts to improve conditions.

Loyalty
Dissatisfaction expressed by passively waiting for conditions to improve.

Neglect
Dissatisfaction expressed through allowing conditions to worsen.

- **Exit**. The **exit response** directs behavior toward leaving the organization, including looking for a new position or resigning. To measure the effects of this response to dissatisfaction, researchers study individual terminations and *collective turnover*—the total loss to the organization of employee knowledge, skills, abilities, and other characteristics.[63]
- **Voice**. The **voice response** includes actively and constructively attempting to improve conditions, including suggesting improvements, discussing problems with superiors, and undertaking union activity.
- **Loyalty**. The **loyalty response** means passively but optimistically waiting for conditions to improve, including speaking up for the organization in the face of external criticism and trusting the organization and its management to "do the right thing."
- **Neglect**. The **neglect response** passively allows conditions to worsen and includes chronic absenteeism or lateness, reduced effort, and an increased error rate.

Exit and neglect behaviors are linked to performance variables such as productivity, absenteeism, and turnover. But this model expands employee responses to include voice and loyalty—constructive behaviors that allow individuals to tolerate unpleasant situations or improve working conditions. Furthermore, some researchers have suggested the framework be expanded to include retaliatory responses, many of which are described in the next section.[64] As helpful as this framework is, it is quite general.

Counterproductive Work Behavior (CWB)

Substance abuse, stealing at work, undue socializing, gossiping, absenteeism, and tardiness are examples of behaviors that are destructive to organizations. They are indicators of a broader syndrome called **counterproductive work behavior (CWB)**, also termed deviant behavior in the workplace, or simply employee withdrawal (see Chapter 1: What Is Organizational Behavior?).[65] Like other behaviors we have discussed, CWB does not just happen—the behaviors often follow negative and sometimes long-standing attitudes. Therefore, if we can identify the predictors of CWB, we may lessen the probability of its effects.

Generally, job dissatisfaction predicts CWB.[66] People who are not satisfied with their work become frustrated, which lowers their performance[67] and makes them more likely to commit CWB.[68] One important point about CWB is that dissatisfied employees often choose one or more specific behaviors due to idiosyncratic factors. One worker might quit. Another might use work time to browse Reddit. Another might take work supplies home for personal use. In short, workers who do not like their jobs "get even" in various ways. Because those ways can be quite creative, controlling only one behavior with policies and punishments leaves the root cause untouched. Employers should seek to correct the source of the problem—the dissatisfaction—rather than try to control the different responses.

As a manager, you can take steps to mitigate CWB. You can poll employee attitudes, for instance, and identify areas for workplace improvement. Furthermore, creating strong teams, integrating supervisors with them, providing formalized team policies, and introducing team-based incentives may help lower the CWB "contagion" that lowers the standards of the group.[69]

ABSENTEEISM We find that unsatisfied employees tend to be absent more often, but the relationship is not very strong.[70] Generally, when numerous alternative jobs are available, dissatisfied employees have high absence rates, but when there are few alternatives, dissatisfied employees have the same (low) rate of absence as satisfied employees.[71]

TURNOVER The relationship between job satisfaction and turnover is stronger than between satisfaction and absenteeism.[72] Overall, a pattern of lowered job satisfaction is the best predictor of intent to leave. Turnover has a workplace environment connection too. If the climate within an employee's immediate workplace is one of low job satisfaction leading to turnover, there will be a contagion effect. This suggests managers should consider the job satisfaction (and turnover) patterns of coworkers when assigning workers to a new area.[73]

The satisfaction–turnover relationship is affected by alternative job prospects. If an employee accepts an unsolicited job offer, job dissatisfaction was less predictive of turnover because the employee more likely left in response to "pull" (the lure of the other job) than "push" (the unattractiveness of the current job). Similarly, job dissatisfaction is more likely to translate into turnover when other employment opportunities are plentiful. Furthermore, when employees have high "human capital" (high education, high ability), job dissatisfaction is more likely to translate into turnover because they have, or perceive, many available alternatives.[74]

Some factors help break the dissatisfaction–turnover relationship. Employees' embeddedness—connections to the people or groups one is involved with at work—can help lower the probability of turnover, particularly in collectivist (group-oriented) cultures.[75] Embedded employees seem less likely to want to consider alternative job prospects.

Counterproductive work behavior (CWB)
Actions that actively damage the organization, including stealing, behaving aggressively toward co-workers, or being late or absent.

Managers Often "Don't Get It"

Given the evidence we have just reviewed, it should come as no surprise that job satisfaction can affect the bottom line. One study by a management consulting firm sepa-
rated large organizations into those with high morale (more than 70 percent of employees
expressed overall job satisfaction) and medium or low morale (fewer than 70 percent).
The stock prices of companies in the high-morale group grew 19.4 percent, compared
with 10 percent for the medium- or low-morale group.[76] Furthermore, companies listed
within the "100 Best Companies to Work for in America" generated 2.3%–3.8% higher
stock returns annually than other firms between 1984 and 2011.[77] Despite these results,
many managers are unconcerned about employee job satisfaction.

Others overestimate how satisfied employees are, so they do not think there is a
problem when there is one. For example, in one study of 262 large employers, 86 percent
of senior managers believed their organizations treated employees well, but only 55 percent of employees agreed; another study found 55 percent of managers, compared to only
38 percent of employees, thought morale was good in their organization.[78] Regular surveys
can reduce gaps between what managers *think* employees feel and what they *really* feel. A
gap in understanding can affect the bottom line in small franchise sites as well as in large
companies. As manager of a KFC restaurant in Houston, Jonathan McDaniel surveyed
the employees every three months. Results led McDaniel to make changes, such as giving
employees greater say about which workdays they had off. McDaniel believed the process
itself was valuable. "They really love giving their opinions," McDaniel said. "That's the
most important part of it—that they have a voice and that they're heard." Surveys are no
panacea, but if job attitudes are as important as we believe, organizations need to use every
reasonable method find out how they can be improved.[79]

SUMMARY

Managers should be interested in their employees' attitudes because attitudes influence
behavior and indicate potential problems. Creating a satisfied workforce is hardly a guarantee of successful organizational performance, but evidence strongly suggests managers'
efforts to improve employee attitudes will likely result in positive outcomes, including
greater organizational effectiveness, higher customer satisfaction, and increased profits.

IMPLICATIONS FOR MANAGERS

- Of the major job attitudes—job satisfaction, job involvement, organizational commitment, perceived organizational support, and employee engagement—remember
  that an employee's job satisfaction level is the best single predictor of behavior.
- Pay attention to your employees' job satisfaction levels as determinants of their
  performance, turnover, absenteeism, and withdrawal behaviors.
- Measure employee job attitudes objectively and at regular intervals in order to
  determine how employees are reacting to their work.
- To raise employee satisfaction, evaluate the fit between the employee's work interests and the intrinsic parts of the job; then create work that is challenging and
  interesting to the individual.
- Consider the fact that high pay alone is unlikely to create a satisfying work
  environment.

4

Emotions and Moods

After studying this chapter, you should be able to:

4.1 Differentiate between emotions and moods.

4.2 Identify the sources of emotions and moods.

4.3 Show the impact emotional labor has on employees.

4.4 Describe affective events theory.

4.5 Describe emotional intelligence.

4.6 Identify strategies for emotion regulation.

4.7 Apply concepts about emotions and moods to specific OB issues.

WHAT ARE EMOTIONS AND MOODS?

Emotions can greatly influence our attitudes toward others, our decision making, and our behaviors. It can even spark conflict with potentially disastrous consequences. For example, after being told to "stop being a crybaby," one Florida Taco Bell employee threw a hot bean burrito at his supervisor, snapped his headset in two, and stormed out of the building.[1] In truth, we are human and cannot set aside our emotions, but we *can* acknowledge and work with them. And not all emotions have negative influences on us. For example, when Fausto Martinez found out about Amazon's minimum wage hike, he was extremely happy—he looked forward to a better quality of life, more time with family, and the lack of a need for a second full-time job.[2] By increasing the minimum wage, Amazon was able to improve the quality of life of its employees and stay competitive with regard to retaining them.

First, however, we need to discuss three terms that are closely intertwined: *affect, emotions,* and *moods.* **Affect** is a generic term that covers a broad range of feelings, including both emotions and moods.[3] **Emotions** are intense, discrete, and short-lived feeling experiences that are often caused by a specific event.[4] **Moods** are longer lived and less intense feelings than emotions and often arise without a specific event acting as a stimulus.[5] Exhibit 4-1 shows the relationships among affect, emotions, and moods.

Affect
A term used to describe a broad range of feelings that people experience, including emotions and moods.

Emotions
Intense, discrete, and short-lived feeling experiences that are often caused by a specific event.

Moods
Feelings that tend to be longer lived and less intense than emotions and that lack a contextual stimulus.

EXHIBIT 4-1
Affect,
Emotions, and
Moods

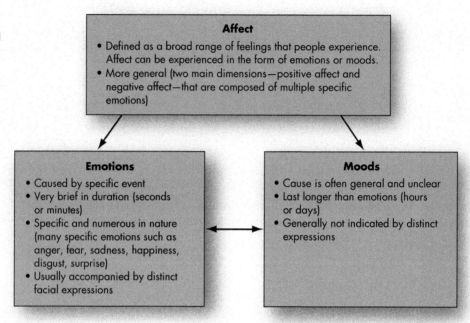

As the exhibit shows, *affect* is a broad term that encompasses emotions and moods. Affect varies by its valence, or the degree to which the feelings are positive (e.g., excited, happy, joyous) or negative (e.g., sad, angry, frustrated). Second, there are differences between emotions and moods. Emotions are more likely to be caused by a specific event and are more fleeting than moods.

Positive affect
A dimension that consists of specific positive emotions such as excitement, enthusiasm, and elation at the high end and boredom, sluggishness, and tiredness at the low end.

Positive and Negative Affect

As a first step toward studying the effect of moods and emotions in the workplace, we classify affect into two broad categories: positive and negative. Positive emotions—such as joy and gratitude—express a favorable evaluation or feeling. Negative emotions—such as anger and guilt—express the opposite. Keep in mind that emotions cannot be neutral. Being neutral is being non-emotional.[6]

The two categories of affect represent overall affective states, known as positive and negative affect (see Exhibit 4-2). So, we can think of **positive affect** as a mood dimension consisting of positive emotions such as excitement, enthusiasm, and elation at the high end (high positive affect). **Negative affect** is a mood dimension consisting of nervousness, stress, and anxiety at the high end (high negative affect).[7]

Negative affect
A dimension that consists of emotions such as nervousness, stress, and anxiety at the high end and relaxation and calmness at the low end.

The Basic Emotions

You might be wondering; how many emotions are there? There are dozens—including anger, contempt, enthusiasm, envy, fear, frustration, disappointment, embarrassment, disgust, happiness, hate, hope, jealousy, joy, love, pride, surprise, and sadness.

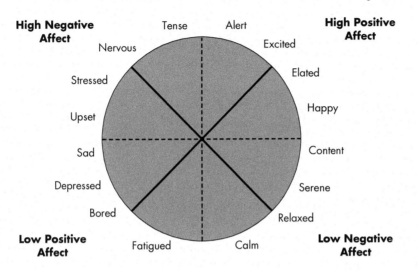

EXHIBIT 4-2
The Affective Circumplex

Numerous researchers have tried to limit them to a fundamental set.[8] Other scholars argue that by thinking in terms of "basic" emotions, we lose sight of the bigger picture because emotions can mean different things in different contexts and may vary across cultures.[9] It is unlikely psychologists or philosophers will ever completely agree on a set of basic emotions, or even on whether there is such a thing. Still, many researchers agree on six universal emotions—anger, fear, sadness, happiness, disgust, and surprise.[10] If you have ever held a job before, you can probably think of times in which you have experienced these emotions in the workplace; for example, after a bad performance review with your supervisor at the department store where you work, you might be angry with your boss, fearful of being let go, or surprised that the supervisor gave you such a poor evaluation.

Psychologists have tried to identify basic emotions by studying how we express them. Facial expressions have proved difficult to interpret.[11] One problem is that some emotions are too complex to be easily represented on our faces. Second, although people can, for the most part, recognize emotions across cultures at better-than-chance levels, this accuracy is worse for cultural groups with less exposure to one another.[12] Employees can also vocally express their emotions, and artificial intelligence is advancing research in this area. For example, one machine learning (see Chapter 1: What Is Organizational Behavior?) study of speeches from one hundred professional actors across various English-speaking countries found that people are better at recognizing the emotions of actors who are from the same country, suggesting that there are dialect differences in verbally expressing emotions.[13] Differentiating the expression of emotions across cultures is quite important in this era of globalization: you may find yourself communicating with people from radically different cultures from you, and understanding the nuances in how they express emotion can be very helpful. Studying how emotions are displayed, educating yourself on culture-specific emotion expressions, and paying attention to cues when interacting with people from other cultures can help you become a better cross-cultural communicator.[14]

Moral Emotions

Moral emotions
Emotions that have moral implications because of our instant judgment of the situation that evokes them.

Some emotions are closely tied to our interpretations of the events that evoke them. One area in which researchers have been furthering this idea is through the study of **moral emotions**, that is, emotions that have moral implications because of our instant judgment of the situation that evokes them.[15]

Say you watched a video of a person making a sexist or racist slur. You might feel disgusted because it offends your sense of right and wrong. In fact, you might feel a variety of emotions based on your moral judgment of the situation.[16] Other examples of moral emotions include sympathy for the suffering of others, guilt about our own immoral behavior, anger about injustice done to others, and contempt for those who behave unethically. Therefore, we need to be aware of the moral aspects of situations that trigger our emotions and make certain we understand the context before we act, especially in the workplace.[17]

Experiencing Moods and Emotions

Positivity offset
The tendency of most individuals to experience a mildly positive mood at zero input (when nothing in particular is going on).

As if it were not complex enough to consider the many distinct emotions a person might experience, the reality is that we each experience moods and emotions differently. For most people, positive moods are somewhat more common than negative moods. Indeed, research finds nearly universal evidence for a **positivity offset**, meaning that at zero input (when nothing in particular is going on), most individuals experience a mildly positive mood.[18] Why is it that we seem to "default" to a positive mood? In general, positive moods enable employees to perform better, be more creative, be more social, as well as improve their health and longevity—for these reasons, humans may have evolved to possess a positivity offset.[19]

The Function of Emotions

In some ways, emotions are a mystery. What function do they serve? As we discussed, a large number of reviews suggest that happy employees tend to have positive job attitudes, engage in fewer withdrawal and counterproductive work behaviors, engage in more task and citizenship performance, and are even more successful than their unhappy counterparts.[20] Individuals who tend to experience positive affect consistently as part of their personalities (see the chapter on personality and values) tend to have positive job attitudes, experience good social integration with their supervisor and coworkers, experience good treatment from their organizations, and engage in more task and citizenship performance.[21]

DO EMOTIONS MAKE US IRRATIONAL? How often have you heard someone say, "Oh, you're just being emotional?" You might have been offended. Observations like this suggest that rationality and emotion are in conflict, and by exhibiting emotion, you are acting irrationally. The perceived association between the two is so strong that some researchers argue displaying emotions such as sadness to the point of crying is so toxic to a career that we should leave the room rather than allow others to witness it.[22] This perspective suggests the demonstration or even experience of emotions can make us seem weak, brittle, or irrational. However, our emotions can make our thinking *more* rational. Why? Because our emotions provide important information about how we understand the world around us and help guide our behaviors. For instance, individuals in a negative mood may be better able to discern truthful from inaccurate information than are people in a happy mood.[23] Furthermore, cold rationality does not acknowledge that *people are, by nature, emotional.* We would do best to recognize and understand our own emotions (as well as others') and use this information in our interactions with others.

When we can identify the sources of emotions and moods, we are better able to predict behavior and manage people well. Let us explore that topic next.

SOURCES OF EMOTIONS AND MOODS

It's 8:15 a.m. on Monday, and you are so incredibly excited to tell your coworker, Jordan, good news about the shiny Pokémon you caught in Pokémon Go. You rush over, but Jordan immediately stops you and says, "Don't even talk to me until I've had my coffee." Defeated, you walk back to your station and continue your opening activities. You wonder where this bad mood originated from and begin to feel angry emotions toward your coworker. You mutter under your breath, "I won't trade the extra shiny Pokémon I caught with Jordan. We'll see who's upset then!" We have all, no doubt, been in a similar situation before. Clearly, these negative emotions and moods are often unavoidable and have an impact on our work. Jordan hurt a coworker's feelings, harming the functioning of the floor team that day, and now you may be preoccupied with what Jordan said and miss one of your opening tasks. We are often left wondering where these emotions and moods originated. Was it really the lack of coffee? Maybe something else was going on? Here we discuss some of the primary influences on emotions and moods.

Personality

Moods and emotions have a personality component, meaning that some people have built-in tendencies to experience certain moods and emotions more frequently than others do. Is Jordan frequently prone to experiencing negative emotions? It could be that Jordan's reaction is a reflection of personality. People also experience the same emotions with different intensities; the degree to which they experience them is called their **affect intensity**.[24] Affectively intense people experience both positive and negative emotions deeply: When they are sad, they are really sad, and when they are happy, they are really happy. Both the tendency to experience positive and negative emotions, as well as the intensity at which we feel them, affects several factors at work, such as our typical moods, job satisfaction, and engagement at work (see the chapter on attitudes and job satisfaction).[25] For example, one review of over one hundred studies suggests that the tendency to experience positive emotions and moods is the strongest predictor of whether an employee is engaged.[26]

Affect intensity
Individual differences in the strength with which individuals experience their emotions.

Time of Day

Maybe it was just too early for Jordan to interact with coworkers? Indeed, research does show that moods vary by the time of day. Furthermore, most of us follow the same pattern. Levels of positive affect tend to peak in the late morning (ten o'clock to noon) and then remain at that level until early evening (around seven o'clock). Starting about twelve hours after waking, positive affect begins to drop until dusk, and then, continues to accelerate until midnight. For those who remain awake, the drop continues until positive mood picks up again after sunrise.[27] As for negative affect, most research suggests it fluctuates less than positive affect,[28] but the general trend is for it to increase over the course of a day, so that it is lowest early in the morning and highest late in the evening.[29] A fascinating study assessed patterns by analyzing millions of Twitter messages from across the globe.[30] The researchers noted the presence of words connoting positive affect (happy, enthused, excited) and negative affect (sad, angry, anxious). You can see the trends they observed in the positive affect part of Exhibit 4-3.

Day of the Week

Was this just a case of the "Mondays" for Jordan? In most cultures, Mondays can be ... "problematic" for employees—for example, as shown in Exhibit 4-3, U.S. adults tend to experience their highest positive affect on Friday, Saturday, and Sunday and their lowest on Monday.[31] This tends to be true in several other cultures. This is not the case in all cultures, however. In Japan, positive affect is higher on Monday than on either Friday or Saturday.[32] As for negative affect, Monday is the highest negative-affect day across most cultures.[33] However, in some countries, negative affect is lower on Friday and Saturday than on Sunday. It may be that while Sunday is enjoyable as a day off (and thus we have higher positive affect), we also get a bit stressed about the week ahead (which is why negative affect is higher). However, these findings may not generalize to cultures that do not follow the Monday-Friday work schedule. For example, many countries observe a Sunday-Thursday work week (e.g., Israel, Malaysia). More research is needed on whether certain days of the week influence affect in these cultures.

Weather

Maybe Jordan was feeling a little ... "under the weather"? Many people believe their mood is tied to the weather, and indeed, there are many self-proclaimed "rain haters" and "summer lovers."[34] However, a large and detailed body of evidence suggests weather has little effect on mood, at least for most people.[35] **Illusory correlation**, which occurs when we associate two events that, in reality, have no connection, explains why people tend to *think* weather influences them. For example, employees may be more productive on bad weather days, as a study in Japan and the United States recently indicated, but not because of mood—instead, the worse weather removed some work distractions.[36]

Illusory correlation
The tendency of people to associate two events when in reality there is no connection.

Stress

Maybe Jordan was anxious about a worrisome meeting with the manager later that afternoon? As you might imagine, stressful events at work (a nasty e-mail, impending deadline, loss of a sale, reprimand from the boss, etc.) negatively affect moods. The effects of stress also build over time. As the authors of one study noted, "A constant diet of even low-level stressful events has the potential to cause workers to experience gradually increasing levels of strain over time."[37] Mounting levels of stress can worsen our moods, as we experience more negative emotions. Although sometimes we thrive on it, most of us find stress usually takes a toll on our mood. In fact, when situations are overly emotionally charged and stressful, we have a natural response to disengage, to literally look away.[38]

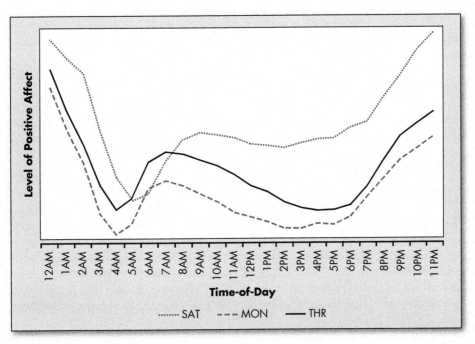

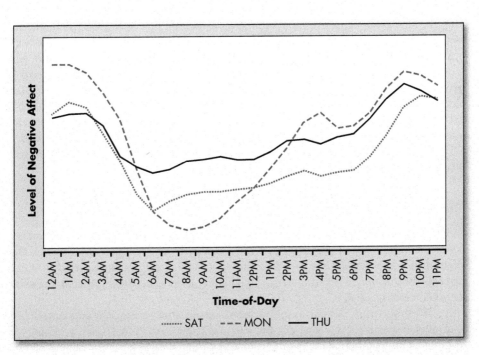

EXHIBIT 4-3
Time-of-Day
Effects on Mood
of U.S. Adults
as Rated From
Twitter Postings

Sources: Based
on S. A. Golder
and M. W. Macy,
"Diurnal and Sea-
sonal Mood Vary
with Work, Sleep,
and Daylength
Across Diverse Cul-
tures," *Science* 333
(2011), 1878–81;
A. Elejalde-Ruiz,
"Seize the Day,"
Chicago Tribune
(September 5,
2012), http://
articles.chicago
tribune.com/

Note: Based on
analysis of U.S.
Twitter post-
ings and coding
of words that
represent positive
feelings (delight,
enthusiasm) and
negative feelings
(fear, guilt). Lines
represent percent
of total words
in Twitter post
that convey these
moods.

Sleep

Maybe Jordan was extremely tired that morning due to a lack of sleep (and, hence, the need for coffee)? Apparently, the world could use more sleep. Adults report sleeping less than adults did a generation ago.[39] Data mined from millions of users of the "Sleep Cycle" application suggest that on average, sleep length and quality has diminished over the years.[40] Sleep quality affects moods and decision making, and increased fatigue puts workers at risk of disease, injury, and depression.[41] Poor or reduced sleep also leads to emotional changes and irritability, makes it difficult to control emotions, and can impair job satisfaction.[42] On the positive side, increased regular sleep can reduce the negative effects of fatigue and stress on employees.[43]

Exercise

To deal with the negative emotions surrounding your interaction with Jordan, have you considered exercising after work (maybe play some more Pokémon Go)? Perhaps you have heard that people should exercise to improve their mood. Does "sweat therapy" really work? It appears so. Research consistently shows exercise enhances people's positive moods and reduces perceptions of fatigue.[44] Exercise can also help protect against persistent negative moods and improve the ability to recover from negative experiences.[45]

Gender

You may think that Jordan's behavior may be attributable to gender differences in emotions. Indeed, many people believe women are more emotional than men, but is there any truth to this? Although there have been several reviews that have found differences in emotion display across genders that tend to increase with age,[46] these tend to be trivial or small, and likely reflect differences in upbringing and stereotypes, or even the way emotions are measured, rather than actual gender differences.[47] Unfortunately, these stereotypical perceptions of women as "emotional" and men as "angry" persist in the workplace, despite little evidence that they are true. For example, a Denver police commander filed a Civil Rights complaint against the city for gender discrimination, noting that the chief told her she was "emotional" and "immature," denying her a promotion to deputy chief.[48]

Let us put together what we have learned about emotions and moods with workplace coping strategies, beginning with emotional labor.

EMOTIONAL LABOR

If you have ever had a job in retail or in sales, or waited on tables in a restaurant, you know the importance of projecting a friendly demeanor and smiling. Even though there were days when you did not feel cheerful, you knew management expected you to be upbeat when dealing with customers, so you either tried to become upbeat and cheerful, or you otherwise faked it.

Emotional labor
An employee's organizationally desired emotions during interpersonal transactions at work.

When you work, you expend physical and mental labor or energy by putting your body and mind, respectively, into your job. But jobs also require **emotional labor**, an employee's expression of organizationally desired emotions during interpersonal transactions at work. Emotional labor is a key component of effective job performance.[49] We expect flight attendants to be cheerful, funeral directors to be sad, and doctors to be emotionally neutral.

Controlling Emotional Displays

The way we experience an emotion is obviously not always the same as the way we show it. To analyze emotional labor, we divide emotions into *felt* or *displayed emotions*.[50] **Felt emotions** are our actual emotions. In contrast, **displayed emotions** are those the organization requires workers to show and considers appropriate in each job. For instance, research suggests that in U.S. workplaces, it is expected that employees should typically display positive emotions like happiness and excitement, and suppress negative emotions like fear, anger, disgust, and contempt.[51]

Displaying fake emotions requires us to suppress real ones. **Surface acting** is hiding feelings and emotional expressions in response to display rules. A worker who smiles at a customer even when they do not feel like it is surface acting. **Deep acting** is trying to modify our true feelings based on display rules. Surface acting deals with *displayed* emotions, and deep acting deals with *felt* emotions.

Displaying emotions we do not really feel can be exhausting. Surface acting is associated with increased stress and decreased job satisfaction.[52] Daily surface acting can also lead to emotional exhaustion at home, work–family conflict, absenteeism, and insomnia.[53] On the other hand, deep acting has a positive relationship with job satisfaction (especially when the work is challenging), job performance, and even better customer treatment and tips.[54]

The disparity between employees having to project one emotion *while feeling another* is called **emotional dissonance**. Bottled-up feelings of frustration, anger, and resentment can lead to emotional exhaustion. Long-term emotional dissonance is a predictor for job burnout, declines in job performance, and lower job satisfaction.[55]

However, research from Germany and Australia suggests that employees who have a high capacity for self-control, who get a good night's sleep every day, and who have strong relationships with their customers or clients tend to be buffered to some degree from the negative side effects of emotional dissonance.[56]

Affective events theory, discussed next, describes how emotions and moods arise from the experience of work events, and how these in turn affect job satisfaction and job performance.

AFFECTIVE EVENTS THEORY

We have seen that emotions and moods are an important part of our personal and work lives. But how do they influence our job performance and satisfaction? **Affective events theory (AET)** proposes that employees react emotionally to things that happen to them at work, and this reaction influences their job performance and satisfaction.[57] For example, Lisamarie, a benefits administrator in North Carolina, began the in-vitro fertilization process after she was unable to conceive a child for six years and halfway through, found out her employer was dropping the benefit—she was "gutted," "lost," and "cried for a week," and undoubtedly did not feel satisfied with her job following such a blow.[58]

Work events trigger positive or negative emotional reactions, to which employees' personalities and moods predispose them to respond with greater or lesser intensity.[59] Furthermore, some events tend to be more impactful than others, on a day-to-day basis. For example, interpersonal mistreatment by customers of part-time workers accounted for nearly 50 percent of negative affective work events.[60]

Felt emotions
An individual's actual emotions.

Displayed emotions
Emotions that are organizationally required and considered appropriate in a given job.

Surface acting
Hiding one's feelings and forgoing emotional expressions in response to display rules.

Deep acting
Trying to modify one's true inner feelings based on display rules.

Emotional dissonance
Inconsistencies between the emotions people feel and the emotions they project.

Affective events theory (AET)
A model that suggests that workplace events cause emotional reactions on the part of employees, which then influence workplace attitudes and behaviors.

In sum, AET offers two important messages.[61] First, emotions provide valuable insights into how workplace events influence employee performance and satisfaction. Second, employees and managers should not ignore emotions or the events that cause them, even when they appear minor, because they accumulate. Emotional intelligence is another framework that may help us understand the impact of emotions on job performance.

EMOTIONAL INTELLIGENCE

As the CEO of an international talent company, Terrie Upshur-Lupberger was at a career pinnacle. So why was she resentful and unhappy? A close friend observed, "Terrie, you were out on the skinny branch—you know, the one that breaks easily in a strong wind. You were so busy and overwhelmed and out of touch with your own values, cares, and guiding beliefs that you failed to pay attention to the branch that was about to break."[62] According to Upshur-Lupberger, she had failed to notice that her moods constantly swung toward frustration and exhaustion. Her job satisfaction, productivity, relationships, and results suffered. Worst, she was too busy to realize the deficiencies until she was completely depleted. She said, "I learned that, as a leader, you either pay attention to and manage the moods (including your own) in the organization, or ... you ignore them and pay the price."[63] Upshur-Lupberger learned the value of emotional intelligence.

Employers value emotional intelligence (EI). In one CareerBuilder survey of over 2,500 hiring managers and HR professionals, 59 percent said they would not hire someone with high cognitive ability (e.g., IQ), but low EI, and 75 percent said they would be more likely to promote a high EI candidate over one with high IQ.[64] In another study that tracked college students from graduation to over ten years after entering the workforce, EI predicted how high the their salary was ten years later, as well as whether the alumni had a mentor.[65]

**Emotional
intelligence (EI)**
The ability to detect
and to manage
emotional cues and
information.

Emotional intelligence (EI) is a person's ability to: (1) perceive emotions in oneself and others; (2) understand the meaning of these emotions; and (3) regulate his or her own emotions accordingly, as shown in Exhibit 4-4.[66] When asked why they value emotional intelligence over cognitive ability, the managers in the Career Builder study noted that persons with high EI are more in tune with their emotions, so they can stay calms under pressure, resolve conflict more effectively, be empathetic with coworkers and team members, and effectively regulate their emotions.[67]

**EXHIBIT 4-4
A Cascading
Model of
Emotional
Intelligence**

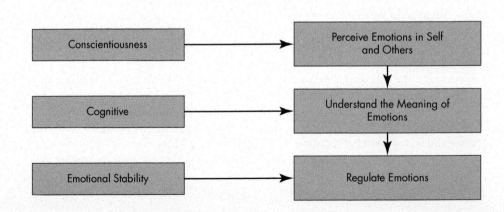

Several studies suggest that EI plays an important role in predicting job attitudes and facilitating academic and job performance, although the survey items are often strikingly similar to other items from personality, intelligence, and self-perception tests.[68] Other reviews suggest that EI is related to improving teamwork effectiveness, organizational citizenship behaviors (OCBs; see Chapter 1: What Is Organizational Behavior?), and career decision making, as well as reducing counterproductive work behaviors (CWBs; see Chapter 1: What Is Organizational Behavior?).[69] South Korean managers with high EI tend to have better sales figures than those with low EI because they were able to create more cohesive stores and improved sales-directed behavior.[70]

For a leadership perspective, one research study examined eleven U.S. presidents—from Franklin Roosevelt to Bill Clinton—and evaluated them on six qualities: communication, organization, political skill, vision, cognitive style, and emotional intelligence. The key quality that differentiated the successful (such as Roosevelt, Kennedy, and Reagan) from the unsuccessful (such as Johnson, Carter, and Nixon) was emotional intelligence.[71] Furthermore, studies of popularity suggest that it is EI, not narcissism, that predicts long-term popularity.[72] As such, leaders and employees alike who are high on EI tend to be more popular and successful because they are able to understand and manage their own, and others', emotions.

However, it appears as if there are limits to the degree to which EI can be helpful in the workplace. For example, one study of Dutch administrative assistants suggests that EI that is focused on the self (e.g., self-understanding) decreases the experience of stress, but with physiological costs, while other-focused EI (e.g., accurately perceiving emotions in others) only weakly explained task performance.[73] This suggests that EI may be costly and not as effective as we think, especially in emotionally demanding contexts. Furthermore, some research suggests that EI might even be related to how well people can fake tests (because they understand what desirable answers are on tests).[74] According to this research, if you use a personality test to screen candidates for a job, those with high EI may be better at faking it.

Although the field is progressing in its understanding of EI, many questions have not been answered.[75] One relates to a better understanding of EI. For example, we need to be precise when we talk about EI—are we referring to EI in general? Or to regulating emotions, understanding emotions, or perceiving emotions specifically? A second question is about the reliability of EI testing and how best to measure emotional intelligence. Several advancements have been made in this area, for example, by having test takers recognize emotions from video clips, and by having them respond with what they would do in emotionally charged situations.[76] A third question is one of the most important for managers in organizations: Can EI be learned? Several reviews of dozens of studies suggest that EI can be trained and developed as a skill—although paradoxically, the people who need it the most are the ones least likely to actually seek it out![77]

All questions aside, EI is wildly popular among consulting firms and in the popular press, and it has accumulated some support in the research literature. Love it or hate it, one thing is for sure—EI is here to stay. So might be our next topic, emotion regulation, which is increasingly studied as an independent concept.[78]

EMOTION REGULATION

Have you ever tried to cheer yourself up when you were feeling down, or calm yourself when you were feeling angry? If so, you have engaged in **emotion regulation**. The central idea behind emotion regulation is to identify and modify the emotions you feel.

Emotion regulation
The process of identifying and modifying felt emotions.

Recent research suggests that emotion regulation is a strong predictor of task performance for some jobs and for OCB.[79]

Emotion Regulation Influences and Outcomes

As you might suspect, not everyone is equally good at regulating emotions.[80] Individuals who are higher in the personality trait of neuroticism (see the chapter on personality and values) have more trouble doing so and often find their moods are beyond their ability to control. Individuals who have lower levels of self-esteem are also less likely to try to improve their moods, perhaps because they are less likely than others to feel they deserve to be in a good mood.[81] Finally, university seniors who are more focused on mastering the job search process were better able to regulate their emotions, and engaged in more job search behaviors as a result.[82]

The workplace environment influences an individual's tendency to employ emotion regulation. In general, diversity in work groups increases the likelihood that you will regulate your emotions. For example, younger employees are likely to regulate their emotions when their work groups include older members.[83] Racial diversity also has an effect. If diversity is low, the minority may engage in emotion regulation, perhaps to "fit in" with the majority race as much as possible; if diversity is high and many different races are represented, the majority race will employ emotion regulation, perhaps to integrate themselves with the whole group.[84] These findings suggest a beneficial outcome of diversity—it may cause us to regulate our emotions more consciously and effectively.

While regulating your emotions might seem beneficial, research suggests there may be a downside to trying to change the way you feel. Changing your emotions takes effort, and as we noted when discussing emotional labor, this effort can be exhausting. Sometimes attempts to change an emotion actually make the emotion stronger; for example, trying to talk yourself out of being afraid can make you focus more on what scares you, which makes you more afraid.[85] From another perspective, research suggests that avoiding negative emotional experiences is less likely to lead to positive moods than does seeking out positive emotional experiences.[86] For example, you are more likely to experience a positive mood if you have a pleasant conversation with a friend than if you avoid an unpleasant conversation with a hostile coworker.

Interestingly, some positions involve more customer incivility and mistreatment directed toward employees than do others—positions with higher levels of customer mistreatment (e.g., call center employees) necessitate more employee emotion regulation and, as a result, can lead to higher levels of employee exhaustion.[87] Do you want to make a customer service employee's life easier? Be nice to them! One study of supermarket checkout operators found that smiling at checkout staff and engaging in short conversations reduces the staff members' emotion regulation needs, and as such reduces their emotional exhaustion and improves their performance.[88]

Emotion Regulation Techniques

Researchers of emotion regulation often study the strategies people employ to change their emotions. One related technique of emotion regulation is *emotional suppression*, literally suppressing—blocking or ignoring—initial emotional responses to situations. This response seems to facilitate practical thinking in the short term, but is generally ineffective when compared with expressing ones' emotions.[89] However, it appears to be helpful only when a strongly negative event would elicit a distressed emotional reaction during a crisis.[90] For example, a portfolio manager might suppress an emotional reaction to a sudden drop in the value of a stock and therefore be able to clearly decide how to plan. *Cognitive reappraisal*, or reframing our outlook on an emotional situation, is one way to regulate emotions effectively.[91] Cognitive reappraisal ability seems to be most helpful to individuals in situations where they cannot control the sources of stress.[92] For example, if you lost your job, reframing it as an opportunity to try the new career you always dreamed about may help you regulate your emotions. Another technique with potential for emotion regulation is *social sharing*, or venting. Research shows that the open expression of emotions can help individuals to regulate their emotions as opposed to keeping emotions "bottled up." Social sharing can reduce anger reactions when people can talk about the facts of a bad situation, their feelings about the situation, or any positive aspects of the situation.[93] For example, venting to your coworker after work about the heated exchange with your manager in the kitchen may help you express your feelings and understand the situation a little better.

While there is much promise in emotion regulation techniques, the best route to a positive workplace is to recruit positive-minded individuals and train employees and leaders alike to manage their moods, job attitudes, and performance.[94] The best leaders manage emotions as much as they do tasks and activities. The best employees can use their knowledge of emotion regulation to decide when to speak up and how to express themselves effectively.[95] The key is to be adaptive: try to be aware of your emotions and use the regulation techniques best suited for the situation.[96]

Now that we have studied the role of emotions and moods in OB, let us consider the opportunities for more specific applications that our understanding provides.

OB APPLICATIONS OF EMOTIONS AND MOODS

Our understanding of emotions and moods can affect many aspects of OB. Let us think through some of them.

Selection

One implication from the evidence on EI is that employers should consider it a factor in hiring employees, especially for jobs that demand a high degree of social interaction. In fact, more employers *are* starting to use EI measures to hire people. For example, a study of U.S. Air Force recruiters showed that top-performing recruiters exhibited high levels of EI. Using these findings, the Air Force revamped its selection criteria. A follow-up investigation found hires who had high EI scores became 2.6 times more successful than those with lower scores. A second implication is that applicant emotions are sometimes, knowingly or not, used in selection decisions. As an example, Hong Kong Chinese applicants are more likely to try to appear calm, rather than excited, during the selection process and Hong Kong Chinese employers were more likely to hire calm applicants.[97]

Decision Making

Moods and emotions have effects on decision making that employees and managers should understand. Positive emotions and moods seem to help people make sound decisions. Positive emotions also enhance problem-solving skills, so positive people find better solutions.[98]

OB researchers continue to debate the role of negative emotions and moods in decision making. One recent study suggested that people who are saddened by events may make the same decisions as before, while people who are angered by events might make stronger (though not necessarily better) choices than before.[99] Another study found that participants made choices reflecting more original thinking when in a negative mood.[100] Still other research indicated that individuals in a negative mood may take higher risks than when in a positive mood.[101] Taken together, these and other studies suggest negative (and positive) emotions impact decision making, but that there are other variables that require further research.[102]

Creativity

As we see throughout this text, one goal of leadership is to maximize employee productivity through creativity. Creativity is influenced by emotions and moods, but there are two schools of thought on the relationship. Much research suggests that people in good moods tend to be more creative than people in bad moods.[103] People in good moods produce more ideas and more options, and others find their ideas original.[104] It seems that people experiencing positive moods or emotions are more flexible and open in their thinking, which may explain why they are more creative.[105] Some researchers, however, do not believe a positive mood makes people more creative. They argue that, when people are in positive moods, they may relax ("If I'm in a good mood, things must be going okay, and I don't need to think of new ideas") and not engage in the critical thinking necessary for some forms of creativity.[106] Individuals who worry more may perform better on creative tasks than those who worry less.

Motivation

Several studies have highlighted the importance of moods and emotions on motivation. Giving people performance feedback—whether real or fake—influences their mood, which then influences their motivation.[107] A cycle can be created in which positive moods cause people to be more creative, leading to positive feedback from those observing their work. The feedback further reinforces the positive mood, which makes people perform even better, and so on. Overall, the findings suggest a manager may enhance employee motivation—and performance—by encouraging good moods.

Leadership

Research indicates that putting people in a good mood makes good sense. Leaders who focus on inspirational goals generate greater optimism, cooperation, and enthusiasm in employees, leading to more positive social interactions with coworkers and customers.[108] A study with Taiwanese military participants indicated that by sharing emotions, transformational leaders inspire positive emotions in their followers that lead to higher task performance.[109]

Leaders are perceived as more effective when they share positive emotions, and followers are more creative in a positive emotional environment. What about when leaders are sad? Research found that leader displays of sadness increased the analytic performance of followers, perhaps because followers attended more closely to tasks to help the leaders.[110] Another interesting study examined over 300 halftime locker room speeches from high school and college basketball teams, finding that leaders' sharing of negative emotions (e.g., anger) can help improve team performance. However, these emotions had to be at the right level of intensity—too negative and intense, and the display would backfire.[111]

Customer Service

Workers' emotional states influence the level of customer service they give, which in turn influences levels of repeat business and customer satisfaction.[112] This result is primarily due to **emotional contagion**—the "catching" of emotions from others.[113] When someone at work experiences positive emotions and laughs and smiles at you, like when they are sending you a funny meme about retail life, you tend to respond positively. Of course, the opposite is true as well.

> **Emotional contagion**
> The process by which people's emotions are caused by the emotions of others.

Studies indicate a matching effect between employee and customer emotions. In the employee-to-customer direction, research finds that customers who catch the positive moods or emotions of employees shop longer. In the other direction, when an employee feels unfairly treated by a customer, it is harder for the employee to display the positive emotions the organization expects.[114] High-quality customer service places demands on employees because it often puts them in a state of emotional dissonance, which can be damaging to the employee and the organization. Managers can interrupt negative contagion by fostering positive moods.

Work–Life Satisfaction

Ever hear the advice "Never take your work home with you," meaning you should forget about work once you go home? That is easier said than done. The good news is that it appears a positive mood at work can spill over to your off-work hours, and a negative mood at work can be restored to a positive mood after a break. Several studies have shown people who had a good day at work tend to be in a better mood at home that evening, and vice versa.[115] Other research has found that although people do emotionally take their work home with them, by the next day the effect is usually gone.[116] The bad news is that the moods of the people in your household may affect yours. As you might expect, one study found if one member of a couple was in a negative mood during the workday, the negative mood spilled over to the spouse at night.[117]

Deviant Workplace Behaviors

Anyone who has spent much time in an organization realizes people can behave in ways that violate established norms and threaten the organization, its members, or both.[118] As we saw in the chapter on attitudes and job satisfaction, these CWBs can be traced to negative emotions and can take many forms. People who feel negative emotions are more likely than others to engage in short-term deviant behavior at work, such as gossiping or surfing the Internet,[119] though negative emotions can also lead to more serious forms of CWB.

For instance, envy is an emotion that occurs when you resent someone for having something you do not have but strongly desire—such as a better work assignment, larger office, or higher salary. It can lead to malicious deviant behaviors. An envious employee could undermine other employees and take all the credit for things others accomplished. Angry people look for other people to blame for their bad mood, interpret other people's behavior as hostile, and have trouble considering others' points of view.[120] It's not hard to see how these thought processes can lead directly to verbal or physical aggression.

One study in Pakistan found that anger correlated with more aggressive CWBs such as abuse against others and production deviance, while sadness did not. Interestingly, neither anger nor sadness predicted workplace deviance, which suggests that managers need to take employee expressions of anger seriously; employees may stay with an organization and continue to act aggressively toward others.[121] Once aggression starts, it is likely that other people will become angry and aggressive, so the stage is set for a serious escalation of negative behavior. Managers therefore need to stay connected with their employees to gauge emotions and emotional intensity levels.

Safety and Injury at Work

Research relating negative affectivity to increased injuries at work suggests employers might improve health and safety (and reduce costs) by ensuring workers are not engaged in potentially dangerous activities when they are in a bad mood. Bad moods can contribute to injury at work in several ways.[122] Individuals in negative moods tend to be more anxious, which can make them less able to cope effectively with hazards. A person who is always fearful will be more pessimistic about the effectiveness of safety precautions because she feels she will just get hurt anyway, or she might panic or freeze up when confronted with a threatening situation. Negative moods also make people more distractable, and distractions can obviously lead to careless behaviors.

Selecting positive team members can contribute toward a positive work environment because positive moods transmit from team member to team member. One study of 130 leaders and their followers found that leaders who are charismatic transfer their positive emotions to their followers through a contagion effect.[123] It makes sense, then, to choose team members predisposed to positive moods.

SUMMARY

Emotions and moods are similar in that both are affective in nature. But they are also different—moods are more general and less contextual than emotions. The time of day, stressful events, and sleep patterns are some of the many factors that influence emotions and moods. OB research on emotional labor, affective events theory, emotional intelligence, and emotional regulation helps us understand how people deal with emotions. Emotions and moods have proven relevant for virtually every OB topic we study, with implications for managerial practices.

IMPLICATIONS FOR MANAGERS

- Recognize that emotions are a natural part of the workplace and good management does not mean creating an emotion-free environment.
- To foster effective decision making, creativity, and motivation in employees, model positive emotions and moods as much as is authentically possible.
- Provide positive feedback to increase the positivity of employees. Of course, it also helps to hire people who are predisposed to positive moods.
- In the service sector, encourage positive displays of emotion, which make customers feel more positive and thus improve customer service interactions and negotiations.
- Understand the role of emotions and moods to significantly improve your ability to explain and predict your coworkers' and others' behavior.

5

Personality and Values

LEARNING OBJECTIVES

After studying this chapter, you should be able to:

5.1 Describe the differences between person–job fit and person–organization fit.

5.2 Describe personality, the way it is measured, and the factors that shape it.

5.3 Describe the strengths and weaknesses of the Myers–Briggs Type Indicator (MBTI) personality framework, the Big Five Model, and the Dark Triad.

5.4 Discuss how the concepts of core self-evaluation (CSE), self-monitoring, and proactive personality contribute to the understanding of personality.

5.5 Describe how the situation affects whether personality predicts behavior.

5.6 Contrast terminal and instrumental values.

5.7 Compare Hofstede's five value dimensions and the GLOBE framework.

LINKING INDIVIDUALS TO THE WORKPLACE

Years ago, organizations were concerned with personality in order to match individuals to specific jobs. That concern has expanded to include how well the individual's personality *and* values (described in more detail later in the chapter) match the organization. Why? Because managers today are less interested in an applicant's ability to perform a *specific* job than with the ability to further the organization's mission and to retain the employee (rather than leaving for another organization). For example, Twegos, a Belgian firm that provides a person–organization value fit assessment, assesses truck driver fit with their carrier, trainers, dispatchers, and managers in order to increase engagement and reduce turnover.[1] Still, one of the first types of fit managers look for is person–job fit.

Person–job fit theory
A theory that identifies six personality types and proposes that the fit between personality type and occupational environment determines satisfaction and turnover.

Person–Job Fit

The effort to match job requirements with personality characteristics is described by John Holland's **person–job fit theory**, one of the most supported OB theories in use internationally.[2] The Vocational Preference Inventory questionnaire contains 160 occupational titles. Respondents indicate which they like or dislike, and their answers form occupation interest profiles. Holland presented six personalities and proposed that satisfaction and the propensity to leave a position depend on how well individuals match their interests to a job. Exhibit 5-1 describes the six types, their personality characteristics, and examples of congruent occupations for each. Notably, this theory tends to be supported, with person–job fit strongly predicting job satisfaction, organizational commitment, and intentions to quit.[3]

There are cultural implications for person–job fit that speak to workers' expectations that jobs will be tailored to them. In individualistic countries where workers expect to be heard and respected by management, increasing person–job fit by tailoring the job to the person increases the individual's job satisfaction. However, in collectivistic countries, person–job fit is a weaker predictor of job satisfaction[4] because people do not expect to have jobs tailored to them, so they value person–job fit efforts less. Therefore, managers in collectivistic cultures should not violate cultural norms by designing jobs for individuals; rather, they should seek people who will likely thrive in jobs that have already been structured.[5]

Person–Organization Fit

Person–organization fit
A theory that people are attracted to and selected by organizations that match their values and leave when there is no compatibility.

Person–organization fit essentially means that people are attracted to and selected by organizations that match their values, and they leave organizations that are not compatible with their personalities.[6] Using the Big Five terminology (discussed later in the next section), for instance, we could expect that extraverts fit well with aggressive and team-oriented cultures; people high on agreeableness match better with a supportive organizational climate; and highly open people fit better in organizations that emphasize innovation rather than standardization.[7] Following these guidelines when hiring should yield employees who fit better with the organization's culture, which should, in turn, result in higher employee satisfaction and reduced turnover.[8] Research on person–organization fit has also looked at whether people's values match the organization's culture. A match predicts job satisfaction, commitment to the organization, and low turnover.[9] Interestingly, new research suggests that people tend to care more about how well an organization's values would be preferred by the typical person, rather than one's own idiosyncratic preferences for values in an organization.[10]

EXHIBIT 5-1
Holland's Typology of Personality and Congruent Occupations

Type	Personality Characteristics	Congruent Occupations
Realistic: Prefers physical activities that require skill, strength, and coordination	Shy, genuine, persistent, stable, conforming, practical	Mechanic, drill press operator, assembly-line worker, farmer
Investigative: Prefers activities that involve thinking, organizing, and understanding	Analytical, original, curious, independent	Biologist, economist, mathematician, news reporter
Artistic: Prefers ambiguous and unsystematic activities that allow creative expression	Imaginative, disorderly, idealistic, emotional, impractical	Painter, musician, writer, interior decorator
Social: Prefers activities that involve helping and developing others	Sociable, friendly, cooperative, understanding	Social worker, teacher, counselor, clinical psychologist
Conventional: Prefers rule-regulated, orderly, and unambiguous activities	Conforming, efficient, practical, unimaginative, inflexible	Accountant, corporate manager, bank teller, file clerk
Enterprising: Prefers verbal activities in which there are opportunities to influence others and attain power	Self-confident, ambitious, energetic, domineering	Lawyer, real estate agent, public relations specialist, small business manager

In pursuit of fit, it is more important than ever for organizations to manage their image online, since job seekers view company websites as part of their pre-application process.[11] Applicants want to see a user-friendly website that provides information about company philosophies and policies. The website is so important to the development of perceived person–organization fit that improvements to its style (usability) and substance (policies) can lead to more applicants.[12]

Other Dimensions of Fit

Although person–job fit and person–organization fit are considered the most salient dimensions for workplace outcomes, other avenues of fit are worth examining. These include *person–group fit* and *person–supervisor fit*.[13] Person–group fit is important in team settings, where the dynamics of team interactions significantly affect work outcomes. Person–supervisor fit has become an important area of research since poor fit in this dimension can lead to lower job satisfaction and reduced performance. All dimensions of fit are sometimes broadly referred to as person–environment fit.

Each dimension can predict work attitudes, which are partially based on culture. A recent meta-analysis of person–environment fit in East Asia, Europe, and North America suggested the dimensions of person–organization and person–job fit are the strongest predictors of positive work attitudes and performance in North America. These dimensions are important to a lesser degree in Europe, and they are least important in East Asia.[14]

PERSONALITY

The needs of a business are broad and varied. People are needed to keep track of accounting and finance, to ensure that the right employees are hired and that training needs are met, to market and sell the products or services the company provides, to research and develop better ways of doing things, and so on. Consider this: if every employee you hired was the same and had identical personalities, would they all be equally effective at meeting these needs?[15] Before we can answer this question, we need to address a more basic one: What is personality?

What Is Personality?

When we speak of someone's personality, we use many adjectives to describe how they act and seem to think; in fact, in one study, research participants used 624 distinct adjectives to describe people they knew.[16] Thinking of one of your coworkers, you might think they are "fun," "outgoing," "nice," "hard-working"; or maybe you think they are "lazy," "aloof," "closed-minded," or "nosy." In organizational behavior (OB) we organize these characteristics into overall traits describing a person's personality.

DEFINING PERSONALITY For our purposes, think of **personality** as the sum of ways in which an individual reacts to and interacts with the world around them. We most often describe personality in terms of the measurable traits a person exhibits.

Early work on personality tried to identify and label all the enduring characteristics, such as the adjectives listed above, that describe an individual's behavior. When someone exhibits these characteristics across many situations and when they are relatively enduring over time, we call them **personality traits**.[17]

Personality
The sum of ways in which an individual reacts to and interacts with the world around them.

Personality traits
Enduring characteristics that describe an individual's behavior.

Research indicates our culture influences the way we describe ourselves and others. Although many personality traits do tend to emerge across cultures (see the Five-Factor Model, later in this chapter),[18] it appears that some traits do not emerge in certain cultures—moreover, certain unique personality traits might emerge.[19] For instance, research in Chinese contexts has uncovered unique traits that focus on interpersonal relatedness, as well as a relative absence of openness traits.[20] As such, when interacting with people from other cultures, it is imperative to keep in mind that there may be cultural differences, *even when it comes to personalities.*

MEASURING PERSONALITY   Personality assessments have been increasingly used in diverse organizational settings. In fact, 89 of the Fortune 100 companies and 57 percent of all large U.S. companies use them,[21] including Xerox, McDonald's, and Lowe's.[22] Schools such as DePaul University have also begun to use personality tests in their admissions process.[23] Personality tests are useful in hiring decisions and help managers forecast who is best for a job.[24]

The most common means of measuring personality is through self-report surveys in which individuals evaluate themselves on a series of factors such as "I worry a lot about the future."[25] In general, when people know their personality scores are going to be used for hiring decisions, they rate themselves much higher on desirable traits (e.g., conscientiousness) than if they are taking the test to learn more about themselves.[26] Another problem is accuracy;[27] for instance, personality ratings from someone who knows you well (e.g., someone you have worked with for five years) might be more accurate than ratings given by a relative stranger to you.[28]

Observer-ratings surveys provide an independent assessment of personality. Here, a coworker or another observer does the rating. Though the results of self-reports and observer-ratings surveys are strongly correlated, research suggests observer-ratings surveys predict job success more than self-ratings alone.[29] However, each can tell us something unique about an individual's behavior, so a combination of self-reports and observer-ratings predicts performance better than any one type of information. What makes for a good observer? Emotion recognition (see the chapter on emotions and moods) may play a role here: One study found that accuracy in judging negative versus positive emotional displays plays a role in how accurately observers judge emotional stability versus extraversion, respectively.[30]

Modern advancements in technology and artificial intelligence (e.g., machine learning, see Chapter 1: What Is Organizational Behavior?) have also improved the ability to score personality tests, reduce faking, and adaptively present items for more accurate personality assessment. For example, machine learning has been used for selecting the most informative questions for traditional personality tests,[31] for detecting people who fake personality tests,[32] and even for scoring personal essays on job applications![33]

PERSONALITY FRAMEWORKS

Throughout history, people have sought to understand what makes individuals behave in different ways. Many of our behaviors stem from our personalities, so understanding the components of personality helps us predict behavior. For example, an employee who is low on tact as a personality trait (a characteristic of "agreeableness") may be more likely to be rude or direct at inappropriate times, which can, in turn, upset or anger coworkers.[34] Theoretical frameworks and assessment tools, discussed next, help us categorize and study these dimensions of personality.

The Myers–Briggs Type Indicator

The **Myers–Briggs Type Indicator (MBTI)** is the most widely used personality-assessment instrument in the world.[35] It is a 100-question personality test that asks people how they usually feel or act in situations. Respondents are classified as extraverted or introverted (E or I), sensing or intuitive (S or N), thinking or feeling (T or F), and judging or perceiving (J or P):

- **Extraverted (E) versus Introverted (I).** Extraverted individuals are outgoing, sociable, and assertive. Introverts are quiet and shy.
- **Sensing (S) versus Intuitive (N).** Sensing types are practical and prefer routine and order, and they focus on details. Intuitives rely on unconscious processes and look at the "big picture."
- **Thinking (T) versus Feeling (F).** Thinking types use reason and logic to handle problems. Feeling types rely on their personal values and emotions.
- **Judging (J) versus Perceiving (P).** Judging types want control and prefer order and structure. Perceiving types are flexible and spontaneous.

The MBTI describes personality by identifying one trait (e.g., extraversion) from each of the four pairs (e.g., extraversion–introversion) and combining them to form a personality type. For example, Introverted/Intuitive/Thinking/Judging people (INTJs) are visionaries with original minds and great drive. They are skeptical, critical, independent, determined, and often stubborn.

There are several potential problems with the use of the MBTI.[36] First, evidence is mixed about its validity as a measure of personality; however, most of the evidence is against it.[37] As Professor Dan Ariely sardonically noted about MBTI results, "Next time, just look at the horoscope. It is just as valid and takes less time."[38] Second, the MBTI forces a person into one type or another; that is, you are either introverted or extraverted. There is no in-between. Third, when people retake the assessment, they often receive different results. An additional problem is in the difficulty of interpretation. There are levels of importance for each of the MBTI facets, and separate meanings for certain combinations of facets, all of which require trained interpretation that can leave room for error. Finally, results from the MBTI tend to be unrelated to job performance. Because results tend to be unrelated to job performance, managers should consider using the Big Five Personality Model, discussed next, as the personality selection test for job candidates instead.

The Big Five Personality Model

The MBTI may lack strong supporting evidence, but an impressive body of research supports the **Big Five Model**, which proposes that five basic dimensions encompass most of the differences in human personality.[39] Test scores of these traits do a very good job of predicting how people behave in a variety of real-life situations[40] and remain relatively stable for an individual over time, with some daily variations.[41] These are the Big Five factors:

- **Conscientiousness.** The **conscientiousness** dimension is a measure of personal consistency and reliability. A highly conscientious person is responsible, organized, dependable, and persistent. Those who score low on this dimension are easily distracted, disorganized, and unreliable.

Myers–Briggs Type Indicator (MBTI)
A personality test that taps four characteristics and classifies people into 1 of 16 personality types.

Big Five Model
A personality model that proposes five basic dimensions encompass most of the differences in human personality.

Conscientiousness
A personality dimension that describes someone who is responsible, dependable, persistent, and organized.

Emotional stability
A personality dimension that characterizes someone as calm, self-confident, and secure (positive) versus nervous, anxious, and insecure (negative).

Extraversion
A personality dimension describing someone who is sociable, gregarious, and assertive.

Openness to experience
A personality dimension that characterizes someone in terms of imagination, artistic sensitivity, and curiosity.

Agreeableness
A personality dimension that describes someone who is good natured, cooperative, and trusting.

- **Emotional stability.** The **emotional stability** dimension taps a person's ability to withstand stress. People with emotional stability tend to be calm, self-confident, and secure. High scorers are more likely to be positive, optimistic, and experience fewer negative emotions (e.g., nervousness, anxiety, insecurity); they are generally happier than low scorers.
- **Extraversion.** The **extraversion** dimension captures our relational approach toward the social world. Extraverts tend to be gregarious, assertive, and sociable. They experience more positive emotions than do introverts, and they more freely express these feelings. On the other hand, introverts (low extraversion) tend to be more thoughtful, reserved, timid, and quiet.
- **Openness to experience.** The **openness to experience** dimension addresses the range of a person's interests and their fascination with novelty. Open people are creative, curious, and artistically sensitive. Those at the low end of the category are conventional and find comfort in the familiar.
- **Agreeableness.** The **agreeableness** dimension refers to an individual's propensity to defer to others. Agreeable people are cooperative, warm, and trusting. You might expect agreeable people to be happier than disagreeable people. They are, but only slightly. When people choose organizational team members, agreeable individuals are usually their first choice. In contrast, people who score low on agreeableness can be cold and antagonistic.

How Do the Big Five Traits Predict Behavior at Work?

There are many relationships between the Big Five personality dimensions and job performance,[42] and we are learning more about them every day. Let us explore one trait at a time, beginning with the strongest predictor of job performance—conscientiousness.

CONSCIENTIOUSNESS AT WORK Researchers have stated, "Personal attributes related to conscientiousness and agreeableness are important for success across many jobs, spanning across low to high levels of job complexity, training, and experience."[43] Employees who score higher in conscientiousness develop higher levels of job knowledge, probably because highly conscientious people learn more (conscientiousness may be related to grade point average [GPA]),[44] and these levels correspond with higher levels of job performance and organizational citizenship behavior (OCB; see Chapter 1: What Is Organizational Behavior?).[45] Conscientious employees are also less likely to engage in counterproductive work behaviors CWB (see the chapter on attitudes and job satisfaction).[46]

Conscientiousness is the best overall predictor of job performance. However, the other Big Five traits are also related to aspects of performance and have other implications for work and for life. Exhibit 5-2 summarizes these other relations.

EMOTIONAL STABILITY AT WORK Of the Big Five traits, emotional stability is most strongly related to life satisfaction and job satisfaction, as well as to reduced burnout and intentions to quit.[47] People with high emotional stability can adapt to unexpected or changing demands in the workplace.[48] At the other end of the spectrum, individuals with low emotional stability, who are unable to cope with these demands, may experience burnout.[49] These people also tend to experience work–family conflict, which can affect

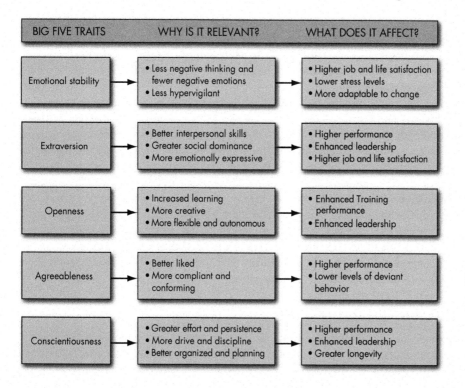

EXHIBIT 5-2
**Model of How
Big Five Traits
Influence OB
Criteria**

work outcomes.[50] Given these straining effects, employees low on emotional stability are more likely to engage in CWBs, less likely to engage in OCDs, and less likely to be motivated at work.[51]

EXTRAVERSION AT WORK   People with extraverted personality traits tend to perform well in jobs that require interpersonal interaction. Extraversion is a relatively strong predictor of leadership emergence and behaviors in groups.[52] Extraverts also experience generally high job satisfaction and reduced burnout.[53] However, extraverts can appear to be dominating, which can be disadvantageous for jobs that do not require frequent social interaction.[54]

OPENNESS AT WORK   Open people tend to be creative and innovative.[55] Open people are more likely to be effective leaders and more comfortable with ambiguity—they cope better with organizational change and are more adaptable.[56] While openness is not related to initial performance on a job, individuals higher in openness are less susceptible to a decline in performance over a longer time period.[57] Open people also experience less work–family conflict.[58]

AGREEABLENESS AT WORK   Agreeable individuals tend to do better in interpersonally oriented jobs such as customer service. They experience less work–family conflict and are less susceptible to turnover.[59] They also engage in a high degree of OCBs and a low degree of CWBs.[60] Lastly, agreeableness is associated with lower levels of career success (especially earnings), perhaps because highly agreeable people consider themselves less marketable and are less willing to assert themselves.[61]

Interestingly, agreeableness might be more important for organizational commitment (see the chapter on attitudes and job satisfaction) in some cultures, more than others. One review of research on nearly 20,000 employees worldwide found that agreeableness was more predictive of organizational commitment in collectivistic cultures, rather than individualistic cultures (see later in this chapter for more information on collectivistic versus individualistic cultures).[62] Furthermore, given that more companies are sending their employees on global assignments, it is important to understand which personality traits are most important for adjusting to living in different cultures. Research suggests that extraversion is the most important trait predicting adjustment.[63] A study on 2,500 international exchange students worldwide corroborated this, with extraversion significantly reducing the stress of being in a new culture and improving cultural adaptation.[64]

Research indicates that the Big Five traits have the most verifiable links to important organizational outcomes, but they are not the only traits a person exhibits, nor are they the only ones with OB implications. Let us discuss some other traits, known collectively as the Dark Triad.

The Dark Triad

Dark Triad
A constellation of negative personality traits consisting of Machiavellianism, narcissism, and psychopathy.

Outside of the Big Five framework, researchers have identified three other socially *undesirable* traits, which we all have in varying degrees: Machiavellianism, narcissism, and psychopathy. Owing to their negative nature, researchers have labeled these the **Dark Triad**—though they do not always occur together.[65] In reviewing these traits, you might remember coworkers or bosses you have had previously that might be characterized by these traits, and the consequences these traits had in your workplace. These traits can literally harm an organization's financial performance. For example, one study of 101 hedge fund managers found that those who were narcissistic and psychopathic tended to have worse financial performance than their peers.[66] These traits might not be far removed as you think; after all, "not all psychopaths are in prison—some are in the board room."[67]

The Dark Triad may sound sinister, but these traits are not clinical pathologies. They might be expressed particularly strongly when an individual is under stress and unable to moderate any inappropriate responses. Sustained high levels of dark personality traits can cause individuals to derail their careers and personal lives.[68]

MACHIAVELLIANISM Aiden is a bank manager in Shanghai. Aiden has received three promotions in the past four years and makes no apologies for using aggressive tactics. "I do whatever I have to do to get ahead," Aiden says. Aiden would be described as Machiavellian.

Machiavellianism
The degree to which an individual is pragmatic, maintains emotional distance, and believes that ends can justify means.

The personality characteristic of **Machiavellianism** (often abbreviated *Mach*) is named after Niccolo Machiavelli, who wrote in the sixteenth century on how to gain and use power. An individual high in Machiavellianism is pragmatic, maintains emotional distance, and believes that ends can justify means. "If it works, use it" is consistent with a high-Mach perspective. High Machs manipulate more, win more, are persuaded less by others, but persuade others more than do low Machs.[69] They are more likely to act aggressively and engage in CWBs as well. Surprisingly, Machiavellianism does not significantly predict overall job performance.[70] High-Mach employees, by manipulating others to their advantage, win in the short term at a job, but lose those gains in the long term because they are not well liked.

NARCISSISM Avery likes to be the center of attention. Avery thinks of Avery as having a very large number of talents ("See, even 'a very' can be found in my name!" Avery says) and as having a grandiose and profound influence on others and is very sensitive to criticism. Avery is a narcissist. The trait is named for the Greek myth of Narcissus, a youth so vain and proud he fell in love with his own image. **Narcissism** describes a person who has a grandiose sense of self-importance, requires excessive admiration, and is arrogant. Narcissists often have fantasies of grand success, a tendency to exploit situations and people, a sense of entitlement, and a lack of empathy.[71] However, narcissists can be hypersensitive and fragile people.[72]

While narcissism seems to have little relationship to job effectiveness or OCB,[73] it is one of the largest predictors of increased CWB in individualistic cultures—but not in collectivist cultures that discourage self-promotion.[74] Narcissists commonly think they are overqualified for their positions.[75] When they receive feedback about their performance, they often tune out information that conflicts with their positive self-perception, but they will work harder if rewards are offered.[76] Narcissist managers are even selective about the relationships they form with their subordinates, often prioritizing those who give positive, noncritical feedback (ultimately, reducing the voice of all subordinates).[77] Research using data compiled over one hundred years has shown that narcissistic CEOs of baseball organizations generate higher levels of manager turnover, although members of external organizations see them as more influential.[78]

On the bright side, narcissists may be more charismatic than others.[79] They also might be found in business more often than in other fields. They are more likely to be chosen for leadership positions, and medium ratings of narcissism (neither extremely high nor extremely low) are positively correlated with leadership effectiveness.[80] Some evidence suggests that narcissists are more adaptable and make better business decisions than others when the issue is complex.[81] Narcissism and its effects are not confined to CEOs or celebrities. Like the effects of Machiavellianism, those of narcissism vary by context, but are evident in all areas of life.

PSYCHOPATHY Psychopathy is part of the Dark Triad, but in OB, it does not connote clinical mental illness. In the OB context, **psychopathy** is defined as a lack of concern for others, and a lack of guilt or remorse when actions cause harm.[82] Measures of psychopathy attempt to assess motivation to comply with social norms, impulsivity, willingness to use deceit to obtain desired ends, and a lack of empathic concern for others.

The literature is not consistent about whether psychopathy is important to work behavior. One review found little correlation between measures of psychopathy and job performance or CWBs.[83] Another found antisocial personality, which is closely related to psychopathy, was positively related to advancement in the organization but unrelated to other aspects of career success and effectiveness.[84] Still other research suggests psychopathy is related to the use of hard influence tactics (threats, manipulation) and bullying work behavior (physical or verbal threatening) and even suggests that they do not feel remorseful when they do it.[85] The cunning displayed by people who score high on psychopathy may thus help them gain power in an organization but keep them from using it toward healthy ends for themselves or their organizations.

Narcissism
The tendency to be arrogant, have a grandiose sense of self-importance, require excessive admiration, and have a sense of entitlement.

Psychopathy
The tendency for a lack of concern for others and a lack of guilt or remorse when actions cause harm.

OTHER FRAMEWORKS   The Dark Triad is a helpful framework for studying the three dominant dark-side traits in current personality research, and researchers are exploring other traits as well. One emerging framework incorporates an additional trait into the Big Five framework. The HEXACO model, which is composed of a new trait— honesty/humility (H)—and emotionality (E; i.e., emotional stability), extraversion (X), agreeableness (A), conscientiousness (C), and openness to experience (O).[86] The addition of the H dimension came from cross-cultural studies that suggest that the English-centric early investigations that produced the Big 5 essentially "missed" a dimension that began to emerge with studies conducted in non-European cultures (e.g., Korean, Hungarian).[87] The H dimension corresponds to people who are sincere, fair, modest, and humble. These individuals are not interested in social status, wealth, or money. Some research suggests that the addition of the H dimension meaningfully adds to the Big 5, and it has been found to predict ethically relevant outcomes, like abstaining from cheating (even in the presence of temptations or prompts to cheat).[88] This additional dimension has implications for OB, considering that dishonesty and cheating are extremely important for organizations (e.g., employees may cut corners, steal from the organization, etc.).[89]

OTHER PERSONALITY ATTRIBUTES RELEVANT TO OB

As we have discussed, studies of traits have much to offer the field of OB. Now we will look at other attributes that are powerful predictors of behavior in organizations: core self-evaluations, self-monitoring, and proactive personality.

Core Self-Evaluation (CSE)

As discussed in the chapter on attitudes and job satisfaction, core self-evaluations (CSEs) are bottom-line conclusions individuals have about their capabilities, competence, and worth as a person. People who have positive CSEs like themselves and see themselves as effective and in control of their environment. Those with negative CSEs tend to dislike themselves, question their capabilities, and view themselves as powerless over their environment.[90] As we discussed in the chapter on atttitudes and job satisfaction, CSEs relate to job satisfaction because people who are positive on this trait see more challenge in their jobs and attain more complex jobs.

People with positive CSEs perform better than others because they set more ambitious goals, are more committed to their goals, and persist longer in attempting to reach them.[91] People who have high CSEs provide better customer service, are more popular coworkers, and may have careers that begin on better footing and ascend more rapidly over time.[92] However, it is possible for one's CSE to be too high—research suggests when CSE is too high, the person may begin to become less popular with coworkers.[93]

CSE also has implications for diversity, globalization, and employee effectiveness in different cultural contexts. Research suggests that employees with positive CSEs tend to more effectively adapt to changes in their careers[94] and to international environments when working in new cultures.[95] As some examples, one study in a Chinese vehicle manufacturing plant found that CSEs were more positively related to job performance when individualism, rather than collectivism, was valued.[96] Furthermore, although one's language proficiency and nationality set employees in multinational teams apart as "different" from the rest of the group, their CSEs compensated for these differentiating factors and they were able to become better leaders in their teams.[97]

Self-Monitoring

Riley is always in trouble at work. Although competent, hardworking, and productive, Riley receives average ratings in performance reviews and seems to have made a career out of irritating the supervisors. Riley's problem is one of political ineptitude and an inability to adjust to changing situations. As Riley says, "I'm true to myself. I don't remake myself to please others." Riley is a low self-monitor.

Self-monitoring describes an individual's ability to adjust behavior to external, situational factors.[98] High self-monitors show considerable adaptability in adjusting their behavior to external situational factors. They are highly sensitive to external cues and can behave differently in varying situations, sometimes presenting striking contradictions between their public personae and their private selves. Low self-monitors like Riley cannot disguise themselves in that way. They tend to display their true dispositions and attitudes in every situation; hence, there is high behavioral consistency between who they are and what they do.

Self-monitoring
A personality trait that measures an individual's ability to adjust their behavior to external, situational factors.

High self-monitor employees show less commitment to their organizations but receive better performance ratings and are more likely to emerge as leaders.[99] High self-monitor managers tend to be more mobile in their careers, receive more promotions (both internal and cross-organizational), and are more likely to occupy central positions in organizations.[100] However, self-monitoring can be considered a mixed blessing: despite the aforementioned positive benefits, self-monitors may be seen as inauthentic, self-serving, or unprincipled.[101]

Proactive Personality

Did you ever notice that some people actively take the initiative to improve their current circumstances or create new ones? These are proactive personalities.[102] Those with a **proactive personality** identify opportunities, show initiative, take action, and persevere until meaningful change occurs, compared to others who generally react to situations. Proactive individuals have many desirable behaviors that organizations covet. They have higher levels of job performance[103] and creativity[104] and do not need much oversight (and are given more autonomy as a result).[105] They tend to be satisfied with their jobs, committed to their organizations, and engaged in their work.[106] Proactive individuals often achieve career success, although they are also more likely to be envied by their coworkers (and prone to social undermining or the withholding of help from coworkers).[107]

Proactive personality
People who identify opportunities, show initiative, take action, and persevere until meaningful change occurs.

In short, these personality traits predict many important organizational outcomes. However, there has been a renewed interest in how personality interacts with the environment, or how traits are affected by the situation or context. The next section will examine how the work environment, including contexts and situations, affect the expression of personality traits.

PERSONALITY AND SITUATIONS

Earlier, we discussed how heredity and the environment interact to form and shape personality. Some personality traits tend to be effective in almost any environment or situation. For example, research indicates conscientiousness is helpful to the performance of most jobs, and extraversion is related to emergence as a leader in most situations. However, we are learning that the effect of traits on behavior depends on the situation.

While advancements have been made in terms of mapping the personality domain, similar progress has been made in how people describe *situations.* One impressive study culled 146.7 *billion* words from several different sources that have been used to describe situations. Using artificial intelligence, these researchers found that situations can be described as either positive–negative, complex, typical, important, or humorous.[108] Each of these characteristics can influence behavior, or even the activation of personality traits. Furthermore, the "importance" dimension clearly has implications for situational strength.

Two theoretical frameworks, situation strength and trait activation, can help describe *how* the context or situations can influence personality and behavior in the workplace.

Situation Strength Theory

Imagine you are in a meeting with your entire office. How likely are you to walk out, shout at a coworker, or turn your back on everyone? Probably highly unlikely. Now imagine working from home. You might work in your pajamas, listen to loud music, or shout at your cat walking across your keyboard. From these examples, you can see that many situations vary in their "strength."

Situation strength theory
A theory indicating that the way personality translates into behavior depends on the strength of the situation.

Situation strength theory proposes that the way personality translates into behavior depends on the strength of the situation. By *situation strength*, we mean the degree to which norms, cues, or standards dictate appropriate behavior.[109] Strong situations show us what the right behavior is, pressure us to exhibit it, and discourage the wrong behavior. In weak situations, conversely, "anything goes," and thus we are freer to express our personality in behavior. Personality traits better predict behavior in weak situations than in strong ones.[110]

COMPONENTS OF SITUATION STRENGTH Researchers have analyzed situation strength in organizations in terms of four elements:[111]

1. *Clarity*, or the degree to which cues about work duties and responsibilities are available and clear. Jobs high in clarity produce strong situations because individuals can readily determine what to do. For example, the job of janitor probably provides higher clarity about each task than that of a Hollywood actor's agent.
2. *Consistency*, or the extent to which cues regarding work duties and responsibilities are compatible with one another. Jobs with high consistency represent strong situations because all the cues point toward the same desired behavior. The job of acute care nurse, for example, probably has higher consistency than the job of manager.
3. *Constraints*, or the extent to which individuals' freedom to decide or act is limited by forces outside their control. Jobs with many constraints represent strong situations because an individual has limited discretion. Bank examiner, for example, is probably a job with stronger constraints than forest ranger.
4. *Consequences*, or the degree to which decisions or actions have important implications for the organization or its members, clients, supplies, and so on. Jobs with important consequences represent strong situations because the environment is probably heavily structured to guard against mistakes. A surgeon's job, for example, has higher consequences than a foreign language teacher.

ORGANIZATIONAL SITUATIONS   Some researchers have speculated that organizations are strong situations because they impose rules, norms, and standards that govern behavior. These constraints are usually appropriate. For example, we would not want an employee to feel free to engage in sexual harassment, follow questionable accounting procedures, or come to work only when the mood strikes.

Beyond the basics, though, it is not always desirable for organizations to create strong situations for their employees for several reasons. The elements of situation strength are often determined by organizational rules and guidelines, which add some objectivity to them. However, it is the perception of these rules that influences how the person will respond to the situation's strength. For instance, imagine having a supervisor who prioritizes safety (creating a strong situation), reduces the impact of construction work insomnia on injuries, and promotes safety behaviors. Their responses (and work attitudes) will reflect their perception of and reaction to the situation.[112] Second, jobs with myriad rules and tightly controlled processes can be dull or demotivating. Third, strong situations may suppress the innovation prized by some organizations. Creating strong rules to govern diverse systems might be not only difficult but also unwise. Fourth, situational strength is not an all-or-nothing characteristic—organizations can be strong in some areas and weak in others. For example, a workplace can have weak norms for how work should be done (low strength) but very strong norms against CWB (high strength).[113] In sum, managers need to recognize the role of situation strength in the workplace and find the appropriate balance.

Trait Activation Theory

Another important theoretical framework toward understanding personality and situations is **Trait Activation Theory (TAT)**. TAT predicts that some situations, events, or interventions "activate" a trait more than others. Using TAT, we can foresee which jobs suit certain personalities. For example, a commission-based compensation plan would likely activate the extraversion trait because extraverts are more reward-sensitive, than, say, open people. Conversely, in jobs that encourage creativity, differences in openness may better predict desired behavior than differences in extraversion. See Exhibit 5-3 for specific examples.

Trait Activation Theory (TAT)
A theory that predicts that some situations, events, or interventions "activate" a trait more than others.

TAT also applies to personality tendencies. For example, a recent study found people learning online responded differently when their behavior was electronically monitored. Those who had a high fear of failure had higher apprehension from the monitoring than others, and consequently learned significantly less. In this case, a feature of the environment (electronic monitoring) activated a trait (fear of failing), and the combination of the two meant lowered job performance.[114] TAT can also work in a positive way. One study found that when your coworkers are supportive, conscientious personality traits are activated so that you have a stronger sense of duty toward your fellow coworkers and, in turn, are more likely to share information with them when conflicted about whether to do so.[115]

Together, situation strength and trait activation theories show that the debate over nature versus nurture might best be framed as nature *and* nurture. Not only do both affect behavior, but they interact with one another. Put another way, personality and the situation both affect work behavior, but when the situation is right, the power of personality to predict behavior is even higher.[116]

EXHIBIT 5-3

Trait Activation Theory: Jobs in Which Certain Big Five Traits Are More Relevant

Note: A plus (+) sign means individuals who score high on this trait should do better in this job. A minus (−) sign means individuals who score low on this trait should do better in this job.

Detail Orientation Required	Social Skills Required	Competitive Work	Innovation Required	Dealing with Angry People	Time Pressure (Deadlines)
Jobs scoring high (the traits listed here should predict behavior in these jobs)					
Air traffic controller	Clergy	Coach/scout	Actor	Correctional officer	Broadcast news analyst
Accountant	Therapist	Financial manager	Systems analyst	Telemarketer	
Legal secretary	Concierge	Sales representative	Advertising writer	Flight attendant	Editor
					Airline pilot
Jobs scoring low (the traits listed here should not predict behavior in these jobs)					
Forester	Software engineer	Postal clerk	Court reporter	Composer	Skincare specialist
Masseuse	Pump operator	Historian	Archivist	Biologist	Mathematician
Model	Broadcast technician	Nuclear reactor operator	Medical technician	Statistician	Fitness trainer
Jobs that score high activate these traits (make them more relevant to predicting behavior)					
Conscientiousness (+)	Extraversion (+) Agreeableness (+)	Extraversion (+) Agreeableness (−)	Openness (+)	Extraversion (+) Agreeableness (+) Neuroticism (−)	Conscientiousness (+) Neuroticism (−)

VALUES

At the heart of all organizations lie a set of values that are central to their mission. Wells Fargo, for instance, values "what's right for customers" and states that they "place customers at the center of everything we do. We want to exceed customer expectations and build relationships that last a lifetime."[117] However, sometimes the values or behaviors of the people who make up organizations do not match the values that they espouse. For example, employees of Wells Fargo, the same organization that values "what's right for customers" opened millions of fake accounts, moved money into these accounts, and signed customers up for online banking without their consent to meet sales goals—opening the company up to legal troubles.[118]

Values represent relatively stable and enduring, basic convictions that "a specific mode of conduct or end-state of existence is personally or socially preferable to an opposite or converse mode of conduct or end-state of existence."[119] Values contain a judgmental element because they carry an individual's ideas about what is right, good, or desirable. They have both content and intensity attributes. The content attribute says a mode of conduct or end-state of existence is *important*. The intensity attribute specifies *how important* it is. When we rank values in terms of intensity, we obtain that person's **value system**. We all have a hierarchy of values according to the relative importance we assign to values such as freedom, pleasure, self-respect, honesty, obedience, and equality.

Many of the values we hold are established in our early years—by parents, teachers, friends, and others. If we question our values, they may change, but more often they are reinforced. There is also evidence linking personality to values, implying our values may be partly determined by our personality traits.[120] Open people, for example, may value pursuing new ideas (e.g., trying a new sales strategy rather than exercising restraint), while agreeable people may place a greater value caring for others and cooperating (e.g., being

Values
Basic convictions that a specific mode of conduct or end-state of existence is personally or socially preferable to an opposite or converse mode of conduct or end-state of existence.

Value system
A hierarchy based on a ranking of an individual's values in terms of their intensity.

attracted to a collaborative, rather than competitive, work environment).[121] To explore the topic further, we will discuss the importance and organization of values first.

Consider this situation: Suppose you enter an organization with the view that allocating pay based on performance is right, while allocating pay based on seniority is wrong. How will you react if you find the organization you have just joined rewards seniority and not performance? You are likely to be disappointed—this can lead to job dissatisfaction and a decision not to exert a high level of effort because "It's probably not going to lead to more money anyway." Would your attitudes and behavior be different if your values aligned with the organization's pay policies? Most likely.

Terminal versus Instrumental Values

How can we organize values? One researcher—Milton Rokeach—argued that we can separate them into two categories.[122] One set, called **terminal values**, refers to desirable end-states. These are the goals a person would like to achieve during a lifetime. The other set, called **instrumental values**, refers to preferable modes of behavior, or means of achieving the terminal values. Each of us places value on both the ends (terminal values) and the means (instrumental values). Some examples of terminal values are prosperity and economic success, freedom, health and well-being, world peace, and meaning in life. Examples of instrumental values are autonomy and self-reliance, personal discipline, kindness, and goal-orientation.

Building upon Rokeach's value theory, Shalom Schwartz organized Rokeach's values into 10 dimensions: achievement, hedonism, stimulation, self-direction, universalism, benevolence, tradition, conformity, security, and power.[123] Shalom provided evidence across twenty separate countries for this framework of values.[124] Perhaps it is easy to see how some of these values are directly relevant to people in organizations, with some (e.g., universalism, benevolence, etc.) promoting effectiveness and treating others well, while others can cling to what is typically done (e.g., tradition, conformity, and security) or value self-enhancement (e.g., power and achievement). Perhaps Wells Fargo, although valuing benevolence toward customers, was composed of employees who valued self-enhancement?

Terminal values
Desirable end-states of existence; the goals a person would like to achieve during their lifetime.

Instrumental values
Preferable modes of behavior or means of achieving one's terminal values.

Generational Values

Researchers have integrated several analyses of work values into groups that attempt to capture the shared views of different cohorts or generations in the U.S. workforce.[125] You will surely be familiar with the labels—for example, baby boomers, gen x'ers, millennials, gen z'ers—some of which are used internationally. Though it is fascinating to think about generational values, remember these classifications lack solid research support. Early research was plagued by methodological problems that made it difficult to assess whether differences exist. Reviews suggest many of the generalizations are either overblown or incorrect.[126] Differences across generations often do not support popular conceptions of how generations differ. For example, the value placed on leisure has increased over generations from the baby boomers to the millennials and work centrality has declined, but research did not find that millennials had more altruistic work values.[127] Another modern criticism of millennials is that they are entitled and remnants of the "participation trophy" generation;[128] however, one study of over 10,000 people in New Zealand suggests that there are no differences between generations in entitlement, and in fact, baby boomers tend to become more entitled as they age![129] Despite the lack of support for the validity of generational values, support has been provided for differences in how people perceive those of other generations—in the workplace, people place

Power distance
A national culture attribute that describes the extent to which a society accepts that power in institutions and organizations is distributed unequally.

others into generational categories and apply stereotypes that affect workplace deci-sions.[130] Although there is little validity to generational differences, nevertheless, these differences are still perpetuated as stereotypes that are often applied in the workplace.

CULTURAL VALUES

Unlike personality, which is largely genetically determined, values are learned. They are passed down through generations, and they vary by cultures. As researchers have sought to understand cultural value differences, two important frameworks have emerged from Geert Hofstede and the GLOBE studies.

Hofstede's Framework

One of the most widely referenced approaches for analyzing variations among cultures was done by Geert Hofstede.[131] Hofstede surveyed more than 116,000 IBM employees in seventy-two countries about their work-related values and found managers and employ-ees varied on five value dimensions of national culture:

Individualism
A national culture attribute that describes the degree to which people prefer to act as individuals rather than as members of groups.

- **Power distance. Power distance** describes the degree to which people in a country accept that power in institutions and organizations is distributed unequally. A high rat-ing on power distance means large inequalities of power and wealth exist and are tol-erated in the culture, as in a class or caste system that discourages upward mobility. A low power-distance rating characterizes societies that stress equality and opportunity.
- **Individualism versus collectivism. Individualism** is the degree to which people pre-fer to act as individuals rather than as members of groups and believe in an individual's rights above all else. **Collectivism** emphasizes a tight social framework in which peo-ple expect others in groups of which they are a part to look after them and protect them.

Collectivism
A national culture attribute that describes a tight social frame-work in which people expect others in groups of which they are a part to look after them and protect them. Col-lectivistic countries/cultures are those in which people see themselves as inter-dependent and seek community and group goals. Collectivistic values are found in Asia, Africa, and South America, for example.

- **Masculinity versus femininity.** Hofstede's construct of **masculinity** is the degree to which the culture favors traditional masculine roles such as achievement, power, and control, as opposed to viewing men and women as equals. A high masculinity rating indicates the culture has separate roles for men and women, with men dominating the society. A high **femininity** rating means the culture sees little differentiation be-tween male and female roles and treats women as the equals of men in all respects.

  It is important to note that when the masculinity/femininity dimension was first uncovered, the sample of IBM employees consisted of mostly male employees surveyed in the 1960s and 1970s.[132] Since then, despite this homogenous sample, these findings have been replicated in more diverse samples from dozens of coun-tries.[133] The masculinity and femininity labels are still used by Hofstede Insights (the consulting firm that administers Hofstede's assessments) and Hofstede has suggested that they focus more on societal gender role expectations than on individuals them-selves.[134] Still, however, many have advocated for the replacement of these terms with alternatives.[135] These alternatives include "achievement versus relational" cultures or even the original terms for this dimension used by Hofstede, "ego versus social." [136]

Masculinity
A national culture attribute that describes the extent to which the culture favors traditional mascu-line work roles of achievement, power, and control. Societal values are character-ized by assertiveness and materialism.

- **Uncertainty avoidance.** The degree to which people in a country prefer structured over unstructured situations defines their **uncertainty avoidance**. In cultures scor-ing high on uncertainty avoidance, people have increased anxiety about uncertainty and ambiguity and use laws and controls to reduce uncertainty. People in cultures low on uncertainty avoidance are more accepting of ambiguity, are less rule ori-ented, take more risks, and more readily accept change.

- **Long-term versus short-term orientation.** The degree of a society's devotion to traditional values. All societies vary in their focus on meeting the challenges of the present and future, as opposed to maintaining a link with its past. **Long-term oriented cultures** tend to assume that preparation for the future is needed because the world is constantly changing. These cultures tend to value thrift, persistence, and pragmatism to prepare for the future. On the other hand, **short-term oriented cultures** prefer to maintain a link to their past by honoring traditions, fulfilling social obligations, and upholding and protecting their image.

In recent years, Hofstede has proposed an additional dimension, *indulgence versus restraint*, which refers to a national culture attribute that emphasizes enjoying life and having fun versus regulating conduct through strict social norms.[137] Although fairly new as a dimension, some research supports its distinction from other values and shows that it is correlated with a society's level of prosociality.[138]

How do different countries score on Hofstede's dimensions? Exhibit 5-4 shows the ratings of the countries for which data are available. For example, power distance is higher in Malaysia than in any other country. The United States is very individualistic; in fact, it's the most individualistic nation of all (closely followed by Australia and Great Britain). Guatemala is the most collectivistic nation. The country with the highest masculinity rank by far is Japan, and the country with the highest femininity rank is Sweden. Greece scores the highest in uncertainty avoidance, while Singapore scores the lowest. Hong Kong has one of the longest-term orientations; Pakistan has the shortest-term orientation.

Research across 598 studies with more than 200,000 respondents has investigated the relationship of Hofstede's cultural values and a variety of organizational criteria at both the individual and national levels of analysis.[139] Overall, the five original culture dimensions were found to be equally strong predictors of relevant outcomes. In sum, this research suggests Hofstede's framework may be a valuable way of thinking about differences among people, but we should be cautious about assuming all people from a country have the same values.

The GLOBE Framework

Founded in 1993, the Global Leadership and Organizational Behavior Effectiveness (GLOBE) research program is an ongoing cross-cultural investigation of leadership and national culture. Using data from 951 organizations in sixty-two countries, the GLOBE team built upon Hofstede's work by identifying nine dimensions on which national cultures differ.[140] Some dimensions—such as power distance, individualism/collectivism, uncertainty avoidance, gender differentiation (like masculinity versus femininity), and future orientation (like long-term versus short-term orientation)—resemble the Hofstede dimensions (although, notably, are defined differently in certain cases). Beyond these, the GLOBE framework added or otherwise split the Hofstede dimensions, such as humane orientation (the degree to which a society rewards individuals for being altruistic, generous, and kind to others) and performance orientation (the degree to which a society encourages and rewards group members for performance improvement and excellence). In Exhibit 5-5, the linkages between dimensions from the GLOBE framework and Hofstede's dimensions are outlined. As can be seen in the exhibit, the GLOBE also differentiated between these dimensions as they relate to practices (what is currently done) and values (what the society idealizes and aspires toward).

Femininity
A national culture attribute that indicates little differentiation between male and female roles; a high rating indicates that women are treated as the equals of men in all aspects of the society.

Uncertainty avoidance
A national culture attribute that describes the extent to which a society feels threatened by uncertain and ambiguous situations and tries to avoid them.

Long-term orientation
A national culture attribute that emphasizes the future, thrift, and persistence.

Short-term orientation
A national culture attribute that emphasizes the present and accepts change.

EXHIBIT 5-4
Hofstede's Cultural Values by Nation

Source: Copyright Geert Hofstede BV, hofstede@bart.nl. Reprinted with permission.
"Index" refers to the given country's score on the dimension, 0 = extremely low to 100 = extremely high. "Rank" refers to the relative ranking of the country compared to the others in Hofstede's database, with 1 = the highest rank.

Country	Power Distance		Individualism versus Collectivism		Masculinity versus Femininity		Uncertainty Avoidance		Long- versus Short-Term Orientation	
	Index	Rank	Index	Rank	Index	Rank	Index	Rank	Index	Rank
Argentina	49	35–36	46	22–23	56	20–21	86	10–15		
Australia	36	41	90	2	61	16	51	37	31	22–24
Austria	11	53	55	18	79	2	70	24–25	31	22–24
Belgium	65	20	75	8	54	22	94	5–6	38	18
Brazil	69	14	38	26–27	49	27	76	21–22	65	6
Canada	39	39	80	4–5	52	24	48	41–42	23	30
Chile	63	24–25	23	38	28	46	86	10–15		
Colombia	67	17	13	49	64	11–12	80	20		
Costa Rica	35	42–44	15	46	21	48–49	86	10–15		
Denmark	18	51	74	9	16	50	23	51	46	10
Ecuador	78	8–9	8	52	63	13–14	67	28		
El Salvador	66	18–19	19	42	40	40	94	5–6		
Finland	33	46	63	17	26	47	59	31–32	41	14
France	68	15–16	71	10–11	43	35–36	86	10–15	39	17
Germany	35	42–44	67	15	66	9–10	65	29	31	22–24
Great Britain	35	42–44	89	3	66	9–10	35	47–48	25	28–29
Greece	60	27–28	35	30	57	18–19	112	1		
Guatemala	95	2–3	6	53	37	43	101	3		
Hong Kong	68	15–16	25	37	57	18–19	29	49–50	96	2
India	77	10–11	48	21	56	20–21	40	45	61	7
Indonesia	78	8–9	14	47–48	46	30–31	48	41–42		
Iran	58	29–30	41	24	43	35–36	59	31–32		
Ireland	28	49	70	12	68	7–8	35	47–48	43	13
Israel	13	52	54	19	47	29	81	19		
Italy	50	34	76	7	70	4–5	75	23	34	19
Jamaica	45	37	39	25	68	7–8	13	52		
Japan	54	33	46	22–23	95	1	92	7	80	4
Korea (South)	60	27–28	18	43	39	41	85	16–17	75	5
Malaysia	104	1	26	36	50	25–26	36	46		
Mexico	81	5–6	30	32	69	6	82	18		
The Netherlands	38	40	80	4–5	14	51	53	35	44	11–12
New Zealand	22	50	79	6	58	17	49	39–40	30	25–26
Norway	31	47–48	69	13	8	52	50	38	44	11–12
Pakistan	55	32	14	47–48	50	25–26	70	24–25	0	34
Panama	95	2–3	11	51	44	34	86	10–15		
Peru	64	21–23	16	45	42	37–38	87	9		
Philippines	94	4	32	31	64	11–12	44	44	19	31–32
Portugal	63	24–25	27	33–35	31	45	104	2	30	25–26
Singapore	74	13	20	39–41	48	28	8	53	48	9
South Africa	49	35–36	65	16	63	13–14	49	39–40		
Spain	57	31	51	20	42	37–38	86	10–15	19	31–32
Sweden	31	47–48	71	10–11	5	53	29	49–50	33	20
Switzerland	34	45	68	14	70	4–5	58	33	40	15–16
Taiwan	58	29–30	17	44	45	32–33	69	26	87	3
Thailand	64	21–23	20	39–41	34	44	64	30	56	8
Turkey	66	18–19	37	28	45	32–33	85	16–17		
United States	40	38	91	1	62	15	46	43	29	27
Uruguay	61	26	36	29	38	42	100	4		
Venezuela	81	5–6	12	50	73	3	76	21–22		
Yugoslavia	76	12	27	33–35	21	48–49	88	8		
Regions:										
Arab countries	80	7	38	26–27	53	23	68	27		
East Africa	64	21–23	27	33–35	41	39	52	36	25	28–29
West Africa	77	10–11	20	39–41	46	30–31	54	34	16	33

Both frameworks have a great deal in common and often lead to similar conclusions. For example, a review of the organizational commitment literature shows that both the Hofstede and GLOBE individualism/collectivism dimensions operated similarly. Specifically, both frameworks showed organizational commitment tends to be lower in individualistic countries.[141] However, GLOBE expands upon the Hofstede framework in a number of ways, methodologically and theoretically. For example, as can be seen in Exhibit 5-5, various aspects of the values are disentangled into narrower dimensions.

Regardless, these dimensions of cultural values are incredibly important to be aware of in this day and age. With the advent of globalization, companies often engage in multinational projects, work in multinational teams, and send their employees to work in different cultures that may be radically different than what they are used to—understanding what is valued (and what is not valued) in each culture is very "valuable" information to have, considering the modern global climate.[142]

EXHIBIT 5-5

Adapted from R. Hadwick, "Should I Use GLOBE or Hofstede? Some Insights That Can Assist Cross-Cultural Scholars, and Others, Choose the Right Study to Support Their Work," Paper presented at *Australian & New Zealand Academy of Management*, Wellington, NZ (December 2011); R. J. House, P. J. Hanges, M. Javidan, P. W. Dorfman, and V. Gupta, *Culture, Leadership, and Organizations: The GLOBE Study of 62 Societies*. Thousand Oaks, CA: Sage, 2004; X. Shi and J. Wang, "Interpreting Hofstede Model and GLOBE Model: Which Way to Go for Cross-Cultural Research?" *International Journal of Business and Management* 6, no. 5 (2011): 93–99.

Hofstede's Dimensions	GLOBE
Power Distance: Extent to which a society accepts an unequal distribution of power.	**Power Distance:** Extent to which a society accepts an unequal distribution of power.
Uncertainty Avoidance: Extent to which a society feels threatened by and avoids ambiguity.	**Uncertainty Avoidance:** Extent to which a society seeks orderliness, structure, and laws to avoid ambiguity.
Long-Term Orientation: Extent to which a society emphasizes the future and persistence (versus the present and change)	**Future Orientation:** Extent to which a society believes their actions can influence the future.
Collectivism: Extent to which a society emphasizes acting as a tight-knit collective (versus as independent individuals)	**Institutional Collectivism:** Extent to which a society supports collective action and resource distribution.
Masculinity: Extent to which a society favors traditional, masculine roles such as power and control (versus little differentiation of gender roles)	**In-Group Collectivism:** Extent to which a society values loyalty, pride, patriotism, and cohesion.
	Gender Egalitarianism: Extent to which a society de-emphasizes traditional gender roles.
	Assertiveness: Extent to which a society emphasizes confidence and advocating for what one wants.
	Humane Orientation: Extent to which a society values caring, friendliness, altruism, fairness, kindness, and generosity.
	Performance Orientation: Extent to which a society values producing results, excellence, and productivity.

SUMMARY

Personality matters to OB. It does not explain all behavior, but it sets the stage. Emerging theory and research reveal how personality matters more in some situations than others. The Big Five has been a particularly important advancement, although the Dark Triad and other traits matter as well. Every trait has advantages and disadvantages for work behavior, and there is no perfect constellation of traits that is ideal in every situation. Personality can help you to understand why people (including yourself!) act, think, and feel the way we do, and the astute employee or manager can put that understanding to use by taking care to place employees in situations that best fit their personalities, or by recognizing personality and value differences in coworkers, in order to work more effectively together.

Values often underlie and explain attitudes, behaviors, and perceptions. Values tend to vary internationally along dimensions that can predict organizational outcomes; however, an individual may or may not hold values that are consistent with the values of the national culture.

IMPLICATIONS FOR MANAGERS

- Consider applicants' and employees' fit to the job and organization in employment decisions. Their personalities, values, and other characteristics may be useful to understanding whether they will flourish in particular assignments, jobs, teams, or organizations.
- Consider screening job candidates for conscientiousness—and the other Big Five traits, depending on the criteria your organization finds most important. Other aspects, such as core self-evaluations or narcissism, may be relevant in certain situations.
- Emphasize the ideal personality and values of your organization in your recruitment materials and practices. This may help attract people whose values and personality types match your organization/or job vacancies.
- Understand that situation strength and the context (e.g., trait activating features) can affect behavior. Take stock of the environmental features in your organization that may influence the behavior of applicants, customers, employees, and even leaders.
- An understanding of differences in cultural values can equip you to interact with others from cultures that are different from your own.

6

Perception and Individual Decision Making

After studying this chapter, you should be able to:

6.1 Explain the factors that influence perception.

6.2 Describe attribution theory.

6.3 Explain the link between perception and decision making.

6.4 Contrast the rational model of decision making with bounded rationality and intuition.

6.5 Explain how individual differences and organizational constraints affect decision making.

6.6 Contrast the three ethical decision criteria.

6.7 Describe the three-stage model of creativity.

WHAT IS PERCEPTION?

Things are not always as they seem, and unfortunately our perceptions can lead to bias. Particularly nefarious, when we perceive another person as belonging to a certain stereotyped group, this can affect how we interact with them. For instance, weight bias and discrimination can affect everyone in the office in hurtful ways, by activating stereotypes that suggest the overweight are unmotivated and the thin are meek and unhealthy.[1] **Perception** is a process by which we organize and interpret sensory impressions in order to give meaning to their environment. What we perceive can be substantially different from objective reality. Why is perception important in the study of organizational behavior (OB)? People's behavior and decisions are based on their perception of what reality is, not on reality itself. In other words, our perception becomes the reality from which we act. For instance, a Brazilian employee interacting with a Japanese employee in a virtual meeting may perceive the silence in the conversation as awkward or something negative—when, in reality, silence is important and conveys good listening in some Asian cultures.[2]

Perception
A process by which individuals organize and interpret their sensory impressions in order to give meaning to their environment.

Factors That Influence Perception

Factors shape and sometimes distort perception. These factors can reside in the *perceiver,* the object or *target* being perceived, or the *situation* in which the perception is made.

PERCEIVER   When you look at a target, your interpretation of what you see is influenced by your personal characteristics—attitudes, personality, motives, interests, past experiences, and expectations.[3] In some ways, we hear what we want to hear[4] and see what we want to see—not because it is the truth, but because it conforms to our thinking. For instance, research indicates that supervisors perceive employees who start work earlier in the day as more conscientious and therefore as higher performers; however, supervisors who are night owls themselves are less likely to make that erroneous assumption.[5]

TARGET   The characteristics of the target also affect what we perceive. Because we do not look at targets in isolation, the relationship of a target to its background influences perception, as does our tendency to group close things and similar things together.[6] We can perceive members of any other group that shares some surface characteristics as alike in other, unrelated ways as well. Often, these assumptions are harmful, as when people who have criminal records are prejudged in the workplace as a result (even when it is known that they were wrongly arrested).[7] Sometimes this can work in the target's favor, in ways that can affect organizations' bottom lines. For example, in over 10,000 microloan transactions, the more pleasant the appearance of the customer (e.g., loan-requester), the more likely the loan was to be approved, and the more quickly the approval occurred.[8] Using artificial intelligence approaches, these researchers applied machine learning techniques and were able to determine that pleasant appearance could predict loan approval with about 60 percent accuracy.[9]

CONTEXT   Context matters, too. The time at which we see an object or event can influence our attention, as can location, light, heat, or situational factors. For instance, if you invite a potential client into your office, and it is messy, they may be more likely to think you are disagreeable, not conscientious, and more neurotic than if your office was neat.[10]

People are usually not aware of the factors that influence their view of reality. In fact, people are not even that perceptive about their *own* abilities.[11] Thankfully, awareness and objective measures can reduce our perceptual distortions. For instance, when people are more aware of their own racial biases, they are more motivated to control their own prejudice.[12] Let us next consider *how* we make perceptions of others.

PERSON PERCEPTION: MAKING JUDGMENTS ABOUT OTHERS

The perception concepts most relevant to OB include *person perceptions,* or the perceptions people form about each other. Many of our perceptions of others are formed by first impressions and small cues that have little supporting evidence. Let us unravel some of our human tendencies that interfere with correct person perception, beginning with the evidence behind attribution theory.

Attribution Theory

When we observe people, we attempt to explain their behavior. Our perception and judgment of a person's actions are influenced by the assumptions we make about that person's state of mind.

Attribution theory tries to explain the ways we judge people differently depending on the meaning we attribute to their behavior.[13] For instance, if your coworker is late to work, you might think it was because they were lazy, or partying too hard the night before—but would you say the same if *you* were late for work (or was it just the bad traffic)?[14] Attributions also try to explain what we do as a result of our attributions. For example, recent research suggests that supervisors are more likely to exploit or treat subordinates poorly (e.g., making them work extra hours, giving them tedious tasks) if they judge them as being "passionate" about their work.[15] In other words, they think it is okay if they make them work harder if they see them as passionate.

Attribution theory
An attempt to explain the ways we judge people differently, depending on the meaning we attribute to a behavior, such as determining whether an individual's behavior is internally or externally caused.

INTERNAL AND EXTERNAL CAUSATION   Attribution theory suggests that when we observe an individual's behavior, we attempt to determine whether it was internally or externally caused. That determination depends largely on three factors: (1) distinctiveness, (2) consensus, and (3) consistency.[16] Let us clarify the differences between internal and external causation, and then we will discuss the determining factors.

Internally caused behaviors are those an observer believes to be under the personal behavioral control of another individual (e.g., coming to work late because the coworker is lazy). *Externally* caused behavior is what we imagine the situation forced the individual to do (e.g., coming to work late because of the bad traffic). New research suggests that there may be another kind of external attribution, where our relationship with the other person is the reason for the behavior.[17] For example, you may think a customer stopped doing business with your company because they are (1) disloyal to the company (e.g., internal), (2) cutting expenditures due to hard financial times (e.g., external), or (3) not getting along with the new employee assigned to their account (e.g., relational).

DISTINCTIVENESS, CONSENSUS, AND CONSISTENCY   Exhibit 6-1 summarizes the key elements in attribution theory, described in this section. *Distinctiveness* refers to whether an individual displays different behavior in different situations. Is the employee who arrives late today also one who regularly "blows off" other kinds of commitments? If no, we are likely to give it an external attribution. If yes, we will probably judge the behavior to be internal.

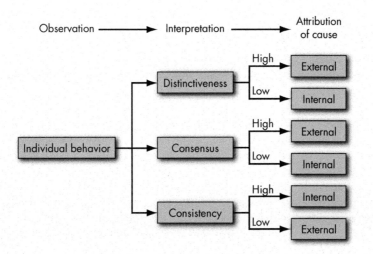

EXHIBIT 6-1
Attribution Theory

If everyone who faces a similar situation responds in the same way, we can say the behavior shows *consensus*. Were all employees who took the same route also late? If yes, you would probably give an external attribution to the employee's tardiness (e.g., traffic or weather). If no, you would be more likely to attribute his lateness to an internal cause.

Finally, an observer looks for *consistency* in a person's actions. Does the person respond the same way over time? Coming in ten minutes late for work is not perceived the same for an employee who has not been late for several months as for an employee who is late three times a week. The more consistent the behavior, the more we are inclined to attribute it to internal causes.

ERRORS AND BIASES   When we make judgments about the behavior of other people, we tend to underestimate the influence of external factors and overestimate the influence of internal or personal factors.[18] This **fundamental attribution error** may explain why we might perceive the wealthy as intelligent, savvy, or innately effective, without considering the external factors that precluded their success (e.g., being born into a wealthy family)— and similarly, to discount the poor as lazy, untalented, or unintelligent.[19]

Fundamental attribution error
The tendency to underestimate the influence of external factors and overestimate the influence of internal factors when making judgments about the behavior of others.

Similarly, people tend to attribute ambiguous information as relatively flattering, accept positive feedback, and reject negative feedback. This is called **self-serving bias**.[20] Although much research focuses on the self-serving bias in business leaders and their negative effects, not all executives are self-serving—many studies suggest that executives who are modest experience better career success and upward mobility, elicit positive investor reactions, and generally lead to higher team and firm performance.[21]

The evidence on cultural differences in perception is mixed, but most suggests there are differences across cultures in the attributions people make, with collectivist cultures making external attributions more frequently than internal attributions.[22] These differences in attributions also influence the degree to whether attributions are made toward individuals or groups. In one study, Asian managers were more likely to blame institutions or whole organizations when things went wrong, whereas Western observers believed individual managers should get blame or praise.[23] This may explain why U.S. newspapers feature the names of individual executives when firms do poorly, whereas Asian media report the firm as a whole has failed.

Self-serving bias
The tendency for individuals to attribute their own successes to internal factors and put the blame for failures on external factors.

Common Shortcuts in Judging Others

Shortcuts for judging others often allow us to make accurate perceptions rapidly and provide valid data for making predictions. However, they can and do sometimes result in significant distortions.

SELECTIVE PERCEPTION   We often choose (sometimes unconsciously) the information we take in from the environment, based on our background, motivations, and characteristics. This is called **selective perception**. For example, organizational leaders are motivated to focus on financial metrics and the bottom line while effectively ignoring employees and their job satisfaction, which we know from the chapter on attitudes and job satisfaction.[24] Some research suggests that if we are directed to focus on more in our environment, we will; for example, if job satisfaction is emphasized as important by the top management team, then other managers will see it as important and will no longer ignore it.[25]

Selective perception
The tendency to selectively interpret what one sees based on one's interests, background, experience, and attitudes.

HALO AND HORNS EFFECTS   When we draw a positive impression about an individual based on a single characteristic, such as intelligence, sociability, or appearance, a **halo effect** is operating.[26] The **horns effect**, on the other hand, is when we draw a *negative* impression from a single characteristic. These effects are easy to demonstrate. Imagine a recruiter meeting with two applicants for an initial interview.[27] One was very friendly and sociable—it is easy for the recruiter to conclude that this applicant will also be clever, smart, or good at their job, even though they may be unrelated (e.g., the halo effect creates a positive, clouded first impression). The other applicant was loud and off-putting—it would be easy, again, to conclude that this applicant will not be clever, smart or good at their job (e.g., the horns effect creates a negative, clouded first impression).

Halo effect
The tendency to draw a positive general impression about an individual based on a single characteristic.

Horns effect
The tendency to draw a negative general impression about an individual based on a single characteristic.

CONTRAST EFFECTS   It is performance appraisal "season," and everyone in your workplace is anxious to receive their evaluation. The boss begins scheduling meetings, and you hear through the grapevine that Regan is going up first—Regan is the star performer in the office and will be a hard act to follow. Everyone in the office will probably look bad in comparison to Regan! This example demonstrates how the **contrast effect** can distort perceptions.[28] We do not evaluate a person in isolation. Our reaction is influenced by other people we have recently encountered.

Contrast effect
Evaluation of a person's characteristics that is affected by comparisons with other people recently encountered who rank higher or lower on the same characteristics.

STEREOTYPING   When we judge someone based on our perception of the group they belong to, we are **stereotyping**.[29] Stereotyping can lead to prejudicial decision making that can mar business processes like selection and promotion. For example, in one study, over 6,500 U.S. professors were sent fake letters by fictitious students asking about graduate school and research opportunities—the contents of these letters were all the same, except the names were changed to correspond with "stereotypically" black, Chinese, Hispanic, Indian, and white names.[30] These professors tended to be significantly more responsive to white males than other students. Furthermore, women and minorities are more likely to be promoted to CEO positions, but only in weakly performing firms (e.g., women and minorities may be given opportunities that set them up to fail)—if the firm performance continues to decline, they tend to be replaced by white men (a glass cliff effect as discussed in the chapter on diversity in organizations).[31]

Stereotyping
Judging someone based on one's perception of the group to which that person belongs.

It should be obvious by now that our perceptions distort our outlook. These perceptions filter into several business processes, such as employment interviews, performance evaluations, and client interactions. Artificial intelligence (AI) has been proving useful in combatting these biases—for example, AI-driven performance assessments can help reduce these common shortcuts in judging others.[32] These types of "mechanical" data analytic methods are very effective—in fact, one review of studies found that mechanical methods were 50 percent more effective than subjective methods at judging job performance.[33] However, this has led many managers and other individuals to worry about AI taking over their jobs, a phenomenon referred to as the **threat of technological unemployment**.[34]

Threat of technological unemployment
A situation in which professional decision makers resist certain decision-making improvements (e.g., AI and structured approaches alike) because they reduce the extent the decision makers are relied on for expert judgment, lessening the value they provide the organization.

Regardless, understanding the link between perception and decision making can help us recognize when our perceptions are interfering with our ability to make effective decisions.

THE LINK BETWEEN PERCEPTION AND INDIVIDUAL DECISION MAKING

Decisions
Choices made from among two or more alternatives.

Problem
A discrepancy between the current state and some desired state.

Individuals make **decisions**, or choices from among two or more alternatives.[35] Ideally, decision making would be objective rather than subjective, but the ways individuals make decisions are largely influenced by their perceptions.

Decision making occurs as a reaction to a **problem**. That is, a discrepancy exists between how things are and how we want them to be, requiring us to consider how we can address this discrepancy. Unfortunately, most problems do not come neatly labeled. One person's *problem* might be another's *desired state.* One manager may view their division's 2 percent decline in quarterly sales to be a serious problem requiring immediate action. The manager's counterpart in another division, who also had a 2 percent sales decrease, may consider it quite acceptable.

Every decision requires us to interpret and evaluate information. We typically receive data from multiple sources that we need to screen, process, and interpret. Which data are relevant to the decision, and which are not? Our perceptions help us, accurately or inaccurately, answer that question. We must consider how our perceptions of the situation influence our decisions, sometimes in ways we would not expect. For example, employees *should* be especially receptive to problems during times of economic instability (times are hard, and they want to do well to keep their jobs!). However, when other employment opportunities are scarce, employees may be motivated to deny or ignore information that there are problems in their organization.[36]

DECISION MAKING IN ORGANIZATIONS

Business schools typically train students to follow rational decision-making models. While such models have merit, they do not always describe how people make decisions. OB improves the way we make decisions in organizations by addressing both perceptual and decision-making errors. First, we describe some decision-making approaches, and then outline a few of the most common errors.

The Rational Model, Bounded Rationality, and Intuition

Rational
A style of decision making characterized by making consistent, value-maximizing choices within specified constraints.

In OB, there are generally accepted approaches to decision making: rational decision making, bounded rationality, and intuition. However, they may not lead to the most accurate (or best) decisions. More importantly, there are times when one strategy may lead to a better outcome than another.

Rational decision-making model
A decision-making model that describes how individuals should behave in order to maximize some outcome.

RATIONAL DECISION MAKING We often think the best decision maker is **rational** and makes consistent, value-maximizing choices within specified constraints.[37] In other words, good decision makers consistently make choices that enable them to enjoy the most benefits, given the situation. Rational decisions follow a six-step **rational decision-making model** (see Exhibit 6-2).[38]

The rational model assumes the decision maker has complete information, can identify all relevant options without bias, and chooses the option with the highest utility.[39] However, most decisions do not follow this model; people are usually content to find an acceptable or reasonable solution to a problem rather than an optimal one. People are remarkably unaware that they are making suboptimal decisions.[40]

1. Define the problem.
2. Identify the decision criteria.
3. Allocate weights to the criteria.
4. Develop the alternatives.
5. Evaluate the alternatives.
6. Select the best alternative.

EXHIBIT 6-2
Steps in the Rational Decision-Making Model

BOUNDED RATIONALITY Often, we do not follow the rational decision-making model for a reason: Our limited abilities to process information make it impossible to assimilate all the information we need, even if it is readily obtainable.[41] Because we cannot solve complex problems with full rationality, we operate within the confines of **bounded rationality**. We take a simplified approach, perceiving and interpreting the essential features of problems without capturing their complexity. We then behave rationally within these boundaries.

Bounded rationality
A simplified process of making decisions by perceiving and interpreting the essential features of problems without capturing their complexity.

One outcome of bounded rationality is a tendency to satisfice or seek solutions that are merely sufficient (e.g., "good enough"). While the satisficing answer is acceptable but not necessarily optimal, it is not always a bad method. Often, a simple process may frequently be more sensible than the traditional rational decision-making model.[42] However, bounded rationality can be a concern in ethical decision making. We are prone to make systematic and predictable errors in ethical decisions,[43] and whether we have the *right* to behave in a particular way is bounded by our *duties* toward the people our actions affect.[44] For example, you *want* to take the last doughnut in the break room but you know that you *shouldn't* in case someone has not had one yet. Researchers have identified ways in which we can address bounded rationality: Be sure to ask multiple questions to understand the situation better, draw on multiple sources of information, evaluate your sources of information, and leave enough time to decide.[45]

INTUITION Perhaps the least rational way of making decisions is **intuitive decision making**, an unconscious process created from distilled experience.[46] Intuitive decision making occurs outside conscious thought; relies on holistic associations, or links between disparate pieces of information; is fast; and is *affectively charged,* meaning it engages the emotions.[47]

Intuitive decision making
An unconscious process created out of distilled experience.

Does intuition help effective decision making? Researchers are divided, but most are skeptical, in part because intuition is hard to measure and analyze. Furthermore, intuition can lead you to "close your eyes to follow your heart," or ignore contradictory information to protect your intuition, even when it is not correct.[48] Much of the research on dozens of decision-making studies suggests that intuition, although it "feels right," does not correspond with rationally made decisions and perhaps leads to inaccurate decisions.[49] Probably the best advice from one expert is: "Intuition can be very useful as a way of setting up a hypothesis but is unacceptable as 'proof.'" Use hunches derived from your experience to speculate, yes, but test those hunches with objective data and rational, dispassionate analysis.[50]

Common Biases and Errors in Decision Making

Systematic biases and errors can creep into the judgments of decision makers.[51] To minimize effort and avoid trade-offs, people tend to rely too heavily on experience, impulses, gut feelings, and convenient rules of thumb. Exhibit 6-3 provides some suggestions for how to avoid falling into these biases and errors.

EXHIBIT 6-3
Reducing Biases and Errors

Source: S. P. Robbins, *Decide & Conquer: Making Winning Decisions and Taking Control of Your Life* (Upper Saddle River, NJ: Financial Times/ Prentice Hall, 2004), 81–84.

Focus on Goals. Without goals, you can't be rational, you don't know what information you need, you don't know which information is relevant and which is irrelevant, you'll find it difficult to choose between alternatives, and you're far more likely to experience regret over the choices you make. Clear goals make decision making easier and help you eliminate options that are inconsistent with your interests.

Look for Information That Disconfirms Your Beliefs. One of the most effective means for counteracting overconfidence and the confirmation and hindsight biases is to actively look for information that contradicts your beliefs and assumptions. When we overtly consider various ways we could be wrong, we challenge our tendencies to think we're smarter than we actually are.

Don't Try to Create Meaning out of Random Events. The educated mind has been trained to look for cause-and-effect relationships. When something happens, we ask why. And when we can't find reasons, we often invent them. You have to accept that there are events in life that are outside your control. Ask yourself if patterns can be meaningfully explained or whether they are merely coincidence. Don't attempt to create meaning out of coincidence.

Increase Your Options. No matter how many options you've identified, your final choice can be no better than the best of the option set you've selected. This argues for increasing your decision alternatives and for using creativity in developing a wide range of diverse choices. The more alternatives you can generate, and the more diverse those alternatives, the greater your chance of finding an outstanding one.

OVERCONFIDENCE BIAS   We tend to be overconfident about our abilities and the abilities of others, but we are usually not aware of this bias.[52] This overconfidence can emerge in organizations, especially during informal interviews. For example, hiring managers may be overconfident about how well they evaluate candidates after an informal interview.[53] Furthermore, some research shows hiring managers can be overconfident in their evaluation of stigmatized candidates (e.g., candidates with facial scars or birthmarks), even when it is clear they were prejudiced in their decisions.[54]

Overconfidence bias
A tendency to be overconfident about our own abilities or the abilities of others.

Overconfidence has a relationship with leadership emergence (which we discuss in the chapter on leadership). People are more likely to select the overconfident as leaders as they tend to ease their sense of ambiguity and overconfidence fits the perceiver's understanding of what it means to be a leader.[55] Furthermore, **overconfidence bias** is more likely to emerge in leaders who are powerful, ambitious, and of a higher social class and, in some cases, lead to higher firm performance.[56] However, despite initial benefits, overconfidence may eventually backfire: as overconfidence is revealed (the person's behaviors are not as good as they say they are or their claims are falsifiable), people begin to perceive the overconfident person negatively, which damages their reputation.[57]

Anchoring bias
A tendency to fixate on initial information, from which one then fails to adequately adjust for subsequent information.

ANCHORING BIAS   **Anchoring bias** is a tendency to fixate on initial information and fail to adequately adjust to subsequent information.[58] The mind appears to disproportionately emphasize the first information it receives. Anchors are widely used by people in professions in which persuasion skills are important—advertising, management, politics, real estate, and law.

Anytime a negotiation takes place, so does anchoring. When a prospective employer asks how much you made in your prior job, your answer typically anchors the employer's offer. (Remember this when you negotiate your salary but set the anchor only as high as you truthfully can.) The more precise your anchor is, the smaller the adjustment. Some research suggests people think of making an adjustment after an anchor is set as rounding off a number: If you suggest a salary of $55,000, your boss will consider

$50,000 to $60,000 a reasonable range for negotiation, but if you mention $55,650, your boss is more likely to consider $55,000 to $56,000 the range of likely values.[59]

CONFIRMATION BIAS   **Confirmation bias** is a case of selective perception: we seek out (and accept) information that reaffirms our past choices and current views, and we discount information that challenges them.[60] We even tend to seek sources most likely to tell us what we want to hear, and we give too much weight to supporting information and too little to contradictory information. The confirmation bias applies to person perception (discussed earlier in this chapter): once we settle on a trait attribution, we seek out and accept information that reaffirms this perception.[61] For example, if your supervisor sees you as unreliable, they are more likely to perceive when you are unreliable than when you are reliable. Confirmation bias may be especially troublesome for entrepreneurs and startups, given the consequences of making faulty decisions in new ventures and failing to learn quickly.[62]

Confirmation bias
The tendency to seek out information that reaffirms past choices and current views, and to discount information that challenges them.

AVAILABILITY BIAS   **Availability bias** is our tendency to base judgments on readily available information. Events that evoke emotions are particularly vivid, and those that are more recent tend to be more available in our memory, leading us to overestimate the chances of unlikely events.[63] Availability bias can help explain why managers give more weight in performance appraisals to recent employee behaviors than to behaviors of six to nine months earlier.[64] Because the challenges people have faced are often more salient than times when things have gone well, employees may also tend to believe they have it worse than others.[65] For example, employees from older generations may discount millennial work experiences as easier because they focus more on their own challenging experiences rather than when things were easier for them.

Availability bias
The tendency for people to base their judgments on information that is readily available to them.

ESCALATION OF COMMITMENT   Another distortion that creeps into decisions is a tendency, often driven by nonrational reasons, to persist even when there is evidence that one should try a different approach or give up.[66] **Escalation of commitment** refers to our staying with a decision even if there is clear evidence it is wrong. When is escalation most likely to occur? Evidence indicates it occurs when individuals view themselves as responsible for the outcome or when they feel like they will eventually succeed.[67] The fear of personal failure even biases the way we search for and evaluate information so that we choose only information that supports our dedication.[68] It does not appear to matter whether we chose the failing course of action or if it was assigned to us—we feel responsible and escalate in either case. Also, the sharing of decision authority—such as when others review the choice we made—can lead to higher escalation.[69]

Escalation of commitment
An increased commitment to a previous decision, despite negative information.

We usually think of escalation of commitment as ungrounded. However, persistence in the face of failure is responsible for a great many of history's greatest feats, including the building of the pyramids, the Great Wall of China, the Panama Canal, and the Empire State Building, among others. Researchers suggest a balanced approach includes frequent evaluation of the spent costs, that is, whether the next step is worth the anticipated costs.[70] As such, what we want to combat is the tendency to *automatically* escalate commitment.

RANDOMNESS ERROR   Our tendency to believe we can predict the outcome of random events is the **randomness error**.

Randomness error
The tendency of individuals to believe that they can predict the outcome of random events.

Decision making suffers when we try to create meaning from random events, particularly when we turn imaginary patterns into superstitions.[71] These can be completely contrived ("I never make important decisions on Friday the 13th") or they can evolve from a reinforced past pattern of behavior (Tiger Woods wears a red shirt playing golf on Sundays because he won many junior tournaments wearing red shirts).[72]

Risk aversion
The tendency to prefer a sure gain of a moderate amount over a riskier outcome, even if the riskier outcome might have a higher expected payoff.

RISK AVERSION   Mathematically speaking, we should find a fifty–fifty flip of the coin for one hundred dollars to be worth as much as a sure promise of fifty dollars. After all, the expected value of the gamble over several trials is fifty dollars. However, nearly everyone would rather have the sure thing than a risky prospect.[73] For many people, a fifty–fifty flip of a coin even for two hundred dollars might not be worth as much as a sure promise of fifty dollars, even though the gamble is mathematically worth twice as much! This tendency to prefer a sure thing over a risky outcome is **risk aversion**. Overall, the framing of a decision has an effect on whether or not people will engage in risk-averse behavior—when decisions are framed positively, such as a potential gain of fifty dollars, people will be more risk averse (conversely, when the decision is framed in a negative manner, such as a loss of fifty dollars, people will engage in riskier behaviors).[74]

Chief executive officers (CEOs) at risk of termination are exceptionally risk averse, even when a riskier investment strategy is in their firms' best interests.[75] Organizations have a stronger hold on employees who are more risk averse because these employees tend to perceive that they have more to lose and are less likely to leave the organization.[76]

Hindsight bias
The tendency to believe falsely, after an outcome of an event is known, that one would have accurately predicted that outcome.

HINDSIGHT BIAS   **Hindsight bias** is the tendency to believe falsely, after the outcome is known, that we would have accurately predicted it.[77] When we have feedback on the outcome, we seem good at concluding it was obvious.

For instance, Or Shani, the founder of Albert Technologies (the maker of the first autonomous digital marketer), notes that marketers this decade sought to create seamlessly digital technologies to replace their cumbersome manual processes—it was easy to conclude in hindsight that *cumbersome* digital systems merely replaced *cumbersome* manual processes.[78] The state of marketing, according to Shani, has not fully realized its digital transformation as a result (although Shani believes AI will be the final "push" that will fully bring marketing into the digital age).[79] While that seems obvious now in hindsight, tempting us to think we could have predicted it, many experts have failed to predict industry trends in advance.

Though criticisms of decision makers may have merit,[80] as Malcolm Gladwell, author of *Blink* and *The Tipping Point,* writes, "What is clear in hindsight is rarely clear before the fact."[81]

INFLUENCES ON DECISION MAKING: INDIVIDUAL DIFFERENCES AND ORGANIZATIONAL CONSTRAINTS

Many factors, such as individual differences and organizational constraints, influence the way people make decisions and the degree to which they are susceptible to errors and biases.

Individual Differences

As we discussed, decision making in practice is characterized by bounded rationality, common biases and errors, and the use of intuition. Individual differences such as personality also create deviations from this rational model.

PERSONALITY   Several personality traits are related to taking on decision-making strategies, or to experiencing errors or biases during decision making. First, employees differ in the extent to which they trust their intuitions, and this can lead them to make riskier decisions or even to be harsher when condemning unethical behavior.[82] Second, employees who are less closed-minded (or higher on openness) tend to be less prone toward selective perception or the confirmation bias, as they are more receptive to contradictory information.[83] Narcissists (see the chapter on personality and values), naturally, tend to be prone to overconfidence or overclaiming and to self-serving biases.[84] Specific facets of conscientiousness—particularly achievement striving and dutifulness—may affect escalation of commitment.[85] Achievement-oriented people hate to fail, so they escalate their commitment, hoping to forestall failure. Dutiful people, however, are more inclined to do what they see as best for the organization, so they are less likely to escalate their commitment. Achievement-striving individuals appear more susceptible to hindsight bias, perhaps because they have a need to justify their actions.[86]

GENDER   Does gender influence decision making? It depends on the situation. When the situation is not stressful, decision making by men and women is about equal in quality. In stressful situations, it appears that men make riskier decisions, while women become more empathetic and their decision making improves.[87] This suggests that it might be best to have gender-diverse corporate boards: In fact, one study of Chinese firms that committed securities fraud found that gender-diverse boards are less likely to commit fraud and enjoy a better stock market response to fraud.[88] Although only focusing on male-female differences here paints an incomplete picture, the state of research is evolving and we expect there to be more research in the future that is more reflective of gender diversity.

GENERAL MENTAL ABILITY   We know people with higher levels of general mental ability (GMA; see the chapter on diversity in organizations) can process information more quickly, solve problems more accurately, and learn faster,[89] so you might expect them to be less susceptible to common decision errors. However, GMA appears to help people avoid only some of them.[90] Smart people are just as likely to fall prey, probably because being smart does not alert you to the possibility you are too confident or emotionally defensive. It is not that intelligence never matters. Once warned about decision-making errors, more intelligent people can probably learn more quickly to avoid them.

CULTURAL DIFFERENCES   The cultural background of a decision maker can significantly influence the selection of problems, the depth of analysis, the importance placed on logic and rationality, and whether organizational decisions should be made autocratically by an individual manager or collectively in groups.[91] Cultures differ in time orientation, the value they place on rationality, their belief in the ability of people to solve problems, and their preference for collective decision making. Second, while rationality is valued in North America, that may not be true elsewhere. In countries such as Iran, where rationality is not paramount to other factors, it is not necessary for efforts to appear rational. Third, some cultures emphasize solving problems, while others focus on accepting situations as they are. Because problem-solving managers believe they can and should change situations to their benefit, U.S. managers might identify a problem long before their Thai or Indonesian counterparts would choose to recognize it as such. Fourth, decision making in Japan, a collectivistic society, is much more group oriented than in the United States, an individualistic society.

Organizational Constraints

Organizations can constrain decision makers, creating deviations from the rational model. For instance, managers make decisions that are influenced by the organization's performance evaluation and reward systems, comply with formal regulations and company precedents, and meet organizationally imposed time constraints.

PERFORMANCE EVALUATION SYSTEMS Managers are influenced by the criteria on which they are evaluated. If a division manager who oversees a group of manufacturing plants, believes they are operating best when there is no negative feedback from staff or auditors; the plant managers will spend a good part of their time ensuring that negative information does not reach him.

REWARD SYSTEMS The organization's reward systems influence decision makers by suggesting which choices have better personal payoffs. For example, for over half a century (the 1930s through the mid-1980s), General Motors consistently gave promotions and bonuses to managers who kept a low profile and avoided controversy. These executives became adept at dodging tough issues and passing controversial decisions on to committees, which harmed the organization over time.

FORMAL REGULATIONS A shift manager at a Taco Bell restaurant in San Antonio, Texas, describes constraints faced on the job: "I've got rules and regulations covering almost every decision I make—from how to make a burrito to how often I need to clean the restrooms. My job doesn't come with much freedom of choice." The manager's situation is not unique. All but the smallest organizations create rules and policies to program decisions and get individuals to act in the intended manner. In doing so, they limit decision choices.

SYSTEM-IMPOSED TIME CONSTRAINTS Almost all important decisions come with explicit deadlines. For example, a report on new product development may have to be ready for executive committee review by the first of the month. Such conditions often make it difficult, if not impossible, for managers to gather all information before making a final choice, thus harming decision performance.[92]

HISTORICAL PRECEDENTS Decisions are not made in a vacuum; they have context. For example, it is common knowledge that the largest determinant of the size of any given year's budget is last year's budget. Choices made today are largely a result of choices made over the years.

DECISION MAKING IN TIMES OF CRISIS During the COVID-19 pandemic of 2020, employees and leaders of businesses alike were forced to make extremely difficult decisions amidst chaos, confusion, and uncertainty.[93] As Anjali Lai, a senior analyst at Forrester, eloquently described, "Unprecedented levels of uncertainty paired with a rapid flow of new information means [people forged] ahead with neither a template to follow, nor the luxury of pondering every decision."[94] Decision-makers are particularly susceptible to biases and distortion during times of crisis. For example, expert credit-rating agencies are more likely to provide negative or pessimistic ratings of creditworthiness during times of crisis, even when the creditworthiness of these target people or organizations would not be affected by the crisis.[95] Furthermore, decisions made during times of crisis are more likely to be emotionally charged and intuitive.[96] Not only does the strain of the crisis add an additional layer of anxiety and negative emotions to typical decisions, but the decisions in and of themselves may become highly charged, such as how doctors and nurses had to make extremely tough decisions as to who would receive treatment during the COVID-19 pandemic.[97] Relatedly, justice and ethics in decision making (see the following section for more discussion) play a huge role in times of crisis. Indeed, perceptions of justice are incredibly important during times of crisis, influencing employee attitudes and customer reactions alike.[98] As Lai noted, "Choices and actions expose the company's priorities and values to ever-watchful consumers. To the business leaders navigating these decisions, our guidance is clear: treat your employers and customers as your North Star."[99]

ETHICS IN DECISION MAKING

As discussed in the prior section, ethical considerations should be important to organizational decision making, but not just during times of crisis. In this section, we present three ways to frame ethical decisions and address the important issue of how lying affects decision making.

Three Ethical Decision Criteria

The first ethical yardstick is **utilitarianism**, which proposes making decisions solely based on their *outcomes,* ideally to provide the greatest good for all.[100] This view dominates business decision making and is consistent with goals such as rationality, efficiency, productivity, and high profits.[101] Keep in mind that utilitarianism is not always as objective as it sounds. One study indicated that the ethicality of utilitarianism is influenced in ways we do not realize. Participants were given a moral dilemma: The weight of five people bends a footbridge, so it is low to some train tracks. A train is about to hit the bridge. The choice is to let all five people perish or push the one heavy man off the bridge to save four people. In the United States, South Korea, France, and Israel, 20 percent of respondents chose to push the man off the bridge, in Spain, 18 percent, and in Korea, none. This might speak to cultural utilitarian values, but a minor change, asking people to answer in a non-native language they knew, caused more participants to push the man overboard: In one group, 33 percent pushed the man, and in another group 44 percent did.[102] The emotional distance of answering in a non-native language seemed to foster a utilitarian viewpoint. It appears that even our view of what we consider pragmatic is changeable.

Another ethical criterion is to make decisions consistent with fundamental liberties and privileges, as set forth in documents such as the U.S. Bill of Rights. An emphasis on *rights* in decision making means respecting and protecting the basic rights of individuals, such as the right to privacy, free speech, and due process.[103] This criterion protects **whistleblowers**[104] when they reveal an organization's unethical practices to the press or government agencies, using their right to free speech.

A third criterion is to impose and enforce rules fairly and impartially to ensure *justice* or an equitable distribution of benefits and costs.[105] This criterion is often approached from a **deonance** standpoint (employees feel as if they *ought* to behave in a certain way,

Utilitarianism
An ethical perspective in which decisions are made to provide the greatest good for all.

Whistleblowers
Individuals who report unethical practices by their employer to outsiders.

Deonance
A perspective in which ethical decisions are made because you "ought to" in order to be consistent with moral norms, principles, standards, rules, or laws.

as laid out in rules, laws, norms, or moral principles).[106] For example, some employees might feel as if they *should not* steal from their workplace because it is ethically "wrong" by moral norms, principles, or standards or it is forbidden by rules or laws. Notably, this "ought force" is present regardless of whether organizational rules exist; often, a decision is regarded as unfair or unjust because it violates a moral norm or principle.

Choosing Between Criteria

Decision makers, particularly in for-profit organizations, feel comfortable with utilitarianism. The "best interests" of the organization and its stockholders can justify a lot of questionable actions, such as large layoffs. However, while raising prices, selling products with questionable effects on consumer health, closing inefficient plants, laying off large numbers of employees, and moving production overseas to cut costs can be justified in utilitarian terms, there may no longer be a single measure by which good decisions are judged. This presents a challenge because satisfying individual rights and social justice creates far more ambiguities than utilitarian effects on efficiency and profits. Indeed, the ethical-decision making process itself is complex, and the traditional perspective of viewing these criteria as completely separate is giving way to one that views them as interrelated and contingent upon whether decisions are made about the self or judging others' behavior.[107]

This is where corporate social responsibility (CSR) makes a difference. As we can see by looking at utilitarian ideals, organizations may approach decisions in a certain way when they are looking only at a balance sheet. However, public pressure on organizations to behave responsibly has meant sustainability issues clearly affect the bottom line: Consumers increasingly choose to purchase goods and services from organizations with effective CSR initiatives, high performers are attracted to work for CSR organizations, governments offer incentives to organizations for sustainability efforts, and so forth.[108]

Behavioral Ethics

Behavioral ethics
Analyzing how people behave when confronted with ethical dilemmas.

Increasingly, researchers are turning to **behavioral ethics**—an area of study that analyzes how people behave when confronted with ethical dilemmas. While ethical standards exist collectively in societies and organizations as well as individually in the form of personal ethics, we do not always follow ethical standards promoted by our organizations. Sometimes, we even violate our own standards. Our ethical behavior varies widely from one situation to the next.

Behavioral ethics research stresses the importance of culture to ethical decision making. There are few global standards for ethical decision making,[109] as contrasts between cultures illustrate. What is ethical in one culture may be unethical in another. For example, because bribery is more common in countries such as China, a Canadian working in China may face a dilemma: Should I pay a bribe to secure business if it is an accepted part of that country's culture? Without sensitivity to cultural differences as part of the definition of ethical conduct, organizations may encourage unethical conduct without even knowing it.

Lying

Although lying might depend on both situational characteristics and individual differences, a large volume of research suggests that lying and dishonest behavior are very common.[110] Perhaps one of the reasons we lie is that lying is difficult for others to detect.[111] In more than 200 studies, individuals correctly identified people who were lying only 47 percent of the time, which is less than random picking.[112] For example, one technique police officers use is based on the theory that people look up and to the right when they lie. Unfortunately, researchers who tested the technique could not substantiate the underlying theory.[113]

Although people often try to justify lying as necessary in certain situations (e.g., sales) or because honesty can be difficult,[114] lying is deadly to decision making. Managers and employees simply cannot make good decisions when facts are misrepresented, and people give false motives for their behaviors. Lying is a big ethical problem as well. From an organizational perspective, using fancy lie-detection techniques and entrapping liars when possible yields unreliable results.[115] The most lasting solution comes from OB, which studies ways to prevent lying by working with our natural propensities to create environments that are not conducive to lying.

CREATIVITY AND INNOVATION IN ORGANIZATIONS

Although alternatives to solving problems may often be clear or readily available, sometimes a decision maker also needs **creativity**, the ability to produce novel and useful ideas. Novel ideas are different from what has been done before but are appropriate for the problem.

Creativity allows the decision maker to appraise and understand problems fully, including seeing problems others cannot see. Although all aspects of OB are complex, this is especially true for creativity. To simplify, Exhibit 6-4 provides a three-stage model of creativity in organizations. The core of the model is *creative behavior*, which has both *causes* (predictors of creative behavior) and *effects* (outcomes of creative behavior).

Creativity
The ability to produce novel and useful ideas.

Creative Behavior

Creative behavior occurs in four steps, each of which leads to the next:[116]

1. **Problem formulation.** Any act of creativity begins with a problem that the behavior is designed to solve. Thus, **problem formulation** is the stage of creative behavior in which we identify a problem or opportunity that requires a solution that is yet unknown. For example, Marshall Carbee and John Bennett founded Eco Safety Products after discovering that even paints declared safe by the Environmental Protection Agency emitted hazardous chemical compounds.[117]

Problem formulation
The stage of creative behavior that involves identifying a problem or opportunity requiring a solution that is yet unknown.

**EXHIBIT 6-4
Three-Stage
Model of
Creativity in
Organizations**

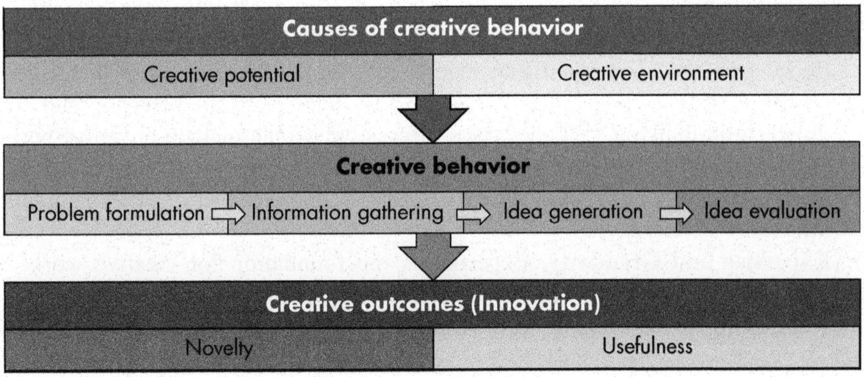

Information gathering
The stage of creative behavior when possible solutions to a problem incubate in an individual's mind.

Idea generation
The process of creative behavior that involves developing possible solutions to a problem from relevant information and knowledge.

Idea evaluation
The process of creative behavior involving the evaluation of potential solutions to problems to identify the best one.

2. **Information gathering.** Given a problem, the solution is rarely clear at the outset. We need time to learn more and to process what we have learned. Thus, **information gathering** is the stage of creative behavior when knowledge is sought and possible solutions to a problem incubate. Information gathering leads us to identifying innovation opportunities.[118] For example, you could have lunch with someone outside your industry to discuss the problem, forcing you to speak about the problem in new terms.[119]

3. **Idea generation. Idea generation** is the process in which we develop possible solutions to a problem from relevant information and knowledge. Curiosity has been found to be a driver of idea generation: when you are curious about something, you are more likely to link earlier ideas or earlier solutions to help solve the current problem.[120]

4. **Idea evaluation.** Finally, it is time to choose from the ideas we have generated. Thus, **idea evaluation** is the process of creative behavior in which we evaluate potential solutions to problems to identify the best one.

Causes of Creative Behavior

Having defined creative behavior, the main stage in the three-stage model, we now look back to the causes of creativity: creative potential and creative environment.

CREATIVE POTENTIAL Is there such a thing as a creative personality? Indeed. While creative genius is rare—whether in science (Stephen Hawking), the performing arts (Martha Graham), or business (Steve Jobs)—most people have some of the characteristics shared by exceptionally creative people. The more of these characteristics we have, the higher our creative potential. Consider these indicators of creative potential:

1. **Intelligence and Creativity.** Intelligence is related to creativity—some research has even shown that some degree of intelligence is necessary in order to be creative.[121] Smart people are more creative because they are better at solving complex problems.[122] However, they may also be more creative because they have greater "working memory," that is, they can recall more information related to the task at hand.[123] Along the same lines, recent research in Europe indicates that an individual's high need for cognition (desire to learn) and cognitive abilities geared toward updating information is correlated with greater creativity.[124]

2. **Personality and Creativity.** The Big Five personality trait of openness to experience (see the chapter on personality and values) correlates with creativity, probably because open individuals are less conformist in behavior and more divergent in thinking.[125] Other traits of creative people include proactive personality, self-confidence, risk taking, tolerance for ambiguity, and perseverance.[126] Hope, self-efficacy (belief in your capabilities), and positive affect also predict an individual's creativity.[127]

3. **Expertise and Creativity.** Expertise is the foundation for creative work. For example, film writer, producer, and director Quentin Tarantino spent his youth working in a video rental store, where he built up an encyclopedic knowledge

of movies. Creative experts, based on this vast knowledge, are able to vividly envision their ideas and forecast what may or may not happen as a result.[128] The expertise of others is important, too. People with larger social networks have greater exposure to diverse ideas and informal access to the expertise and resources of others.[129]

4. **Ethics and Creativity.** Although creativity is linked to many desirable individual characteristics, its relationship with ethicality is unclear. People who cheat may be more creative than those who behave ethically, according to recent research. It may be that dishonesty and creativity can both stem from a rule-breaking desire.[130] Some recent research has found that people who tend to have creative personalities (or who are members of more creative teams) tend to be imaginative concerning moral issues (e.g., able to better envision consequences of their actions) and, as such, are actually *more* ethical.[131]

CREATIVE ENVIRONMENT Most of us have creative potential we can learn to apply, but as important as creative potential is, by itself it is not enough. We need to be in an environment where creative potential can be realized.[132] Perhaps most important, is *motivation*. Intrinsic motivation, or the desire to work on something because it is interesting, exciting, satisfying, and challenging (discussed in more detail in the chapters on motivation), correlates strongly with creative outcomes.[133] As such, environments should foster employees' motivations to be creative.[134] What other environmental factors affect whether creative potential translates into creative behaviors?

First, it is valuable to work in an environment that rewards and recognizes creative work.[135] A study of health care teams found that team creativity translated into innovation only when the climate actively supported innovation.[136] The organization should foster the free flow of ideas, including providing fair and constructive judgment. Freedom from excessive rules also encourages creativity; employees should have the freedom to decide what work is to be done and how to do it. One study in China revealed that both structural empowerment (in which the structure of the work unit allows sufficient employee freedom) and psychological empowerment (which lets the individual feel personally enabled to decide) were related to employee creativity.[137] However, research in Slovenia found that creating a competitive climate where achievement at any cost is valued will stymie creativity.[138]

Second, certain job characteristics can foster creativity. Specifically, jobs that are complex, autonomous, and have clear role expectations for innovation are related to innovative behavior—these job characteristics can be especially important in inspiring creative behavior.[139] Managers and leaders play a large role in establishing these characteristics as a part of the organizational infrastructure and culture. They may be able to heighten innovation when resources are limited by encouraging employees to find resources for their novel ideas and by giving direct attention to appropriate tools when resources are plentiful.[140] Managers also serve as an important bridge role for knowledge transfer. When managers link teams to additional information and resources, radical creativity (introducing creative ideas that break the status quo) is more likely.[141] The weaker ties between team members and manager networks may have more impact on creativity than the direct, stronger ties that team members have with their own networks because the weaker sources provide more divergent thinking.[142]

Creative Outcomes (Innovation)

The final stage in our model of creativity is the outcome. We can define *creative outcomes* as ideas or solutions judged to be novel and useful by relevant stakeholders. Novelty itself does not generate a creative outcome if it is not useful. Thus, "off the wall" solutions are creative only if they help solve the problem. The usefulness of the solution might be self-evident (the iPad), or it might be considered successful by only the stakeholders initially.[143]

An organization may harvest many creative ideas from its employees and call itself innovative. However, as one expert stated, "Ideas are useless unless used." Soft skills help translate ideas into results. One researcher found that in a large agribusiness company, creative ideas were most likely to be implemented when an individual was motivated to translate the idea into practice—and had strong networking ability.[144] These studies highlight an important fact: Creative ideas do not implement themselves; translating them into creative outcomes is a social process that requires utilizing other concepts addressed in this text, including power and politics, leadership, and motivation.

SUMMARY

Individuals base their behavior not on their external environment, but rather on the way they see it or believe it to be. An understanding of the way people make decisions can help us explain and predict behavior, but few important decisions are simple or unambiguous enough for the rational model's assumptions to apply. We find individuals looking for solutions that satisfice rather than optimize, injecting biases and prejudices into the decision process, and relying on intuition. Managers should encourage ethicality and creativity in employees as well as teams to create a route to effective decision making.

IMPLICATIONS FOR MANAGERS

- Behavior follows perception, so to influence behavior at work, assess how people perceive their work. Often behaviors we find puzzling can be explained by understanding the initiating perceptions.
- Make better decisions by recognizing perceptual biases and decision-making errors we tend to commit. Learning about these problems does not always prevent us from making mistakes, but it does help.
- Adjust your decision-making approach to the national culture you are operating in and to the criteria your organization values. If you are in a country that does not value rationality, do not feel compelled to follow the decision-making model or to try to make your decisions appear rational. Adjust your decision approach to ensure compatibility with the organizational culture.
- Combine rational analysis with intuition. These are not conflicting approaches to decision making. By using both, you can improve your decision-making effectiveness.
- Try to enhance your creativity. Actively look for novel solutions to problems, attempt to see problems in new ways, use analogies, and hire creative talent. Try to remove work and organizational barriers that might impede creativity.

7
Motivation Concepts

After studying this chapter, you should be able to:

7.1 Describe the three key elements of motivation.

7.2 Compare the early theories of motivation.

7.3 Contrast the elements of self-determination theory and goal-setting theory.

7.4 Demonstrate the differences among self-efficacy theory, reinforcement theory, and expectancy theory.

7.5 Describe the forms of organizational justice, including distributive justice, procedural justice, informational justice, and interactional justice.

7.6 Identify the implications of employee job engagement for managers.

7.7 Describe how the contemporary theories of motivation complement one another.

MOTIVATION

Millions of people each year spend money in the hopes that they will become more "motivated." In the U.S. alone, self-improvement and motivational services is a $9.9-billion market, that is expected to grow 5.6 percent on average until 2022, when it is projected to be worth $13.2 billion.[1] In the following chapters, you will see how important motivation is to performance, as well as how it is linked to well-being in the workplace.

As we analyze the concept of motivation, keep in mind that levels of motivation can vary from moment-to-moment, but also be a meaningful individual difference (see the chapter on personality and values). We define **motivation** as the processes that account for an individual's *intensity, direction*, and *persistence* of effort toward attaining a goal.[2] While general motivation is concerned with effort toward *any* goal, we will narrow the focus to *organizational* goals.

Intensity describes how hard a person tries. This is the element most of us focus on when we talk about motivation. However, high intensity is unlikely to lead to favorable job performance outcomes unless the effort is channeled in a *direction* that benefits the organization. Finally, motivation has a *persistence* dimension. This measures how long a person can maintain effort. Motivated individuals work intensely on an appropriate task, long enough to achieve their goals.

Motivation
The processes that account for an individual's intensity, direction, and persistence of effort toward attaining a goal.

EARLY THEORIES OF MOTIVATION

Three theories of employee motivation formulated during the 1950s are probably the best known. Although they are now of questionable validity (as we will discuss), they represent a foundation of motivation theory, and many practicing managers still use their terminology.

Hierarchy of Needs Theory

Hierarchy of needs
Abraham Maslow's hierarchy of five needs—physiological, safety, social, esteem, and self-actualization—in which, as each need is well-satisfied, the next need becomes dominant.

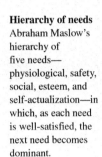

The best-known theory of motivation is Abraham Maslow's **hierarchy of needs**,[3] which hypothesizes that there is a hierarchy of five needs humans are motivated to meet. Recently, a sixth need has been proposed for a highest level—intrinsic values—but it has yet to gain widespread acceptance.[4] The original five needs are:

1. **Physiological.** Hunger, thirst, shelter, sex, and other bodily needs.
2. **Safety-security.** Security and protection from physical and emotional harm.
3. **Social-belongingness.** Affection, belongingness, acceptance, and friendship.
4. **Esteem.** Internal factors such as self-respect, autonomy, and achievement as well as external factors such as status, recognition, and attention.
5. **Self-actualization.** Drive to become what we can become; includes growth, achievement of our potential, and self-fulfillment.

According to Maslow, as each need becomes well-satisfied, the next one becomes dominant. If you want to motivate someone, you need to understand what level of the hierarchy that person is on and focus on satisfying needs at or above that level. We depict the hierarchy as a pyramid in Exhibit 7-1.

Maslow's theory has broadly received long-standing recognition, particularly among practicing managers. It is intuitively logical and easy to understand, and some research supports it.[5] Unfortunately, however, most research does not, and it has not been frequently researched since the 1960s.[6] Nonetheless, it is important to be aware of the prevailing public acceptance of the hierarchy when discussing motivation.

Two-Factor Theory

Two-factor theory
A theory that relates intrinsic factors to job satisfaction and associates extrinsic factors with dissatisfaction. Also called motivation–hygiene theory.

Believing an individual's relationship to work is basic, and that the attitude toward work can determine success or failure, psychologist Frederick Herzberg wondered, "What do people want from their jobs?" He asked people to describe, in detail, situations in which they felt exceptionally *good* or *bad* about their jobs. The responses differed significantly and led Herzberg to his **two-factor theory** (also called *motivation–hygiene theory*, but this term is not used much today).[7]

EXHIBIT 7-1
Maslow's Hierarchy of Needs

Source: H. Skelsey, "Maslow's Hierarchy of Needs—the Sixth Level," *Psychologist* (2014): 982–83.

As shown in Exhibit 7-2, intrinsic factors such as advancement, recognition, responsibility, and achievement seem related to job satisfaction. Respondents who felt good about their work tended to attribute these factors to their situations, while dissatisfied respondents tended to cite extrinsic factors such as supervision, pay, company policies, and work conditions. To Herzberg, the data suggest that the opposite of satisfaction is not dissatisfaction, as was traditionally believed (see Exhibit 7-2). Removing dissatisfying characteristics from a job does not necessarily make the job satisfying; managers would be placating, rather than motivating, the employees.

Conditions such as quality of supervision, pay, company policies, physical work conditions, relationships with others, and job security are **hygiene factors**. When they are adequate, people will not be dissatisfied; neither will they be satisfied. If we want to *motivate* people on their jobs, we should emphasize factors associated with the work itself or with outcomes directly derived from it such as promotional opportunities, personal growth opportunities, recognition, responsibility, and achievement. These are the characteristics people find intrinsically rewarding.

Two-factor theory has not been well supported in research. Criticisms center on Herzberg's original methodology and his assumptions, such as how the participants may be biased in thinking back to times when they felt good or bad about their jobs.[8] Furthermore, if hygiene and motivational factors are equally important to a person, both should be capable of motivating.

Regardless of the criticisms, Herzberg's theory has been quite influential and has been used in many studies in Asian countries such as Japan and India.[9] Most managers worldwide are familiar with its recommendations.

Hygiene factors
Factors—such as company policy and administration, supervision, and salary—that, when adequate in a job, placate workers and limit job dissatisfaction.

McClelland's Theory of Needs

Imagine that you are a sales manager in a well-known mountaineer outfitting company reviewing the bonus memo you received earlier in the day. If you meet the easier, Level one sales goal, you will get a $2,000 bonus. If you meet the Level two sales goal (which only 80 percent of the people who try will attain), you will get a $4,000 bonus. Level three pays $8,000, which only half the people who try will attain. Finally, Level four pays

Traditional view

Satisfaction   Dissatisfaction

Herzberg's view

Motivators

Satisfaction   No satisfaction

Hygiene factors

No dissatisfaction   Dissatisfaction

EXHIBIT 7-2
Contrasting Satisfaction and Dissatisfaction

$32,000, but it is almost impossible to achieve. Which would you try for? If you selected level three, you are likely a high achiever.

McClelland's theory of needs, unlike Maslow's hierarchy, suggests that needs are more like motivating factors than strict needs for survival.[10] In McClelland and colleagues' theory, there are three primary needs:

- **Need for achievement (nAch)** is the need to excel or achieve to a set of standards.
- **Need for power (nPow)** is the need to make others behave in a way they would not have otherwise.
- **Need for affiliation (nAff)** is the need to establish friendly and close interpersonal relationships.

McClelland and subsequent researchers focused most of their attention on nAch.[11] In general, high achievers perform best when they perceive their probability of success as 0.5—that is, a fifty–fifty chance. They dislike gambling with high odds because they get no achievement satisfaction from success that comes by pure chance. Similarly, they dislike low odds (high probability of success) because then there is no challenge to their skills. Based on prior nAch research, we can predict some relationships between nAch and job performance. First, when employees have a high level of nAch, they tend to exhibit more positive moods and be more interested in the task at hand.[12] Second, employees high on nAch tend to perform very well in high-stakes conditions on the job, like work walkthroughs or sales encounters.[13]

The other needs within the theory also have research support. First, the nPow concept also has research support, but it may be more familiar to people in broad terms than in relation to the original definition.[14] We will discuss power much more in the chapter on power and politics. Second, the nAff concept is also well established and accepted in research—for example, one study of 145 teams suggests that groups composed of employees with a high nAff tend to perform the best, exhibit the most open communication, and experience the least amount of conflict (compared with the other needs).[15] Additional research suggests that our individual differences (discussed in the chapter on personality and values) may affect whether we can satisfy these needs. For example, a high degree of neuroticism can prevent one from fulfilling the nAff, whereas agreeableness supports fulfillment of this need; interestingly, extraversion had no significant effect.[16] Furthermore, some evidence suggests that women may be more likely to have more nAff needs than men.[17]

The degree to which we have each of the three needs is difficult to measure, and therefore the theory is difficult to put into practice. A behavior may satisfy many different needs, and many different behaviors may be directed at satisfying one given need, making needs difficult to isolate and examine.[18] Therefore, the concepts are helpful, but they are not often used objectively.

CONTEMPORARY THEORIES OF MOTIVATION

Contemporary theories of motivation have a reasonable degree of evidence supporting them. We call them "contemporary theories" because they represent the latest thinking in explaining employee motivation. This does not mean they are unquestionably right, however.

Need for achievement (nAch)
The need to excel or achieve to a set of standards.

Need for power (nPow)
The need to make others behave in a way in which they would not have behaved otherwise.

Need for affiliation (nAff)
The need to establish friendly and close interpersonal relationships.

Self-Determination Theory

"It's strange," said Jordan. "I started work at the Humane Society as a volunteer. I put in fifteen hours a week helping people adopt pets. And I loved coming to work. Then, three months ago, they hired me full-time at eleven dollars an hour. I am doing the same work I did before. But I'm not finding it as much fun."

Does Jordan's reaction seem counterintuitive? One explanation can be found in **self-determination theory**, which proposes that employees' well-being and performance are influenced by their motivation for certain job activities, including the sense of choice over what they do, how motivating the task is in and of itself, how rewards influence motivation, and how work satisfies psychological needs.[19] This *meta-theory* (or a collection of related theories behind a common theme) is widely used and contains several sub-theories, including cognitive evaluation theory and self-concordance theory, discussed next.

COGNITIVE EVALUATION THEORY Much research on self-determination theory in organizational behavior (OB) has focused on **cognitive evaluation theory (CET)**, a sub-theory that suggests that extrinsic rewards will reduce intrinsic interest in a task.[20] When people are paid for work, it feels less like something they *want* to do and more like something they *must* do. For example, if a computer programmer values writing code out of a love for solving problems, a bonus for writing a certain number of lines of code every day could feel coercive, and the programmer's intrinsic motivation could suffer.

CET suggests that some caution in the use of extrinsic rewards to motivate is wise, and that pursuing goals from intrinsic motives (such as a strong interest in the work itself) is more sustaining to human motivation than are extrinsic rewards. In support, research confirms that intrinsic motivation contributes to the quality of work, while incentives contribute to the quantity of work. Also, effects of intrinsic motivation may be weaker when incentives are directly tied to performance (such as a monetary bonus for each call made in a call center).[21]

SELF-CONCORDANCE An outgrowth of self-determination theory is **self-concordance theory**, which considers how strongly people's reasons for pursuing goals are consistent with their interests and core values. OB research suggests that people who pursue work goals that align with their interests and values are more satisfied with their jobs, feel they fit into their organizations better, and perform better.[22] Across cultures, if individuals pursue goals because of intrinsic interest, they are more likely to attain goals, are happier when they do, and are happy even if they are unable to attain them.[23] Why? Because they feel like they are more competent at accomplishing the goal and like they fit better with their organization.[24]

BASIC PSYCHOLOGICAL NEEDS Similar to Maslow's and McClelland's theories, discussed in the prior section, self-determination theory also suggests that there are several basic psychological needs that affect work motivation. When they are satisfied, we tend to be more motivated; when they are frustrated, we tend to be less motivated. *Need for relatedness* is very similar to nAff, discussed in the prior section. However, **need for autonomy** and **need for competence** are two newer needs that correspond with the need to feel in control and autonomous at work and the need to feel like we are good at what we

---

Self-determination theory
A meta-theory of motivation at work that is concerned with autonomy, intrinsic motivation, extrinsic motivation, and the satisfaction of psychological work needs.

Cognitive evaluation theory
A sub-theory of self-determination theory in which extrinsic rewards for behavior tend to decrease the overall level of motivation, if the rewards are seen as controlling or reduce their sense of competence.

Self-concordance
The degree to which people's reasons for pursuing goals are consistent with their interests and core values.

Need for autonomy
The need to feel in control and autonomous at work.

Need for competence
The need to feel like we are good at what we do and be proud of it.

do and are proud of it.[25] Of all the three needs, however, the autonomy need is the most important for attitudinal and affective outcomes, whereas the competence need appears to be most important for predicting performance.[26] Also, when using extrinsic rewards, need satisfaction matters less for performance when the rewards are directly salient and clear.[27]

What does all this mean? Managers need to design jobs so that they are motivating, provide recognition, and support employee growth and development. Employees who feel autonomous and free in what they choose to do are likely to be more motivated by their work and committed to their employers. Furthermore, employees can satisfy many of these needs through helping others.[28] As Walmart leadership coach, Lucy Duncan, suggests about Walmart associates, if you take the time to incorporate self-determination theory in your workplace, "you will be blown away with associate satisfaction."[29]

Goal-Setting Theory

Goal-setting theory
A theory that specific and difficult goals, with feedback, lead to higher performance.

You've likely heard this a number of times: "Just do your best. That's all anyone can ask." But what does "do your best" mean? Do we ever know whether we have achieved that vague goal? Research on **goal-setting theory** reveals the impressive effects of goal specificity, challenge, and feedback on performance. Under the theory, intentions to work toward a goal are considered a major source of work motivation.[30]

SPECIFICITY, DIFFICULTY, AND FEEDBACK   Goal-setting theory is well supported. Evidence strongly suggests that *specific* goals increase performance; that *difficult* goals, when accepted, produce higher performances than do easy goals; and that *feedback* leads to higher performance than does non-feedback.[31] Why? First, goals that are specific explicitly direct attention toward what needs to be accomplished. Second, once a difficult task has been accepted, we can expect the employee to exert a high level of effort to try to achieve it. Third, people do better when they get feedback on how well they are progressing toward their goals—that is, feedback guides behavior. But all feedback is not equally potent. Self-generated feedback—with which employees can monitor their own progress or receive feedback from the task process itself—is more powerful than externally generated feedback.[32]

If employees can participate in the setting of their own goals, will they try harder? The evidence is mixed, although across studies it appears that they will not perform any better.[33] In some studies, participatively set goals yielded superior performance; in others, individuals performed best when assigned goals by their boss. If goals are not set by the employee, then the manager needs to ensure that the employee clearly understands its purpose and importance.[34]

GOAL COMMITMENT, TASK CHARACTERISTICS, AND NATIONAL CULTURE   Three factors influence the goals–performance relationship: *goal commitment, task characteristics*, and *national culture*.

1. **Goal commitment**. Goal-setting theory assumes an individual is committed to the goal and determined not to shirk or abandon it. The individual (1) believes they can achieve the goal and (2) wants to achieve it.[35] Goal commitment is most likely to occur when employees expect that their efforts will pay off in goal attainment, when people of higher status are watching and aware of the goal, and when accomplishing the goal is attractive to them.[36]

2. **Task characteristics.** Goals themselves seem to affect performance more strongly when tasks are simple rather than complex, and when the tasks are independent rather than interdependent.[37] On interdependent tasks, group goals along with delegation of tasks are preferable. Unplanned disturbances also play a role. If distractions or events outside your control limit how quickly you can make progress, chances are you will become frustrated and less enthusiastic.[38] For example, co-workers who constantly slow down progress on projects can be very frustrating.

3. **National culture.** In collectivistic and high power-distance cultures, achievable moderate goals can be more motivating than difficult ones.[39] Assigned goals appear to generate greater goal commitment in high than in low power-distance cultures.[40] More research is needed to assess how goal constructs might differ across cultures.

Although goal setting can be positive, employees and managers should be careful not to overdo it.[41] For example, goals might impede learning because we become too focused on achievement, we may choose the wrong type or form of goal which may impede performance, and we may fall prey to escalation of commitment (see the chapter on perception and individual decision making) if we are not careful. If you want to maximize the extent to which goal setting is successful, recent research suggests that setting a cadence of accountability can help, and monitoring of goals can lead to more frequent goal attainment, especially when goal progress is publicly announced.[42]

INDIVIDUAL AND PROMOTION FOCI   Research has found that people differ in the way they regulate their thoughts and behaviors during goal pursuit.[43] Generally, people fall into one of two categories, though they can belong to both. Those with a **promotion focus** strive for advancement and accomplishment, and approach conditions that move them closer toward desired goals. Those with a **prevention focus** strive to fulfill duties and obligations, as well as avoid conditions that pull them away from desired goals. Although you would be right to note that both strategies are in the service of goal accomplishment, the way they get there is quite different. As an example, consider studying for an exam. You could engage in promotion-focused activities such as reading class materials, or you could engage in prevention-focused activities such as refraining from doing things that would get in the way of studying, such as playing video games.

You may ask, "Which is the better strategy?" Well, the answer depends on the outcome you are striving for. A promotion (but not a prevention) focus is related to higher levels of task performance, citizenship behavior, well-being, and innovation; a prevention (but not a promotion) focus is related to safety performance. Ideally, it is probably best to be both promotion *and* prevention oriented, depending upon the situation.[44] Employees and managers should set achievable goals, remove distractions, and provide structure for these individuals.[45] Furthermore, research suggests that if an individuals' focus matches their supervisor's, they will report higher relationship quality and be more committed to the relationship.[46]

Promotion focus
A self-regulation strategy that involves striving for goals through advancement and accomplishment.

Prevention focus
A self-regulation strategy that involves striving for goals by fulfilling duties and obligations.

GOAL-SETTING IMPLEMENTATION   How do managers set goals in their organizations? That is often left up to the individual manager. Some managers set aggressive performance targets—what General Electric called "stretch goals." For example, Motorola once sought to reduce how long it took to close their year-end books from *six weeks* to *four days*.[47] Some leaders, such as the CEO of Telltale Games, are known for their demanding performance goals—some of which even suggest game developers to weather the "crunch," a sudden spike in work hours that require them to work as many as 20 hours a day. But many managers do not set goals. When asked whether their jobs had clearly defined goals, a minority of respondents to a survey said yes.[48]

Management by objectives (MBO)
A program that encompasses specific goals, participatively set, for an explicit time period and including feedback on goal progress.

A more systematic way to utilize goal setting is with **management by objectives (MBO)**, an initiative most popular in the 1970s but still used today.[49] MBO emphasizes participatively set goals that are tangible, verifiable, and measurable. As Exhibit 7-3 shows, the organization's overall objectives are translated into specific cascading objectives for each level (divisional, departmental, individual). Because lower-unit managers jointly participate in setting their own goals, MBO works from the bottom up as well as from the top down. The result is a hierarchy that links objectives at one level to those at the next.

You will find MBO programs in many organizations from different industries, and many of these have led to performance gains.[50] A version of MBO, called *management by objectives and results* (MBOR), has been used for over thirty years in the governments of Denmark, Norway, and Sweden.[51] However, the popularity of these programs does not mean they always work.[52] When MBO fails, the culprits tend to be unrealistic expectations, lack of commitment by top management, and inability or unwillingness to allocate rewards based on goal accomplishment.

GOAL SETTING AND ETHICS If we emphasize the attainment of goals, what is the cost? The answer is probably found in the standards we set for goal achievement. For example, when money is tied to goal attainment (e.g., getting money), we may focus on the money and become willing to compromise ourselves ethically. Moreover, a focus on the outcome (especially if the goal is difficult) may make unethical behavior more likely.[53] Time pressure also increases as we are nearing a goal, which can tempt us to act unethically to achieve it.[54] Goal setting can lead to unethical behavior in a different way: through depletion.[55] For example, if the kitchen staff is exhausted and overloaded, they might be more prone to take shortcuts in food preparation and cleaning that put food safety in danger.

EXHIBIT 7-3
Cascading of Objectives

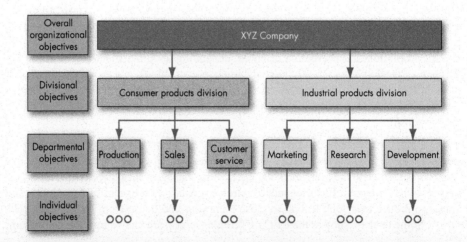

OTHER CONTEMPORARY THEORIES OF MOTIVATION

Self-determination theory and goal-setting theory are well supported contemporary theories of motivation. But they are far from the only noteworthy OB theories on the subject. Self-efficacy, reinforcement, and expectancy theories reveal different aspects of our motivational processes and tendencies.

Self-Efficacy Theory

Self-efficacy theory, a component of *social cognitive theory* or *social learning theory,* refers to an individual's belief of being capable of performing a task.[56] For example, professional basketball players with high self-efficacy believe they can play very well. In difficult situations people with low self-efficacy are more likely to lessen their effort or give up altogether, while those with high self-efficacy will try harder to master the challenge.[57]

> **Self-efficacy**
> An individual's belief of being capable of performing a task.

Self-efficacy can (but not always) create a positive spiral in which those with high efficacy become more engaged in their tasks and then, in turn, increase performance, which increases efficacy further.[58] Intelligence and personality are linked to higher self-efficacy.[59] People who are intelligent, conscientious, and emotionally stable are so much more likely to have high self-efficacy that some researchers argue self-efficacy is less important than prior research suggested.[60]

INFLUENCING SELF-EFFICACY IN OTHERS   How can managers help their employees achieve high levels of self-efficacy? By bringing goal-setting theory and self-efficacy theory together. As Exhibit 7-4 shows, employees whose managers set difficult goals for them (and, by extension, communicate their confidence in the employees) will have a higher level of self-efficacy and set higher goals for their own performance.

Research also suggests that there are four ways to increase self-efficacy: (1) Give employees relevant experiences with the task (i.e., *enactive mastery*), (2) Enable them to watch someone else do the task (i.e., *vicarious modeling*), (3) Reassure the employees, letting them know that they have "what it takes" to do the task (i.e., *verbal persuasion*), and (4) Tell them to "get psyched up" (i.e., *arousal*)—getting energized will enable the employees to approach the task more positively (although this last step is probably not a good idea if the task is "low key," like writing a sales report.[61]

One of the best ways for a manager to use verbal persuasion is through the *Pygmalion effect,* a term based on the Greek myth about a sculptor (Pygmalion) who fell in love with a statue he carved. The Pygmalion effect is a form of *self-fulfilling prophecy* in which believing something can make it true. Here, it is often used to describe "that what one person expects can come to serve a self-fulfilling prophecy."[62] For example, if we identify those in the office with the highest leadership potential, we may treat them in such a way where they eventually become a leader.[63] However, we may find leaders in unexpected places, as "diamonds in the rough"—Dov Frohman notes, "Leaders are found in the strangest places. Often the best candidates turn out to be people from outside the mainstream ... who at first glance one would never expect would have leadership potential."[64] The Pygmalion approach can be effective in the workplace, with replicable results and enhanced effects when leader–subordinate relationships are strong.[65]

Training programs often make use of enactive mastery by having people practice and build their skills. In fact, one reason training works is that it increases self-efficacy,

EXHIBIT 7-4

Joint Effects of Goals and Self-Efficacy on Performance

Source: Based on E. A. Locke and G. P. Latham, "Building a Practically Useful Theory of Goal Setting and Task Motivation: A 35-Year Odyssey," *American Psychologist* 57, no. 9 (2002): 705–17.

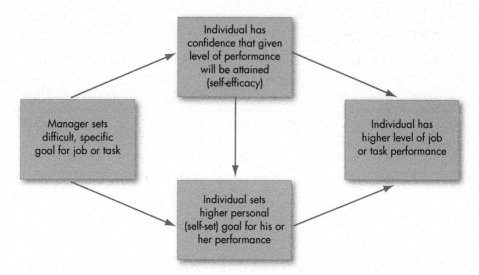

particularly when the training is interactive and feedback is given afterward.[66] However, some research suggests that if the employee is unable to see their own improvement, then they will not experience enhanced self-efficacy.[67] Regardless, individuals with higher levels of self-efficacy appear to reap more benefits from training programs and are more likely to use their training on the job.[68]

Reinforcement Theory

Reinforcement theory
A theory that behavior is a function of its consequences.

Reinforcement theory takes a behaviorist approach, arguing that reinforcement conditions behavior.[69] Reinforcement theorists see behavior as environmentally caused. You need not be concerned, they would argue, with internal cognitive events (e.g., goal setting); what controls behavior are reinforcers—any consequences that, when they immediately follow responses, increase the probability that the behavior will be repeated. For example, when you are given a compliment for doing something at work, you might be more likely to do it again.

Reinforcement theory ignores the inner state of the individual and concentrates solely on what happens when the individual acts. Although it is not strictly a motivation theory, it does provide a powerful means of analyzing what controls behavior, and therefore we typically consider reinforcement concepts in discussions of motivation.

Behaviorism
A theory that behavior follows stimuli in a relatively unthinking manner.

OPERANT CONDITIONING/BEHAVIORISM AND REINFORCEMENT *Operant conditioning* suggests that people *learn* to behave a certain way to either get something they want or to avoid something they do not want. Operant conditioning was part of B. F. Skinner's broader concept of **behaviorism**, which argues that behavior follows stimuli in a relatively unthinking manner. In short, under behaviorism people learn to associate stimulus and response, but their conscious awareness of this association is irrelevant.[70] For instance, a commissioned salesperson wanting to earn a sizable income finds doing so is contingent on generating high sales, so the salesperson sells as much as possible.

SOCIAL LEARNING THEORY   Individuals can learn by observing what happens to other people, as well as through direct experience. Much of what we have learned comes from watching models—coworkers, bosses, and so forth.[71] The view that we can learn through both observation and direct experience is called **social learning theory**.[72]

Social learning theory, like operant conditioning, assumes behavior is a function of consequences—but it also clarifies the effects of observation and perception. People respond to the way they perceive and define consequences, not to the objective consequences themselves.

Social learning theory
The view that we can learn through both observation and direct experience.

Expectancy Theory

One of the most widely accepted explanations of motivation is Victor Vroom's **expectancy theory**.[73] Although it has critics, most evidence supports the theory.[74] Expectancy theory argues that the strength of our tendency to act a certain way depends on the strength of our expectation of a given outcome and its attractiveness. In practical terms, employees will be motivated to exert a high level of effort when they believe that it will lead to a good performance appraisal, that a good appraisal will lead to organizational rewards such as salary increases and/or intrinsic rewards, and that the rewards will satisfy their personal goals. The theory, therefore, focuses on three relationships (see Exhibit 7-5).

Expectancy theory
A theory that the strength of a tendency to act in a certain way depends on the strength of an expectation that the act will be followed by a given outcome and on the attractiveness of that outcome to the individual.

1. **Expectancy.** The effort–performance relationship. The probability perceived by the individual that exerting a given amount of effort will lead to performance.
2. **Instrumentality.** The performance–reward relationship. The degree to which the individual believes performing at a certain level will lead to the attainment of a desired outcome.
3. **Valence.** The rewards–personal goals relationship. The degree to which organizational rewards satisfy an individual's personal goals or needs and the attractiveness of those potential rewards for the individual.[75]

Expectancy theory helps explain why a lot of workers are not motivated on their jobs and do only the minimum necessary to get by. It can also explain employees' efforts toward goal accomplishment. For example, let us consider a work contest: the prize? An employee of the month parking spot. Some may really want this, others could not care less (valence). Maybe if the business shares a parking lot with Trader Joe's (and is, thus, frequently crowded), this spot would be more coveted. Next, what is the contest itself? Let us say it is whoever solicits the most donations to the company charity that year.

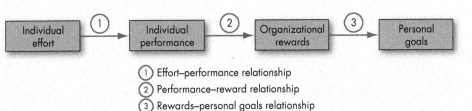

EXHIBIT 7-5
Expectancy Theory

Individual effort → ① → Individual performance → ② → Organizational rewards → ③ → Personal goals

① Effort–performance relationship
② Performance–reward relationship
③ Rewards–personal goals relationship

If an employee puts forth the effort to elicit donations, will they actually receive donations (expectancy)? Maybe people would be more likely to donate in one-dollar increments than in fifty-dollar increments. Finally, if you do get several people to donate, how likely is it that you will win the parking spot (instrumentality)? Are there multiple parking spots up for grabs? Or just one that Avery wins every year (maybe Avery knows someone who donates a ton of money every year to this contest)? Several factors play into decisions to put forth effort, and expectancy theory suggests that these may be in part explained by valence, instrumentality, and expectancy.

ORGANIZATIONAL JUSTICE

Equity Theory

Ainsley is a student working toward a bachelor's degree in finance. Ainsley has accepted a summer internship in the finance department at a pharmaceutical company and is pleased with the pay: twenty dollars an hour is more than other students in the cohort receive for their summer internships. At work Ainsley meets Kai, a recent graduate working as a middle manager in the same finance department. Kai makes thirty dollars an hour and is dissatisfied. Specifically, Kai tells Ainsley that, compared to managers at other pharmaceutical companies, this position pays much less. "It isn't fair. I work just as hard as they do, yet I do not make as much. Maybe I should go work for the competition?"

Equity theory
A theory stating that individuals compare their job inputs and outcomes with those of others and then respond to eliminate any inequities.

How could someone making thirty dollars an hour be less satisfied with their pay than someone making twenty dollars an hour and be less motivated as a result? The answer lies in **equity theory** and, more broadly, in principles of organizational justice.[76] According to equity theory, employees compare what they get from their jobs (their outcomes such as pay, promotions, recognition, or a bigger office) to what they put into it (their inputs such as effort, experience, and education). They take the ratio of their Outcomes (O) to their Inputs (I) and compare it to the ratio of others, usually someone similar like a coworker or someone doing the same job.[77] This is shown in Exhibit 7-5. If we believe our ratio is equal to those with whom we compare ourselves, a state of equity exists, and we perceive our situation as fair. However, some research suggests that inputs and outputs matter as a function of age: the older you become, the more you focus on task contributions (inputs) than what you get from them (outputs).[78]

Based on equity theory, employees who perceive inequity will make one of six choices:[79]

1. **Change inputs** (exert less effort if underpaid or more if overpaid).
2. **Change outcomes** (individuals paid on a piece-rate basis can increase their pay by producing a higher quantity of units of lower quality).
3. **Distort perceptions of self** ("I used to think I worked at a moderate pace, but now I realize I work a lot harder than everyone else").
4. **Distort perceptions of others** ("Mike's job isn't as desirable as I thought").
5. **Choose a different referent** ("I may not make as much money as my brother-in-law, but I'm doing a lot better than my dad did when he was my age").
6. **Leave the field** (quit the job).

Equity theory has support from some researchers, but not from all.[80] As some examples demonstrate, it seems that some employees are more sensitive to equity, with some feeling more entitled and others feeling more benevolent.[81] Also, if someone feels like they are being overpaid on the job, would you expect them to give back part of their salary? Although equity theory's propositions have not all held up, the hypothesis served as an important precursor to the study of **organizational justice**, or more simply fairness, in the workplace.[82] Organizational justice is concerned broadly with how employees feel authorities and decision makers at work treat them. Research over the past several decades consistently shows that justice is critically important for maintaining the employee–organization relationship.[83] For the most part, employees evaluate how fairly they are treated, as shown in Exhibit 7-6.

Distributive Justice

Distributive justice is concerned with the fairness of outcomes, such as pay and recognition, that employees receive.[84] Outcomes can be allocated in many ways. For example, raises can be distributed equally among employees, or they can be based on which employees need money the most. As we said in our discussion about equity theory, however, employees tend to perceive their outcomes are fairest when they are distributed equitably. Distributive injustice can also occur at a broader level—for example, the black–white pay gap in the U.S. has been steadily getting larger from year to year and exists even when they share educational backgrounds and come from affluent families.[85]

The way we have described things so far, individuals appear to gauge distributive justice and equity in a rational, calculative way as they compare their outcome–input ratios to those of others. But the experience of justice, and especially of injustice, is often not so cold and calculated. Instead, people base distributive judgments on a feeling or an emotional reaction to the way they think they are being treated relative to others, and their reactions are often "hot" and emotional rather than cool and rational.[86] For example, during the 2018 U.S. government shutdown, one TSA employee noted that while others "get to stay home, enjoy their personal time with their families, and still get paid, we have to struggle and suffer ... most of us live paycheck to paycheck and cannot afford to be unpaid and still go to work for long. It is not fair."[87]

Procedural Justice

While distributive justice looks at *what* outcomes are allocated, **procedural justice** examines *how*.[88] For one, employees perceive that procedures are fairer when they are given a say in the decision-making process or when decision makers follow several rules:

Organizational justice
An overall perception of what is fair in the workplace, composed of distributive, procedural, informational, and interpersonal justice.

Distributive justice
Perceived fairness of the amount and allocation of rewards among individuals.

Procedural justice
The perceived fairness of the process used to determine the distribution of rewards.

Ratio Comparisons*	Perception
$\dfrac{O}{I_A} < \dfrac{O}{I_B}$	Inequity due to being underrewarded
$\dfrac{O}{I_A} = \dfrac{O}{I_B}$	Equity
$\dfrac{O}{I_A} > \dfrac{O}{I_B}$	Inequity due to being overrewarded

*Where $\dfrac{O}{I_A}$ represents the employee and $\dfrac{O}{I_B}$ represents relevant others

EXHIBIT 7-6
Equity Theory

making decisions in a timely, consistent manner (across people and over time), avoiding bias (not favoring one group or person over another), using accurate information, considering the groups or people that their decisions affect, and remaining open to appeals.[89]

If the process is judged to be fair, then employees are more accepting of unfavorable outcomes.[90] For example, If you are hoping for a raise and your manager informs you that you did not receive one, you will probably want to know how raises were determined. If it turns out your manager allocated raises based on merit and you were simply outperformed by a coworker, then you are more likely to accept your manager's decision than if raises were based on favoritism.

Interactional Justice

Interactional justice
Sensitivity to the quality of interpersonal treatment.

Beyond outcomes and procedures, research has shown that employees care about two other types of fairness that have to do with the way they are treated during interactions with others. Both of these fall within the category of **interactional justice** (see Exhibit 7-7).[91]

Informational justice
The degree to which employees are provided truthful explanations for decisions.

INFORMATIONAL JUSTICE The first type is **informational justice**, which reflects whether managers provide employees with explanations for key decisions and keep them informed of important organizational matters. The more detailed and candid managers are with employees, the more fairly treated those employees feel.

It may seem obvious that managers should be honest with their employees and not keep them in the dark about organizational matters; however, many managers are hesitant

EXHIBIT 7-7
Model of Organizational Justice

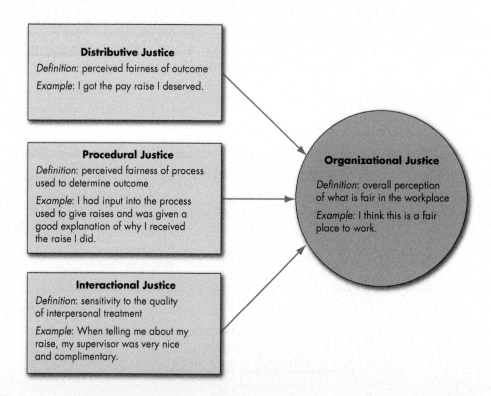

Distributive Justice
Definition: perceived fairness of outcome
Example: I got the pay raise I deserved.

Procedural Justice
Definition: perceived fairness of process used to determine outcome
Example: I had input into the process used to give raises and was given a good explanation of why I received the raise I did.

Interactional Justice
Definition: sensitivity to the quality of interpersonal treatment
Example: When telling me about my raise, my supervisor was very nice and complimentary.

Organizational Justice
Definition: overall perception of what is fair in the workplace
Example: I think this is a fair place to work.

to share information. This is especially the case with bad news, which is uncomfortable for both the manager delivering it and the employee receiving it. Explanations for bad news are beneficial when they take the form of excuses after the fact ("I know this is bad, and I wanted to give you the office, but it wasn't my decision") rather than justifications ("I decided to give the office to Sam, but having it isn't a big deal").[92]

INTERPERSONAL JUSTICE **Interpersonal justice** reflects whether employees are treated with dignity and respect. Compared to the other forms of justice, interpersonal justice is unique in that it can occur in everyday interactions between managers and employees.[93] This quality allows managers to take advantage of (or miss out on) opportunities to make their employees feel fairly treated. Unfortunately, some research suggests that even when minority leaders adhere to interpersonal justice rules, they can still be treated with bias in return, as stereotypes are activated.[94]

Interpersonal justice
The degree to which employees are treated with dignity and respect.

Justice Outcomes

How much does justice really matter to employees? A great deal, as it turns out. When employees feel fairly treated, they respond in a number of positive ways. All the types of justice discussed in this section have been linked to higher levels of task performance and citizenship behaviors such as helping coworkers, as well as lower levels of counterproductive behaviors such as shirking job duties.[95] Distributive and procedural justice are more strongly associated with task performance, while informational and interpersonal justice are more strongly associated with citizenship behavior. Even physiological outcomes, such as how well employees sleep and the state of their health, have been linked to fair treatment.[96]

Interestingly, your coworkers' reactions to injustice can be just as important as your own. Research is beginning to suggest that *third-party*, or observer, reactions to injustice can have a substantial effect. Let us say that you read about massive, unannounced layoffs at a restaurant chain you frequent. You find out that employees were let go without any warning and were not given any assistance in finding alternative arrangements. Would you continue to go to this restaurant? Research suggests that you may not.[97] People also make attributions when judging justice rule violations. Research suggests that violation of justice norms is gendered: Women are judged more harshly when they violate interactional norms than when they violate procedural norms.[98]

Despite all attempts to enhance fairness, perceived injustices are still likely to occur. Fairness is often subjective: What one person sees as unfair, another may see as perfectly appropriate. In general, people see allocations or procedures favoring themselves as fair.[99] However, if an organization is not consistent in how justly it treats its employees and employees feel like they are on a roller coaster of abuse and fair treatment, then they are more likely to become detached, cooperate less, and have lower job attitudes.[100]

Culture and Justice

Across nations, the same basic principles of procedural justice are respected: Workers around the world prefer rewards based on performance and skills over rewards based on seniority.[101] However, inputs and outcomes are valued differently in various cultures.[102]

We may think of justice differences in terms of Hofstede's cultural dimensions (see the chapter on personality and values). One large-scale study of over 190,000 employees in thirty-two countries and regions suggested that justice perceptions are most important to people in countries with individualistic, feminine, uncertainty-avoidance, and low power-distance values.[103] Indeed, research demonstrates that employees react differently (e.g., with reduced trust or effort) to perceived injustice, like abusive supervision, in different ways depending upon their culture: Employees in Confucian societies that are high power distance tend to be less affected.[104]

Organizations can tailor programs to meet these justice expectations. For example, in countries that are highest in individualism, such as Australia and the United States, competitive pay plans and rewards for superior individual performance may enhance feelings of justice. In countries dominated by uncertainty avoidance, such as France, fixed-pay compensation and employee participation may help employees feel more secure. The dominant dimension in Sweden is femininity, so organizations may therefore want to provide work–life balance initiatives and social recognition. Austria, in contrast, has a strong low power-distance value. Ethical concerns may be foremost to individuals in perceiving justice in Austrian organizations, so organizations there may want to openly justify inequality between leaders and workers and provide symbols of ethical leadership.

JOB ENGAGEMENT

When Addison reports to work as a hospital nurse, it seems that everything else melts away. Addison becomes completely absorbed in the job: all emotions, thoughts, and behavior are all directed toward patient care. In fact, Addison can get caught up in work to the point of not even being aware of the time. As a result of this state, Addison is more effective in providing patient care and feels uplifted by the work.

Job engagement
The investment of an employee's physical, cognitive, and emotional energies into job performance.

Addison has a high level of **job engagement**, the investment of an employee's physical, cognitive, and emotional energies into job performance.[105] Practicing managers and scholars have been interested in facilitating job engagement, given that disengaged employees cost U.S. businesses up to $550 billion annually in lost productivity.[106] Job engagement appears to matter for organizations, and has been found to predict higher levels of task performance and citizenship behavior.[107] However, the construct is partially redundant with job attitudes like job satisfaction, organizational commitment, and job involvement.[108]

What makes people more likely to be engaged in their jobs? One review of over 40,000 employees suggests that apart from a proactive personality, conscientiousness, and extraversion, one key trait predicts job engagement: employees' tendencies to experience positive moods and emotions (e.g., positive affectivity; see the chapter on emotions and moods).[109] Context factors also play a role. For example, job characteristics and access to sufficient resources to work effectively, person–organization value fit, and inspirational leadership all affect job engagement as well.[110]

INTEGRATING CONTEMPORARY THEORIES OF MOTIVATION

Our job might be simpler if, after presenting a half-dozen theories, we could say only one was found valid. But many of the theories in this chapter are complementary. We now tie them together to help you understand their interrelationships. Exhibit 7-8 integrates much of what we know about motivation. Its foundation is the expectancy model that was shown in Exhibit 7-7. Let us walk through Exhibit 7-8. (We will look at job design closely in the chapter on motivation.)

We begin by explicitly recognizing that opportunities can either aid or hinder individual effort. Note that the individual effort box on the left also has another arrow leading into it, from the person's goals. Consistent with goal-setting theory, the goals–effort loop is meant to remind us that goals direct behavior.

Expectancy theory predicts employees will exert a high level of effort if they perceive strong relationships between effort and performance, performance and reward, and rewards and satisfaction of personal goals. Each of these relationships is, in turn, influenced by other factors. For effort to lead to good performance, the individual must have the ability to perform and perceive the performance appraisal system as fair and objective. The performance–reward relationship will be strong if the individual perceives that performance (rather than seniority, personal favorites, or other criteria) is rewarded. If cognitive evaluation theory were fully valid in the actual workplace, we would predict that basing rewards on performance should decrease the individual's intrinsic motivation. The final link in expectancy theory is the rewards–goals relationship. Motivation is high if the rewards for high performance satisfy the dominant needs consistent with individual goals.

A closer look at Exhibit 7-8 also reveals that the model considers achievement motivation, job design, reinforcement, and equity theories/organizational justice. A high achiever is not motivated by an organization's assessment of performance or

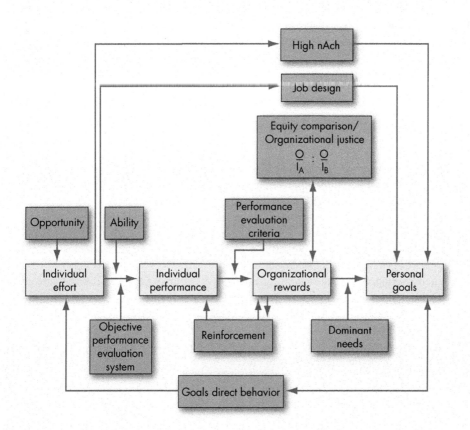

EXHIBIT 7-8
Integrating Contemporary Theories of Motivation

organizational rewards, hence the jump from effort to personal goals for those with high nAch. Remember, high achievers are internally driven if their jobs provide them with personal responsibility, feedback, and moderate risks. They are not as concerned with the effort–performance, performance–reward, or rewards–goal linkages.

Reinforcement theory enters the model by recognizing that the organization's rewards reinforce the individual's performance. If employees see a reward system as "paying off" for good performance, the rewards will reinforce and encourage good performance. Rewards also play a key part in organizational justice research. Individuals will judge the favorability of their outcomes (for example, their pay) relative to what others receive but also with respect to how they are treated: When people are disappointed by their rewards, they are likely to be sensitive to the perceived fairness of the procedures used and the consideration given to them by their supervisors. Some modern approaches to establishing reward systems might include using fair, objective, artificial-intelligence driven processes to improve employee fairness perceptions.[111]

SUMMARY

Motivation describes the processes underlying how employees and other individuals in the workplace direct their efforts toward a goal. Although not well supported, many early foundational theories of motivation focused on the needs that employees have along with the consequences of need satisfaction. More contemporary theories focus on topics such as intrinsic and extrinsic motivation, setting goals in organizations, self-efficacy, reinforcement, and our expectancies. Beyond these theories, various forms of organizational justice, all deriving from equity theory, are important in motivating employees. Motivation is key to understanding employees' contributions to their work, including their job engagement. Overall, motivation underlies employees exert effort to engage in performance activities, which in turn meet personal or organizational goals.

IMPLICATIONS FOR MANAGERS

- Make sure extrinsic rewards for employees are not viewed as coercive but instead provide information about competence and relatedness.
- Either set or inspire your employees to set specific, difficult goals and provide quality, developmental feedback on their progress toward those goals.
- Try to align or tie employee goals to the goals of your organization.
- Model the types of behaviors you would like to see performed by your employees.
- Expectancy theory offers a powerful explanation of performance variables such as employee productivity, absenteeism, and turnover.
- When making decisions regarding resources in your organization, make sure to consider how the resources are being distributed (and who is affected), the fairness of the decision, and whether your actions demonstrate that you respect those involved.
- Try to foster conditions that help improve job engagement and harness your employees' traits to facilitate job engagement.

8

Motivation: From Concepts to Applications

After studying this chapter, you should be able to:

8.1 Describe how the job characteristics model (JCM) motivates by changing the work environment.

8.2 Compare the main ways jobs can be redesigned.

8.3 Explain how specific alternative work arrangements can motivate employees.

8.4 Describe how employee involvement measures can motivate employees.

8.5 Demonstrate how the different types of variable-pay programs can increase employee motivation.

8.6 Show how flexible benefits turn benefits into motivators.

8.7 Identify the motivational benefits of intrinsic rewards.

MOTIVATING BY JOB DESIGN: THE JOB CHARACTERISTICS MODEL (JCM)

The way work is structured has a bigger impact on an individual's motivation than it seems. For example, one survey of nearly 3,000 working parents (despite having children to care for) in the UK found that 78 percent were working beyond their contracted hours, mainly for workload reasons, or because it was part of the culture to work overtime.[1] Commenting on the results, one manager noted that employers should "really rethink job design to tackle the problem of overworking. Parents need more human-sized jobs."[2] Indeed, there may be some truth to when an employee exclaims, "this job is (literally) killing me"—one study of over 3,000 employees over a twenty-year period found that job demands are linked to mortality, with effective job design as one way in which these negative effects are buffered.[3]

Job design suggests that the way elements in a job are organized can influence employee effort,[4] and the model discussed next can serve as a framework to identify opportunities for changes to those elements. The **job characteristics model (JCM)** describes jobs in terms of five core job dimensions:[5]

Job design
The way the elements in a job are organized.

Job characteristics model (JCM)
A model that proposes that any job can be described in terms of five core job dimensions: skill variety, task identity, task significance, autonomy, and feedback.

121

Skill variety
The degree to which a job requires a variety of activities using different skills or talents.

Task identity
The degree to which a job requires completion of a whole and identifiable piece of work.

Task significance
The degree to which a job has a substantial impact on the lives or work of other people.

Autonomy
The degree to which a job provides substantial freedom and discretion to the individual in scheduling the work and in determining the procedures to be used in carrying it out.

Feedback
The degree to which carrying out the work activities required by a job results in the individual obtaining direct and clear information about the effectiveness of their performance.

1. **Skill variety** is the degree to which a job requires a variety of activities using different skills or talents. The work of a garage owner–operator who does electrical repairs, rebuilds engines, does bodywork, and interacts with customers scores high on skill variety. The job of a body shop worker who sprays paint eight hours a day scores low on this dimension.
2. **Task identity** is the degree to which a job requires completion of a whole and identifiable piece of work. A cabinetmaker who designs furniture, selects the wood, builds the objects, and finishes them has a job that scores high on task identity. A job scoring low on this dimension is operating a lathe solely to make table legs.
3. **Task significance** is the degree to which a job affects the lives or work of other people. The job of a nurse helping patients in a hospital intensive care unit scores high on task significance; sweeping floors in a hospital scores low.
4. **Autonomy** is the degree to which a job provides the worker freedom, independence, and discretion in scheduling work and determining the procedures for carrying it out. Sales managers who schedule their own work and tailor their sales approach to each customer without supervision have highly autonomous jobs. An account representative who is required to follow a standardized sales script with potential customers has a job low on autonomy.
5. **Feedback** is the degree to which carrying out work activities generates direct and clear information about your own performance. A job with high feedback would be testing and inspecting iPads. Installing components of iPads as they move down an assembly line provides low feedback.

Elements of the JCM

Exhibit 8-1 presents the JCM. Note how the first three dimensions—skill variety, task identity, and task significance—combine to create meaningful work the employee will view as worthwhile. Jobs with high autonomy give employees a feeling of responsibility for the outcomes of work; and feedback shows them how effectively they are performing. The more these three psychological states (e.g., meaningfulness, responsibility, and knowledge of results) are present, the greater will be employees' motivation, performance, and satisfaction, and the lower their absenteeism and likelihood of leaving. As Exhibit 8-1 indicates, individuals with a high growth need are more likely to experience the critical psychological states when their jobs are enriched—and respond to them more positively.

Efficacy of the JCM

Much evidence supports the relationship between the presence of these job characteristics and higher job satisfaction and organizational commitment through increased motivation.[6] Furthermore, although employees have noticed that jobs are becoming more autonomous, interdependent, and require more skills than before; the relationship with job satisfaction has not changed since the 1970s, suggesting that employees still value enriched work.[7] In general, research supports the JCM, although some personality and context differences exist. For example, studies suggest that the link between job characteristics and satisfaction are highest when employees tend to regularly experience positive moods (i.e., trait positive affect; see the chapter on emotions and moods).[8] Other research

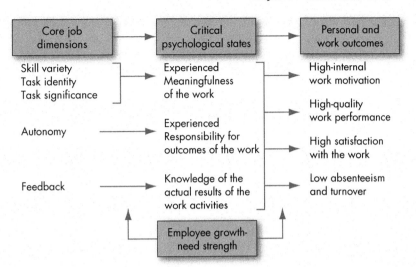

EXHIBIT 8-1
The Job Characteristics Model

Source: J. R. Hackman and G. R. Oldham, "Development of Job Diagnostic Survey," *Journal of Applied Psychology* 60, no. 2 (1975): 159–70.

has explored the JCM in unique settings such as virtual work situations, finding that if individuals work together online but not in person, their experience of meaningfulness, responsibility, and knowledge of results can suffer. [9] Thankfully, managers can mitigate these outcomes for employees by consciously developing personal relationships with them and increasing their sense of task significance, autonomy, and feedback.[10]

Motivating Potential Score (MPS)

We can combine the core dimensions of the JCM into a single predictive index, called the **motivating potential score (MPS)** and calculated as follows:

$$\text{MPS} = \frac{\text{Skill} + \text{Task identity} + \text{Task significance}}{3} \times \text{Autonomy} \times \text{Feedback}$$

Motivating potential score (MPS)
A predictive index that reflects the motivating potential in a job.

To be high on motivating potential, jobs must be high on at least one of the three factors that lead to experienced meaningfulness and high on both autonomy and feedback. If jobs score high on motivating potential, the model predicts that motivation, performance, and satisfaction will improve, and that absence and turnover will be reduced. Think about your job (or one you had in the past). Could you work on different tasks, or was there more of a routine? Could you work independently, or did you constantly have a supervisor or coworker looking over your shoulder? Your answers might indicate this job's motivating potential.

JOB REDESIGN

"Every day was the same thing," Cameron said. "Stand on that assembly line. Wait for an instrument panel to be moved into place. Unlock the mechanism and drop the panel into the Jeep Cherokee as it moved by on the line. Then I plugged in the harnessing wires. I repeated that for eight hours a day. I don't care that they were paying me twenty-four dollars an hour. I was going crazy. Finally, I just said this isn't going to be the way I'm going to spend the rest of my life. My brain was turning to JELL-O. So, I quit. Now I work in a print shop, and I make less than fifteen dollars an hour. But let me tell you, the work I do is interesting. The job changes all the time, I'm continually learning new things, and the work really challenges me! I look forward every morning to going to work again."

The repetitive tasks in Cameron's job at the Jeep plant provided little variety, autonomy, or motivation. In contrast, Cameron's job in the print shop is challenging and stimulating. From an organizational perspective, the failure of Cameron's first employer to redesign the job into a more satisfying one led to increased turnover. Redesigning jobs therefore has important practical implications—reduced turnover and increased job satisfaction among them.[11]

Furthermore, societies and organizations are looking to job design as one way to improve inclusiveness in organizations. Consider Mohsin Khan, a seventy-five-year-old aircraft repair technician. As Khan's eyesight deteriorated, the company invested in an expensive laser-marker machine with a large screen to assist Khan in how he does his job embossing numbers on metal plates.[12] Singapore is helping businesses assist and retain older employees through a job redesign grant, available since 2016.[13] This grant has enabled the government and businesses to care for the needs of the aging population and provide a source of life enrichment for older workers. Let us look at other ways that jobs can be re-designed to motivate employees.

Job Rotation and Job Enrichment

JOB ROTATION If employees suffer from over-routinization of their work, one alternative is **job rotation**, or the periodic shifting of an employee from one task to another with similar skill requirements at the same organizational level (also called *cross-training*).[14] One survey of millennial managers and professionals suggests that job rotation is an important aspect of modern work, with roughly 70 percent of respondents rating it as important.[15] Manufacturers also use job rotation as needed to respond more flexibly to the volume of incoming orders, while also enjoying reduced boredom and increased motivation.[16] It may also increase safety and reduce repetitive-based work injuries, but that is currently a topic of much study and debate, with mixed findings.[17]

Job rotation
The periodic shifting of an employee from one task to another.

New managers are sometimes rotated through jobs, too, to help them get a picture of a whole organization.[18] For these reasons, job rotation can be applied in any setting where cross-training is feasible, from manufacturing floors to hospital wards. At Singapore Airlines, for instance, a ticket agent may temporarily take on the duties of a baggage handler, both for cross-training and to get exposure to different aspects of the organization.[19]

Job rotation does have drawbacks. Training costs increase when each rotation necessitates a round of training. Second, moving a worker into a new position reduces overall productivity for that role. Third, job rotation creates disruptions when members of the work group must adjust to new employees. Fourth, supervisors may have to spend more time answering questions and monitoring the work of recently rotated employees.

Job enrichment
Adding high-level responsibilities to a job to increase intrinsic motivation.

JOB ENRICHMENT The major focus of self-determination theory (see the chapter on motivation concepts) can be put into action through the process of job enrichment. In **job enrichment**, high-level responsibilities are added to the job to increase a sense of purpose, direction, meaning, and intrinsic motivation.[20] Enriching a job in this way is different from enlarging it (adding more tasks and requirements). It involves adding another layer of responsibility and meaning. Job enrichment has its roots in Herzberg's theories (see the chapter on motivation concepts) of providing hygiene, or motivating factors, to the job to increase motivation.

Early reviews suggest that job enrichment can be effective at reducing turnover, almost twice as effective as giving employees a "realistic preview" of the work before they join the organization.[21] In a survey of over 20,000 British employees, job enrichment practices were related to organizations' financial performance, labor productivity, absenteeism, and output quality through improvements in job satisfaction.[22] Regardless of these benefits, managers who are high on openness (see the chapter on personality and values) and are in autonomous jobs themselves, tend to be more likely to *design* jobs that are enriching.[23] Regardless of personality, managers should consider the benefits of job enrichment and work against natural inclinations to micro-manage.

Relational Job Design

While redesigning jobs based on job characteristics theory is likely to make work more intrinsically motivating, research is also exploring how to make jobs more *prosocially* motivating to people. In other words, how can managers design work so employees are motivated to promote the well-being of the organization's beneficiaries (customers, clients, patients, and employees)? This view, **relational job design**, shifts the spotlight from the employee to those whose lives are affected by the job that the employee performs.[24] It also motivates individuals toward increased job performance and job satisfaction, especially when coupled with autonomy.[25]

One way to make jobs more prosocially motivating is to connect employees more closely with the beneficiaries of their work by relating stories from customers who have found the company's products or services to be helpful. For example, researchers found that when university fundraisers briefly interacted with the undergraduates who would receive the scholarship money they raised, they persisted 42 percent longer and raised nearly twice as much money as those who did not interact with potential recipients.[26] The positive impact was apparent even when fundraisers met with just a single scholarship recipient.

Relational job design
Constructing jobs so employees see the positive difference they can make in the lives of others directly through their work.

ALTERNATIVE WORK ARRANGEMENTS

Another approach to motivation is to consider alternative work arrangements such as flextime, job sharing, and telecommuting.[27] These are likely to be especially important for a diverse workforce of dual-earner couples, single parents, and employees caring for a sick or aging relative. For example, flextime and telework can help women continue to advance their careers after childbirth.[28]

Flextime

Jim Ware, founder of Focus Consulting Group, notes that "if you're trying to build a first-rate culture that attracts and retains people, you better make sure you get the rewards piece right and part of that is autonomy."[29] Flexibility is a key, attractive benefit that organizations can offer employees that helps make life easier for employees.[30] For example, Polen Capital Management institute doubled its workforce in three years after instituting a **flextime**, or "flexible work time," policy.[31]

Flextime
Flexible work hours.

In one arrangement, flextime employees work a specific number of hours per week but may vary their hours of work within limits. As in Exhibit 8-2, each day consists of a common core, usually six hours, with a flexibility band surrounding it. The core may be 9:00 a.m. to 3:00 p.m., with the office opening at 6:00 a.m. and closing at 6:00 p.m. Employees should be at their jobs during the common core period, but they may accumulate their other two hours around that. Some flextime programs allow employees to accumulate extra hours and turn them into days off. Some, like the Sterling-Rice Group, even allow employees to craft the nature of flexible work: they propose, after being hired, how, when and where they would like to complete the work and adjust accordingly as they work.[32]

Flextime has become extremely popular. According to recent surveys, a majority (57 percent) of U.S. organizations offer some form of flextime[33]—and reap benefits from it as well. Thirty-three percent of organizations report an increase in participation, and 23 percent indicate an increase in productivity (conversely, 5 percent or less indicated a decrease in participation and productivity).[34] It appears as if flextime has become an important job design element for many employees—53 percent of employees cite

---

**EXHIBIT 8-2
Possible
Flextime Staff
Schedules**

Schedule 1

Percent Time:	100% = 40 hours per week
Core Hours:	9:00 A.M.–5:00 P.M., Monday through Friday (1-hour lunch)
Work Start Time:	Between 8:00 A.M. and 9:00 A.M.
Work End Time:	Between 5:00 P.M. and 6:00 P.M.

Schedule 2

Percent Time:	100% = 40 hours per week
Work Hours:	8:00 A.M.–6:30 P.M., Monday through Thursday (1/2-hour lunch)
	Friday off
Work Start Time:	8:00 A.M.
Work End Time:	6:30 P.M.

Schedule 3

Percent Time:	90% = 36 hours per week
Work Hours:	8:30 A.M.–5:00 P.M., Monday through Thursday (1/2-hour lunch)
	8:00 A.M.–Noon, Friday (no lunch)
Work Start Time:	8:30 A.M. (Monday–Thursday); 8:00 A.M. (Friday)
Work End Time:	5:00 P.M. (Monday–Thursday); Noon (Friday)

Schedule 4

Percent Time:	80% = 32 hours per week
Work Hours:	8:00 A.M.–6:00 P.M., Monday through Wednesday (1/2-hour lunch)
	8:00 A.M.–11:30 A.M. Thursday (no lunch)
	Friday off
Work Start Time:	Between 8:00 A.M. and 9:00 A.M.
Work End Time:	Between 5:00 P.M. and 6:00 P.M.

flexible arrangements as a very important aspect of their job satisfaction, 55 percent of employees were unlikely to seek job opportunities elsewhere within the year, and 34 percent stated that they would remain with their current employer because of flexible arrangements.[35] In countries such as Germany, Belgium, the Netherlands, and France, by law employers are not allowed to refuse an employee's request for either a part-time or a flexible work schedule as long as the request is reasonable, such as to care for an infant child.[36]

Most of the evidence for flextime stacks up favorably. One review of over forty studies suggests that flextime is related to positive work outcomes in general, but only weakly—the effects are much stronger when considering reductions in absenteeism and, to a lesser degree, improvements in productivity and schedule satisfaction.[37] Much less promising, the empirical evidence from over 100,000 employees suggests that although flextime is weakly effective at reducing the extent to which work interferes with family, it does not affect situations in which family interferes with work.[38]

However, flextime's effects on work–life balance are more nuanced than they might appear. For example, two studies of German employees suggest that, although flextime leads employees to set stronger work–life boundaries (which in turn makes them happier), these boundaries are not truly "set" unless the employees complete their daily goals at work.[39] Flextime's major drawback is that it is not applicable to every job or every worker; for example, some research suggests both young, healthy employees and older, unhealthy employees benefit the most from flextime.[40] It also appears that people who have a strong desire to separate their work and family lives are less apt to use flextime.[41] Those who ask for it are often stigmatized, which may be avoided if the majority of the organization's leaders adopt flexible hours to signal that flextime is acceptable.[42]

Job Sharing

Job sharing allows two or more individuals to split a traditional full-time job. One employee might perform the job from 8:00 a.m. to noon, perhaps, and the other from 1:00 p.m. to 5:00 p.m., or the two could work full but alternate days. For example, actor-puppeteers Lizzie Wort and Ruth Calkin are now able to tour Britain doing what they love: performing as the Twirlywoos, puppets from a popular UK children's TV program.[43] This is now possible due to a theatre job share arrangement, which has the "potential to revolutionize" how actors approach touring, and "open up possibilities ... for performers with children."[44]

Job sharing
An arrangement that allows two or more individuals to split a traditional full-time job.

Only 18 percent of U.S. organizations offered job sharing in 2014, a 29 percent decrease since 2008.[45] Reasons it is not more widely adopted include the difficulty of finding compatible partners to job share and the historically negative perceptions of job share individuals as not completely committed to their jobs and employers. However, eliminating job sharing for these reasons might be short-sighted. Job sharing allows an organization to draw on the talents of more than one individual for a given job. It opens the opportunity to acquire skilled workers—for instance, parents with young children and retirees—who might not be available on a full-time basis. From employees' perspectives, job sharing can increase motivation and satisfaction if they can work when they would not normally be able to do so.

An employer's decision to use job sharing is often based on policy and financial reasons. Two part-time employees sharing a job can be less expensive in terms of salary and benefits than one full-timer, but this may not be the case because training, coordination, and administrative costs can still be high. Ideally, employers should consider each employee and job separately, seeking to match the skills, personality, and needs of the employee with the tasks required for the job and considering that individual's motivating factors.

Telecommuting

With the COVID-19 pandemic of 2020, working from home might be the "new normal."[46] During this time, a large portion of the nearly 9,000 employees from the Gallup panel indicated that they were working from home during the pandemic, especially those of middle to upper class backgrounds.[47] Furthermore, a Gartner survey suggested that 74 percent of the executives surveyed would keep at least a portion of their work force remote after the pandemic.[48]

Telecommuting
Working from home at least two days a week through virtual devices that are linked to the employer's office.

Although people rarely had a choice in the matter during the COVID-19 pandemic, is working from home effective? Do employees like working from home? For some, it might be close to the ideal job: no rush hour traffic, flexible hours, freedom to dress as you please, and few interruptions. **Telecommuting** refers to working at home—or anywhere else the employee chooses that is outside the workplace—at least two days a week on a computer linked to the employer's office.[49] (A closely related concept— working from a *virtual office*—describes working outside the workplace on a relatively permanent basis.)

Telecommuting has several benefits. It increases performance and job satisfaction (especially for complex, independent jobs, with low social interaction requirements); to a lesser degree, it reduces role stress and turnover intentions.[50] Employees who work virtually more than 2.5 days a week tend to experience the benefits of reductions in work–family conflict more intensely than those who are in the office the majority of their workweek.[51] Beyond the benefits to organizations and their employees, telecommuting has potential benefits to society. One study estimated that if people in the United States telecommuted half the time, carbon emissions would be reduced by approximately fifty-one metric tons per year. Environmental savings could come from lower office energy consumption, fewer traffic jams that emit greenhouse gases, and a reduced need for road repairs.[52]

From the employee's standpoint, telecommuting can increase feelings of isolation and reduce job satisfaction and coworker relationship quality.[53] On the other hand, it can help you "get away from them all" if your working situation is emotionally exhausting.[54] Research indicates that if you are forced to work from home, although you may experience less work–family conflict in general, you might still experience it if you work hours beyond the contracted workweek and are constantly "on call."[55] Telecommuters are also vulnerable to the "out of sight, out of mind" effect: Employees who are not at their desks, miss impromptu meetings in the office, and do not share in day-to-day informal workplace interactions may be at a disadvantage when it comes to raises and promotions because they are perceived as not putting in the requisite face time unless telework is the norm with the organization, there is still common contact with the supervisor, and it is clear that the employee is working (e.g., they have a heavy workload and are productive).[56]

If telecommuting is here to stay, what can employees and employers do to ensure the arrangements are effective? Apart from ensuring the arrangement is right for the position (as described above),[57] self-leadership, including proactive, goal-setting, and personal performance management are related to success in telework.[58] Further, using smart collaboration tools, communicating frequently, clear and transparent policies, and building trust among virtual team members can help improve the effectiveness of telework for the whole team.[59]

EMPLOYEE INVOLVEMENT

Employee involvement and participation (EIP)[60] is a process that uses employees' input to increase their commitment to organizational success. If workers are engaged in decisions that increase their autonomy and control over their work lives, they will become more motivated, committed to the organization, productive, and satisfied with their jobs (and less likely to leave their jobs).[61] These benefits do not stop with individuals—when teams are given more control over their work, morale and performance increase as well.[62]

> **Employee involvement and participation (EIP)**
> A participative process that uses the input of employees to increase employee commitment to organizational success.

Cultural EIP

To be successful, EIP programs should be tailored to local and national norms.[63] A study of four countries, including India and the United States, confirmed the importance of modifying practices to reflect national culture.[64] While U.S. employees readily accepted EIP programs, managers in India who tried to empower their employees were rated low by those employees. These reactions are consistent with India's high power-distance culture, which accepts and expects differences in authority. The work culture in India may not be in as much transition as it is in China, in which some employees are becoming less high power-distance oriented. In one study, Chinese workers who were very accepting of traditional Chinese cultural values showed few benefits from participative decision making. However, Chinese workers who were less traditional were more satisfied and had higher performance ratings under participative management.[65] These differences within China may well reflect the current transitional nature of that culture. Research in urban China indicated that some EIP programs, namely, those that favor consultation and expression but not participation in decision making, yielded higher job satisfaction.[66]

Examples of Employee Involvement Programs

Let's look at two major forms of employee involvement—participative management and representative participation—in more detail.

PARTICIPATIVE MANAGEMENT Common to all **participative management** programs is joint decision making, in which subordinates share a significant degree of decision-making power with their immediate superiors.[67] This sharing can occur either formally through, say, briefings or surveys, or informally through daily consultations, as a way to enhance motivation through trust and commitment.[68] For example, emergency medical service staff can meet to provide improvement opportunities based on their medical specialty areas—improvements to the process that can literally save lives.[69] Participative management has, at times, been considered a panacea for poor morale and low productivity—indeed, evidence suggests that participative management reduces the negative effects of job insecurity on satisfaction and turnover intentions.[70] For participative management to be effective, followers must have trust and confidence in

> **Participative management**
> A process in which subordinates share a significant degree of decision-making power with their immediate superiors.

their leaders and be prepared for the change in management style, whereas leaders should avoid coercive techniques, stress the organizational consequences of decision making to their followers, and review progress periodically.[71]

Studies of the participation–performance relationship have yielded mixed findings.[72] Organizations that institute participative management may realize higher stock returns, lower turnover rates, and higher labor productivity, although these effects are typically not large.[73]

Representative participation
A system in which workers participate in organizational decision making through a small group of representative employees.

REPRESENTATIVE PARTICIPATION Most countries in western Europe require companies to practice **representative participation**.[74] Representative participation redistributes power within an organization, putting labor's interests on a more equal footing with the interests of management and stockholders by including a small group of employees as participants in decision making. In the United Kingdom, Ireland, Australia, and New Zealand, representative participation was originally the only EIP program; it was formed to allow employee representatives to discuss issues outside union agreements and the representatives were all from the union. However, representative groups are now increasingly a mix of union and non-union, or separate from the union arrangement.[75]

The two most common forms of representation are works councils and board representatives. Works councils are groups of nominated or elected employees who must be consulted when management makes decisions about employees. Board representatives are employees who sit on a company's board of directors and represent employees' interests.

The influence of representative participation on working employees seems to be mixed, but generally employees would need to feel that their interests were well represented and make a difference to the organization for motivation to increase.

USING EXTRINSIC REWARDS TO MOTIVATE EMPLOYEES

As we saw in the chapter on attitudes and job satisfaction, pay is not the only factor driving job satisfaction. However, it does motivate people, and companies often underestimate its importance. Although not as important as enjoyment of one's work and the job fitting well with other areas of an employee's life, approximately 60 percent of respondents to an American Psychological Association survey indicated that they were staying with their current employer because of the pay and benefits.[76]

In this section, we consider (1) how much employees should be paid (establishing a pay structure), and (2) how to pay individual employees (through variable-pay plans).

What to Pay: Establishing a Pay Structure

There are many ways to pay employees. The process of initially setting pay levels entails balancing *internal equity*—the worth of the job to the organization (usually established through a technical process called job evaluation), and *external equity*—the competitiveness of an organization's pay relative to pay in its industry (usually established through pay surveys). Obviously, the best pay system reflects what the job is worth, while also staying competitive relative to the labor market.

Pay more, and you may get better-qualified, more highly motivated employees who will stay with the organization longer, and perhaps be more likely to perform and innovate.[77] A study covering 126 large organizations found employees who believed they were receiving a competitive pay level had higher morale and were more productive, and customers were more satisfied as well.[78] But pay is often the highest single operating cost for an organization, which means paying too much can make the organization's products or services too expensive. Furthermore, the salience of money may even motivate employees toward self-serving behavior. For example, one study of NHL and NBA players found that during the final contract year, players engage in more self-serving behaviors while in play.[79] It's a strategic decision an organization must make, with clear trade-offs.

In the case of Walmart, it appears that its strategic decision on pay did not work. While annual growth in U.S. stores slowed to around 1 percent in 2011, one of Walmart's larger competitors, Costco, grew around 8 percent. The average worker at Costco made approximately $45,000, compared to approximately $17,500 for the average worker at Walmart-owned Sam's Club. Costco's strategy was that it will get more if it pays more— and higher wages resulted in increased employee productivity and reduced turnover. Given the subsequent Walmart decision to increase worker wages throughout the organization, perhaps its executives agree.[80]

How to Pay: Rewarding Individual Employees Through Variable-Pay Programs

"Why should I put any extra effort into this job?" asked Anne, a fourth-grade elementary schoolteacher in Denver, Colorado. "I can excel, or I can do the bare minimum. It makes no difference. I get paid the same. Why do anything above the minimum to get by?" Comments like Anne's have been voiced by schoolteachers for decades because pay increases were tied to seniority. Recently, however, many states have altered their compensation systems to motivate teachers by linking pay to results in the classroom, and other states are considering such programs.[81]

Piece rate, merit based, bonus, profit sharing, and employee stock ownership plans are all forms of a **variable-pay program** (also known as *pay-for-performance*), which bases a portion of an employee's pay on some individual and/or organizational measure of performance.[82] The variable portion may be all or part of the paycheck, and it may be paid annually or upon attainment of benchmarks. It can also be either optional for the employee or an accepted condition of employment.[83] Globally, around 84 percent of companies offer some form of variable-pay plan.[84] Variable-pay plans have long been used to compensate salespeople and executives, but the scope of variable-pay jobs has broadened.

Variable-pay program
A pay plan that bases a portion of an employee's pay on some individual and/or organizational measure of performance.

Not all employees see a strong connection between pay and performance, although it seems that the type of plan matters. As we stated, teacher pay-for-performance plans are starting to be used more frequently, particularly those that are based on student test scores. Recent research on thousands of teachers in the United States has shown that these programs (1) are not having a positive impact on teacher motivation or teaching practices and (2) have actually led to higher levels of stress, along with counterproductive work behaviors such as cheating and even bullying of students to perform better on tests.[85] A similar effect has been found in other workplaces: When managers are subject to pay-for-performance, it leads to employer–employee relationship strain and can increase employee turnover.[86] Employees in these situations may also compete with their coworkers, and may actively try to harm one another.[87] Also, some employees react more negatively to pay-for-performance. For example, employees with disabilities in Britain tend to react more negatively to pay-for-performance than others.[88]

The results of pay-for-performance plans vary by several conditions. For instance, group-based pay-for-performance plans may have a strong positive effect on organizational performance, but they may only be effective in stable economic environments and in organizations that have fair policies.[89] On the other hand, research in Canada indicated that variable-pay plans increase job satisfaction only if employee *effort* is rewarded as well as performance.[90] There are cultural differences as well: when *guanxi* (e.g., specific, personal connections between subordinates, supervisors, and coworkers) plays a role in human resources (HR) practices, pay-for-performance plans tend to be less effective.[91]

Secrecy also plays a role in the motivational success of variable-pay plans. In some government and not-for-profit agencies, pay amounts are either specifically or generally made public, but most U.S. organizations encourage or require pay secrecy.[92] Is this good or bad? Unfortunately, it is bad: Pay secrecy has a detrimental effect on job performance. Even worse, it adversely affects high performers more than other employees. It very likely increases employees' perception that pay is subjective, which can be demotivating. Individual pay amounts may not need to be broadcast to restore the balance, if general pay categories are made public and employees feel variable pay is linked objectively to their performance, the motivational effects of variable pay can be retained.[93]

Piece-rate pay plan
A pay plan in which workers are paid a fixed sum for each unit of production completed.

PIECE-RATE PAY The **piece-rate pay plan** has long been popular as a means of compensating production workers with a fixed sum for each unit of production completed, but it can be used in any organizational setting where the outputs are similar enough to be evaluated by quantity.[94] A pure piece-rate plan provides no base salary and pays the employee only for what they produce. Ballpark workers selling peanuts and soda are frequently paid piece-rate. If they sell forty bags of peanuts at one dollar each for their earnings, their take is forty dollars. The more peanuts they sell, the more they earn. Alternatively, piece-rate plans are sometimes distributed to sales teams, so a ballpark worker makes money on a portion of the total number of bags of peanuts sold by the group during a game.

Piece-rate plans are known to produce higher effort, productivity and wages, so they can be attractive to organizations and motivating for workers.[95] In fact, one major Chinese university increased its piece-rate pay for articles by professors and realized 50 percent increased research productivity.[96] The chief concern of both individual and team piece-rate workers is financial risk. A recent experiment in Germany found that 68 percent of risk-averse (see the chapter on perception and individual decision making) individuals prefer an individual piece-rate system and that lower performers prefer team piece-rate pay. Why? The authors suggested risk-averse and high-performing individuals would rather take their chances on pay based on what they can control (their own work) because they are concerned others will slack off in a team setting.[97] What about using both? Recent work suggests that doing so might address the limitations of using either in isolation: across more than 22,000 European establishments, using both plans (combined with an EIP approach like described earlier) led to stark increases in employee innovation.[98]

Organizations, on the other hand, should verify that their piece-rate plans are indeed motivating to individuals. European research has suggested that when the pace of work is determined by uncontrollable outside factors such as customer requests, rather than internal factors such as coworkers, targets, and machines, a piece-rate plan is not motivating.[99] Either way, managers must be mindful of the motivation for workers to decrease quality in order to increase their speed of output.

MERIT-BASED PAY   A **merit-based pay plan** pays for individual performance based on performance appraisal ratings.[100] If designed correctly, merit-based plans let individuals perceive a strong relationship between their performance and their rewards.[101]

Merit-based pay plan
A pay plan based on performance appraisal ratings.

Most large organizations have merit-based pay plans, especially for salaried employees. Merit pay is slowly taking hold in the public sector. For example, New York City's public hospital system pays doctors based on how well they reduce costs, increase patient satisfaction, and improve the quality of care.[102] A move away from merit pay, on the other hand, is coming from some organizations that do not feel it separates high and low performers enough. When the annual review and raise are months away, the motivation of this reward for high performers diminishes. Even companies that have retained merit pay are rethinking the allocation.[103] However, some data from a service-related organization suggests that when merit pay and bonuses are used in tandem, merit raises tend to be most effective at increasing job performance and preventing turnover—although bonuses may affect future performance to a larger extent.[104]

Despite their intuitive appeal, merit-based pay plans have several limitations. One is that they are typically based on an annual performance appraisal and thus are only as valid as the performance ratings, which are often subjective. This brings up issues of discrimination, as we discussed in the chapter on diversity in organizations. Research indicates that black employees receive lower performance ratings than white employees, women's ratings are higher than men's, and there are demographic differences in the distribution of salary increases, even with all other factors being equal.[105] Another limitation is that the pay-raise pool of available funds fluctuates on economic or other conditions that have little to do with individual performance. Lastly, unions typically resist merit-based pay plans. For example, relatively few U.S. teachers are covered by merit pay for this reason. Instead, seniority-based pay, which gives all employees the same raises, predominates.

BONUS   An annual **bonus** is a significant component of total compensation for many jobs.[106] Once reserved for upper management, bonus plans are now routinely offered to employees in all levels of the organization. The incentive effects should be higher than those of merit pay because rather than paying for previous performance now rolled into base pay, bonuses reward recent performance (merit pay is cumulative, but the increases are generally much smaller than bonus amounts). When times are bad, firms can cut bonuses to reduce compensation costs. Firms may even cut executive bonuses when in the face of scandal, often to signal to shareholders that they are taking the scandal seriously and working to address the situation.[107]

Bonus
A pay plan that rewards employees for recent performance rather than historical performance.

Bonus plans have a clear upside: They are motivating for workers. As an example, a recent study in India found that when a higher percentage of overall pay was reserved for the potential bonuses of managers and employees, productivity increased.[108] This example also highlights the downside of bonuses: They leave employees' pay more vulnerable to cuts. This is problematic, especially when employees depend on bonuses or take them for granted. "People have begun to live as if bonuses were not bonuses at all but part of their expected annual income," said Jay Lorsch, a Harvard Business School professor.

Profit-sharing plan
An organization-wide program that distributes compensation based on some established formula designed around a company's profitability.

PROFIT-SHARING PLAN   A **profit-sharing plan** distributes compensation based on some established formula designed around a company's profitability.[109] Compensation can be direct cash outlays or, particularly for top managers, allocations of stock options. When you read about executives like Mark Zuckerberg, who accepts an absurdly modest one-dollar salary, remember that many executives are granted generous stock options. In fact, Zuckerberg made as much as $8.8 million in 2017 after considering other income.[110] Of course, most profit-sharing plans are not so grand in scale. For example, Fiat Chrysler automobile workers averaged $7,280 in profit-sharing income in 2019.[111]

Studies generally support the idea that organizations with profit-sharing plans have higher levels of profitability than those without them.[112] These plans have also been linked to higher levels of employee commitment, especially in small organizations.[113] Profit sharing at the organizational level appears to have positive impacts on employee attitudes: Employees report a greater feeling of psychological ownership.[114] Recent research indicates that profit-sharing plans motivate individuals to higher job performance when they are used in combination with other pay-for-performance plans.[115] Obviously, profit sharing does not work when there is no reported profit *per se*, such as in nonprofit organizations, or often in the public sector.

Employee stock ownership plan (ESOP)
A company-established benefits plan in which employees acquire stock, often at below-market prices, as part of their benefits.

EMPLOYEE STOCK OWNERSHIP PLAN   An **employee stock ownership plan (ESOP)** is a company-established benefit plan in which employees acquire stock, often at below-market prices, as part of their benefits.[116] Research on ESOPs indicates they increase firm performance as well as employee innovation and organizational identification.[117] ESOPs have the potential to increase job satisfaction, but only when employees psychologically experience ownership.[118] Even so, ESOPs may not inspire lower absenteeism or greater motivation,[119] and may also lead managers to allocate money in a way that maximizes managerial payoffs in either the long or short run, perhaps because the employee's actual monetary benefit comes with cashing in the stock at a later date.[120] Relatedly, in a study of nearly three thousand Chinese firms, ESOPs were not as strongly related with firm performance when combined with executive stock ownership plans and when employees had no control rights (e.g., no "say" in the management of the business).[121] Furthermore, a study of nearly two thousand European firms suggested that the stock-ownership predicts return-on-investment only when the employees trusted the managers and were culturally low on uncertainty avoidance (see the chapter on personality and values).[122] Thus, employees need to be kept regularly informed of the status of the business and can positively influence it in order to feel motivated toward higher personal performance.[123]

USING BENEFITS TO MOTIVATE EMPLOYEES

Flexible benefits
A benefits plan that allows each employee to put together a benefits package individually tailored to their own needs and situation.

Like pay, benefits are both a provision and a motivator. Consistent with expectancy theory's thesis that organizational rewards should be linked to each employee's goals, **flexible benefits** individualize rewards by allowing each employee to choose the compensation package that best satisfies their own current needs and situation. Flexible benefits can accommodate differences in employee needs based on age, marital status, partner's benefit status, and number and age of dependents.

Benefits in general can be a motivator for a person to go to work, and for a person to choose one organization over another. But are flexible benefits more motivating than traditional plans? It is difficult to tell. Some organizations that have moved to flexible plans report increased employee retention, job satisfaction, and productivity. However, flexible benefits may not substitute for higher salaries when it comes to motivation.[124] As more organizations worldwide adopt flexible benefits, the individual motivation they produce will likely decrease (the plans will be seen as a standard work provision). The downsides of flexible benefit plans may be obvious: They may be costlier to manage and identifying the motivational impact of different provisions is challenging.

USING INTRINSIC REWARDS TO MOTIVATE EMPLOYEES

We have discussed motivating employees through job design and by the extrinsic rewards of pay and benefits. On an organizational level, are those the only ways to motivate employees? Not at all! We would be remiss if we overlooked intrinsic rewards organizations can provide, such as employee recognition programs.

Employee Recognition Programs

Let us start with an example. Dakota makes nine dollars per hour working at a fast-food job in Pensacola, Florida, and the job is not very challenging or interesting. Yet Dakota talks enthusiastically about the job, the boss, and the company Dakota works for. "What I like is the fact that Carroll [the supervisor] appreciates the effort I make. Carroll compliments me regularly in front of the other people on my shift, and I've been chosen as Employee of the Month twice in the past six months. Did you see my picture on that plaque on the wall?"

Organizations are increasingly realizing what Dakota knows: Recognition programs increase an employee's intrinsic motivation. An **employee recognition program** is a plan to encourage specific behaviors by formally appreciating specific employee contributions.[125] Employee recognition programs range from a spontaneous and private thank-you to widely publicized formal programs in which the procedures for attaining recognition are clearly identified.

Employee recognition program
A plan to encourage specific employee behaviors by formally appreciating specific employee contributions.

As companies and government organizations face tighter budgets, nonfinancial incentives become more attractive. Everett Clinic in Washington State uses a combination of local and centralized initiatives to encourage managers to recognize employees.[126] Employees and managers give "Hero Grams" and "Caught in the Act" cards to colleagues for exceptional accomplishments at work. Part of the incentive is simply to receive recognition, but there are also drawings for prizes based on the number of cards a person receives. Multinational corporations like Symantec Corporation, Intuit, and Panduit have also increased their use of recognition programs. Symantec, which had employees in 280 locations across fifty countries, claims it increased engagement 14 percent in less than a year due to the Applause recognition program administered by Globoforce, a corporation that implements employee recognition programs.[127] Centralized programs across multiple offices in different countries can help ensure that all employees, regardless of where they work, can be recognized for their contribution to the work environment.[128]

Research suggests financial incentives may be more motivating in the short term, but in the long run nonfinancial incentives work best.[129] Surprisingly, there is not a lot of research on the motivational outcomes or global usage of employee recognition programs. However, studies indicated that employee recognition programs are associated with self-esteem, self-efficacy, and job satisfaction.[130]

An obvious advantage of recognition programs is that they are inexpensive: Praise is free![131] With or without financial rewards, they can be highly motivating to employees. Despite the increased popularity of such programs, though, critics argue they are highly susceptible to political manipulation by management. When applied to jobs for which performance factors are relatively objective, such as sales, recognition programs are likely to be perceived by employees as fair. In most jobs, however, performance criteria are not self-evident, which allows managers to manipulate the system and recognize their favorites. Abuse can undermine the value of recognition programs, demoralize employees, and even cause the person recognized to be ostracized. As one study in a northern Chinese manufacturing company showed, once a top performer was recognized, other members of the team whose contributions were not recognized may begin to distance themselves from that member.[132] These members may have unfair procedural justice perceptions (see the chapter on motivation concepts) and begin to ostracize that employee as a result. Therefore, where formal recognition programs are used, care must be taken to ensure fairness. Where they are not, it is important to motivate employees by consistently recognizing their performance efforts.

SUMMARY

As we have seen in the chapter, understanding what motivates individuals is ultimately key to organizational performance. Employees whose differences are recognized, who feel valued, and who can work in jobs tailored to their strengths and interests will be motivated to perform at the highest levels. Employee participation can also increase employee productivity, commitment to work goals, motivation, and job satisfaction. However, we cannot overlook the powerful role of organizational rewards in influencing motivation. Pay, benefits, and intrinsic rewards must be carefully and thoughtfully designed in order to enhance employee motivation.

IMPLICATIONS FOR MANAGERS

- Recognize individual differences. Spend the time necessary to understand what is important to each employee. Design jobs to align with individual needs to maximize their motivation potential.
- Use goals and feedback. You should give employees firm, specific goals, and employees should get feedback on how well they are faring in pursuit of those goals.
- Allow employees to participate in decisions that affect them. Employees can contribute to setting work goals, choosing their own benefits packages, and solving productivity and quality problems.
- Link rewards to performance. Rewards should be contingent on performance, and employees must perceive the link between the two.
- Check the system for equity. Employees should perceive that individual effort and outcomes explain differences in pay and other rewards.

9
Foundations of Group Behavior

After studying this chapter, you should be able to:

9.1 Distinguish between the different types of groups.

9.2 Describe the punctuated equilibrium model of group development.

9.3 Show how role requirements change in different situations.

9.4 Demonstrate how norms exert influence on an individual's behavior.

9.5 Show how status and size differences affect group performance.

9.6 Describe how issues of cohesiveness and diversity can be integrated for group effectiveness.

9.7 Contrast the strengths and weaknesses of group decision making.

DEFINING AND CLASSIFYING GROUPS

In organizational behavior (OB), a **group** consists of two or more individuals, interacting and interdependent, who have come together to achieve certain objectives. For example, consider a sales group from a regional office of a large insurance company: The group is responsible for selling insurance to local citizens, each person on the team has come together to sell insurance for their organization.[1] We belong to many groups throughout our lifetime, but some are more salient than others at certain times, and some group roles can even conflict (e.g., being a parent and a manager).[2]

Groups can be either formal or informal. A **formal group** is defined by the organization's structure, with designated work assignments and established tasks. In formal groups, the behaviors members should engage in are stipulated by and directed toward organizational goals. The six members of an airline flight crew are a formal group, for example. In contrast, an **informal group** is neither formally structured nor organizationally determined, and often meets to fulfills social needs or to bind employees with common interests. Three employees from different departments who regularly have lunch or coffee together are an informal group. These types of interactions among individuals, though informal, deeply affect their behavior and performance.

Group
Two or more individuals, interacting and interdependent, who have come together to achieve certain objectives.

Formal group
A designated work group defined by an organization's structure.

Informal group
A group that is not defined by an organization's structure; such a group appears in response to other needs, such as social clubs or interest groups.

Social Identity

People often feel strongly about their groups, partly because shared experiences amplify our perception of events, and can increase our sense of a bond and trust toward others.[3] For example, consider Tom's Marine Sales, a local business in Crawfordsville, Indiana.[4] Celebrating their fiftieth anniversary, the company threw a party with their closest friends and employees in attendance. The employees not only appreciate the history of the company and identify with its successes and losses (including the loss of Tom's wife and co-founder, Joy), but also identify as a part of the Crawfordsville community. In fact, the mayor and county commissioners were on hand to present Tom's with a plaque to commemorate their service to the community. Our tendency to personally invest in the accomplishments of a group can be explained by **social identity theory**.

Social identity theory proposes that people have emotional reactions to the failure or success of their group because their self-esteem gets tied to whatever happens to the group.[5] Employees might feel proud of the company's successes, angry and threatened when the company is threatened, or even *schadenfreude* (i.e., pleasure due to another's misfortune) when competitors suffer.[6] Wendy's social media group, for example, harnesses these emotions with Twitter "roasting wars" with fast food rivals (sassy put-downs of other companies and their products).[7] Twitter fans and employees of Wendy's, alike, feel especially proud and identify with when Wendy's "burns" a competitor. One of our colleagues knew someone who identified so much with Wendy's that he had a poster of Wendy's in his room and would get furiously angry when anyone tried to say that other fast food restaurants are better!

Within our organizations and work groups, we can develop many identities through (1) *relational* identification, when we connect with others because of our roles, and (2) *collective* identification, when we connect with the aggregate characteristics of our groups. In the workplace, our identification with our workgroups is often stronger than with our organizations, but both are important to positive outcomes in attitudes and behaviors.[8] If we have low identification with both our work groups and organizations, we may experience decreased satisfaction and engage in fewer organizational citizenship behaviors (OCBs; see Chapter 1: What Is Organizational Behavior?).[9] Immigrant workers, for example, often experience strained and threatened identities when they do not have inclusive, supportive supervisors or when they do not feel like they are a part of the local community. This often leads to high turnover rates for immigrants and migrants.[10] Even the words leaders use matter—when CEOs use "we" or "us" language (instead of "I" language), this signals to employees and stakeholders alike that they are a part of a group. One study of German organizations spanning sixteen years found that use of collective language was correlated with increased sales and return-on-investment.[11]

Ingroups and Outgroups

An **ingroup** consists of the members of a group we belong to. We tend to "play favorites" or see our ingroup as better than other people.[12] Favoritism can influence discrimination and prejudice in the workplace. For example, some research suggests that favoritism and not hostility, might cause most discriminatory behaviors: "hostility isn't integral to the definition of discrimination; you can treat people differently without being hostile to anyone."[13] For example, when a person from our ingroup does something unethical, we are more likely to respond by repairing the relationship than by punishing them, *even*

Social identity theory
A perspective that considers when and why individuals consider themselves members of groups.

Ingroup
The members of a group we belong to. We tend to play favorites with our ingroup.

if it is for a heinous crime.[14] By playing favorites with your own ingroup (e.g., people of the same race/ethnicity, gender identity, etc.), employees and managers alike may be complicit in discrimination.

Whenever there is an ingroup, there is by necessity an **outgroup**, which is sometimes "everyone else," but it is usually an identified group known by the ingroup's members. For example, if my ingroup as a fast food employee is Wendy's, my outgroup might be McDonald's, Burger King, or Taco Bell. We tend to see members of the outgroup as being "all the same" or ignore characteristics that make them different from one another. For example, voters and politicians alike are falling into the dangerous trap of believing that people who belong to different, outgroup parties are "all the same" and that "they just don't understand us," contributing to the polarization of people in democratic societies around the world.[15] Unfortunately, research suggests that people may be more likely to be disgusted with outgroup members, derogate them, and treat them as if they have little worth.[16] One of the most powerful sources of ingroup–outgroup derogation regards the practice of religion, even in the workplace. One global study, for instance, found that when groups became heavily steeped in religious rituals and discussions, they became especially discriminatory toward outgroups and aggressive if the outgroups had more resources,[17] likely because these outgroups threaten their sense of identity and worldview.[18]

On a final note, you may remember discussing *the threat of technological unemployment* in the chapter on perception and individual decision making. Despite fear of job loss to automation, recent research suggests that the rise of automation and a robot workforce may lead to a *less prejudiced workforce*. By classifying employees into human and non-human, a new *panhumanist social identity* (i.e., seeing humanity as a common social identity, where humans are a part of the ingroup) may emerge that can reduce human-to-human prejudice, discrimination, and inequality.[19]

Outgroup
The inverse of an ingroup; an outgroup can mean anyone outside the group, but more usually it is an identified other group. We tend to see anyone outside of our group as "all the same" and can derogate them or treat them as if they have little worth.

STAGES OF GROUP DEVELOPMENT

Temporary groups with finite deadlines pass through a unique sequencing of actions (or inaction) called the **punctuated equilibrium model**, shown in Exhibit 9-1:

1. The first meeting sets the group's direction.
2. The first phase of group activity is one of inertia and thus makes slower progress.
3. A transition takes place when the group has used up half its allotted time.
4. This transition initiates major changes.
5. A second phase of inertia follows the transition.
6. The group's last meeting is characterized by markedly accelerated activity.[20]

Punctuated equilibrium model
A set of phases that temporary groups go through that involve transitions between inertia and activity.

At the first meeting, the group's general purpose and direction is established, and then a framework emerges of behavioral patterns and assumptions through which the group will approach its project, sometimes in the first few seconds of the group's existence. Once set, the group's direction is solidified and is unlikely to be reexamined throughout the first half of its life. This is a period of inertia—the group tends to stand still or become locked into a fixed course of action, even if it gains new insights that challenge initial patterns and assumptions.

Groups experience a transition halfway between the first meeting and the official deadline—whether members spent an hour on their project or six months. The midpoint

EXHIBIT 9-1
The Punctuated Equilibrium Model

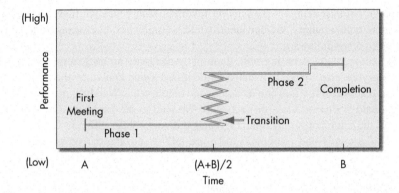

appears to work like an alarm clock, heightening members' awareness that their time is limited and that they need to get moving. This transition ends Phase 1 and is characterized by a concentrated burst of changes, dropping of old patterns, and adoption of new perspectives. The transition sets a revised direction for Phase 2, a new equilibrium or period of inertia in which the group executes plans created during the transition period. The group's last meeting is characterized by a final burst of activity to finish its work.

There are many models of group stages, but the punctuated equilibrium model tends to be a dominant theory with strong support. Keep in mind, however, that this model does not apply to all groups, but is suited to the finite quality of temporary task groups working under a time deadline.[21] Alternative models suggest that teams progress through a formation stage, a conflict resolution or "storming" stage, a "norming" stage where members agree on roles and make decisions, and a "performing" stage where members begin to work collaboratively. The forming, storming, norming, and performing stages may occur at phase one of the punctuated equilibrium model, while a second performing and conforming stage may occur in the second phase, following a short period of reforming group norms and expectations.[22]

Apart from the identity bestowed by group membership and the ways in which groups are formed, there are several other defining properties that are important to understanding groups in organizations: *roles, norms, status, size, cohesiveness*, and *diversity*. We will discuss each in the sections that follow.

GROUP PROPERTY 1: ROLES

The Independent Group was formed (and dissolved) in 2019 after eleven British members of Parliament resigned from their political parties, forming a new group dedicated to reaching across party divides to further centrist political interests in the UK.[23] Each member of the group brought something different to the table. As another example, in the *Ocean's* movie series, each con-artist has a different role in contributing to pulling off the heist (e.g., the "drivers," the "electronics," the "traps," the "grease," etc.). All members play a **role**, a function assumed by someone occupying a given position in a group.

Role
A function assumed by someone occupying a given position in a group.

We all take on several diverse roles, both on and off our jobs (e.g., wife, mother, poker champion, editor, professor). Different groups impose different role requirements on individuals. Many of these roles are compatible; some create conflicts. For example, if you were offered a job in Phoenix, but your family wanted to stay in Orlando—can the demands of the parent–professional role be reconciled? Furthermore, how do we come to understand others' role requirements? We draw upon our *role perceptions* to frame our ideas of appropriate behaviors and learn the *expectations* of our groups. We also seek to understand the parameters of our roles to minimize *role conflict*. Let us discuss each of these facets.

Role Perception

Our view of how we are supposed to act in a given situation is a **role perception**. We get role perceptions from stimuli all around us (e.g., our family, office, YouTube). For example, working, married parents identify strongly with their family roles, and positively translate these roles into work roles, such as their leadership expectations.[24] However, research on marines in the U.S. military suggests that even though some role perceptions translate from context to context, some do not (with marines "protecting" their work roles from becoming a part of their family life, for example).[25]

Role perception
An individual's view of how they are supposed to act in a given situation.

Role Expectations

Role expectations are the way others believe you should act in a given context. A U.S. federal judge is viewed as having propriety and dignity, while a football coach is seen as aggressive, dynamic, and inspiring to the players. Role expectations can influence the way people perform their work. For example, creative role expectations can lead people to be more creative in their work.[26]

Role expectations
How others believe a person should act in a given situation.

In the workplace, we often look at role expectations through the perspective of the **psychological contract**: an unwritten agreement between employees and employers (including senior management, supervisors, coworkers, and recruiters) that establishes mutual expectations.[27] Management is expected to treat employees justly, provide acceptable working conditions, clearly communicate what is a fair day's work, and give feedback on how well an employee is doing. Employees are expected to demonstrate a good attitude, follow directions, and show loyalty to the organization. Unfortunately, employees can even be expected to be unethical by their employers—if they do not comply, they are often met with sanctions (e.g., insults, pressure) and may be perceived as being less warm.[28]

Psychological contract
An unwritten agreement between employees and employers that establishes mutual expectations.

What happens if management is derelict in its part of the bargain? We can expect negative effects on employee performance, turnover, and satisfaction.[29] Why might employees not play their part? Loss of resources, workload, stress (e.g., family interfering with work), a sense of wanting more than what the contract can offer, and other obstacles can limit the extent to which employees can fulfill their part of the bargain, causing their performance at work to suffer, and causing them to be potentially passed up for promotions.[30] What happens if the organization fulfills its part of the bargain? Employees are likely to feel grateful and identify with their organization and will be more willing to go above and beyond by performing OCBs.[31]

Role Conflict

When compliance with one role requirement makes it difficult to comply with another, the result is **role conflict**.[32] At the extreme, two or more role expectations may be clashing, like when professors are expected to be excellent teachers *and* researchers, when they normally only have enough time for one.[33]

Role conflict
A situation in which an individual is confronted by divergent role expectations.

Interrole conflict
A situation in which the expectations of an individual's different, separate groups are in opposition.

Similarly, we can experience **interrole conflict**[34] when the expectations of the different groups we belong to are in direct opposition. As a primary example, many people hold multiple jobs, perhaps one that is primary (e.g., software engineer) and a secondary job (e.g., guitarist in a metal band). These jobs might inevitably come into conflict, and indeed, research supports that jobs like this can interfere with the primary job.[35] As a more common example, family/life roles can often conflict with work roles. For instance, one American mother described how she was "scrambling after her son was born to accomplish two tasks: 'knitting back together' from her C-section and assembling a patchwork of enough disability leave, vacation and sick days, and unpaid time off, to rest briefly and care for her infant son before returning to work."[36] Roles can often conflict within jobs, such as when nurses unexpectedly find themselves in a disaster (e.g., a hurricane or mass shooting) where they are required to calmly provide aid for someone (their professional role) who is close to them, regulating emotions they are experiencing that stem from their attachment to that person (the relational role).[37]

Indeed, research demonstrates that role conflict is a significant source of stress for most employees.[38] Furthermore, during global mergers and acquisitions, employees can be torn between their identities as members of their original organization and of the new parent company.[39] Multinational mergers can lead to dual identification—with the employee splitting identification with the local division and with the international organization.[40]

GROUP PROPERTY 2: NORMS

San Francisco startup, Gusto, designed their office as if it were a living room, with a "no shoes" policy (although sandals and slippers are permitted, if you must).[41] Why do we wear shoes indoors to begin with, and why do we take them off in some environments (Gusto, some people's houses) and not in others (Best Buy)? The answer can be found in norms.

Norms
Acceptable standards of behavior within a group that are shared by the group's members.

All groups have established **norms**—acceptable standards of behavior shared by members that express what they ought to do and ought not to do under certain circumstances. Different groups, communities, and societies have different norms, but they all have them.[42] Norms are established through the social perception of group members, such as when a group leader says, "This is what we should do" and rewards the practices when they happen and the rest of the group unanimously puts the suggestion into practice.[43] Norms are not just leader-established, opinion-driven policies: For them to be adopted (and not abandoned after several days), they need to be accepted by all.[44]

Norms and Emotions

The emotions of group members, especially those who work together daily, can amplify the power of norms. Coworkers, for example, may react negatively to you coming in sick for work and may be angry and uncivil toward you.[45] Norms can even dictate which emotions individuals and their groups experience—in other words, people may grow to interpret their shared experiences in the same way.[46] Employees may also see through attempts to comply with office norms, even though you may not be doing so for genuine reasons.

Norms and Conformity

As a member of a group, you desire acceptance and stability. Thus, you may conform to group norms when you perceive that others are doing so or if you experience conflict or frustration.[47] Considerable evidence suggests that groups can place strong pressures on members to change in order to match the group's standard.[48]

The impact that group pressures for **conformity** can have on an individual member's judgment was demonstrated in studies by Solomon Asch and others.[49] Asch formed groups of seven to eight people who were asked to compare two cards. One card had one line, and the other had three lines of varying length, one of which was identical to the line on the one-line card, as Exhibit 9-2 shows. The difference in line length was obvious; in fact, participants were incorrect less than 1 percent of the time in announcing which of the three lines matched the single line.

Conformity
The adjustment of one's behavior to align with the norms of the group.

The experiment began with two rounds of matching exercises, where each participant was called upon to match the card to its identical counterpart. Everyone gave the right answers. On the third round, however, the first participant, who was part of the research team, gave an obviously wrong answer—for example, saying "C" in Exhibit 9-2. The next participant, also on the research team, gave the same wrong answer, and so forth. Now the dilemma confronting the participant, who did not know the others were on the research team, was this: publicly state a perception that differed from the position of the others or give an incorrect answer that agreed with the others.

The results over many experiments showed 75 percent of subjects gave at least one answer that conformed—that they knew was wrong but was consistent with the replies of other group members—and the average conformer gave wrong answers 37 percent of the time. But does that mean we are mere robots? Certainly not. Do individuals conform to the pressures of all groups to which they belong? Again, obviously not. When they *do* conform, it is most likely to their **reference groups**, important groups in which a person is aware of other members, defines themself as a member or would like to be a member, and feels group members are significant. Conformity effects are not always bad; for example, people can conform to prosocial norms, such as generosity in donating and can even feel more empathy as a result.[50]

Reference groups
Important groups to which individuals belong or hope to belong and which adopt norms with which individuals are most likely to conform.

Norms and Behavior

Norms can cover any aspect of group behavior.[51] As we have mentioned, norms in the workplace significantly influence employee behavior. This may seem intuitive, but full appreciation of the influence of norms on worker behavior did not occur until the Hawthorne Studies, conducted between 1924 and 1932 at the Western Electric Company's Hawthorne Works in Chicago.[52]

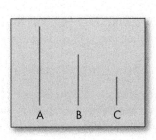

**EXHIBIT 9-2
Examples of Cards Used in Asch's Study**

In the studies, the researchers first examined the relationship between the physical environment—specifically, the amount of light on the shop floor—and productivity. As they increased the light level for the experimental group of workers, output rose for that unit and the control group. But as they dropped the light level, productivity continued to increase. In fact, productivity in the experimental group decreased only when the light intensity had been reduced to that of moonlight, leading researchers to believe that group dynamics, rather than the environment, influenced behavior.

The researchers next isolated a small group of women assembling telephones so their behavior could be more carefully observed. Over the next several years, this small group's output increased steadily, and the number of personal and sick absences was approximately one-third of that in the regular production department. It became evident this group's performance was significantly influenced by its "special" status. The members thought they were in an elite group, and that management showed concern about their interests by engaging in experimentation. Workers in both the illumination and assembly experiments were really reacting to the increased attention they received.

Finally, the researchers implemented a wage-incentive plan for employees in the bank wiring observation room. The most important finding was that employees did not individually maximize their output. Rather, their role performance became controlled by a group norm. Members were afraid that if they significantly increased their output, the unit incentive rate might be cut, the expected daily output might be increased, layoffs might occur, or slower workers might be reprimanded. So, the group established its idea of a fair output—neither too much nor too little. Members helped each other ensure their reports were nearly level, and the norms the group established included several behavioral "don'ts." *Don't* be a rate buster—turning out too much work. *Don't* be a chiseler—turning out too little work. *Don't* squeal on any of your peers. The group enforced its norms with name calling, ridicule, and even punches to the upper arms of violators. The group thus operated well below its capability, using norms that were tightly established and strongly enforced.

Positive Norms and Group Outcomes

Positive group norms may very well beget positive outcomes, but only if other factors are present, too. Overall, evolutionary explanations of norms suggest they were developed so that we can observe positive outcomes: for example, groups facing a high degree of threat develop strong interaction and cooperation norms, and norms to punish deviants.[53] This may be why we observe differences in cultural norms across the globe.

As an example of the positive effect of positive norms, one goal of every organization with corporate social responsibility (CSR; see the chapter on attitudes and job satisfaction) initiatives is for its values to hold normative sway over employees.[54] After all, if employees aligned their thinking with positive norms, these norms would become stronger and the probability of positive impact would grow exponentially. Some research in Germany indicates that this may be a function of how satisfied people are with their groups, with more satisfied employees more likely to adopt the CSR norms.[55]

Negative Norms and Group Outcomes

Deviant workplace behavior
Voluntary behavior that violates significant organizational norms and, in so doing, threatens the well-being of the organization or its members. Also called antisocial behavior or workplace incivility.

As we discussed in the chapter on attitudes and job satisfaction, work behavior (CWB), or **deviant workplace behavior**, is voluntary behavior that violates significant organizational norms and, in so doing, threatens the well-being of the organization or its members. Exhibit 9-3 provides a typology of deviant workplace behaviors, with examples of each.

Negative norms operate to facilitate poor group outcomes and deviant behavior. As some examples, group member and supervisor absences set the tone for the office: If the team members do not show up, and if the boss does not show up, most employees will probably not show up.[56] One study of firefighters and nurses found that even though family-friendly benefits were intended to be used and are effective in reducing work–family conflict, the firefighters were less likely to use these benefits if they perceived that others in their work group did not use them.[57] Interestingly, some research suggests that when trying to promote diversity in the workplace, raising awareness for the prevalence of stereotyping can backfire and can actually lead toward more stereotype-consistent behavior.[58]

Few organizations will admit to creating or condoning conditions that encourage or sustain deviant behaviors. Yet they exist. For one, as we discussed before, a work-group can become characterized by positive or negative attributes. When those attributes are negative, CWBs or deviant behaviors may be observed more frequently: As some researchers suggest, "bad apples" come from "bad barrels."[59] Second, employees can be mistreated by their supervisors, their coworkers, and even their customers, which can cause them to engage in unethical behaviors as a result.[60] Mistreatment of this type is important to organizational retention efforts, as nearly half of employees who have suffered this incivility say it has led them to think about changing jobs; 12 percent actually quit because of it.[61] Finally, as organizations have tried to do more with less and are pushing their employees to work extra hours, they may indirectly be facilitating deviant behavior.[62]

Category	Examples
Production	Leaving early Intentionally working slowly Wasting resources
Property	Sabotage Lying about hours worked Stealing from the organization
Political	Showing favoritism Gossiping and spreading rumors Blaming coworkers
Personal aggression	Sexual harassment Verbal abuse Stealing from coworkers

EXHIBIT 9-3

Typology of Deviant Workplace Behavior

Sources: S. H. Appelbaum, G. D. Iaconi, and A. Matousek, "Positive and Negative Deviant Workplace Behaviors: Causes, Impacts, and Solutions," *Corporate Governance* 7, no. 5 (2007), 586–98; R. W. Griffin and A. O'Leary-Kelly, *The Dark Side of Organizational Behavior* (New York: Wiley, 2004).

Norms and Culture

Do people in collectivist cultures have different norms than people in individualist cultures? Of course, they do—even to the extent that some norms are undetectable or not understood by outgroup members.[63] But did you know that our orientation may be momentarily changed within a group context, even after years of living in one society? In one recent experiment, an organizational role-playing exercise was given to a neutral group of subjects; the exercise stressed either collectivist or individualist (see the chapter on personality and values) norms. Subjects were then given a task of their personal choice or were assigned one by an ingroup or outgroup person. When the individualist-primed subjects were allowed personal choice of the task, or the collectivist-primed subjects were assigned the task by an ingroup person, they became more highly motivated.[64]

Regardless of these temporary shifts, cultural norms can affect many behaviors in the workplace, such as which negotiation strategy to select (aggressive strategies are more often used in honor and face cultures, like Qatar and China, relative to dignity cultures like the U.S.).[65] The negotiation results are surprising, considering that Asian cultures value harmony and cooperation in interpersonal interactions, but will do what they can to compete and save face in professional contexts. Cultural norms can even influence how people respond to those who violate the norm. For instance, norm violators in collectivist cultures (see the chapter on personality and individual differences) are seen as less powerful and evoke more moral outrage than individualistic cultures.[66]

GROUP PROPERTY 3: STATUS, AND GROUP PROPERTY 4: SIZE AND DYNAMICS

Have you ever noticed how groups tend to stratify into higher- and lower-status members? Sometimes the status of members reflects their status outside the group setting, but not always. Groups can also vary by size in ways that affect members' behaviors, dynamics, and group outcomes. Let's examine how these factors affect a workgroup's efficacy.

Group Property 3: Status

Status
A socially defined position or rank given to groups or group members by others.

Status—a socially defined position or rank given to groups or group members by others—permeates every society. Even the smallest group will show differences in member status over time. Status is a significant motivator and has major behavioral consequences when individuals perceive a disparity between what they believe their status is and what others perceive it to be.

Status characteristics theory
A theory that states that differences in status characteristics create status hierarchies within groups.

WHAT DETERMINES STATUS? According to **status characteristics theory**, status tends to derive from one of three sources:[67]

1. **The power a person wields over others.** Because they likely control the group's resources, people who control group outcomes tend to be perceived as high status.
2. **A person's ability to contribute to a group's goals.** People whose contributions are critical to the group's success tend to have high status.
3. **An individual's personal characteristics.** Someone whose personal characteristics are positively valued by the group (good looks, intelligence, money, or a friendly personality) typically has higher status than someone with fewer valued attributes.

STATUS AND NORMS High-status individuals may be more likely to deviate from norms when they have low identification (social identity) with the group.[68] They also eschew pressure from lower-ranking members of other groups. High-status people are also better able to resist conformity pressures than are their lower-status peers. An individual who is highly valued by a group but does not need or care about the group's social rewards is particularly able to disregard conformity norms.[69] In general, bringing high-status members into a group may improve performance, but only up to a point, perhaps because these members may introduce counterproductive norms.[70] They do not control everything, though: gossip can both confer status and damage reputations.[71]

STATUS AND GROUP INTERACTION People tend to become more assertive when they *seek* to attain higher status in a group.[72] They speak out more often, criticize more, state more commands, and interrupt others more often. Conversely, some evidence suggests that those who *do* have higher status tend to conceal it to promote harmony.[73] Lower-status members participate less actively in group discussions; when they possess insights that could aid the group, failure to fully utilize these members reduces the group's overall performance. Supervisors can help here by encouraging these employees to speak up.[74] But that does not mean a group of only high-status individuals would be preferable. Adding *some* high-status individuals to a group of mid-status individuals may be advantageous because group performance suffers when too many high-status people are in the mix.[75] Regardless of one's status, however, accurate knowledge of the status hierarchy (i.e., "who is who in my group") leads to better performance and results in effective within-group networking.[76]

STATUS INEQUITY It is important for group members to believe the status hierarchy is equitable. Perceived inequity creates disequilibrium, which inspires various types of corrective behaviors. Hierarchy can lead to negative emotions and resentment among those at the lower end of the status continuum.[77] Large differences in status within groups are also associated with poorer individual performance, lower health, and higher intentions for the lower-status members to leave the group.[78] Generally, inequity in power-based forms of status tends to have more negative effects: It tends to drive interpersonal conflict, whereas other forms promote healthy competition for status advancement.[79]

STATUS AND STIGMATIZATION Miriam O'Reilly sued the BBC for age discrimination, and immediately afterwards became a pariah. While being ostracized at a professional dinner, one of Miriam's colleagues told her, "I am so sorry ... but I really can't be seen with you. My agent said that it could have an effect on my career."[80] Although it is clear that status affects the way people perceive you, the status of people with whom you are affiliated can also affect others' views of you. People who are stigmatized can "infect" others with their stigma.[81] This "stigma by association" effect can result in negative opinions and evaluations of the person affiliated with the stigmatized individual, even if the association is brief and purely coincidental. Even if the low status, stigmatized person calls the group members out for doing so, other low status members will still tend to legitimize their beliefs and continue to withhold support to the stigmatized.[82]

GROUP STATUS Early in life, we acquire an "us and them" mentality.[83] Culturally, sometimes ingroups represent the dominant forces in a society and are given high status, which can create discrimination against their outgroups. Low-status groups, perhaps in response to this discrimination, are likely to leverage ingroup favoritism to compete for higher status.[84] When high-status groups then feel the discrimination from low-status groups, they may increase their bias against the outgroups.[85] With each cycle, the groups become more polarized.

Group Property 4: Size and Dynamics

Does the size of a group affect the group's overall behavior? Yes, but the effect depends on the outcomes we are interested in.[86] Groups with a dozen or more members are good for gaining diverse input.[87] If the goal is fact-finding or idea-generating, then larger groups should be more effective.[88] Smaller groups of about seven members are better at doing something productive.[89] We even hold group size stereotypes that affect our behaviors (e.g., smaller groups are more trustworthy, larger groups are more difficult to help).[90]

Social loafing
The tendency for individuals to expend less effort when working collectively than when working individually.

Group dynamics are also important for characterizing groups. One of the most important findings concerning group dynamics involves **social loafing**, the tendency for individuals to expend less effort when working collectively than when alone.[91] Social loafing directly challenges the assumption that the productivity of the group as a whole should at least equal the sum of the productivity of the individuals in it, no matter what the group size.

Social loafing appears to have a Western bias.[92] It is consistent with individualistic cultures, such as those found in the United States and Canada, which are dominated by self-interest. It is *not* consistent with collectivistic societies, in which individuals are motivated by group goals. When research is compared across cultures, groups from Eastern cultures had significantly lower rates of social loafing.

Research indicates that the stronger an individual's work ethic is, the less likely that person is to engage in social loafing.[93] Also, the greater the level of conscientiousness and agreeableness (see the chapter on personality and values) in a group, the more likely that performance will remain high whether there is social loafing or not.[94] Virtual groups also may have issues with social loafing, especially if members are dissimilar and have a number of family responsibilities that detract their attention away from group performance.[95] There are ways to prevent social loafing:

1. Set group goals, so the group has a common purpose to strive toward.
2. Increase intergroup competition, which focuses on the shared group outcome.
3. Engage in peer evaluations.
4. Select members who have high motivation and prefer to work in groups.
5. Base group rewards in part on each member's unique contributions, and structure work so that each member's contribution can be identified.[96]

GROUP PROPERTY 5: COHESIVENESS, AND GROUP PROPERTY 6: DIVERSITY

For a group to be highly functioning, it must act cohesively as a unit. Furthermore, certain types of diversity can enable teams to perform better in different ways. Let us discuss the importance of group cohesiveness first.

Group Property 5: Cohesiveness

Groups differ in their **cohesiveness**—the shared bond driving group members to work together and to stay in the group.[97] Some workgroups are cohesive because the members have spent a great deal of time together, the group's small size or purpose facilitates high interaction, or external threats have brought members close together.

Cohesiveness affects group productivity, and vice versa.[98] However, studies consistently show that the relationship between cohesiveness and productivity depends on the group's performance-related norms.[99] If norms for quality, output, and cooperation with outsiders are high, a cohesive group will be more productive than a less cohesive group. But if cohesiveness is high and performance norms are low, productivity will be low. If cohesiveness is low and performance norms are high, productivity increases, but less than in the high-cohesiveness/high-norms situation. When cohesiveness and performance-related norms are both low, productivity tends to fall into the low-to-moderate range. These conclusions are summarized in Exhibit 9-4.

Beyond playing Fortnite, Minecraft, or other video games with your group;[100] what can you do to encourage group cohesiveness?

1. Make the group smaller.
2. Encourage agreement with group goals.
3. Increase the time members spend together.
4. Increase the group's status and the perceived difficulty of attaining membership.
5. Stimulate competition with other groups.
6. Give rewards to the group rather than to individual members.
7. Physically isolate the group.[101]

Cohesiveness
The shared bond driving group members to work together and to stay in the group.

Group Property 6: Diversity

The final group property we consider is **diversity** in the group's membership, or the degree to which members of the group are alike, or different from, one another. Overall, studies tend to be inconclusive, depend upon several contextual factors, and depend on how diversity is indexed and conceptualized.[102] Interestingly, there is only a modest link between *actual* diversity and *perceived* diversity (and even differences between majority and minority perceptions of diversity!),[103] and some research suggests that members seek to balance a need to belong and a need to be distinctive in group membership. This disconnect could also be because people tend to develop perceptions' of their groups diversity and perpetuate the status quo. For example, one study of the S&P 1500 boards

Diversity
The extent to which members of a group are similar to, or different from, one another.

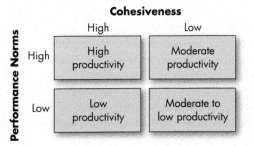

EXHIBIT 9-4
The Impact of Cohesiveness and Performance Norms on Productivity

found that there was a status quo norm across organizations to have two women, what the researchers referred to as "twokenism."[104]

Furthermore, perceived self-to-team dissimilarity and splits lead to negative effects, and perceived group heterogeneity lead to both positive and negative effects.[105] In other words, maybe the effect of diversity is more contingent on how it is framed or perceived, such as when executives adopt a "value-in-diversity" perspective.[106] Despite the mixed state of things, artificial intelligence research is, yet again, helping move this area forward, and a recent application to multicultural manufacturing teams has produced a new way to assess how salient social categories (e.g., race, gender) are to individual team members' perceptions.[107]

TYPES OF GROUP DIVERSITY   Surface-level diversity (e.g., gender, race; see the chapter on diversity in organizations) appears to increase group conflict, especially in the early stages of a group's tenure, which often lowers group morale and raises dropout rates.[108] One study compared groups that were culturally diverse and homogeneous (composed of people from the same country). On a virtual wilderness survival test, the groups performed equally well, but the members from the diverse groups were less satisfied with their groups, were less cohesive, and had more conflict.[109] Outsiders are even more likely to be biased toward racially heterogenous groups and allocate less resources toward them.[110]

At a deeper level, groups in which members' values or opinions differ tend to experience more conflict, but leaders who can get the group to focus on the task at hand and encourage group learning are able to reduce these conflicts and enhance discussion of group issues.[111] Research in Korea indicates that putting people with a high need for power (nPow; see the chapter on motivation concepts) with those with a low need for power can reduce unproductive group competition, whereas putting individuals with a similar need for achievement may increase task performance.[112] Furthermore, diversity in propensity to trust can cause downward trust spirals, which fuels conflict and further erodes trust over time.[113]

On the other hand, *functional* diversity, or differences in skills, abilities, or other characteristics needed for the job, may improve team performance and innovation, but these effects are contingent on several factors.[114] For example, functional diversity can influence team creativity by facilitating knowledge sharing.[115] Leadership plays a substantial role in maximizing the benefits of functional diversity—great leaders bring disparate skills together to do great work.[116]

CHALLENGES OF GROUP DIVERSITY   Although differences can lead to conflict, they also provide an opportunity to solve problems in unique ways. One study of jury behavior found diverse juries were more likely to deliberate longer, share more information, and make fewer factual errors when discussing evidence. Altogether, it is difficult to be in a diverse group in the short term. They tend to homogenize over time, they are fragile, and they tend to be prone to fragmentation.[117] However, if members can weather their differences, over time diversity may help them to be more open-minded and creative and to do better. For example, research into the development of identification in diverse United Nations peacebuilding teams across the world shows that team members develop a sense of identification, but that this evolves over time.[118]

Faultlines
The perceived divisions that split groups into two or more subgroups based on individual differences such as sex, race, age, work experience, language, and education.

One possible negative effect of diverse teams—especially those that are diverse in terms of surface-level characteristics—is **faultlines**, or perceived divisions that split groups into two or more subgroups based on individual differences such as sex, race, age, work experience, language, and education.[119]

For example, let us say Group A is composed of three black and three Hispanic employees. The three Hispanic employees have approximately the same amount of work experience and backgrounds in marketing. The three black employees have about the same amount of work experience and backgrounds in finance. Group B has three Hispanic and three black employees, but they all differ in terms of their experience and backgrounds. Two of the black employees are experienced, while the other is new. One of the Hispanic employees has worked at the company for several years, while the other two are new. In addition, two of the black and one of the Hispanic employees in Group B have backgrounds in marketing, while the others have backgrounds in finance. It is thus likely that a faultline will result in the subgroups of black and Hispanic employees in Group A but not in Group B, based on the differentiating characteristics.

Research on faultlines has shown that splits are generally detrimental to group functioning and performance. Subgroups may compete, which takes time away from core tasks and harms group performance. Groups that have subgroups learn more slowly, make more risky decisions, are less creative, and experience higher levels of conflict. Subgroups may not trust each other and may have low levels of cohesion.[120] Finally, satisfaction within subgroups is generally high, but the overall group's satisfaction is lower when faultlines are present.[121] Are faultlines ever a good thing? One study suggested that faultlines regarding skill, knowledge, and expertise may be beneficial in a results-driven organizational culture. Why? A results-driven culture focuses people's attention on what is important to the company rather than on problems arising from subgroups.[122]

How can faultlines be addressed or harnessed for good within organizations? Studies show that problems stemming from diversity and strong faultlines may be overcome when their roles are crosscut, the group is given a common goal to strive for, and similar pairs are recruited within a diverse group. Altogether, forced collaboration between members of subgroups and a focus on accomplishing a goal may boost performance in certain organizations.[123] Pro-diversity beliefs and open-mindedness norms also help (and training can help improve this, when they are low):[124] for example, one study of international diplomats with the German Ministry of Foreign Affairs suggest that diplomat and team pro-diversity beliefs reduce the negative effect of faultlines on performance.[125] Similarly, research on multicultural groups suggests that policies, practices, and procedures that welcome and accept diversity, and that assume a diversity in thought, lead to an effective exchange of thoughts and to more effective teams.[126] Finally, there may be cultural differences in how group diversity affects performance: a study of over 5,000 Himalayan climbing expeditions found that collectivist values (see the chapter on personality and individual differences) blur the lines between groups, which can lead to diversity either hurting or helping the group, depending upon the task.[127]

GROUP DECISION MAKING

The belief—characterized by juries—that two heads are better than one has long been accepted as a basic component of the U.S. legal system and those of many other countries. Many decisions in organizations are made by groups, teams, or committees. We will discuss the advantages of group decision making, along with the unique challenges group dynamics bring to the decision-making process. Finally, we will offer some techniques for maximizing the group decision-making opportunity.

Groups Versus the Individual

Decision-making groups may be widely used in organizations, but are group decisions preferable to those made by an individual alone? The answer depends on several factors. Let us begin by looking at the strengths, weaknesses, and benefits of group decision making.

STRENGTHS OF GROUP DECISION MAKING Groups generate *more complete information and knowledge.* By aggregating the resources of several individuals, groups bring more input as well as heterogeneity into the decision process (as long as this information is reliable).[128] They offer *increased diversity of views.* This opens the opportunity to consider more approaches and alternatives.[129] Finally, groups lead to increased *acceptance of a solution.* During decision making, members are more likely to be accepting when dissenting opinions are framed as debates rather than disagreements.[130] Group members who participate in deciding are more likely to enthusiastically support and encourage others to accept it later.

WEAKNESSES OF GROUP DECISION MAKING Group decisions are time-consuming because groups typically take more time to reach a solution, especially for virtual groups.[131] There are *conformity pressures.* The desire by group members to be accepted and considered an asset to the group can squash any overt disagreement and cause group members to settle for less.[132] Group discussion can be *dominated by one or a few members.* If they are low- and medium-ability members, the group's overall effectiveness will suffer. Interestingly, in virtual contexts, this may be addressed by allowing minority members to have secret conversations and lead to improved decision quality.[133] Also, setting a norm that allows "lone dissenters," or group members who have divergent opinions, can reduce conformity and the influence of dominating members.[134] Finally, group decisions suffer from *ambiguous responsibility.* In an individual decision, it is clear who is accountable for the outcome. In a group decision, the responsibility of any single member is diluted.

EFFECTIVENESS AND EFFICIENCY Whether groups are more effective than individuals depends on how you define effectiveness and who is making the evaluation. As discussed in the chapter on perception and individual decision making, the accuracy of evaluators can be affected by general perceptions of group cohesion and trust.[135] Group decisions are generally more *accurate* than the decisions of the average individual in a group, but generally less accurate than the judgments of the most accurate person.[136] In terms of *speed*, individuals are superior. If *creativity* is important, groups tend to be more effective. And if effectiveness means the degree of *acceptance* of achievable solutions, the nod again goes to the group.[137]

We cannot consider effectiveness without also assessing efficiency. With few exceptions, group decision making consumes more work hours than does having an individual tackle the same problem. The exceptions tend to be instances in which, to achieve comparable quantities of diverse input, the single decision maker must spend a great deal of time reviewing files and talking to other people who have unique information that could lead to a better solution.[138] Research suggests that groups may be inefficient in decision making if information is heavily dispersed among group members and effectively "hidden." It is very difficult to compile this information to make the best decision, and groups in these situations are encouraged to openly and collaboratively share information to solve the problem.[139] In deciding whether to use groups, then, managers must assess whether increases in effectiveness are more than enough to offset the reductions in efficiency.

Groupthink and Groupshift

Two by-products of group decision making, groupthink and groupshift, can affect a group's ability to appraise alternatives objectively and achieve high-quality solutions.

GROUPTHINK **Groupthink** describes situations in which group pressures for conformity deter the group from critically appraising unusual, minority, or unpopular views. Groupthink attacks many groups and can dramatically hinder their performance.[140] Groupthink appears closely aligned with the conclusions Solomon Asch drew in his experiments with a lone dissenter. Groups that are more focused on performance than on learning are especially likely to fall victim to groupthink and to suppress the opinions of those who do not agree with the majority.[141] Groupthink seems to occur most often early in the group's tenure, when there is a clear group identity, when members hold a positive image of their group they want to protect, and when the group perceives a collective threat to its positive image.[142]

What can managers do to minimize groupthink?[143] First, they can monitor group size. People grow more intimidated and hesitant as group size increases. Managers should also encourage group leaders to play an impartial role. In addition, managers should appoint one group member to play the role of devil's advocate, overtly challenging the majority position and offering divergent perspectives. Yet another suggestion is to use exercises that stimulate active discussion of diverse alternatives without threatening the group or intensifying identity protection. Have group members delay discussion of possible gains so they can first talk about the dangers or risks inherent in a decision.

GROUPSHIFT **Groupshift**, or group polarization, describes the way group members tend to exaggerate their initial positions when discussing a given set of alternatives to arrive at a solution. We can view this group polarization as a special case of groupthink. The group's decision reflects the dominant decision-making norm—toward greater caution or more risk—that develops during discussion.[144] In groups, discussion leads members toward a more extreme view of the position they already held.[145]

The shift toward polarization has several explanations.[146] It has been argued, for instance, that discussion is persuasive and makes members more comfortable with each other and thus more willing to express extreme versions of their original positions. Another argument is that the group diffuses responsibility. Group decisions free any single member from accountability for the group's final choice, so a more extreme position can be taken. It is also likely that people take extreme positions because they want to demonstrate how different they are from the outgroup.[147]

We now turn to the techniques by which groups make decisions. These reduce some of the dysfunctional aspects of group decision making.

Group Decision-Making Techniques

The most common form of group decision making takes place in **interacting groups**.[148] Members rely on both verbal and nonverbal interactions to communicate. But as our discussion of groupthink demonstrated, interacting groups often censor themselves and pressure individual members toward conformity of opinion. Brainstorming and the nominal group technique (discussed below) can reduce problems inherent in the traditional interacting group.

Groupthink
A phenomenon in which the norm for consensus overrides the realistic appraisal of alternative courses of action.

Groupshift
A change between a group's decision and an individual decision that a member within the group would make; the shift can be toward either conservatism or greater risk, but it generally is toward a more extreme version of the group's original position.

Interacting groups
Typical groups in which members interact with each other, relying on both verbal and nonverbal communication.

Brainstorming
An idea-generation process that specifically encourages any and all alternatives while withholding any criticism of those alternatives.

BRAINSTORMING **Brainstorming** can overcome the pressures for conformity that dampen creativity[149] by encouraging any and all alternatives while withholding criticism. In a typical brainstorming session, the group leader states the problem in a clear manner so all group members understand. Members then freewheel as many alternatives as they can in a given length of time. To encourage members to "think the unusual," no criticism is allowed, even of the most bizarre suggestions, and all ideas are recorded for later discussion and analysis.

Brainstorming may indeed generate ideas—but not very efficiently. Research consistently shows individuals working alone generate more ideas than a group in a brainstorming session. One reason for this is "production blocking." When people are generating ideas in a group, many are talking at once, which blocks individuals' thought processes and eventually impedes the sharing of ideas.[150]

Nominal group technique
A group decision-making method in which individual members meet face to face to pool their judgments in a systematic but independent fashion.

NOMINAL GROUP TECHNIQUE   The **nominal group technique** may be more effective. This technique restricts discussion and interpersonal communication during the decision-making process. Group members are all present, as in a traditional meeting, but they operate independently. Specifically, a problem is presented and then the group takes the following steps:

1. Before any discussion takes place, each member independently writes down ideas about the problem.
2. After this silent period, each member presents one idea to the group. No discussion takes place until all ideas have been presented and recorded.
3. The group discusses the ideas for clarity and evaluates them.
4. Each group member silently and independently rank-orders the ideas. The idea with the highest aggregate ranking determines the final decision.

The chief advantage of the nominal group technique is that it permits a group to meet formally but does not restrict independent thinking. Research generally shows nominal groups outperform brainstorming groups.[151]

Each of the group-decision techniques has its own set of strengths and weaknesses. The choice depends on the criteria you want to emphasize and the cost–benefit trade-off. As Exhibit 9-5 indicates, an interacting group is good for achieving commitment to a solution; brainstorming develops group cohesiveness; and the nominal group technique is an inexpensive means for generating many ideas.

| | Type of Group | | |
Effectiveness Criteria	Interacting	Brainstorming	Nominal
Number and quality of ideas	Low	Moderate	High
Social pressure	High	Low	Moderate
Money costs	Low	Low	Low
Speed	Moderate	Moderate	Moderate
Task orientation	Low	High	High
Potential for interpersonal conflict	High	Low	Moderate
Commitment to solution	High	Not applicable	Moderate
Development of group cohesiveness	High	High	Moderate

EXHIBIT 9-5
Evaluating Group Effectiveness

SUMMARY

We can draw several implications from our discussion of groups. First, norms control behavior by establishing standards of right and wrong. Second, status inequities create frustration and can adversely influence productivity and willingness to remain with an organization. Third, the impact of size on a group's performance depends on the type of task. Fourth, cohesiveness may influence a group's level of productivity, depending on the group's performance-related norms. Fifth, diversity appears to have a mixed impact on group performance, with some studies suggesting that diversity can help performance and others suggesting the opposite. Sixth, role conflict is associated with job-induced tension and job dissatisfaction.[152] Groups can be carefully managed toward positive organizational outcomes and optimal decision making. The next chapter will explore several of these conclusions in greater depth.

IMPLICATIONS FOR MANAGERS

- Recognize that groups can have a dramatic impact on individual behavior in organizations, to either a positive or negative effect. Therefore, pay special attention to roles, norms, and cohesion—to understand how these are operating within a group is to understand how the group is likely to behave.
- To decrease the possibility of deviant workplace activities, ensure that group norms do not support antisocial behavior.
- Pay attention to the status aspect of groups. Because lower-status people tend to participate less in group discussions, groups with high-status differences are likely to inhibit input from lower-status members and reduce their potential.
- Use larger groups for fact-finding activities and smaller groups for action-taking tasks. With larger groups, provide measures of individual performance.
- To increase employee satisfaction, ensure people perceive their job roles accurately.

10

Understanding Work Teams

After studying this chapter, you should be able to:

10.1 Contrast groups and teams.

10.2 Contrast the five types of team arrangements.

10.3 Identify the characteristics of effective teams.

10.4 Explain how organizations can create team players.

10.5 Decide when to use individuals instead of teams.

SoaPen, a product that has received a $50,000 grant from Toyota and numerous awards from organizations like UNICEF, is the product of teamwork and the entrepreneurial spirit.[1] The founders (Amanat Anand, Shubham Issar, and Maria Putri), a diverse all-female minority team, designed the product (soap in the form of a thick colored pen that children can draw with) in order to make hand hygiene more accessible to children. Building their team was incredibly important, and Shubham notes that discovering people with complimentary expertise and different perspectives was critical to their success as a startup.[2]

Teams can sometimes achieve feats an individual could never accomplish.[3] Teams are more flexible and responsive to changing events than traditional departments can be. They can quickly assemble, deploy, refocus, and disband. And finally, research indicates that our involvement in teams positively shapes the way we think as individuals, introducing a collaborative mindset about even our own personal decision making.[4]

The fact that organizations have embraced teamwork does not necessarily mean teams are always effective. Team members, being human, can be swayed by errors in decision-making processes and dynamics (see, for example, the chapter on foundations of group behavior) that can lead them astray from the best decisions. What conditions affect their potential? How do members work together? To answer these questions, let us first distinguish between groups and teams.

DIFFERENCES BETWEEN GROUPS AND TEAMS

According to some scholars, groups and teams are not the same thing (although, functionally, they are often used to refer to the same thing).[5] In the chapter on foundations of group behavior, we defined a *group* as two or more individuals, interacting and interdependent, who come together to achieve certain objectives. A **work group** is a group that interacts primarily to share information and make decisions to help all members perform within their respective areas of responsibility.

Work groups have no need or opportunity to engage in collective work with joint effort, so the group's performance is merely the summation of each member's individual contribution. There is no positive synergy that would create an overall level of performance greater than the sum of the inputs. A work group is a collection of individuals doing their work, albeit with some interaction and/or dependency.

A **work team**, on the other hand, generates positive synergy through coordination.[6] The individual efforts result in a level of performance greater than the sum of the individual inputs. Teams are more likely to be constantly changing and adapting rather than static entities—seeing teams as dynamic systems in this way has led many to focus more on *teaming* as a verb (e.g., on the processes or actions involved in engaging as a team) rather than on the team itself.[7]

In both work groups and work teams, there are often behavioral expectations of members, collective normalization efforts, active group dynamics, and some level of decision making (even if only informally). Both may generate ideas, pool resources, or coordinate logistics such as work schedules; for the work group, however, this effort will be limited to information gathering for decision makers outside the group. Whereas we can think of a work team as a subset of a work group, the team is constructed to be purposeful (symbiotic) in its member interaction. Exhibit 10-1 highlights the differences between them.

The definitions help clarify why organizations structure work processes in the way they do. The extensive use of teams creates the *potential* for an organization to generate greater outputs with no increase in employee headcount. There is nothing magical, however, that ensures the achievement of positive synergy in the creation of teams. Merely calling a *group* a *team* does not automatically improve its performance. As we show later, effective teams have certain common characteristics. If management hopes to gain increases in organizational performance by teams, these teams should possess these characteristics.

Work group
A group that interacts primarily to share information and make decisions to help all members perform within their respective areas of responsibility.

Work team
A group whose individual efforts result in performance that is greater than the sum of the individual inputs.

Work Groups		Work Teams
Share information	◄— Goal —►	Collective performance
Neutral (sometimes negative)	◄— Synergy —►	Positive
Individual	◄— Accountability —►	Individual and mutual
Random and varied	◄— Skills —►	Complementary

EXHIBIT 10-1
Comparing
Work Groups
and Work Teams

TYPES OF TEAMS

Teams can make products, provide services, negotiate deals, coordinate projects, offer advice, and make decisions.[8] In this section, we first describe four common types of teams in organizations: *problem-solving teams, self-managed work teams, cross-functional teams*, and *virtual teams* (see Exhibit 10-2). Then we will discuss *multiteam systems*, which utilize a "team of teams" and are becoming increasingly widespread as work increases in complexity.

Problem-Solving Teams

Problem-solving teams
Groups of five to twelve employees from the same department who meet for a few hours each week to discuss ways of improving quality, efficiency, and the work environment.

Problem-solving teams such as quality-control teams have been in use for many years. Originally seen most often in manufacturing plants, these were permanent teams that generally met at a regular time, sometimes weekly or daily, to address quality standards and any problems with the products made. For example, direct-to-consumer watchmaker Vincero employs a full-time quality-control team that hand-checks every manufactured watch.[9] The use of quality-control teams has since expanded into other arenas such as the medical field, where they are used to improve patient care services. Problem-solving teams like these rarely have the authority to unilaterally implement their suggestions, but if their recommendations are paired with implementation processes, some significant improvements can be realized.

Self-Managed Work Teams

As we discussed, problem-solving teams only make recommendations. Some organizations have gone further and created teams that also implement solutions and take responsibility for outcomes. For example, self-managed teams are used in the thirteen practices of the O'Brien Veterinary Group in Chicago, where they autonomously decide how to solve problems that arise and share what they have learned from their experiences with the other work teams.[10]

Self-managed work teams
Groups of ten to fifteen people who autonomously implement solutions and take responsibility for the outcomes (responsibilities normally given to supervisors).

    Self-managed work teams are groups of employees (typically ten to fifteen in number) who perform highly related or interdependent jobs; these teams take on some supervisory responsibilities.[11] Typically, the responsibilities include planning and scheduling work, assigning tasks to members, making operating decisions, acting on problems, and working with suppliers and customers. Fully self-managed work teams even select their own members who evaluate each other's performance.

    When these teams are established, former supervisory positions become less important and are sometimes eliminated. However, with a lack of authority and accountability, teams may spend valuable time and resources aligning team member values and goals to "get on the same page."[12] Greg O'Brien, founder of O'Brien Veterinary Group, notes

EXHIBIT 10-2
Four Types of Teams

  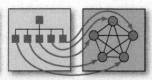 

Problem-solving   Self-managed   Cross-functional   Virtual

that it is often difficult for managers to give up this kind of control: "It requires building a team of adults who want to handle problems and staying the course when things go sideways. The temptation to grab control back is big."[13]

Research on the effectiveness of self-managed work teams has not been uniformly positive. Some research indicates that the effectiveness of self-managed teams is contingent on the degree to which team-promoting behaviors are rewarded. For example, when team members perceive that economic rewards such as pay are dependent on input from their teammates, performance improves for both the individuals and the team.[14]

A second area of research focus has been the impact of conflict on self-managed team effectiveness. Some research indicates that self-managed teams are not effective when there is conflict. When disputes arise, members often stop cooperating and power struggles ensue, which leads to lower group performance.[15] However, other research indicates that conflict can be beneficial and boost team performance when members feel they can speak up without being embarrassed, rejected, or punished by other team members.[16]

Thirdly, research has explored the effect of self-managed work teams on member behavior. Here again the findings are mixed. Although individuals on teams report higher levels of job satisfaction than other individuals, studies indicate they sometimes also have higher absenteeism and turnover rates. Furthermore, one large-scale study of labor productivity in British establishments found that no evidence supported the claim that self-managed teams performed better than traditional teams with less decision-making authority.[17] Finally, some research suggests that in the absence of controlled supervision, leaders may "over-emerge": in other words, people who are not very effective as leaders can take control more readily.[18]

Cross-Functional Teams

Tech companies like ExtraHop and Ixia have been working to implement teams that bring employees from information technology and security operations to work together. As a result, they can meet cyber security objectives and, in so doing, consolidate their toolsets, break down silos, and formalize and automate their collaboration.[19] These examples illustrate the use of **cross-functional teams**: teams made up of employees from about the same hierarchical level, but from different work areas, who come together to accomplish a task.

Cross-functional teams are an effective means of allowing people from diverse areas within or even between organizations to exchange information, develop new ideas, solve problems, and coordinate complex projects. However, due to the high need for coordination, cross-functional teams are not simple to form and manage. Why? First, different expertise is needed because the members are at roughly the same level in the organization, which creates leadership ambiguity. A climate of trust thus needs to be developed before leadership shifts can happen without undue conflict.[20] Second, the early stages of development are often long since members need to learn to work with higher levels of diversity and complexity. Third, it takes time to build trust and teamwork, especially among people with different experiences and perspectives.

Virtual Teams

The teams described in the preceding section do their work face-to-face, whereas **virtual teams** use technology to unite physically dispersed members to achieve a common goal.[21] Members collaborate online using communication links such as wide-area networks, corporate social media, videoconferencing, and e-mail; whether members are

Cross-functional teams
Employees from about the same hierarchical level, but from different work areas, who come together to accomplish a task.

Virtual teams
Teams that use technology to tie together physically dispersed members in order to achieve a common goal.

nearby or continents apart. As an example, Cisco relies on teams to identify and capital-ize on new trends in several areas of the software market. Its teams are the equivalent of social-networking groups of employees from different areas that collaborate in real time to identify new business opportunities and implement them from the bottom up.[22]

Virtual teams should be managed differently than face-to-face teams in an office, partially because virtual team members may not interact in the same ways. For instance, virtual environments differ from face-to-face environments in the ways they con-vey social cues and foster a sense of distance between people.[23] As another example, although virtual teams may share more unique information with one another than face-to-face teams, managers should be aware that they may be less open to sharing information with one another.[24] As such, for virtual teams to be effective, trust is very important.[25] Management should ensure that (1) trust is established among members (one inflamma-tory remark in an e-mail can severely undermine team trust), (2) progress is monitored closely (so the team does not lose sight of its goals and no team member "disappears"), and (3) the efforts and products of the team are publicized throughout the organization (so the team does not become invisible).[26]

Multiteam Systems

The types of teams we have described so far are typically smaller, standalone teams, though their activities relate to the broader objectives of the organization. As tasks become more complex, teams often grow, which is accompanied by higher coordina-tion demands. This creates a tipping point at which the addition of another member does more harm than good. To solve this problem, organizations use **multiteam systems**, col-lections of two or more interdependent teams that share a superordinate goal. In other words, a multiteam system is a "team of teams."[27]

Multiteam system
A collection of two or more interdependent teams that share a superordinate goal; a team of teams.

To picture a multiteam system, consider NASA's plans to send a team of astronauts to Mars.[28] In order to make this mission a success, countless teams of researchers, sci-entists, professors, engineers, operations employees, groundcrews, and psychologists are needed. Although the research and operations teams, for example are technically indepen-dent, their activities are interdependent, and the success of one depends on the success of the others. Why? Because they all share the higher goal of sending the astronauts to Mars.

Some factors that make smaller, more traditional teams effective do not necessarily apply to multiteam systems and can even hinder their performance. One study showed that multiteam systems performed better when they had "boundary spanners" whose jobs were to coordinate efforts with all constituents. This reduced the need for some team member communication, which was helpful because it reduced coordination demands.[29] Some people ("boundary spoilers") and teams within a multiteam system may also *hin-der* effective communication and coordination;[30] in these instances, these teams could benefit from training in which all teams adopt the same perspectives or assumptions (e.g., "getting on the same page").[31] In some cases, employees can even identify with either their own team or the multiteam system as a whole. When multiteam systems are first established, strong identification to one's own team can lead to conflicts between teams—by developing an identification with the multiteam system as a whole, conflicts can be reduced and the performance of the whole system can be improved.[32]

Leadership of multiteam systems is also much different than for standalone teams. While leadership of all teams affects team performance, a multiteam leader must both facilitate coordination between teams and lead them.[33] Research indicated teams that received more attention and engagement from the organization's leaders felt more empowered, which made them more effective as they sought to solve their own problems.[34]

CREATING EFFECTIVE TEAMS

Teams are often created deliberately but sometimes evolve organically. For example, tech startup teams are often started naturally by friends. In Noam Wasserman's research of over ten thousand tech startups, nearly 40 percent of founders were friends before going into business.[35] Interestingly, being friends increases the likelihood of failure, and for each additional friend on the founding team, Wasserman suggests, the likelihood of the founders leaving the startup increases by nearly 30 percent.[36]

Many people have tried to identify factors related to team effectiveness. To help, some studies have organized what was once a large list of characteristics into a relatively focused model.[37] Exhibit 10-3 summarizes what we currently know about what makes teams effective. As you will see, it builds on many of the group concepts introduced in the chapter on foundations of group behavior. We can organize the key components of effective teams into three general categories. First are resources and other *contextual* influences that make teams effective. The second relates to the team's *composition*.

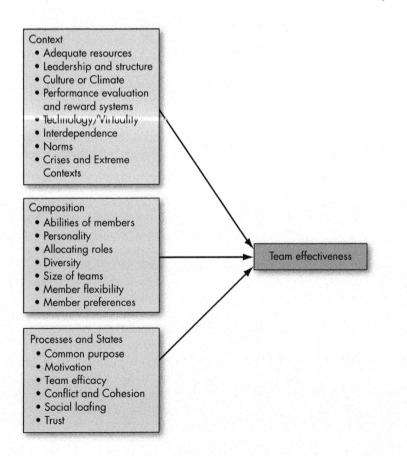

EXHIBIT 10-3
Team
Effectiveness
Model

Finally, *process* and *state* variables are events within the team that influence effectiveness. We will explore each of these components next.

Team Context

The five contextual factors most significantly related to team performance, discussed next, are *adequate resources, leadership and structure, culture or climate,* a *performance evaluation and reward system* that reflects team contributions, and *crises and extreme contexts.* (Technology/virtuality was discussed earlier in this chapter; interdependence was also discussed earlier in this chapter in our discussion of self-managed teams; norms, defined as acceptable standards of behavior within a group that are shared by the group's members, were discussed in the previous chapter).

ADEQUATE RESOURCES   Teams are part of a larger organization system; every work team relies on resources outside the group to sustain it. A scarcity of resources directly reduces the ability of a team to perform its job effectively and achieve its goals. As one study concluded after looking at thirteen factors related to group performance, "perhaps one of the most important characteristics of an effective work group is the support the group receives from the organization."[38] Important resources include timely information, proper equipment, adequate staffing, encouragement, and administrative assistance.

LEADERSHIP AND STRUCTURE   Teams function well if they properly allocate roles and ensure the workload is shared by all team members. This requires leadership and structure, either from management or from team members themselves. Beyond initiating structure for team members, leaders play critical motivational roles for team members. For example, well-performing teams tend to have leaders who are transformational (see the chapter on leadership) and empowering.[39] Furthermore, the relationship between the leader and their team member followers has been found to be more important for job attitudes, job performance, and turnover intentions than the relationships between team members themselves.[40]

CULTURE OR CLIMATE   As will be discussed in the chapter on organizational culture, culture (e.g., organizational values, beliefs, and assumptions) and climate (e.g., organizational policies, practices, and procedures) are very important in organizations. However, teams can have their own cultures and climates that influence their effectiveness. For example, one study of teams within a Hong Kong multinational bank found that citizenship behaviors improved team performance in those that valued collectivism, as opposed to individualism.[41]

Earlier research on team climates specifically focused on policies, practices, and procedures related to team effectiveness and innovation. These studies suggest that a shared sense of vision; a sense of being able to share and collaborate in a nonthreatening environment; a concern for performance quality; encouragement of creative and innovative solutions; and regular, frequent interaction are the most important factors for team climate.[42] Research in bank teams in Spain and research and development teams in Australia have supported the importance of these factors for teams, with strong team climates leading to increased team financial performance (e.g., sales made) as well as innovation performance (e.g., speed to innovation, project completion).[43] Over the past decade, more research has examined the effects of different climates in teams. For example, perceptions of fair and just policies, practices, and procedures have proved very important for team attitudes, conflict, and performance.[44]

PERFORMANCE EVALUATION AND REWARD SYSTEM Individual performance evaluations and incentives may interfere with the development of high-performance teams. So, in addition to evaluating and rewarding employees for their individual contributions, management should utilize hybrid performance systems that incorporate an individual member component to recognize individual contributions, and a group reward to recognize positive team outcomes.[45] Group-based appraisals, profit sharing, small-group incentives, and other system modifications can reinforce team effort and commitment. Furthermore, when instituting a performance management system, constructive feedback can have a positive effect on team performance.[46] However, one should take care to avoid bias and discrimination in implementing a team reward system: research demonstrates that teams composed of primarily black employees tend to be stigmatized to a greater degree (and paid less) than those composed of white employees.[47]

CRISES AND EXTREME CONTEXTS Crises and extreme contexts are a crucible in which the merits of teams can be put to the test. These contexts can unlock the potential of team members who do truly great things under stress. They can also lead to the unraveling of the team fabric, resulting in disaster. As an example, in the Mann Gulch fire of 1949, dozens of smokejumpers (i.e., elite firefighters who are airlifted to fight wildfires) led by foreman "Wag" Dodge were dispatched to an area south of the Mann Gulch valley in Montana after a lightning storm caused a wildfire.[48] Illustrating how quickly crises can escalate and unravel a team, Dodge saw the fire was moving toward them at 610 feet per minute with thirty-foot-high flames. The team turned around and headed up the 76 percent grade mountain toward the ridge. They were quickly losing ground, and Dodge yelled for everyone to drop their tools, lit a fire in front of them, and told them to lie down in the area he had burned. No one listened, and they all ran for the ridge. Dodge lived by lying down in the ashes of his escape fire.[49]

Disasters and extreme contexts alike have attracted a lot of research attention from OB researchers in the past several decades. From astronauts in long-duration space missions to health professional teams responding to crises during a worldwide pandemic, teams may find themselves in extreme, disastrous contexts and must act quickly together to perform their duties.[50] Research on multiteam systems in disaster environments demonstrate that people tend to default to gathering information rather than taking action—when they do take action, they do so without deliberately considering the context or options or even forming a plan.[51] Several factors play a role in influencing team success during crises. Leaders are extremely important in these contexts (just consider Dodge's role in the Mann Gulch fire). Leaders are most effective during disasters when they support team problem solving, are supportive of the team members, initiate structure and planning, delegate, and coordinate as well as help team members make sense of the situation.[52] Structure also plays an important role. *Team scaffolds* (i.e., fluid, underlying structures that establish role types, shared responsibilities, and boundaries in teams) have been shown to help support coordination during crises because they establish accountability, a shared understanding, and a sense of identity or belonging.[53] Indeed, this fluidity and flexibility are important for teams in crisis, as higher-performing teams tend to be adaptable and exhibit few, short, and simple interaction patterns.[54] As for individual team members during times of crisis, positive affectivity (PA; see the chapter on personality and individual differences) can help buffer the negative impact of the strain of the crisis situation.[55] Finally, informed decision-making is critical, as team members should know where to target decision making (e.g., toward the problem or the coordination of team members), how to share information effectively with team members, and when to reflect on team objectives, processes, and strategies before acting.[56]

Team Composition

Maria Contreras-Sweet, former head of the U.S. Small Business Administration, said, "When I'm building a team, I'm looking for people who are resourceful. I need people who are flexible, and I really need people who are discreet... . Discreetness also speaks to integrity."[57] These are good qualities, but not all that we should consider when staffing teams. The team composition category includes variables that relate to how teams should be staffed: the *abilities* and *personalities* of team members, *allocation of roles, diversity* (see the chapter on foundations of group behavior), *cultural differences, size* of the team, and *members' preferences* for teamwork.

ABILITIES OF MEMBERS   It is true we occasionally read about an "underdog" team of mediocre players who, because of excellent coaching, determination, and precision teamwork, beat a far more talented group. But such cases make the news precisely because they are unusual. A team's performance depends in part on the knowledge, skills, and abilities of individual members.[58] Abilities set limits on what members can do and how effectively they will perform on a team. Research suggests that a number of groups of abilities are helpful to be an effective team member, namely conflict resolution, collaborative problem solving, communication, goal setting, and planning abilities/skills.[59] In general, despite being weakly related to team performance, complementary backgrounds (e.g., education level, area of expertise, and abilities) also tend to be more strongly related to innovation and creativity in practice.[60] It is also worth noting that, over time, the experiences of the team members add up to improve performance by enhancing the way problems are solved as members learn to work together.[61] In other words, team members learn how to work with one another over time.

PERSONALITY OF MEMBERS   We demonstrated in the chapter on personality and values that personality significantly influences individual behavior. Some dimensions identified in the Big Five personality model are particularly relevant to team effectiveness.[62] Conscientiousness is especially important to teams.[63] Conscientious people are good at backing up other team members and sensing when their support is truly needed.

What about the other traits? Teams that are more agreeable tend to perform better. The level of team member agreeableness matters, too: Teams do worse and are less cohesive when they have disagreeable members, and a wide span in individual levels of agreeableness can lower productivity.[64] Open team members are willing to share more ideas with one another, which makes teams with open people more creative and innovative.[65] Teams confronted with task conflict will likely perform better when they are composed of members with high levels of emotional stability.[66] It's not so much that the conflict itself improves performance for these teams, but that teams characterized by emotional stability are able to handle conflict and leverage it to improve performance. Research is not clear on the outcomes of extraversion, but one study indicated that a high mean level of extraversion in a team can increase the level of helping behaviors, particularly in a team climate of cooperation.[67] Beyond the Big Five, recent research has suggested that team proactive personality (see the chapter on personality and individual differences) is important for team innovation.[68] Thus, the personality traits of individuals are as important to teams as the overall personality characteristics of the team.

ALLOCATION OF ROLES   Teams have different needs, and members should be selected to ensure all the various roles are filled.[69] A study of 778 major league baseball teams over a twenty-one-year period highlighted the importance of assigning roles appropriately.[70] As you might expect, teams with more skilled members performed better. However, the skill of those in core roles—those who handled more of the workflow of the team and were central to all work processes (in this case, pitchers and catchers)—were especially vital.[71]

   We can identify nine potential team member roles (see Exhibit 10-4). Successful work teams have selected people to play all these roles based on their skills and preferences (On many teams, individuals will play multiple roles). To increase the likelihood team members will work well together, managers need to understand the individual strengths each person can bring to a team, select members with their strengths in mind, and allocate work assignments that fit with members' preferred styles.

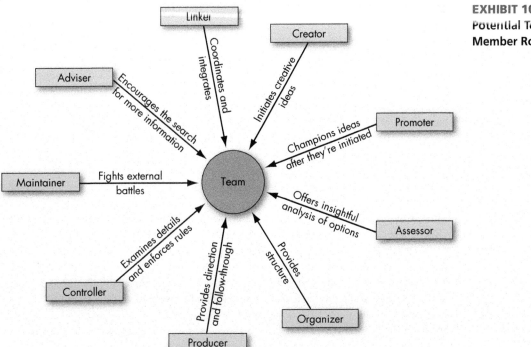

**EXHIBIT 10-4
Potential Team
Member Roles**

DIVERSITY OF MEMBERS   In the chapter on foundations of group behavior, we discussed the effect of diversity on groups. How does *team* diversity affect *team* performance? The degree to which members of a work unit (group, team, or department) share a common demographic attribute, such as age, sex, race, educational level, or length of service in the organization, is the subject of **demography**. Demography research suggests that turnover will be greater among those with dissimilar experiences, as communication may be more difficult and conflict more likely.[72] However, the conclusion from reviews of hundreds of studies suggests that demographic diversity has a negative (but very small) effect on team performance and creativity.[73] Many of us hold the optimistic view that diversity should be a good thing—diverse teams should benefit from differing perspectives.[74] But as reviewed in the chapter on foundations of group behavior, we realize that the picture is complicated by several issues, and there is not a straight answer to whether diversity is always a good thing.

Demography
The degree to which members of a work unit share a common demographic attribute; such as age, sex, race, educational level, or length of service in an organization.

CULTURAL DIFFERENCES   We have discussed research on team diversity regarding several differences. But what about cultural differences? Evidence indicates cultural diversity interferes with team processes, at least in the short term,[75] but let us dig a little deeper. What about differences in cultural status? Researchers in the United Kingdom, for example, found that cultural status differences affected team performance, noting that teams with more high-cultural-status members than low-cultural-status members realized improved performance—for *every* member on the team.[76] This suggests not that diverse teams should be filled with individuals who have high cultural status in their countries, but that we should be aware of how people identify with their cultural status even in diverse group settings. In general, cultural diversity seems to be an asset for tasks that call for a variety of viewpoints. But culturally heterogeneous teams have more difficulty learning to work with each other and solving problems. The good news is that these difficulties seem to dissipate with time.

SIZE OF TEAMS   Many experts believe that keeping teams small is key to improving group effectiveness.[77] Amazon CEO Jeff Bezos uses the "two-pizza" rule, saying, "If it takes more than two pizzas to feed the team, the team is too big."[78] Author and *Forbes* publisher Rich Karlgaard writes, "Bigger teams almost never correlate with a greater chance of success" because the potential connections between people grow exponentially as team size increases, complicating communications and leading to decreased perceptions of support.[79]

Experts suggest using the smallest number of people who can do the task. Unfortunately, managers often err by making teams too large because they believe more people means more benefits (while increasingly underestimating the number of hours required to complete projects, and other losses associated with adding more people).[80] When teams have excess members, cohesiveness and mutual accountability decline, social loafing increases, and people communicate less.[81] Members of large teams have trouble coordinating with one another, especially under time pressure. When a natural working unit is larger and you want a team effort, consider breaking the group into sub-teams.[82] The most effective teams have about five to nine members.

MEMBER PREFERENCES   Not every employee is a team player. Given the option, many employees will select themselves *out* of team participation. When people who prefer to work alone are required to team up, there is a direct threat to the team's morale and to individual member satisfaction.[83] This suggests that, when selecting team members, managers should consider individual preferences along with abilities, personalities, and skills. High-performing teams are likely to be composed of people who prefer working as part of a group.

Team Processes and States

The final category related to team effectiveness includes process variables and team states such as member commitment to a *common plan and purpose, specific team goals, team efficacy, team identity, team cohesion, mental models, conflict, cohesion, social loafing,* and *trust.* These characteristics tend to be excellent predictors of team performance and team member attitudes and are especially important in larger teams and in teams that are highly interdependent.[84]

Why are processes important to team effectiveness? Teams should create outputs greater than the sum of their inputs. Exhibit 10-5 illustrates how group processes can have an impact on a group's actual effectiveness.[85]

COMMON PLAN AND PURPOSE Effective teams begin by analyzing the team's mission, developing goals to achieve that mission, and creating strategies for achieving the goals. Teams that consistently perform better have a clear sense of what needs to be done and how.[86] This sounds obvious, but many teams ignore this fundamental process. Effective teams show **reflexivity**, meaning they reflect on and adjust their purpose when necessary.[87] A team must have a good plan, but it needs to be willing and able to adapt when conditions call for it.[88] As some examples, reflexivity can help improve psychological well-being in manufacturing teams, help startup teams learn from their setbacks, and help improve performance in extreme environments like hospital emergency rooms.[89] Interestingly, some evidence suggests that teams high in reflexivity are better able to adapt to conflicting plans and goals among team members.[90]

> **Reflexivity**
> A team characteristic of reflecting on and adjusting their purpose or plan when necessary.

MOTIVATION Successful teams translate their common purpose into specific, measurable, and difficult (yet realistic) performance goals that align with team objectives.[91] So, for instance, goals for quantity tend to increase quantity, goals for accuracy increase accuracy, and so on.[92] Furthermore, setting goals intended to improve team member performance (instead of team performance as a whole) has the tendency to *undermine* group performance.[93] As such, individual goals should be linked to the actual goals of the group. Furthermore, motivational factors beyond goals matter. For instance, beyond goal setting, the actual experience of striving toward a goal involves wins, setbacks, and conservation of energy. Teams that are geared toward achievement tend to perform better over time.[94] Furthermore, teams that are strategic in how they allocate their resources and energy tend to perform better. For example, one study of five National Hockey League (NHL) seasons suggest that teams that are strategic in when they bench their most valuable players predicts their end-of-season record.[95]

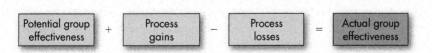

EXHIBIT 10-5
Effects of Group Processes

Team efficacy
A team's collective belief among team members that they can succeed at their tasks.

TEAM EFFICACY   Effective teams have confidence in themselves; they believe they can succeed. We call this **team efficacy**.[96] Teams that have been successful raise their beliefs about future success, which, in turn, motivates them to work harder. Prior research has demonstrated that team efficacy is strongly predictive of team performance, especially when team members are dependent upon one another to contribute to team goals.[97] In addition, teams that have a shared knowledge of individual capabilities can strengthen the link between team members' self-efficacy and their individual creativity because members can more effectively solicit informed opinions from their teammates.[98]

What can be done to increase team efficacy? Two ways might be found in helping the team achieve small successes that build confidence and providing training to improve members' technical and interpersonal skills. The greater the abilities of team members, the more likely the team will develop confidence and the ability to deliver on that confidence.

Team identity
Team members' affinity for and sense of belongingness to their teams.

TEAM IDENTITY   In the chapter on foundations of group behavior, we discussed the important role of social identity in people's lives. When people connect emotionally with the groups they are in, they are more likely to invest in their relationship with those groups. It is the same with teams.[99] For example, research with soldiers in the Netherlands indicated that individuals who felt included and respected by team members became more willing to work hard for their teams, even though as soldiers they were already called upon to be dedicated to their units.[100] Therefore, by recognizing individuals' specific skills and abilities, as well as creating a climate of respect and inclusion, leaders and members can foster positive **team identity** and realize improved team outcomes.[101]

Organizational identity is important, too. Although team identification is often stronger than other types of identification, rarely do teams operate in a vacuum—they are part of a larger organization and interact with other units, teams, and people.[102] Individuals with a positive team identity but without a positive organizational identity can become fixed to their teams and unwilling to coordinate with other teams within the organization.[103] In general, however, team identity serves an instrumental role in affecting team performance, attitudes, and cooperation; in other words, more positive organizational identification tends to lead to more positive team identification, which is beneficial for team outcomes.[104]

Team cohesion
When team members are emotionally attached and bonded to one another and committed toward the team.

TEAM COHESION   Have you ever been a member of a team that really "gelled," one in which team members felt connected? The term **team cohesion** means members are emotionally attached and bonded to one another and committed toward the team. Experiments on astronauts (to prepare for an eventual mission to Mars) in isolated, confined, and extreme environments such as those outside of Hawaiian volcanoes has found that cohesion tends to break down over several months into missions.[105] By studying factors that lead to these breakdowns in cohesion, researchers hope to improve astronaut team functioning.

Cohesive teams tend to perform better than non-cohesive teams—evidence also suggests the reverse can be true (better performing teams can become more cohesive as a result of their successes).[106] Several factors can increase team cohesion, such as shared leadership responsibilities, open information sharing among team members, and interdependence among team members.[107] Recent research also suggests that the effects of team cohesion can last even after the team has disbanded—particularly cohesive teams may develop friendships and networks that they draw on for the rest of their lives.[108]

MENTAL MODELS The members of an effective team share accurate **mental models**—organized mental representations of the key elements within a team's environment (team mission and goals pertain to *what* a team needs to be effective, while mental models pertain to *how* a team does its work).[109] If team members have the wrong mental models, which is particularly likely in teams under acute stress, their performance suffers.[110] One review found that teams with shared mental models engaged in more frequent interactions with one another, were more motivated, had more positive attitudes toward their work, and had higher levels of objectively rated performance.[111] If team members have different ideas about how to do things, however, the team will fight over methods rather than focus on what needs to be done.[112]

> **Mental models**
> Team members' knowledge and beliefs about how the work gets done by the team.

Teams should also develop *transactive memory systems*, which represent a shared model of information relevant to the team. For example, these types of teams enable team members to know "who knows what and is best at what" so that the most-skilled members are assigned tasks they are best suited for and the most knowledgeable are consulted for advice on issues they are experts in.[113] Transactive memory systems are important for performance, especially in collectivist and high power distance cultures and in environments that are particularly volatile (e.g., times of crisis).[114]

An anesthetic team in a hospital is one example of an action team with shared mental models. Research in Switzerland found that anesthetic teams communicated two distinct types of messages while in an operation: vocally monitoring each other's performance (not to criticize but to keep a vocal record of events) and "talking to the room" (announcements to everyone such as "Patient's blood pressure is dropping"). The study found that high- and low-performing teams communicated in these ways equally often; what mattered to performance was the sequencing of the communication to maintain a shared mental model. High-performing teams followed up monitoring dialogue with assistance, instructions, and talking-to-the-room dialogue.[115] The message seems simple: to maintain shared mental models and to share in conversations about what is happening while the team is in operation!

TEAM CONFLICT Conflict has a complex relationship with team performance, and it is not necessarily bad (see the chapter on conflict and negotiation).[116] *Relationship conflicts*—those based on interpersonal incompatibility, tension, and animosity toward others—are almost always dysfunctional. However, when teams are performing nonroutine activities, disagreements about task content—called *task conflicts*—stimulate discussion, promote critical assessment of problems and options, and can lead to better team decisions. According to one study conducted in China, moderate levels of task conflict during the initial phases of team performance were positively related to team creativity, but both very low and very high levels of task conflict were negatively related to team performance.[117] In other words, both too much and too little disagreement about how a team should initially perform a creative task can inhibit performance.

SOCIAL LOAFING As we noted in the chapter on foundations of group behavior, individuals can engage in social loafing and coast on the group's effort when their contributions (or lack thereof) cannot be identified. Effective teams undermine this tendency by making members individually and jointly accountable for the team's purpose, goals, and approach.[118] Therefore, members should be clear on what they are individually and jointly responsible for on the team.

TEAM TRUST   During the COVID-19 pandemic, it was clear just how important trust is to the successful operation of teams. Lindsay Kaplan, co-founder and CEO of Chief, recounts life as a virtual manager during this time after a household emergency with her baby: "I text the marketing team that I'll likely be late to our team meeting . . . trust in my team is what's getting me through. I believe in hiring slowly, and it's rewarding to see our carefully curated team operate self-sufficiently."[119] Trust in teams entails a mutual, positive state of positive expectations between team members. When you trust a team member, you believe in their reliability and dependability and are genuinely concerned for their welfare (and vice versa). Trust can be broken, but it can also be repaired.[120] Team trust has been shown to have a sizeable effect on team performance, especially in virtual teams.[121] Team trust evolves over time as members share with one another, put effort into the team, and monitor one another's performance.[122]

TURNING INDIVIDUALS INTO TEAM PLAYERS

Many organizations have historically gone to great lengths to hire, train, and reward team players given how important teams are to the success of organizations. As some examples, Don Yaeger (author and associate editor at *Sports Illustrated*), notes that organizations wish to hire people "who think team first"—instead of those who engage in self-centered behavior.[123] Search and rescue teams have also engaged in team training in order to hone team processes that lead to successful search and rescue missions.[124] Dental teams have also implemented team bonus plans in order to reward team performance.[125]

Selecting: Hiring Team Players

Some people already possess the interpersonal skills to be effective team players. Therefore, managers, when hiring team members, can make certain that candidates can fulfill their team roles as well as technical requirements.[126] Creating teams often means resisting the urge to hire the best talent no matter what. For example, the New York Knicks professional basketball team pays Carmelo Anthony well because he scores a lot of points for his team; but statistics show he takes more shots than other highly paid players in the league, which means fewer shots for his teammates.[127] As discussed in this chapter, a number of personality traits, abilities, and other characteristics lead to effective team performance—managers should be sure to hire applicants who have the highest potential to perform well in a team, and strategically place them in teams where they are most likely to work well with the other team members.[128]

Training: Creating Team Players

Training specialists conduct exercises that enable teams to perform more effectively by learning relevant team skills and practices. A large body of research suggests that team training is effective at improving team member attitudes, team processes, and cognitive aspects like developing shared mental models; and that these findings generalize to particularly important industries (e.g., medical services).[129] Workshops help employees improve their problem-solving, communication, negotiation, conflict-management, and coaching skills. L'Oréal, for example, found that successful sales teams required much more than a staff of high-ability salespeople. "What we didn't account for was that many members of our top team in sales had been promoted because they had excellent technical and executional skills," said L'Oréal's senior VP David Waldock. As a result of introducing purposeful team training, Waldock said, "We are no longer a team just on paper, working independently. We have a real group dynamic now, and it's a good one."[130] An effective team does not develop overnight—it takes time.

Rewarding: Providing Incentives to Be a Good Team Player

A traditional organization's reward system must be reworked to encourage cooperative efforts rather than competitive ones.[131] Hallmark Cards Inc. added to its basic individual-incentive system an annual bonus based on the achievement of team goals. Whole Foods directs most of its performance-based rewards toward team performance. As a result, teams select new members carefully so they will contribute to team effectiveness (and, thus, team bonuses).[132] Promotions, pay raises, and other forms of recognition should be given to individuals who work effectively as team members by training new colleagues, sharing information, helping resolve team conflicts, and mastering needed new skills. Team-based rewards have been shown to positively influence team performance, especially when they are distributed based on individual's level of contribution (rather than equally distributed).[133] This does not mean individual contributions should be ignored; rather, they should be balanced with selfless contributions to the team.

Finally, do not forget the intrinsic rewards, such as camaraderie, that employees can receive from teamwork. The opportunity for personal development of self and teammates can be a very satisfying and rewarding experience. Ben Affleck and Oscar Isaac, while filming *Triple Frontier* (about former Special Forces operatives and their difficulties in acclimating to civilian life), commented on the sense of loyalty, camaraderie, and teamwork they experienced in playing those roles (even permeating into their own lives).[134]

BEWARE! TEAMS ARE NOT ALWAYS THE ANSWER

Teamwork takes more time and often more resources than individual work. Teams have increased communication demands, conflicts to manage, and meetings to run. So, the benefits of using teams must exceed the costs, and that is not always possible.[135]

How do you know whether the work of your group would be better done in teams? You can apply three tests.[136] First, can the work be done better by more than one person? Good indicators are the complexity of the work and the need for different perspectives. Simple tasks that do not require diverse inputs are probably better left to individuals. Second, does the work create a common purpose or set of goals for the people in the group that is more than the aggregate of individual goals? Many service departments of new vehicle dealers have introduced teams that link customer-service people, mechanics, parts specialists, and sales representatives. Such teams can better manage collective responsibility for ensuring customer needs are properly met. The final test is to determine whether the members of the group are interdependent. Using teams makes sense when there is interdependence among tasks—the success of the whole depends on the success of each one, *and* the success of each one depends on the success of the others. Soccer, for instance, is an obvious *team* sport. Success requires a great deal of coordination among interdependent players. Conversely, except possibly for relays, swim teams are not really teams. They are groups of individuals performing individually, whose total performance is merely the aggregate summation of their individual performances.

SUMMARY

Working on teams requires employees to cooperate with others, share information, confront differences, and sublimate personal interests for the greater good of the team. Understanding the distinctions between problem-solving, self-managed, cross-functional, and virtual teams as well as multiteam systems helps determine the appropriate applications for team-based work. Concepts such as reflexivity, team efficacy, team identity, team cohesion, and mental models bring to light important issues relating to team context, composition, and processes. For teams to function optimally, careful attention must be given to hiring, creating, and rewarding team players. Still, effective organizations recognize that teams are not always the best method for getting the work done efficiently. Careful discernment and an understanding of organizational behavior are needed.

IMPLICATIONS FOR MANAGERS

- Effective teams have adequate resources, effective leadership, positive cultures and climates, and a performance evaluation and reward system that reflects team contributions. These teams have individuals with technical expertise, and the right traits and skills.
- Effective teams tend to be small. They have members who fill role demands and who prefer to be part of a group.
- Effective teams have members who believe in the team's capabilities, are committed to a common plan and purpose, and have an accurate shared mental model of what it is to be accomplished.
- Select individuals who have the interpersonal skills to be effective team players; provide training to develop teamwork skills; and reward individuals for cooperative efforts.
- Do not assume that teams are always needed. When tasks will not benefit from interdependency, individuals may be the better choice.

11

Communication

After studying this chapter, you should be able to:

11.1 Describe the functions and process of communication.

11.2 Contrast downward, upward, and lateral communication through small-group networks and the grapevine.

11.3 Contrast oral, written, and nonverbal communication.

11.4 Describe how channel richness underlies the choice of communication channel.

11.5 Differentiate between automatic and controlled processing of persuasive messages.

11.6 Identify common barriers to effective communication.

11.7 Discuss how to overcome potential problems of cross-cultural communication.

Communication is the primary means through which people connect with one another. Communication is not only used to transmit a message or impart meaning—it is also used to bond and forge connections with others. For instance, Shelley Zalis (CEO of The Female Quotient [FQ]) has created The FQ Lounge, which has connected more than 17,500 women in the corporate world.[1] According to Jocelyn Greenky, CEO of Sider Road, this network has enabled women to find their voice and "build circles of trust with one another."[2]

It may surprise you that **communication** includes both the *transfer* and the *understanding* of meaning. Communicating is more than merely imparting meaning; that meaning must also be understood. Though it sounds elementary, perfect communication is never achieved in practice due to poor delivery of messages, misunderstandings, and other obstacles.

Communication
The transfer and the understanding of meaning.

FUNCTIONS OF COMMUNICATION

Communication serves five major functions within a group or organization: *management, feedback, emotional sharing, persuasion*, and *information exchange*.[3]

MANAGING BEHAVIOR Communication acts to *manage* member behavior in several ways.[4] Organizations have formal hierarchies and guidelines for employees that guide communication. When employees comply with company policies, communication performs a management function. Informal communication can also manage behavior. When work groups tease or harass a member who produces too much (and makes the rest of the members look bad), they are informally communicating, and managing, the member's behavior.

FEEDBACK Communication can be used to convey *feedback* (see the chapter on motivation concepts), such as by clarifying to employees what they must do, how well they are doing it, and how they can improve their performance. Formation of goals, feedback on progress, and reward for desired behavior all require communication and stimulate motivation. Feedback is not merely a one-way supervisor-to-subordinate transaction. Supervisors may also seek feedback from subordinate employees,[5] employees may informally give feedback about organizations (e.g., on websites such as *Glassdoor*),[6] and customers provide feedback about providers' service (e.g., on websites like *Yelp*).[7]

EMOTION SHARING Communication is a fundamental mechanism by which members show satisfaction and frustration. Communication, therefore, provides for the *sharing* of feelings to fulfill social needs. For instance, Lisa Jennings, a Canadian paramedic, started a campaign in which she reached out to other first responders to share their emotions concerning how they have been affected by traumatic events at work, to raise awareness among legislators for first responder mental-health injury.[8] As a second example, Starbucks had baristas write "Race Together" on coffee cups to start conversations about race relations. In both cases, the initial communications were awkward, so awkward that Starbucks pulled the campaign, but Jennings and others have forged solid relationships from their emotional sharing.[9]

PERSUASION Like emotional sharing, *persuasion* can be good or bad depending on whether, say, a leader is trying to persuade a workgroup to commit to the organization's corporate social responsibility initiatives or to, conversely, persuade the workgroup to break the law to meet an organizational goal. These may be extreme examples, but it is important to remember that persuasion can benefit or harm an organization.

INFORMATION EXCHANGE The final function of communication is *information exchange* to facilitate decision making. Communication provides the information (e.g., context, situation, norms, available choices) individuals and groups need to make decisions.

The Communication Process

Before communication can occur, it needs a purpose, a message to be conveyed between a sender and a receiver. The sender encodes the message (converts it to a symbolic form) and passes it through a medium (channel) to the receiver, who decodes it. The result is a transfer of meaning from one person to another.[10]

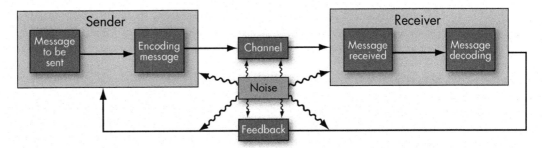

EXHIBIT 11-1
The Communication Process

Exhibit 11-1 depicts this **communication process**. The key parts of this model are (1) the sender, (2) encoding, (3) the message, (4) the channel, (5) decoding, (6) the receiver, (7) noise, and (8) feedback.

The *sender* initiates a message by encoding a thought. The *receiver* is the person(s) to whom the message is directed, who must first translate the symbols into understandable form.

The *message* is the actual physical product of the sender's *encoding*. When we speak, the speech is the message. When we write, the writing (e.g., a letter) is the message. When we gesture, the movements of our arms and the expressions on our faces are the message.

The *channel* is the medium through which the message travels. The sender selects it, determining whether to use a formal or informal channel. **Formal channels** are established by the organization and transmit messages that are related to the professional activities of members. For example, a formal resignation letter conveys an employee's intentions to quit. Other forms of messages, such as those that are personal or social, follow **informal channels**, which are spontaneous and subject to individual choice.[11] For example, throwing your apron off and storming out of the restaurant in which you work is a more informal way of conveying an employee's intentions to quit.

Once received, the message should be *decoded*. Certain factors muddle the decoding of the message, so that it is not decoded in the way it was intended. *Noise* represents communication barriers that distort the clarity of the message, such as perceptual problems, information overload, semantic difficulties, or cultural differences.

The final link in the communication process is a feedback loop. *Feedback* is the check on how successful we have been in transferring our messages as originally intended. It determines whether understanding has been achieved. This final link may or may not be achieved, depending upon whether the receiver engages in closed-loop communication (i.e., when the receiver acknowledges, verbally or nonverbally, that they heard and/or understood the message).[12]

Communication process
The steps between a source and a receiver that result in the transfer and understanding of meaning.

Formal channels
Communication channels established by an organization to transmit messages related to the professional activities of members.

Informal channels
Communication channels that are created spontaneously and that emerge as responses to individual choices.

DIRECTION OF COMMUNICATION

Communication can flow vertically or laterally, through formal small-group networks or the informal grapevine. We subdivide the vertical dimension into downward and upward directions.[13] For instance, you may think of a CEO or founder establishing a vision for an entire organization (see the next chapter)—however, in reality, communication transforms this vision as it travels downward, laterally, and upward throughout the organization, resulting in separate sub-visions.[14]

Downward Communication

Communication that flows from one level of a group or organization to a lower level is *downward communication*. In downward communication, the delivery mode and the context of the information are of high importance. Group leaders and managers use it to assign goals, provide job instructions, explain policies and procedures, point out problems that need attention, and offer feedback. More informally, group leaders and managers may also convey signals of their rank (e.g., prestige or dominance) through downward communication.[15]

Consider the ultimate downward communication: the performance review. Automated performance reviews have allowed managers to review their subordinates without discussions, which is efficient but misses critical opportunities for growth, motivation, and relationship building.[16] In general, employees subjected to indirect, impersonal communications are less likely to understand the intentions of the message correctly. The best communicators explain the reasons behind their downward communications but also solicit communication from the employees they supervise.[17]

Upward Communication

Upward communication flows to a higher level in the group or organization.[18] It is used to provide feedback to higher-ups, inform them of progress toward goals, and relay current problems. Upward communication keeps managers aware of how employees feel about their jobs, coworkers, and the organization in general. Managers also rely on upward communication for ideas on how conditions can be improved. When employees remain silent, they are withholding potentially useful organization for their superiors. In general, managers should consider what might get in the way of employees upwardly communicating needed information (e.g., personality, stressors, fear, rigid organizational hierarchies, detachment),[19] especially if the managers are not perceived as very open to suggestions.[20]

Given that most managers' job responsibilities have expanded, upward communication is increasingly difficult because managers can be overwhelmed and easily distracted. To engage in effective upward communication, try to communicate in short summaries rather than long explanations, support your summaries with actionable items, and prepare an agenda to make sure you use your boss's attention well.[21] Your delivery can be as important as the content of your communication.

Lateral Communication

When communication occurs between members of the same workgroup, members at the same level in separate workgroups, or any other horizontally equivalent workers, we describe it as *lateral communication*.[22]

Lateral communication saves time and facilitates coordination. Some lateral relationships are formal, such as when project teams at Social Native meet to discuss the team objectives and solve problems. (No one at Social Native has their own office, to

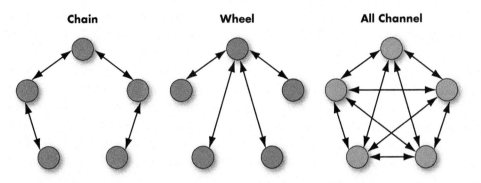

Chain   **Wheel**   **All Channel**

EXHIBIT 11-2
Three Common
Small Group
Networks

inspire lateral communication!)[23] On the other hand, some lateral communication can also be informal, such as when coworkers witness the emotional expression of another coworker.[24] For example, witnessing a crying coworker leaving the manager's office can be a powerful message to the rest of the office. Lateral communication occurring with management's knowledge and support can be beneficial. But dysfunctional conflict can result when formal vertical channels are ignored, such as when managers find actions have been taken or decisions made without their knowledge. Therefore, both lateral and vertical communication should be used in organizations.

Formal Small-Group Networks

Formal organizational networks can be complicated, including hundreds of people and a half-dozen or more hierarchical levels.[25] We have condensed these networks into three common small groups of five people each (see Exhibit 11-2): chain, wheel, and all channel.

The *chain* rigidly follows the formal chain of command; this network approximates the communication channels you might find in a rigid three-level organization. The *wheel* relies on a central figure to act as the conduit for all group communication; it simulates the communication network you might find on a team with a strong leader. The *all-channel* network permits group members to actively communicate with each other; it is most often characterized by self-managed teams, in which group members are free to contribute and no one person takes on a leadership role. Many organizations today like to consider themselves all channel, meaning that anyone can communicate with anyone (but sometimes they should not).

As Exhibit 11-3 demonstrates, the effectiveness of each network is determined by the outcome you are interested in. The structure of the wheel facilitates the emergence of a leader, the all-channel network is best if you desire high member satisfaction, and the chain is best if accuracy is most important.

The Grapevine

The informal communication network in a group or organization is called the **grapevine**.[26] Typically, the grapevine and gossip are viewed negatively by most people. Indeed, research shows that untrustworthy gossip can cause people to unfairly judge and dislike others.[27] Overall, the grapevine is a mixed blessing, leading to positive performance because of the sense of social pressure it produces while also undermining

Grapevine
An organization's informal communication network.

EXHIBIT 11-3
Small Group
Networks and
Effectiveness
Criteria

| | | Networks | |
Criteria	Chain	Wheel	All Channel
Speed	Moderate	Fast	Fast
Accuracy	High	High	Moderate
Emergence of a leader	Moderate	High	None
Member satisfaction	Moderate	Low	High

employee well-being.[28] Furthermore, rumors and gossip transmitted through the grape-vine may be an important source of information for employees and job applicants.[29] Grapevine or word-of-mouth information from peers about a company has important effects on whether job applicants join an organization,[30] even over and above informal ratings on websites like Glassdoor. For employers, it is also a way to recruit from within the employees' own networks: for example, the TWT Group (a Canadian information technology firm) recruits potential applicants from within their own networks, who they know and trust.[31]

The grapevine is an important part of any group or organization communication network. It serves employees' needs: Small talk creates a sense of closeness and friend-ship among those who share information, although often at the expense of those in the outgroup.[32] Managers can study the gossip driven largely by employee social networks to learn more about how positive and negative information is flowing through the organiza-tion.[33] Furthermore, managers can identify influencers (highly networked people trusted by their coworkers[34]) by noting which individuals are small talkers (those who regularly communicate about insignificant, unrelated issues). Small talkers tend to be influencers and are significantly more likely to retain their jobs during layoffs.[35] Furthermore, one study used artificial intelligence to detect small talk and follow-up questions during one-on-one conversations, and was able to demonstrate that follow-up questions predicted liking and intentions to continue to have conversations with that person in the future.[36]

However, the way "small talkers" go about their deeds matters: Collaborating and helping with others, rather than gossip, tends to be related to earning a "central posi-tion" in the network.[37] Regardless, being an active, helpful participant in the grapevine appears to help. It can even help entrepreneurs doing business in new countries face the challenges of being labeled as an "outsider," gaining legitimacy through attempting to be a part of local networks and communities.[38] Thus, while the grapevine may not be sanc-tioned or controlled by the organization, it can be understood and leveraged a bit.

MODES OF COMMUNICATION

The choice between modes of communication can greatly enhance or detract from the way the perceiver reacts to the message. For example, consider a doctor at a hospital in California who informed a seventy-eight-year-old (surrounded by family) that he was unlikely to survive his illness. You may picture the doctor gently comforting the family of the dying man. However, the family was outraged that the doctor sent a rolling video technology robot to deliver the news instead.[39] Clearly, certain modes are highly pre-ferred for specific types of communication. Aside from issues of whether to virtually or corporeally communicate, we must also draw upon oral, written, and nonverbal modes to communicate with others. We will cover the latest thinking and practical application.

Oral Communication

A primary means of conveying messages is oral communication. Speeches, formal one-on-one and group discussions, and the informal grapevine are popular forms of oral communication.

The advantages of oral communication are *speed, feedback,* and *exchange.* Regarding *speed,* we can convey a verbal message and receive a response in minimal time. If the receiver is unsure of the message, rapid *feedback* allows the sender to quickly detect and correct it. Unfortunately, we should acknowledge that we are usually bad listeners. Researchers indicate that we are prone to "listener burnout" in which we tune the other person out and rush to offer advice. "Good listeners overcome their natural inclination to fix the other's problems and to keep the conversation brief," said Professor Graham Bodie.[40] Active listening—in which we remove distractions, lean in, make eye contact, paraphrase, and encourage the talker to continue[41]—helps us learn more and build trust if we are genuine and not judgmental.[42] The *exchange* given through oral communication has social, cultural, and emotional components. Cultural social exchange, in which we purposefully share exchanges that transcend cultural boundaries, can build trust, cooperation, and agreement between individuals and teams.[43]

One major disadvantage of oral communication surfaces whenever a message must pass through several people: the more people, the greater the potential distortion. If you have ever played "Telephone," you know the problem. Each person who receives a whispered message in this pass-along game interprets the message in their own way. The message's content, when it reaches its destination, is often very different from the original, even when we think the message is simple and straightforward. For example, in product development teams, the engineers may often be so far removed from the customers that they end up building something (often quite well) that does not match the customers' expectations.[11] In these situations, the teams receive communications filtered through a number of layers without ever meeting with the customers themselves—prompting many organizations to turn to engineer teams who can effectively work with clients *and* be savvy engineers.

Written Communication

Written communication includes letters, e-mail, instant messaging, organizational periodicals, and any other method that conveys written words or symbols. Written business communication today is usually conducted via letters, PowerPoint®, e-mail, instant messaging, text messaging, social media, apps, and blogs. Some of these create a digital or physical long-term record, while the advantage of others is quick, fleeting information exchange. The disadvantages are also specific to each written mode.

Data mining and artificial intelligence approaches to analyzing (and learning from) data have benefited greatly from written business communication repositories. Through *natural language processing,* researchers can train algorithms to incorporate the actual words people use in e-mail, instant messages, social media, and other written communication media (including hashtags) to measure emotions, moods, personality traits, stress, and other characteristics of employees.[45] The business applications have been nearly endless, with companies using natural language processing to better understand the types of products customers may be interested in (and to advertise accordingly) as well as customer sentiment and intentions in real time, to detect fraud and compliance in accounting, to improve patient experience and diagnostic power in medical contexts, to intelligently detect sensitive information (and improve cybersecurity protection efforts), and to even create digital assistants to help teams manage tasks.[46] The market outlook has been immense as well: The market is said to exceed 26.4 billion dollars by 2024 and to grow at a rate of 21 percent between 2019 and 2024.[47]

Nonverbal Communication

When we deliver a message, we also impart an unspoken message.[48] No discussion of communication would thus be complete without consideration of *nonverbal communication*; which includes body movements, the intonations or emphasis we give to words, and facial expressions.[49] We could argue that every *body movement* has meaning, and no movement is accidental (though some are unconscious). We smile to project trustworthiness, uncross our arms to appear approachable, and stand to signal authority.[50] We may also engage in nonverbal communication unconsciously and automatically—when events happen, we react and express our emotions—the bystanders perceiving our emotions then make appraisals based on the emotional expressions.[51]

   If you read the minutes of a meeting, you would not grasp the impact of what was said the same way as if you had been there or could see the meeting on video. Why not? There is no record of nonverbal communication, and the emphasis given to words or phrases (*intonation*) is missing. Intonations can change the meaning of a message. *Facial expressions* also convey meaning. Facial expressions, along with intonations, can show arrogance, aggressiveness, fear, shyness, and other emotions. For example, nonverbal behaviors (e.g., handshaking) of both interviewers and applicants in job interviews suggests that this form of communication is important for molding and managing impressions.[52] Nonverbal communication can affect the behavior of communication receivers. For example, racial bias can also be contagious through nonverbal communication:[53] In one research study, merely watching videos of white individuals subtly treating black individuals poorly prompted observers to adopt negative racial stereotypes and form negative impressions of the black person.[54]

CHOICE OF COMMUNICATION CHANNEL

Why do people choose one channel of communication over another? A model of channel (or media) richness helps explain channel selection among managers.[55]

Channel Richness

Channels differ in their capacity to convey information.[56] Some are *rich* in that they can (1) handle multiple cues simultaneously, (2) facilitate rapid feedback, and (3) be very personal. Others are *lean*, in that they score low on these factors. Face-to-face conversation scores highest in **channel richness** because it transmits the most information per communication episode—multiple information cues (words, postures, facial expressions, gestures, intonations), immediate feedback (both verbal and nonverbal), and the personal touch of being present. Other examples of media with high channel richness (in descending order) include video conferences, telephone conversations, live speeches, and voice mail. Impersonal written media such as formal reports and bulletins score lowest in richness.

Channel richness
The amount of information that can be transmitted during a communication episode.

Choosing Communication Methods

The choice of channel depends on whether the message is routine. Routine messages tend to be straightforward and have minimal ambiguity; channels low in richness can carry them efficiently. Nonroutine communications are likely to be complicated and have the potential for misunderstanding. Managers can communicate them effectively only by selecting the appropriate channel for the message.[57] In the sections that follow, we describe when it is appropriate to choose oral, written, and nonverbal communication.

CHOOSING ORAL COMMUNICATION   Whenever you need to gauge the receiver's receptivity, *oral communication* is usually the better choice. The marketing plan for a new product, for instance, may need to be worked out with clients in person, so you can see their reactions to each idea you propose. Also consider the receiver's preferred mode of communication; some individuals focus on content better in written form and others prefer discussion. For example, if your manager requests a meeting with you, you may not want to ask for an e-mail exchange instead. The pace of your work environment matters too. A fast-paced workplace may thrive on pop-by meetings, while a deadline-heavy team project may progress faster with scheduled Zoom videoconferences.

Much of what we communicate face-to-face is in the delivery, so also consider your speaking skills when choosing your communication method. Research indicates the sound of your voice is twice as important as what you are saying. A good speaking voice, clear and moderated, can be a help to your career. Your work teams can help you raise your awareness so you can make changes, or you may benefit from the help of a voice coach.[58]

CHOOSING WRITTEN COMMUNICATION   *Written communication* is generally the most reliable mode for complex and lengthy communications, and it can be the most efficient method for short messages when, for instance, a two-sentence text can take the place of a ten-minute phone call. But keep in mind that written communication can be limited in its emotional expression.

Choose written communication when you want the information to be tangible, verifiable, and "on the record." *Letters* are used in business primarily for networking and record-keeping purposes, and when signatures need to be authentic. Also, a handwritten thank-you note is never a wrong choice for an applicant to send after an employment interview, and handwritten envelopes are often put right on the receiver's desk unopened by administrative staff. *E-mails* are often less formal forms of written communication and perhaps used the most frequently in business contexts. Use e-mails to informally communicate information that does not require a meeting but are too long or information-dense to be conveyed through a text or instant message. However, beware of how you word your message—nonverbal cues are often lost in these messages, and you could be perceived as rude, egocentric, or even culturally insensitive.[59] In general, you should respond to *instant messages* only when they are professional and initiate them only when you know they will be welcome. *Texts* are cheap to send and receive, and the willingness to be available for quick communications from clients and managers is conducive to good business. Some of the most spectacular gains in *social media* are in the sales arena, both business-to-public and business-to-business. For instance, one sales representative for virtual meetings company PGi landed his fastest sale ever by instantly connecting with a potential client after TweetDeck alerted him that a CEO was tweeting his frustration about Web conferencing.[60] But be careful with your posting and commenting activity; both options are more public than you may think, and your posts may leave negative impressions on hiring managers.[61]

CHOOSING NONVERBAL COMMUNICATION It is important to be aware of the *nonverbal* aspects of our communication. You should particularly be aware of contradictions between messages. For example, someone who frequently glances at their wristwatch is giving the message that they would prefer to terminate the conversation. We misinform others when we express one message verbally, such as trust, but nonverbally communicate a contradictory message that reads, "I don't have confidence in you." Research suggests that organizational leaders send similar mixed messages when they state that they value gender diversity, yet have male-dominated corporate boards (and, as a result, are less attractive to potential applicants).[62]

Information Security

Security is a huge concern for nearly all organizations with private or proprietary information about clients, customers, and employees. Organizations worry about the security of the electronic information they need to protect, such as hospital patient data.[63] Most companies actively monitor employee Internet use and e-mail records, and some even use video surveillance and record phone conversations. Necessary though they may be, such practices can seem invasive to employees, who may lash out as a result.[64] An organization can relieve employee concerns by engaging them in the creation of information-security policies and giving them some control over how their personal information is used.[65]

PERSUASIVE COMMUNICATION

We have discussed several communication methods up to this point. Now we turn our attention to one of the functions of communication—persuasion—and the features that might make messages persuasive to an audience.

Automatic and Controlled Processing

To understand the process of persuasion, it is useful to consider two different ways we process information.[66] Think about the last time you were browsing a social networking website and came across an ad. Moments later, you did not expect to be buying a Harry Potter t-shirt that also had your college's sports mascot on it, did you? Instead of making a concerted effort to research different t-shirt designs, you made an impulse buy that was the result of appealing advertising and a highly intelligent machine learning algorithm. If we are honest, we will admit flashy marketing can have an influence on our choices as consumers, and research shows that in this environment, we tend to operate in an "automatic" mode, with heart rate and skin conductance data to support.[67] We often rely on **automatic processing**, a relatively superficial consideration of evidence and information that takes little time or effort, making use of heuristics like those we discussed in the chapter on perception and individual decision making. The disadvantage is that it lets us be easily fooled by a variety of tricks, like a cute jingle or glamorous photo.

Automatic processing
A relatively superficial consideration of evidence and information that takes little time or effort and makes use of heuristics.

Now consider the last time you chose a place to live. You probably sourced experts who knew something about the area, gathered information about pricing, and considered the costs and benefits of renting versus buying. You were engaging in more effortful **controlled processing**, a detailed consideration of evidence and information, relying on facts, figures, and logic. Controlled processing requires effort and energy, and it is harder to fool someone who has taken the time and effort to engage in it.

Controlled processing
A detailed consideration of evidence and information relying on facts, figures, and logic.

IMPORTANCE/INTEREST LEVEL One of the best predictors of whether people will use an automatic or controlled process for reacting to a persuasive message is their level of interest in it.[68] When people are very interested in the outcome of a decision, or if the decision has important implications, they are more likely to process information carefully. That is probably why people look for so much more information when deciding about something important (like where to live) than something relatively unimportant (like an impulse t-shirt buy).

One way you can enhance interest in what a sender is communicating is through storytelling. For example, even though structured job interviews are much more valid than unstructured ones, HR professionals tend to use unstructured interviews more often. Some have found that stories or testimonials about the successes of structured interviews can persuade HR professionals to adopt more structured approaches.[69]

PRIOR KNOWLEDGE People who are well informed about a subject area are more likely to use controlled processing strategies. They have already thought through various arguments for or against a specific course of action, and therefore will not readily change their position unless very good, thoughtful reasons are provided. On the other hand, people who are poorly informed about a topic can change their minds more readily, even in the face of superficial arguments presented without a great deal of evidence. A better-informed audience is likely to be much harder to persuade.[70]

PERSONALITY Do you always read countless reviews on Amazon before purchasing any product? Perhaps you even go to multiple online stores, or review websites, before deciding. If so, you are probably high in **need for cognition**, a personality trait of individuals who are most likely to be persuaded by evidence and facts.[71] Those who are lower in their need for cognition are more likely to use automatic processing strategies, relying on intuition and emotion to guide their evaluation of persuasive messages.

Need for cognition
A personality trait of individuals depicting the ongoing desire to think and learn.

MESSAGE CHARACTERISTICS Another factor that influences whether people use an automatic or controlled processing strategy is the characteristics of the message itself. For example, readers of an online blog are more likely to report increased trust in the blogger (and to evaluate the blogger more favorably) when there is a conflict of interest disclosure, but when they are prompted to think about the disclosure (priming controlled processing), they become more skeptical.[72]

Messages provided through relatively lean communication channels, with little opportunity for users to interact with the content of the message, encourage automatic processing. Conversely, messages provided through richer communication channels encourage more deliberative processing. These messages vary through nuanced pitch, volume, intonation, and speech rate, which can convey confidence (and thus lead the messages to be perceived as more persuasive).[73]

Choosing the Message

The most important implication is to match your persuasive message to the type of processing your audience is likely to use.[74] When the audience is not interested in a persuasive message topic, when they are poorly informed, when they are low in need for cognition, and when information is transmitted through relatively lean channels, they will be more likely to use automatic processing. In these cases, use messages that are more emotionally laden and associate positive images with your preferred outcome. On the other hand, when the audience is interested in a topic, when they are high in need for cognition, or when the information is transmitted through rich channels, then it is a better idea to focus on rational arguments and evidence to make your case.

BARRIERS TO EFFECTIVE COMMUNICATION

Several barriers can slow or distort effective communication. In this section, we highlight the most important.

Filtering

Filtering
The manipulation of information so that it will be seen more favorably by the receiver.

Filtering refers to the purposeful manipulation of information so the receiver will see it more favorably. Telling the boss what the boss wants to hear is filtering information.

The more vertical levels in the organization's hierarchy, the more opportunities there are for filtering. But some filtering will occur wherever there are status differences. Factors such as fear of conveying bad news and the desire to please the boss often lead employees to tell their superiors what they think they want to hear, thus distorting upward communications.[75]

Selective Perception

Selective perception is important because the receivers in the communication process selectively see and hear based on their needs, motivations, experience, background, and other personal characteristics. Receivers also project their interests and expectations into communications as they decode them. For example, an employment interviewer who expects a female job applicant to put her family ahead of her career is likely to see that characteristic in all female applicants, regardless of whether any of the women feel that way. As we said in the chapter on perception and individual decision making, we do not see reality; we interpret what we see and call it reality.

Information Overload

Information overload
A condition in which information inflow exceeds an individual's processing capacity.

Although people integrate information from multiple sources to effectively make sense of information,[76] individuals have a finite capacity for processing data. When the information we must work with exceeds our processing capacity, the result is **information overload**.

What happens when individuals have more information than they can sort and use? They tend to select, ignore, pass over, or forget it. Or they may put off further processing until the overload situation ends. In any case, lost information and less effective communication results, making it more important to deal well with overload.

More generally, as an Intel study shows, it may make sense to connect less frequently to technology, to, in the words of one article, "avoid letting the drumbeat of digital missives constantly shake up and reorder to-do lists."[77] One radical way is to limit the number of devices you access. For example, Coors Brewing executive Frits van Paasschen jettisoned his desktop computer in favor of mobile devices only, and Eli Lilly & Co. moved its sales teams from laptops plus other devices to just iPads. Both these moves have resulted in increased productivity.[78]

Emotions

Your emotion regulation and expression of emotion can have an impact on how effectively you can communicate. For example, one review of dozens of studies interestingly found that intentional, nonverbal communication displays had a positive effect on communication performance, whereas those that were more spontaneous had no effect.[79] This suggests that you can alter your nonverbal communication to become an effective communicator. Furthermore, although suppressing your emotions is generally hurtful (causing negative first impressions and social outcomes), expressing negative emotions such as anger can also lead to poor social outcomes. However, the benefit to expressing your negative emotions is that others may have a better understanding of how you feel.[80] What is perhaps most important is how you express your negative emotions. Ruminating or dwelling on your negative emotions might not be the best way of processing your negative emotions; research suggests that when you process your emotions productively (e.g., rethinking or examining how you *really* feel), you may experience a sense of closure and experience better social outcomes than when you ruminate.[81]

You may also interpret the same message differently when you are angry or distraught than when you are happy. For example, individuals in positive moods are more confident about their opinions after reading a persuasive message, so well-designed arguments have a stronger impact on their opinions.[82] People in negative moods are more likely to scrutinize messages in greater detail, whereas those in positive moods tend to accept communications at face value.[83] Extreme emotions such as fury are most likely to hinder effective communication.[84] In such instances, we are most prone to disregard our controlled thinking processes.

Language

Even when we are communicating in the same language, words mean different things to different people. Age and jargon are two of the biggest factors that influence such differences. Sometimes the meaning of these words can change over time. For example, older employees are becoming more-and-more incensed at the use of words that bring undue attention to their age and which many consider patronizing.[85] As a manager, it is prudent to be aware of the appropriate terms and vocabulary to use to effectively communicate with all members of the organization. Furthermore, it is important to select language and terminology that can connect with the most people.[86] Jargon might not be accessible to everyone, as not everyone comes from the same context or background. When communicating with diverse audiences, often, simpler is better.

Silence

It is easy to ignore silence or lack of communication because it is defined by the absence of information. This is often a mistake—silence itself can be the message, communicating non-interest or inability to deal with a topic.[87] Silence can also be a simple outcome of information overload, or a delaying period for considering a response. For whatever reasons (and there are many of them, including fear, resignation, and even prosocial motives),[88] research suggests using silence and withholding communication are common and problematic.[89] Recent research has sought to understand *why* employees and managers are silent when they probably should speak up. This research has found that perceptions of target openness and employee sense of powerlessness as well as a tendency to experience negative emotions (especially fear) tend to influence the decision to stay silent.[90] Managers and employees alike should try to forge an environment where people are comfortable sharing and are open to other thoughts and opinions, or even to bad news.

Communication Apprehension

Communication apprehension
Undue tension and anxiety about oral communication, written communication, or both.

An estimated 5 to 20 percent of the population suffers debilitating **communication apprehension**.[91] These people experience undue tension and anxiety in oral communication, written communication, or both.[92] They may find it extremely difficult to talk with others face-to-face or become extremely anxious when they have to use the phone, relying on memos or e-mails when a phone call would be faster and more appropriate.

Oral-communication apprehensives avoid situations, such as teaching, for which oral communication is a dominant requirement.[93] But almost all jobs require *some* oral communication. Of greater concern is evidence that high oral-communication apprehensives may distort the communication demands of their jobs in order to minimize the need for communication.

Lying

Outright misrepresentation of information, or lying, is a barrier to effective information. (It literally involves information distortion.)[94] People differ in their definition of a lie. For example, is deliberately withholding information about a mistake a lie, or do you have to actively deny your role in the mistake to pass the threshold? While the definition of a lie befuddles ethicists and social scientists, there is no denying the prevalence of lying. People may tell one to two lies per day, with some individuals telling considerably more.[95] Compounded across a large organization, this is an enormous amount of deception happening every day.

Communicating in Times of Crisis

The final barrier to effective communication can be found in the underlying context: communication becomes more challenging during times of crisis.[96] As an example, the devastation of Hurricane Katrina in August 2005 has been frequently viewed as an exemplary case in how crises can be fraught with ineffective and inefficient communication.[97] Government agencies at all levels were taken by surprise when confronted with the threat of Hurricane Katrina approaching the United States and had difficulty in coordinating a response to the crisis as well as coping with the uncertainty and ambiguity of the situation.

Effective communication during times of crisis involves breaking down crisis response into several stages: (1) communicating in anticipation of or preparation for crises, (2) managing responses to the crises while they are occurring, (3) communicating with stakeholders after the crisis and catalyzing shared learning.[98] Collective motivations underlying communication change throughout these stages: people become driven to take control and dominate during times of war, whereas crises during times of peace tend to drive people toward being self-critical and fear of negative consequences.[99] These shifting motivations need to be accounted for in crisis communication—control, domination, anxiety, and fear are not directly aligned with reassurance and grace under pressure.

What can be done to improve communication during times of crisis? Effective messaging that focuses on sharing facts, sharing interpretations of the facts, and projections for consequences of actions at all stages can be beneficial.[100] Furthermore, although motivations tend to shift more toward power and responsibility, people should try to work together in times of crisis, instead of independently. For example, research shows that people, when trying to solve a problem separately (e.g., developing a vaccine for a virus), may become overcome by confusion and an inability to learn from one another's failures—by coordinating and collaborating, they may be able to overcome the confusion and learn from one another.[101] Finally, technology can help communicate information rapidly and accurately to all those who may be (imminently) affected by a disaster, including apps that help provide information quickly to response teams.[102] Technology can also be used to sound the crisis alarm: for instance, a Twitter alert was issued in 2018 for a potential ballistic missile threat. However, this alert proved to be a false alarm and an analysis of the 1.2 million tweets that followed suggested that anxiety remained heightened throughout the week as a result.[103] Therefore, people should remain sensitive to the impact of their communications on people during crises.

CULTURAL FACTORS

Effective communication is difficult under the best of conditions. Cross-cultural factors clearly create the potential for increased communication problems. A communication approach that works for one culture may not work for another. For example, a U.S. pharmaceutical company was having trouble distributing vaccines in an area of California that was predominantly first-generation Asian American. They found that the sales and marketing team did not consider that the prospective client's spouse was usually the decision maker in the prevailing culture, as the spouse in these contexts tended to act as the office manager. After adjusting their sales approach, they were able to improve their sales in that region.[104]

Cultural Barriers

Several problems are related to difficulties in cross-cultural communications.

First are *barriers caused by semantics*. Words mean different things to different people, particularly people from different national cultures. Some words do not translate between cultures. For instance, the Finnish word *sisu* means something akin to "guts" or "dogged persistence" but is essentially untranslatable into English. In 1945, Kantaro Suzuki (prime minister of Japan), following an Allied ultimatum days before Hiroshima, was translated as saying "silent contempt" when he actually meant "no comment. We need more time."[105] Similarly, differences can be observed for some communicative behaviors beyond language, such as how people culturally differ in the expression of gratitude, such as the use of bodily contact in individualist cultures.[106]

Second are *barriers caused by word connotations*. Words imply different things in different languages. Negotiations between U.S. and Japanese executives can be difficult because the Japanese word *hai* translates as "yes," but its connotation is "Yes, I'm listening" rather than "Yes, I agree."

Third are *barriers caused by tone differences.* In some cultures, language is formal; in others, it is informal. In some cultures, the tone changes depending on the context: People speak differently at home, in social situations, and at work.[107] For example, Mexicans are relatively formal in their dress and communication in the tire industry, compared with other countries—they also tend to use the formal version of you (*usted*) in the workplace rather than the informal version (*tú*).[108] Using a personal, informal style when a more formal style is expected can be inappropriate.

Fourth are *differences in tolerance for conflict and methods for resolving conflicts.* People from individualist cultures tend to be more comfortable with direct conflict and will make the source of their disagreements overt. Collectivists are more likely to acknowledge conflict only implicitly and avoid emotionally charged disputes. They may attribute conflicts to the situation more than to the individuals and therefore may not require explicit apologies to repair relationships, whereas individualists prefer explicit statements, accepting responsibility for conflicts and public apologies to restore relationships.

Cultural Context

High-context cultures
Cultures that rely heavily on nonverbal and subtle situational cues in communication.

Low-context cultures
Cultures that rely heavily on words to convey meaning in communication.

Cultures tend to differ in the degree to which context influences the meaning individuals take from communication.[109] In **high-context cultures** such as China, Korea, Japan, and Vietnam, people rely heavily on nonverbal and subtle situational cues in communicating with others, and a person's official status, place in society, and reputation carry considerable weight. What is *not* said may be more significant than what *is* said. In contrast, people from Europe and North America reflect their **low-context cultures**. They rely essentially on spoken and written words to convey meaning; body language and formal titles are secondary (see Exhibit 11-4).

Contextual differences mean quite a lot in terms of communication. Communication in high-context cultures implies considerably more trust by both parties. What may appear to be casual and insignificant conversation, in fact reflects the desire to build a relationship and create trust. Oral agreements imply strong commitments in high-context cultures. And who you are—your age, seniority, rank in the organization—is highly valued and

EXHIBIT 11-4
Continuum of Countries With High and Low Context Cultures

High context → Chinese, Korean, Japanese, Vietnamese, Arab, Greek, Spanish, Italian, English, North American, Scandinavian, Swiss, German ← Low context

heavily influences your credibility. Managers can therefore "make suggestions" rather than give orders. But in low-context cultures, enforceable contracts tend to be in writing, precisely worded, and highly legalistic. Similarly, low-context cultures value directness. Managers are expected to be explicit and precise in conveying intended meaning.

A Cultural Guide

There is much to be gained from business intercultural communications. It is safe to assume every one of us has a different viewpoint that is culturally shaped. Because we do have differences, we have an opportunity to reach the most creative solutions possible with the help of others if we communicate effectively.

According to Fred Casmir, a leading expert in intercultural communication research, we often do not communicate well with people outside of our culture because we tend to generalize from only their cultural origin. This can be insensitive and potentially disastrous, especially when we make assumptions based on observable characteristics. Also, attempts to be culturally sensitive to another person are often based on stereotypes propagated by media. These stereotypes usually do not have a correct or current relevance.

Casmir noted that because there are far too many cultures for anyone to understand completely, and individuals interpret their own cultures differently, intercultural communication should be based on sensitivity and pursuit of common goals. He found the ideal condition is an ad hoc "third culture" where a group can form when they seek to incorporate aspects of each member's cultural communication preferences. The norms this subculture establishes through appreciating individual differences create a common ground for effective communication. Intercultural groups that communicate effectively can be highly productive and innovative.

When communicating with people from a different culture, what can you do to reduce misinterpretations? Casmir and other experts offer the following suggestions:

1. *Know yourself.* Recognizing your own cultural identity and biases is critical to understanding the unique viewpoints of other people.
2. *Foster a climate of mutual respect, fairness, and democracy.* Clearly establish an environment of equality and mutual concern. This will be your "third culture" context for effective intercultural communication that transcends each person's cultural norms.
3. *State facts, not your interpretation.* Interpreting or evaluating what someone has said or done draws more on your own culture and background than on the observed situation. If you state only facts, you will have the opportunity to benefit from the other person's interpretation. Delay judgment until you have had enough time to observe and interpret the situation from the differing perspectives of all concerned.
4. *Consider the other person's viewpoint.* Before sending a message, put yourself in the recipient's shoes. What are their values, experiences, and frames of reference? What do you know about their education, upbringing, and background that can give you added insight? Try to see the people in the group as they really are first and take a collaborative problem-solving approach whenever potential conflicts arise.

5. ***Proactively maintain the identity of the group.*** Like any culture, the establishment of a common-ground "third culture" for effective intercultural communication takes time and nurturing. Remind members of the group of your common goals, mutual respect, and need to adapt to individual communication preferences.[110]

SUMMARY

Communication is what keeps organizations running—by managing the transmission and understanding of information, organizations can improve their processes and ultimately achieve better outcomes. In this chapter, you discovered that communication follows a specific process that fulfills multiple functions. Communication can be directed downward, upward, or laterally. It can also occur more formally through established connections in a network, or more informally through the office grapevine. There are also several communication channels (e.g., oral, written, and verbal) that vary in their degree of richness, with some being more appropriate than others, given the situation. Finally, in considering the perspective of the message receiver, it is important to understand that some messages are received automatically and require little thought, whereas others involve more cognitive effort to decode on the part of the receiver. Communication, overall, also is limited by several barriers and cultural considerations that you should be aware of if you want to become an effective communicator.

IMPLICATIONS FOR MANAGERS

- Remember that your communication mode will partly influence communication effectiveness.
- Obtain feedback to make certain your messages—regardless of how they are communicated—are understood.
- Remember that written communication creates more misunderstandings than oral communication does; communicate with employees through in-person meetings when possible.
- Make sure you use communication strategies appropriate to your audience and the type of message you are sending.
- Keep in mind communication barriers such as gender and culture.

12
Leadership

After studying this chapter, you should be able to:

12.1 Summarize the conclusions of trait theories of leadership.

12.2 Identify the central tenets and main limitations of behavioral theories.

12.3 Contrast contingency theories of leadership.

12.4 Describe the contemporary theories of leadership and their relationship to foundational theories.

12.5 Discuss the roles of leaders in creating ethical organizations.

12.6 Describe how leaders can have a positive impact on their organizations through building trust and mentoring.

12.7 Identify the challenges to our understanding of leadership.

TRAIT THEORIES OF LEADERSHIP

Gloria Boyland (vice president of Operations and Service Support at FedEx) has been referred to as one of the most powerful women in corporate America. Gloria spends much of her time coaching and guiding her direct reports, inspiring them, and re-affirming their vital role to FedEx. She also gives much autonomy to her followers: One of her guiding principles is, "Step back so others can step up."[1] She notes she has learned a lot from the FedEx founder and CEO, Fred Smith, who leads by example as a transformational, motivational leader. As a black woman, the cards are stacked against her: Corporate leadership is dominated by white men, and women are compelled by leader stereotypes to be both warm and tough at the same time.[2]

Surely, you have noticed, though, that not all leaders are managers, nor are all managers leaders. *Nonsanctioned leadership*—the ability to influence that arises outside the formal structure of the organization—is sometimes more important than formal influence. For example, Marcy Shinder (now chief marketing officer at Work Market) builds relationships with coworkers at work and informally emerged as a leader shortly after being hired.[3] What makes a person a leader? Gloria Boyland exhibits many of the characteristics and behaviors of a leader, while also highlighting some of the modern challenges facing leadership (e.g., a lack of ethnic and gender diversity).[4] Although it

Leadership
The act of influencing a group toward the achievement of a vision or set of goals.

Trait theories of leadership
Theories that consider personal qualities and characteristics that differentiate leaders from nonleaders.

has been defined in several ways and involves traits, behaviors, and other factors; we define **leadership** as the act of influencing a group toward the achievement of a vision or set of goals.

Personality Traits and Leadership

What constitutes a great leader? To begin, the **trait theories of leadership** focus on personal qualities, including personality traits like those in the Big Five (see the chapter on personality and individual differences), and characteristics that predict two distinct outcomes: leadership emergence and leadership effectiveness.[5] Since strong leaders have been described by their traits throughout history, leadership research has sought to identify the personality, social, physical, or intellectual attributes that differentiate leaders from nonleaders. Keep in mind that just because someone exhibits the right traits and others consider that person a leader does not necessarily mean they will be effective or successful at influencing the group to achieve its goals. Echoing the person-situation approach we discussed in the chapter on personality, leader behavior is a function of traits and the situation.[6] In support, researchers and HR practitioners have used machine learning and AI approaches to try to predict leader effectiveness from several leader characteristics and found that both traits and situational features are important predictors of leader effectiveness.[7]

BIG FIVE TRAITS   In examining personality traits, researchers have consistently found extraversion to be important for several leadership outcomes. Despite being the strongest predictor of leader emergence,[8] extraversion also predicts several leadership behaviors or styles. For example, extraverted leaders are more likely to use transformational leadership styles and consideration behaviors (as described later in this chapter).[9] As such, they are likely to be considered more effective leaders, although it is the *agentic*, bold, or assertive aspects of extraversion that account for this, not necessarily the warm, sociable, *affiliative* aspects.[10] So although extraversion can predict effective leadership, the relationship may be due to unique facets of the trait. As a caveat, however, being "too bold" or "too warm" can also hurt your chances of emerging as a leader.[11]

Although agreeableness and emotional stability are important to some aspects of leadership (e.g., they predict follower satisfaction with the leader), openness to experience appears to be less important as a trait, despite being a modest predictor of leader effectiveness.[12] Conscientiousness, on the other hand, appears to be important for several leadership behaviors and outcomes. For example, conscientiousness predicts initiating structure behaviors *as well as* consideration behaviors (as described later in this chapter).[13] Conscientiousness is also a moderate predictor of leader effectiveness and the strongest leader trait predictor of group performance.[14]

DARK-TRIAD TRAITS   What about the Dark-Triad personality traits (see the chapter on personality and values)? Research indicates they are not all bad for leadership: normative (mid-range) scores on Dark-Triad personality traits (even psychopathy) were optimal, and low (and high) scores were associated with ineffective leadership.[15] Thankfully, both this study and other international research indicate that building self-awareness and self-regulation skills may be helpful for leaders to control the effects of their Dark-Triad traits.[16] This self-awareness may be difficult for leaders to achieve, especially since narcissists tend to engage in self-enhancement (e.g., perceive themselves more positively than others see them) and be selective in the feedback they elicit and listen to when it comes to leadership.[17]

Emotional Intelligence (EI) and Leadership

Another trait that may indicate effective leadership is emotional intelligence (EI), which was discussed in the chapter on emotions and moods. A core component of EI is empathy. Empathetic leaders can sense others' needs, listen to what followers say (and do not say), and read the reactions of others. A leader who effectively displays and manages emotions will find it easier to influence the feelings of followers by expressing genuine sympathy and enthusiasm for good performance, and by showing irritation when employees fail to perform.[18] Although the association between leaders' self-reported EI and transformational leadership (to be discussed later in this chapter) is moderate, it is much weaker when followers rate their leaders' leadership behaviors.[19] Research has also demonstrated that people high in EI are more likely to emerge as leaders, even after taking cognitive ability and personality into account.[20]

Based on the latest research literature, we offer two conclusions about personality traits and leadership: One, traits can predict leadership; and two, traits do a better job in predicting the emergence of leaders and the appearance of leadership than in distinguishing between effective and ineffective leaders.[21]

BEHAVIORAL THEORIES

Trait theories provide a basis for *selecting* the right people for leadership. **Behavioral theories of leadership,** in contrast, imply we can *train* people to be leaders.[22]

The most comprehensive behavioral theories of leadership resulted from the Ohio State Studies,[23] which sought to identify independent dimensions of leader behavior. Beginning with more than a thousand dimensions, the studies narrowed the list to two that substantially accounted for most of the leadership behavior described by employees: *initiating structure* and *consideration.*

Initiating Structure

Initiating structure is the extent to which leaders define and structure their roles and those of their subordinates in pursuit of goal attainment. It includes behavior that attempts to organize work, work relationships, and goals. A leader high in initiating structure is someone who assigns followers tasks, sets definite standards of performance, and emphasizes deadlines (you may now see why, as we mentioned earlier, conscientiousness would be an important personality trait to have here!). According to a review of hundreds of leadership studies, initiating structure is more strongly related to higher levels of group and organization productivity, and to more positive performance evaluations.[24]

Consideration

Consideration is the extent to which a person's work relationships are characterized by mutual trust, respect for employees' ideas, and regard for their feelings. A leader high in consideration helps employees with personal problems, is friendly and

Behavioral theories of leadership
Theories proposing that specific behaviors differentiate leaders from nonleaders.

Initiating structure
The extent to which leaders define and structure their roles and those of their subordinates in pursuit of goal attainment.

Consideration
The extent to which a leader is likely to have job relationships characterized by mutual trust, respect for subordinates' ideas, and regard for their feelings.

approachable, treats all employees as equals, and expresses appreciation and support (people oriented). Most of us want to work for considerate leaders—according to one study by the National Bureau of Economic Research consisting of millions of responses over several years, working with a boss like this was "equivalent to the increased satisfaction that comes from more than doubling your household income"![25] Indeed, research suggests that the followers of leaders high in consideration were more satisfied with their jobs, were more motivated, and had more respect for their leaders.[26]

Cultural Differences

Mixed results from behavioral theory tests may lie partly in follower preferences, particularly cultural preferences. Research from the program (discussed in the chapter on personality and values) suggested there are international differences in the preference for initiating structure and consideration.[27] The study found that leaders high in consideration succeeded best in countries where cultural values did not favor unilateral decision making, such as Brazil. As one Brazilian manager noted, "We do not prefer leaders who take self-governing decisions and act alone without engaging the group. That's part of who we are." A U.S. manager leading a team in Brazil would therefore need to be high in consideration—team oriented, participative, and humane—to be effective. In contrast, the French have a more bureaucratic view of leaders and are less likely to expect them to be humane and considerate. A leader high in initiating structure (relatively task-oriented) will do best there and can make decisions in a relatively autocratic manner. A manager who scores high in consideration (people-oriented) may find that the style backfires in France. In other cultures, both dimensions may be important—for example, Chinese culture emphasizes being polite, considerate, and unselfish, but it has a high-performance orientation. Thus, both consideration and initiating structure may be important for a manager to be effective in China. Interestingly, however, research on thousands of managers in dozens of countries suggests that culture is much less important than the organization or managers themselves in determining whether they practice consideration or initiating structure behaviors.[28]

CONTINGENCY THEORIES

Some leaders gain a lot of admirers when they take over struggling companies and lead them out of crises. For example, Alfred Glancy III saved the Detroit Symphony Orchestra (DSO) as they teetered on the edge of failing. However, predicting leadership success is more complex than merely leading a group out of crisis. Alfred Glancy dealt with a lot of this complexity: refusing to spend beyond the DSO's means, negotiating labor agreements, resolving the debt burden, and amplifying fundraising efforts—all while staying true to the art. Importantly, the leadership style that works in very bad times does not necessarily translate into long-term success. For example, after times got better, Glancy turned to more innovative approaches to developing the DSO: upgrading the technology of their global webcast series and improving lighting and electronics in the Orchestra Hall, among other innovative approaches. As you can see, being an effective leader can be highly contingent upon situational demands.[29]

The Fiedler Model

Fred Fiedler developed the first comprehensive contingency model for leadership.[30] The **Fiedler contingency model** proposes that group performance depends on the proper match between the leader's style and the degree to which the situation gives the leader control. With the model, the individual's leadership style is assumed to be permanent.

As a first step, the **least preferred coworker (LPC) questionnaire** identifies whether a person is *task* or *relationship oriented* by asking respondents to think of all the coworkers they ever had and describe the one they *least enjoyed* working with. If you describe this person in favorable terms (a high LPC score), you are relationship oriented. If you see your least-preferred coworker in unfavorable terms (a low LPC score), you are primarily interested in productivity and are task oriented.

After finding a score, a fit must be found between the organizational situation and the leader's style for leadership effectiveness to be predicted. We can assess the situation in terms of three contingency or situational dimensions:

1. **Leader–member relations** is the degree of confidence, trust, and respect members have in their leader.
2. **Task structure** is the degree to which job assignments follow a specific procedure (that is, they are structured or unstructured).
3. **Position power** is the degree of influence a leader has over power variables such as hiring, firing, discipline, promotions, and salary increases.

According to the model, the higher the task structure becomes, the more procedures are added; and the stronger the position power, the more control the leader has. The favorable situations are on the left side of the model in Exhibit 12-1. A very favorable situation (in which the leader has a great deal of control) might include a payroll manager who has the respect and confidence of the employees (good leader–member relations), activities that are clear and specific, such as wage computation, check writing, and report filing (high task structure); and considerable freedom to reward and punish employees (strong position power). An unfavorable situation, to the right in the model, might be that of the disliked chairperson of a volunteer United Way fundraising team (low leader–member relations, low task structure, low position power). In this job, the leader has very little control. When faced with a category I, II, III, VII, or VIII situation, task-oriented leaders perform better. Relationship-oriented leaders, however, perform better in moderately favorable situations—categories IV, V, and VI.

Studies testing the overall validity of the Fiedler model were initially supportive, but the model has not been studied much in recent years.[31] While it provides some insights we should consider, its strict practical application is problematic.

Situational Leadership Theory

Situational leadership theory (SLT) suggests that successful leadership depends on selecting the right leadership style contingent on the followers' *readiness*: the extent to which followers are willing and able to accomplish a specific task.[32] A leader should choose one of four behaviors depending on follower readiness.

If followers are *unable* and *unwilling* to do a task, the leader needs to give clear and specific directions; if they are *unable* but *willing*, the leader needs to display a high task orientation to compensate for followers' lack of ability, and a high relationship

Fiedler contingency model
The theory that effective groups depend on a proper match between a leader's style of interacting with subordinates and the degree to which the situation gives control and influence to the leader.

Least preferred coworker (LPC) questionnaire
An instrument that measures whether a person is task or relationship oriented.

Leader–member relations
The degree of confidence, trust, and respect subordinates have in their leader.

Task structure
The degree to which job assignments follow a specific procedure.

Position power
Influence derived from one's formal structural position in the organization; includes power to hire, fire, discipline, promote, and give salary increases.

Situational leadership theory (SLT)
A contingency theory that focuses on followers' readiness, or the extent to which they are willing and able to accomplish a specific task.

EXHIBIT 12-1
**Findings From
the Fiedler
Model**

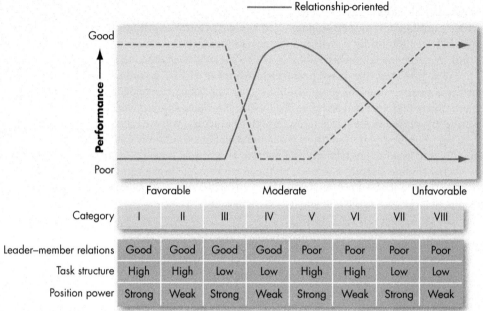

Category	I	II	III	IV	V	VI	VII	VIII
Leader–member relations	Good	Good	Good	Good	Poor	Poor	Poor	Poor
Task structure	High	High	Low	Low	High	High	Low	Low
Position power	Strong	Weak	Strong	Weak	Strong	Weak	Strong	Weak

orientation to get them to "buy into" the leader's desires. If followers are *able* but *unwilling,* the leader needs to use a supportive and participative style; if they are both *able* and *willing*, the leader does not need to do much.

SLT has intuitive appeal. It acknowledges the importance of followers and builds on the logic that leaders can compensate for followers' limited ability and motivation. Yet research efforts to test and support the theory have generally been disappointing.[33] Why? Possible explanations include internal ambiguities and inconsistencies in the model itself as well as problems with research methodology.

Path–Goal Theory

Path–goal theory
A theory that states that it is the leader's job to assist followers by providing the necessary resources to achieve their goals, to ensure that the path to accomplishing these goals is understandable or clear, and to reduce any roadblocks that may be making goal accomplishment difficult.

Path–goal theory combines elements of initiating structure and consideration with the expectancy theory of motivation.[34] Path–goal theory suggests it is the leader's job to provide followers with information, support, or other resources necessary to achieve goals (the term *path–goal* implies that effective leaders clarify followers' paths to their work goals and make the journey easier by reducing roadblocks).
The theory makes the following predictions:

- Directive leadership yields greater employee satisfaction when tasks are ambiguous or stressful than when they are highly structured and well laid out.
- Supportive leadership results in high employee performance and satisfaction when employees are performing structured tasks.
- Directive leadership is likely to be perceived as redundant among employees with high ability or considerable experience.

Like SLT, path–goal theory has intuitive appeal, especially from a goal attainment perspective. For example, research on high school principals and the high school teachers they supervise suggests that principals who engage in transactional leadership behaviors (see later in this chapter) can help provide clarity on the path toward goal accomplishment.[35] Also like SLT, the theory can be only cautiously adopted for application, but it is a useful framework in examining the important role of leadership.[36]

Leader-Participation Model

The final contingency theory we cover argues that *the way* the leader makes decisions is as important as *what* is decided. The **leader-participation model** relates leadership behavior to subordinate participation in decision making.[37] Like path–goal theory, this model suggests that leader behavior must adjust to reflect the task structure (such as routine, nonroutine, or in between). However, it does not cover all leadership behaviors and is limited to recommending what types of decisions might be best made with subordinate participation. It lays the groundwork for the situations and leadership behaviors most likely to elicit acceptance from subordinates. For example, Steve Kerr, coach of the Golden State Warriors, notes that it is not enough to be a leader and manage the players—he relies on them to be involved and set examples as well, when the situation calls for it.[38]

The theories we have covered to this point assume leaders use a homogeneous style with everyone in their work units. Think about your past experiences. Did leaders often act very differently toward different people?

Leader-participation model
A leadership theory that provides a set of rules to determine the form and amount of participative decision making in different situations.

CONTEMPORARY THEORIES OF LEADERSHIP

The understanding of leadership is a constantly evolving science. Contemporary theories have built upon the foundation we have just established to discover the unique ways leaders emerge, influence, and guide their employees and organizations. Let us explore some of the leading current concepts and look for aspects of the theories we have discussed already.

Leader–Member Exchange (LMX) Theory

Think of a leader you know. Does this leader have favorites who make up an ingroup? If you answered "yes," you are acknowledging **leader–member exchange (LMX) theory**.[39] LMX suggests leaders and followers have unique, one-on-one relationships that vary with each follower (e.g., some are higher quality than others). It also suggests that leaders establish a special relationship with a small group of their followers. These followers make up the ingroup—they are trusted, get a disproportionate amount of the leader's attention, and are more likely to receive special privileges. Other followers fall into the outgroup.

For the relationship to remain intact, the leader and the follower must invest in the relationship (see Exhibit 12-2). Competent, conscientious, proactive, and positive employees tend to have higher quality relationships with their leaders and are more likely to be placed in the ingroup (as well as those who are ingratiating and self-promoting).[40]

Leader–member exchange (LMX) theory
A theory that suggests (1) leaders and followers have unique relationships that vary in quality and (2) these followers comprise ingroups and outgroups; subordinates with ingroup status will likely have higher performance ratings, less turnover, and greater job satisfaction.

EXHIBIT 12-2
Similarity With and Interactions Between the Leader, Ingroup, and Outgroup

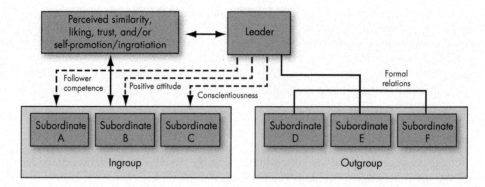

Leaders induce higher quality LMX perceptions by engaging in transformational leadership behaviors, ingratiating their followers, rewarding employees with whom they want a closer linkage, and punishing those with whom they do not.[41] When leaders and followers interact with one another, research suggests that leaders and followers build social capital with one another—they contribute more to the relationship when they feel obligated to and will withhold contribution when they believe they have "done enough."[42] In general, however, leaders and followers tend to develop high-quality relationships over time when the supervisor has high expectations for the follower, when they see themselves as similar, when they like each other, and when they trust each other.[43] Leaders and followers of the same gender tend to have closer (higher LMX) relationships than those of different genders.[44] Regardless of LMX quality perceptions, it is also true that LMX more or less varies in importance for leaders and followers. (Some employees value LMX less than others.)[45]

Research to test LMX theory has been generally supportive, with substantive evidence that leaders do differentiate among followers; these disparities are far from random; and followers with ingroup status receive higher performance ratings, objectively perform better, engage in more helping or organizational citizenship behaviors (OCBs) at work, engage in less deviant behaviors, and report greater satisfaction with their superiors.[46]

Furthermore, the extent to which leaders "play favorites" and create explicit in- and outgroups tends to have a negative effect on group or team outcomes.[47] Although LMX only has a weak effect on group performance, it negatively affects team attitudes, collective efficacy, justice climate, and coordination, and can lead to conflict in teams.[48] On the other hand, the overall level of LMX quality among members of the team (how strongly followers tend to see their relationships with their leaders) tends to matter more for work group or team outcomes.[49] Similar to substitutes for leadership theory (discussed later in the chapter), the quality of exchange between coworkers and colleagues can often substitute for or offset the negative impacts of low LMX in teams.[50]

There are some boundary conditions for the effects of LMX, however. For example, it appears as if LMX's relationship with perceptions of trust, job satisfaction, and justice, as well as with OCBs and turnover intentions, depends in part on the culture—in a study of nearly 70,000 employees from twenty-three countries, the researchers found that it matters more in individualistic rather than collectivistic cultures.[51] Another limitation is that the agreement between leaders and followers on their relationship quality (e.g., a boss might think the relationship is great, the follower might not) is not very strong—when there is disagreement between the two, this can hurt employee engagement (regardless of who perceives the relationship as stronger).[52]

Charismatic, Transformational, and Transactional Leadership Styles

There is just "something" about certain leaders that cause people to be drawn toward them. There is an undeniable presence to leaders like Rev. Martin Luther King Jr., Mahatma Gandhi, and former president Barack Obama, which can be explained in part by their abilities to unite and transform people.[53] Two contemporary leadership theories—charismatic leadership and transformational leadership—share a common theme in the great leader debate: They view leaders as individuals who inspire followers through words, ideas, and behaviors.

WHAT IS CHARISMATIC LEADERSHIP? Sociologist Max Weber defined *charisma* (from the Greek for "gift") as "a certain quality of an individual personality, by virtue of which the leader is set apart from ordinary people and treated as endowed with supernatural, superhuman, or at least specifically exceptional powers or qualities. These are not accessible to the ordinary person and are regarded as of divine origin or as exemplary, and based on them the individual concerned is treated as a leader."[54]

According to **charismatic leadership theory**, followers attribute heroic or extraordinary leadership abilities when they observe certain behaviors (e.g., those that are values driven, symbolic, or emotion laden), and tend to give these leaders power.[55] A number of studies have attempted to identify the characteristics of charismatic leaders: they have a vision, are willing to take personal risks to achieve that vision, are sensitive to followers' needs, and exhibit extraordinary behaviors[56] (see Exhibit 12-3). Some research has also linked intelligence, extraversion, and agreeableness to the motivational and influential factors of charismatic leadership.[57] Charismatic leadership theory suggests that these personality traits enable leaders to react to work events with a positive attitude, and their emotional intelligence enables them to influence followers to unite and constructively confront the adverse work event.[58]

HOW CHARISMATIC LEADERS INFLUENCE FOLLOWERS Charismatic leadership has a positive effect on follower outcomes: They can, for instance, enhance follower task performance and OCB as well as reduce/reframe follower turnover and stressors.[59] But how do charismatic leaders influence followers? By articulating an appealing **vision**, a long-term strategy for attaining a goal by linking the present with a better future for the organization.

1. *Vision and articulation.* Has a vision—expressed as an idealized goal—that proposes a future better than the status quo; and is able to clarify the importance of the vision in terms that are understandable to others.
2. *Personal risk.* Willing to take on high personal risk, incur high costs, and engage in self-sacrifice to achieve the vision.
3. *Sensitivity to follower needs.* Perceptive of others' abilities and responsive to their needs and feelings.
4. *Unconventional behavior.* Engages in behaviors that are perceived as novel and counter to norms.

Charismatic leadership theory
A leadership theory that states that followers make attributions of heroic or extraordinary leadership abilities when they observe certain behaviors.

Vision
A long-term strategy for attaining a goal or goals.

EXHIBIT 12-3 Key Characteristics of Charismatic Leaders

Source: Based on J. A. Conger and R. N. Kanungo, *Charismatic Leadership in Organizations* (Thousand Oaks, CA: Sage, 1998), p. 94.

Desirable visions fit the times and circumstances, as well as reflect the uniqueness of the organization. Thus, followers are inspired not only by how passionately the leader communicates and their nonverbal cues (e.g., extended eye contact)[60] but also by an appealing message. For example, research on Israeli schools suggests that charismatic principals that promote a shared vision among teachers can improve the organizational climate (see the chapter on organizational culture) and, as a result, improve school outcomes.[61]

Vision statement
A formal articulation of an organization's vision or mission.

A vision needs an accompanying **vision statement**, a formal articulation of an organization's vision or mission. Charismatic leaders may use vision statements to imprint on followers an overarching goal and purpose. These leaders also set a tone of cooperation and mutual support. They build followers' self-esteem and confidence with high performance expectations and the belief that followers can attain them. Through words and actions, the leader conveys a new set of values and sets an example for followers to imitate. Finally, the charismatic leader engages in emotion-inducing and often unconventional behavior to demonstrate courage and conviction about the vision.

Research indicates that charismatic leadership works as followers "catch" the emotions their leader is conveying.[62] One study found employees had a stronger sense of personal belonging at work when they had charismatic leaders which, in turn, increased their willingness to engage in helping and compliance-oriented behavior.[63]

DOES EFFECTIVE CHARISMATIC LEADERSHIP DEPEND ON THE SITUATION? Charismatic leadership has positive effects across many contexts. There are, however, characteristics of followers, and of the situation, that enhance or somewhat limit its effects.

One factor that enhances charismatic leadership is stress. People are especially receptive to charismatic leadership when they sense a crisis, when they are under stress, or when they fear for their lives. We may be more receptive to charismatic leadership under crises because we think bold leadership is needed. Some of it, however, may be more primal. When people are psychologically aroused, even in laboratory studies, they are more likely to respond to charismatic leaders, especially when they use language that is constructive and "promotion-oriented" rather than that which does not propose solutions and focuses on the negative.[64] Stress matters for leaders, too: When leaders are under stress, they may not have the resources to engage in charismatic behaviors.[65]

Another factor is ambiguity: when we cannot accurately assess or observe how someone is doing, we rely more on cues (e.g., charismatic behaviors) to assess whether they are being effective as a leader. For example, one study of both U.S. presidents and CEOs found that charisma was more likely to predict whether a leader is selected or appointed, especially when the situation was ambiguous.[66]

Some personalities are especially susceptible to charismatic leadership.[67] For instance, individuals who lack self-esteem and question their self-worth are more likely to absorb a leader's direction rather than establish an individual way of leading or thinking. For these people, the situation may matter much less than the desired charismatic qualities of the leader.

THE DARK SIDE OF CHARISMATIC LEADERSHIP   Unfortunately, charismatic leaders who are larger than life do not necessarily act in the best interests of their organizations.[68] Commensurate with this observation, studies have indicated that individuals who are narcissistic are higher in some behaviors associated with charismatic leadership.[69] Furthermore, research suggests that charismatic leadership can unduly distort follower fairness perceptions: Because they see the charismatic leader in a positive light, they may be (consciously or not) more willing to perceive them as fair.[70]

Many charismatic—but corrupt—leaders have allowed their personal goals to override the goals of their organizations. For example, leaders at Enron, Tyco, WorldCom, and HealthSouth recklessly used organizational resources for their personal benefit, violated laws and ethics to inflate stock prices, and then cashed in millions of dollars in personal stock options. It is not that charismatic leadership is not effective; overall, it is. But a charismatic leader is not always the answer. Success depends, to some extent, on the situation and on the leader's vision, and on the organizational checks and balances in place to monitor the outcomes.

BECOMING A CHARISMATIC LEADER   Anyone can develop, within our own limitations, a more charismatic leadership style. If you stay active and central in your leadership roles, you will naturally communicate your vision for achieving goals to your followers, which increases the likelihood you will be charismatic.[71] To further develop an aura of charisma, use your passion as a catalyst for generating enthusiasm. Speak in an animated voice, reinforce your message with eye contact, emphatic gestures, and facial expressions. Bring out the potential in followers by tapping into their emotions and forging a unifying bond among the team. But do not *overdo* it: Research suggests that you can be *too* charismatic and be so focused on your vision that you neglect operational behavior, like initiating structure![72]

Transactional and Transformational Leadership

According to a survey by Right Management, only 17 percent of employees report that their supervisors are actively engaged in developing them, and 68 percent report that their supervisors are not engaged in this way at all.[73] Those in the 68 percent likely have leaders who primarily use transactional leadership styles.

Transactional leaders guide their followers toward established goals by clarifying role and task requirements, allocating rewards and punishment where needed, and (passively or actively) intervening when the situation calls for it.[74] Some of the earlier leadership approaches we discussed, including path–goal theory, tend to focus on a transactional approach. Sometimes, transactional leadership approaches are needed.[75] For example, research on offshore rig employees suggests that leaders who actively intervene when the situation calls for it led employees to become more engaged in safety behaviors, especially given the high likelihood of accidents.[76]

Transformational leaders, on the other hand, inspire followers to transcend their self-interests for the good of the organization.[77] Transformational leaders can have an extraordinary effect on their followers.[78] Exhibit 12-4 briefly identifies and defines characteristics that differentiate transactional from transformational leaders. In her book, *Leadership in Turbulent Times*, Doris Kearns Goodwin describes the transformational qualities of past presidents such as Abraham Lincoln, Theodore Roosevelt, and Lyndon Johnson who personally appealed to Americans and inspired followers to make sacrifices to pursue goals for the country.[79] There is evidence that whether leaders engage in transformational behaviors depends to a large extent on culture and industry. For example, one review of dozens of studies from eighteen different countries suggests that transformational leadership may be used more often in the health and security industries, as well as in cultures worldwide that value assertiveness and egalitarianism and that are lower on power distance.[80]

Transactional leaders
Leaders who guide or motivate their followers in the direction of established goals by clarifying role and task requirements, allocating rewards and punishment where needed, and (passively or actively) intervening when the situation calls for it.

Transformational leaders
Leaders who inspire followers to transcend their own self-interests for the good of the organization.

EXHIBIT 12-4

Characteristics of Transactional and Transformational Leaders

Source: B. M. Bass, "From Transactional to Transformational Leadership: Learning to Share the Vision," *Organizational Dynamics* 18, no. 3 (1990): 19–31.

Transactional Leader

Contingent Reward: Contracts exchange of rewards for effort, promises rewards for good performance, recognizes accomplishments.

Management by Exception (active): Watches and searches for deviations from rules and standards, takes corrective action.

Management by Exception (passive): Intervenes only if standards are not met.

Laissez-Faire: Abdicates responsibilities, avoids making decisions.

Transformational Leader

Idealized Influence: Provides vision and sense of mission, instills pride, gains respect and trust.

Inspirational Motivation: Communicates high expectations, uses symbols to focus efforts, expresses important purposes in simple ways.

Intellectual Stimulation: Promotes intelligence, rationality, and careful problem solving.

Individualized Consideration: Gives personal attention, treats each employee individually, coaches, advises.

Full range of leadership model
A model that depicts seven leadership styles on a continuum: laissez-faire, management by exception, contingent reward leadership, individualized consideration, intellectual stimulation, inspirational motivation, and idealized influence.

FULL RANGE OF LEADERSHIP MODEL Exhibit 12-5 shows the **full range of leadership model**. Laissez-faire, which literally means "let it be" (do nothing), is the most passive and therefore least effective of leader behaviors.[81] Management by exception, in which leaders primarily "put out fires" during crises, monitor employee performance for errors, and interact with followers only when something is wrong, is generally ineffective as a style of leadership.[82] Notably, management by exception can be utilized either actively or passively, with the passive form tending to be more ineffective.[83] Contingent reward leadership, which gives predetermined rewards for employee efforts, can be an effective style of leadership but will not get employees to go above and beyond the call of duty.[84]

Only with the four remaining styles—all aspects of transformational leadership—are leaders able to motivate followers to perform above expectations and transcend their self-interest for the sake of the organization. Individualized consideration, intellectual stimulation, inspirational motivation, and idealized influence (known as the "four I's") all result in extra effort from workers, higher productivity, higher creativity, higher well-being, higher morale and satisfaction, higher organizational effectiveness, lower turnover, lower absenteeism, and greater organizational adaptability.[85]

Interestingly, it appears certain traits are more important than others, depending upon the transformational leadership style. For example, most of the Big Five traits (except emotional stability) appear to be important for idealized influence, but only openness and agreeableness appear to consistently predict inspirational motivation and individualized consideration. Curiously, none of the Big Five predict intellectual stimulation, but perhaps this dimension is more influenced by intelligence than personality.[86]

HOW TRANSFORMATIONAL LEADERSHIP WORKS Overall, an exhaustive program of research has sought to discover why transformational is so effective.[87] Researchers have

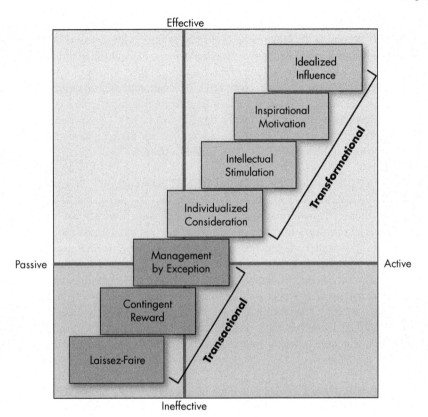

Effective

Idealized
Influence

Inspirational
Motivation

Intellectual
Stimulation

Individualized
Consideration

Management
by Exception

Contingent
Reward

Laissez-Faire

Transformational

Transactional

Passive   Active

Ineffective

EXHIBIT 12-5
Full Range of Leadership Model

Source: Adapted from B. M. Bass and B. J. Avolio, *Improving Organizational Effectiveness Through Transformational Leadership* (Thousand Oaks, CA: Sage, 1994).

found that transformational leadership is, in general, effective for five reasons (many of which correspond with various chapters in this book):[88]

1. **Affective or Attitudinal Mechanism:** Transformational approaches promote positive employee moods, emotions, job satisfaction, organizational commitment, and feelings of well-being.
2. **Motivational Mechanism:** Transformational approaches motivate employees—they become more confident and engaged.
3. **Identification Mechanism:** Transformational approaches lead employees to personally identify with the leader and the leader's values and identity, as well as with the team or organization.
4. **Social Exchange Mechanism:** Transformational approaches improves the quality of exchange and relationship between leaders and followers (i.e., LMX, see earlier in this chapter). Followers are also more likely to perceive that they are supported by the leader, team, and/or organization.
5. **Justice Enhancement Mechanism:** Transformational approaches improve employee fairness perceptions, motivating followers to contribute more and to trust the leader, team, and organization more.

Research suggests that the "social exchange mechanism" is the primary "reason" for why leadership behaviors and styles influence outcomes: Behaviors that improve perceptions of leader–follower relationship quality, in turn, result in improved follower performance.[89] Although the other reasons are just as important, it seems as if they operate *through* improved social exchange. In other words, (1) transformational leadership approaches improve the leader–follower relationship, (2) *then,* this improved relationship paves the way for positive affective, attitudinal, motivational, identification, and justice-related changes. However, we should note that a limitation here is that it is often very difficult to differentiate transformational leadership from LMX—regardless, they should not change the mechanisms (e.g., affect, identification, justice, motivation) through which transformational leadership has been found to operate.[90]

TRANSFORMATIONAL VERSUS TRANSACTIONAL LEADERSHIP Transactional and transformational leadership complement each other; they are not opposing approaches to getting things done.[91] Transformational leadership *builds on* transactional leadership and produces levels of follower effort and performance beyond what transactional leadership alone can do. Although both tend to be important, it appears that transformational leadership is more important for group performance, OCBs, and satisfaction with the leader, whereas transactional leadership (primarily contingent reward) is more important for leader effectiveness, follower performance, and follower job satisfaction.[92] Also, as mentioned earlier, transformational leadership and management-by-exception (active) are both important in their own right for safety behaviors in organizations.[93] However, the distinction between the two is not as clear-cut as it seems. The full range of leadership model shows a clear division between transactional and transformational leadership that may not fully exist in practice, and prior reviews of the research suggest that transformational leadership and contingent reward are very highly related—even to the point where researchers have begun questioning whether they are, in fact, identical.[94]

TRANSFORMATIONAL VERSUS CHARISMATIC LEADERSHIP In considering transformational and charismatic leadership, you surely noticed some commonalities. There are differences, too. As discussed in a prior section, charismatic leaders are those that make value-based appeals and communicate through symbolic and emotion-laden means.[95] Charismatic leadership places somewhat more emphasis on the way leaders communicate (are they passionate and dynamic?), while transformational leadership focuses more on what they are communicating (is it individualized, intellectually stimulating, inspirational, and influential?). At their heart, both focus on the leader's ability to inspire followers, and sometimes they do so in the same way.

EVALUATION OF TRANSFORMATIONAL LEADERSHIP In general, organizations perform better when they have transformational leaders. However, transformational leadership is not without its critics, some of who boldly claim that transformational leadership behaviors can be construed as manipulative and unduly granting power to inspirational people.[96] Others have noted that transformational leadership theory could benefit from understanding which dimensions are most important, exactly "how" these combine to form transformational leadership, and "how" the dimensions of transformational leadership lead to different outcomes.[97] More importantly, researchers have criticized the surveys with which transformational leadership is measured, and suggest that transformational leadership is often confounded with outcomes. (For example, are individual attention, intellectual stimulation, inspiration, and influence behaviors performed by the leader, or are they perceptions of the follower?)[98]

RESPONSIBLE LEADERSHIP

Although theories have increased our understanding of effective leadership, they do not explicitly deal with the roles of ethics and trust, which some argue are essential to complete the picture. Here, we consider contemporary concepts that explicitly address the role of leaders in creating ethical organizations.

Authentic Leadership

Authentic leaders are self-aware (e.g., they know what is important to them, including their own strengths/weaknesses), are anchored by their mission and principles, consider others' opinions and all relevant information before acting, and display their true selves when interacting with employees.[99] The result: People have faith in them. For example, Nick Sarillo of Nick's Pizza and Pub is authentic in how he runs his business—when one of the locations was not doing too well, he was publicly open and transparent about it, along with the need to close the store.[100] Unfortunately, there appears to be a double-standard for women when it comes to authenticity: In general, women are perceived to be more authentic, especially when they engage in traditionally "feminine" hobbies and when they engage in "warm" leadership styles.[101] However, if they engage in more assertive, transactional approaches (e.g., initiating structure, directive leadership behaviors), this goes against the stereotype and may lead some to label them as inauthentic.[102] These stereotypes have led many to comment on how Hillary Clinton was mocked as "Saint Hillary" when she stood behind her message of "politics of meaning" in the 1990s, but was branded as inauthentic when she adopted more traditionally masculine approaches to leadership during her presidential campaign decades later.[103]

> **Authentic leaders**
> Leaders who are self-aware and anchored by their mission, consider others' opinions and all relevant information before acting, and display their true selves when interacting with employees.

Authentic leadership strongly predicts outcomes such as group performance, OCBs, LMX, satisfaction and trust in the leader, ratings of leader effectiveness, follower attitudes and empowerment, and, to a lesser degree, follower creativity, engagement, deviance, turnover intentions, and burnout.[104] Furthermore, research suggests that leaders who "practice what they preach" observe improved follower outcomes because their followers begin to trust them and become more committed to the organization.[105] Authentic leaders can inspire their employees to be better: For example, research on Pakistani communications employees suggests that the awareness of one's own strengths and weaknesses that comes from authentic leadership, predicts followers' intentions to improve themselves.[106]

Despite these interesting findings concerning the nature of authentic leadership, reviews of the leadership literature point to how transformational and authentic leadership are extremely similar in practice, to the point where many researchers consider them to be identical.[107] However, some work does suggest that authentic leadership is more important for explaining team performance and whether employees engage in OCBs, because they have an internalized mission that propels the group forward.[108]

(Un)ethical Leadership

(Un)ethical leadership, although it has been conceptualized in many ways, refers to how leaders serve as ethical role models to followers, and thus demonstrate normatively appropriately (or inappropriate) behavior by using their power in (un)ethical ways and by treating others fairly (or unfairly).[109] (Un)ethical leadership tends to affect employees in a number of ways. First, (un)ethical leadership has a direct influence on how employees

> **(Un)ethical leadership**
> The idea that leaders serve as ethical role models to followers, and thus demonstrate appropriate (or inappropriate) behavior by using their power in (un)ethical ways and/or by treating others fairly (or unfairly).

think about moral issues.[110] Second, ethical leadership tends to improve follower job attitudes, job performance and perceptions of follower leaders—indeed, ethical leadership tends to increase followers' trust in their leaders, which in turn can lead to these positive outcomes.[111] Third, ethical leadership sets the example for how employees should treat one another: It can lead employees to use less intimidation, fewer justifications, and fewer excuses for their behavior, and it can even improve customer service performance by clarifying moral reasons for treating customers right.[112]

Unfortunately, (un)ethical leadership tends to run into similar criticisms as authentic leadership because it is hard to disentangle it from transformational leadership in practice.[113] Furthermore, it is hard to be consistently ethical: leaders who were ethical on one day were more likely to be abusive the next day, often because of stressful circumstances, mental depletion, and a feeling that one has built up "credits" to behave in an unethical way.[114] However, followers do not necessarily act negatively to leader unethical behavior: if the followers' values align with the leader's and they have a sense of mutual trust, they may be more likely to continue to support the leader.[115] Furthermore, there are certain situations that reduce the effectiveness of ethical leadership. When there are too many followers, when the followers do not share the same moral perspectives as the leader (what if leaders and followers disagree on what is right and wrong?), and when followers are not in a state of mindfulness (see the chapter on organizational change and stress management), ethical leadership tends to be less effective at improving follower behaviors.[116] Although every member of an organization is responsible for ethical behavior, many initiatives aimed at increasing organizational ethical behavior are focused on the leaders.

When considering corporate scandals, like Wells Fargo's unethical sales practices in 2016, it is clear that ethics-based leadership is crucial at all levels of organizations.[117] Ethical top leadership influences not only direct followers, but all the way down the command structure as well, because top leaders create an ethical culture and expect lower-level leaders to behave along ethical guidelines.[118] Ethical leadership has implications for financial outcomes as well. For example, one study of 111 U.S. retail stores found that ethical leadership can reduce "retail shrink," or the loss of merchandise primarily due to theft and shoplifting, because ethical leadership can reduce incivility among employees and customers.[119]

Servant Leadership

Servant leadership
A leadership style marked by going beyond the leader's own self-interest and instead focusing on opportunities to help followers grow and develop.

Servant leadership involves going beyond self-interest to focus on opportunities that help followers grow and develop.[120] Characteristic behaviors include listening, empathizing, persuading, accepting stewardship, and actively developing followers' potential.[121] Because servant leadership is based on the value of serving the needs of others, research has focused on its outcomes for the well-being of followers. Indeed, servant leadership is strongly related to followers' job attitudes, as well as their trust in leadership and LMX perceptions.[122] In turn, servant leadership predicts both job performance and OCB, albeit to a lesser degree than well-being and leadership quality.[123] This may be due to follower feelings of gratitude that engender prosocial behavior and a need to reciprocate.[124] Similar to authentic leadership, there appears to be an advantage for women who are servant leaders because the leadership style stereotypically matches the gender role prototype. In other words, women who draw on servant leadership techniques tend to inspire their use in their followers, which leads to higher performance than men servant leaders.[125]

Research also suggests that servant leadership may "fuel the service fire." Research on hairstylists suggests that servant leaders help promote their sense of identity with the salon and their confidence, which in turn leads customers to rate their performance more highly.[126] Furthermore, research suggests that there is a trickle-down effect: High-level managers who are servant leaders can influence low-level managers to practice servant leadership, which in turn improves employee performance.[127] Although servant leadership is highly related to transformational, authentic, and ethical leadership (particularly the latter), research suggests that it holds the most promise "of standing on its own" as a unique leadership style in practice, when compared with authentic and ethical leadership.[128]

POSITIVE LEADERSHIP

In each of the theories we have discussed, you can see opportunities for the practice of good, bad, or mediocre leadership. Now let us think about the intentional development of positive leadership states.

Trust

Trust (see also our discussion in the groups and teams chapters) is a psychological state of mutual positive expectations between people—both depend on each other and are genuinely concerned for each other's welfare.[129] Although you are not completely in control of the situation and sometimes under time pressures that *force* you to trust another,[130] you are willing to take a chance that the other person will come through for you. Trust can be focused on *competence* (e.g., faith in the leaders' technical skills, experience) or *integrity* (e.g., faith in a leaders' motives, honesty, and character). So naturally, integrity-based trust is much more effective at reducing the costs associated with building new relationships (at least for establishing business connections between organizations).[131]

Trust is a primary attribute associated with leadership; breaking it can have serious adverse effects on a group's performance.[132] Followers who trust a leader are confident their rights and interests will not be abused.[133] Leaders who trust their followers are confident that they will follow through and completing their duties effectively.[134] Felt trust matters as well—when the leader feels trusted and the followers actually trust the leader, leaders are more effective.[135]

THE OUTCOMES OF TRUST Trust between supervisors and employees has several specific advantages. Here are just a few from research:

- **Trust encourages taking risks.** Whenever employees decide to deviate from the usual way of doing things, or to take their supervisor's word on a new direction, they are taking a risk. In both cases, a trusting relationship can facilitate that leap.[136]
- **Trust facilitates information sharing.** When managers demonstrate they will give employees' ideas a fair hearing and actively make changes, employees are more willing to speak out.[137]
- **Trusting groups are more effective.** When a leader sets a trusting tone in a group, members are more willing to help each other and exert extra effort, which increases trust.[138]
- **Trust enhances productivity.** Employees who trust their supervisors tend to receive higher performance ratings, indicating higher productivity.[139]

Trust
A psychological state of mutual positive expectations between people—both depend on each other and are genuinely concerned for each other's welfare.

EXHIBIT 12-6
Model of Trust in Organizations

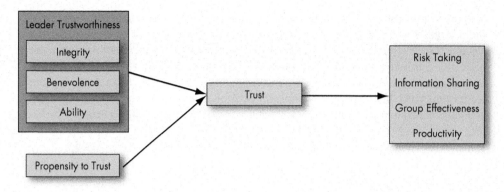

TRUST DEVELOPMENT What key characteristics lead us to believe a leader is trustworthy? Evidence has identified three: *integrity, benevolence,* and *ability* (see Exhibit 12-6).[140]

Integrity refers to honesty and truthfulness. When 570 white-collar employees were given a list of twenty-eight attributes related to leadership, they rated honesty the most important by far.[141] Integrity also means maintaining consistency between what you do and say (see prior section on authentic leadership).

Benevolence means the trusted person has your interests at heart, even if your interests are not necessarily in line with theirs. Caring and supportive behavior is part of the emotional bond between leaders and followers.

Ability encompasses an individual's technical and interpersonal knowledge and skills. You are unlikely to depend on someone whose abilities you do not believe in, even if the person is highly principled and has the best intentions.

Trust propensity
How likely an employee is to trust a leader.

TRUST PROPENSITY **Trust propensity** refers to how likely an employee is to trust a leader. Some people are simply more likely to believe others can be trusted.[142] Trust propensity is closely linked to the personality trait of agreeableness, and people with lower self-esteem are less likely to trust others.[143] When teams are composed of members with different propensities to trust leaders or other team members, they are more prone to spiral downward when conflict arises.[144]

TRUST AND CULTURE Trust in an employment relationship may be built on very different perceptions from culture to culture. For example, a study in Taiwan indicated that employees responded to paternalistic leadership, when it was benevolent and ethical, with increased trust.[145] This positive response to paternalism may be unique to the collectivistic context of Taiwan, where the Confucian values of hierarchy and relationship predominate. In individualistic societies (see the chapter on personality and values), we might expect that paternalistic leadership will rankle many employees who prefer not to see themselves as part of a hierarchical family work group.

THE ROLE OF TIME We come to trust people by observing their behavior over time, such as when you are developing new relationships with people when you start a new job.[146] For example, employees in newly acquired companies develop trust toward top managers in the acquiring company (especially when they institute fair procedures and when they are seen as competent).[147] To help, leaders need to demonstrate integrity, benevolence, and ability in situations where trust is important—say, where they could behave opportunistically or let employees down. Second, research with one hundred companies around the world suggested that leaders can build trust by shifting their communication style from top-down commands to ongoing organizational dialogue. Third, when leaders regularly create interpersonal conversations with their employees that are intimate, interactive, and inclusive, and that intentionally follow an agenda, followers demonstrate trust with high levels of engagement.[148] Finally, followers can experience a breach of trust when leaders replace transformational leadership with laissez-faire leadership or when they are furious in response to an unethical behavior—this breach of trust can cause followers to rate leaders as less effective as a result.[149]

REGAINING TRUST Managers who break the psychological contract with workers, demonstrating they are not trustworthy leaders, will find employees are less satisfied and less committed, have a higher intent toward turnover, engage in fewer OCBs, and have lower levels of task performance.[150]

Once it has been violated, trust can be regained through long-term and short-term strategies,[151] but only in certain situations and depending on the type of violation.[152] If the cause is lack of ability, it is usually best to apologize and recognize you should have done better. When lack of integrity is the problem, apologies do not do much good. Regardless of the violation, saying nothing or refusing to confirm or deny guilt is never an effective strategy for regaining trust.[153]

Trust can be restored when we observe a consistent pattern of trustworthy behavior by the transgressor, although time is of the essence when issuing an apology: Quicker apologies tend to be better than those that come late.[154] However, if the transgressor used deception, trust never fully returns, not even after apologies, promises, or a consistent pattern of trustworthy actions.[155]

Mentoring

Leaders often take responsibility for developing future leaders. A **mentor** is a senior employee who sponsors and supports a less-experienced employee—a protégé.[156] Mentoring relationships serve career and psychosocial functions.[157] Successful mentors build personal relationships with protégés that are characterized by mutual trust; instill accountability and build confidence and adaptability in protégés; and seek to improve protégés' competence and career progression (e.g., through networking).[158]

Are all employees in an organization likely to participate in a mentoring relationship? Unfortunately, no. However, research continues to indicate that employers should establish mentoring programs because they benefit both mentors and protégés,[159] although informal programs tend to work better.[160] Furthermore, there are some gender differences: Males tend to be more likely to serve as a mentor, while females tend to both give and receive more psychosocial support in a mentoring relationship.[161]

You might assume mentoring is valuable for objective outcomes like compensation and job performance, but research suggests the gains are primarily psychological.[162] Thus, while mentoring can have an impact on career success, it is not as much of a contributing factor.

Mentor
A senior employee who sponsors and supports a less-experienced employee, called a protégé.

Leading in Times of Crisis

A popular English proverb states, "Cometh the hour, cometh the [wo]man," suggesting that during times of crisis, leaders will emerge to bring order and understanding to the chaos.[163] Indeed, leaders can and do emerge during times of crisis, although there is variability in how effective they are at handling the situation. For example, during the COVID-19 outbreak of 2020, German Chancellor Angela Merkel has been praised for her impressive, decisive, firm, evidence-based, and effective leadership—and these are not merely attributions; under her leadership, Germany had one of the lowest fatality rates in the world when the virus broke out.[164] During times of peace and stability, women leaders tend to under-emerge due to the *glass cliff* phenomenon (see the chapter on diversity for more discussion).[165] Because of this *think female-think crisis* effect, women are not seen as leaders during status-quo periods, often due to leader stereotypes of not being agentic enough that prevent their emergence (despite little evidence indicating that they are more or less effective than men). This phenomenon is just one of the many indicators that leadership in crisis is not as simple as the "cometh the hour" proverb would suggest—not to mention the time pressure, complexity, and strain from the threat these stressful situations impose.[166]

Leaders in times of crisis, such as decorated combat heroes of World War II, are often thought of in mythical, heroic terms: eager, loyal, risk-taking, transformational, and so on.[167] Interestingly, one review of historical leadership incidents across several decades suggested that much of the successful leadership episodes involved *transactional* behaviors, such as strategizing (e.g., analyzing the situation, delegating, planning) and coordinating (e.g., orchestrating action, managing information flow).[168] Analyzing the situation appears to be particularly important, and research demonstrates that leaders managing crisis teams move quickly toward a shared mental model (see the chapter on teams) of the crisis with followers over time.[169] Emotions also play a large role: for example, in one study, a leader responsible for a product recall that cost an organization a lot of money was rated more favorably when accepting responsibility and expressing sadness (as opposed to denial and anger).[170] Furthermore, research in this area has yet to fully cover how gender identity relates to leadership emergence in times of crisis, but we expect progress to be made in this area moving forward.

Of all the leadership styles during times of crisis, charismatic leadership has been studied the most frequently. During times of crisis, charismatic leadership can be *visionary* (e.g., starting with establishing a vision and then making a plea for action) or *crisis-responsive* (e.g., starting with a plea for action and, over time, justifying this action by communicating their effective results).[171] Both forms can be effective in different ways, although the crisis-responsive approach tends to be used less frequently once the crisis ends.[172] Followers are also highly attuned to the crisis, and this affects their leadership attributions. For example, analyses of presidential elections suggest that perceptions of crisis predict voters' attributions of candidate charisma and their intentions to vote for candidates who are charismatic.[173] The effects of charismatic and transformational leadership during times of crisis may even reverberate after the crisis is over. For example, in a study of U.S. Army unit leaders suggests that transformational leaders observe less unit turnover after the crisis is over and that these soldiers feel more embedded in their unit due to their shared experiences.[174]

CHALLENGES TO OUR UNDERSTANDING OF LEADERSHIP

Management expert Jim Collins said, "In the 1500s, people ascribed all events they didn't understand to God. Why did the crops fail? God. Why did someone die? God. Now our all-purpose explanation is leadership."[175] This may be an astute observation from management consulting, but of course much of an organization's success or failure is due to factors outside the influence of leadership. In this section, we present challenges to the accepted beliefs about the value of leadership.

Leadership as an Attribution

As you may remember from the chapter on perception and individual decision-making, attribution theory examines how people try to make sense of cause-and-effect relationships. The **attribution theory of leadership** says leadership is merely an attribution people make about other individuals.[176] We attribute the following to leaders: intelligence, outgoing personality, strong verbal skills, aggressiveness, understanding, and industriousness.[177] We also, in our day-to-day interactions with our leaders, tend to make attributions toward our relationships (e.g., my supervisors gave me a terrible performance appraisal because they *hate me*).[178] At the organizational level, we tend, rightly or wrongly, to see leaders as responsible for both extremely negative and extremely positive performance.[179]

> **Attribution theory of leadership**
> A leadership theory that states that leadership is merely an attribution that people make about other individuals.

Perceptions of leaders by their followers strongly affect leaders' ability to be effective. A study of more than three thousand employees from western Europe, the United States, and the Middle East found that people who tended to "romanticize" leadership in general were more likely to believe their own leaders were transformational.[180] Attribution theory suggests what is important is projecting the *appearance* of being a leader rather than focusing on *actual accomplishments*. Leader-wannabes who can shape the perception that they are smart, personable, verbally adept, aggressive, hardworking, and consistent in their style can increase the probability their bosses, colleagues, and employees will view them as effective leaders. It works both ways as well—coworkers and leaders alike can see a follower engaging in OCB toward the leader as being ingratiating or "sucking up."[181] Similarly, attributions that suggest the leader was only acting fairly for non-benevolent motives (e.g., desiring to exercise control or maintain their image) do not influence trust in the leader like a more benevolent motive would.[182]

Neutralizers of and Substitutes for Leadership

One theory of leadership suggests that in many situations, leaders' actions are irrelevant.[183] **Neutralizers**, such as indifference to rewards, make it impossible for leader behavior to make any difference to follower outcomes (see Exhibit 12-7). On the other

> **Neutralizers**
> Attributes that make it impossible for leader behavior to make any difference to follower outcomes.

Defining Characteristics	Relationship-Oriented Leadership	Task-Oriented Leadership
Individual		
Experience/training	No effect on	Substitutes for
Professionalism	Substitutes for	Substitutes for
Indifference to rewards	Neutralizes	Neutralizes
Job		
Highly structured task	No effect on	Substitutes for
Provides its own feedback	No effect on	Substitutes for
Intrinsically satisfying	Substitutes for	No effect on
Organization		
Explicit formalized goals	No effect on	Substitutes for
Rigid rules and procedures	No effect on	Substitutes for
Cohesive work groups	Substitutes for	Substitutes for

EXHIBIT 12-7

Neutralizers of and Substitutes for Leadership

Source: Based on S. Kerr and J. M. Jermier, "Substitutes for Leadership: Their Meaning and Measurement," *Organizational Behavior and Human Performance* (1978), p. 378."

Substitutes
Attributes, such as experience and training, that can replace the need for a leader's support or ability to create structure.

hand, experience and training are among the **substitutes** that can replace the need for a leader's support or ability to create structure. Organizations such as video game producer Valve Corporation, Gore-Tex maker W. L. Gore, and collaboration-software firm GitHub have experimented with eliminating leaders and management. Governance in the "bossless" work environment is achieved through accountability to coworkers, who determine team composition and sometimes even pay.[184] Organizational characteristics such as explicit formalized goals, rigid rules and procedures, and cohesive workgroups can replace formal leadership. At the same time, leadership can also substitute for the effects of policies, practices, and procedures. For example, ethical leadership can substitute for actual justice enactment, such that perceiving your leader as ethical matters more to you than them actually enacting and enforcing justice.[185]

It's simplistic to think employees are guided to goal accomplishments solely by the actions of their leaders.[186] We have introduced several variables—such as attitudes, personality, ability, and group norms—that affect employee performance and satisfaction. Leadership is simply another variable in our overall organizational behavior model.

SUMMARY

Leadership plays a central part in understanding group behavior because it is the leader who usually directs us toward our goals. Knowing what makes a good leader should thus be valuable toward improving group performance. The Big Five personality framework shows strong and consistent relationships between personality and leadership. The behavioral approach's major contribution was narrowing leadership into task-oriented (initiating structure) and people-oriented (consideration) styles. By evaluating the situation in which a leader operates, contingency theories promised to improve on the behavioral approach. Contemporary theories have made major contributions to our understanding of leadership effectiveness, and studies of ethics and positive leadership offer exciting promise.

IMPLICATIONS FOR MANAGERS

- For maximum leadership effectiveness, ensure that your preferences on the initiating structure and consideration dimensions are a match for your work dynamics and culture.
- Hire candidates who exhibit transformational leadership qualities and who have demonstrated success in working through others to meet a long-term vision. Personality tests can reveal candidates higher in extraversion and conscientiousness, which may indicate leadership readiness.
- Hire candidates whom you believe are ethical and trustworthy for management roles and train current managers in your organization's ethical standards in order to increase leadership effectiveness.
- Seek to develop trusting relationships with followers because, as organizations have become less stable and predictable, strong bonds of trust are replacing bureaucratic rules in defining expectations and relationships.
- Consider investing in leadership training such as formal courses, workshops, and mentoring.

13
Power and Politics

After studying this chapter, you should be able to:

13.1 Contrast leadership and power.

13.2 Explain the three bases of formal power and the two bases of personal power.

13.3 Explain the role of dependence in power relationships.

13.4 Identify power or influence tactics and their contingencies.

13.5 Identify the causes and consequences of abuse of power.

13.6 Describe how politics work in organizations.

13.7 Identify the causes, consequences, and ethics of political behavior.

POWER AND LEADERSHIP

In organizational behavior (OB), **power** simply refers to the capacity, discretion, and means to enforce one's will over others.[1] Someone can thus have power but not use it; a powerful person has discretion over when to exercise their power. Probably the most important aspect of power is that it is a function of **dependence**.[2] The more people rely or depend upon the powerful person (who controls something the others rely on or want), the more powerful that person becomes. When people begin to have more alternatives and options, or begin to rely on themselves or different people, the powerful person loses power.

 Unfortunately, we all too often hear about people using their power to unethical ends. For example, people depend upon executives, managers, and even employee "superstars" (e.g., a partner in a law firm who brings in lucrative clients) for promotions, pay raises, or bringing in customers/clientele. These powerful leaders are thus unjustly empowered to enforce their will over others in several ways, including sexual harassment.[3] Sexual harassment is a huge problem, adversely affecting employees' mental and physical health and opportunities for advancement as well as costing organizations millions of dollars in legal fees and employee turnover.[4]

 A careful comparison of our description of power with our description of leadership in the previous chapter reveals that the concepts are closely intertwined. How are the two terms different? Power does not require goal compatibility, just dependence. Leadership, on the other hand, requires some congruence between the goals of the leader and those being led. A second difference relates to the direction of influence. Power

Power
The capacity, discretion, and means to enforce one's will over others.

Dependence
The extent to which people depend or rely upon a powerful person.

focuses more so on the downward influence on followers. It minimizes the importance of lateral and upward relationships, which are important in leadership. For a third difference, leadership research often emphasizes style. It seeks answers to questions such as: How supportive should a leader be? How much decision making should be shared with followers? In contrast, the research on power focuses on tactics for gaining compliance.

Power relationships are possible in all areas of life, not just leadership positions, and power can be obtained in many ways. Let us explore the various sources of power next.

BASES OF POWER

Where does power come from? We answer this question by dividing the bases (or sources) of power into two general groupings, formal and personal, and breaking each of these down into more specific categories.[5]

Formal Power

Formal power is based on an individual's position in an organization. It can come from the ability to coerce or reward, or from legitimate authority.

Coercive power
A power base that is dependent on fear of the negative results from failing to comply.

COERCIVE POWER   The **coercive power** base depends on the target's fear of negative results from failing to comply, or acting in a way that would anger the power holder.[6] Sales consultants may remain silent after witnessing their supervisors falsify their team's sales numbers for fear of being terminated or demoted, being assigned to undesirable regions or clients, and/or being treated in an embarrassing way in front of the rest of the team. Coercive power comes also from withholding key information. People in an organization who have data or knowledge others need can make others dependent on them. For example, the sales team lead may have valuable information on client leads—anything that might threaten obtaining this information may lead the consultant to remain silent.

Reward power
Power based on the ability to distribute rewards that others view as valuable.

REWARD POWER   The opposite of coercive power is **reward power**, with which people comply because it produces positive benefits; someone who can distribute rewards that others view as valuable will have power over them. These rewards can be financial—such as controlling pay rates, raises, and bonuses—or nonfinancial, including recognition, promotions, interesting work assignments, friendly colleagues, and preferred work shifts or sales territories.[7] Using the same example, the sales team lead who rewards compliant team members with lead information is exercising reward power.

Legitimate power
Power based on a person's position in the formal hierarchy of an organization.

LEGITIMATE POWER   The most common way to access one or more of the power bases is probably through **legitimate power**. It represents the formal authority to control and use organizational resources based on the person's structural position in the organization. In general, when school principals, bank presidents, or army captains speak, teachers, tellers, and first lieutenants usually comply. Legitimate power includes members' acceptance of the authority of a hierarchical position.[8] We associate power so closely with the concept of hierarchy that just drawing longer lines in an organization chart leads people to infer the leaders are especially powerful.[9] Furthermore, legitimate power can also reduce the effect of others' power; for example, research suggests that when an employee stands up against something unethical, they are less likely to suffer the consequences of others' coercive power (e.g., sanctioning, ostracism, etc.) when they, themselves, are high in legitimate power.[10]

Personal Power

Personal power comes from an individual's unique characteristics.[11] There are two bases of personal power: expertise and the respect and admiration of others. Some people might only have personal power, but others can also have formal power. For example, many consultants have personal power but have no formal power if they are not managers. Conversely, a sales team lead may not only have formal power bases but can also be well-liked and respected.

EXPERT POWER   Expert power is based on influence wielded as a result of expertise, special skills, or knowledge.[12] As jobs become more specialized, we become dependent on experts to achieve goals. It is generally acknowledged that physicians have expertise and hence expert power: Most of us follow our doctor's advice. Returning to our sales consultant example, some of the team members may wield expert power due to their strong sales skills or expertise in the area.

> **Expert power**
> Power based on influence through possessing expertise, special skills, or knowledge.

REFERENT POWER   Referent power is based on identification with a person who has desirable resources or personal traits.[13] If I like, respect, and admire you; you can exercise power over me because I want to please you. Some people who are not in formal leadership positions have referent power and exert influence over others because of their charismatic dynamism, likability, and emotional appeal.[14]

> **Referent power**
> Power based on identification with a person who has desirable resources or personal traits.

Referent power develops out of admiration of another and a desire to be like that person. It helps explain, for instance, why celebrities are paid millions of dollars to endorse products in commercials. Marketing research shows people such as LeBron James have the power to influence your choice of athletic shoes and credit cards.[15]

Which Bases of Power Are Most Effective?

Of the bases of power, which are most effective? This is a complicated question. Regarding the dependents in the power relationship, different bases of power are effective depending upon the perceptions and characteristics of the dependent. For example, dependents view angry leaders as higher on formal power, and in turn are more loyal toward these leaders and perceive them as more effective.[16] On the other hand, dependents are likely to perceive coercive and low-referent leaders as ineffective, become less loyal toward these leaders, and even engage in deviant behaviors directed at these leaders.

It does appear though, that referent power can be an especially powerful motivator. Consider Steve Stoute's company, Translation, which matches pop-star spokespersons with corporations that want to promote their brands. Stoute has paired Justin Timberlake with McDonald's, Mary J. Blige with Apple Music, and several famous rappers with shoe companies (e.g., Jay-Z and 50 Cent).[17] Translation's approach has changed with the times as well. As more/frequent content is needed in today's day and age, Translation has worked on creating an online mini-series to promote products and to discuss culture, which has reached 42.5 million people. Partnering with Dr. Dre (Beats by Dre),

Translation created "The Shop," a series where NBA all-stars (e.g., Kevin Durant, LeBron James) and hip-hop artists (e.g., Future) alike, all with large bases of referent power, discuss several topics (e.g., sneakers, music, the game) amid a barbershop backdrop.[18]

DEPENDENCE: THE KEY TO POWER

The most important aspect of power is that it is a function of dependence. In this section, we show how understanding dependence helps us understand degrees of power.

The General Dependence Postulate

Let us begin with a general postulate: *The greater* B*'s dependence on* A, *the more power* A *has over* B. When you possess anything others require that you alone control, you make them dependent on you, and therefore you gain power over them.[19] But if something is plentiful, possessing it will not increase your power. Therefore, the more you can expand your own options, the less power you place in the hands of others. This explains why most organizations develop multiple suppliers rather than give their business to only one.

What Creates Dependence?

Dependence increases when a resource you control is important, scarce, and nonsubstitutable.[20]

IMPORTANCE   If nobody wants what you have, it is not going to create dependence. However, note that there are many degrees of importance, from needing the resource for survival to wanting a resource that is in fashion or adds to convenience.

SCARCITY   When the supply of labor is low relative to demand, workers can negotiate compensation and benefits packages that are far more attractive than those in occupations with an abundance of candidates. For example, college administrators have no problem today finding English instructors since there is a high supply and low demand. The market for network systems analysts, in contrast, is comparatively tight, with demand high and supply limited. The resulting bargaining power of computer-engineering faculty allows them to negotiate higher salaries, lighter teaching loads, and other benefits.

NONSUBSTITUTABILITY   The fewer viable substitutes for a resource, the more power a person controlling that resource has. Advancements in artificial intelligence (AI) have brought economic and philosophical issues of labor nonsubstitutability to the forefront. For example, employees with skilled trades are at risk for losing power as their skills become more efficiently and automatically handled by robotics: In other words, their skills are becoming "substitutable" (see the threat of technological unemployment in the chapter on perception and individual decision-making). Despite this fear, some economists and theorists suggest that new jobs are created as the need arises for labor that requires nonsubstitutable abilities, and we are merely enhancing productivity and making work easier through AI.[21]

Social Network Analysis: A Tool for Assessing Resources

One tool to assess the exchange of resources and dependencies within an organization is *social network analysis*.[22] This method examines patterns of communication among organizational members to identify how information flows between them. Within a social network, or connections between people who share professional interests, each individual or group is called a node, and the links between nodes are called ties. When nodes communicate or exchange resources frequently, they are said to have very strong ties. Other nodes that are not engaged in direct communication with one another achieve resource flows through intermediary nodes. In other words, some nodes act as brokers between otherwise unconnected nodes. A graphical illustration of the associations among individuals in a social network is called a *sociogram,* which functions like an informal version of an organization chart. The difference is that a formal organization chart shows how authority is supposed to flow, whereas a sociogram shows how resources *really* flow in an organization. An example of a sociogram is shown in Exhibit 13-1.

Networks can create substantial power dynamics. Those in the position of brokers tend to have more power because they can leverage the unique resources they can acquire from different groups. In other words, many people are dependent upon brokers, which gives the brokers more power. Data from the United Kingdom's National Health Service shows that change agents, people entrusted with helping an organization to make a significant change, have more success if they are information brokers.[23] However, it is

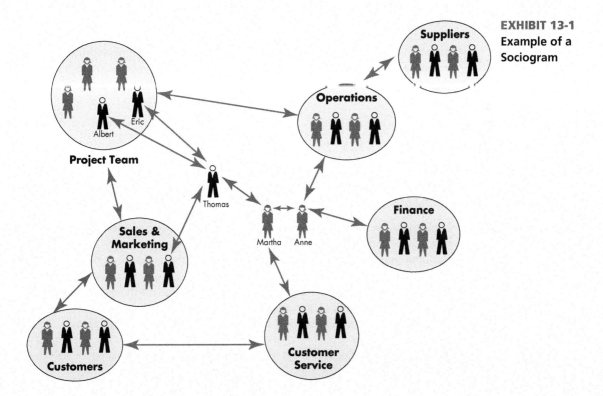

EXHIBIT 13-1
Example of a Sociogram

paradoxical how powerful brokers within marketing agency networks, even though they are more willing to leverage their power, often fail to perceive opportunities to do so.[24]

Some of the most powerful people within social networks are able to amass power because of their personality traits—for example, their insensitivity to rewards (making them resistant to others' influence), extraversion, and even dark triad traits (see the chapter on personality and values) is positively related to their social network position and power.[25] Stereotype threat (see the chapter on diversity), however, can also influence the effectiveness of women in brokerage positions. Because the agency, power, and assertiveness (that come with the brokerage position) contradict with the feminine stereotype, women are more likely to experience anxiety about their performance and fear of negative evaluation in these positions.[26]

The relationships brokers form within networks are also extremely important. People form relationships with their leaders and coworkers, such as friendships and partnerships, which nurture mutual reliance and obligation.[27] These "ties" are important not only for getting things done in organizations, but also for employees' well-being—employees who do not nurture these ties or who lose them over time are more likely to leave their organization (although these ties can remain dormant, even after the employee leaves!).[28]

There are many ways to implement a social network analysis in an organization.[29] Some organizations keep track of the flow of e-mail communications or document sharing across departments. These big data tools are an easy way to gather objective information about how individuals exchange information. Other organizations look at data from human resources (HR) information systems, analyzing how supervisors and subordinates interact with one another. These data sources can produce sociograms showing how resources and power flow. Leaders can then identify powerful brokers who exert the strongest influence on many groups and address these key individuals. Newer applications of AI have enabled organizations and researchers to use machine learning algorithms to model the flow of information in social networks over time (and learn from events).[30]

INFLUENCE TACTICS

Influence tactics
Ways in which individuals translate power bases into specific actions.

What **influence tactics** do people use to translate power bases into specific action? What options do they have for influencing their bosses, coworkers, or employees? Research has identified nine distinct influence tactics:[31]

- **Legitimacy.** Relying on your authority position or saying a request accords with organizational policies or rules.
- **Rational persuasion.** Presenting logical arguments and factual evidence to demonstrate a request is reasonable.
- **Inspirational appeals.** Developing emotional commitment by appealing to a target's values, needs, hopes, and aspirations.
- **Consultation.** Increasing support by involving the target in deciding how to accomplish your plan.
- **Exchange.** Rewarding the target with benefits or favors in exchange for agreeing to a request.

- **Personal appeals.** Asking for compliance based on friendship or loyalty.
- **Ingratiation.** Using flattery, praise, or friendly behavior prior to making a request.
- **Pressure.** Using warnings, repeated demands, and threats.
- **Coalitions.** Enlisting the aid or support of others to persuade the target to agree.

Using Influence Tactics

Some tactics are more effective than others. Rational persuasion, inspirational appeal, and consultation tend to be equally effective in influencing performance at work.[32] Rational persuasion, although still effective at helping build relationships at work, tends to not be as superbly effective as inspirational appeal and consultation.[33] The pressure tactic tends to backfire and is typically the least effective.[34] Using ingratiation can improve relational outcomes of influence at work (e.g., during job interviews),[35] but perhaps only when the audience does not really care about the outcome of the request or if it is routine.[36]

Let us consider the most effective way of getting a raise. You can start with a rational approach—figure out how your pay compares to that of your organizational peers, land a competing job offer, gather data that testify to your performance, or use salary calculators like Salary.com to compare your pay with others in your occupation—then share your findings with your manager. The results can be impressive. Kitty Dunning, a senior vice president at Don Jagoda Associates, once landed a 16 percent raise when she e-mailed her boss numbers showing she had increased sales.[37] Using rational persuasion to make a case to your supervisor about a possible raise or even an alternative work arrangement (see the chapter on motivation applications) may be effective because it fosters a mutual sense of respect between you and your supervisor.[38]

While rational persuasion may work in this situation, the effectiveness of some influence tactics depends to some extent on the direction of influence[39] and, of course, on the audience. As Exhibit 13-2 shows, rational persuasion is the only tactic effective at both upwardly and downwardly influencing, although it is stronger when it is used for downward influence attempts.[40] Inspirational appeals work best as a downward-influencing tactic with subordinates.[41] Ingratiation is most effective as lateral influence, although it can also be effective in downward influence.[42] Other factors relating to the effectiveness of influence include the sequencing of tactics, a person's skill in using the tactic, and the organizational culture. In general, you are more likely to be effective if you begin with "softer" tactics that rely on personal power, such as personal and inspirational appeals, rational persuasion, and consultation. If these fail, you can move to "harder" tactics, such as exchange and coalitions, which emphasize formal power and incur greater costs and risks.[43]

Upward Influence	Downward Influence	Lateral Influence	
Rational persuasion	Rational persuasion	Rational persuasion	**EXHIBIT 13-2**
	Inspirational appeals	Consultation	**Preferred**
	Ingratiation	Ingratiation	**Influence Tactics**
	Legitimacy	Exchange	**by Influence**
		Legitimacy	**Direction**
		Personal appeals	
		Coalitions	

As we mentioned, the effectiveness of tactics depends on the audience.[44] People especially likely to comply with soft influence tactics tend to be more reflective and intrinsically motivated; they have high self-esteem and a greater desire for control. Those likely to comply with hard influence tactics are more action-oriented and extrinsically motivated and are more focused on getting along with others than on getting their own way. Interestingly, prior research does not support differences between men and women in the effectiveness of use of influence tactics—both men and women benefit from soft or neutral tactics, as opposed to harder tactics.[45]

Cultural Preferences for Influence Tactics

Preference for influence tactics varies across cultures.[46] Those from individualistic countries tend to see power in personalized terms and as a legitimate means of advancing their personal ends, whereas those in collectivistic countries see power in social terms and as a legitimate means of helping others.[47] Managers in the United States seem to prefer rational appeal, whereas Chinese managers may prefer coalition tactics.[48] Reason-based tactics are consistent with the U.S. preference for direct confrontation and rational persuasion to influence others and resolve differences, while coalition tactics align with the Chinese preference for meeting difficult or controversial requests with indirect approaches.

Applying Influence Tactics

Political skill
The ability to influence others in such a way as to enhance one's objectives.

People differ in their **political skill**, or their ability to influence others to enhance their own objectives.[49] The politically skilled are more effective users of influence tactics and draw on their knowledge of others' demands, resources, and preferences to do so.[50] Political skill is also more effective when social skills are required to do well in your job, such as in leadership positions, sales consultants, real estate agents, and other relationship-oriented occupations.[51] The politically skilled can exert their influence without others detecting it, a key element in effectiveness (it is damaging to be labeled political).[52]

We know cultures within organizations differ markedly; some are warm, relaxed, and supportive; others are formal and conservative. Some encourage participation and consultation, some encourage reason, and still others rely on pressure. People who fit the culture of the organization tend to obtain more influence.[53] Specifically, extraverts tend to be more influential in team-oriented organizations, and highly conscientious people are more influential in organizations that value working alone on technical tasks. People who fit the culture are influential because they can perform especially well in the domains deemed most important for success. Thus, the organization itself will influence which subset of influence tactics is viewed as acceptable for use. Regardless of the cultural fit, however, evidence suggests that in general, extraverts tend to be more prone to develop political skills, although agreeableness and conscientiousness are also important to some degree.[54] But beware: political skill has been found to camouflage some negative dark triad traits, such as Machiavellianism (see the chapter on personality and values).[55]

Overall, political skill leads to several positive individual outcomes for employees.[56] Developing political skill can help you build self-efficacy and become more satisfied with your job and committed to your organization, and lead you to experience less stress, to a small degree. Furthermore, developing political skill can boost your performance and productivity, as well as enable you to engage in more organizational citizenship behaviors (OCBs). Probably the most important are the career outcomes: Being politically skilled can improve your reputation and career success as you earn a higher income and a more prestigious position and are more satisfied with your career. Research suggests the reasons *why* political skill leads to these positive outcomes are through the reputation and confidence boosts that come along with building these skills.[57]

HOW POWER AFFECTS PEOPLE

To this point, we have discussed what power is and how it is acquired. But we have not yet answered one important question: Does power corrupt? For one, it is clear that power affects the power holder: It energizes people, on the one hand, but can cause the power holder to rely more on gut feelings and to become self-serving and potentially more corrupt.[58] So all forms of power can lead to the downside of getting "caught up" in the feeling of power.

There is certainly evidence that there are corrupting aspects of power. Power leads people to place their own interests ahead of others' needs or goals.[59] Why does this happen? Interestingly, power not only leads people to focus on their self-interests because they can; it also liberates them to focus inward and thus come to place greater weight on their own aims and interests. Power also appears to lead individuals to "objectify" others (to see them as tools to obtain their instrumental goals) and to see relationships as more peripheral.[60]

That is not all. Powerful people react—especially negatively—to any threats to their competence. People in positions of power hold on to it when they can, and individuals who face threats to their power are exceptionally willing to take actions to retain it whether their actions harm others or not.[61] Possessing formal power can alter how you perceive others' emotions (e.g., the powerful are quicker to detect anger because this threatens their power) and cause you to behave in an ineffective way.[62] Those given power are more likely to make self-interested decisions when faced with a moral hazard (such as when hedge fund managers take more risks with other people's money because they are rewarded for gains but punished less often for losses). People in power are also more willing to denigrate others. Power also leads to overconfident decision making (although firm leader overconfidence may actually result in positive firm outcomes).[63]

What We Can Do About Power

Power does not affect everyone in the same way, and there are even positive effects of power. Power can cause others to view you more positively.[64] Power energizes and increases motivation to achieve goals. It also can enhance our motivation to help others. One study found, for example, that a desire to help others translated into actual work behavior when people felt a sense of power.[65] In general, power has been studied based on how it affects peoples' thoughts, emotions, and behaviors.[66]

Power affects the cognition, or thought, as the powerful tend to simplify how they process information, rely on single sources, and use information that is easier to retrieve.[67] This means that the powerful are more likely to rely on stereotypes and heuristic forms of processing. For example, a start-up founder who has built several successful businesses in the past may look past certain aspects of the market or the process because of the previous successes enjoyed. Although not much research has been conducted on how power affects emotions, some work suggests that the powerful are more inclined to express genuine positive emotions without repercussions, but less likely to "mirror" others' emotions (e.g., not feeling distressed at witnessing another person's distress).[68] Finally, powerful people (due to enhanced confidence and a sense of volition) tend to display personal initiative and be more sensitive to potential rewards or benefits (e.g., are personally selfish), and are less sensitive to normative behaviors.[69] For example, graduate students at professional academic conferences often note that they can tell who has "made it" in their careers, because they are the ones showing up to presentations in jeans, rather than business attire.

So, what can we *do* about power? Are we "powerless" in its wake? First, the toxic effects of power depend on the wielder's personality. Research suggests that if you have an anxious personality, power does not corrupt you because you are less likely to think that using power benefits yourself.[70] Second, the corrosive effect of power can be contained by organizational systems. For example, one study found that while power made people behave in a self-serving manner, the self-serving behavior stopped when accountability for the behavior was initiated. Third, we have the means to blunt the negative effects of power. One study showed that simply expressing gratitude toward powerful others makes them less likely to act aggressively against us. Finally, remember the saying that those with little power abuse what little they have. There seems to be some truth to this in that the people most likely to abuse power are those who start low in status and gain power. Why is this the case? It appears that having low status is threatening, and the fear this creates is used in negative ways if power is given later.[71]

Sexual Harassment: Unequal Power in the Workplace

Sexual harassment
Any unwanted activity of a sexual nature that affects an individual's employment and creates a hostile work environment.

Sexual harassment is defined as any unwanted activity of a sexual nature that affects an individual's employment or creates a hostile work environment.[72] According to the U.S. Equal Employment Opportunity Commission (EEOC), sexual harassment happens when a person encounters "unwelcome sexual advances, requests for sexual favors, and other verbal or physical conduct of a sexual nature" on the job that disrupts work performance or that creates an "intimidating, hostile, or offensive" work environment.[73] Worldwide, 35 percent of women have experienced physical or sexual violence, and even larger numbers (for some countries, well over 50 percent) across the world have experienced sexual harassment.[74] For example, a study in Pakistan found that up to 93 percent of female workers were sexually harassed.[75] Although the definition changes from country to country, most nations have at least some policies to protect workers. Whether the policies or laws are followed is another question, however. Equal employment opportunity legislation is established in Pakistan, Bangladesh, and Oman, for example, but studies suggest it might not be well implemented.[76] Sexual harassment is disproportionately prevalent for women in certain types of jobs. In the restaurant industry, for instance, 80 percent of female waitstaff in a study reported having been sexually harassed by coworkers or customers, compared to 70 percent of male waitstaff.[77] It goes without saying that the effects of sexual harassment are deplorable and nefarious and, in large part, due to the prevailing climate in the team, organization, or region.[78]

Most studies confirm that power is central to understanding sexual harassment.[79] This seems true whether the harassment comes from a supervisor, coworker, or employee, although it is especially pronounced for employees who have newly acquired power.[80] Sexual harassment is more likely to occur when there are large power differentials. The supervisor–employee dyad best characterizes an unequal power relationship, where formal power gives the supervisor the capacity to reward and coerce. Because employees want favorable performance reviews, salary increases, and the like, supervisors control resources most employees consider important and scarce. When there are not effective controls to detect and prevent sexual harassment, abusers are more likely to act. Relatedly, if there are not effective controls to give voice to whistleblowers and protect them from retaliation, abusers are more likely to act and continue to act.[81] The #MeToo and Time's Up movements were formed to establish a coalition giving voice to sexual harassment and abuse survivors to quell the tide of sexual harassment in organizations and communities.[82]

Sexual harassment can have a detrimental impact on individuals and the organization, but it can be avoided. The manager's commitment to the process and responsibility is critical:[83]

- *Make sure an active policy defines what constitutes sexual harassment, informs employees they can be fired for inappropriate behavior, and establishes procedures for making complaints.*
- *Reassure employees that they will not encounter retaliation if they file a complaint.*
- *Investigate every complaint and inform the legal and HR departments.*
- *Make sure offenders are disciplined or terminated.*
- *Set up in-house training to raise employee awareness of sexual harassment issues.*

POLITICS: POWER IN ACTION

Whenever people get together in groups, power will be exerted. People in organizations want to carve out a niche to exert influence, earn rewards, and advance their careers. If they convert their power into action, we describe them as being engaged in *politics*. Those with good political skills will likely use their bases of power effectively.[84] Politics are not only inevitable; they might be essential, too.

Political Behavior

Essentially, *organizational politics* focus on the use of power to affect decision making in an organization, sometimes for self-serving and organizationally unsanctioned behaviors.[85] For our purposes, **political behavior** in organizations consists of activities that are not required as part of an individual's formal role but that influence, or attempt to influence, the distribution of advantages and disadvantages within the organization.[86]

Political behavior is outside specified job requirements. It requires some attempt to use power bases. It includes efforts to influence the goals, criteria, or processes used for decision making. Our definition is broad enough to include varied political behaviors such as withholding key information from decision makers, joining a coalition, whistleblowing,

Political behavior
Activities that are not required as part of a person's formal role in the organization but that influence, or attempt to influence, the distribution of advantages and disadvantages within the organization.

spreading rumors, leaking confidential information to the media, exchanging favors with others for mutual benefit, and lobbying on behalf of or against a particular individual or decision alternative.[87] In this way, political behavior is often negative, but not always.

The Reality of Politics

Research has demonstrated that there are multiple ways people construe politics: (1) some are *reactive,* believing that it involves engaging in destructive and manipulative behavior; some are (2) *reluctant,* viewing it as a necessary evil; still, others are (3) *strategic,* and view politics as a useful way of getting things done; and finally, some have more of an (4) *integrated* perception, viewing politics as central to the reality of decision making.[88]

Indeed, interviews with experienced managers show most believe political behavior is a major part of organizational life.[89] Many managers report some use of political behavior is ethical, if it does not directly harm anyone else. They describe politics as necessary and believe someone who never uses political behavior will have a hard time getting things done. Although those with lower incomes also believe political behavior is necessary, they are more reluctant to engage in it and thus have a harder time of advancing their careers.[90]

But why, you may wonder, must politics exist? Is it not possible for an organization to be politics-free? It is *possible*—if all members of that organization hold the same goals and interests, if organizational resources are not scarce, and if performance outcomes are completely clear and objective. But that does not describe the organizational world in which most of us live. Regardless, it appears as if people, although often reluctant to politick, will do so when it is done through prosocial means and with the goal of helping others.[91]

Maybe the most important factor leading to politics within organizations is the realization that most of the "facts" used to allocate limited resources are open to interpretation. When allocating pay based on performance, for instance, what is *good* performance? What is an *adequate* improvement? What constitutes an *unsatisfactory* job? It is in this large and ambiguous middle ground of organizational life—where the facts do not speak for themselves—that politics flourish.

Finally, because most decisions must be made in a climate of ambiguity—where facts are rarely objective and thus are open to interpretation—people within organizations will use whatever influence they can to support their goals and interests. That, of course, creates the activities we call *politicking.* One person's "selfless effort to benefit the organization" is seen by another as a "blatant attempt to further his or her interest."[92]

CAUSES AND CONSEQUENCES OF POLITICAL BEHAVIOR

Now that we have discussed the constant presence of politicking in organizations, let us discuss the causes and consequences of these behaviors.

Factors Contributing to Political Behavior

Not all groups or organizations are equally political. In some organizations, politicking is overt and rampant, while in others, politics play a small role in influencing outcomes. What causes this variation? Research and observation have identified several factors that

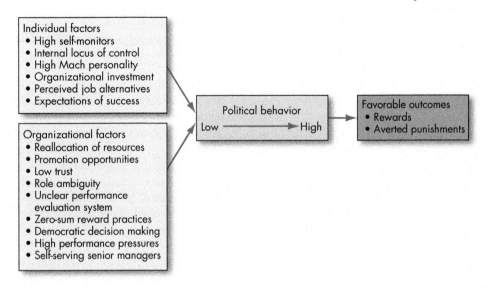

EXHIBIT 13-3
Antecedents
and Outcomes
of Political
Behavior

appear to encourage political behavior. Some are individual characteristics, derived from the qualities of the people the organization employs; others are a result of the organization's culture or internal environment. Exhibit 13-3 illustrates how both individual and organizational factors can encourage political behavior and provide favorable outcomes (increased rewards and averted punishments) for individuals and groups in the organization.

INDIVIDUAL FACTORS   At the individual level, researchers have identified certain personality traits, needs, and other factors likely to be related to political behavior. In terms of traits, we find that employees who are high self-monitors, possess an internal locus of control, and have a high need for power (nPow; see the chapter on motivation concepts) are more likely to engage in political behavior. The high self-monitor is more sensitive to social cues, exhibits higher levels of social conformity, and is more likely to be skilled in political behavior than the low self-monitor. Because they believe they can control their environment, individuals with an internal locus of control are more prone to take a proactive stance and attempt to manipulate situations in their favor. Not surprisingly, the Machiavellian personality (see the chapter on personality and values)—characterized by the will to manipulate and the desire for power—is consistent with using politics to further personal interests.

An individual's investment in the organization and perceived alternatives influence the degree to which they will pursue illegitimate means of political action.[93] The more a person expects increased future benefits from the organization, and the more that person has to lose if forced out, the less likely they are to use illegitimate means. Conversely, the more alternate job opportunities an individual has—due to a favorable job market, possession of scarce skills or knowledge, prominent reputation, or influential contacts outside the organization—the more likely the person is to employ politics.

Finally, some individuals engage in political behavior simply because they are better at it. Such individuals read interpersonal interactions well, fit their behavior to situational needs, and excel at networking.[94] These people are often indirectly rewarded for their political efforts. For example, a study of a construction firm in southern China found that politically skilled subordinates were more likely to receive recommendations for rewards from their supervisors, and politically oriented supervisors were especially likely to respond positively to politically skilled subordinates.[95] Other studies from countries around the world have similarly shown that higher levels of political skill are associated with higher levels of perceived job performance.[96]

ORGANIZATIONAL FACTORS   Although we acknowledge the role individual differences can play, the evidence more strongly suggests that certain situations and cultures promote politics. Specifically, when an organization's resources are declining, when the existing pattern of resources is changing, and when there is opportunity for promotions, politicking is more likely to surface.[97] When resources are reduced, people may engage in political actions to safeguard what they have. Also, *any* changes, especially those implying a significant reallocation of resources within the organization, are likely to stimulate conflict and increase politicking.

Cultures characterized by low trust, role ambiguity, unclear performance evaluation systems, win–lose reward allocation practices, democratic decision making, high pressure for performance, and self-serving senior managers will create breeding grounds for politicking.[98] Because political activities are not required as part of the employee's formal role, the greater the role ambiguity, the more employees can engage in unnoticed political activity. Role ambiguity means the prescribed employee behaviors are not clear. In this situation, there are fewer limits to the scope and functions of the employee's political actions.

Additionally, the more an organizational culture emphasizes the zero-sum or win–lose approach to reward allocations (which often begins as a result of financial vulnerability), the more employees will be motivated to engage in politicking.[99] The **zero-sum approach** treats the reward "pie" as fixed, so any gain one person or group achieves comes at the expense of another person or group. For example, if fifteen thousand dollars is distributed among five employees for raises, any employee who gets more than three thousand dollars takes money away from one or more of the others. Such a practice encourages making others look bad and increasing the visibility of what you do.

Zero-sum approach
An approach to reward allocation that treats the reward "pie" as fixed, so any gain one person or group achieves comes at the expense of another person or group.

How Do People Respond to Organizational Politics?

For most people who have modest political skills or who are unwilling to play the politics game, outcomes tend to be predominantly negative in terms of decreased job satisfaction, increased anxiety and stress, increased turnover, and reduced performance. Research has demonstrated that the more politics play a role in one's environment, organization, or team, the more negative outcomes will be experienced (e.g., increased stress and turnover intentions as well as decreased morale and performance), regardless of how necessary people perceive them to be.[100] Politics may lead to self-reported declines in employee performance, perhaps because employees perceive political environments to be unfair, which demotivates them.[101] Other research suggests that it may be a "double-edged sword" (e.g., beneficial on the one hand, but detrimental on the other), meaning that political behaviors can empower people to do well, while at the same time draining them from emotional exhaustion.[102]

The politics–performance relationship appears to be moderated by an individual's understanding of the "hows" and "whys" of organizational politics. Researchers have noted, "An individual who has a clear understanding of who is responsible for making decisions and why they were selected to be the decision makers would have a better understanding of how and why things happen the way they do than someone who does not understand the decision-making process in the organization."[103] When both politics and understanding are high, performance is likely to increase because these individuals see political activity as an opportunity. This is consistent with what you might expect for individuals with well-honed political skills. But when understanding is low, individuals are more likely to see politics as a threat, which can have a negative effect on job performance.[104]

When employees see change as a threat, they may respond with **defensive behaviors**—reactive and protective behaviors to avoid action, blame, or change.[105] (Exhibit 13-4 provides some examples.) These behaviors can be a part of politicking, but in a destructive, negative sense. Instead of attempting to influence people in

Defensive behaviors Reactive and protective behaviors to avoid action, blame, or change.

Avoiding Action

Overconforming. Strictly interpreting your responsibility by saying things like "The rules clearly state ..." or "This is the way we've always done it."

Buck passing. Transferring responsibility for the execution of a task or decision to someone else.

Playing dumb. Avoiding an unwanted task by falsely pleading ignorance or inability.

Stretching. Prolonging a task so that one person appears to be occupied—for example, turning a two-week task into a four-month job.

Stalling. Appearing to be more or less supportive publicly while doing little or nothing privately.

Avoiding Blame

Bluffing. Rigorously documenting activity to project an image of competence and thoroughness, known as "covering your rear."

Playing safe. Evading situations that may reflect unfavorably. It includes taking on only projects with a high probability of success, having risky decisions approved by superiors, qualifying expressions of judgment, and taking neutral positions in conflicts.

Justifying. Developing explanations that lessen one's responsibility for a negative outcome and/or apologizing to demonstrate remorse, or both.

Scapegoating. Placing the blame for a negative outcome on external factors that are not entirely blameworthy.

Misrepresenting. Manipulation of information by distortion, embellishment, deception, selective presentation, or obfuscation.

Avoiding Change

Prevention. Trying to prevent a threatening change from occurring.

Self-protection. Acting in ways to protect one's self-interest during change by guarding information or other resources.

EXHIBIT 13-4 Defensive Behaviors

"soft," bond-affirming ways, these behaviors protect self-interests through aggressive or avoidant means, such as withholding ideas or contributions.[106] In the short run, employees may find that defensiveness protects their self-interests, but in the long run it wears them down.

Impression Management

We know people have an ongoing interest in how others perceive and evaluate them. Being perceived positively by others has benefits in an organizational setting. It might, for instance, help us initially to get the jobs we want in an organization and, once hired, to get favorable evaluations, superior salary increases, and more rapid promotions. Managing how others perceive you is especially important, for example, to expatriates representing their organizations in other countries, and requires them to adapt to cultural norms.[107] The process by which individuals attempt to control the impression others form of them is called **impression management (IM)**.[108] See Exhibit 13-5 for examples. This process can be conscious or unconscious and can be perceived as authentic or disingenuous. When perceived as inauthentic or disingenuous, IM can lead to decrements in performance, increased anxiety, and negative feelings.[109] When perceived as modest, authentic, and genuine (e.g., disclosing something negative and humorous about yourself to relate with another person), IM can lead others to see you more positively and lead to better relationship outcomes.[110]

Impression management (IM)
The process by which individuals attempt to control the impression others form of them.

IM research has linked IM to two criteria: interview success and performance evaluations. Let us consider each of these.

INTERVIEWS AND IM   The evidence indicates most job applicants and interviewers alike use IM techniques in interviews and that they work, in part because they increase interviewer perceptions of the applicants' warmth and competence.[111] To develop a sense of how effective different IM techniques are in interviews, one study grouped data from thousands of recruiting and selection interviews into appearance-oriented efforts (efforts toward looking professional), explicit tactics (such as flattering the interviewer or talking up your own accomplishments), and verbal cues (such as using positive terms and showing general enthusiasm).[112] Across all the dimensions, it was quite clear that IM was a powerful predictor of how well people did. However, there was a twist. When interviews were highly structured, meaning the interviewer's questions were written out in advance and focused on applicant qualifications, the effects of IM were substantially weaker. Manipulative behaviors like IM are more likely to have an effect in ambiguous and unstructured interviews.

PERFORMANCE EVALUATIONS AND IM   In terms of performance evaluations, the picture is quite different. Ingratiation is positively related to performance ratings, meaning those who ingratiate with their supervisors get higher performance evaluations. However, self-promotion appears to backfire: Those who self-promote may receive *lower* performance ratings.[113] There is an important qualifier to these general findings. It appears that individuals high in political skill are able to translate IM into higher performance appraisals, whereas those lower in political skill are more likely to be hurt by their IM attempts.[114] One study of 760 boards of directors found that individuals who ingratiated themselves to current board members (expressed agreement with the director, pointed out shared attitudes and opinions, complimented the director) increased their chances of landing on a board.[115] Another study found that interns who attempted to use

Conformity

Agreeing with someone else's opinion to gain his or her approval is a form of *ingratiation.*

Example: A manager tells his boss, "You're absolutely right on your reorganization plan for the western regional office. I couldn't agree with you more.

Favors

Doing something nice for someone to gain that person's approval is a form of *ingratiation.*

Example: A salesperson says to a prospective client, "I've got two tickets to the theater tonight that I can't use. Take them. Consider it a thank-you for taking the time to talk with me."

Excuses

Explaining a predicament-creating event aimed at minimizing the apparent severity of the predicament is a *defensive IM technique.*

Example: A sales manager says to her boss, "We failed to get the ad in the paper on time, but no one responds to those ads anyway."

Apologies

Admitting responsibility for an undesirable event and simultaneously seeking to get a pardon for the action is a *defensive IM technique.*

Example: An employee says to his boss, "I'm sorry I made a mistake on the report. Please forgive me."

Self-Promotion

Highlighting your best qualities, downplaying your deficits, and calling attention to your achievements is a *self-focused IM technique.*

Example: A salesperson tells his boss, "Matt worked unsuccessfully for three years to try to get that account. I sewed it up in six weeks. I'm the best closer this company has."

Enhancement

Claiming that something you did is more valuable than most other members of the organizations would think is a *self-focused IM technique.*

Example: A journalist tells his editor, "My work on this celebrity divorce story was really a major boost to our sales" (even though the story only made it to page 3 in the entertainment section).

Flattery

Complimenting others about their virtues in an effort to make yourself appear perceptive and likeable is an *assertive IM technique.*

Example: A new sales trainee says to her peer, "You handled that client's complaint so tactfully! I could never have handled that as well as you did."

Exemplification

Doing more than you need to in an effort to show how dedicated and hardworking you are is an *assertive IM technique.*

Example: An employee sends e-mails from his work computer when he works late so that his supervisor will know how long he's been working.

EXHIBIT 13-5

Impression Management (IM) Techniques

Source: Based on B. R. Schlenker, *Impression Management* (Monterey, CA: Brooks/Cole, 1980); M. C. Bolino, K. M. Kacmar, W. H. Turnley, and J. B. Gilstrap, "A Multi-Level Review of Impression Management Motives and Behaviors," *Journal of Management* 34, no. 6 (2008), 1080–109; R. B. Cialdini, "Indirect Tactics of Image Management Beyond Basking," in R. A. Giacalone and P. Rosenfeld (eds.), *Impression Management in the Organization* (Hillsdale, NJ: Lawrence Erlbaum, 1989), 45–71.

ingratiation with their supervisors were usually disliked—unless they had high levels of political skill. For those who had this ability, ingratiation led to higher levels of liking from supervisors, and higher performance ratings.[116]

The Ethics of Behaving Politically

Although there are no clear-cut ways to differentiate ethical from unethical politicking, there are some questions you should consider. For example, what is the utility of engaging in politicking? Sometimes we do it for little good reason. Another question is this: How does the utility of engaging in the political behavior balance out the harm (or potential harm) it will do to others? Finally, does the political activity conform to justice and fairness standards?

Unfortunately, powerful people can become very good at explaining self-serving behaviors in terms of the organization's best interests. They can persuasively argue that unfair actions are fair and just. Those who are powerful, articulate, and persuasive are most vulnerable to ethical lapses because they are more likely to get away with them. When faced with an ethical dilemma regarding organizational politics, try to consider whether playing politics is worth the risk and whether others might be harmed in the process. If you have a strong power base, recognize the ability of power to corrupt. Remember it is a lot easier for people who are in a powerless position to act ethically, if for no other reason than they typically have very little political discretion to exploit.

Mapping Your Political Career

As we have seen, politics are not just for politicians. You can use the concepts presented in this chapter in some very tangible ways we have outlined in your organization. However, they also have another application: You.

One of the most useful ways to think about power and politics is in terms of your own career.[117] What are your ambitions? Who has the power to help you achieve them? What is your relationship to these people? The best way to answer these questions is with a political map, which can help you sketch out your relationships with the people upon whom your career depends. Exhibit 13-6 contains such a political map.[118] Let us walk through it.

Assume your future promotion depends on five people, including Jamie, your immediate supervisor. As you can see in the exhibit, you have a close relationship with Jamie (you would be in real trouble otherwise). You also have a close relationship with Zack in finance. However, with the others you have either a loose relationship (Lane) or none (Jia, Marty). One obvious implication of this map is the need to formulate a plan to gain more influence over, and a closer relationship with, these people. How might you do that?

One of the best ways to influence people is indirectly. What if you played in a tennis league with Mark, Jamie's former coworker who you know remains friends with Jamie? To influence Mark, in many cases, may also be to influence Marty. You can complete a similar analysis for the other four decision makers and their networks.

All of this may seem a bit Machiavellian to you. However, remember that only one person gets the promotion, and your competition may have a map of their own. As we noted in the early part of the chapter, power and politics are a part of organizational life.

SUMMARY

Few employees relish being powerless in their jobs and organizations. People respond differently to the various power bases. Expert and referent power are derived from an

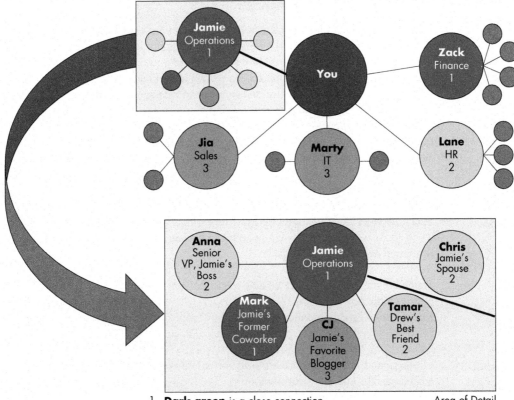

1 - **Dark green** is a close connection.
2 - **Light green** is a loose connection.
3 - **Medium green** is no connection at all.

Area of Detail

EXHIBIT 13-6

Drawing Your Political Map

Source: Based on D. Clark, "A Campaign Strategy for Your Career," *Harvard Business Review,* November 2012, 131–134.

individual's personal qualities. In contrast, coercion, reward, and legitimate power are essentially organizationally granted. Competence especially appears to offer wide appeal, and its use as a power base results in high performance by group members.

An effective manager accepts the political nature of organizations. Some people are more politically astute than others, meaning they are aware of the underlying politics and can manage impressions. Those who are good at playing politics can be expected to get higher performance evaluations and, hence, larger salary increases and more promotions than the politically naïve or inept. The politically astute are also likely to exhibit higher job satisfaction and be better able to neutralize job stressors. However, politics may be a double-edged sword, leading to both positive and negative outcomes.

A political map can provide a good schematic from which to identify positive politicking opportunities. Finally, power and politics present significant ethical considerations. To accept the reality of these dimensions in organizations is to accept the responsibility for awareness and ethical behavior.

IMPLICATIONS FOR MANAGERS

- When attempting to build and use power to further your teams' or organizations' interests (or, perhaps, your own), recognize that certain power bases tend to be more effective than others. You should be aware of these power bases and use them when the situation calls for it (but stay within ethical guidelines).
- In the same way, various tactics and impression management strategies are effective at influencing others to comply with your requests. In general, note that you may have more success with rational persuasion, inspirational appeal, and consultation, and the least success with pressure and self-promotion.
- Be aware that power arises from dependence. If you feel a lack of control because you depend too much on another for resources (e.g., a supplier who charges too much), try to maximize your alternatives and seek ways to find a substitution for these resources.
- Social network positions affect power: to promote change and exercise influence, try to serve as a bridge between people and broker connections, resources, and information across these boundaries.
- Recognize that power affects people in several ways. By being aware of power-granted blind spots, you may be able to circumvent some of the negative effects of power on the powerholder.
- Make sure to establish policy regarding how your organization handles sexual harassment, investigate and report complaints, and appropriately discipline offenders.
- By assessing behavior in a political framework, you can better predict the actions of others and use that information to formulate political strategies that will gain advantages for you and your work unit.

14
Conflict and Negotiation

After studying this chapter, you should be able to:

14.1 Describe the three types of conflict and the three loci of conflict.

14.2 Outline the conflict process.

14.3 Contrast distributive and integrative bargaining.

14.4 Apply the five steps of the negotiation process.

14.5 Show how individual differences influence negotiations.

14.6 Describe the social factors that influence negotiations.

14.7 Assess the roles and functions of third-party negotiations.

A DEFINITION OF CONFLICT

Tesla, an American automotive and energy company, along with their founder and CEO, Elon Musk, have experienced conflict on several fronts. From issues with Musk's candid Twitter posts, lawsuits, and feuds with the Securities and Exchange Commission, as well as musicians Azealia Banks and Claire Boucher (a.k.a. Grimes), Tesla, along with the board of directors and employees, have witnessed their fair share of interorganizational conflict.[1]

What is interesting, however, is where Tesla has *not* experienced conflict: within the board of directors.[2] Many have accused the board of being "asleep at the wheel," not willing to cause conflict where some might be needed. This might be due to loyalty to Musk, lack of time and resources (most board members are part-time), and because all the corporate information they receive that affects their decision making is filtered through Musk. This has even led some to suggest using artificial intelligence in corporate board decision making, which is not limited by lack of time and resources and is perhaps more impartial.[3] The case of Tesla illustrates that conflict can arise in a number of different organizational arenas, and that even the *absence* of conflict altogether can be a signal that perhaps important issues are not being discussed or that controversial ideas are not being challenged.

There has been no shortage of definitions of *conflict*,[4] but common to most is the idea that conflict is a perception of differences or opposition. We define **conflict** broadly as a process that begins when one party perceives another party has negatively affected or is about to negatively affect something the first party cares about. People experience a

Conflict
A process that begins when one party perceives that another party has negatively affected, or is about to negatively affect, something that the first party cares about.

wide range of conflicts in organizations over an incompatibility of goals, differences in interpretations of facts, disagreements over behavioral expectations, and the like.

Functional conflict
Conflict that supports the goals of the group and improves its performance.

Contemporary perspectives classify conflict based on its effects.[5] **Functional conflict** supports the goals of the group, improves its performance, and, as such, is a constructive form of conflict. For example, a debate among members of a corporate board (see opening example) about the most efficient way to improve production can be functional if unique points of view are discussed and compared openly. Conflict that hinders group performance is destructive or **dysfunctional conflict**. A highly personal struggle for control that distracts from the task at hand in a team is dysfunctional. Exhibit 14-1 provides an overview depicting the effect of levels of conflict.

Dysfunctional conflict
Conflict that hinders group performance.

Types of Conflict

One means of understanding conflict is to identify the *type* of disagreement, or what the conflict is about. Is it a disagreement about goals? Is it about people who just rub one another the wrong way? Or is it about the best way to get things done? Although

EXHIBIT 14-1
Conflict and Unit Performance

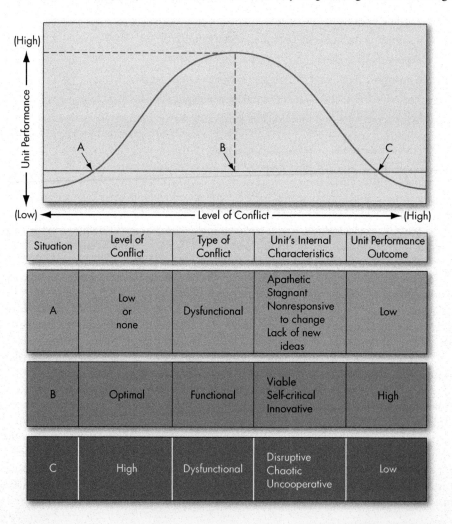

Situation	Level of Conflict	Type of Conflict	Unit's Internal Characteristics	Unit Performance Outcome
A	Low or none	Dysfunctional	Apathetic Stagnant Nonresponsive to change Lack of new ideas	Low
B	Optimal	Functional	Viable Self-critical Innovative	High
C	High	Dysfunctional	Disruptive Chaotic Uncooperative	Low

each conflict is unique, researchers have classified conflicts into three categories: relationship, task, or process.[6] **Relationship conflict** focuses on interpersonal relationships. **Task conflict** relates to the content and goals of the work. **Process conflict** is about how the work gets done.

RELATIONSHIP CONFLICT   Studies demonstrate that relationship conflicts, at least in work settings, are almost always dysfunctional.[7] Why? The friction and interpersonal hostilities inherent in relationship conflict increases interpersonal clashes and decreases mutual understanding. Of the three types, relationship conflict also appears to be the most psychologically exhausting to individuals. It tends to derail team processes by reducing the extent to which people are open toward working with one another to work collaboratively toward solutions, while increasing the extent to which they avoid and compete with one another.[8] As a result, relationship conflict strongly depletes trust, cohesion (see the chapter on understanding work teams), satisfaction, job attitudes, and positive affect (see the chapter on emotions and moods) and can even lead to a reduction in organizational citizenship behaviors (OCBs) paired with an increase in deviant behavior.[9] However, relationship conflict itself is only weakly related to how well the team performs—so it appears its most nefarious affects are in how it affects people psychologically, and how it reduces OCBs and increases deviance.[10]

TASK CONFLICT   While scholars agree that relationship conflict is dysfunctional, there is considerably less agreement about whether task conflict is functional. Early research suggested that task conflict within groups correlated to *higher* group performance, but a review of ninety-five studies found that task conflict was essentially unrelated to group performance (although it did appear to be correlated to *lower* group performance in nonmanagement positions, and *higher* group performance in decision-making teams).[11] Despite these findings, research suggests that task conflict slightly reduces the extent to which people collaborate, and moderately increases the degree to which they compete with one another.[12] This, in turn, has a strong negative effect on their trust and job attitudes and, like relationship conflict, leads to a reduction in OCBs paired with an increase in deviant behavior.[13]

PROCESS CONFLICT   Process conflicts are often about delegation and roles. Conflicts over delegation often revolve around the perception that some members are shirking, and conflicts over roles can leave some group members feeling marginalized. Thus, process conflicts often become highly personalized and quickly devolve into relationship conflicts. It is also true, of course, that arguing about how to do something takes time away from doing it. Although relatively less research has been conducted on process conflict, research suggests that it has a strong negative effect on team member trust and attitudes, as well as a weak effect on team performance (like that of relationship conflict).[14]

COMPLICATING CONFLICT   It also appears to matter whether other types of conflict occur at the same time. If task and relationship conflict occur together, relationship conflict is more likely to have a negative effect, whereas if task conflict occurs by itself, it is more likely to have a positive effect.[15] How often does this occur in practice? Research from one entrepreneurial venture suggests that although the two are initially co-occurring, over time, they tend to stabilize after some time.[16] This suggests that one might expect

Relationship conflict
Conflict based on interpersonal relationships.

Task conflict
Conflict over content and goals of the work.

Process conflict
Conflict over how work gets done.

relationship and task conflict to co-occur at the beginning of the relationship. In support, research in the Netherlands indicates that even the mere perception of relationship conflict during task conflict is enough to cause people to hold onto their initial preferences regarding the task conflict.[17]

Other scholars have argued that the perception of conflict is important. If task conflict is perceived as being very low, people are not really engaged or addressing the important issues; if task conflict is too high, infighting will quickly degenerate into relationship conflict. Moderate levels of task conflict may thus be optimal.[18] Furthermore, *who* perceives conflict also matters. Incompatibilities between work styles or dominating personalities with little space for compromise can lead to "too many cooks in the kitchen," resulting in relationship conflict and even abusive supervision.[19] Research suggests that conflict is more likely to have a positive effect on performance when a few members perceive strong task disagreement, whereas most others on the team perceive weak task disagreement. This is because those in the minority are much more likely to present their disagreements in a careful, cooperative, open manner.[20]

Loci of Conflict

Dyadic conflict
Conflict that occurs between two people.

Intergroup conflict
Conflict between different groups or teams.

Intragroup conflict
Conflict that occurs within a group or team.

Another way to understand conflict is to consider its *locus*, or the framework within which conflict occurs. Here, too, there are three basic types. **Dyadic conflict** is conflict between two people. **Intragroup conflict** occurs *within* a group or team. **Intergroup conflict** is conflict *between* groups or teams.[21]

Nearly all the research on relationship, task, and process conflicts considers intragroup conflict (within the group). However, it does not necessarily tell us all we need to know about the context and outcomes of conflict. For example, research has found that for intragroup task conflict to positively influence performance within the team, it is important that the team has a supportive climate in which mistakes are not penalized and every team member "[has] the other's back."[22] But is this concept applicable to the effects of intergroup conflict? Think about, say, NFL football. For a team to adapt and improve, perhaps a certain amount of intragroup conflict (but not too much) is good for team performance, especially when the team members support one another. But would we care whether members from one team conflicted with members from another team? Probably not. Still, it must be managed. Intense intergroup conflict can be quite stressful to group members and might well affect the way they interact.

It may surprise you that a group member's network position (see the chapter on power and politics) is important during intergroup conflicts. One study that focused on intergroup conflict found an interplay between an individual's position within a group and the way that individual managed conflict between groups. Group members who were relatively peripheral in their own group were better at resolving conflicts between their group and another one. But this happened only when those peripheral members were still accountable to their groups.[23] Thus, being at the core of your work group does not necessarily make you the best person to manage conflict with other groups.

Altogether, understanding functional and dysfunctional conflict requires not only that we identify the type of conflict; we also need to know where it occurs. It is possible that while the concepts of relationship, task, and process conflicts are useful in understanding intragroup or even dyadic conflict, they are less useful in explaining the effects of intergroup conflict.

THE CONFLICT PROCESS

The conflict process has five stages: potential opposition or incompatibility, cognition and personalization, intentions, behavior, and outcomes (see Exhibit 14-2).[24]

Stage I: Potential Opposition or Incompatibility

The first stage of conflict is the appearance of conditions—causes or sources—that create opportunities for it to arise.[25] These conditions *need not* lead directly to conflict, but one of them is necessary if it is to surface. Apart from the obvious, which would be behaviors directly *intended* to provoke conflict,[26] we group the conditions into three general categories: communication, structure, and personal variables.

COMMUNICATION Communication can be a source of conflict in group interactions and dyadic exchanges.[27] There are opposing forces that arise from semantic difficulties, misunderstandings, and "noise" in the communication channel (see the chapter on communication). These factors, along with jargon and insufficient information, can be barriers to communication and potential antecedent conditions to conflict. Even the way communication is framed can have an effect; for example, research suggests that framing task conflict as a debate increases receptivity to others' opinions.[28] The potential for conflict has also been found to increase with too little or *too much* communication. Communication is functional up to a point, after which it is possible to overcommunicate, increasing the potential for conflict.

STRUCTURE The term *structure* in this context includes variables such as size of group, degree of specialization in tasks assigned to group members, role clarity, member–goal compatibility, leadership styles, reward systems, and degree of dependence between groups or group members. The larger the group and the more specialized its activities, the greater the likelihood of intragroup conflict. Tenure and conflict are inversely related, meaning that the longer a person stays with an organization, the less likely intragroup conflict becomes.[29] Therefore, the potential for intragroup conflict is greatest when group members are newer to the organization and when turnover is high. However, as far as intergroup conflict is concerned, it can self-perpetuate, actually imbuing *meaning*

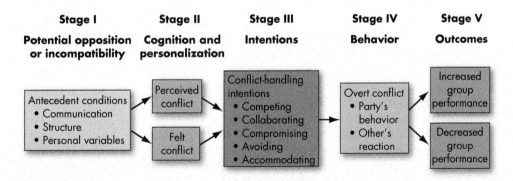

Stage I	Stage II	Stage III	Stage IV	Stage V
Potential opposition or incompatibility	Cognition and personalization	Intentions	Behavior	Outcomes

EXHIBIT 14-2
The Conflict Process

and *identity* to the groups experiencing conflict.[30] Anyone familiar with the Big Ten one-hundred-plus-year rivalry between The Ohio State University and the University of Michigan can attest to this.[31]

PERSONAL VARIABLES   Our last category of potential sources of conflict is personal variables, which include personality, emotions, and values. People high in the personality traits of disagreeableness, neuroticism, or self-monitoring (see the chapter on personality and values) are prone to spar with other people more often—and to react poorly when conflicts occur.[32] Emotions can cause conflict even when they are not directed at others. For example, an employee who shows up to work irate from the hectic morning commute may carry that anger into the workday, which can result in a tension-filled meeting.[33] Incompatibilities in emotions can also lead to conflict—for example, if your supervisor is more optimistic than you about your work, you are more likely (than if you had similar optimistic-pessimistic outlooks) to experience more conflict, become less engaged, and perform poorly.[34] Furthermore, differences in preferences and values can generate increased levels of conflict. For example, a study in Korea found that when group members did not agree about their desired achievement levels, there was more task conflict; when group members did not agree about their desired interpersonal closeness levels, there was more relationship conflict; and when group members did not have similar desires for power, there was more conflict over status.[35] Furthermore, people differ with regard to their beliefs about conflict, and which strategies of managing conflict are the best or worst, and these beliefs shape the types of conflict they perceive as well as how they react.[36]

Stage II: Cognition and Personalization

If the conditions cited in Stage I negatively affect something one party cares about, then the potential for opposition or incompatibility becomes actualized in the second stage.

As we noted in our definition of conflict, one or more of the parties must be aware that antecedent conditions exist. However, just because a disagreement is a **perceived conflict** does not mean it is personalized. It is at the **felt conflict** level, when individuals become emotionally involved, that they experience anxiety, tension, frustration, or hostility. By making sense of the preceding events, employees perceive conflict (e.g., label it as an offense) and then recognize that the other party violated norms or did something wrong.[37] Following these processes of *naming* and *blaming*, employees naturally *feel* the negative emotions surrounding conflict.

Perceived conflict Awareness by one or more parties of the existence of conditions that create opportunities for conflict to arise.

Felt conflict Emotional involvement in a conflict that creates anxiety, tension, frustration, or hostility.

Stage II is important because it is where conflict issues tend to be defined, where the parties decide what the conflict is about.[38] For example, the employee who was irate from the traffic jam may cause others around the office to perceive that something is up—but this conflict is not "felt" until a sour interaction with this employee (e.g., "it's not fair the boss took the long commute out on me with extra work!"). Emotions play a major role in shaping perceptions.[39] Negative emotions lead us to oversimplify issues, lose trust, and put negative interpretations on the other party's behavior.[40] When you perceive conflict, sometimes you may turn to a confidant within your group to vent or talk about what you are feeling. Paradoxically, if this person is responsive and reaffirming, your confidant may validate your perspective, which might undermine the resolution of conflict as a result.[41] In contrast, positive feelings increase our tendency to see potential relationships among elements of a problem, take a broader view of the situation, and develop innovative solutions.[42] Negative emotions are natural and perhaps inevitable—before conflict escalates, taking time to reflect and reappraise how you are feeling may help you approach the conflict more constructively (but don't ruminate!).[43] Ultimately, a state of mindfulness (see the chapter on organizational change and stress management) might be a good emotional state to aspire toward, given that it facilitates constructive conflict management.[44]

Stage III: Intentions

Intentions intervene between people's perceptions and emotions and their overt behavior. They are decisions to act in a particular way.[45] Although we may decide to act in a certain way, our intentions do not always line up with what we actually do. Furthermore, intentions are not always fixed. During a conflict, intentions might change if a party is able to see the other's point of view or respond emotionally to the other's behavior.

      Using two dimensions—*assertiveness* (the degree to which one party attempts to satisfy their own concerns) and *cooperativeness* (the degree to which one party attempts to satisfy the other party's concerns)—we can identify five conflict-handling intentions: *competing* (assertive and uncooperative), *collaborating* (assertive and cooperative), *avoiding* (unassertive and uncooperative), *accommodating* (unassertive and cooperative), and *compromising* (mid-range on both assertiveness and cooperativeness).[46]

COMPETING When one person seeks to satisfy their own interests regardless of the impact on the other parties in the conflict, that person is **competing**.[47] We are more apt to compete when resources are scarce, when we have competition-prone personalities, when we are close to satisfying our own interests (e.g., the "finish line is near"), or when the culture or climate supports competition.[48]

COLLABORATING When parties in conflict each desire to fully satisfy the concerns of all parties, there is cooperation and a search for a mutually beneficial outcome. In **collaborating**, parties intend to solve a problem by clarifying differences rather than by accommodating various points of view.[49] If you attempt to find a win–win solution that allows both parties' goals to be completely achieved, that is collaborating. Collaboration is more likely if the party is seen as competent, rational, and open to collaborating.[50]

AVOIDING A person may recognize a conflict exists and want to withdraw from or suppress it. Examples of **avoiding** include trying to ignore a conflict and keeping away from others with whom you disagree.

ACCOMMODATING A party who seeks to appease a negotiation partner may be willing to place the negotiation partner's interests above their own, sacrificing to maintain the relationship. We refer to this intention as **accommodating**. Supporting someone else's opinion despite your reservations about it, for example, is accommodating.

COMPROMISING In **compromising**, there is no winner or loser. Rather, there is a willingness to ration the object of the conflict and accept a solution with incomplete satisfaction of both parties' concerns. The distinguishing characteristic of compromising, therefore, is that each party intends to give up something.

Intentions
Decisions to act in a particular way.

Competing
A desire to satisfy one's interests, regardless of the impact on the other party to the conflict.

Collaborating
A situation in which the parties to a conflict each desires to satisfy fully the concerns of all parties.

Avoiding
The desire to withdraw from or suppress a conflict.

Accommodating
The willingness of one party in a conflict to place the negotiation partner's interests above his or her own.

Compromising
A situation in which each party to a conflict is willing to give up something.

A review that examined the effects of the sets of behaviors across multiple studies found that collaborating was associated with superior group performance and team attitudes, whereas avoiding and competing strategies were associated with significantly worse group performance.[51] This further demonstrates that it is not just the existence of conflict or even the type of conflict that creates problems, but rather the ways people respond to conflict and manage the process once conflicts arise.

Stage IV: Behavior

Stage IV is a dynamic process of interaction. For example, you make a demand on me, I respond by arguing with you, you shout at me, I yell at you back, and so on. Exhibit 14-3 provides a way of visualizing conflict behavior. All conflicts exist somewhere along this continuum. At the lower end are conflicts characterized by subtle, indirect, and highly controlled forms of tension, such as a student challenging a point the instructor has made. Conflict intensities escalate as they move upward along the continuum until they become highly destructive. Strikes, riots, and wars clearly fall in this upper range. Conflicts that reach the upper range of the continuum are almost always dysfunctional. Functional conflicts are typically confined to the lower range of the continuum.

Stage V: Outcomes

The action–reaction interplay between conflicting parties creates consequences. As our model demonstrates (see Exhibit 14-1), these outcomes may be functional if the conflict improves the group's performance, or dysfunctional if it hinders performance. Realistically, however, many researchers suggest that although workplace conflict can be beneficial, this usually happens under special circumstances, and most of the time the dysfunctional outcomes outweigh the functional outcomes in severity.[52] This suggests that managers will likely spend most of their time reducing dysfunctional conflict, rather than stimulating functional conflict.

EXHIBIT 14-3
Dynamic Escalation of Conflict

Sources: Based on S. P. Robbins, *Managing Organizational Conflict: A Nontraditional Approach* (Upper Saddle River, NJ: Prentice Hall, 1974): 93–97; and F. Glasi, "The Process of Conflict Escalation and the Roles of Third Parties," in G. B. J. Bomers and R. Peterson (eds.), *Conflict Management and Industrial Relations* (Boston: Kluwer-Nijhoff, 1982): 119–40.

FUNCTIONAL OUTCOMES Conflict is constructive when it improves the quality of decisions, stimulates creativity and innovation, encourages interest and curiosity among group members, provides the medium for problems to be aired and tensions released, and fosters self-evaluation and change. Indeed, research on organizations in Taiwan suggests that, over time, the right amount of task conflict (not relational conflict) can cause teams to improve their relations, the quality of social interaction, and meaningful communication.[53] Mild conflicts also may generate energizing emotions, so members of groups become more active and engaged in their work.[54] However, groups that are extremely polarized do not manage their underlying disagreements effectively and tend to accept suboptimal solutions, or they avoid making decisions altogether rather than work out the conflict.[55] As mentioned earlier in this chapter, conflict severity plays a large role.

Conflict is an antidote for groupthink (see the chapter on foundations of group behavior). Conflict does not allow the group to passively rubber-stamp decisions that may be based on weak assumptions, inadequate consideration of relevant alternatives, or other weaknesses. Conflict challenges the status quo and furthers the creation of new ideas, promotes reassessment of group goals and activities, and increases the probability that the group will respond to change.

DYSFUNCTIONAL OUTCOMES The destructive consequences of conflict on the performance of a group or an organization are generally well known. A substantial body of research documents how dysfunctional conflicts can reduce group effectiveness.[56] Among the undesirable consequences are poor communication, reductions in group cohesiveness, and subordination of group goals to the primacy of infighting among members. All forms of conflict—even the functional varieties—appear to reduce group member satisfaction and trust.[57] At the extreme, conflict can bring group functioning to a halt and threaten the group's survival.

MANAGING CONFLICT If a conflict is dysfunctional, what can the parties do to de-escalate it? Or, conversely, what options exist if conflict is too low to be functional and needs to be increased? In these situations, people can use resolution and stimulation techniques to achieve the desired level of conflict, a process known as **conflict management**.[58] In anticipating and managing conflict, organizations can target three specific domains: *strategy* (e.g., designing conflict management activities with an understanding of their effect on the organization system, garnering managerial support for and application of conflict management strategies), *function* (e.g., encouraging the systemic adoption of conflict management practices, understanding employees' needs, job design to reduce conflict), and *worker* (e.g., improving employee perceptions of conflict, fostering ties and cohesion between people, adaptively addressing conflict as it emerges).[59] For example, if the conflict is expected to be perpetual and ongoing, a strategic conflict management strategy might not target resolving the conflict completely but rather how people can adaptively address the conflict over time.[60]

Under ideal conditions, a person's intentions should translate into comparable behaviors. However, conditions are not always ideal, and the findings from research on conflict management have been inconsistent.[61] First, strategies appropriate for resolving one form of conflict may backfire and cause more conflict in another area.[62] For example, adopting a shared identity and improving relationship quality may unintentionally backfire by causing blurred distinctions between people's roles, stimulating task conflict.

Conflict management
The use of resolution and stimulation techniques to achieve the desired level of conflict.

Second, strategies appropriate for managing one form of conflict may spill over into another domain.[63] For example, clearly outlining differences in what people do in the presence of task conflict can spill over to stimulate relational conflict. This is where strategic conflict management (as mentioned earlier) may come into play.

One of the keys to minimizing counterproductive conflicts is recognizing when there really is a disagreement. Perhaps the most successful conflict management recognizes different views and attempts to resolve them by encouraging open, frank discussions focused on views rather than issues, listening and understanding opposing views, and then integrating them constructively.[64] Another approach is to have opposing groups pick parts of the solution that are most important to them and then focus on how each side can get its top needs satisfied. Neither side may get exactly what it wants, but each side will achieve the most important parts of its agenda.[65] Third, groups that resolve conflicts successfully discuss differences of opinion openly and are prepared to manage conflict when it arises.[66] An open discussion makes it much easier to develop a shared perception of the problems at hand; it also allows groups to work toward a mutually acceptable solution. Fourth, managers need to emphasize shared interests in resolving conflicts, so groups that disagree with one another do not become too entrenched in their points of view and start to take the conflicts personally. Groups with cooperative conflict styles and a strong underlying identification with the overall group goals are more effective than groups with a competitive style.[67]

CULTURAL INFLUENCES Differences across countries in conflict resolution strategies may be based on collectivist versus individualist (see the chapter on personality and values) tendencies and motives. One study suggests that top management teams in Chinese high-technology firms prefer collaboration even more than compromising and avoiding. Collectivists may also be more interested in demonstrations of concern and working through third parties to resolve disputes, whereas individualists will be more likely to confront differences of opinion directly and openly.

Cross-cultural negotiations can lead to trust issues.[68] One study of Indian and U.S. negotiators found that respondents reported having less trust in their cross-culture negotiation counterparts. The lower level of trust was associated with less discovery of common interests between parties, which occurred because cross-culture negotiators were less willing to disclose and solicit information. Another study found that both U.S. and Chinese negotiators tended to have an ingroup bias, which led them to favor negotiating partners from their own cultures. For Chinese negotiators, this was particularly true when accountability requirements were high.

Having considered conflict—its nature, causes, and consequences—we now turn to negotiation, which often resolves conflict.

NEGOTIATION

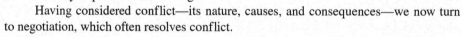

Negotiation
A process in which two or more parties exchange goods or services and attempt to agree on the exchange rate for them.

Negotiation permeates the interactions of almost everyone in groups and organizations. There is the obvious: Labor bargains with management. There is the not-so-obvious: Managers negotiate with employees, peers, and bosses; salespeople negotiate with customers; purchasing agents negotiate with suppliers. Then there is the subtle: An employee agrees to cover for a colleague for a few minutes in exchange for a future favor. Clearly, negotiation skills are important in today's workplace.

We can define **negotiation** as a process that occurs when two or more parties decide how to allocate scarce resources.[69] Although we commonly think of the outcomes of negotiation in one-shot transactional terms, like negotiating over one's salary before accepting a job offer, every negotiation in organizations also affects the relationship between negotiators and the way negotiators feel about themselves.[70] Depending on how much the parties are going to interact with one another, sometimes maintaining the social relationship and behaving ethically will be just as important as achieving an immediate outcome of bargaining. (Note that we use the terms *negotiation* and *bargaining* interchangeably.)

Bargaining Strategies

There are two general approaches to negotiation—*distributive bargaining* and *integrative bargaining*.[71] As Exhibit 14-4 shows, they differ in their goals and motivation, focus, interests, information sharing, and duration of relationship. Let us define each and illustrate the differences.

DISTRIBUTIVE BARGAINING   Your team was not aware of a change in policy until it was already happening.[72] This policy meant that your team would receive 20 percent fewer resources next fiscal year. There is nothing you can do to stop the policy from being implemented, so you negotiate with the executive team regarding these provisions. Both parties believe that any gain is made at the others' expense, and when you try to negotiate halving this reduction in resources, the executives counter with an offer of 15 percent. The negotiating strategy you are engaging in is called **distributive bargaining**. Its identifying feature is that it operates under zero-sum conditions—that is, any gain I make is at your expense, and vice versa (see the chapter on power and politics). The essence of distributive bargaining is negotiating who gets what share of a fixed pie. By **fixed pie**, we mean a set amount of goods or services to be divvied up. When the pie is fixed, or the parties believe it is, they tend to bargain distributively.

The essence of distributive bargaining is depicted in Exhibit 14-5. Parties A and B represent two negotiators. Each has a *target point* that defines what he or she would like to achieve. Each also has a *resistance point,* which marks the lowest acceptable outcome—the point beyond which the party would break off negotiations rather than accept a less favorable settlement. The area between these two points makes up each party's *aspiration range*. If there is some overlap between A's and B's aspiration ranges, there exists a settlement range in which each one's aspirations can be met.

Distributive bargaining
Negotiation that seeks to divide up a fixed amount of resources; a win–lose situation.

Fixed pie
The belief that there is only a set amount of goods or services to be divvied up between the parties.

Bargaining Characteristic	Distributive Bargaining	Integrative Bargaining
Goal	Get as much of the pie as possible	Expand the pie so that both parties are satisfied
Motivation	Win–lose	Win–win
Focus	Positions ("I can't go beyond this point on this issue.")	Interests ("Can you explain why this issue is so important to you?")
Interests	Opposed	Congruent
Information sharing	Low (Sharing information will only allow other party to take advantage)	High (Sharing information will allow each party to find ways to satisfy interests of each party)
Duration of relationship	Short term	Long term

EXHIBIT 14-4
Distributive Versus Integrative Bargaining

EXHIBIT 14-5
Staking Out the
Bargaining Zone

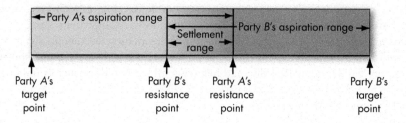

When you are engaged in distributive bargaining, you may want to consider making the first offer. Making the first offer can put you at an advantage because of the anchoring bias, mentioned in the chapter on perception and individual decision making. People tend to fixate on initial information. Once that anchoring point has been set, they fail to adequately adjust it based on subsequent information. A savvy negotiator sets an anchor with the initial offer, and scores of negotiation studies show that such anchors greatly favor the person who sets them.[73] However, if you have a negotiation partner who is motivated to maximize their own return, a disadvantage of making the first offer is that you are conveying information about your priorities that the individual can use against you.[74] Furthermore, framing matters: if you frame the first proposal as a *request* (i.e., I request your B for my A) instead of an *offer* (i.e., I offer my A for your B), it can be detrimental to your negotiation success by highlighting a "loss" rather than a "gain" for the negotiation partner.[75]

In distributive bargaining, should you engage in *hardline* strategies, in which you minimize your own concessions and make extreme offers, or should you engage in *softline* strategies, where you elicit concessions from the other party through your own concessions? One review suggests that it depends on the outcome you want: If it is important to preserve the relationship, softline strategies might be better.[76] If you want a higher economic return, than hardline strategies may be better. When is each strategy most effective? The hardline approach tends to be most effective if you are physically interacting with the other negotiator, when the other party is male, when both are motivated to maximize individual outcomes, and when they know what they can and cannot bargain (although, people's perception of the bargaining zone itself is often distorted[77]).[78] The softline approach is more effective only when you are able to adequately give concessions to the other party. Furthermore, some research suggests that *phantom anchors* (e.g., "I was going to ask for $10,000, but since you are making that concession, I will ask for $8,000 instead) can be an effective softline strategy that communicates your concession (even if the concession is overstated).[79] Another soft tactic that builds upon the first offer effect mentioned earlier is the use of *multiple equivalent simultaneous offers* (MESOs). MESOs involve presenting multiple, equivalent first offers to the negotiating partner to choose from. This may lead the negotiation partner to perceive the offeror as flexible and sincerely trying to reach an agreement as well as increase the likelihood of the negotiation partner finding an option they like right away.[80]

INTEGRATIVE BARGAINING During her first pregnancy, one woman who worked for the federal government knew that she wanted to be able to be with her child but did not think she could do so while working full time.[81] She did her research on the policies and procedures for part-time work to see how she might be able to make it happen. She then went to her supervisor and discussed possibilities for an alternative work arrangement and was successfully able to negotiate time with her child a couple of times each week. This employee's attitude shows the promise of **integrative bargaining**. In contrast to distributive bargaining, integrative bargaining assumes that one or more of the possible settlements can create a win–win solution rather than an all-or-nothing, win–lose situation. Of course, both parties must be engaged for integrative bargaining to work.

Integrative bargaining Negotiation that seeks one or more settlements that can create a win–win solution.

CHOOSING BARGAINING METHODS In terms of intraorganizational behavior, integrative bargaining is preferable to distributive bargaining because the former builds long-term relationships.[82] Integrative bargaining bonds negotiators and allows them to leave the bargaining table feeling they have achieved a victory. Distributive bargaining, however, leaves one party a loser. It tends to build animosity and deepen divisions when people must work together on an ongoing basis. Research shows that over repeated bargaining episodes, a losing party who feels positively about the negotiation outcome is much more likely to bargain cooperatively in subsequent negotiations.

Why, then, do not we see more integrative bargaining in organizations? The answer lies in the conditions necessary for it to succeed. Evidence from a study of nearly 200,000 people found that the financially vulnerable are more likely to construe the negotiation in zero-sum terms, curtailing their ability to come to integrative solutions.[83] Furthermore, negotiating parties who are open with information and candid about concerns, are sensitive to the other's needs and trust, and maintain flexibility tend to foster integrative bargaining. Although more traditional organizations may not foster these conditions, organizations with psychologically safe, open environments with positive cultures and climates and negotiating partners with integrative mindsets may perhaps do so.

THE NEGOTIATION PROCESS

Exhibit 14-6 provides a simplified model of the negotiation process. It views negotiation as comprised of five steps: (1) preparation and planning, (2) definition of ground rules, (3) clarification and justification, (4) bargaining and problem solving, and (5) closure and implementation.[84]

EXHIBIT 14-6
The Negotiation Process

PREPARATION AND PLANNING This may be the most important part of the process. Before you start negotiating, do your homework. What is the nature of the conflict? What is the history leading up to this negotiation? Who is involved and what are their perceptions of the conflict? Then consider your goals, in writing, with a range of outcomes from "most helpful" to "minimally acceptable." If you are a supply manager at Dell, for instance, and your goal is to get a significant cost reduction from your keyboard supplier, make sure this goal stays paramount in discussions and does not get overshadowed by other issues. Next, assess what you think are the other party's goals. What intangible or hidden interests may be important to them? On what might they be willing to settle? Think carefully about what the other side might be willing to give up. People who underestimate their negotiating partner's willingness to give on key issues before the negotiation even starts end up with lower outcomes.[85]

BATNA
The best alternative to a negotiated agreement; the least the individual should accept.

Once you have gathered your information, develop a strategy. You should determine your and the other side's **b**est **a**lternative **t**o a **n**egotiated **a**greement, or **BATNA**. Your BATNA determines the lowest value acceptable to you for a negotiated agreement. Any offer you receive that is higher than your BATNA is better than an impasse. Conversely, you should not expect success in your negotiation effort unless you are able to make the other side an offer it finds more attractive than its BATNA.

In nearly all cases, the party with superior alternatives will do better in a negotiation, so experts advise negotiators to solidify their BATNA prior to any interaction.[86] Therefore, be equipped to counter arguments with facts and figures that support your position. There is an interesting exception to this general rule—negotiators with absolutely no alternative to a negotiated agreement sometimes "go for broke" since they do not even consider what would happen if the negotiation falls through.[87] Even though this is a safeguard against an inferior agreement, it is not a way to reach the optimal agreement—some suggest that although it is good to have this information ahead of time, you should focus on your mutual dependence (not alternatives) and positively frame the way you think about the negotiation (e.g., a learning experience with hidden potential, not a "frightening minefield").[88] Furthermore, just as phantom anchors are possible, so are *phantom BATNAs*. Setting a BATNA before a negotiation does not guarantee that the BATNA is probable or even possible. Those who hold a phantom BATNA may find themselves in the undesirable position of having to accept or reject a final offer from a negotiation partner, where their chosen BATNA was not possible to begin with.[89]

DEFINITION OF GROUND RULES Once you have done your planning and developed a strategy, you are ready to define with the other party the ground rules and procedures of the negotiation itself. Who will do the negotiating? Where will it take place? What time constraints, if any, will apply? To what issues will negotiation be limited? Will you follow a specific procedure if an impasse is reached? During this phase, the parties will exchange their initial proposals or demands.

CLARIFICATION AND JUSTIFICATION When you have exchanged initial positions, you and the other party will explain, amplify, clarify, bolster, and justify your original demands. This step need not be confrontational. Rather, it is an opportunity for educating each other on the issues, why they are important, and how you arrived at your initial demands. Provide the other party with any documentation that supports your position. It might be useful to think back to what you learned in the previous chapter (the chapter on power and politics) on influence, as framing can be important here. For example, some research suggests that the other party will be less likely to make concessions if you frame your position (and subsequent offers) as a request rather than an offer on your part (see earlier discussion of requests in first offers).[90]

BARGAINING AND PROBLEM SOLVING The essence of the negotiation process is the actual give-and-take in trying to hash out an agreement. This is where both parties need to make concessions. Relationships change as a result of negotiation, so take that into consideration. If you could "win" a negotiation but push the other side into resentment or animosity, it might be wiser to pursue a more compromising style.[91] As an example, of how the tone of a relationship in negotiations matters, people who feel good about the *process* of a job offer negotiation are more satisfied with their jobs and less likely to turn over a year later regardless of their actual *outcomes* from these negotiations.[92]

CLOSURE AND IMPLEMENTATION The final step in the negotiation process is formalizing your agreement and developing procedures necessary for implementing and monitoring it.[93] For major negotiations—from labor–management negotiations to bargaining over lease terms—this requires hammering out the specifics in a formal contract. For other cases, closure of the negotiation process is nothing more formal than a handshake.

INDIVIDUAL DIFFERENCES IN NEGOTIATION EFFECTIVENESS

Are some people better negotiators than others? The answer is complex. Although recent research suggests that the situation or relationship tends to account more for negotiation outcomes, individual differences explain to a great degree how people perceive these outcomes.[94] In other words, if you tend to be low on emotional stability, you will probably view an unsuccessful negotiation as much more catastrophic than it actually was. Research suggests that extraverted, open, and honest negotiators tend to have better experiences than others.[95]

Four factors influence how effectively individuals negotiate: personality, mood/emotions, culture, and gender.

PERSONALITY TRAITS IN NEGOTIATIONS Can you predict a negotiation partner's negotiating tactics if you know something about their personality? Because personality and negotiation outcomes are related but only weakly, the answer is, at best, "sort of."[96] Recent research on marketing managers, lawyers, and construction supervisors suggests that when it comes to negotiation effectiveness, people who are ambitious and likeable tend to fare the best.[97] But most research has focused on the Big Five trait of agreeableness, for obvious reasons—agreeable individuals are cooperative, compliant, kind, and conflict averse. We might think such characteristics make agreeable individuals easy prey in negotiations, especially distributive ones. This prediction may come true, if the agreeable negotiator is bargaining with a partner who is low on honesty or humility. Furthermore, if the agreeable person seeks to preserve relationships at all costs and avoids straining them, than the person may be more likely to fare worse in a distributive negotiation.[98] Overall, agreeableness is weakly related to negotiation outcomes.[99]

Interestingly, what seems to be more important is whether the negotiators have *similar* personalities (even if these traits are perceived by most people as *negative*!); when they do, they tend to reach agreement faster, perceive less conflict, display more positive emotions, and have better impressions of the other negotiation partner.[100] Furthermore, when both parties seek to preserve relationships at all costs (as an element of agreeableness), they tend to fare much better in integrative negotiation.[101]

Self-efficacy (see the chapter on motivation concepts) is one individual-difference variable that consistently seems to relate to negotiation outcomes.[102] This is an intuitive finding—it is not too surprising to hear that those who believe they will be more successful in negotiation situations tend to perform more effectively. It may be that individuals who are more confident stake out stronger claims, are less likely to back down from their positions, and exhibit confidence that intimidates others. Although the exact mechanism is not yet clear, it does seem that negotiators may benefit from trying to get a boost in confidence before going to the bargaining table. However, do not be too confident: If you have a supervisor who will be judging your performance and you are expected to do well, it would be prudent to try to prevent negative outcomes (because you have more to lose).[103]

Finally, some research suggests that emotional intelligence and emotion recognition ability is linked to gains in negotiation performance as well as to perceptions of being more cooperative and likeable.[104] In the next section, we describe how specific emotions and moods affect negotiations.

MOODS/EMOTIONS IN NEGOTIATIONS Do moods and emotions influence negotiation? They do, but the way they work depends on the emotion as well as the context.

A negotiator who shows anger can induce concessions, for instance, because the other negotiator believes no further concessions from the angry party are possible. One factor that governs this outcome, however, is power—you should show anger in negotiations only if you have at least as much power as your counterpart. If you have less, showing anger actually seems to provoke "hardball" reactions from the other side.[105] "Faked" anger, or anger produced from surface acting, is not effective, but showing anger that is genuine (deep acting) is (see the chapter on emotions and moods).[106] However, maybe you should not hold it in either: Suppressing anger hurts performance because it is distracting to the negotiator, but only when the anger is integral to the negotiation.[107] Having a history of showing anger induces more concessions because the other party perceives the negotiator as "tough."[108] Research suggests if you use anger to "win" a negotiation, even though the tactic might be effective, you might *lose* in the long run as the other party is less likely to follow through with the deal and less likely to work with you again.[109] Regardless of strictly positive or negative effects, your anger could lead the negotiating partner to try to seek more information about your preferences and priorities, leading to higher joint gains for both parties.[110] The effects of anger in negotiations varies across cultures. For instance, one study found that when East Asian participants showed anger, it induced more concessions than when the negotiator expressing anger was from the United States or Europe, perhaps because of the stereotype of East Asians as refusing to show anger.[111]

Several other emotions also have effects on negotiation performance. For instance, anxiety may impact negotiation. One study found that individuals who experienced more anxiety about a negotiation used more deceptions in dealing with others.[112] Another study found that anxious negotiators expect lower outcomes, respond to offers more quickly, and exit the bargaining process more quickly, leading them to obtain worse outcomes.[113]

Relatedly, the expression of sadness can elicit more concessions, but only when the other negotiator perceives the expresser as lower in power and anticipates future interactions with this person, and when the relationship is collaborative.[114] This illustrates why it is important in both types of negotiation for parties to display sympathy for their counterparts, when needed, as this appeals to perceptions of rationality and fairness.[115]

Even emotional unpredictability affects outcomes: Researchers have found that negotiators who express positive and negative emotions in an unpredictable way extract more concessions because this behavior makes the other party feel less in control.[116] As one negotiator put it, "Out of the blue, you may have to react to something you have been working on in one way, and then something entirely new is introduced, and you have to veer off and refocus."[117] However, emotional ambivalence tends to be related to more integrative agreements and concession making, as the ambivalent person is perceived as submissive.[118]

CULTURE AND RACE IN NEGOTIATIONS Do people from different cultures negotiate differently? The simple answer is the obvious one: Yes, they do. In general, people negotiate more effectively within cultures than between them. For example, a Colombian is apt to do better negotiating with a Colombian than with a Sri Lankan.

It appears that for successful cross-cultural negotiations, it is especially important that the negotiators be high in openness. This suggests a good strategy is to choose cross-cultural negotiators who are high on openness, and it helps to avoid factors, such as time pressure, that tend to inhibit learning about the other party.[119] Second, because emotions are culturally sensitive, negotiators need to be especially aware of the emotional dynamics in cross-cultural negotiation. For example, individuals from East Asian cultures may feel that using anger to get their way in a negotiation is not a legitimate tactic, so they refuse to cooperate when their negotiation partners become upset.[120]

Some research on negotiations in the United States and Egypt suggest that the same language that leads to integrative agreements in Western cultures can backfire in others.[121] For example, in the U.S., language that emphasizes cognitive, rational, and logical gains and losses tends to promote integrative bargaining. However, in other cultures, such as Egypt, this language can backfire and what is preferable would be language that emphasizes honor, moral integrity, and protecting one's image and strength. Furthermore, some idiosyncratic rituals that differ across cultures can improve the success of integrative bargaining; for example, in Western cultures, a handshake promotes integrative dealmaking because it acts as a signal of cooperative intent.[122]

Although not much research has examined the role of race in negotiations, a recent study has found that black job seekers in America are (1) expected to negotiate less than white job seekers, (2) penalized in negotiations when they do try to negotiate, and (3) penalized more heavily when the negotiator is more racially biased.[123]

GENDER IN NEGOTIATIONS With regard to gender in negotiations, one stereotype is that women are more cooperative and pleasant in negotiations than men and, as a result, obtain worse outcomes. However, decades of research tends to suggest that the influence of gender in negotiations is highly context dependent.[124] For example, women may be more effective negotiators in collectivist cultures with high harmony and low assertiveness norms.[125]

The influence of gender on both negotiation behavior and negotiation outcomes has been examined (although more research is needed on the influence of gender identity and sexual orientation). Compared to men, women tend to behave in a slightly less assertive, less self-interested, and more cooperative manner.[126] However, these differences are reduced when there are restrictions on communication. The research also suggests that women can actually be *more* competitive than men when the other negotiator engages in a "tit-for-tat" strategy.[127] However, when it comes to *initiating* negotiations, women are less likely to initiate than men, especially when the situation is ambiguous and when gender-role reinforcing information is present in the situational context.[128] A study of MBA students at Carnegie-Mellon University found that the male students took the step of negotiating their first salary offer 57 percent of the time, compared to 4 percent for the female students. The net result? A four thousand dollar difference in starting salaries.[129] Although earlier research concluded that there was a slight benefit for men in negotiation outcomes,[130] an updated meta-analysis has found no significant difference between men and women. Although men achieved better outcomes, on average, these differences were reduced when controlling for negotiation experience, knowledge of the zone of bargaining, when negotiating on behalf of others, and when gendered role norms were not activated in the context.[131]

NEGOTIATING IN A SOCIAL CONTEXT

We have mostly been discussing negotiations that occur among parties that meet only once, and in isolation from other individuals. However, in organizations, many negotiations are open-ended and public. When you are trying to figure out who in a work group should do a tedious task, negotiating with your boss to get a chance to travel internationally, or asking for more money for a project; there is a social component to the negotiation. You are probably negotiating with someone you already know and will work with again, and the negotiation and its outcome are likely to be topics people will talk about. To really understand negotiations in practice, then, we must consider the social factors of reputation and relationships.

Reputation

Your reputation is the way other people think and talk about you. When it comes to negotiation, having a reputation for being trustworthy matters. In short, trust in a negotiation process opens the door to many forms of integrative negotiation strategies that benefit both parties.[132] The most effective way to build trust is to behave in an honest way across repeated interactions. Then, others feel more comfortable making open-ended offers with many different outcomes. This helps to achieve win–win outcomes, since both parties can work to achieve what is most important to themselves while still benefiting the other party.

Sometimes we either trust or distrust people based on word of mouth about a person's characteristics. What characteristics help a person develop a trustworthy reputation? Individuals who have a reputation for integrity can also be more effective in negotiations.[133] They are seen as more likely to keep their promises and present information accurately, so others are more willing to accept their promises as part of a bargain. This opens many options for the negotiator that would not be available to someone who is not seen as trustworthy. Finally, individuals who have higher reputations are better liked and have more friends and allies—in other words, they have more social resources, which may give them more understood power in negotiations.

Relationships

There is more to repeated negotiations than just reputation. The social, interpersonal component of relationships with repeated negotiations means that individuals go beyond valuing what is simply good for themselves and instead start to think about what is best for the other party and the relationship as a whole.[134] Repeated negotiations built on a foundation of trust also broaden the range of options, since a favor or concession today can be offered in return for some repayment further down the road.[135] Repeated negotiations also facilitate integrative problem solving. This occurs partly because people begin to see their negotiation partners in a more personal way over time and come to share emotional bonds.[136] Repeated negotiations also make integrative approaches more workable because a sense of trust and reliability has been built up.[137]

THIRD-PARTY NEGOTIATIONS

To this point, we have discussed bargaining in terms of direct negotiations. Occasionally, however, individuals or group representatives reach a stalemate and are unable to resolve their differences through direct negotiations. In such cases, they may turn to a third party to help them find a solution. There are three basic third-party roles: mediator, arbitrator, and conciliator.

A **mediator** is a neutral third party who facilitates a negotiated solution by using reasoning and persuasion, suggesting alternatives, and the like. Mediators are widely used in labor–management negotiations and in civil court disputes. Their overall effectiveness is impressive. For example, the Equal Employment Opportunity Commission (EEOC) reported a settlement rate through mediation of 72.1 percent.[138] But the situation is the key to whether mediation will succeed: The conflicting parties must be motivated to bargain and resolve their conflict. In addition, conflict intensity cannot be too high; mediation is most effective under moderate levels of conflict. Finally, perceptions of the mediator are important; to be effective, the mediator must be perceived as neutral and noncoercive.

Mediator
A neutral third party who facilitates a negotiated solution by using reasoning, persuasion, and suggestions for alternatives.

An **arbitrator** is a third party with the authority to dictate an agreement. Arbitration can be voluntary (requested by the parties) or compulsory (forced on the parties by law or contract). The big plus of arbitration over mediation is that it always results in a settlement. Whether there is a downside depends on how heavy-handed the arbitrator appears. If one party is left feeling overwhelmingly defeated, that party is certain to be dissatisfied and the conflict may resurface later.

Arbitrator
A third party to a negotiation who has the authority to dictate an agreement.

A **conciliator** is a trusted third party who provides an informal communication link between the negotiator and the negotiation partner. Agreeable individuals with a concern for others tend to adopt the role of conciliator, and they tend to be respected and admired by their peers as a result.[139] This role was made famous by Robert Duval in the first *Godfather* film. As Don Corleone's adopted son and a lawyer by training, Duval acted as an intermediary between the Corleones and the other Mafioso families. Comparing conciliation to mediation in terms of effectiveness has proven difficult because the two overlap a great deal. In practice, conciliators typically act as more than mere communication conduits. They also engage in fact finding, interpret messages, and persuade disputants to develop agreements.

Conciliator
A trusted third party who provides an informal communication link between the negotiator and the negotiation partner.

SUMMARY

While many people assume conflict lowers group and organizational performance, this assumption is frequently incorrect. Conflict can be either constructive or destructive to the functioning of a group or unit. Levels of conflict can be either too high or too low to be constructive. Either extreme hinders performance. An optimal level is one that prevents stagnation, stimulates creativity, allows tensions to be released, and initiates the seeds of change without being disruptive or preventing the coordination of activities.

IMPLICATIONS FOR MANAGERS

- Always try to be aware of potential conflict between people, within teams, and between groups. Recognize that relational and process conflict tends to be nefarious, while some task conflict may be beneficial in certain circumstances. You should try to maximize functional conflict and minimize the negative effects of dysfunctional conflict.
- Try to identify ahead of time conditions that can cause conflict. Engage in conflict handling behaviors that are constructive, like the collaborating approach, but realize that conflict management strategies are often tricky as they can cause unintended conflict in other areas. One of the most effective conflict management strategies, however, is open, interest-based discussion.
- When it comes to negotiation, we often believe that distributive bargaining is the only option; try to determine whether there are opportunities for integrative bargaining, as this approach is better for maintaining relationships over time. Also select hardline or softline strategies, depending upon what your goals are and what the situation calls for.
- When you expect negotiations, be sure to follow the steps of preparing, setting ground rules, clarifying and justifying your arguments, bargaining, and implementing. Consider developing a "best alternative to a negotiated agreement," or BATNA, before negotiating (but make sure it is realistic).
- When selecting individuals for negotiating roles or assignments, remember that negotiators do well when they are similar to the person they are negotiating with; as well as reputable, confident, ambitious, and likeable. Also, emotionally intelligent negotiators who can recognize, understand, and express emotions to their advantage tend to do well in negotiations. The negotiator should also be aware of the culture within which they are negotiating.

15

Foundations of Organization Structure

LEARNING OBJECTIVES

After studying this chapter, you should be able to:

15.1 Identify seven elements of an organization's structure.

15.2 Identify the characteristics of the simple structure, bureaucracy, and the matrix structure.

15.3 Identify the characteristics of the virtual structure, the team structure, and the circular structure.

15.4 Describe the effects of downsizing on organizational structures and employees.

15.5 Contrast the reasons for mechanistic and organic structural models.

15.6 Analyze the behavioral implications of different organizational designs.

WHAT IS ORGANIZATIONAL STRUCTURE?

Google is a company that "does organizational structure right."[1] Its structure supports the innovative culture, competitiveness, and growth of the company. Although it might not seem like it at first, structure is very important for different aspects of business.[2] For example, Dr. Timothy Giardino, the human resources (HR) director at Cantata Health and Meta Healthcare IT solutions suggests, "structure follows strategy ... structure controls behavior ... [and] structure supports execution."[3] Structure can also stand in the way of organizations fulfilling their social mission. For example, systematic biases and structural barriers can prevent women and minorities from advancing in their careers.[4] Organizations have a responsibility to consider the need for organizational change and identify barriers that formally (and informally) limit their advancement.

An **organizational structure** defines how job tasks are formally divided, grouped, and coordinated.[5] Seven key elements should be considered when designing an organization's structure: work specialization, departmentalization, chain of command, span of control, centralization and decentralization, formalization, and boundary spanning.[6]

Organizational structure
The way in which job tasks are formally divided, grouped, and coordinated.

EXHIBIT 15-1	The Key Question	The Answer Is Provided by
Key Design Questions and Answers for Designing the Proper Organizational Structure	1. To what degree are activities subdivided into separate jobs?	Work specialization
	2. On what basis will jobs be grouped together?	Departmentalization
	3. To whom do individuals and groups report?	Chain of command
	4. How many individuals can a manager efficiently and effectively direct?	Span of control
	5. Where does decision-making authority lie?	Centralization and decentralization
	6. To what degree will there be rules and regulations to direct employees and managers?	Formalization
	7. Do individuals from different areas need to regularly interact?	Boundary spanning

Exhibit 15-1 presents each element as the answer to an important structural question, and the following sections describe each one.

Work Specialization

Early in the twentieth century, Henry Ford became rich by building automobiles on an assembly line. Every worker was assigned a specific, specialized task such as installing the right front door. By dividing jobs into small standardized tasks that could be performed over and over, Ford was able to produce a car every 10 seconds using employees with relatively limited skills.[7]

Work specialization The degree to which tasks in an organization are subdivided into separate jobs.

Work specialization, or *division of labor,* describes the degree to which activities in any organization are divided into separate jobs, each completed by a separate individual.[8] Overall, specialization is a means of making the most efficient use of employee skills and even successfully improving them through repetition. Amazon's Mechanical Turk program, TopCoder, and others like it have facilitated a new trend in *microspecialization* in which extremely small pieces of programming, data processing, or evaluation tasks are delegated to a global network of individuals by a program manager who then assembles the results.[9]

By the 1960s, it seemed that the good news of specialization could be carried too far. Human diseconomies began to surface in the form of boredom, fatigue, stress, low productivity, poor quality, increased absenteeism, and high turnover, which more than offset the economic advantages (see Exhibit 15-2).[10] Productivity could be increased now by enlarging, rather than narrowing, the scope of job activities. Giving employees a variety of activities to do, allowing them to do a whole and complete job, and putting them into teams with interchangeable skills often achieved significantly higher output with increased employee satisfaction.[11]

Departmentalization The basis by which jobs in an organization are grouped together.

Departmentalization

Once jobs have been divided through work specialization, they must be grouped so common tasks can be coordinated and complexity can be reduced. The basis by which jobs are grouped is called **departmentalization**.[12]

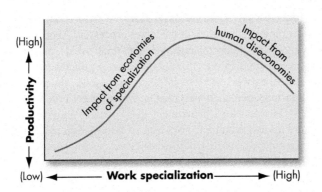

EXHIBIT 15-2
Economies and
Diseconomies
of Work
Specialization

FUNCTIONAL DEPARTMENTALIZATION One of the most popular ways to group activities is by the *functions* performed. A manufacturing manager might organize a plant into engineering, accounting, manufacturing, HR, and supply chain departments. Functional departmentalization allows efficiencies to be gained from putting specialists who focus on similar areas together. Furthermore, the functional structure allows specialists to become experts more easily than if they worked in diversified units. Employees can also be motivated by a clear career path to the top of the organization chart specific to their specialties. The functional structure works well if the organization is focused on one product or service. However, coordination among these diverse units is a problem, and infighting in units and between units can lead to reduced motivation.

PRODUCT OR SERVICE DEPARTMENTALIZATION Jobs can also be departmentalized by the type of *product* or *service* the organization produces.[13] Procter & Gamble places each major product—such as Tide, Pampers, Charmin, and Febreeze—under an executive who has complete global responsibility for it. The major advantage here is increased accountability for performance, but for this type of departmentalization to be effective, it is also important for the department or team to have a broader understanding of the organization outside their own product specialization (e.g., knowing what the other teams and departments work on over time).[14]

GEOGRAPHICAL DEPARTMENTALIZATION When a firm is departmentalized based on *geography* (or territory), each function (for example, sales) may have western, southern, northern, and eastern regions.[15] This form is valuable when an organization's customers are scattered over a large geographic area and have similar needs within their locations. For this reason, Toyota changed its management structure into geographic regions "so that they may develop and deliver ever better products," said CEO Akio Toyoda.[16] When organizations departmentalize by region, these departments and co-located teams form their own identities and practices.[17] These regional teams affect the coordination and performance across locations as well as how information is acquired and shared throughout the organization.[18] Organizations with geographical departmentalization should pay special care toward inter-region communication and knowledge sharing, which can be made easier through virtual communications and knowledge management systems.

PROCESS AND CUSTOMER DEPARTMENTALIZATION *Process* departmentalization involves structuring employee, product, or customer processes.[19] For example, information security firms may have (1) a policy management department that works with HR, legal, and project management functions to set information security policies; (2) a network security department that oversees network security, intrusion prevention, and event management; (3) an identity and access management department to oversee user credentialing, identification, and access; and (4) an operations department that oversees implementing changes and ensuring systems are up and running.[20] As a user of information technology (IT) services, you often start by agreeing to an acceptable use policy, requesting access to the system as well as an online identity, and then interacting with the network, while being notified of security breaches and relevant system maintenance/outages. A final category of departmentalization uses the customer the organization seeks to reach. For example, an assessment organization may departmentalize according to government, industrial, or private consumers.

IMPLICATIONS FOR OB   Organizations do not always stay with the departmentalization they adopted first. Microsoft, for instance, used customer departmentalization for years, organizing around its customer bases: consumers, large corporations, software developers, and small businesses. In June 2013, Microsoft announced a restructuring to functional departmentalization, citing a need to foster continuing innovation. The new departments grouped jobs by traditional functions including engineering, marketing, business development, strategy and research, finance, HR, and legal.[21] Since then, Microsoft has restructured yet again to primarily departmentalize by product type, with smaller groups organized by function and geographic segment (U.S. and international).[22]

The more *divisional* structures (e.g., product, geographical, process, customer departmentalization) have the opposite benefits and disadvantages of the functional structure. They facilitate coordination in units to achieve on-time completion, budget targets, and development and introduction of new products to market, while addressing the specific concerns of each unit. They provide clear responsibility for all activities related to a product, but with duplication of functions and costs. Sometimes this is helpful, say, when the organization has a unit in Spain and another in China, and a marketing strategy is needed for a new product. Marketing experts in both places can incorporate the appropriate cultural perspectives into their region's marketing campaigns. However, having marketing function employees in two different countries may represent an increased cost for the organization, in that they are doing basically the same task in two different places.

As we see throughout this text, whenever changes are deliberately made in organizations to align practices with organizational goals, particularly the goals of strong leaders, a good execution of the changes creates a much higher probability for improvement.

Chain of Command

Chain of command
The unbroken line of authority that extends from the top of the organization to the lowest echelon and clarifies who reports to whom.

While the chain of command was once a basic cornerstone in the design of organizations, it has far less importance today. But managers should still consider its implications, particularly in industries that deal with potential life-or-death situations when people need to quickly rely on decision makers. The **chain of command** is an unbroken line of authority that extends from the top of the organization to the lowest echelon and clarifies who reports to whom. But first, we cannot discuss the chain of command without also discussing *authority* and *unity of command*.

AUTHORITY **Authority** refers to the rights inherent in a position to give orders and expect them to be obeyed.[23] To facilitate coordination, each position is given a place in the chain of command, and each person is given a degree of authority in order to meet their responsibilities. In chains of command in which most of the authority is vested in one person, LMX (see the chapter on leadership) becomes more important, as the leader's "buy-in" becomes more important to getting things done.[24]

Authority
The rights inherent in a position to give orders and to expect the orders to be obeyed.

UNITY OF COMMAND **Unity of command** states that a person should have one and only one superior to whom they are directly responsible. If the unity of command is broken, an employee might have to cope with conflicting demands or priorities from several superiors.[25] Although unity of command is more common than having multiple supervisors, if you do find yourself in the situation where you report to multiple people, be aware of your own workload, conflicting messages, who has the "final say" in disputes, and loyalty expectations.[26] Furthermore, you should try to be proactive about your workload, foster communication between your supervisors, and set up boundaries and norms for effective communication and workflow.

Unity of command
The idea that a subordinate should have only one superior to whom he or she is directly responsible.

IMPLICATIONS FOR OB Times change, and so do the basic tenets of organizational design. A low-level employee today can access information in seconds that was available only to top managers a generation ago, and many employees are empowered to make decisions previously reserved for management.[27] Considering the popularity of self-managed and cross-functional teams (see the chapter on understanding work teams), you can see why authority and unity of command may appear to hold less relevance.

Yet many organizations still find they can be most productive by enforcing the chain of command. Indeed, one survey of more than one thousand managers found that 59 percent agreed with the statement "There is an imaginary line in my company's organizational chart. Strategy is created by people above this line, while strategy is executed by people below the line." However, this same survey found that lower-level employees' buy-in (agreement and active support) to the organization's overall, big picture strategy was inhibited by their reliance on the hierarchy for decision making.[28] Maybe instead of viewing the chain of command as a line, it should be seen more as a pyramid? Indeed, one study found that people who see the chain of command in this way are more likely to acknowledge the collective contributions of lower-level employees as well as experience enhanced group performance and social relationships.[29]

Span of Control

How many employees can a manager direct efficiently and effectively? The **span of control** describes the number of levels (also referred to as layers) and managers in an organization.[30] All things being equal, the wider or larger the span, the fewer the levels, and the more employees at each level, the more efficient the organization.[31]

Span of control
The number of subordinates a manager can efficiently and effectively direct.

Narrow or small spans have their advocates. By keeping the span of control to five or six employees, a manager can maintain close control.[32] But narrow spans have three major drawbacks.[33] First, they are expensive because they add levels of management. Assume two organizations each have about 4,100 operative-level employees. One has a uniform span of four and the other a span of eight. As Exhibit 15-3 illustrates, the wider span of eight will have two fewer levels and approximately 800 fewer managers. If the

EXHIBIT 15-3

Contrasting Spans of Control

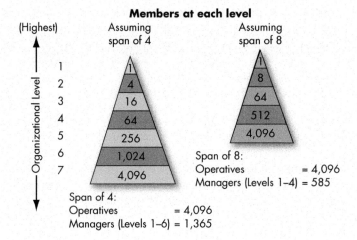

Members at each level

(Highest)

Organizational Level

1
2
3
4
5
6
7

Assuming span of 4

1
4
16
64
256
1,024
4,096

Assuming span of 8

1
8
64
512
4,096

Span of 8:
Operatives   = 4,096
Managers (Levels 1–4) = 585

Span of 4:
Operatives   = 4,096
Managers (Levels 1–6) = 1,365

average manager makes $60,000 a year, the wider span will save $48 million a year in management salaries! Second, they make vertical communication in the organization more complex. The added levels of hierarchy slow down decision making and can isolate upper management. Third, narrow spans encourage overly tight supervision and discourage employee autonomy. Supervisors no longer have time to provide subordinates with the necessary leadership and support; thus, employee performance suffers.[34]

The trend in recent years has been toward wider spans of control.[35] However, to ensure performance does not suffer because of these wider spans, organizations have been investing heavily in employee training, because managers recognize they can handle a wider span best when employees know their jobs inside and out or can turn to coworkers with questions.

Centralization and Decentralization

Centralization
The degree to which decision making is concentrated at a single point in an organization.

Centralization refers to the degree to which decision making is concentrated at a single point in the organization.[36] In *centralized* organizations, top managers make all the decisions, and lower-level managers merely carry out their directives. In organizations at the other extreme, *decentralized* decision making is pushed down to the managers closest to the action or to workgroups.[37] The concept of centralization includes only formal authority—that is, the rights inherent to a position. Management centralization efforts are often directed toward decision making by lower-level managers, who are closer to the action and typically have more detailed knowledge about problems than top managers. When Procter & Gamble empowered small groups of employees to make decisions about new-product development independent of the usual hierarchy, it was able to rapidly increase the proportion of new products ready for market.[38]

IMPLICATIONS FOR OB   A decentralized organization can act more quickly to solve problems, more people provide input into decisions,[39] and employees are less likely to feel alienated from those who make decisions that affect their work lives.[40] Centralized organizations are better for avoiding commission errors (bad choices), while decentralized organizations are better for avoiding omission errors (lost opportunities).[41] Concerning creativity, research investigating a large number of Finnish organizations demonstrated that companies with decentralized research and development (R&D) offices in multiple locations were better at producing innovation than companies that centralized all R&D in a single office.[42] Decentralization is often necessary for companies with offshore sites because localized decision making is needed to respond to each region's profit opportunities, client base, and specific laws, while centralized oversight is needed to hold regional managers accountable. Failure to successfully balance these priorities can harm not only the organization, but also its relationships with foreign governments.[43] Sometimes, however, decentralization can be a double-edged sword—one study of nearly three thousand U.S. Air Force officers suggests that there can sometimes be negative effects of decentralization in organizations with multiteam systems, including excessive risk seeking and coordination failures.[44]

Formalization

Formalization refers to the degree to which a job is standardized.[45] If a job is highly formalized, the employee has a minimal amount of discretion over what to do (e.g., there are explicit job descriptions) and when and how to do it, resulting in consistent and uniform output. Clerical workers at a publishing firm, for example, generally have very formalized jobs in which there are standard procedures and expectations for what they do. Conversely, where formalization is low, job behaviors are relatively unprogrammed and employees have a great deal of freedom to exercise discretion in their work. For example, publishing representatives who call on college professors to inform them of their company's new publications have a great deal of freedom in their jobs. They have only a general sales pitch, which they tailor as needed, and rules and procedures governing their behavior may be little more than suggestions on what to emphasize about forthcoming titles and the requirement to submit a weekly sales report.

> **Formalization**
> The degree to which a job is standardized.

Research suggests that sometimes formalization can be a detriment. For example, ninety-four Chinese firms indicated that formalization is a detriment to team flexibility in decentralized organization structures, suggesting that formalization does not work as well where duties are inherently interactive, or where there is a need to be flexible and innovative.[46] On the other hand, sometimes it is beneficial; for instance, formalizing pay determinations for jobs reduces gender inequality in most circumstances.[47]

Boundary Spanning

If there is too much division within an organization, attempts to coordinate across groups can be disastrous. One way to overcome compartmentalization and retain the positive elements of structure is to encourage or create boundary-spanning roles. **Boundary spanning** occurs when individuals form relationships with people outside their formally assigned groups.[48] For instance, an HR executive who frequently engages with the IT group is engaged in boundary spanning. These activities help prevent formal structures from becoming too rigid and, not surprisingly, enhance team creativity, decision making, knowledge sharing, and performance.[49] Boundary spanning can be an excellent tool for expatriates and local workers to collaborate. For example, one global study of aid workers from nearly sixty humanitarian aid organizations found that office leaders play a boundary spanning role that serves to connect groups and facilitate joint learning and creativity.[50]

> **Boundary spanning**
> When individuals form relationships outside their formally assigned groups.

Organizations can use formal mechanisms to facilitate boundary-spanning activities. One method is to assign formal liaison roles or develop committees of individuals from different areas of the organization.[51] Development activities can also facilitate boundary spanning. Employees with experience in multiple functions, such as accounting and marketing, are more likely to engage in boundary spanning.[52] Many organizations try to set the stage for these sorts of positive relationships by creating job rotation programs so new hires get a better sense of different areas of the organization.

COMMON ORGANIZATIONAL FRAMEWORKS AND STRUCTURES

Organizational designs are known by many names and are constantly evolving in response to changes in the way work is done. We start with three of the more common organizational frameworks: the *simple structure,* the *bureaucracy,* and the *matrix structure.*

The Simple Structure

Simple structure
An organization structure characterized by a low degree of departmentalization, wide spans of control, authority centralized in a single person, and little formalization.

A **simple structure** is common in many startups, such as those found in Silicon Valley. The modern tech startup is driven by an entrepreneurial founder, supported by a core set of loyal employees who work long hours, that enacts a unifying vision.[53] The simple structure has a low degree of departmentalization, wide spans of control (e.g., a flat organization), authority centralized in a single person, and little formalization.[54]

Simple structures are strong because they are, well, simple. They are fast, flexible, and inexpensive to operate, and accountability is clear. One major weakness is that it becomes increasingly inadequate as an organization grows because its low formalization and high centralization tend to create information overload at the top. Decision making typically becomes slower as the single executive tries to continue doing it all. This proves the undoing of many small businesses. If the structure is not changed and made more elaborate, the firm often loses momentum and can eventually fail.[55] The simple structure's other weakness is that it is risky—everything depends on one person. If the founder/manager becomes ill, it can literally halt the organization's information and decision-making capabilities.[56]

The Bureaucracy

Standardization! That is the key aspect underlying all bureaucracies. Consider the government offices that collect taxes, enforce health regulations, or provide local fire protection. They all rely on standardized work processes for coordination and control.

Bureaucracy
An organization structure with highly routine operating tasks achieved through specialization, very formalized rules and regulations, departmentalization, centralized authority, narrow spans of control, and decision making that follows the chain of command.

The **bureaucracy** is characterized by highly routine operating tasks achieved through specialization, strictly formalized rules and regulations, departmentalization (into functional, divisional, or other structures), centralized authority, narrow spans of control, and decision making that follows the chain of command.[57]

Bureaucracy is a dirty word in many people's minds. However, it does have advantages, primarily the ability to perform standardized activities very efficiently. Putting like specialties together in units results in economies of scale, minimum duplication of people and equipment, and a common language that employees all share. Bureaucracies can get by with less talented—and hence less costly—middle- and lower-level managers because rules and regulations substitute for managerial discretion. There is little need for innovative and experienced decision makers below the level of senior executives, and innovative employees often do not mesh well with bureaucracy.[58]

The other major weakness of a bureaucracy is something we have all witnessed: obsessive concern with following the rules. When cases do not precisely fit the rules, there is no room for modification. The bureaucracy is efficient only if employees confront familiar problems with programmed decision rules.[59] However, the standardization and rule adherence that benefit it also result in drawbacks: bureaucratic structures may result in diminished autonomy and motivation for employees within these systems, making it difficult to develop and maintain motivation.[60]

The Matrix Structure

The **matrix structure** combines functional and product departmentalization, and we find these types of structures in a multitude of organizations.[61] Organizations with a matrix structure create a dual line of authority, so that there are multiple people accountable, depending upon their function and product. One survey by Gallup found that 84 percent of employees in the United States are in matrixed organizations.[62] Companies that use matrix-like structures include Samsung, BASF, and L'Oréal.[63]

Matrix structure
An organization structure that creates dual lines of authority and combines functional and product departmentalization.

The most obvious structural characteristic of the matrix is that it breaks the unity-of-command concept discussed earlier. Exhibit 15-4 shows the matrix for a college of business administration. The academic departments of accounting, decision and information systems, marketing, and so forth are functional units. Overlaid on them are specific programs (that is, services). Employees in the matrix have two bosses: their functional department managers and their product managers. A professor of accounting teaching an undergraduate course may report to the director of undergraduate programs as well as to the chairperson of the accounting department.

Matrices can help facilitate coordination when the organization has several complex and interdependent activities.[64] Consider the case of the terrible snow during the winter of 2018. Boston's Logan International Airport was best equipped to deal with this disaster as a result of their matrix structure, whereas John F. Kennedy International Airport (JFK) in New York City was left with delays for days that made news worldwide due to over-delegated authority and reliance on third-party contractors.[65] The matrix reduces so-called "bureaupathologies"—its dual lines of authority limit people's tendency to protect their territories at the expense of the organization's goals.[66] A matrix also achieves

Programs / Academic Departments	Undergraduate	Master's	Ph.D.	Research	Executive Development	Community Service
Accounting						
Finance						
Decision and Information Systems						
Management						
Marketing						

EXHIBIT 15-4
Matrix Structure for a College of Business Administration

economies of scale and facilitates the allocation of specialists by both providing the best resources and ensuring that they are efficiently used.[67] However, some disadvantages of the matrix structure are found in the confusion it creates, its tendency to foster power struggles, and the stress it places on individuals.[68] For individuals who desire security and less ambiguity, this work climate can be stressful.

Some of these disadvantages can be offset through culture (see the chapter on organizational culture), especially one that values agility, flexibility, fluidity, collaboration, and a clear direction. For example, Spotify espouses these key values, while organizing individuals into "squads," "guilds," "chapters," and "tribes" that fulfill the mission of Spotify through so-called *agile matrices*.[69] Loosely speaking, the "tribes" and the teams that comprise them (e.g., "squads") are focused on specific products or services Spotify provides. "Chapters" are made up of people who do similar jobs across products/services (e.g., database administrators, front office developers). The cross-section of tribes and chapters make up the traditional matrix, like the one in Exhibit 15-4. However, where things truly get interesting is with the formation of "guilds." "Guilds" are amorphous collections of members who merely share the same interests and want to consistently improve upon their shared interests. Organizing in this way has enabled Spotify to quickly throw together squads to accomplish temporary objectives, without needing to worry about who reports to whom.

ALTERNATE DESIGN OPTIONS

With the increasing trend toward flatter structures, many organizations have been developing alternative options with fewer layers of hierarchy and more emphasis on opening the boundaries of the organization.[70] In this section, we describe three such designs: the *virtual structure*, the *team structure,* and the *circular structure.*

The Virtual Structure

Virtual structure
A small, core organization that outsources major business functions.

Why own when you can rent? That question captures the essence of the **virtual structure** (also sometimes called the *network,* or *modular,* structure), typically a small, core organization that outsources its major business functions.[71] The virtual structure is highly centralized, with little or no departmentalization.

Exhibit 15-5 shows a virtual structure in which management outsources all the primary functions of the business. The core of the organization is a small group of executives whose job is to oversee directly any activities done in-house and to coordinate relationships with organizations that manufacture, distribute, and perform other crucial functions.

Network organizations often take many forms.[72] Some of the more traditional forms include the *franchise* form, in which there are managers, systems, and other experts in the central node (i.e., executive group), and customer sales and services are carried out by franchise units. This popular form of network organization is very common in service business models such as 7-Eleven, McDonald's, Jimmy John's, and Dunkin' Donuts. In this form, however, franchisees do not tend to collaborate or coordinate with one another, are difficult to influence by the executive group, and may even be in direct competition for resources from the executive group. For instance, one study of franchises found that there is variability in how mission statements are formed at each franchise along with

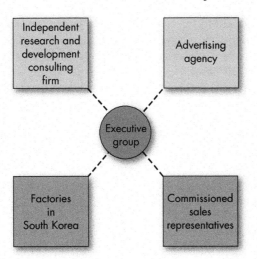

EXHIBIT 15-5
A Virtual Organization

how well they consider ethical standards. These differences subsequently impact how much discrimination is experienced at each franchise.[73] Another example is the *starburst* form, in which a parent firm splits off one of its functions into a spinoff firm.[74] For example, in 2012, Netflix split off its DVD function into a separate entity, now DVD.com.[75]

Virtual structures offer flexibility, which allows individuals with an innovative idea and little money to successfully compete against larger, more established organizations. The structure also saves a great deal of money by eliminating permanent offices and hierarchical roles for outsourced functions.[76] On the other hand, the drawbacks have become increasingly clear as popularity has grown.[77] Virtual organizations are in a state of perpetual flux and reorganization, which means roles, goals, and responsibilities are unclear, setting the stage for political behavior. Looking back to the earlier example of the winter of 2018 snow emergency, JFK utilized more of a virtual organization structure, which (during crisis), limited communication and agility.[78]

The Team Structure

The **team structure** seeks to eliminate the chain of command and replace departments with empowered teams.[79] This structure removes vertical and horizontal boundaries in addition to breaking down external barriers between the company and its customers and suppliers.

By removing vertical boundaries, management flattens the hierarchy and minimizes status and rank. A recent review of nearly 14,000 teams suggests that hierarchy can engender conflict, which can, in turn, limit how effective teams can be.[80] Cross-hierarchical teams (which include top executives, middle managers, supervisors, and operative employees), participative decision-making practices, and the use of 360-degree performance appraisals (in which peers and others evaluate performance) can be used. For example, at the Danish firm Oticon A/S, the world's largest hearing aid manufacturer, all traces of hierarchy have disappeared.[81] Everyone works at uniform mobile workstations, and project teams, not functions or departments, coordinate work.

When fully operational, the team structure may break down geographic barriers. Today, most large U.S. companies see themselves as team-oriented global corporations;

Team structure
An organizational structure that replaces departments with empowered teams, and that eliminates horizontal boundaries and external barriers between customers and suppliers.

many, like Coca-Cola and McDonald's, do as much business overseas as in the United States, and some struggle to incorporate geographic regions into their structure. In other cases, the team approach is need based. Such is the case with Chinese companies that, together, made ninety-three acquisitions in the oil and gas industry in five years—incorporating each acquisition as a new team unit—to meet forecasted demand that their resources in China could not meet.[82] The team structure provides a solution because it considers geography as more of a tactical, logistical issue than a structural one. In short, the goal may be to break down cultural barriers and open opportunities. Some organizations create teams incorporating their employees and their customers or suppliers. For example, to ensure important product parts are reliably made to exacting specifications by its suppliers, Honeywell International partners some of its engineers with managers at those suppliers.

The Circular Structure

Picture the concentric rings of an archery target. In the center are the executives; radiating outward in rings grouped by function are the managers, then the specialists, then the workers. This is the **circular structure**.[83] There is still a hierarchy, but top management is at the very heart of the organization, with its vision spreading outward.

    The circular structure has intuitive appeal for creative entrepreneurs, and some small innovative firms have claimed it. However, as in many of the current hybrid approaches, employees are apt to be unclear about whom they report to and who is running the show. We are still likely to see the popularity of the circular structure spread. The concept may have intuitive appeal for spreading a vision of corporate social responsibility (CSR) initiatives, for instance.

Circular structure
An organizational structure in which executives are at the center, spreading their vision outward in rings grouped by function (managers, then specialists, then workers).

THE LEANER ORGANIZATION: DOWNSIZING

The goal of some organizational structures we have described is to improve agility by creating a lean, focused, and flexible organization. **Downsizing** is a systematic effort to make an organization leaner by closing locations, reducing staff, de-layering (e.g., narrowing of span of control by reducing the number of levels in a hierarchy), or selling off business units that do not add value.[84]

    Some firms downsize to direct all their efforts toward their core competencies. American Express claims to have been doing this in a series of layoffs over more than a decade; each layoff was accompanied by a restructuring to reflect changing customer preferences, away from personal customer service and toward online customer service. According to former CEO Ken Chennault, "Our business and industry continue to become transformed by technology. As a result of these changes, we have the need and the opportunity to evolve our organization and cost structure."[85] However, other firms do not have a choice and implement downsizing measures because of outside forces. For example, organizations may engage in downsizing, along with work restructuring, wage, and employment freezes during times of natural disaster, pandemics (such as those that occurred during the COVID-19 pandemic), and economic recessions.[86]

    Despite the advantages of being a lean organization, the impact of downsizing on organizational performance is not without controversy. Reducing the size of the workforce perhaps has positive outcomes in the long run, although most of the evidence

Downsizing
A systematic effort to make an organization leaner by closing locations, reducing staff, or selling off business units that do not add value.

suggests that downsizing has a negative impact on stock returns the year of downsizing. However, this may be contingent on the organization's goals for downsizing along with other contextual factors).[87] An example of these contingencies can be found in the case of Russia's Gorky Automobile Factory, which realized a profit for the first time in many years after President Bo Andersson fired fifty thousand workers, half the workforce.[88] Eventually, however, the rampant downsizing policy caught up with Andersson when he was CEO of Russia's largest car maker, AvtoVAZ. From 2014 to 2016, downsizing at its plant in Togliatti led to tens of thousands of workers losing their jobs. At the time, Sergei Chemezov, an ally of President Vladmir Putin, told Andersson that he was "playing with fire."[89] Eventually, Andersson was removed as CEO for his tactics in 2016—what tended to be standard practice in the West (downsizing) was frowned upon in Russia, where the auto industry is revered with nationalistic pride and jobs tend to be preserved rather than cut.[90]

Part of the problem is the effect of downsizing on employee attitudes.[91] From a broad perspective, many have argued that the prominence of downsizing has led employees across the world to be insecure about their jobs and uncertain about their careers.[92] Employees who remain often feel worried about future layoffs, may be less committed to the organization, and may experience a greater amount of stress and strain.[93] Downsizing can also lead to more voluntary turnover, so vital human capital is lost.[94] The result is a company that is more anemic than lean.

WHY DO STRUCTURES DIFFER?

Exhibit 15-6 differentiates between two extreme models of organizational design.[95] One is the **mechanistic model**, which is generally synonymous with the bureaucracy in that it has highly standardized processes for work, high formalization, and more managerial hierarchy. The other extreme is the **organic model**, which is flat, has fewer formal procedures for making decisions, has multiple decision makers, and favors flexible practices.[96] Whether the organization is more mechanistic or organic has implications for which behaviors are most effective. For example, research suggests that political behaviors tend to be more effective in mechanistic organizations,[97] whereas transformational leadership and empowerment tend to be more effective in organic organizations.[98]

With these two models in mind, why are some organizations more mechanistic whereas others are more organic? What forces influence the choice of design? In this section, we present major causes or determinants of an organization's structure.[99]

Organizational Strategies

Because structure is a means to achieve objectives, and objectives derive from the organization's overall strategy, it is only logical that structure should follow strategy. If management significantly changes the organization's strategy or its values, the structure must also change to accommodate. For example, recent research indicates that aspects of organizational culture may influence the success of CSR initiatives.[100] If the culture is supported by the structure, the initiatives are more likely to have clear paths toward application. Regarding strategy, most current frameworks focus on three dimensions—innovation, cost minimization, and imitation—and a structural design that works best with each.[101]

Mechanistic model
A structure characterized by extensive departmentalization, high formalization, a limited information network, and centralization.

Organic model
A structure that is flat, uses cross-hierarchical and cross-functional teams, has low formalization, possesses a comprehensive information network, and relies on participative decision making.

The Mechanistic Model

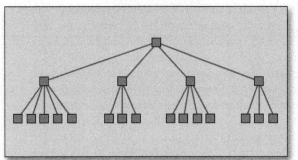

- High specialization
- Rigid departmentalization
- Clear chain of command
- Narrow spans of control
- Centralization
- High formalization

The Organic Model

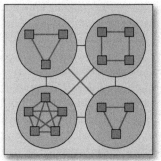

- Cross-functional teams
- Cross-hierarchical teams
- Free flow of information
- Wide spans of control
- Decentralization
- Low formalization

EXHIBIT 15-6
Mechanistic Versus Organic Models

Innovation strategy
A strategy that emphasizes the introduction of major new products and services.

INNOVATION STRATEGY   To what degree does an organization introduce major new products or services? An **innovation strategy** strives to achieve meaningful and unique innovations.[102] Innovative firms use competitive pay and benefits to attract top candidates and motivate employees to take risks. Some degree of the mechanistic structure can benefit innovation. Well-developed communication channels, policies for enhancing long-term commitment, and clear channels of authority all may make it easier for rapid changes to occur smoothly. Obviously, not all firms pursue innovation. Tesla, Amazon, and Netflix do,[103] but some other firms do not.

Arguably, some degree of innovation is needed if the firm is to stay ahead of the competition. We can recall several instances in which companies failed to innovate, causing them to lose position in the market (e.g., Kodak, Blockbuster).[104] Steve Sasson, an engineer at Kodak, invented the first digital camera in 1975. When Sasson showed the camera to management, their response was, "That's cute—but don't tell anyone about it." Former Kodak executives noted that although they developed this, leadership was too focused on the success of film to notice the digital revolution and too afraid of how this innovation would affect the film market.[105] However, sometimes innovation does not work out in the face of competitors. For instance, My Space's response to Facebook's popularity in the mid-2000s was to change its niche to entertainment and music, eventually leading to its decline as a social network.[106]

Cost-minimization strategy
A strategy that emphasizes tight cost controls, avoidance of unnecessary innovation or marketing expenses, and price cutting.

COST-MINIMIZATION STRATEGY   An organization pursuing a **cost-minimization strategy** tightly controls costs, refrains from incurring unnecessary expenses, and cuts prices in selling a basic product.[107] For example, India's Jet Airways did away with the first class section in its Boeing 777 planes, enabling it to increase revenue by adding an additional fifty-four seats per plane in 2019.[108] But sometimes, cost minimization can hurt customer loyalty and perceptions of product quality, such as when you notice the paper products in restrooms are of low quality (as one marketing author notes).[109] But even further, sometimes the public is unaware of these cost-cutting measures or remains "blissfully ignorant," as is the case with historical ethical and quality concerns levied toward major American meat suppliers.[110] Regardless, with the advent of machine learning and artificial intelligence (AI), thought leaders have proposed a new philosophy that is not so focused on price cutting.[111] This strategy, *cost-optimization*, focuses on looking at the bigger picture and making sure expenditures maximize long-term growth and profits. AI can empower organizations to quickly collect, process, and learn from mountains of data, all while forecasting future returns.

IMITATION STRATEGY Organizations following an **imitation strategy** try to both minimize risk and maximize opportunity for profit, moving new products or entering new markets only after innovators have proven their viability.[112] On a smaller scale, companies within the same industry share best practices and benchmarking data in order to advance the industry. More overt imitation strategies suggest organizations follow smaller and more innovative competitors with superior products, but only after competitors have demonstrated the market is there. One modern example is how Instagram released its own version of "Stories," a feature nearly identical to the one Snapchat introduced: Since its release, Instagram added 250 million users.[113]

> **Imitation strategy**
> A strategy that seeks to move into new products or new markets only after their viability has already been proven.

However, the imitation strategy does have its drawbacks. As some examples, imitation can cause firms to imitate the effects of success rather than its causes, imitation often ignores the luck and serendipity that caused the imitated to become successful, and imitation can lead to long-term decline if the imitating company does not have the capacity or resources to scale.[114] Interestingly, there appears to be an ethical component as well: Imitation can lead some companies today to get a "bad reputation" for partnering up with firms, learning from them, and then "stabbing them in the back" once they have developed their own version of the product or service.[115]

STRUCTURAL MATCHES Exhibit 15-7 describes the structural option that best matches each strategy. Innovators need the flexibility of the organic structure (although, as we noted, they may use some elements of the mechanistic structure as well), whereas cost minimizers seek the efficiency and stability of the mechanistic structure. Imitators combine the two structures. They use a mechanistic structure to maintain tight controls and low costs in their current activities but create organic subunits in which to pursue new opportunities.

Strategy	Structural Option
Innovation	**Organic:** A loose structure; low specialization, low formalization, decentralized
Cost minimization	**Mechanistic:** Tight control; extensive work specialization, high formalization, high centralization
Imitation	**Mechanistic and organic:** Mix of loose with tight properties; tight controls over current activities and looser controls for new undertakings

EXHIBIT 15-7
The Strategy-Structure Relationship

Organization Size

An organization's size significantly affects its structure.[116] Organizations that employ two thousand or more people tend to have more specialization, more departmentalization, more vertical levels, and more rules and regulations than do small organizations. However, size becomes less important as an organization expands. Why? At around two thousand employees, an organization is already mechanistic; 500 more employees will not have much of an impact. But adding 500 employees to an organization of only 300 is likely to significantly shift it toward a more mechanistic structure.

Technology

Technology
The way in which an organization transfers its inputs into outputs.

Technology describes the way an organization transfers inputs into outputs.[117] Every organization has at least one technology for converting financial, human, and physical resources into products or services. For example, the Chinese consumer electronics company Haier (the owners of GE Appliances) uses an assembly-line process for mass-produced products, which is complemented by more flexible and innovative structures to respond to customers and design new products.[118] Regardless, organizational structures adapt to their technology—and vice versa.[119] Organizational structure and culture can become inscribed in the data structure, software, and hardware that an organization uses.[120]

Environment

Environment
Forces outside an organization that potentially affect the organization's structure.

An organization's **environment** includes outside institutions or forces that can affect its structure, such as suppliers, customers, competitors, and public pressure groups.[121] Dynamic environments create significantly more uncertainty for managers than do static ones. To minimize uncertainty in key market arenas, managers may broaden their structure to sense and respond to threats. For example, most companies have added social networking departments not only to promote their products/services to more people, but to also find and respond to negative information (e.g., reviews) posted online.[122]

Any organization's environment has three dimensions: capacity, volatility, and complexity.[123] Let us discuss each separately.

CAPACITY   *Capacity* refers to the degree to which the environment can support growth. Rich and growing environments generate excess resources, which can buffer the organization in times of relative scarcity. One example of how capacity plays a role in strategic decisions is how Amazon sought to build a second headquarters in a major US city, considering several environmental factors (including capacity) in its decision.[124]

VOLATILITY   *Volatility* describes the degree of instability in the environment. A dynamic environment with a high degree of unpredictable change makes it difficult for management to make accurate predictions. Because information technology changes at such a rapid pace, most organizations' environments are volatile. The characteristics of firms, their teams, and their leaders often affect how well firms weather the storms of volatility.[125] For example, research on top executives in China point to the Chinese concept of *negotiable fate* (i.e., the belief that personal actions can shape outcomes); when executives hold this belief, they tend to be more entrepreneurial in how they approach volatility, which in turn predicts' their firm's innovation and financial performance.[126]

COMPLEXITY Finally, *complexity* is the degree of heterogeneity and concentration among environmental elements. Environments characterized by heterogeneity and dispersion are complex and diverse, with numerous competitors. For example, information security firms operate in an incredibly complex environment: Competitors are widely dispersed and different from one another, the way people interact with technology and the Internet is diverse, and adversaries (e.g., attackers, hackers, and cyber-criminals) also use several methods to complete their work.[127]

THREE-DIMENSIONAL MODEL Exhibit 15-8 summarizes our definition of the environment along its three dimensions. The arrows indicate movement toward higher uncertainty. Thus, organizations that operate in environments characterized as scarce, dynamic, and complex face the greatest degree of uncertainty because they have high unpredictability, little room for error, and a diverse set of elements in the environment to monitor constantly. Given this three-dimensional definition of *environment*, we can offer some general conclusions about environmental uncertainty and structural arrangements. The more scarce, dynamic, and complex the environment, the more organic a structure should be. The more abundant, stable, and simple the environment, the more the mechanistic structure will be preferred.

Institutions

Another factor that shapes organizational structure is **institutions**. These are cultural factors that act as guidelines for appropriate behavior.[128] Institutional theory describes some of the forces that lead many organizations to have similar structures and, unlike the theories we have described so far, focuses on pressures that are not necessarily adaptive. In fact, many institutional theorists try to highlight the ways corporate behaviors sometimes *seem* to be performance oriented but are really guided by unquestioned social norms and conformity.

The most obvious institutional factors come from regulatory pressures; certain industries under government contracts, for instance, must have clear reporting relationships and strict information controls. Sometimes simple inertia determines an organizational form—companies can be structured in a particular way just because that is the way things have always been done, or what others are doing. Organizations in countries

Institutions
Cultural factors, especially those factors that might not lead to adaptive consequences, that lead many organizations to have similar structures.

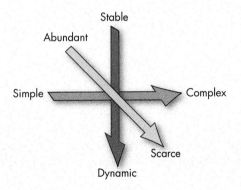

EXHIBIT 15-8

The Environment Along Three Dimensions

with high power distance might have a structural form with strict authority relationships because it is seen as more legitimate in that culture. Some have attributed problems in adaptability in Japanese organizations to the institutional pressure to maintain authority relationships.

ORGANIZATIONAL DESIGNS AND EMPLOYEE BEHAVIOR

A review of the evidence on how organizational designs affects employees leads to a clear conclusion:[129] You cannot generalize! Not everyone prefers the freedom and flexibility of organic structures. Several factors stand out in different structures as well. In highly formalized, heavily structured, mechanistic organizations, the level of fairness in formal policies and procedures (organizational justice) is a very important predictor of satisfaction. In more personal, individually adaptive organic organizations, employees value interpersonal justice more.[130] Some people are most productive and satisfied when work tasks are standardized and ambiguity is minimized—that is, in mechanistic structures. So, any discussion of the effect of organizational design on employee behavior must address individual differences.[131]

Span of Control

It is probably safe to say no evidence supports a relationship between *span of control* and employee satisfaction or performance. Although it is intuitively attractive that large spans might lead to higher employee performance because they provide more distant supervision and more opportunity for personal initiative, research fails to support this notion.[132] Some people like to be left alone; others prefer the security of a boss who is always quickly available. Consistent with several of the contingency theories of leadership discussed in the leadership chapter, we would expect factors such as employees' experiences and abilities, and the degree of structure in their tasks, to explain when wide or narrow spans of control are likely to contribute to performance and job satisfaction. However, some evidence indicates that a *manager's* job satisfaction increases as the number of employees supervised increases.[133]

Centralization

We find fairly strong evidence linking *centralization* and job satisfaction.[134] In general, less centralized organizations have a greater amount of autonomy, and autonomy appears positively related to job satisfaction. But again, while one employee may value freedom, another may find autonomous environments frustratingly ambiguous.

Predictability Versus Autonomy

We can draw one obvious insight: People do not select employers randomly. They are attracted to, are selected by, and stay with organizations that suit their personal characteristics.[135] Thus, the effect of structure on employee behavior is undoubtedly reduced when the selection process facilitates proper matching of individual characteristics with organizational characteristics. Furthermore, companies should strive to establish, promote, and maintain the unique identity of their structures since skilled employees may quit as a result of dramatic changes.[136]

National Culture

Research suggests national culture influences the preference for structure.[137] Organizations that operate with people from high power-distance cultures, such as Greece, France, and most of Latin America, often find their employees are much more accepting of mechanistic structures than are employees from low power-distance countries. So, consider cultural differences along with individual differences when predicting how structure will affect employee performance and satisfaction.

SUMMARY

The theme of this chapter is that an organization's internal structure contributes to explaining and predicting behavior. That is, in addition to individual and group factors, the structural relationships in which people work have a bearing on employee attitudes and behavior. What is the basis for this argument? To the degree that an organization's structure reduces ambiguity for employees and clarifies concerns such as "What am I supposed to do?" "How am I supposed to do it?" "To whom do I report?" and "To whom do I go if I have a problem?" it shapes their attitudes and facilitates and motivates them to higher levels of performance.

IMPLICATIONS FOR MANAGERS

- Design the structure of your organization, unit, or team so that it follows strategy, supports execution, and elicits desired behaviors and outcomes. In other words, your structure should be purpose driven.
- Consider the design features that relate to specialization, departmentalization, authority, formalization, and boundary spanning to implement your strategy.
- There are several common organizational structures that you can implement, and most organizations today use hybrid structures with a matrix format. However, you should always match your decision to your strategy (for example, flatter organizations tend to elicit more innovation) and what you expect to encounter in the organization's environment (e.g., scarcity, volatility, complexity).
- Downsize only if necessary, because downsizing can have a significant negative impact on employee attitudes/motivation and customer perceptions.
- Generally, aim for an organic structure if your strategy prioritizes innovation, a mechanistic structure if your strategy prioritizes cost minimization, and a combination of the two if your strategy prioritizes imitation.

16
Organizational Culture

LEARNING OBJECTIVES

After studying this chapter, you should be able to:

16.1 Describe the common characteristics of organizational culture.

16.2 Show how culture is transmitted to employees.

16.3 Identify the factors that create and sustain an organization's culture.

16.4 Compare the functional and dysfunctional effects of organizational culture on people and the organization.

16.5 Describe the similarities and differences in creating an ethical culture, a positive culture, and a spiritual culture.

16.6 Show how national culture can affect the way organizational culture is interpreted in another country.

WHAT IS ORGANIZATIONAL CULTURE?

Would you spend $10,000 on a guitar without even playing it? Customers of Chicago-based Reverb.com, an online musical instrument marketplace, are willing to do so. Why do they keep coming back, rather than going to competitors such as eBay? The answer may be found in its organizational culture.[1]

We have all felt an indescribable essence about the organizations we have experienced. This pervasive atmosphere can have a strong and measurable impact on behavior. Reverb.com has created an organization and a brand, founded on a passion for music and a drive to create a wonderful customer experience for musicians. Employees and customers alike share values, beliefs, and traditions centered around music and its performance.[2] As you will see in this chapter, organizational culture can have a profound effect on organizational effectiveness. Notably, 88 percent of millennials surveyed by Gallup (a polling company) stated that they would remain in their jobs *for more than five years* if they were satisfied with the company's purpose, or mission.[3]

A Definition of Organizational Culture

Organizational culture refers to a system of shared meaning held by members that distinguishes the organization from other organizations.[4] This system of shared meaning includes values, beliefs, material symbols, and assumptions that characterize the organization.[5] These values, beliefs, and assumptions, when put into practice, (1) filter what employees pay attention to, (2) are physically manifested as *material symbols* (for example, uniforms, statues) and *stories*, and (3) form the foundation for shared meaning amongst members of an organization.[6]

Organizational culture shows how employees perceive the essence of an organization, not whether they like them—that is, it is a *descriptive* term. Research on organizational culture has sought to measure how employees see their organization: Does it encourage teamwork? Does it reward innovation? Does it stifle initiative? In contrast, job satisfaction is an *evaluative* term: it seeks to measure how employees feel about the organization's expectations, reward practices, and the like. See Exhibit 16-1 for a contrast of two companies with very different organizational cultures.

> **Organizational culture**
> A system of shared meaning held by members that distinguishes the organization from other organizations. This system is characterized by values, beliefs, and underlying assumptions that serve several purposes.

Organization A

This organization is a manufacturing firm. Managers are expected to fully document all decisions, and "good managers" are those who can provide detailed data to support their recommendations. Creative decisions that incur significant change or risk are not encouraged. Because managers of failed projects are openly criticized and penalized, managers try not to implement ideas that deviate much from the status quo. One lower-level manager quoted an often-used phrase in the company: "If it ain't broke, don't fix it."

There are extensive rules and regulations in this firm that employees are required to follow. Managers supervise employees closely to ensure there are no deviations. Management is concerned with high productivity, regardless of the impact on employee morale or turnover.

Work activities are designed around individuals. There are distinct departments and lines of authority, and employees are expected to minimize formal contact with other employees outside their functional area or line of command. Performance evaluations and rewards emphasize individual effort, although seniority tends to be the primary factor in the determination of pay raises and promotions.

Organization B

This organization is also a manufacturing firm. Here, however, management encourages and rewards risk taking and change. Decisions based on intuition are valued as much as those that are well rationalized. Management prides itself on its history of experimenting with new technologies and its success in regularly introducing innovative products. Managers or employees who have a good idea are encouraged to "run with it." And failures are treated as "learning experiences." The company prides itself on being market driven and rapidly responsive to the changing needs of its customers.

There are few rules and regulations for employees to follow, and supervision is loose because management believes that its employees are hardworking and trustworthy. Management is concerned with high productivity but believes that this comes through treating its people right. The company is proud of its reputation as being a good place to work.

Job activities are designed around work teams, and team members are encouraged to interact with people across functions and authority levels. Employees talk positively about the competition between teams. Individuals and teams have goals, and bonuses are based on achievement of these outcomes. Employees are given considerable autonomy in choosing the means by which the goals are attained.

EXHIBIT 16-1
Contrasting Organizational Cultures

Organizational cultures are extremely difficult to define and characterize, and over the years, many people sought to understand the meaning of culture in organizations.[7] Many have asked, do organizations *have* cultures? These researchers have tried to figure out what makes cultures different from one another. Still others have asked, what *are* organizations' cultures? These researchers are more concerned with describing specific cultures and understanding what makes one particular organization tick. As an example, followers of the *have* perspective might try to figure out what values and beliefs that descriptively separate Reverb.com from, say, eBay. On the other hand, followers of the *are* perspective would only try to understand what Reverb.com is, for what it is, by studying the stories, rituals, material symbols, and language used at Reverb.com. Notably, these latter forms (described later in the next section) are notoriously hard to measure and interpret. Although sometimes observable by outsiders, they tap into deep underlying assumptions that are sometimes only capable of being fully grasped and experienced by an "insider."[8]

Regardless of the many ways of conceptualizing varying "types" of culture by values or beliefs, one of the most common frameworks describes organizational cultures as possessing several competing values.[9]

- **"The Clan."** A culture based on human affiliation. Employees value attachment, collaboration, trust, and support.
- **"The Adhocracy."** A culture based on change. Employees value growth, variety, attention to detail, stimulation, and autonomy.
- **"The Market."** A culture based on achievement. Employees value communication, competence, and competition.
- **"The Hierarchy."** A culture based on stability. Employees value communication, formalization, and routine.

The differences between these cultures are reflected in their internal versus external focus and their flexibility and stability.[10] For instance, clans are internally focused and flexible, adhocracies are externally focused and flexible, markets are externally focused and stable, and hierarchies are internally focused and stable. Reviews of hundreds of studies have helped summarize the findings on the cultures from the competing values framework.[11] As shown in Exhibit 16-2, the various cultures differ regarding how they influence organizational outcomes. Although we note that many of these outcomes are also heavily influenced by leadership and organizational structure (see their respective chapters for more information), culture adds more to the picture than leadership or structure. A strategic approach to culture would suggest that cultures would ideally match one's objectives. Although most cultures have a positive effect on employee attitudes, performance, innovation, product/service quality, and operational efficiency, it is clear that a clan or market culture is perhaps best aligned with customer-oriented outcomes and that a hierarchical culture is best for profitability and revenue growth.

Although the competing values approach is one of the most frequently studied ways of examining organizational culture, other frameworks have been introduced. For example, the *Organizational Culture Inventory* groups cultures into three categories: (1) *constructive cultures* that value affiliation, encouragement, and achievement; (2) *passive-defensive cultures* that avoid accountability, seek validation and approval from others, and are conventional; and (3) *aggressive-defensive cultures* that are competitive, perfectionist, and power-oriented.[12]

EXHIBIT 16-2
The Effect of Culture on Organizational Outcomes

Culture	Employee Attitudes & Performance	Innovation	High Quality Products/Services & Operational Efficiency	Customer Satisfaction & Market Share	Profitability & Revenue Growth
Clan	+*	+*	0	+*	-
Adhocracy	+*	+	+*	-	0
Market	0	+	+*	+*	0
Hierarchy	+*	-	+*	0	+*

Note: + corresponds with a positive effect on the outcome, - corresponds with a negative effect on the outcome, 0 corresponds with a zero, or null, effect on the outcome, * suggests the culture is strongly related to the outcome.

Sources: Based on findings from C. A. Hartnell, A. Y. Ou, A. J. Kinicki, D. Choi, and E. P. Karam, "A meta-analytic test of organizational culture's association with elements of an organization's system and its relative predictive validity on organizational outcomes," *Journal of Applied Psychology* 104, no. 6 (2019): 832–850.

Another widely used framework is the *Organizational Culture Profile* (OCP).[13] The OCP draws upon a novel survey method in which employees sort a set of values based on how closely they represent their organization. The OCP suggests an organizational culture can be described by eight dimensions: (1) *innovation,* (2) *attention to detail,* (3) *decisiveness*, (4) *team orientation*, (5) *outcome orientation*, (6) *aggressiveness*, (7) *supportiveness*, and (8) *rewards emphasis.*

Do Organizations Have Uniform Cultures?

Organizational culture represents a perception that the organization's members hold in common. Statements about organizational culture are valid only if individuals with different backgrounds or at different levels in the organization describe the culture in similar terms.[14]

The **dominant culture** expresses the **core values** most members share and that give the organization its distinct personality.[15] **Subcultures** tend to develop in large organizations in response to common problems or experiences a group of members face in the same department or location.[16] Most large organizations have a dominant culture and numerous subcultures.[17] Sometimes the subcultures can be so strong, however, that they subtly reject the "official" culture and do not conform.[18] If organizations were composed only of subcultures, the dominant organizational culture would be significantly less powerful. It is this "shared meaning" aspect of culture (in both dominant and subcultures) that makes it a potent device for guiding and shaping behavior. Subcultures have even been detected at the country or nation level, with subcultures forming because of immigration, assimilation of new immigrants, or class differences amongst the people.[19]

Strong Versus Weak Cultures

It is possible to differentiate between strong and weak cultures.[20] If most employees (responding to surveys) have the same opinions about the organization's mission and values, the culture is strong; if opinions vary widely, the culture is weak.

Dominant culture
A culture that expresses the core values that are shared by most of the organization's members.

Core values
The primary or dominant values that are accepted throughout the organization.

Subcultures
Minicultures within an organization, typically defined by department designations or geographical separation.

Strong culture
A culture in which the core values are intensely held and widely shared.

In a **strong culture**, the organization's core values are both intensely held and widely shared.[21] The more members who accept the core values and the greater their commitment, the stronger the culture and the greater its influence on member behavior. David Rodriguez, Marriott executive vice president and chief human resources officer, emphasizes that it really is the people who forge a strong culture: "If you don't have the courage and wisdom to release control of the culture to your associates and employees, it won't work." Instead, Marriott enlists the help of over 15,000 volunteer employees to champion the company's culture.[22]

A strong culture should reduce employee turnover because it demonstrates high agreement about what the organization represents. Such unanimity of purpose builds cohesiveness, loyalty, and organizational commitment. These qualities, in turn, lessen employees' propensity to leave. Indeed, a study of nearly 90,000 employees from 137 organizations found that culture strength or consistency was related to numerous financial outcomes when there was a strong sense of mission and high employee involvement.[23] A strong culture has enabled companies like Ace Hardware to thrive in an extremely competitive market, a market in which many other companies have folded or declared bankruptcy.[24]

HOW EMPLOYEES LEARN CULTURE

Culture is transmitted in several forms, the most potent being stories, rituals, material symbols, and language.

Stories

When Henry Ford II was chairman of Ford Motor Company, you would have been hard pressed to find a manager who had not heard how he reminded his executives when they got too arrogant, "It's my name that's on the building." The message was clear: Henry Ford II ran the company.

Today, several senior Nike executives spend much of their time serving as corporate storytellers.[25] When they tell how cofounder (and Oregon track coach) Bill Bowerman went to his workshop and poured rubber into a waffle iron to create a better running shoe, they are talking about Nike's spirit of innovation. The elderly man running in their first commercial in 1988 marks the first use of their slogan "just do it," and continues the story that anyone, despite their differences, can strive for and achieve their athletic goals.[26]

Rituals
Repetitive sequences of activities that express and reinforce the key values of the organization, which goals are most important, which people are important, and which are expendable.

Stories such as these circulate through many organizations, anchoring the present to the past and legitimizing current practices.[27] They typically include narratives about the organization's founders, rule breaking, rags-to-riches successes, workforce reductions, relocations of employees, reactions to past mistakes, and organizational coping.[28] Employees also create their own narratives about how they came to either fit or not fit with the organization during the process of socialization, including first days on the job, early interactions with others, and first impressions of organizational life.[29]

Rituals

Rituals are repetitive sequences of activities that express and reinforce the key values of the organization—what goals are most important and/or which people are important versus which are expendable.[30] Some companies have nontraditional rituals to help support the values of their cultures. Kimpton Hotels & Restaurants, one of *Fortune*'s 100 Best

Companies to Work For, maintains its customer-oriented culture with traditions like a Housekeeping Olympics that includes blindfolded bedmaking and vacuum races.[31] Some companies have also been using rituals to "convert" potential customers, clients, and investors. For example, Ontario cool climate wineries have been using rituals in order to inspire and rouse emotional experiences among wine enthusiasts to identify with the winery and their product.[32] Why do rituals work in reinforcing values and placating supervisors, employees, and customers alike? Recent research suggests that rituals work because they inspire a sense of control in their participants and, as a result, reduce anxiety.[33]

Symbols

The layout of corporate headquarters, the types of automobiles top executives are given, and the presence or absence of corporate aircraft are a few examples of **material symbols**, sometimes also known as artifacts.[34] Others include the size of offices, the elegance of furnishings, perks, and attire.[35] These convey to employees who is important, the degree of egalitarianism top management desires, and the kinds of behavior that are appropriate, such as risk taking, conservative, authoritarian, participative, individualistic, or social behavior. Material symbols also offer a sense of connection and stir emotions in employees who make sense of the symbols.[36]

Material symbols Physical objects, or artifacts, that symbolize values, beliefs, or assumptions inherent in the organization's culture.

At some firms, like Chicago shirt maker Threadless, an "anything goes" atmosphere helps emphasize a creative culture. Threadless meetings are held in an Airstream camper parked inside the company's converted FedEx warehouse, while employees in shorts and flip-flops work in bullpens featuring disco balls and garish decorations chosen by each team.[37] As another example, the Palo Alto office of IDEO has an airplane wing sticking out of one of the walls—which may symbolize IDEO's playful experimentation and free expression values.[38]

Some cultures are known for the perks in their environments, such as Google's bocce courts, FACTSET Research's onsite pie/cheese/cupcake trucks, software designer Autodesk's bring-your-dog office, SAS's free health care clinic, Microsoft's organic spa, and adventure-gear specialist REI's free equipment rentals. Other companies communicate the values of their cultures through the gift of time to think creatively, either with leaders or offsite. For instance, Biotech leader Genentech and many other top companies provide paid sabbaticals. Genentech offers every employee six weeks' paid leave for every six years of service to support a culture of equitability and innovative thinking.[39]

Language

Many organizations and subunits within them use language to help members identify with the culture, attest to their acceptance of it, and help preserve it.[40] Unique terms describe equipment, officers, key individuals, suppliers, customers, or products that relate to the business. New employees may at first be overwhelmed by acronyms and jargon that, once assimilated, act as a common denominator to unite members of a given culture or subculture. As an idea of how expansive the terminology used in the U.S. government is, one librarian created a comprehensive dictionary and guide (*GovSpeak*) to non-military acronyms, abbreviations, and terms.[41]

Despite providing a unique, descriptive window into the culture of organizations, values and beliefs can be conveyed *through* stories, rituals, material symbols, and language. For example, in one study of *Fortune* 500 mission statements, organizations that

communicated that they believe people can grow and improve tended to have more positive culture ratings on Glassdoor than companies that believe people do not change. In
subsequent studies of employees at *Fortune* 1000 companies, this perception of culture
impacted employee trust and commitment.[42]

CREATING AND SUSTAINING CULTURE

An organization's culture does not pop out of thin air, and once established it rarely fades
away. What influences the creation of a culture? What reinforces and sustains it once in place?

How a Culture Begins

An organization's customs, traditions, and general way of doing things are largely due to
what it has done before and how successful it was in doing it. This leads us to the ultimate
source of an organization's culture: the founders.[43] Founders have a vision of what the
organization should be, and a firm's initially small size makes it easy to enact that vision
with all members.

Culture creation occurs in three ways.[44] First, founders hire and keep only employees
who think and feel the same way they do. Second, they socialize employees to their way of
thinking and feeling. And finally, the behavior of the founder(s) encourages employees to
identify with them and internalize their beliefs, values, and assumptions. When the organization succeeds, the personality of the founder(s) becomes embedded in the culture.

For example, the fierce, competitive style and disciplined, authoritarian nature of
Hyundai, the giant Korean conglomerate, exhibits the same characteristics often used to
describe founder Chung Ju-Yung.[45] Other founders with sustaining impact on their organization's culture include Bill Gates at Microsoft, Ingvar Kamprad at IKEA, Herb Kelleher at
Southwest Airlines, Fred Smith at FedEx, and Richard Branson at the Virgin Group.

Exhibit 16-3 summarizes how an organization's culture is established and sustained. The original culture derives from the founders' philosophy and strongly influences hiring criteria as the firm grows.[46] The success of socialization depends on the
deliberateness of matching new employees' values to those of the organization in the
selection process and on top management's commitment to socialization programs. Top
managers' actions signal what is valued, including what is acceptable behavior and what
is not, thus directly influencing the socialization process and the culture.[47] The culture
then becomes linked and entrenched within the organizational structures and systems and
is perpetuated by leadership. In the most comprehensive study of organizational culture
to-date (an impressive study of more than 500,000 employees from over 26,000 organizations), culture was found to be strongly related to the current leadership, practices, and
structures that comprise the organization.[48]

EXHIBIT 16-3
How
Organizational
Cultures Form

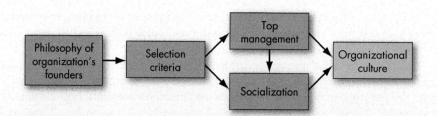

Keeping a Culture Alive

Once a culture is in place, practices within the organization maintain it by giving employees a set of similar experiences.[49] The selection process, performance evaluation criteria, training and development activities, and promotion procedures ensure those hired fit in with the culture, reward those employees who support it, and penalize (or even expel) those who challenge it.[50] Three forces play a particularly important part in sustaining a culture: selection practices, actions of top management, and socialization methods (e.g., onboarding, teaching, and including new employees).

SELECTION   The explicit goal of the selection process is to identify and hire individuals with the knowledge, skills, and abilities to perform successfully. The final decision, because it is significantly influenced by the decision maker's judgment of how well candidates will fit into the organization, identifies people whose values are consistent with at least a good portion of the organization's.[51] The selection process also provides information to applicants. Those who perceive a conflict between their values and those of the organization may remove themselves from the applicant pool or even fake their way into the organization by feigning that they share the organization's values.[52] Selection thus becomes a two-way street, with both employers and applicants as active participants in determining the value fit between the applicant and the organization. For example, in W. L. Gore & Associate's selection process, teams put job applicants through extensive interviews to ensure that they can deal with the level of uncertainty, flexibility, and teamwork that is normal in Gore plants. Not surprisingly, W. L. Gore appears regularly on *Fortune's* list of "100 Best Companies to Work For" (number eighty-three in 2020) partially because of its selection process emphasis on culture fit.[53]

TOP MANAGEMENT   The actions of top management have a major impact on the organization's culture.[54] Through words and behavior, senior executives establish norms that filter through the organization about, for instance, whether risk taking is desirable; how much freedom managers give employees; the uniforms employees should wear; and what behavior is desired and rewarded. Interestingly, research on hundreds of CEOs and top management team members suggests that organizational culture and leadership can be complementary: It is not always best if they focus on the same values.[55] In other words, one can fill in where the other fails.

SOCIALIZATION   No matter how good a job the organization does in recruitment and selection, new employees need help adapting to the prevailing culture. This help comes in the form of **socialization**.[56] Socialization can help alleviate the problem many employees report when their new jobs are different than they expected. For example, Clear Channel Communications, Facebook, Google, and other companies are adopting fresh onboarding (new hire assimilation) procedures, including assigning "peer coaches," holding socializing events, personalizing orientation programs, and giving out immediate work assignments. "When we can stress the personal identity of people, and let them bring more of themselves at work, they are more satisfied with their job and have better results," researcher Francesca Gino of Harvard said.[57]

Socialization
A process that enables new employees to acquire the social knowledge and necessary skills in order to adapt to the organization's culture.

We can think of socialization as a process with three stages: prearrival, encounter, and metamorphosis.[58] This process, shown in Exhibit 16-4, has an impact on the new employee's work productivity, commitment to the organization's objectives, and decision to stay with the organization.

EXHIBIT 16-4
A Socialization
Model

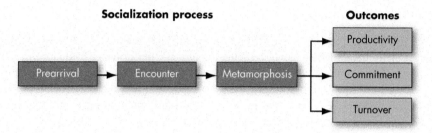

Socialization process   **Outcomes**

Prearrival → Encounter → Metamorphosis → Productivity / Commitment / Turnover

Prearrival stage
The period of learning
in the socialization
process that occurs
before a new
employee joins the
organization.

Encounter stage
The stage in the
socialization process
in which a new
employee sees what
the organization is
really like and con-
fronts the possibility
that expectations
and reality may diverge.

**Metamorphosis
stage**
The stage in the
socialization process
in which a new
employee changes
and adjusts to the
job, workgroup, and
organization.

1. *Prearrival stage*. The **prearrival stage** recognizes that everyone arrives with a set of values, attitudes, and expectations about both the work and the organization. One major purpose of a business school, for example, is to socialize students to the attitudes and behaviors companies want. Newcomers to high-profile organizations with strong market positions have their own assumptions about what it is like to work there.[59] Most new recruits will expect Nike to be dynamic and exciting and a stock brokerage firm to be high in pressure and rewards. How accurately people judge an organization's culture before they join the organization, and how positive, adaptive, and proactive their personalities are, become critical predictors of how well they adjust.[60]

2. *Encounter stage*. The selection process can help inform prospective employees about the organization. Upon entry into the organization, the new member enters the **encounter stage** and confronts the possibility that expectations—about the job, coworkers, boss, and organization in general—may differ from reality.[61] If expectations were accurate, this stage merely cements earlier perceptions. However, this is not often the case. At the extreme, a new member may become disillusioned enough to resign. Proper recruiting and selection should significantly reduce this outcome, along with encouraging friendship ties in the organization—newcomers are more committed when friendly coworkers help them "learn the ropes."[62] For better or worse, learning, unlearning, and relationship building are key during this stage:[63] If newcomers are not proactive enough in learning about the organization and helping out where they can, if supervisors and coworkers do not do their due diligence in socializing the newcomer and fulfilling promises made during recruitment, or if the exchange between the newcomer and the employees is not good, newcomers may become disillusioned.[64] However, it is also possible for undesirable behaviors that may be an aspect of the organization's culture such as CWBs to be transmitted to employees during the encounter stage. For example, one study of manufacturing sales departments in southern China found employees may model undesirable behaviors, such as heavy drinking with clients, that may result in increased work-family conflict and turnover risk over time.[65]

3. *Metamorphosis stage*. Finally, to work out any problems discovered during the encounter stage, the new member changes or goes through the **metamorphosis stage**.[66] The options presented in Exhibit 16-5 are alternatives designed to bring about metamorphosis. Most research suggests two major "bundles" of socialization practices.[67] The more management relies on formal, collective, fixed, and serial socialization programs while emphasizing divestiture, the more likely newcomers' differences will be stripped away and replaced by standardized predictable

Formal Versus Informal The more a new employee is segregated from the ongoing work setting and differentiated in some way to make explicit their newcomer's role, the more socialization is formal. Specific orientation and training programs are examples. Informal socialization puts the new employee directly into the job, with little or no special attention.

Individual Versus Collective New members can be socialized individually. This describes how it is done in many professional offices. They can also be grouped together and processed through an identical set of experiences, as in military boot camp.

Fixed Versus Variable This refers to the time schedule in which newcomers make the transition from outsider to insider. A fixed schedule establishes standardized stages of transition. This characterizes rotational training programs. It also includes probationary periods, such as the eight- to ten-year "associate" status used by accounting and law firms before deciding on whether or not a candidate is made a partner. Variable schedules give no advance notice of their transition timetable. Variable schedules describe the typical promotion system, in which one is not advanced to the next stage until one is "ready."

Serial Versus Random Serial socialization is characterized by the use of role models who train and encourage the newcomer. Apprenticeship and mentoring programs are examples. In random socialization, role models are deliberately withheld. New employees are left on their own to figure things out.

Investiture Versus Divestiture Investiture socialization assumes that the newcomer's qualities and qualifications are the necessary ingredients for job success, so these qualities and qualifications are confirmed and supported. Divestiture socialization tries to strip away certain characteristics of the recruit. Fraternity and sorority "pledges" go through divestiture socialization to shape them into the proper role.

**EXHIBIT 16-5
Entry
Socialization
Options**

behaviors. These *institutional* practices are common in police departments, fire departments, and other organizations that value rule following and order. Programs that are informal, individual, variable, and random while emphasizing investiture are more likely to give newcomers a sense of their roles and methods of working. Creative fields such as research and development, advertising, and filmmaking rely on these *individual* practices.[68] Most research suggests that high levels of institutional practices encourage person–organization fit, high levels of commitment, and improved role clarity, whereas individual practices produce more role innovation, improve motivation, and lead to social integration.[69]

Researchers examine how employee attitudes change during socialization by measuring it at several time points over the first few months. Several studies have now documented patterns of "honeymoons" and "hangovers" for new workers, showing that the period of initial adjustment is often marked by decreases in job satisfaction as idealized hopes come into contact with the reality of organizational life.[70] Newcomers may find that the level of social support they receive from supervisors and coworkers is gradually withdrawn over the first few weeks on the job, as everyone returns to "business as usual."[71] Role conflict and role overload may rise for newcomers over time, and workers with the largest increases in these role problems experience the largest decreases in commitment and satisfaction.[72] It may be that the initial adjustment period for newcomers presents increasing demands and difficulties, at least in the short term. What can supervisors and coworkers do to address "hangovers"? Research suggests that "too many" socialization practices can make things worse but providing a great deal of social support helps newcomers deal with their increasing demands and decreasing attitudes.[73]

WHAT DO CULTURES DO?

The Functions of Culture

Culture defines "the rules of the game." First, it has a boundary-defining role: It creates distinctions between organizations. Second, it conveys a sense of identity for organization members. Third, culture facilitates commitment to something larger than individual self-interest. Fourth, it enhances the stability of the social system. Culture is the social glue that helps hold the organization together by providing standards for what employees should say and do. Finally, it is a sense-making and control mechanism that guides and shapes employees' attitudes and behavior. This last function is of interest to us in the study of OB.[74]

A strong culture ensures employees will act in a relatively uniform and predictable way. For example, research has shown that a positive organizational culture improves employee job attitudes and, as such, bolsters talent attraction and retention.[75] As another example, a study of the top 100 Taiwanese financial enterprises in 2005 demonstrated that those companies that valued innovation as a component of their culture were able to learn more and more quickly in order to drive innovation.[76]

Today's trend toward decentralized organizations makes culture more important than ever, but ironically, it also makes establishing a strong culture more difficult. When formal authority and control systems are reduced through decentralization, culture's *shared meaning* can point everyone in the same direction. Decentralization also highlights the role climate plays in linking organizational culture to organizational and employee outcomes.

Culture Creates Climate

Organizational climate
The shared perceptions organizational members have about their organization's policies, procedures, and practices.

Organizational climate refers to the shared perceptions organizational members have about their organization's policies, procedures, and practices.[77] Although it may appear difficult on the surface to distinguish organizational culture from climate, culture and climate are "two crucial building blocks for organizational description."[78] In our discussion of culture so far, we have referred to culture as something that is difficult to measure and somewhat esoteric. For instance, an employee of an organization for many years may have a much better understanding of an organization's culture than someone who just found out about the organization. Today, researchers agree that organizational climate represents the more readily observable "behavioral evidence" for an organization's culture.[79] It directly links what the organization values and believes with explicit practices, policies, and procedures. In other words, it puts the "what we believe and value" (like what you would find in a mission statement) and links it to what employees perceive is *actually* supported, rewarded, and practiced. If an organization is like an onion, the culture is at the core, and the climates are on the surface layers.

An example might help illustrate this culture–climate distinction.[80] Let us say the captain of a cargo ship was running behind in departing from port. The captain tried to increase speed and take a more direct course to make up for the delay. On its way to the destination, the ship ran aground and was damaged, and thousands of dollars in expensive cargo was damaged. If we were to interview the captain, the captain might say, "I feel a tremendous sense of pressure to make sure the cargo gets to where it needs to be on time. Our company values timeliness above everything else, and top management constantly reiterates this to us." These statements reflect the underlying value of timeliness that underlies the company's culture. "Besides, we are rewarded for getting to the port on time, policy permits us to increase speed and alter routes to get to port on time, and every other captain I work with at this company makes similar decisions when we're running behind!" These statements reflect the policies, practices, and procedures that reflect a timeliness climate. At the same time, when asked about safety, the captain's shoulder shrug and "it's just not important to them" says a lot. An organization with a strong safety culture (valuing safety and believing safety matters) and a strong safety climate (prohibiting speed and direction changes, incorporating technology to detect and prevent collisions, using proper safety equipment, and requiring safety training for captains) may have avoided this incident altogether.

Dozens of dimensions of climate have been studied, including innovation, creativity, communication, warmth and support, involvement, safety, justice, diversity, and customer service.[81] For example, strong safety climates (like the one described earlier) lead to high levels of job satisfaction, organizational commitment, and healthier employees.[82] Climate influences the habits people adopt. In an organization with a strong safety climate, everyone wears safety gear and follows safety procedures even if individually they would not normally think very often about being safe—indeed, many studies have shown that a safety climate decreases the number of documented injuries on the job.[83] In general, one meta-analysis found that across dozens of different samples, positive climates (e.g., innovation, warmth and support, etc.) were strongly related to individuals' levels of job satisfaction, involvement, commitment, and motivation.[84] Positive workplace climates have also been linked to higher customer satisfaction and organizational financial performance.[85]

Exhibit 16-6 depicts the impact of organizational culture. Employees form an overall subjective perception of the organization based on leader and member behaviors, the organizational structure, and the organization's values and beliefs as well as artifacts, stories, and symbols. This overall perception represents, in effect, the organization's culture, which varies in its strength (or degree to which others perceive the culture in the same way). The culture is then revealed through organizational climates, which manifest the culture's underlying values and beliefs. The climates then affect employee performance and satisfaction, along with other outcomes relevant to organization.

In the following sections, we describe several cultures (and their corresponding climates) that affect attitudes and behavior in organizations.

EXHIBIT 16-6

How Organizational Cultures Have an Impact on Employee Performance and Satisfaction

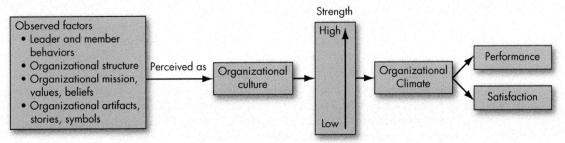

The Ethical Dimension of Culture

Ethical culture
The shared concept of right and wrong behavior in the workplace that reflects the true values of the organization and shapes the ethical decision making of its members.

Organizational cultures are not neutral in their ethical orientation, even when they are not openly pursuing ethical goals. **Ethical culture** develops over time as the shared concept of right and wrong behavior in the workplace. Ethical culture reflects the true values of the organization and shapes the ethical decision making of its members.[86] Research on public sector organizations in Finland suggests that ethical culture is important for organizations to reduce employee burnout and bolster employee engagement, in *both* managers and employees.[87]

Researchers have developed *ethical climate theory* (*ECT*) to measure the shared perceptions of ethical policies, practices, and procedures.[88] Ethical climates are heavily influenced by the values and beliefs leaders hold about ethical behavior as well as the collective sense of identity people forge around their shared ethics[89] manual. Organizations often progress through different categories as they move through their business life cycle.

An organization's ethical climate powerfully influences the way its individual members feel they should behave, so much so that researchers have been able to predict organizational outcomes.[90] Ethical climates that emphasize self-interest are negatively associated with employee job satisfaction and organizational commitment, even though those climates appeal to helping oneself vs. others. These climates are also positively associated with turnover intentions, workplace bullying, and deviant behavior.[91] Ethical climates that emphasize caring for one another and establishing rules may bring greater job satisfaction, as well as reduce employee turnover intentions, workplace bullying, and dysfunctional behavior. Research also suggests ethical climates have a strong influence on sales growth over time when there is also a customer service climate to support it.[92]

Culture and Sustainability

Sustainability
Organization practices that can be sustained over a long period of time because the tools or structures that support them are not damaged by the processes.

Sustainability refers to maintaining practices over very long periods of time, because the tools or structures that support the practices are not damaged by the processes.[93] Jeffrey Hollender created an organization that literally embodies the concept of sustainability: Seventh Generation. Founded in 1988, the company's name is based on an Iroquois proverb: In our every deliberation, we must consider the impact of our decisions on the next seven generations."[94] The name serves as a symbol reflecting the value of sustainability to Seventh Generation. When we engage in business practices (e.g., enacting a sustainability climate), we do so sustainably when we ensure that our practices can be continued and that we use resources responsibly, minimizing waste, maximizing reusability, and ensuring continued efficiency. *Social sustainability* practices address the ways social systems are affected by an organization's actions over time and, in turn, how changing social systems may affect the organization. Here, organizations should consider the effect of their labor practices on people over time, such as how job design (e.g., working hours) affects stress and health, how layoff policies and health insurance affect employees' well-being, etc.[95]

One survey found that a great majority of executives saw sustainability as an important part of future success.[96] Indeed, research has demonstrated that sustainability practices can affect organizations' reputation, productivity, talent acquisition, retention, engagement, cost efficiency, innovation, and financial performance.[97] Concepts of sustainable management have their origins in the environmental movement, so processes that are in harmony with the natural environment are encouraged. For example, farmers in Australia have been working collectively to increase water use efficiency, minimize soil erosion, and implement tilling and harvesting methods that ensure long-term viability for their farm businesses.[98] In a very different context, Siemens has a comprehensive sustainability strategy that uses the United Nation's sustainable development goals as a guideline, focusing on improving peoples' health and well-being, taking action for clean energy and climate, as well as furthering education, peace, and justice across the globe.[99] With such a comprehensive focus on sustainability, it is no wonder that Siemens was ranked in the Top Ten Most Sustainable Companies in the world in 2018, according to *Forbes*.[100]

To create a truly sustainable business, an organization must develop a long-term culture and put its values into practice through climate.[101] In other words, there needs to be a sustainable system for creating sustainability! In one study, a company seeking to reduce energy consumption found that soliciting group feedback reduced energy use significantly more than simply issuing reading materials about the importance of conservation.[102] In other words, talking about energy conservation and building the value into the organizational culture resulted in positive employee behavioral changes. The leader plays a large role, too: In one study of British and Italian firms in the cultural/creative industry, leaders can engage in several behaviors to help build a sustainable culture.[103] Like other cultural practices we have discussed, sustainability needs time and nurturing to grow.

Culture and Innovation

The most innovative companies are often characterized by their open, unconventional, collaborative, vision-driven, and accelerating cultures.[104] Start-up firms often have innovative cultures because they are usually small, agile, and focused on solving problems in order to survive and grow. Consider ad agency Droga5, recently bought by Accenture. As a start-up, Droga5 sought to "redefine advertising, making it viral and into a union of marketing and entertainment instead of a 'disruption model of uninvited guests'" (e.g., intrusive or annoying commercials, ad spots).[105] Both Accenture and Droga5 have been listed on most innovative company lists, so the fit seemed to be a good one.[106] Because of the similar organizational cultures, the two may be able to continue their start-up level of innovation. Research on companies such as these has found that innovation-friendly practices (support for new ideas, openness to change, and providing resources to be creative) leads to boosts in creativity at work, the creation and implementation of novel ideas, and increased performance.[107]

At the other end of the start-up spectrum, consider Netflix. They went from a traditional mail-order DVD service to video-on-demand, even when they were the leader in their already large business. Netflix embodies, as Gary Pisano (professor at Harvard) notes, the "no, it doesn't have to be that way" culture. When others were predicting their downfall when trying to innovate while they already "had a good thing going," they succeeded.[108] Innovation can also come from *subcultures*. For example, during the 2013–2018 period, researchers at NASA's Johnson Space Center documented a subculture group that became known as the "Pirates." They were known for directly opposing NASA's early values of hierarchy, and revolutionizing the way employees ran mission control, resulting in an innovative and cost-focused culture.[109]

Culture as an Asset

As we have discussed, organizational culture can foster a positive environment, with organizational climates that put values in action. Culture can also significantly contribute to an organization's bottom line in many ways.[110]

One strong example can be found in the case of ChildNet.[111] ChildNet is a nonprofit child welfare agency in Florida whose organizational culture was described as "grim" from 2000 (when one of its foster children disappeared) through 2007 (when the CEO was fired amid FBI allegations of fraud and forgery). "We didn't know if we would have jobs or who would take over," employee Maggie Tilelli said. However, after intense turn-around efforts aimed at changing the organizational culture, ChildNet became Florida's top-ranked agency within four years and *Workforce Management*'s Optima award winner for General Excellence in 2012.

While ChildNet demonstrates how an organizational culture can positively affect outcomes, Dish Network illustrates the elusiveness of matching a particular culture to an industry or organization.[112] By every measure, Dish Network is a business success story—it is the second-largest U.S. satellite TV provider and it has made its founder one of the richest men in the world. Yet Dish had been ranked as the worst U.S. company to work for at one point, and employees say that this is due to the culture. Employees recounted various practices that suggest undesirable climates, including arduous manda-tory overtime, fingerprint scanners to record work hours to the minute, public berating from leadership, management condescension and distrust, quarterly "bloodbath" layoffs, and no working from home. One employee advised another online, "You're part of a poisonous environment . . . go find a job where you can use your talents for good rather than evil."

At ChildNet, positive changes to the organization's performance have been clearly attributed to the transformation of its organizational culture. Dish, on the other hand, may have succeeded *despite* its culture. We can only wonder how much more successful it could be if it reformed its toxic culture. There are many more cases of business success stories due to excellent organizational cultures than there are of success stories despite bad cultures, and almost no success stories because of bad ones. Research suggests that part of the reason why culture affects an organization's performance is through customer satisfaction: One study of nearly one hundred automobile dealerships over a six-year timeframe found that a positive culture leads to improved sales performance because it increases customer satisfaction.[113]

Culture as a Liability

Culture can enhance organizational commitment and increase the consistency of employee behavior, which clearly benefits an organization. Culture is valuable to employ-ees too, because it spells out what is important. But we should not ignore the potentially dysfunctional aspects of culture, especially a strong one, on an organization's effective-ness. Hewlett-Packard, once known as a premier computer manufacturer, rapidly lost market share and profits as dysfunction in its top management team trickled down, leav-ing employees disengaged, uncreative, unappreciated, or in a polarized environment.[114] Let us unpack some of the major factors that signal a negative organizational culture, beginning with institutionalization.

Institutionalization
A condition that occurs when an organization takes on a life of its own, apart from any of its mem-bers, and acquires immortality.

INSTITUTIONALIZATION When an organization undergoes **institutionalization**—that is, it becomes valued for itself and not for the goods or services it produces—it takes on a life of its own, apart from its founders or members.[115] Institutionalized organizations often do not go out of business even if the original goals are no longer relevant. Acceptable modes of behavior become largely self-evident to members, and although this is not entirely negative, it does mean behaviors and habits go unquestioned, which can stifle innovation and make maintaining the organization's culture an end in itself.

BARRIERS TO CHANGE   Culture is a liability when shared values are not aligned with those that further the organization's effectiveness. This is most likely when an organization's environment is undergoing rapid change and its entrenched culture may no longer be appropriate.[116] Consistency of employee behavior, which is an asset in a stable environment, may then burden the organization and make it difficult to respond to changes. Cultural change is possible, however.[117] Consider the case of the joint auto plant where GM, whose workforce was struggling, teamed up with Toyota. Within just a year's time, GM's product quality increased, absenteeism dropped by 18 percent to near-zero levels, strikes stopped, counterproductive work behaviors were squelched, and employees passionately embraced the change.[118]

BARRIERS TO DIVERSITY   Hiring new employees who differ from the majority in race, age, gender, disability, or other characteristics creates a paradox:[119] Management wants to demonstrate support for the differences these employees bring to the workplace, but newcomers who wish to fit in are usually pressured to accept the organization's core culture. Second, because diverse behaviors and unique strengths are likely to diminish as people assimilate, strong cultures can become liabilities when they effectively eliminate the advantages of diversity. Third, a strong culture that condones prejudice, supports bias, or becomes insensitive to differences can undermine formal corporate diversity policies or the positive effects of demographic diversity.[120] It seems that these barriers to diversity can start at the community level: One study of nearly 150 retail bank locations in the United States found that the demographic composition of the community serves as an important signal in setting the diversity norms that are adopted and made part of an organization's culture and climate.[121] Barriers to diversity can, in part, be addressed through cultures and climates of inclusion—by showing the organization values and enacts an inclusive environment, diversity may flourish within the organization, and employees may be more committed to the organization.[122] On the other hand, people from various backgrounds may perceive the culture and climates differently, undermining the effect positive cultures and climates may have on organizational outcomes.[123]

TOXICITY AND DYSFUNCTIONS   We have discussed cultures that generally cohere around a positive set of values and beliefs. This consensus can create a powerful forward momentum. However, coherence around negative and dysfunctional values in a corporation can produce downward forces that are equally powerful yet toxic. For example, research on 862 bank employees in about 150 branches of a large bank in the United States suggests that branch managers model conflict management styles, which then shape conflict cultures within each branch.[124] Collaborative cultures (i.e., encouraging proactive, constructive, and collaborative conflict resolution) tended to increase the cohesion and satisfaction of the branch and decrease levels of burnout. Dominating cultures (i.e., encouraging active confrontation and aggressive competition among employees when there is conflict) tend to reduce branch cohesion and customer service performance. Avoidance cultures (i.e., those that passively avoid conflict) tended to be less creative.

BARRIERS TO ACQUISITIONS AND MERGERS   Historically, when management looked at acquisition or merger decisions, the key decision factors were potential financial advantage and product synergy. In recent years, cultural compatibility has become the primary concern.[125] All things being equal, whether the acquisition works seems to have much to do with how well the two organizations' cultures match up. When they do not mesh well, the organizational cultures of both become a liability to the whole new organization. A study conducted by Bain and Company found that 70 percent of mergers failed to increase shareholder values, and Hay Group found that more than 90 percent of mergers in Europe failed to reach financial goals.[126] Considering this dismal rate of success, Lawrence Chia from Deloitte Consulting observed, "One of the biggest failings is people. The people at Company A have a different way of doing things from Company B . . . you can't find commonality in goals." For example, one employee (of a creative company acquired by a larger one), who was transplanted from the East Village to Wall Street (in New York City), suggested the move was "more than physical, representing the scrappy creative adolescent putting on a tie."[127] In order for mergers or acquisitions to be successful, cultural integration is essential, as well as flexibility and complementarity in employee skills (think back to the chapters on foundations of group behavior and understanding work teams and what we know about team diversity).[128]

INFLUENCING ORGANIZATIONAL CULTURE

As we discussed, the culture of an organization is set by its founders and is often difficult to change. It is true that the ideal scenario is a strong founder (or founders) who carefully plans the organization's culture beforehand. That is seldom the case, though; organizational culture usually grows organically over time. When we think of the development of culture as ongoing and conducted through each employee, we can see ways to increase the ethical, positive, and/or spiritual aspects of the environment, as discussed next.

Ethical Cultures

Despite differences across industries and cultures, ethical organizational cultures share some common values and processes.[129] Therefore, managers can create a more ethical culture and more ethical climates by adhering to the following principles:[130]

- **Be a visible role model.** Employees will look to the actions of top management as a benchmark for appropriate behavior, but everyone can be a role model to positively influence the ethical atmosphere. Send a positive message.
- **Communicate ethical expectations.** Whenever you serve in a leadership capacity, minimize ethical ambiguities by sharing a code of ethics that states the organization's primary values and the judgment rules employees must follow.
- **Provide ethical training.** Set up seminars, workshops, and training programs to reinforce the organization's standards of conduct, clarify what practices are permissible, and address potential ethical dilemmas.
- **Visibly reward ethical acts and punish unethical ones.** Evaluate subordinates on how their decisions measure up against the organization's code of ethics. Review the means as well as the ends. Visibly reward those who act ethically and conspicuously punish those who do not.

- **Provide protective mechanisms.** Seek formal mechanisms so everyone can discuss ethical dilemmas and report unethical behavior without fear of reprimand. These might include identifying ethical counselors, ombudspeople, or ethical officers for liaison roles.

A widespread positive ethical climate must start at the top of the organization.[131] When top management emphasizes strong ethical values, supervisors are more likely to practice ethical leadership. Clear expectations transfer down to line employees, who show lower levels of deviant behavior and higher levels of cooperation and assistance. Several other studies have come to the same general conclusion: The values of top management are a good predictor of ethical behavior among employees. For example, one study involving auditors found perceived pressure from organizational leaders to behave unethically was associated with increased intentions to engage in unethical practices.[132] Clearly, the wrong type of organizational culture can negatively influence employee ethical behavior. Conversely, ethical leadership has been shown to improve group ethical voice, or the extent to which employees feel comfortable speaking up about issues that seem unethical to them, through improvements in ethical culture.[133] Finally, employees whose ethical values are similar to those of their department are more likely to be promoted, so we can think of ethical culture as flowing from the bottom up as well.[134]

Positive Cultures

At first blush, creating a positive culture may sound hopelessly naïve or like a Dilbert-style conspiracy. The one thing that makes us believe this trend is here to stay, however, are signs that management practice and OB research are converging. A **positive organizational culture** values building on employee strengths, rewards more than it punishes, and encourages individual vitality and growth.[135] Let us consider each of these areas.

> **Positive organizational culture**
> A culture that values building on employee strengths, rewards more than it punishes, and encourages individual vitality and growth.

BUILDING ON EMPLOYEE STRENGTHS Although a positive organizational culture does not ignore problems, it does emphasize showing workers how they can capitalize on their strengths. As management guru Peter Drucker said, "Most Americans do not know what their strengths are. When you ask them, they look at you with a blank stare, or they respond in terms of subject knowledge, which is the wrong answer." Wouldn't it be better to be in an organizational culture that helped you discover your strengths and how to make the most of them?

REWARDING MORE THAN PUNISHING Although most organizations are sufficiently focused on extrinsic rewards such as pay and promotions, they often forget about the power of smaller (and cheaper) rewards such as praise. Part of creating a positive organizational culture is "catching employees doing something right." Many managers withhold praise because they are afraid employees will coast or because they think praise is not valued. Employees generally do not ask for praise, and managers usually do not realize the costs of failing to give it.

ENCOURAGING VITALITY AND GROWTH No organization will get the best from employees who see themselves as mere cogs in the machine. A positive culture recognizes the difference between a job and a career. It supports not only what the employee contributes to organizational effectiveness but how the organization can make the employee more effective—personally and professionally.

LIMITS OF POSITIVE CULTURE Is a positive culture a cure-all? Though many companies have embraced aspects of a positive organizational culture, it is a new enough idea for us to be uncertain about how and when it works best.

Not all national cultures value being positive as much as the U.S. culture does and, even within U.S. culture, there surely are limits to how far organizations should go. The limits may need to be dictated by the industry and society. For example, Admiral, a British insurance company, has established a Ministry of Fun in its call centers to organize poem writing, foosball, conkers (a British game involving chestnuts), and fancy-dress days, which may clash with an industry value of more serious cultures.[136] When does the pursuit of a positive culture start to seem coercive? As one critic notes, "Promoting a social orthodoxy of positiveness focuses on a particular constellation of desirable states and traits but, in so doing, can stigmatize those who fail to fit the template."[137] There may be benefits to establishing a positive culture, but an organization also needs to be objective and not pursue it past the point of effectiveness.

Spiritual Cultures

What do Southwest Airlines, Hewlett-Packard, Ford, The Men's Wearhouse, Tyson Foods, Wetherill Associates, and Tom's of Maine have in common? They are among a growing number of organizations that have embraced workplace spirituality.

Workplace spirituality
The recognition that people have an inner life that nourishes and is nourished by meaningful work that takes place in the context of community.

WHAT IS SPIRITUALITY? Workplace spirituality is *not* about organized religious practices. It is not about God or theology. **Workplace spirituality** recognizes that people have an inner life that nourishes and is nourished by meaningful work in the context of community.[138] Organizations that support a spiritual culture recognize that people seek to find meaning and purpose in their work and desire to connect with other human beings as part of a community. Many of the topics we have discussed—ranging from job design to corporate social responsibility (CSR)—are well matched to the concept of organizational spirituality. When a company emphasizes its commitment to paying third-world suppliers a fair (above-market) price for their products to facilitate community development—as did Starbucks—or encourages employees to share prayers or inspirational messages through e-mail—as did Interstate Batteries—it may encourage a more spiritual culture and climate.[139]

WHY SPIRITUALITY NOW? As noted in our discussion of emotions in the chapter on emotions and moods, the myth of rationality assumed the well-run organization eliminated people's feelings. Concern about an employee's inner life had no role in the perfectly rational model. But just as we realize that the study of emotions improves our understanding of OB, an awareness of spirituality can help us better understand employee behavior.

Of course, employees have always had an inner life. So why has the search for meaning and purposefulness in work surfaced now? We summarize the reasons in Exhibit 16-7.

- Spirituality can counterbalance the pressures and stress of a turbulent pace of life. Contemporary lifestyles—single-parent families, geographic mobility, the temporary nature of jobs, new technologies that create distance between people—underscore the lack of community many people feel and increase the need for involvement and connection.

- Formalized religion hasn't worked for many people, and they continue to look for anchors to replace a lack of faith and to fill a growing feeling of emptiness.

- Job demands have made the workplace dominant in many people's lives, yet they continue to question the meaning of work.

- People want to integrate personal life values with their professional lives.

- An increasing number of people are finding that the pursuit of more material acquisitions leaves them unfulfilled.

EXHIBIT 16-7
Reasons for the Growing Interest in Spirituality

CHARACTERISTICS OF A SPIRITUAL ORGANIZATION The concept of workplace spirituality draws on our previous discussions of values, ethics, motivation, and leadership. Although research remains preliminary, several cultural values tend to be evident in spiritual organizations:[140]

- **Benevolence.** Spiritual organizations value kindness toward others and the happiness of employees and other organizational stakeholders.
- **Strong sense of purpose.** Spiritual organizations build their cultures around a meaningful purpose. Although profits may be important, they are not the primary value.
- **Trust and respect.** Spiritual organizations are characterized by mutual trust, honesty, and openness. Employees are treated with esteem and are valued, consistent with the dignity of each individual.
- **Open-mindedness.** Spiritual organizations value flexible thinking and creativity among employees.

ACHIEVING SPIRITUALITY IN THE ORGANIZATION Many organizations have grown interested in spirituality but have had trouble putting principles into practice. Several types of practices can facilitate a spiritual climate,[141] including those that support work–life balance. Leaders can demonstrate values, attitudes, and behaviors that trigger intrinsic motivation and a sense of fulfilling a calling through work.[142] Encouraging employees to consider how their work provides a sense of purpose can help achieve a spiritual workplace; often this is done through group counseling and organizational development, a topic we take up in the chapter on organizational change and stress management. Third, a growing number of companies, including Taco Bell, offer employees the counseling services of corporate chaplains. Many chaplains are employed by agencies, such as Marketplace Chaplains USA, while some corporations, such as Tyson Foods, employ chaplains directly. The workplace presence of corporate chaplains, who are often ordained Christian ministers, is obviously controversial, although their role is not to increase spirituality but to help human resources departments serve the employees who already have Christian beliefs.[143] Similar roles for leaders of other faiths certainly must be encouraged.

CRITICISMS OF SPIRITUALITY   Critics of the spirituality movement in organizations[144] have focused on three issues. First is the question of scientific foundation. What is workplace spirituality, exactly? Is it just a buzzword? Second, an emphasis on spirituality can clearly make some employees uneasy. Critics have argued that secular institutions, especially business firms, should not impose spiritual values on employees.[145] This criticism is undoubtedly valid when spirituality is defined as bringing religion and God into the workplace. However, it seems less stinging when the goal is limited to helping employees find meaning and purpose in their work lives. Finally, whether spirituality and profits are compatible objectives is a relevant concern for managers and investors in business. Although there has been relatively little research on this topic in recent years, some research does suggest that it can help address some of the negative effects of emotional labor in Chinese service workers.[146] In another study, organizations that provided their employees with opportunities for spiritual development outperformed those that did not.[147] Other studies reported that spirituality in organizations was positively related to creativity, employee satisfaction, job involvement, and organizational commitment.[148]

THE GLOBAL CONTEXT

We considered global cultural values (collectivism–individualism, power distance, and so on) in the chapter on personality and values. Here our focus is a bit narrower: How is organizational culture affected by the global context? Organizational culture is so powerful that it often transcends national boundaries.[149] But that does not mean organizations should ignore national and local culture.

One of the primary things U.S. employees can do is be culturally sensitive. The United States is a dominant force in business and in culture—and with that influence comes a reputation. "We are broadly seen throughout the world as arrogant people, totally self-absorbed and loud," says one U.S. executive. Some ways in which U.S. employees can be culturally sensitive include being aware of one's actions and how they may be perceived by others and to consider others' backgrounds, perspectives, and emotions before speaking or acting.

The management of ethical behavior is one area where national culture can rub against corporate culture.[150] U.S. managers and employees often endorse the supremacy of anonymous market forces as a moral obligation for business organizations. This worldview sees bribery, nepotism, and favoring personal contacts as highly unethical. They also value profit maximization, so any action that deviates from profit maximization may suggest inappropriate or corrupt behavior. In contrast, managers in developing economies are more likely to see ethical decisions as embedded in the social environment. That means doing special favors for family and friends is not only appropriate but possibly even an ethical responsibility. Managers in many nations view capitalism skeptically and believe the interests of workers should be put on a par with the interests of shareholders, which may limit profit maximization. Creating a multinational organizational culture can initiate strife between employees of traditionally competing countries. As national organizations seek to employ workers in overseas operations, top management must decide whether to standardize many facets of organizational culture. At this point, there is no clear consensus on the best course of action, but the first step is for companies to be sensitive to differing standards.

SUMMARY

Organizational cultures have an immense impact on behavior in organizations. Although the "essence" of an organization is often hard to describe, we can peer into the world of organizational life by examining an organization's shared values and beliefs, material symbols, rituals, stories, and language. Several culture frameworks have demonstrated that values and beliefs can have a substantial effect on organizational outcomes and that different cultural values affect different strategic outcomes. Cultures can also cut across organizations because employees differ in how strongly they agree on their organization's culture—these differences can lead to the creation of subcultures, which have implications for why people do things differently in different branches, departments, or teams.

The influence of founders on organizations' cultures is strong and undeniable. Founders set the tone and establish the foundation for what is valued, which leads them to hire people who share these values (and exclude those who do not). Over time, support from top management and socialization processes perpetuate the organizational culture, making it very difficult to change.

Cultures serve several functions for organizations. They define boundaries, convey a sense of identity, facilitate commitment to something larger than the self, and enhance the stability of the organizational system (acting as the "glue that holds the organization together"). The way the culture establishes tangible, concrete roots in organizations is through the establishment of climates, or policies, practices, and procedures that reinforce cultural values and beliefs. These climates then influence organizational outcomes such as performance and attitudes. Notably, a plethora of types of cultures and climates have been studied in OB to date. Of these, safety, ethical, sustainable, and innovation cultures and climates are particularly important and relevant for organizations. Furthermore, cultures and climates can be construed as both assets and liabilities, depending upon the values and practices considered. To enhance their value as assets, managers and employees alike can seek to foster positive, ethical, and spiritual cultures and climates that may help make their organization a reaffirming and positive place to work. As a caveat, you should always be aware of how national and organizational cultures may sometimes clash, especially when it comes to ethical issues.

IMPLICATIONS FOR MANAGERS

- Realize that organizational culture is a complex, descriptive, and information-rich aspect of organizations that has a major influence on important outcomes, although is relatively fixed in the short term. To affect change, involve top management and strategize a long-term plan for culture and climate transformation.
- Hire individuals whose values align with those of the organization (unless the objective is to introduce a diversity of perspectives); these employees will tend to remain committed and satisfied. Not surprisingly, "misfits" have considerably higher turnover rates.
- Understand that employees' performance and socialization depend to a considerable degree on their knowing what is valued and what is practiced in the organization. Train your employees well and keep them informed of changes to their job roles.

- You can shape the culture of your work environment, sometimes as much as it shapes you. All managers can do their part to create the desired culture by focusing on establishing policies, practices, and procedures that reinforce the desired or emphasized values.
- Realize that although culture change often begins with managers, it is most directly a function of the people who make up the company. You must involve and engage employees to be active participants in the organizational culture to create, sustain, or change culture.
- Be aware that your company's organizational culture may not be "transportable" to other countries. Understand the cultural relevance of your organization's norms before introducing new plans or initiatives overseas.

17
Organizational Change and Stress Management

LEARNING OBJECTIVES

After studying this chapter, you should be able to:

17.1 Contrast the forces for change and planned change.

17.2 Describe ways to overcome resistance to change.

17.3 Compare the four main approaches to managing organizational change.

17.4 Demonstrate three ways of facilitating change.

17.5 Identify the potential environmental, organizational, and personal sources of stress at work as well as the role of individual and cultural differences.

17.6 Identify the physiological, psychological, and behavioral symptoms of stress at work.

17.7 Describe individual and organizational approaches to managing stress at work.

CHANGE

During the fourth quarter of 2016, 77 million iPhones were sold, compared with 76.8 million Samsung sales.[1] Contrast this with the fourth quarter of 2015, in which considerably fewer (71.5 million) iPhones were sold versus considerably more (83.4 million) Samsung phones.[2] At the same time, the Chinese mobile phone company Oppo and its parent company, BBK Electronics, had been moving rapidly into the market: Collectively they held only 6 percent less market share than either Samsung or Apple.[3] A look just a few years further back shows formerly dominant players like Nokia or Research in Motion (makers of the Blackberry) shrinking dramatically in size. In this and many markets, competitors are constantly entering and exiting the field, gaining and losing ground quickly. It seems that change is a constant in this and many other environments.

Forces for Change

There are several forces that drive change in today's modern workplace. Below, we summarize six of these forces that stimulate change:

1. **The changing nature of the workforce** is evident across industries. As we have discussed throughout the text, almost every organization must adjust to a multicultural environment, demographic changes, immigration, and outsourcing.

2. **Technology** is continually changing jobs and organizations.[4] For example, machine learning and artificial intelligence are revolutionizing many aspects of organizations: how business is conducted, how decisions are made, how information is collected and acted on, even how organizations structure themselves.[5] And with advancements in virtual communication, it is not difficult to imagine the idea of an office soon becoming an antiquated concept.[6]

3. **Economic shocks** also have a huge impact on organizations, leading to job loss, the death of organizations, and a long road to recovery, such as with the Great Recession of 2007–2009.[7] Economic shocks are a serious driver for change in organizations and society at large: For example, economic shocks are the primary force behind food shortages and insecurity for over 10 million people, such as those in Sudan, Burundi, and Zimbabwe.[8] Often, as the name suggests, these are difficult to forecast and happen suddenly: As former Federal Chairman Ben Bernanke stated, "I don't think economic expansions just die of old age ... they get murdered."[9] Some of the culprits here are international and national crises (such as the COVID-19 pandemic), overbuilding, rising inflation, speculative pricing, and debt accumulation (and its resulting spending cuts).[10]

4. **Competition** precipitates change. Today, competitors are as likely to be across the ocean as across town. Successful organizations are fast on their feet, capable of developing new products rapidly and getting them to market quickly. In other words, they are flexible and require an equally flexible and responsive workforce. Juliet Bourke, Deloitte partner, recently has articulated that the right kind of diversity approaches can help organizations become more flexible and agile (they are six times more likely to be innovative and agile).[11]

5. **Social trends** do not remain static. Organizations must therefore continually adjust product and marketing strategies to be sensitive to changing social trends. For example, most consumers nowadays want personalized experiences.[12] One survey found that 80 percent of consumers are more likely to make a purchase when the experience is personalized to them.[13] Dunkin' Donuts used geofencing to deliver personalized ads and coupons to people near competitor's coffee shops—they found that over a third of recipients clicked on the offer, with some saving the coupon or redeeming it right away.[14] Consumers, employees, and organizational leaders are also becoming increasingly sensitive to environmental concerns. "Green" practices seem like they are now expected rather than optional.[15]

6. **World politics** also affect changes in organizations. Not even globalization's strongest proponents could have imagined the change in world politics in recent years. We have seen a major set of financial crises that have rocked global markets, a worldwide pandemic,[16] a dramatic rise in the power and influence of China, and intense shakeups in governments across the Arab world. For example, Britain's exit from the European Union (and the political turmoil surrounding it) have led to changes that affect organizations across the globe.[17]

Reactionary Versus Planned Change

Change is simply when things become different than the way they are. Oftentimes, changes are unplanned and happen naturally—however, certain situations involve proactive, intentional, and goal-oriented efforts to realize change, which all describe **planned change**.[18]

What are the goals of planned change? First, it seeks to improve the ability of the organization to adapt to changes in its environment. Second, it seeks to change employee behavior.

Who in organizations are responsible for managing change activities? The answer is **change agents**.[19] They see a future for the organization others have not identified, and they are able to motivate, invent, and implement this vision.[20] Change agents can be managers or non-managers, current or new employees, or outside consultants. Some change agents look to transform old industries to meet new capabilities and demands. For instance, Sandy Jen, Cameron Ring, Monica Lo, and Seth Sternberg are working together to apply social marketplace concepts to online business—a concept exemplified by crowdfunding firm Kickstarter. The group has created an innovative service for senior care called Honor.[21] In contrast to older methods of matching seniors and their families with services through nursing facilities, Honor uses an online marketplace.

Change
When things become different from the way they were.

Planned change
Change activities that are proactive, intentional, and goal oriented.

Change agents
People who act as catalysts and assume the responsibility for managing change activities.

RESISTANCE TO CHANGE

Our egos are fragile, and we often see change as threatening. Even when employees are shown data that suggest they need to change; they latch onto whatever information they can find that suggests they are okay and do not need to change.[22] Employees who feel negatively about a change cope by not thinking about it or even leaving the organization. These reactions can sap the organization of vital energy when it is most needed.[23] Indeed, resisting change can be emotionally exhausting for employees.[24]

Resistance to change does not just come from lower levels of the organization. In many cases, higher-level managers will resist changes proposed by subordinates, especially if these leaders are focused on immediate performance. Conversely, when leaders are more focused on mastery and exploration, they are more willing to hear and adopt subordinates' suggestions for change.[25] Furthermore, during an acquisition, employee and middle manager resistance to change can be reduced through a slow, rather than fast, transition.[26]

Resistance to change can be positive if it leads to open discussion and debate.[27] These responses are usually preferable to apathy or silence and can indicate that members of the organization are engaged in the process, providing change agents an opportunity to explain the change effort. Change agents can also monitor resistance in order to modify the approach to fit the preferences of members of the organization.

Resistance does not necessarily surface in standardized ways. It can be overt, implicit, immediate, or deferred.[28] It is easiest for management to deal with overt and immediate resistance such as complaints, a work slowdown, or a strike threat. The greater challenge is managing resistance that is implicit or deferred because these responses—loss of loyalty or motivation, increased errors, or absenteeism—are more subtle and more difficult to recognize for what they are. Deferred actions also cloud the link between the change and the reaction to it, sometimes surfacing weeks, months, or even years later. Or a single change of little inherent impact may be the straw that breaks the camel's back because resistance to earlier changes has been deferred and stockpiled.

EXHIBIT 17-1 **Sources of Resistance to Change**	**Individual Sources** *Habit*—To cope with life's complexities, we rely on habits or programmed responses. But when confronted with change, this tendency to respond in our accustomed ways becomes a source of resistance. *Security*—People with a high need for security are likely to resist change because it threatens their feelings of safety. *Economic factors*—Changes in job tasks or established work routines can arouse economic fears if people are concerned that they will not be able to perform the new tasks or routines to their previous standards, especially when pay is closely tied to productivity. *Fear of the unknown*—Change substitutes ambiguity and uncertainty for the unknown. *Selective information processing*—Individuals are guilty of selectively processing information in order to keep their perceptions intact. They hear what they want to hear, and they ignore information that challenges the world they have created. **Organizational Sources** *Structural inertia*—Organizations have built-in mechanisms—such as their selection processes and formalized regulations—to produce stability. When an organization is confronted with change, this structural inertia acts as a counterbalance to sustain stability. *Limited focus of change*—Organizations consist of a number of interdependent subsystems. One cannot be changed without affecting the others. So limited changes in subsystems tend to be nullified by the larger system. *Group inertia*—Even if individuals want to change their behavior, group norms may act as a constraint. *Threat to expertise*—Changes in organizational patterns may threaten the expertise of specialized groups. *Threat to established power relationships*—Any redistribution of decision-making authority can threaten long-established power relationships within the organization.

Exhibit 17-1 summarizes major forces for resistance to change, categorized by their sources. Individual sources reside in human characteristics such as perceptions, personalities, and needs. Organizational sources reside in the structural makeup of organizations themselves.

Overcoming Resistance to Change

Eight tactics can help change agents deal with resistance to change.[29] Let us review them briefly.

COMMUNICATION Communication is more important than ever in times of change. One study of German companies revealed changes are most effective when a company communicates a rationale that balances the interests of various stakeholders (shareholders, employees, community, customers) rather than those of shareholders only.[30] Other research on a changing organization in the Philippines found that formal information sessions decreased employees' anxiety about the change, and that providing high-quality information about the change increased their commitment to it.[31] Framing may also play a role, as research in France and Spain suggests that if the changes are framed (and perceived) as threatening, people may not comply, whereas if they are seen as a challenge, they are more likely to champion the change, comply with it, and become engaged with their work.[32]

PARTICIPATION   It is difficult to resist a change decision in which we have participated. Assuming participants have the expertise to make a meaningful contribution, their involvement can reduce resistance, obtain commitment, and increase the quality of the change decision. One study of the Sicilian anti-Mafia organization, the Addiopizzo, found that by involving organizations in directly questioning the *pizzo* (i.e., paying protection money to the Mafia) through an appeal to values (e.g., critical consumption, integrity, pride) they were able to successfully challenge the Mafia.[33] However, against these advantages are the negatives: the potential for a poor solution and a great consumption of time.

BUILDING SUPPORT AND COMMITMENT   When managers or employees have low emotional commitment to change, they resist it and favor the status quo.[34] Employees are also more accepting of changes when they are committed to the organization as a whole.[35] So, providing organizational support (e.g., coaching and training programs to cope with the change) and developing a positive climate can enable employees to emotionally commit to the change rather than embrace the status quo.[36] Counseling and therapy, new-skills training, or a short paid leave of absence may facilitate adjustment to change when employees' fear and anxiety are high.

DEVELOPING POSITIVE RELATIONSHIPS   People are more willing to accept changes if they trust the managers implementing them and see them as legitimate.[37] One study surveyed 235 employees from a large housing corporation in the Netherlands that was experiencing a merger. Those who had a more positive relationship with their supervisor, and who felt that the work environment supported development, were much more positive about the change process.[38] There is also a contrast effect, with research at a large Chinese hospitality organization showing that people are more willing to accept changes from a *new* leader when the older leader was ineffective, abusive, or too hands-off.[39] Underscoring the importance of social context, other work shows that even individuals who are generally resistant to change will be more willing to accept new and different ideas when they feel supported by their coworkers and believe the environment is safe for taking risks.[40]

IMPLEMENTING CHANGES FAIRLY   One way organizations can minimize negative impact is to make sure change is implemented fairly for coworkers, the organization, and other parties.[41] As we saw in the chapter on motivation concepts, procedural fairness is especially important when employees perceive an outcome as negative, so it is crucial that employees see the reason for the change and perceive its implementation as consistent and fair.[42]

MANIPULATION AND COOPTATION   *Manipulation* refers to covert influence attempts.[43] Twisting facts to make them more attractive, hiding behind false truisms, withholding information, and creating false rumors to get employees to accept change are all examples of manipulation. For example, when Billy McFarland (co-founder of the Fyre Festival) was exposed for fraudulent practices, he told them that "work is your family." As one employee recounted, "We're not a family. You won't even tell me anything!"[44] *Cooptation*, on the other hand, combines manipulation and participation. It seeks to buy off members of a resisting group by giving them a key role, seeking their advice not to find a better solution but to get their endorsement. For example, the "right to repair" movement opposes manufacturing companies' monopolization of product repairs: Companies like Samsung co-opt by allowing customers to seek out "authorized repair providers," but they still can block repairs or decide the terms for the repair. As Nathan Proctor, director of the Right to Repair campaign, emphasizes, "First they ignore you, then they laugh at you, then they fight you . . . but then, as a last-ditch effort, *they co-opt you.*" Both manipulation and cooptation are relatively inexpensive ways to gain the support of adversaries, but they can backfire if the targets become aware they are being tricked or used. Once that is discovered, the change agent's credibility may drop to zero.

SELECTING PEOPLE WHO ACCEPT CHANGE Research suggests the ability to easily accept and adapt to *change* is related to personality—some people simply have more positive attitudes toward change.[45] Individuals who are open to experience, are willing to take risks, and are flexible in their behavior are prime candidates.[46] One study of managers in the United States, Europe, and Asia found those with a positive self-concept and high risk tolerance coped better with organizational change. Individuals higher in general mental ability are also better able to learn and adapt to changes in the workplace.[47] In sum, an impressive body of evidence shows organizations can facilitate change by selecting people predisposed to accept it.

COERCION Last on the list of tactics is *coercion*, the application of direct threats or force on dissenters (see the chapter on power and politics).[48] Examples include threatening employees with forced transfers, blocked promotions, negative performance evaluations, and poor letters of recommendation. Coercion is most effective when some force or pressure is enacted on at least some resisters—for instance, if an employee is publicly refused a transfer request, the threat of blocked promotions will become a real possibility in the minds of other employees.

The Politics of Change

No discussion of resistance would be complete without a mention of the politics of change. Because change invariably threatens the status quo, it inherently implies political activity.

Politics suggests the impetus for change is more likely to come from outside change agents, employees new to the organization (who have less invested in the status quo), or managers who are slightly removed from the main power structure. Managers who have spent a long time with an organization and achieved a senior position in the hierarchy are often major impediments to change. Of course, as you might guess, these longtime power holders tend to implement incremental changes when they are forced to introduce change. This explains why boards of directors that recognize the imperative for rapid and radical change frequently turn to outside candidates for new leadership.[49]

APPROACHES TO MANAGING ORGANIZATIONAL CHANGE

We now turn to several approaches to managing change: Lewin's classic three-step model of the change process, Kotter's eight-step plan, action research, and organizational development.

Lewin's Three-Step Model

Kurt Lewin argued that successful change in organizations should follow three steps: *unfreezing* the status quo, *movement* to a desired end state, and *refreezing* the new change to make it permanent[50] (see Exhibit 17-2).

EXHIBIT 17-2
Lewin's Three-Step Change Model

By definition, status quo is an equilibrium state. To move from equilibrium—to overcome the pressures of both individual resistance and group conformity—unfreezing must happen in one of three ways (see Exhibit 17-3). For one, the **driving forces**, which direct behavior away from the status quo, can be increased. For another, the **restraining forces**, which hinder movement away from equilibrium, can be decreased. A third alternative is to combine the first two approaches. Companies that have been successful in the past are likely to encounter restraining forces because people question the need for change.[51]

Once the movement stage begins, it is important to keep the momentum going. Organizations that build up to change do less well than those that get to and move through the movement stage quickly. When change has been implemented, the new situation must be refrozen so it can be sustained over time. Without this last step, change will likely be short lived, and employees will attempt to revert to the previous equilibrium state.

Scholars in recent years have criticized Lewin's model for several reasons.[52] First, like Maslow's hierarchy of needs (see the chapter on motivation concepts), Lewin assumes that change happens sequentially, in order, always progressing. Second, the model implies a sense of perfect agency for managers; in other words, do change agents really know where they are, where the people in the organization are, and where they are going? Organizations are so fluid that it may be impossible to do this in real life. Still others have mentioned that the "freezing" language is somewhat problematic: Time keeps moving, freezing may never really happen, and new changes interrupt current changes dynamically. Indeed, more modern approaches to understanding change in organizations consider issues such as timing, pacing, rhythm, and the nature of the change agents involved.[53]

Driving forces
Forces that direct behavior away from the status quo.

Restraining forces
Forces that hinder movement from the existing equilibrium.

Kotter's Eight-Step Plan

John Kotter built on Lewin's three-step model to create a more detailed approach for implementing change.[54] Kotter began by listing common mistakes managers make when trying to initiate change. They may fail to create a sense of urgency about the need for change, a coalition for managing the change process, or a vision for change. They also may fail to effectively communicate it, and/or to anchor the changes into the organization's culture. They also may fail to remove obstacles that could impede the vision's achievement and/or provide short-term and achievable goals. Finally, they may declare victory too soon.

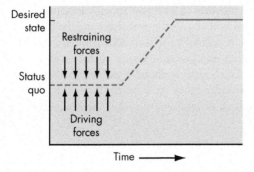

EXHIBIT 17-3
Unfreezing the Status Quo

1. Establish a sense of urgency by creating a compelling reason for why change is needed.
2. Form a coalition with enough power to lead the change.
3. Create a new vision to direct the change and strategies for achieving the vision.
4. Communicate the vision throughout the organization.
5. Empower others to act on the vision by removing barriers to change and encouraging risk taking and creative problem solving.
6. Plan for, create, and reward short-term "wins" that move the organization toward the new vision.
7. Consolidate improvements, reassess changes, and make necessary adjustments in the new programs.
8. Reinforce the changes by demonstrating the relationship between new behaviors and organizational success.

EXHIBIT 17-4

Kotter's Eight-Step Plan for Implementing Change

Source: Based on M. du Plessis, "Re-implementing an Individual Performance Management System as a Change Intervention at Higher Education Institutions Overcoming Staff Resistance," *Proceedings of the 7th European Conference on Management Leadership and Governance,* 2011, 105–15.

Kotter established eight sequential steps to overcome these problems. They are listed in Exhibit 17-4. Notice how Kotter's first four steps essentially extrapolate Lewin's "unfreezing" stage. Steps 5, 6, and 7 represent "movement," and the final step works on "refreezing." Kotter's contribution lies in providing managers and change agents with a more detailed guide for successfully implementing change.

Action Research

Action research
A change process based on the systematic collection of data and the selection of a change action based on what the analyzed data indicate.

Action research is a change process based on the systematic collection of data and selection of a change action based on what the analyzed data indicate.[55] Its value is in providing a scientific methodology for managing planned change. Action research consists of five steps (note how they closely parallel the scientific method): diagnosis, analysis, feedback, action, and evaluation. Applications of action research in Britain have been successful at improving the engagement of nursing staff,[56] as well as in making supply chain systems more sustainable.[57] In the United States, action research has been utilized by Optum, a health care company, through involving customer service specialists in determining more effective ways of engaging with customers.[58]

Action research provides at least two specific benefits. First, it is problem focused. The change agent objectively looks for problems, and the type of problem determines the type of change action. A second benefit of action research is the lowering of resistance. Because action research engages employees so thoroughly in the process, it reduces resistance to change. Once employees have actively participated in the feedback stage, the change process typically takes on a momentum of its own. However, organizations may resist participating in action research when their legitimacy is potentially or already at risk.[59]

Organizational Development

Organizational development (OD) is a collection of change methods that try to improve organizational effectiveness and employee well-being.[60]

OD methods value human and organizational growth, collaborative and participative processes, and a spirit of inquiry.[61] Contemporary OD borrows heavily from postmodern philosophy in placing heavy emphasis on the subjective ways people see and make sense of their work environment. The change agent may take the lead in OD, but there is a strong emphasis on collaboration.

What are some OD techniques or interventions for bringing about change? Here are six.

SENSITIVITY TRAINING A variety of names—**sensitivity training**, laboratory training, encounter groups, and T-groups (training groups)—all refer to an early method of changing behavior through unstructured group interaction.[62] Current organizational interventions such as diversity training, executive coaching, and team-building exercises are descendants of this early OD intervention technique. With all forms of OD, caution must be taken so the unstructured groups are not intimidating, chaotic, and damaging to work relationships.

SURVEY FEEDBACK One tool for assessing the attitudes of organizational members, identifying discrepancies among member perceptions, and solving differences is the **survey feedback** technique.[63] Basically, data collected from strategic surveys in work units is then used as a springboard to spur problem identification and discussion. Answers should lead the group to commit to various remedies for the problems.

The survey feedback approach can be helpful to keep decision makers informed about the attitudes of employees toward the organization. However, individuals are influenced by many factors when they respond to surveys, which may make some findings unreliable. Managers who use the survey feedback approach should therefore monitor their organization's current events and employee response rates.

PROCESS CONSULTATION Managers often sense their unit's performance can be improved but are unable to identify what to improve and how. The purpose of **process consultation (PC)** is for an outside consultant to assist a client, usually a manager, through crafting "a relationship through a continuous effort of 'jointly deciphering what is going on' . . . to make co-authored choices about how to go on."[64] These events might include those surrounding the workflow, informal relationships among unit members, and formal communication channels.

PC is similar to sensitivity training in assuming we can improve organizational effectiveness by dealing with interpersonal problems and in emphasizing involvement. But PC is more task directed, and consultants do not solve the organization's problems, but rather guide or coach the client to solve their own problems after *jointly* diagnosing what needs improvement. The client develops the skill to analyze processes within their unit and can therefore use the skill long after the consultant is gone. Because the client actively participates in both the diagnosis and the development of alternatives, they arrive

Organizational development (OD)
A collection of planned change interventions, built on humanistic–democratic values, that seeks to improve organizational effectiveness and employee well-being.

Sensitivity training
Training that seeks to change behavior through unstructured group interaction.

Survey feedback technique
The use of questionnaires to listen to members and identify discrepancies among member perceptions; discussion follows and remedies are suggested.

Process consultation (PC)
A meeting in which a consultant assists clients in understanding process events with which they must deal and identifying processes that need improvement.

at a greater understanding of the process and the remedy and becomes less resistant to the action plan chosen.

Team building
High interaction among team members to increase trust and openness.

TEAM BUILDING   We have noted throughout this text that organizations increasingly rely on teams to accomplish work tasks. **Team building** uses high-interaction group activities to increase trust and openness among team members, improve coordination efforts, and increase team performance.[65] For example, a number of companies are turning to "escape rooms" as a team-building method (where members have to work together and solve puzzles in order to escape a themed room).[66] As one Baltimore employee who participated in an escape room team-building exercise noted, "what comes out of an experience like that is a depended sense of relationship and community . . . once inside, it's when fun and team building intersect at a high level."[67]

Team building typically includes goal setting, development of interpersonal relations among team members, role analysis to clarify each member's role and responsibilities, and team process analysis. It may emphasize or exclude certain activities, depending on the purpose of the development effort and the specific problems the team is confronting. Basically, however, team building uses high interaction among members to increase trust and openness. In these times when organizations increasingly rely on teams, team building is an important topic.

Intergroup development
Organizational development efforts to change the attitudes, stereotypes, and perceptions that groups have of each other.

INTERGROUP DEVELOPMENT   A major area of concern in OD is dysfunctional conflict among groups. **Intergroup development** seeks to change groups' attitudes, stereotypes, and perceptions about each other.[68] Here, training sessions closely resemble diversity training, except rather than focusing on demographic differences, they focus on differences among occupations, departments, or divisions within an organization. Once they have identified the causes of discrepancies, the groups move to the integration phase—developing solutions to improve relations between them. Subgroups can be formed of members from each of the conflicting groups to conduct further diagnoses and formulate alternative solutions.

Among several approaches for improving intergroup relations, a popular one emphasizes problem solving.[69] Each group meets independently to list its perceptions of itself and another group and how it believes the other group perceives it. The groups then share their lists, discuss similarities and differences, and look for causes of disparities.

Appreciative inquiry
An approach that seeks to identify the unique qualities and special strengths of an organization, which can then be built on to improve performance.

APPRECIATIVE INQUIRY   Most OD approaches are problem centered. They identify a problem or set of problems, then look for a solution. **Appreciative inquiry** instead accentuates the positive.[70] Rather than looking for problems to fix, it seeks to identify the unique qualities and special strengths of an organization, which members can build on to improve performance. It has been demonstrated to be an effective change strategy in organizations such as GTE, Roadway Express, American Express, and the U.S. Navy.[71] The U.S. dairy industry used it to transform their sustainability efforts, resulting in nearly $300 million in projects that were singled out as models for other industries.[72]

The appreciative inquiry process consists of four steps—discovery, dreaming, design, and destiny—often played out in a large-group meeting over two to three days and overseen by a trained change agent. *Discovery* sets out to identify what people think are the organization's strengths. Employees recount times they felt the organization worked best or when they specifically felt most satisfied with their jobs. In *dreaming*, employees use information from the discovery phase to speculate on possible futures, such as what the organization will be like in five years. In *design*, participants find a common vision of how the organization will look in the future and agree on its unique qualities. For the fourth step, participants seek to define the organization's *destiny* or how to fulfill their dream, and they typically write action plans and develop implementation strategies.

FACILITATING CHANGE

We have considered how organizations can *adapt* to change. But recently, some OB scholars have focused on a more proactive approach—how organizations can *embrace* change by transforming their cultures. In this section, we review three approaches: managing paradox, stimulating innovation, and creating a learning organization. We also address the issue of organizational change and stress.

Managing Paradox

Managers can learn a few lessons from **paradox theory**,[73] which states the key paradox in management is that there is no final optimal status for an organization.[74] In a *paradox* situation, we are required to balance tensions across various courses of action, which are caused by resource scarcity.[75] There is a constant process of finding a balancing point, a dynamic equilibrium, among shifting priorities over time.[76] The first lesson is that as the environment and members of the organization change, different elements take on importance. For example, sometimes a company needs to acknowledge past success and learn how it worked, while at other times looking backward will only hinder progress. There is some evidence that managers who think holistically and recognize the importance of balancing paradoxical factors are more effective, especially in generating adaptive and creative behaviors in those they are managing.[77] However, leaders who adopt paradoxical approaches may fall into the trap of escalation of commitment (see the chapter on perception and decision making) given that they may be more optimistic that the current state of affairs will swing toward a more desirable one.[78]

Paradox theory
The theory that the key paradox in management is that there is no final optimal status for an organization.

Stimulating Innovation

How can an organization become more innovative? Although there is no guaranteed formula, certain characteristics—in structure, culture, and climate—surface repeatedly when researchers study innovative organizations (see the chapter on organizational culture). Let us first clarify what we mean by innovation.

DEFINITION OF *INNOVATION* We said change refers to making things different. **Innovation**, a specialized kind of change, is applied to initiating or improving a product, process, or service.[79] So all innovations imply change, but not all changes introduce new ideas or lead to significant improvements. Innovations can range from incremental improvements, such as tablets, to radical breakthroughs, such as the electric car.

Innovation
A new idea applied to initiating or improving a product, process, or service.

SOURCES OF INNOVATION   Structural variables are one potential source of innovation.[80] A comprehensive review of the structure–innovation relationship leads to the following conclusions:

1. **Organic structures positively influence innovation**. Because they are lower in vertical differentiation, formalization, and centralization; organic organizations facilitate the flexibility, adaptation, and cross-fertilization that make the adoption of innovations easier.[81]

2. **Contingent rewards positively influence innovation.** When creativity is rewarded, firms tend to become more innovative—especially when employees are given feedback on their performance in addition to autonomy in doing their jobs.[82]

3. **Innovation is nurtured when there are slack resources**. Having an abundance of resources allows an organization to afford to purchase or develop innovations, bear the cost of instituting them, and absorb failures.[83]

4. **Interunit communication is high in innovative organizations**. These organizations are heavy users of committees, task forces, cross-functional teams, and other mechanisms that facilitate interaction across departmental lines.[84]

CONTEXT AND INNOVATION   National cultures have an effect on innovation in organizations.[85] One study using global data from a crowdsourcing company suggests that the more a country is characterized by strong social norms and low tolerance for any deviation from the norm, innovation tends to be stifled more often.[86] Cultural diversity at the local level also has an impact. Having close, interpersonal relationships (both romantic and friendship) with those from different culture backgrounds (such as those from international assignments) sparks innovation and entrepreneurship.[87]

As described in the chapter on culture, innovative organizations encourage experimentation and reward both successes and failures.[88] Unfortunately, in too many organizations, people are rewarded for the absence of failures rather than for the presence of successes. Such cultures extinguish risk taking and innovation.[89] Innovative organizations have a shared sense of purpose[90] and also tend to be cohesive, mutually supportive, and encouraging of innovation.[91] Innovative organizations actively promote the training and development of their members so they keep current, offer high job security so employees do not fear getting fired for making mistakes, and encourage individuals to become champions of change.[92] These practices should be mirrored for workgroups as well. One study of 1,059 individuals on over 200 different teams in a Chinese high-tech company found that work systems emphasizing commitment to employees increased creativity in teams.[93] These effects were even greater in teams where there was cohesion among coworkers. Furthermore, research from Spain suggests that hotel teams deliver better customer service when innovation is supported by their organization, perhaps because they are empowered to provide the best service to accommodate each guest.[94]

Idea champions
Individuals who take an innovation and actively and enthusiastically promote the idea, build support, overcome resistance, and ensure that the idea is implemented.

IDEA CHAMPIONS AND INNOVATION   Once a new idea has been developed, **idea champions** actively and enthusiastically promote it, build support, overcome resistance, and ensure it is implemented.[95] Champions often have similar personality characteristics:[96] extremely high self-confidence, persistence, energy, and a tendency to take risks. They may display traits associated with transformational leadership—they inspire and energize others with their vision of an innovation's potential and their strong personal conviction about their mission. Managers and change agents alike should also be aware of the other types of reactions employees can have to the idea over time. For example, doubters will probably never get on board with the new idea, converts will start to like the idea more and more, and defectors are more likely to dislike the idea over time.[97] Keeping in mind these audiences, change agents can vary their message to try to obtain the best result.

Situations can also influence the extent to which idea champions are forces for change. For example, passion for change among entrepreneurs is greatest when work roles and the social environment encourage them to put their creative identities forward. On the flip side, work roles that push creative individuals to do routine management and administration tasks will diminish both the passion for and successful implementation of change.[98] Idea champions are good at gaining the commitment of others, and their jobs should provide considerable decision-making discretion. This autonomy helps them introduce and implement innovations when the context is supportive.[99]

Do successful idea champions do things differently in varied cultures? Generally, people in collectivist cultures prefer appeals for cross-functional support for innovation efforts; people in high power-distance cultures prefer champions to work closely with those in authority to approve innovative activities before work has begun; and the higher the uncertainty avoidance of a society, the more champions should work within the organization's rules and procedures to develop the innovation.[100]

Creating a Learning Organization

Another way an organization can proactively manage change is to make continuous growth part of its culture—to become a learning organization.[101]

WHAT'S A LEARNING ORGANIZATION?   Just as individuals learn, so do organizations. A **learning organization** has developed the continuous capacity to adapt and change. The Dimensions of the Learning Organization Questionnaire has been adopted and adapted internationally to assess the degree of commitment to learning organization principles.[102]

Exhibit 17-5 summarizes the five basic characteristics of a learning organization—one in which people put aside their old ways of thinking, learn to be open with each other, understand how their organization really works, form a plan or vision everyone can agree on, and work together to achieve that vision.[103]

> **Learning organization**
> An organization that has developed the continuous capacity to adapt and change.

MANAGING LEARNING What can managers do to make their firms learning organizations? Here are some suggestions:

- **Establish a strategy.** Management needs to make explicit its commitment to change, innovation, and continuous improvement.
- **Redesign the organization's structure.** The formal structure can be a serious impediment to learning. Flattening the structure, eliminating or combining departments, and increasing the use of cross-functional teams reinforces interdependence and reduces boundaries.
- **Reshape the organization's culture.** To become a learning organization, managers must demonstrate by their actions that taking risks and admitting failures are desirable. This means rewarding people who take chances and make mistakes. Management needs to encourage functional conflict.

1. There exists a shared vision that everyone agrees on.

2. People discard their old ways of thinking and the standard routines they use for solving problems or doing their jobs.

3. Members think of all organizational processes, activities, functions, and interactions with the environment as part of a system of interrelationships.

4. People openly communicate with each other (across vertical and horizontal boundaries) without fear of criticism or punishment.

5. People sublimate their personal self-interest and fragmented departmental interests to work together to achieve the organization's shared vision.

EXHIBIT 17-5

Characteristics of a Learning Organization

Source: Based on P. M. Senge, *The Fifth Discipline: The Art and Practice of the learning Organization* (New York: Doubleday, 2006).

Organizational Change and Stress

Think about the times you have felt stressed during your work life. Look past the every-day stress factors that can spill over to the workplace, like a traffic jam that makes you late for work. What have been your more memorable and lasting stressful times at work? For many people, they were those caused by organizational change. Researchers are increasingly studying the effects of organizational change on employees. We are interested in determining the specific causes and mitigating factors of stress to learn how to manage organizational change effectively.[104] The overall findings demonstrate that organizational changes that incorporate OB knowledge of how people react to stressors may yield more effective results than organizational changes that are managed only objectively through goal-setting plans.[105]

STRESS AT WORK

Stress comes in many forms at work. Racial prejudice is one particularly nefarious form that has left professionals such as Jessica Jackson, a black, female clinical psychologist with the Department of Veterans Affairs, strained. Ever since her high school days, when her teacher said she was in the wrong room and gave her lower grades than the other classmates (even on group projects), Jackson has had the stressful and frustrating task of proving her place.[106]

Stress is (quite literally) a killer, and the statistics on workplace stress are shocking.[107] One compilation of statistics suggests that (1) 83 percent of workers in the U.S. are stressed, (2) stress results in $300 billion in losses annually, (3) it accounts for 60 to 80 percent of workplace accidents, (4) it causes one million people to miss work daily, and (5) 29 percent of workers (that is almost a third!) have admitted to wanting to punch a coworker because of stress.[108] Harris, Rothenberg International, a leading provider of employee assistance programs, finds that employees are having mental breakdowns and needing professional help at higher rates than ever.[109] Indeed, as Exhibit 17-6 shows, work is a major source of stress in most people's lives. (Recent surveys also show that access to health care and the threat of sexual harassment are also major sources of stress.)[110] What are the causes and consequences of stress, and what can individuals and organizations do to reduce it?

What area of your life causes you the most stress?

Area	Causes Most Stress
Nation's future	63%
Money	62%
Work	61%
Political climate	57%
Crime (e.g., violence)	51%

EXHIBIT 17-6

Work Is a Top Source of Stress

Source: "Stress in America: The State of Our Nation," *American Psychological Association*, November 1, 2017, https://www.apa.org/news/press/releases/stress/2017/state-nation.pdf

What Is Stress?

Stress is a psychological process in which an individual is confronted with an opportunity, demand, or resource related to what the individual desires and for which the outcome is perceived to be both uncertain and important (e.g., *stressors*).[111] Then, as a result, an individual experiences **strain**, or a psychological and physical unpleasant response due to an appraisal of the stressor.[112] In a nutshell, stress is a process in which we are exposed to stressors that cause us to experience strain. Although stress is typically discussed in a negative fashion (as most of the time it is harmful), it can serve positive purposes, such as supplying you with a boost to cope with stressful situations (e.g., when professional athletes are "down to the wire") or enhancing the quality of your work when you are up against a challenge.

STRESSORS Researchers have argued that **challenge stressors**—or stressors associated with workload, pressure to complete tasks, and time urgency—operate quite differently from **hindrance stressors**—or stressors that keep you from reaching your goals (for example, red tape, office politics, confusion over job responsibilities).[113] Evidence suggests that both challenge and hindrance stressors lead to strain, although hindrance stressors lead to increased levels of strain.[114] Challenge stressors (when they are stable over time) lead to more motivation, engagement, and performance than hindrance stressors.[115] Hindrance stressors, on the other hand, appear to have more of a negative effect on safety compliance and participation, employee engagement, job satisfaction, organizational commitment, performance, and withdrawal than do challenge stressors.[116]

Researchers have sought to clarify the conditions under which each type of stress exists. It appears that time pressure and learning demands both act as challenge stressors that can help employees learn and thrive in organizations.[117] Unnecessary tasks block the potentially positive, challenging nature of the normally challenging stressors, such as time pressure.[118] Hindrances (e.g., a lack of resources to complete your job) serve to block goal attainment and should be distinguished from threats, which can result in personal harm (e.g., corrections officers fearing harm from inmates).[119] Interestingly, recent research suggests that each type of stressor is amplified by given risk factors to produce negative health effects: Challenge stressors are amplified when coupled with alcohol consumption, and hindrance stressors are amplified when coupled with food consumption and smoking.[120]

Stress
A psychological process in which an individual is confronted with an opportunity, demand, or resource related to what the individual desires and for which the outcome is perceived to be both uncertain and important (e.g., stressors).

Strain
A psychological and physical unpleasant response due to an appraisal of the stressor.

Challenge stressors
Stressors associated with workload, pressure to complete tasks, and time urgency.

Hindrance stressors
Stressors that keep you from reaching your goals (for example, red tape, office politics, confusion over job responsibilities).

Demands
Responsibilities, pressures, obligations, and even uncertainties that individuals face in the workplace.

Resources
Things within an individual's control that can be used to resolve demands.

DEMANDS AND RESOURCES Typically, stress is associated with demands and resources. **Demands** are responsibilities, pressures, obligations, and uncertainties individuals face in the workplace. **Resources** are things within an individual's control that they can use to resolve the demands. Let us discuss what this demands–resources model means.[121]

When you undergo your annual performance review at work, you feel stress because you confront opportunities and performance pressures. A good performance review may lead to a promotion, greater responsibilities, and a higher salary. A poor review may prevent you from getting a promotion. An extremely poor review might even result in your being fired. To the extent you can apply resources to the demands on you—such as preparing for the review, putting the review in perspective (it's not the end of the world), or obtaining social support—you will feel less stress.[122] In fact, this last resource—social support—may be more important on an ongoing basis than anything else. Overall, under the demands–resources perspective, having resources to cope with stress is just as important in offsetting stress as demands are in increasing it.[123]

Allostasis
Working to change behavior and attitudes to find stability.

ALLOSTASIS So far, what was discussed may give you the impression that individuals are seeking a steady state in which demands perfectly match resources. While early research tended to emphasize such a *homeostatic*, or balanced equilibrium, perspective; it has now become clear that no single ideal state exists. Instead, it is more accurate to talk about *allostatic* models, in which demands shift, resources shift, and systems of addressing imbalances shift.[124] Through **allostasis**, we work to find stability by changing our behaviors and attitudes. It all depends on the allostatic load, or the cumulative effect of stressors on us given the resources we draw upon.[125] For example, if you are feeling especially confident in your abilities and have lots of support from others, you may increase your willingness to experience strain and be better able to mobilize coping resources. This would be a situation where the allostatic load was not too great; in other cases where the allostatic load is too great and too prolonged, we may experience psychological or physiological stress symptoms.

Potential Sources of Stress at Work

What causes stress? Let's examine the model in Exhibit 17-7.

ENVIRONMENTAL FACTORS Just as environmental uncertainty influences the design of an organization's structure; it also influences stress levels among employees in that organization. Indeed, uncertainty is the biggest reason people have trouble coping with organizational changes, and why decisions made under stress deteriorate decision quality.[126] There are three main types of environmental uncertainty: economic, political, and technological.

Changes in the business cycle create *economic uncertainties*. When the economy is contracting, for example, people become increasingly anxious about their job security. *Political uncertainties* do not tend to create stress among North Americans as much as they do for employees in countries such as Haiti or Venezuela. The obvious reason is that the United States and Canada have more stable political systems, in which change is typically implemented in an orderly manner. Yet political threats and changes in all countries can induce stress. Because innovations can make an employee's skills and experience obsolete

Potential sources   **Consequences**

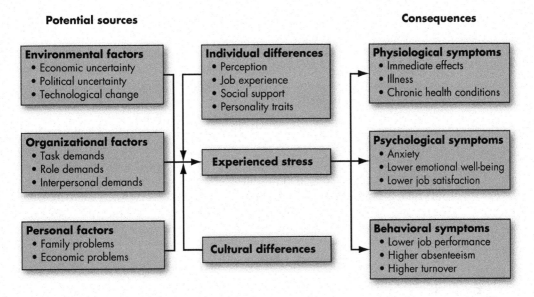

EXHIBIT 17-7
A Model of Stress

in a very short time, keeping up with new computer programs, robotics, automation, and similar forms of *technological change* are a further challenge to many people at work that cause them stress. However, newer research suggests that people are *most* uncomfortable with technological changes and uncertainty when artificial intelligence replaces jobs that require some form of emotion or feeling.[127] Interestingly people also prefer when more "cognitively demanding" jobs are *outsourced* to people in other countries.[128]

ORGANIZATIONAL FACTORS   There is no shortage of factors within an organization that can cause stress. Pressures to avoid errors or complete tasks in a limited time, work overload, a demanding and insensitive boss, and unpleasant coworkers are a few examples. We have categorized these factors around task, role, and interpersonal demands.

1. *Task demands* relate to a person's job. They include the design of the job (including its degree of autonomy, task variety, and automation), the working conditions, and the physical work layout. The single factor most consistently related to stress in the workplace is the amount of work that needs to be done, followed closely by the presence of looming deadlines.[129] Working in an overcrowded room or visible location where noise and interruptions are constant can also increase anxiety and stress.[130]

2. *Role demands* relate to pressures placed on a person as a function of the role they play in the organization.[131] Role conflicts create expectations that may be hard to reconcile or satisfy. Role overload occurs when the employee is expected to take on too much. Role ambiguity means role expectations are not clearly understood and the employee is not sure what to do. Unfortunately, individuals who face high situational constraints in their roles (such as fixed work hours or demanding job

responsibilities) are less able to engage in proactive coping behaviors, like taking a break, which can reduce stress levels.[132]

3. *Interpersonal demands* are pressures created by other employees. Some pressures are expected, but a rapidly growing body of research has shown that negative co-worker and supervisor behaviors, including fights, bullying, incivility, racial harassment, and sexual harassment, are especially and strongly related to stress at work.[133] Interpersonal mistreatment can have effects at a physiological level, with one study finding that unfair treatment in a controlled setting triggers the release of cortisol, a hormone involved in the stress-reaction process.[134] Individuals who believe they are experiencing a social climate of discrimination or social exclusion from multiple sources over time have higher levels of psychological strain, even after accounting for differing baseline levels of well-being.[135] Interpersonal demands from outside of work can also have a reciprocal effect: In other words, your family can interfere with your work and your work can interfere with your family, causing strain all-around.[136]

PERSONAL FACTORS   The typical individual may work between 40 and 50 hours a week. But the experiences and problems people encounter in the other 120-plus hours in the week can spill over to the job. For example, the quality and quantity of sleep an individual gets can adversely affect the amount of strain they experience.[137] The final category of sources of stress at work includes factors of an employee's personal life: family issues and personal economic problems.

National surveys consistently show people hold their families dear.[138] *Family issues*, even good ones, can cause stress that significantly impacts individuals.[139] Family issues are often closely related to work–life conflict, and work–life conflict is a major source of strain.[140]

Regardless of income level, financial issues can be a major source of stress. People who make $100,000 per year seem to have as much trouble handling their finances as those who earn $20,000, although recent research indicates that those who make under $50,000 per year do experience more stress.[141] The *personal economic problems* of over-extended financial resources create stress and siphon attention away from work.

STRESSORS ARE ADDITIVE   When we review stressors individually, it is easy to overlook that stress is an additive phenomenon—it builds up.[142] For example, when you experience incivility from customers or coworkers, this can lead you to have a poor night's sleep and experience additional strain beyond the incivility you just experienced.[143] Each new and persistent stressor adds to an individual's stress level. A single stressor may be relatively unimportant in and of itself, but if added to an already high level of stress, it can be too much. To appraise the total amount of stress an individual is under, we must sum up all the sources and severity levels of that person's stress. Since this cannot be easily quantified or observed, managers should remain aware of the potential stress loads from organizational factors. Many employees are willing to express their perceived stress load at work to a caring manager.

Individual Differences in Stress

Some people thrive on stressful situations, while others are overwhelmed by them. What differentiates people in terms of their ability to handle stress? What individual variables moderate the relationship between *potential* stressors and *experienced* stress? At least four are relevant—perception, job experience, social support, and personality traits.

PERCEPTION   In the chapter on perception and individual decision making, we demonstrated that employees react in response to their perception of reality, rather than to reality itself. *Perception*, therefore, will moderate the relationship between a potential stress condition and an employee's reaction to it. Layoffs may cause one person to fear losing a job, while another sees it as an opportunity to get a large severance allowance and start a new business. Those who perceive a stressful event as a small blip in an otherwise long timeline (and who take to heart phrases such as "this, too, shall pass" and "time heals all wounds") tend to cope better than those who focus on immediate circumstances.[144] So, stress potential does not lie in objective conditions; rather, it lies in an employee's interpretation of those conditions.

JOB EXPERIENCE   *Experience* on the job tends to be negatively related to work stress. Why? Two explanations have been offered.[145] First is selective withdrawal. Voluntary turnover is more probable among people who experience more stress. Therefore, people who remain with an organization longer are those with more stress-resistant traits or those more resistant to the stress characteristics of the organization. Second, people eventually develop coping mechanisms to deal with stress. Because this takes time, senior members of the organization are more likely to be fully adapted and should experience less stress.

SOCIAL SUPPORT   *Social support*—collegial relationships with coworkers or supervisors—can buffer the impact of stress.[146] This is one of the best-documented relationships in the stress literature. Social support acts as a palliative, mitigating the negative effects of even high-strain jobs.[147]

PERSONALITY TRAITS   Stress symptoms expressed on the job may originate from the person's personality.[148] Perhaps the most widely studied *personality trait* in research on stress is emotional stability, which we discussed in the chapter on personality and values. As you might expect, individuals low on emotional stability are more prone to experience psychological strain.[149] Evidence suggests that they are more likely to find stressors in their work environments, so they believe their environments are more threatening. They also tend to select less adaptive coping mechanisms, relying on avoidance as a way of dealing with problems rather than attempting to resolve them.[150] Workaholism is another personal characteristic related to stress levels.[151] Workaholics are people obsessed with their work; they put in an enormous number of hours, think about work even when not working, and create additional work responsibilities to satisfy an inner compulsion to work more.

Cultural Differences

Research suggests that the job conditions that cause stress show some differences across cultures. One study revealed that whereas U.S. employees were stressed by a lack of control, Chinese employees were stressed by job evaluations and lack of training.[152] It does not appear that personality effects on stress are different across cultures, however. A study of 5,270 managers from twenty countries found individuals from individualistic countries such as the United States, Canada, and the United Kingdom experienced higher levels of stress due to work interfering with family than did individuals from collectivist countries in Asia and Latin America.[153] The authors proposed that this may occur because, in collectivist cultures, working extra hours is seen as a sacrifice to help the family, whereas in individualistic cultures, work is seen as a means to personal achievement that takes away from the family.

CONSEQUENCES OF STRESS AT WORK

Strain manifests in several ways, such as high blood pressure, ulcers, irritability, difficulty making routine decisions, changes in appetite, accident proneness, and the like. Refer to Exhibit 17-7. These symptoms fit under three general categories: physiological, psychological, and behavioral symptoms.

PHYSIOLOGICAL SYMPTOMS Most early concerns with stress were directed at physiological symptoms because most researchers were specialists in the health and medical sciences. Their work led to the conclusion that stress could create changes in metabolism, increase heart and breathing rates and blood pressure, bring on headaches, and induce heart attacks.[154] Evidence now clearly suggests stress may have other harmful physiological effects, including backaches, headaches, eye strain, sleep disturbances, dizziness, fatigue, loss of appetite, and gastrointestinal problems.[155] Other research has found that stress, in general, impairs episodic memory (but enhances memory after a stressful event).[156]

PSYCHOLOGICAL SYMPTOMS Job dissatisfaction is an obvious symptom of stress. But strain manifests itself in other psychological states—for instance, tension, anxiety, irritability, boredom, and procrastination. One study that tracked physiological responses of employees over time found that stress due to high workloads was related to lower emotional well-being.[157]

Jobs that make multiple and conflicting demands or that lack clarity about the incumbent's duties, authority, and responsibilities increase both strain and dissatisfaction.[158] Similarly, the less control people have over the pace of their work, the greater their strain and dissatisfaction. Jobs that provide a low level of variety, significance, autonomy, feedback, and identity appear to create strain and reduce satisfaction and involvement in the job.[159] Not everyone reacts to autonomy in the same way, however. For those with an external locus of control, increased job control increases the tendency to experience strain and exhaustion.[160]

BEHAVIORAL SYMPTOMS Research on behavior and stress has been conducted across several countries and over time, and the relationships appear relatively consistent. Behavior-related stress symptoms include reductions in productivity; increases in absences and turnover; and personal changes in eating habits, increased smoking or consumption of alcohol, rapid speech, fidgeting, and sleep disorders.[161] As we mentioned earlier, researchers have begun to differentiate challenge and hindrance stressors, showing that these two forms of stress have opposite effects on job behaviors, especially job performance. A meta-analysis of responses from more than 35,000 individuals showed role ambiguity, role conflict, role overload, job insecurity, environmental uncertainty, and situational constraints were all consistently and negatively related to job performance.[162] There is also evidence that challenge stress improves job performance in a supportive work environment, whereas hindrance stress reduces job performance in all work environments.[163]

MANAGING STRESS

It is not unlikely for employees and management to have different notions of what constitutes an acceptable level of stress on the job. What management may consider to be "a positive stimulus that keeps the adrenaline running" is very likely to be seen as "excessive pressure" by the employee. Keep this in mind as we discuss individual and organizational approaches toward managing stress.[164]

Individual Approaches

An employee can effectively take personal responsibility for reducing stress levels through coping practices and recovery experiences, and doing so can have a downstream effect on performance, OCB, CWB, attitudes, and health at work.[165] Developing *resilience,* or a resistance to the adverse effects of stress and strain, has been shown to be possible over time through practice, coaching, and training.[166] Individual strategies within a resilience program that have proven effective include time-management techniques, physical exercise, relaxation techniques, and social support networks.[167] But before we proceed, it is important to note that the way you approach stress management matters: You should not be trying to actively prevent or avoid stress, but instead, you should be trying to actively recover, relax, and refresh.[168]

TIME-MANAGEMENT TECHNIQUES   Many people manage their time poorly. The well-organized employee can often accomplish twice as much as the person who is poorly organized. Time-management skills can help minimize procrastination by focusing efforts on immediate goals and boosting motivation even in the face of tasks that are less enjoyable.[169] Furthermore, psychological techniques such as self-distancing from future stressors can help you adaptively cope with time pressure.[170]

PHYSICAL EXERCISE   Physicians have recommended noncompetitive *physical exercise*, such as aerobics, walking, jogging, swimming, and riding a bicycle, to deal with excessive stress levels. These activities decrease the detrimental physiological responses to stress and allow us to recover from stress more quickly.[171]

RELAXATION TECHNIQUES   Individuals can teach themselves to reduce tension through *relaxation techniques* such as mindfulness, meditation, hypnosis, and deep breathing.[172] The objective is to reach a state of deep physical relaxation, in which you focus all your energy on the release of muscle tension.[173] Interestingly, the body's natural response of crying may help induce a state of self-soothing through deep breathing and heart rate regulation.[174] Deep relaxation for fifteen or twenty minutes a day releases strain and provides a pronounced sense of peacefulness, as well as significant changes in heart rate, blood pressure, and other physiological factors.[175] A growing body of research shows that simply taking breaks from work at routine intervals (e.g., lunch breaks, walks in the park) can facilitate psychological recovery and reduce stress significantly and may improve job performance, and these effects are even greater if relaxation techniques are employed.[176] Indeed, reviews of research on thousands of employees suggest relaxation techniques can help manage stress and reduce burnout.[177] Furthermore, use of relaxation techniques during the day (and a lack of frustrating events) can help you relax when you get home—otherwise, you may have trouble doing so.[178]

SOCIAL SUPPORT NETWORKS   As we have noted, friends, family, or work colleagues can provide an outlet when stress levels become excessive.[179] Expanding your *social support network* provides someone to hear your problems and offer a more objective perspective on a stressful situation than your own. Sometimes, however, these networks produce the opposite effect: If you do not try to expand your network and instead ruminate with similarly stressed friends, you can get caught in a vicious cycle.[180] That is why it is so important to be proactive and try to address your stress head on. But apart from rumination, support from family, friends, or spouses who help you recover from stressful work experiences can be mutually beneficial.[181]

Organizational Approaches

Several organizational factors that cause stress—particularly task and role demands—are controlled by management. Strategies to consider include improving employee selection and job placement, training, goal setting, redesigning jobs, increasing organizational communication and involvement, and providing employee sabbaticals and corporate wellness programs.

SELECTION, PLACEMENT, AND TRAINING   Certain jobs are more stressful than others, but as we have seen, individuals differ in their response to stressful situations. We know individuals with little experience or an external locus of control tend to be more prone to stress. Obviously, management should not hire only experienced individuals with an internal locus, but such individuals may adapt better to high-stress jobs and perform those jobs more effectively. Similarly, *training* can increase an individual's resilience and thus lessen job strain.[182]

GOAL SETTING   As discussed in the chapter on motivation concepts, individuals perform better when they have specific and challenging goals and receive feedback on their progress toward these goals. Goals can reduce stress as well as provide motivation.[183] Employees who are highly committed to their goals and see purpose in their jobs experience less stress because they are more likely to perceive stressors as challenges rather than hindrances. The type of goal also matters: When given a developmental, learning goal after negative feedback, employees tend to experience less tension and better performance than when they are given a performance target goal.[184] The employee's personality also matters: Goal setting and goal-focused leadership tend to be more successful in reducing stress for the conscientious but not for those who are low on emotional stability.[185]

REDESIGNING JOBS   *Redesigning jobs* to give employees more responsibility, more meaningful work, more autonomy, and increased feedback can reduce stress because these factors give employees greater control over work activities and lessen dependence on others.[186] But not all employees want enriched jobs. The right redesign for employees with a low need for growth might include less responsibility and increased specialization. If individuals prefer structure and routine, reducing skill variety should reduce uncertainties and stress levels.

EMPLOYEE INVOLVEMENT   Role stress is detrimental to a large extent because employees feel uncertain about goals, expectations, how they will be evaluated, and the like. By giving these employees a voice in the decisions that directly affect their job performance, management can increase employee control and reduce role stress. Thus, managers should consider increasing *employee involvement* in decision making because evidence clearly shows that increases in employee empowerment reduce psychological strain.[187]

ORGANIZATIONAL COMMUNICATION Increasing formal *organizational communication* with employees reduces uncertainty by lessening role ambiguity and role conflict.[188] Given the importance that perceptions play in moderating the stress–response relationship, management can also use effective communication to shape employee perceptions. Remember that what employees categorize as demands, threats, or opportunities at work is an interpretation; that interpretation can be affected by the symbols and actions communicated by management.

EMPLOYEE SABBATICALS Some employees need an occasional escape from the frenetic pace of their work. Companies including Genentech, the Container Store, REI, PricewaterhouseCoopers, Goldman Sachs, The Cheesecake Factory Inc., VMware, and Adobe Systems have begun to provide extended voluntary leaves.[189] These *sabbaticals*—ranging in length from a few weeks to several months—allow employees to travel, relax, or pursue personal projects that consume time beyond normal vacations. One study of university faculty members suggests that sabbaticals increase job resources and well-being, especially when they have greater autonomy in how they spend their sabbatical.[190]

WELLNESS PROGRAMS Our final suggestion is to create organizationally supported **wellness programs**. These typically provide workshops to help people quit smoking, control alcohol use, lose weight, eat better, and develop a regular exercise program; they focus on the employee's total physical and mental condition.[191] Some programs help employees improve their psychological health as well. A meta-analysis of thirty-six programs designed to reduce stress (including wellness programs) showed that interventions that helped employees reframe stressful situations and use active coping strategies appreciably reduced stress levels.[192] Most wellness programs assume employees need to take personal responsibility for their physical and mental health and that the organization is merely a means to that end.

> **Wellness programs**
> Organizationally supported programs that focus on the employee's total physical and mental condition.

Most firms that have introduced wellness programs have observed significant benefits. Johnson & Johnson reported that their wellness program has saved the organization $250 million in health care costs in ten years, and research has indicated that effective wellness programs significantly decreased turnover rates for most organizations.[193] Indeed, the accumulated research suggests that organizations that implement wellness programs (1) observe a $5.93 to $1.00 savings-to-cost ratio, (2) reduce health costs by 26 percent and workers' compensation claims by 30 percent, and (3) observe a 28 percent reduction in sick days used.[194] However, the benefits workers experience appear to be contingent on how much they put into the program, the extent to which they participate, and their attitudes upon entering the program.[195]

SUMMARY

The need for change has been implied throughout this text. For instance, think about attitudes, motivation, work teams, communication, leadership, organizational structures, and organizational cultures. Change was an integral part in our discussion of each. If environments were perfectly static, if employees' skills and abilities were always up to date and incapable of deteriorating, and if tomorrow were always the same as today, organizational change would have little or no relevance to managers. But the real world is turbulent, requiring organizations and their members to undergo dynamic change if they are to perform at competitive levels. Coping with all these changes can be a source of stress, but with effective management, challenge can enhance engagement and fulfillment, leading to the high performance that is one major goal of the study of organizational behavior (OB), as you have discovered in this text.

IMPLICATIONS FOR MANAGERS

- You are a change agent in your organization. The decisions you make and your role-modeling behaviors will help shape the organization's change culture.
- Management policies and practices will determine the degree to which the organization learns and adapts to changing environmental factors.
- Some stress is good. Increasing challenges brought by autonomy and responsibility at work will lead to some stress but also increase feelings of accomplishment and fulfillment. Hindrance stressors like bureaucracy and interpersonal conflicts, on the other hand, are entirely negative and should be eliminated.
- You can help alleviate harmful workplace stress for your employees by accurately matching workloads to employees, providing employees with stress-coping resources, and responding to their concerns.
- You can identify extreme stress in your employees when performance declines, turnover increases, health-related absenteeism increases, and engagement declines. However, by the time these symptoms are visible, it may be too late to be helpful, so stay alert for early indicators and be proactive.

EPILOGUE

The end of a book typically has the same meaning to an author that it has to the reader: it generates feelings of both accomplishment and relief. As both of us rejoice at having completed our tour of the essential concepts in organizational behavior, this is a good time to examine where we've been and what it all means.

The underlying theme of this book has been that the behavior of people at work is not a random phenomenon. Employees are complex entities, but their attitudes and behavior can nevertheless be explained and predicted with a reasonable degree of accuracy. Our approach has been to look at organizational behavior at three levels: the individual, the group, and the organization system.

We started with the individual and reviewed the major psychological contributions to understanding why individuals act as they do. We found that many of the individual differences among employees can be systematically labeled and categorized, and therefore generalizations can be made. For example, we know that individuals with a conventional type of personality are better matched to certain jobs in corporate management than are people with investigative personalities. So placing people into jobs that are compatible with their personality types should result in higher-performing and more satisfied employees.

Next, our analysis moved to the group level. We argued that the understanding of group behavior is more complex than merely multiplying what we know about individuals by the number of members in the group, because people act differently in a group than when they are alone. We demonstrated how roles, norms, leadership styles, power relationships, and other similar group factors affect the behavior of employees.

Finally, we overlaid system-wide variables on our knowledge of individual and group behavior to further improve our understanding of organizational behavior. Major emphasis was given to showing how an organization's structure, design, and culture affect both the attitudes and the behavior of employees.

It may be tempting to criticize the stress this book placed on theoretical concepts, but as noted psychologist Kurt Lewin is purported to have said, "There is nothing so practical as a good theory." Of course, it's also true that there is nothing so impractical as a good theory that leads nowhere. To avoid presenting theories that lead nowhere, this book included a wealth of examples and illustrations and we regularly stopped to inquire about the implications of theory for the practice of management. The result has been the presentation of numerous concepts that, individually, offer some insights into behavior; but when taken together, provide a complex system to help you explain, predict, and control organizational behavior.

ENDNOTES

CHAPTER 1

1. B. Schneider, "The People Make the Place," *Personnel Psychology* 40, no. 3, (1987): 437–53.

2. J. Bersin, L. Collins, D. Mallon, J. Moir, and R. Straub, "People Analytics: Gaining Speed," in B. Pelster and J. Schwartz (eds.), *The New Organization: Different by Design* (London, UK: Deloitte University Press, 2016): 87–96.

3. R. Umoh, "The CEO of LinkedIn Shares the No. 1 Job Skill American Employees are Lacking," *CNBC*, April 26, 2018, https://www.cnbc.com/2018/04/26/linkedin-ceo-the-no-1-job-skill-american-employees-lack.html

4. M. Ward, "The 5 Soft Skills That Will Get You Hired—And How to Learn Them," *CNBC,* April 26, 2017, https://www.cnbc.com/2017/04/26/the-5-soft-skills-that-will-get-you-hired-and-how-to-learn-them.html

5. "Survey: Few CFOs Plan to Invest in Interpersonal Skills Development for Their Teams," Accountemps press release, June 19, 2013, http://accountemps.rhi.mediaroom.com/2013-06-19-Survey-Few-CFOs-Plan-to-Invest-in-Interpersonal-Skills-Development-for-Their-Teams

6. Y.-M. Lim, T. H. Lee, C. S. Yap, and C. C. Ling, "Employability Skills, Personal Qualities, and Early Employment Problems of Entry-Level Auditors: Perspectives from Employers, Lecturers, Auditors, and Students," *Journal of Education for Business* 91, no. 4 (2016): 185–92.

7. J. Gassam, "The Best Places to Work in 2019," *Forbes,* December 7, 2018, https://www.forbes.com/sites/janicegassam/2018/12/07/the-best-places-to-work-for-2019/#770f0bf6528f

8. I. S. Fulmer, B. Gerhart, and K. S. Scott, "Are the 100 Best Better? An Empirical Investigation of the Relationship between Being a 'Great Place to Work' and Firm Performance," *Personnel Psychology* 56, no. 4, (2003): 965–93.

9. S. E. Humphrey, J. D. Nahrgang, and F. P. Morgeson, "Integrating Motivational, Social, and Contextual Work Design Features: A Meta-Analytic Summary and Theoretical Extension of the Work Design Literature," *Journal of Applied Psychology* 92, no. 5 (2007): 1332–56.

10. E. R. Burris, "The Risks and Rewards of Speaking Up: Managerial Responses to Employee Voice," *Academy of Management Journal* 55, no. 4 (2012): 851–75.

11. T. L. Miller, C. L. Wesley II, and D. E. Williams, "Educating the Minds of Caring Hearts: Comparing the Views of Practitioners and Educators on the Importance of Social Entrepreneurship Competencies," *Academy of Management Learning & Education* 2, no. 3 (2012): 349–70.

12. H. Aguinis and A. Glavas, "What We Don't Know about Corporate Social Responsibility: A Review and Research Agenda," *Journal of Management* 38, no. 4 (2012): 932–68.

13. "The Bottom Line- Necessity of Training Your Managers," *HR Professionals Magazine*, July 16, 2012, http://hrprofessionalsmagazine.com/train-your-managers/

14. D. Meinert, "Background on Bosses," *HR Magazine,* August 2014, 29.

15. Ibid.

16. Ibid.

17. For the original study, see F. Luthans, "Successful vs. Effective Real Managers," *Academy of Management Executive,* 2, no. 2 (1988): 127–32.

A great deal of research has been built by Fred Luthans and others from this study. See, for example, M. M. Hopkins, D. A. O'Neil, and J. K. Stoller, "Distinguishing Competencies of Effective Physician Leaders," *Journal of Management Development* 34, no. 5 (2015): 566–84.

18. P. Wu, M. Foo, and D. B. Turban, "The Role of Personality in Relationship Closeness, Developer Assistance, and Career Success," *Journal of Vocational Behavior* 73, no. 3 (2008): 440–48.

19. L. Dragoni, H. Park, J. Soltis, and S. Forte-Trammell, "Show and Tell: How Supervisors Facilitate Leader Development Among Transitioning Leaders," *Journal of Applied Psychology* 99, no. 1 (2014): 66–86.

20. For a review of what one researcher believes *should* be included in organizational behavior, based on survey data, see J. B. Miner, "The Rated Importance, Scientific Validity, and Practical Usefulness of Organizational Behavior Theories: A Quantitative Review," *Academy of Management Learning & Education* 2, no. 3 (2003): 250–68.

21. D. M. Rousseau, *The Oxford Handbook of Evidence-Based Management* (New York: Oxford University Press, 2014).

22. W. M. Grove, D. H. Zald, B. S. Lebow, B. E. Snitz, and C. Nelson, "Clinical Versus Mechanical Prediction: A Meta-Analysis," *Psychological Assessment* 12, no. 1 (2000): 19-30; A. McAfee, "The Future of Decision Making: Less Intuition, More Evidence," *Harvard Business Review,* January 7, 2010, https://hbr.org/2010/01/the-future-of-decision-making

23. J. M. Logg, J. A. Minson, and D. A. Moore, "Algorithm Appreciation: People Prefer Algorithmic to Human Judgment," *Organizational Behavior and Human Decision Processes* 151 (2019): 90–103.

24. J. Welch and S. Welch, "When to Go with Your Gut," *LinkedIn Pulse* (blog post), November 12, 2013, https://www.linkedin.com/pulse/20131112125301-86541065-when-to-go-with-your-gut

25. Z. Karabell, "Everyone Has a Data Point," *The Wall Street Journal,* February 19, 2014, A11.

26. I. Adjerid and K. Kelley, "Big Data in Psychology: A Framework for Research Advancement," *American Psychologist* 73, no. 7 (2018): 899-917; E. E. Chen and S. P. Wojcik, "A Practical Guide to Big Data Research in Psychology," *Psychological Methods* 21, no. 4 (2016): 458-474; L. L. Harlow and F. L. Oswald, "Big Data in Psychology: Introduction to the Special Issue," *Psychological Methods* 21, no. 4 (2016): 447–57.

27. E. Morozov, "Every Little Byte Counts," *The New York Times Book Review,* May 18, 2014, 23.

28. M. Taves, "If I Could Have More Data...," *The Wall Street Journal,* March 24, 2014, R5.

29. J. Hugg, "Fast Data: The Next Step after Big Data," InfoWorld, June 11, 2014, http://www.infoworld.com/article/2608040/big-data/fast-data-the-next-step-after-big-data.html; A. Lorentz, "Big Data, Fast Data, Smart Data," Wired, April 17, 2013, https://www.wired.com/insights/2013/04/big-data-fast-data-smart-data/; and J. Spencer, "Which Do We Need More: Big Data or Fast Data?," Entrepreneur, March 12, 2015, https://www.entrepreneur.com/article/243123

30. N. Bloom, R. Sadun, and J. Van Reenan, "Does Management Really Work? How Three Essential Practices Can Address Even the Most Complex Global Problems," *Harvard Business Review,* November 2012, 77–82.

31. K. Kersting and U. Meyer, "From Big Data to Artificial Intelligence?" *Künstliche Intelligenz* 32, no. 1 (2018): 3–8.

32. Dell Technologies, "The Difference Between AI, Machine Learning, & Robots," *Dell Technologies: Perspectives* [Blog], January 7, 2019, https://www.delltechnologies.com/en-us/perspectives/the-difference-between-ai-machine-learning-and-robotics/

33. M. Beane and W. J. Orlikowski, "What Difference Does a Robot Make? The Material Enactment of Distributed Coordination," *Organization Science* 26, no. 6 (2015): 1553–804.

34. Dell Technologies, "The Difference Between AI, Machine Learning, & Robots."

35. J. Bughin, E. Hazan, S. Ramaswamy, M. Chui, T. Allas, P. Dahlström, N. Henke, and M. Trench, "Artificial Intelligence: The Next Digital Frontier?" *McKinsey Global Institute* [Discussion Paper], June 2017, https://www.mckinsey.com/mgi/overview/2017-in-review/whats-next-in-digital-and-ai/artificial-intelligence-the-next-digital-frontier

36. Ibid.

37. E. E. Chen and S. P. Wojcik, "A Practical Guide to Big Data Research in Psychology."

38. E. Dwoskin, "Big Data Knows When You Turn off the Lights," *The Wall Street Journal,* October 21, 2014, B1–B2.

39. S. Lohr, "Unblinking Eyes Track Employees," *The New York Times,* June 22, 2014, 1, 15.

40. D. B. Bhave, "The Invisible Eye? Electronic Performance Monitoring and Employee Job Performance," *Personnel Psychology* 67, no. 3 (2003): 605–35.

41. R. Karlgaard, "Danger Lurking: Taylor's Ghost," *Forbes,* May 26, 2014, 34.

42. I. Adjerid and K. Kelley, "Big Data in Psychology: A Framework for Research Advancement"; E. E. Chen and S. P. Wojcik, "A Practical Guide to Big Data Research in Psychology."

43. E. Broadbent, "Interactions with Robots: The Truths We Reveal About Ourselves," *Annual Review of Psychology* 68 (2017): 627–52.

44. I. Adjerid and K. Kelley, "Big Data in Psychology: A Framework for Research Advancement."

45. O. Rudgard, "Admiral to Use Facebook Profile to Determine Insurance Premium," *The Telegraph,* November 2, 2016, https://www.telegraph.co.uk/insurance/car/insurer-trawls-your-facebook-profile-to-see-how-well-you-drive/

46. J. J. Arnett, "The Psychology of Globalization," *American Psychologist* 57 (2002): 774–83.

47. K. Schwab, "Globalization 4.0 – What It Means and How It Could Benefit Us All," *World Economic Forum,* November 5, 2018, https://www.weforum.org/agenda/2018/11/globalization-4-what-does-it-mean-how-it-will-benefit-everyone/

48. M. N. Thompson and J. J. Dahling, "Employment and Poverty: Why Work Matters in Understanding Poverty," *American Psychologist* 74, no. 6 (2019): 673–684.

49. K. Schwab, "The Fourth Industrial Revolution: What It Means, How to Respond," *World Economic Forum,* January 14, 2016, https://www.weforum.org/agenda/2016/01/the-fourth-industrial-revolution-what-it-means-and-how-to-respond/

50. C. Karmin and S. Chaturvedi, "Grosvenor House Is Seized," *The Wall Street Journal,* March 4, 2015, C8.

51. V. McGrane, "The Downside of Lower Unemployment," *The Wall Street Journal,* February 3, 2014, A2.

52. A. Lowrey, "Long Out of Work, and Running Out of Options," *The New York Times,* April 4, 2014, B1, B4.

53. L. Weber and R. E. Silverman, "On-Demand Workers: 'We Are Not Robots,'" *The Wall Street Journal,* January 28, 2015, B1, B7.

54. C. Porter and M. Korn, "Can This Online Course Get Me a Job?" *The Wall Street Journal,* March 4, 2014, B1.

55. D. Belkin and M. Peters, "For New Grads, Path to a Career Is Bumpy," *The Wall Street Journal,* May 24–25, 2014, A5.

56. N. Kitsantonis, "A Hands-On Approach to the Greek Economy," *The New York Times,* March 25, 2014, B3.

57. World Health Organization, *Global Health Observatory (GHO) Data: Life Expectancy,* Accessed January 18, 2019, https://www.who.int/gho/en/

58. United Nations, Gender Equality, Accessed April 16, 2020, https://www.un.org/en/sections/issues-depth/gender-equality/index.html

59. A. Joshi, B. Neely, C. Emrich, D. Griffiths, and G. George, "Gender Research in AMJ: An Overview of Five Decades of Empirical Research and Calls to Action," Academy of Management Journal 58, no. 5 (2015): 1459–75.

60. J. Greenwald, "Tips for Dealing with Employees Whose Social Media Posts Reflect Badly on Your Company," *Forbes,* March 6, 2015, http://www.forbes.com/sites/entrepreneursorganization/2015/03/06/tips-for-dealing-with-employees-whose-social-media-posts-reflect-badly-on-your-company/

61. See, for example, M. Carpentier, G. Van Hoye, and B. Weitjers, "Attracting Applicants Through the Organization's Social Media Page," Journal of Vocational Behavior 115 (in press).

62. E. Jaffe, "Using Technology to Scale the Scientific Mountain," *Observer* 27, no. 6 (2014): 17–19.

63. N. Fallon, "No Face Time? No Problem: How to Keep Virtual Workers Engaged," *Business News Daily,* October 2, 2014, http://www.businessnewsdaily.com/7228-engaging-remote-employees.html

64. E. J. Hirst, "Burnout on the Rise," *Chicago Tribune,* October 19, 2012, http://articles.chicagotribune.com/2012-10-29/business/ct-biz-1029-employee-burnout-20121029_1_employee-burnout-herbert-freudenberger-employee-stress

65. F. Luthans and C. M. Youssef, "Emerging Positive Organizational Behavior," *Journal of Management* 33, no. 3 (2007): 321–49; C. M. Youssef and F. Luthans, "Positive Organizational Behavior in the Workplace: The Impact of Hope, Optimism, and Resilience," *Journal of Management* 33, no. 5 (2007): 774–800; J. E. Dutton and S. Sonenshein, "Positive Organizational Scholarship," in C. Cooper and J. Barling (eds.), *Encyclopedia of Positive Psychology* (Thousand Oaks, CA: Sage, 2007): 3–13.

66. "Five Jobs That Won't Exist in 10 Years... And One New Title You'll Start to See," *HR Magazine,* February 2014, 16.

67. Editorial Board, "NCAA Should Punish the University of North Carolina for Cheating Scandal," *Chicago Tribune,* November 7, 2014, http://www.chicagotribune.com/news/opinion/editorials/ct-north-carolina-sports-scandal-edit-1108-20141107-story.html, accessed March 11, 2015.

68. D. M. Mayer, M. Kuenzi, R. Greenbaum, M. Bardes, and R. Salvador, "How Low Does Ethical Leadership Flow? Test of a Trickle-Down Model," *Organizational Behavior and Human Decision Processes* 108, no. 1 (2009): 1–13; A. Ardichvili, J. A. Mitchell, and D. Jondle, "Characteristics of Ethical Business Cultures," *Journal of Business Ethics* 85, no. 4 (2009): 445–51.

69. D. Meinert, "Managers' Influence," *HR Magazine,* April 2014, 25.

70. K. Xie, L. Kwok, and W. Wang, "Monetizing Managerial Responses on TripAdvisor: Performance Implications Across Hotel Classes," *Cornell Hospitality Quarterly* 58, no. 3 (2017): 240–52.

71. W. F. Cascio and H. Aguinis, "Research in Industrial and Organizational Psychology from 1963 to 2007: Changes, Choices, and Trends," *Journal of Applied Psychology* 93, no. 5 (2008): 1062–81; G. George, J. Howard-Grenville, A. Joshi, and L. Tihanyi, "Understanding and Tackling Societal Grand Challenges through Management Research," *Academy of Management Journal* 59, no. 6 (2016): 1880–95; L. W. Porter and B. Schneider, "What Was, What Is, and What May Be in OP/OB," *Annual Review of Organizational Psychology and Organizational Behavior* 1, no. 1 (2014): 1–21.

72. B. Schneider, "The People Make the Place."

CHAPTER 2

1. G. T. Chao and H. Moon, "The Cultural Mosaic: A Metatheory for Understanding the Complexity of Culture," *Journal of Applied Psychology* 90, no. 6 (2005): 1128–40.

2. "Taj Mahal," *History Channel,* June 13, 2011, https://www.history.com/topics/india/taj-mahal; S. Das, "Impact of Ethnic Diversity and Multiculturalism in Corporate Culture," *Entrepreneur India,* July 10, 2018, https://www .entrepreneur.com/article/316482

3. M. Toossi, "A Century of Change: The U.S. Labor Force, 1950–2050," Bureau of Labor Statistics, May 2002, http:// www.bls.gov/opub/2002/05/art2full.pdf

4. U.S. Census Bureau, DataFerrett, *Current Population Survey,* December 2016; S. Ricker, "The Changing Face of U.S. Jobs," *CareerBuilder,* March 26, 2015, http://www.thehir ingsite.careerbuilder.com/2015/03/26/9-findings-diversity-americas-workforce.

5. L. Colley, "Not Codgers in Cardigans! Female Workforce Participation and Ageing Public Services," *Gender Work and Organization* 20, no. 3 (2013): 327–48; M. Toossi and T. L. Morisi, "Women in the Workforce Before, During, and After the Great Recession," *U.S. Bureau of Labor Statistics: Spotlight on Statistics,* July 2017, https://www .bls.gov/spotlight/2017/women-in-the-workforce-before-during-and-after-the-great-recession/pdf/women-in-the-workforce-before-during-and-after-the-great-recession .pdf

6. W. H. Frey, *Diversity Explosion: How New Racial Demographics are Remaking America* (Washington, DC: Brookings Institution Press, 2014).

7. M. Toossi, "Labor Force Projections to 2024: The Labor Force is Growing, but Slowly," *Monthly Labor Review,* U.S. Bureau of Labor Statistics, December 2015, https://doi .org/10.21916/mlr.2015.48

8. A. H. Eagly and J. L. Chin, "Are Memberships in Race, Ethnicity, and Gender Categories Merely Surface Characteristics?" *American Psychologist* 65, no. 9 (2010): 934–35.

9. W. J. Casper, J. H. Wayne, and J. G. Manegold, "Who Will We Recruit? Targeting Deep- and Surface-Level Diversity with Human Resource Policy Advertising," *Human Resource Management* 52, no. 3 (2013): 311–32.

10. D. Schuler, "Research Examines Conflicts Within Professional Kitchens," Pennsylvania State University Press Release, April 6, 2016, https://phys.org/news/2016-04-conflicts-professional-kitchens.html

11. Ibid.

12. A. Murrell, "On the Tennis Court and in the Workplace: When Unconscious Bias Isn't Unconscious," *Forbes,* September 20, 2018, https://www.forbes.com/sites/audreymurrell/2018/09/20/on-the-tennis-court-and-in-the-workplace-when-unconscious-bias-isnt-unconscious/#1a3d190f5aa4; S. Gleeson, "Serena Williams Accuses US Open Chair Umpire Carlos Ramos of Sexism," *USA Today,* September 8, 2018, https://www.usatoday.com/story/sports/tennis/2018/09/08/serena-williams-accuses-us-open-chair-umpire-carlos-ramos-sexism/1243767002/

13. Ibid.

14. A. M. Grant (AdamMGrant), "When a man argues with an umpire, it's passion. When a woman does it, it's a meltdown. When a black woman does it, it's a penalty" [Tweet], September 8, 2018, 6:29 p.m., https://twitter.com/AdamMGrant/status/1038600245389799425

15. S. J. Spencer, C. Logel, and P. G. Davies, "Stereotype Threat," *Annual Review of Psychology* 67 (2016): 415–37.

16. G. M. Walton, M. C. Murphy, and A. M. Ryan, "Stereotype Threat in Organizations: Implications for Equity and Performance," *Annual Review of Organizational Psychology and Organizational Behavior* 2 (2015): 523–50.

17. O. R. Shewach, P. R. Sackett, and S. Quint, "Stereotype Threat Effects in Settings with Features Likely Versus Unlikely in Operational Test Settings: A Meta-Analysis," Journal of Applied Psychology (in press).

18. G. Czukor and M. Bayazit, "Casting a Wide Net? Performance Deficit, Priming, and Subjective Performance Evaluation in Organizational Stereotype Threat Research," *Industrial and Organizational Psychology* 7, no. 3 (2014): 409–12; K. S. Jones and N. C. Carpenter, "Toward a Sociocultural Psychological Approach to Examining Stereotype Threat in the Workplace," *Industrial and Organizational Psychology* 7, no. 3 (2014): 429–32; C. T. Kulik, "Spotlight on the Context: How a Stereotype Threat Framework Might Help Organizations to Attract and Retain Older Workers," *Industrial and Organizational Psychology* 7, no. 3 (2014): 456–61; C. T. Kulik, S. Perera, and C. Cregan, "Engage Me: The Mature-Age Worker and Stereotype Threat," *Academy of Management Journal* 59, no. 6 (2016): 2132–56.

19. L. M. Cortina, "Unseen Injustice: Incivility as Modern Discrimination in Organizations," *Academy of Management Review* 33, no. 1 (2008): 55–75; K. P. Jones, C. I. Peddie, V. L. Gilrane, E. B. King, and A. L. Gray, "Not so Subtle: A Meta-Analytic Investigation of the Correlates of Subtle and Overt Discrimination," *Journal of Management* 42, no. 6 (2016): 1588–613; P. P. Lui and L. Quezada, "Associations Between Microaggression and Adjustment Outcomes: A Meta-Analytic and Narrative Review," *Psychological Bulletin* 145, no. 1 (2019): 45–78.

20. J. P. Jamieson, K. Koslov, M. K. Nock, and W. B. Mendes, "Experiencing Discrimination Increases Risk Taking," *Psychological Science* 24, no. 2 (2012): 131–39; L. Y. Dhanani, J. M. Beus, and D. L. Joseph, "Workplace Discrimination: A Meta-Analytic Extension, Critique, and Future Research Agenda," *Personnel Psychology* 71 (2018): 147–79; Jones et al., "Not So Subtle."

21. C. T. Kulik, S. Ryan, S. Harper, and G. George, "Aging Populations and Management," *Academy of Management Journal* 57, no. 4 (2014): 929–35.

22. T. Morisi, "Why More People Ages 55+ Are Working," *U.S. Department of Labor* [Blog], November 18, 2016, https://blog.dol.gov/2016/11/18/why-more-people-ages-55-are-working

23. Lewis Silkin, LLP, "International Age Discrimination," *AgeDiscrimination.Info* [Website], Accessed January 22, 2019, http://www.agediscrimination.info/international/

24. G. Bronshtein, J. Scott, J. B. Shoven, and S. N. Slavov, *The Power of Working Longer* [NBER Working Paper No. 24226], National Bureau of Economic Research, January 2018; S. O'Brien, "More Than Half of 60-somethings say They're Delaying Retirement," *CNBC: Personal Finance,* April 27, 2018, https://www.cnbc.com/2018/04/27/delayed-retirement-is-in-the-cards-for-more-than-half-of-60-somethings.html

25. P. M. Bal, A. H. de Lange, B. I. J. M. Van der Heijden, H. Zacher, F. A. Oderkerk, and S. Otten, "Young at Heart, Old at Work? Relations Between Age, (Meta-)Stereotypes, Self-Categorization, and Retirement Attitudes," *Journal of Vocational Behavior* 91(2015): 35–45.

26. M. Chand and R. L. Tung, "The Aging of the World's Population and Its Effects on Global Business," *Academy of Management Perspectives* 28, no. 4 (2014): 409–29.

27. S. Shellenbarger, "Work & Family Mailbox," *The Wall Street Journal,* January 29, 2014, D2.

28. N. E. Wolfson, T. M. Cavanaugh, and K. Kraiger, "Older Adults and Technology-Based Instruction: Optimizing Learning Outcomes and Transfer," *Academy of Management Learning & Education* 13, no. 1 (2014): 26–44.

29. A. Tergesen, "Why Everything You Know About Aging Is Probably Wrong." *The Wall Street Journal* (November 30, 2014).

30. Ibid.

31. Ibid;

32. A. Burmeister, M. Wang, and A. Hirschi, "Understanding the Motivational Benefits of Knowledge Transfer for Older and Younger Workers in Age-Diverse Coworker Dyads: An Actor-Partner Interdependence Model," Journal of Applied Psychology (in press); Y. Li, Y. Gong, A. Burmeister, M. Wang, V. Alterman, A. Alonso, and S. Robinson, "Leveraging Age Diversity for Organizational Performance: An Intellectual Capital Perspective," Journal of Applied Psychology (in press).

33. T. W. H. Ng and D. C. Feldman, "The Relationship of Age with Job Attitudes: A Meta-Analysis," *Personnel Psychology* 63, no. 3 (2010): 677–718.

34. S. D. Riza, Y. Ganzach, and Y. Liu, "Time and Job Satisfaction: A Longitudinal Study of the Differential Roles of Age and Tenure," *Journal of Management* 44, no. 7 (2018): 2558–79.

35. E. Zell, Z. Krizan, and S. R. Teeter, "Evaluating Gender Similarities and Differences Using Metasynthesis," *American Psychologist* 70, no. 1 (2015): 10–20.

36. A. Joshi, J. Son, and H. Roh, "When Can Women Close the Gap? A Meta-analytic Test of Sex Differences in Performance and Rewards," *Academy of Management Journal* 58, no. 5 (2015): 1516–45; T. W. H. Ng, S. S. K. Lam, and D. C. Feldman, "Organizational Citizenship Behavior and Counterproductive Work Behavior: Do Males and Females Differ?" *Journal of Vocational Behavior* 93 (2016): 11–32; P. L. Roth, K. L. Purvis, and P. Bobko, "A Meta-Analysis of Gender Group Differences for Measures of Job Performance in Field Studies," *Journal of Management* 38, no. 2 (2012): 719–39.

37. R. E. Silverman, "Study Suggests Fix for Gender Bias on the Job," *The Wall Street Journal,* January 9, 2013, D4.

38. A. J. Koch, S. D. D'Mello, and P. R. Sackett, "A Meta-Analysis of Gender Stereotypes and Bias in Experimental Simulations of Employment Decision Making," *Journal of Applied Psychology* 100, no. 1 (2015): 128–61.

39. E. B. King et al., "Benevolent Sexism at Work: Gender Differences in the Distribution of Challenging Developmental Experiences," *Journal of Management* 38, no. 6 (2012): 1835–66.

40. C. Hymowitz and T. D. Schellhardt, "The Glass Ceiling," The Wall Street Journal (March 24, 1986): D1, 4–5; K. S. Lyness and D. E. Thompson, "Above the Glass Ceiling? A Comparison of Matched Samples of Female and Male Executives," Journal of Applied Psychology 82 (1997): 359–375; B. Zimmer, "The Phrase 'Glass Ceiling' Stretches Back Decades," The Wall Street Journal (April 3, 2015), https://www.wsj.com/articles/the-phrase-glass-ceiling-stretches-back-decades-1428089010

41. Catalyst, List: Women CEOs of the S&P 500, accessed April 16, 2020, https://www.catalyst.org/research/women-ceos-of-the-sp-500/

42. L. Gartzia, M. K. Ryan, N. Balluerka, and A. Aritzeta, "Think Crisis-Think Female: Further Evidence," *European Journal of Work and Organizational Psychology* 21, no. 4 (2014): 603–28; M. K. Ryan and S. A. Haslam, "The Glass Cliff: Evidence That Women Are Overrepresented in Precarious Leadership Positions," British Journal of Management 16, no. 2 (2005): 81–90; M. K. Ryan and S. A. Haslam, "The Glass Cliff: Exploring the Dynamics Surrounding the Appointment of Women to Precarious Leadership Positions," Academy of Management Review 32, no. 2 (2007): 549–72.

43. P. Wechsler, "58 Women CFOs in the Fortune 500: Is This Progress?" *Fortune,* February 24, 2015, http://fortune .com/2015/02/24/58-women-cfos-in-the-fortune-500-is-this-progress/

44. F. M. Cheung and D. F. Halpern, "Women at the Top: Powerful Leaders Define Success at Work + Family in a Culture of Gender," American Psychologist 65, no. 3 (2010): 182–193.

45. K. L. Badura, E. Grijalva, D. A. Newman, T. Taiyi Yan, and G. Jeon, "Gender and Leadership Emergence: A Meta-Analysis and Explanatory Model," Personnel Psychology 71 (2018): 335–367; J. M. Hoo-

bler, J. Hu, and M. Wilson, "Do Workers Who Experience Conflict Between the Work and Family Domains Hit a 'Glass Ceiling?': A Meta-Analytic Examination," Journal of Vocational Behavior 77, no. 3 (2010): 481–494.

46. S. C. Paustian-Underdahl, A. A. Eaton, A. Mandeville, and L. M. Little, "Pushed Out or Opting Out? Integrating Perspectives on Gender Differences in Withdrawal Attitudes During Pregnancy," Journal of Applied Psychology 104, no. 8 (2019): 985–1002.

47. J. M. Hoobler, C. R. Masterson, S. M. Nkomo, and E. J. Michel, "The Business Case for Women Leaders: Metaanalysis, Research Critique, and Path Forward," Journal of Management 44, no. 6 (2018): 2473–2499; S. C. Paustian-Underdahl, L. Slattery Walker, and D. J. Woehr, "Gender and Perceptions of Leadership Effectiveness: A Meta-Analysis of Contextual Moderators," Journal of Applied Psychology 99, no. 6 (2014): 1129–45.

48. L. Turner and A. Suflas, "Global Diversity—One Program Won't Fit All," *HR Magazine,* May 2014, 59–61.

49. K. A. Appiah, "Race in the Modern World: The Problem of the Color Line," *Foreign Affairs,* March 1, 2015, https://www.foreignaffairs.com/articles/united-states/2015-03-01/race-modern-world?cid=int-lea&pgtype=hpg

50. L. Turner and A. Suflas, "Global Diversity—One Program Won't Fit All."

51. T. Vega, "With Diversity Still Lacking, Industry Focuses on Retention," *The New York Times,* September 4, 2012, B3.

52. P. Bobko and P. L. Roth, "Reviewing, Categorizing, and Analyzing the Literature on Black-White Mean Differences for Predictors of Job Performance: Verifying Some Perceptions and Updating/Correcting Others," *Personnel Psychology* 66 (2013): 91–126; S. Y. Lee, M. Pitesa, S. Thau, and M. M. Pillutla, "Discrimination in Selection Decisions: Integrating Stereotype fit and Interdependence Theories," *Academy of Management Journal* 58, no. 3 (2015): 789–812; A. Luksyte, E. Waite, D. R. Avery, and R. Roy, "Held to a Different Standard: Racial Differences in the Impact of Lateness on Advancement Opportunity," *Journal of Occupational and Organizational Psychology* 86 (2013): 142–65.

53. M. A. McCord, D. L. Joseph, L. Y. Dhanani, and J. M. Beus, "A Meta-analysis of sex and Race Differences in Perceived Workplace Mistreatment," *Journal of Applied Psychology* 103, no. 2 (2018): 137–63; M. D-C. Triana, M. Jayasinghe, and J. R. Pieper, "Perceived Workplace Discrimination and Its Correlates: A Meta-analysis," *Journal of Organizational Behavior* 36 (2015): 491–513.

54. J. M. Sacco, C. R. Scheu, A. M. Ryan, and N. Schmitt, "An Investigation of Race and Sex Similarity Effects in Interviews: A Multilevel Approach to Relational Demography," *Journal of Applied Psychology* 88, no. 5 (2003): 852–65; P. F. McKay and M. A. McDaniel, "A Reexamination of Black-White Mean Differences in Work Performance: More Data, More Moderators," *Journal of Applied Psychology* 91, no. 3 (2006): 538–54.

55. S. Mullainathan, "The Measuring Sticks of Racial Bias," *The New York Times,* January 4, 2015, 6.

56. M. Bertrand and S. Mullainathan, "Are Emily and Brendan More Employable Than Latoya and Tyrone? Evidence on Racial Discrimination in the Labor Market from a Large Randomized Experiment," American Economic Review 94 (2004): 991–1013.

57. L. Turner and A. Suflas, "Global Diversity—One Program Won't Fit All."

58. Information on the Americans with Disabilities Act can be found on its website at www.ada.gov

59. S. G. Goldberg, M. B. Killeen, and B. O'Day, "The Disclosure Conundrum: How People with Psychiatric Disabilities Navigate Employment," *Psychology, Public Policy, and Law* 11, no. 3 (2005): 463–500;

M. L. Ellison, Z. Russinova, K. L. MacDonald-Wilson, and A. Lyass, "Patterns and Correlates of Workplace Disclosure Among Professionals and Managers with Psychiatric Conditions," *Journal of Vocational Rehabilitation* 18, no. 1 (2003): 3–13; C. Hunter, M-L. Verreynne, N. Pachana, and P. Harpur, "The Impact of Disability-Assistance Animals on the Psychological Health of Workplaces: A Systematic Review," Human Resource Management Review 29 (2019): 400–417.

60. B. S. Bell and K. J. Klein, "Effect of Disability, Gender, and Job Level on Ratings of Job Applicants," *Rehabilitation Psychology* 46, no. 3 (2001): 229–46; and E. Louvet, "Social Judgment Toward Job Applicants with Disabilities: Perception of Personal Qualities and Competences," *Rehabilitation Psychology* 52, no. 3 (2007): 297–303.

61. L. R. Ren, R. L. Paetzold, and A. Colella, "A Meta-Analysis of Experimental Studies on the Effects of Disability on Human Resource Judgments," *Human Resource Management Review* 18, no. 3 (2008): 191–203; J. E. Beatty, D. C. Baldridge, S. A. Boehm, M. Kukarni, and A. J. Colella, "On the Treatment of Persons with Disabilities in Organizations: A Review and Research Agenda," Human Resource Management 58 (2019): 119–137; S. Bonaccio, C. E. Connelly, I. R. Gellatly, A. Jetha, and K. A. Martin Ginis, "The Participation of People with Disabilities in the Workplace Across the Employment Cycle: Employer Concerns and Research Evidence," Journal of Business and Psychology 35 (2020): 135–158.

62. D. J. G. Dwertmann and S. A. Boehm, "Status Matters: The Asymmetric Effects of Supervisor-Subordinate Disability Incongruence and Climate for Inclusion," *Academy of Management Journal* 59, no. 1 (2016): 44–64.

63. S. Almond and A. Healey, "Mental Health and Absence from Work: New Evidence from the UK Quarterly Labour Force Survey," *Work, Employment, and Society* 17, no. 4 (2003): 731–42.

64. P. Button, "Expanding Employment Discrimination Protections for Individuals with Disabilities: Evidence From California," *Industrial and Labor Relations Review* 71, no. 2 (2018): 365–393; P. T. J. H. Nelissen, K. Vornholt, G. M. C. Van Ruitenbeek, U. R. Hülsheger, and S. Uitdewilligen, "Disclosure or Nondisclosure—Is This the Question?" *Industrial and Organizational Psychology* 7, no. 2 (2014): 231–35.

65. A. M. Santuzzi, P. R. Waltz, and L. M. Finkelstein, "Invisible Disabilities: Unique Challenges for Employees and Organizations," *Industrial and Organizational Psychology* 7, no. 2 (2014): 204–19.

66. Ibid.

67. T. D. Johnson and A. Joshi, "Dark Clouds or Silver Linings? A Stigma Threat Perspective on the Implications of an Autism Diagnosis for Workplace Well-Being," *Journal of Applied Psychology* 101, no. 3 (2015): 430–49.

68. R. A. Schriber, R. W. Robins, and M. Solomon, "Personality and Self-Insight in Individuals with Autism Spectrum Disorder," *Journal of Personality and Social Psychology* 106, no. 1 (2014): 112–30.

69. C. L. Nittrouer, R. C. E. Trump, K. R. O'Brien, and M. Hebl, "Stand Up and Be Counted: In the Long Run, Disclosing Helps All," *Industrial and Organizational Psychology* 7, no. 2 (2014): 235–41.

70. L. Turner and A. Suflas, "Global Diversity—One Program Won't Fit All."

71. S. Lucas, "Hilton's $21 Million Reason to Honor a Dishwasher's Religious Schedule Request," *Inc.*, January 17, 2019, https://www.inc.com/suzanne-lucas/hilton-21-million-reason-to-honor-a-dishwashers-religious-schedule-request.html

72. A. Liptak, "In a Case of Religious Dress, Justices Explore the Obligations of Employers," *The New York Times,* February 25, 2015, http://www.nytimes.com/2015/02/26/us/in-a-case-of-religious-dress-justices-explore-the-obligations-of-employers.html?

73. E. B. King and A. S. Ahmad, "An Experimental Field Study of Interpersonal Discrimination Toward Muslim Job Applicants," *Personnel Psychology* 63, no. 4 (2010): 881–906.

74. M. Gold, "The ABCs of L.G.B.T.Q.I.A.+," *The New York Times,* June 24, 2018, F6; V. Priola, D. Lasio, S. De Simone, and F. Serri, "The Sound of Silence: Lesbian, Gay, Bisexual, and Transgender Discrimination in 'Inclusive Organizations,'" *British Journal of Management* 25, no. 3 (2012): 488–502.

75. A. Tilcsik, "Pride and Prejudice: Employment Discrimination against Openly Gay Men in the United States," *American Journal of Sociology* 117, no. 2 (2011): 586–626.

76. Z. Henry, "Tesla and Instacart Among the Most LGBT-friendly Companies in America," *Inc.,* Dec 5, 2016, https://www.inc.com/zoe-henry/the-most-lgbt-friendly-companies-in-america.html

77. N. Legate, R. M. Ryan, and R. D. Rogge, "Daily Autonomy Support and Sexual Identity Disclosure Predicts Daily Mental and Physical Health Outcomes," *Personality and Social Psy- chology Bulletin* 43, no. 6 (2017): 860–73; L. R. Martinez, K. B. Sawyer, C. N. Thoroughgood, E. N. Ruggs, and N. A. Smith, "The Importance of Being 'Me': The Relation Between Authentic Identity Expression and Transgender Employees' Work-Related Attitudes and Experiences," *Journal of Applied Psychology* 102, no. 2 (2017): 215–26; R. L. Williamson, A. Beiler-May, L. R. Locklear, and M. A. Clark, "Bringing Home What I'm Hiding at Work: The Impact of Sexual Orientation Disclosure at Work for Same-Sex Couples," *Journal of Vocational Behavior* 103, Part A (2017): 7–22;

78. The International Lesbian, Gay, Bisexual, Trans and Intersex Association (ILGA), Sexual Orientation Laws in the World—Overview, December 2019, https://ilga.org/sites/default/files/ENG_ILGA_World_map_sexual_orientation_laws_dec2019_update.png

79. L. Hurley, "In Landmark Ruling, Supreme Court Bars Discrimination Against LGBT Workers," Reuters, June 15, 2020, https://www.reuters.com/article/us-usa-court-lgbt-idUSKBN23M20N

80. L. Turner and A. Suflas, "Global Diversity—One Program Won't Fit All."

81. B. Polakowski, "America's LGBT 2015 Buying Power Estimated at $917 Billion," Witeck Communications [Press Release], July 20, 2016, https://www.nlgja.org/outnewswire/2016/07/20/americas-lgbt-2015-buying-power-estimated-at-917-billion/

82. A. E. Jackson, "20 Companies That Champion LGBTQ Equality Hiring Now," *Glassdoor* [Blog], June 6, 2018, https://www.glassdoor.com/blog/companies-lgbtq-equality/

83. Z. Henry, "Tesla and Instacart Among the Most LGBT-friendly Companies in America."

84. V. Priola, D. Lasio, S. De Simone, and F. Serri, "The Sound of Silence: Lesbian, Gay, Bisexual, and Transgender Discrimination in 'Inclusive Organizations,'" *British Journal of Management* 25, no. 3 (2014): 488–502.

85. C-R. Lee, *Native Speaker* (New York: Riverhead Books, 1996); I. Sung, "Korean American's Journey for Cultural Identity," *The Korea Times,* January 23, 2019, https://www .koreatimes.co.kr/www/art/2018/07/142_252586.html

86. M. W. Morris, K. Savani, S. Mor, and J. Cho, "When in Rome: Intercultural Learning and Its Implications for Training," *Research in Organizational Behavior* 34 (2014): 189–215.

87. K. Leung, S. Ang, and M. Ling Tan, "Intercultural Competence," Annual Review of Organizational Psychology and Organizational Behavior 1 (2014): 489–519.

88. E. Gonzalez-Mulé, M. K. Mount, and I-S. Oh, "A Meta-Analysis of the Relationship Between General Mental Ability and Nontask Performance," *Journal of Applied Psychology* 99, no. 6 (2014): 1222–43; T. W. H. Ng and D. C. Feldman, "Human Capital and Objective

Indicators of Career Success: The Mediating Effects of Cognitive Ability and Conscientiousness," *Journal of Occupational and Organizational Psychology* 83 (2010): 207–35; F. L. Schmidt and J. Hunter, "General Mental Ability in the World of Work: Occupational Attainment and Job Performance," *Journal of Personality and Social Psychology* 86, no. 1 (2004): 162–73.

89. P. A. Freund and N. Kasten, "How Smart Do You Think You Are? A Meta-Analysis of the Validity of Self-Estimates of Cognitive Ability," *Psychological Bulletin* 138, no. 2 (2012): 296–321.

90. R. E. Nisbett et al., "Intelligence: New Findings and Theoretical Developments," *American Psychologist* 67, no. 2 (2012): 130–59.

91. L. S. Gottfredson, "The Challenge and Promise of Cognitive Career Assessment," *Journal of Career Assessment* 11, no. 2 (2003): 32–34.

92. Wonderlic, "The NFL Wonderlic Test and the NFL Scouting Combine: The Top 7 Questions," *Wonderlic* [Blog], April 25, 2017, https://www.wonderlic.com/blog/nfl-wonderlic-test-nfl-scouting-combine/

93. M. D. Dunnette and E. A. Fleishman, eds., *Human Performance and Productivity: Human Capability Assessment* (New York and London: Psychology Press/Taylor & Francis Group, 2014).

94. R. T. Warne and C. Burningham, "Spearman's *g* Found in 31 Non-Western Nations: Strong Evidence That *g* is a Universal Phenomenon," *Psychological Bulletin* 145, no. 3 (2019): 237–272.

95. N. Barber, "Educational and Ecological Correlates of IQ: A Cross-National Investigation," *Intelligence* 33, no. 3 (2005): 273–84; G. Meisenberg and M. A. Woodley, "Are Cognitive Differences Between Countries Diminishing? Evidence From TIMSS and PISA," *Intelligence* 41, no. 6 (2013): 808–16; R. T. Warne and C. Burningham, Spearman's *g* Found in 31 Non-Western Nations: Strong Evidence That *g* is a Universal Phenomenon."

96. "What Companies Will Make You Take a Wonderlic Test?" *Beat the Wonderlic* [Blog] December 31, 2014, http://www .beatthewonderlic.com/blog/2014/12/31/what-companies-will-make-you-take-a-wonderlic-test

97. Y. Ganzach, "Intelligence and Job Satisfaction," *Academy of Management Journal* 41, no. 5 (1998): 526–39; and Y. Ganzach, "Intelligence, Education, and Facets of Job Satisfaction," *Work and Occupations* 30, no. 1 (2003): 97–122.

98. Y. Ganzach, "Intelligence, Education, and Facets of Job Satisfaction," *Work and Occupations* 30, no. 1 (2003): 97–122.

99. J. J. Caughron, M. D. Mumford, and E. A. Fleishman, "The Fleishman Job Analysis Survey: Development, Validation, and Applications," in M. A. Wilson, W. Bennett Jr., S. G. Gibson, and G. M. Alliger (eds.), *The Handbook of Work Analysis: Methods, Systems, Applications and Science of Work Measurement in Organizations* (New York: Routledge/Taylor & Francis Group, 2012): 231–46; P. D. Converse, F. L. Oswald, M. A. Gillespie, K. A. Field, and E. B. Bizot, "Matching Individuals to Occupations Using Abilities and the O*Net: Issues and an Application in Career Guidance," *Personnel Psychology* 57, no. 2 (2004): 451–87.

100. P. R. Sackett, F. Lievens, C. H. Van Iddekinge, and N. R. Kuncel, "Individual Differences and Their Measurement: A Review of 100 Years of Research," *Journal of Applied Psychology* 102, no. 3 (2017): 254–73.

101. N. D. Henderson, "Predicting Long-Term Firefighter Performance From Cognitive and Physical Ability Measures," *Personnel Psychology* 63 (2010): 999–1039.

102. S. H. Courtright, B. W. McCormick, B. E. Postlethwaite, C. J. Reeves, and M. K. Mount, "A Meta-Analysis of Sex Differences in Physical Ability: Revised Estimates and Strategies for Reducing Differences in Selection Contexts," *Journal of Applied Psychology* 98, no. 4 (2013): 623–41.

103. S. S. Wang, "Companies Find Autism Can Be a Job Skill," *The Wall Street Journal*, March 28, 2014, B1–B2.

104. Q. M. Roberson, "Diversity in the Workplace: A Review, Synthesis, and Future Research Agenda," Annual Review of Organizational Psychology and Organizational Behavior 6 (2019): 69–88.

105. N. Wingfield, "Microsoft Chief Backpedals on Women's Pay," *The Wall Street Journal*, October 10, 2014, B1, B7.

106. D. R. Avery, "Reactions to Diversity in Recruitment Advertising: Are the Differences Black and White?" *Journal of Applied Psychology* 88, no. 4 (2003): 672–79; P. F. McKay and D. R. Avery, "What Has Race Got to Do with It? Unraveling the Role of Racioethnicity in Job Seekers' Reactions to Site Visits," *Personnel Psychology* 59, no. 2 (2006): 395–429; D. R. Avery and P. F. McKay, "Target Practice: An Organizational Impression Management Approach to Attracting Minority and Female Job Applicants," *Personnel Psychology* 59, no. 1 (2006): 157–87.

107. M. R. Buckley, K. A. Jackson, M. C. Bolino, J. G. Veres, and H. S. Field, "The Influence of Relational Demography on Panel Interview Ratings: A Field Experiment," *Personnel Psychology* 60, no. 3 (2007): 627–46; J. M. Sacco, C. R. Scheu, A. M. Ryan, and N. Schmitt, "An Investigation of Race and Sex Similarity Effects in Interviews: A Multilevel Approach to Relational Demography," *Journal of Applied Psychology* 88, no. 5 (2003): 852–65; and J. C. Ziegert and P. J. Hanges, "Employment Discrimination: The Role of Implicit Attitudes, Motivation, and a Climate for Racial Bias," *Journal of Applied Psychology* 90, no. 3 (2005): 553–62.

108. S. T. Bell, "Deep-Level Composition Variables as Predictors of Team Performance: A Meta-Analysis," *Journal of Applied Psychology* 92, no. 3 (2007): 595–615; S. T. Bell, A. J. Villado, M. A. Lukasik, L. Belau, and A. L. Briggs, "Getting Specific About Demographic Diversity Variable and Team Performance Relationships: A Meta-Analysis," *Journal of Management* 37, no. 3 (2011): 709–43; S. K. Horwitz and I. B. Horwitz, "The Effects of Team Diversity on Team Outcomes: A Meta-Analytic Review of Team Demography," *Journal of Management* 33, no. 6 (2007): 987–1015; H. van Dijk, M. L. van Engen, and D. van Knippenberg, "Defying Conventional Wisdom: A Meta-Analytical Examination of the Differences Between Demographic and Job-Related Diversity Relationships With Performance," *Organizational Behavior and Human Decision Processes* 119 (2012): 38–53.

109. G. Andrevski, O. C. Richard, J. D. Shaw, and W. J. Ferrier, "Racial Diversity and Firm Performance: The Mediating Role of Competitive Intensity," *Journal of Management* 40, no. 3 (2014): 820–44.

110. S. T. Bell, "Deep-Level Composition Variables as Predictors of Team Performance: A Meta-Analysis"; D. J. Devine and J. L. Philips, "Do Smarter Teams Do Better: A Meta-Analysis of Cognitive Ability and Team Performance," *Small Group Research* 32, no. 5 (2001): 507–32; M. S. Prewett, A. A. G. Walvoord, F. R. B. Stilson, M. E. Rossi, and M. T. Brannick, "The Team Personality-Team Performance Relationship Revisited: The Impact of Criterion Choice, Pattern of Workflow, and Method of Aggregation," *Human Performance* 22 (2009): 273–96.

111. S. T. Bell, A. J. Villado, M. A. Lukasik, L. Belau, and A. L. Briggs, "Getting Specific About Demographic Diversity Variable and Team Performance Relationships: A Meta-Analysis."

112. D. C. Lau and J. K. Murnighan, "Interactions Within Groups and Subgroups: The Effects of Demographic Faultlines," *Academy of Management Journal* 48, no. 4 (2005): 645–59; T. M. Spoelma and A. P. J. Ellis, "Fuse or Fracture? Threat as a Moderator of the Effects of Diversity Faultlines in Teams," *Journal of Applied Psychology* 102, no. 9 (2017): 1344–59.

113. A. C. Homan, J. R. Hollenbeck, S. E. Humphrey, D. van Knippenberg, D. R. Ilgen, and G. A. Van Kleef, "Facing Differences with an Open Mind: Openness to Experience, Salience of Intragroup Differences, and Performance of Diverse Work Groups," *Academy of Management Journal* 51, no. 6 (2008): 1204–22; R. Rico, M. Sánchez-Manzanares,

M. Antino, and D. Lau, "Bridging Team Faultlines by Combining Task Role Assignment and Goal Structure Strategies," *Journal of Applied Psychology* 97, no. 2 (2012): 407-420.

114. H. Huettermann, S. Doering, and S. Boerner, "Understanding the Development of Team Identification: A Qualitative Study in UN Peacebuilding Teams," *Journal of Business and Psychology* 32 (2017): 217–34.

115. D. van Knippenberg and J. N. Mell, "Past, Present, and Potential Future of Team Diversity Research: From Compositional Diversity to Emergent Diversity," *Organizational Behavior and Human Decision Processes* 136 (2016): 135–45.

116. K. Srikanth, S. Harvey, and R. Peterson, "A Dynamic Perspective on Diverse Teams: Moving From the Dual-Process Model to a Dynamic Coordination-based Model of Diverse Team Performance," *Academy of Management Annals* 10, no. 1 (2016): 453–93.

117. A. Hajro, C. B. Gibson, and M. Pudelko, "Knowledge Exchange Processes in Multicultural Teams: Linking Organizational Diversity Climates to Teams' Effectiveness," *Academy of Management Journal* 60, no. 1 (2017): 345–72; K. Srikanth, S. Harvey, and R. Peterson, "A Dynamic Perspective on Diverse Teams: Moving From the Dual-Process Model to a Dynamic Coordination-based Model of Diverse Team Performance."; M. Williams, "Being Trusted: How Team Generational age Diversity Promotes and Undermines Trust in Cross-Boundary Relationships," *Journal of Organizational Behavior* 37 (2016): 346–73; Y. Zhang and M-Y. Huai, "Diverse Work Groups and Employee Performance: The Role of Communication Ties," *Small Group Research* 47, no. 1 (2016): 28–57.

118. K. Bezrukova, C. S. Spell, J. L. Perry, K. A. Jehn, "A Meta-Analytical Integration of Over 40 Years of Research on Diversity Training Evaluation," *Psychological Bulletin* 142, no. 11 (2016): 1227–74; Z. T. Kalinoski, D. Steele-Johnson, E. J. Peyton, K. A. Leas, J. Steinke, and N. A. Bowling, "A Meta-Analytic Evaluation of Diversity Training Outcomes," *Journal of Organizational Behavior* 34 (2013): 1076–104.

119. C. L. Holladay and M. A. Quiñones, "The Influence of Training Focus and Trainer Characteristics on Diversity Training Effectiveness," *Academy of Management Learning and Education* 7, no. 3 (2008): 343–54; R. Anand and M. Winters, "A Retrospective View of Corporate Diversity Training from 1964 to the Present," *Academy of Management Learning and Education* 7, no. 3 (2008): 356–72.

120. A. M. Konrad, Y. Yang, and C. C. Maurer, "Antecedents and Outcomes of Diversity and Equality Management Systems: An Integrated Institutional Agency and Strategic Human Resource Management Approach," *Human Resource Management* 55, no. 1 (2016): 83–107.

121. A. Rattan and C. S. Dweck, "What Happens After Prejudice is Confronted in the Workplace? How Mindsets Affect Minorities' and Women's Outlook on Future Social Relations," *Journal of Applied Psychology* 103, no. 6 (2018): 676–87.

122. E. B. King, L. M. V. Gulick, and D. R. Avery, "The Divide Between Diversity Training and Diversity Education: Integrating Best Practices," *Journal of Management Education* 34, no. 6 (2010); 891–906.

123. A. Sippola and A. Smale, "The Global Integration of Diversity Management: A Longitudinal Case Study," *International Journal of Human Resource Management* 18, no. 11 (2007): 1895–916.

CHAPTER 3

1. Robert Half International, "CPA Job Satisfaction: It's Not Just About Money," *Robert Half* [Blog], March 12, 2015, https://www.roberthalf.com/blog/management-tips/cpa-job-satisfaction-its-not-just-about-money

2. A. Barsky, S. A. Kaplan, and D. J. Beal, "Just Feelings? The Role of Affect in the Formation of Organizational Fairness Judgments,"

Journal of Management 37, no. 1 (2011): 248–79; J. A. Mikels, S. J. Maglio, A. E. Reed, and L. J. Kaplowitz, "Should I Go with My Gut? Investigating the Benefits of Emotion-Focused Decision Making," *Emotion* 11, no. 4 (2011): 743–53; A. J. Rojas Tejada, O. M. Lozano Rojas, M. Navas Luque, and P. J. Pérez Moreno, "Prejudiced Attitude Measurement Using the Rasch Scale Model," *Psychological Reports* 109, no. 2 (2011): 553–72.

3. O. N. Solinger, J. Hofmans, and W. van Olffen, "The Dynamic Microstructure of Organizational Commitment," *Journal of Occupational and Organizational Psychology* 88 (2015): 773–96.

4. See L. S. Glasman and D. Albarracín, "Forming Attitudes That Predict Future Behavior: A Meta-Analysis of the Attitude-Behavior Relation," *Psychological Bulletin* 132, no. 5 (2006): 778–822; M. Riketta, "The Causal Relation Between Job Attitudes and Performance: A Meta-Analysis of Panel Studies," *Journal of Applied Psychology* 93, no. 2 (2008): 472–81.

5. L. S. Glasman and D. Albarracin, "Forming Attitudes That Predict Future Behavior: A Meta-Analysis of the Attitude-Behavior Relation."

6. M. J. Somers, "Thinking Differently: Assessing Nonlinearities in the Relationship Between Work Attitudes and Job Performance Using a Bayesian Neural Network," *Journal of Occupational and Organizational Psychology* 74 (2001): 47–61.

7. S. K. Johnson, J. Kirk, and K. Keplinger, "Why We Fail to Report Sexual Harassment," *Harvard Business Review,* October 4, 2016, https://hbr.org/2016/10/why-we-fail-to-report-sexual-harassment; C. Tavris and E. Aronson, *Mistakes Were Made (but not by me): Why We Justify Foolish Beliefs, Bad Decisions, and Hurtful Acts* (New York, NY: Houghton Mifflin Harcourt, 2015).

8. See L. Festinger, *A Theory of Cognitive Dissonance* (Stanford, CA: Stanford UP: 1957); L. Festinger and J. M. Carlsmith, "Cognitive Consequences of Forced Compliance," *Journal of Abnormal and Social Psychology* 58 (1959): 203–10.

9. See, for instance, L. R. Fabrigar, R. E. Petty, S. M. Smith, and S. L. Crites, "Understanding Knowledge Effects on Attitude-Behavior Consistency: The Role of Relevance, Complexity, and Amount of Knowledge," *Journal of Personality and Social Psychology* 90, no. 4 (2006): 556–77; D. J. Schleicher, J. D. Watt, and G. J. Greguras, "Reexamining the Job Satisfaction-Performance Relationship: The Complexity of Attitudes," *Journal of Applied Psychology* 89, no. 1 (2004): 165–77.

10. J. Cloutier, P. L. Denis, and H. Bilodeau, "The Dynamics of Strike Votes: Perceived Justice During Collective Bargaining," *Journal of Organizational Behavior* 34 (2013): 1016–38.

11. J. K. Caird, S. M. Simmons, K. Wiley, K. A. Johnston, and W. J. Horrey, "Does Talking on a Cell Phone, With a Passenger, or Dialing Affect Driving Performance? An Updated Systematic Review and Meta-Analysis of Experimental Studies," *Human Factors* 60, no. 1 (2018): 101–33.

12. L. Festinger, *A Theory of Cognitive Dissonance.*

13. Ibid.

14. J. E. Dutton, J. M. Dukerich, and C. V. Harquail, "Organizational Images and Member Identification," *Administrative Science Quarterly* 39 (1994): 239–63.

15. E-S. Lee, T-Y. Park, and B. Koo, "Identifying Organizational Identification as a Basis for Attitudes and Behaviors: A Meta-Analytic Review," *Psychological Bulletin* 141, no. 5 (2015): 1049–80.

16. V. R. Lane and S. G. Scott, "The Neural Network Model of Organizational Identification," *Organizational Behavior and Human Decision Processes* 104 (2007): 175–92.

17. D. A. Harrison, D. A. Newman, and P. L. Roth, "How Important Are Job Attitudes? Meta-analytic Comparisons of Integrative Behavioral Outcomes and Time Sequences," *Academy of Management Journal* 49 (2006): 305–25; D. A. Newman, D. L. Joseph, and C. L. Hulin,

"Job Attitudes and Employee Engagement: Considering the Attitude 'A-Factor,'" in S. L. Albrecht (ed.), *Handbook of Employee Engagement: Perspectives, Issues, Research and Practice* (Northampton, MA: Edward Elgar, 2010): 43–61.

18. D. J. Schleicher, S. D. Hansen, and K. E. Fox, "Job Attitudes and Work Values," in *APA Handbook of Industrial and Organizational Psychology,* ed. S. Zedeck (Washington, D.C.: APA, 2011), 137–89.

19. S. P. Brown, "A Meta-Analysis and Review of Organizational Research on Job Involvement," *Psychological Bulletin* 120, no. 2 (1996): 235–55; T. M. Lodahl and M. Kejner, "The Definition and Measurement of Job Involvement," *Journal of Applied Psychology* 49, no. 1 (1965): 24–33.

20. S. P. Brown, "A Meta-Analysis and Review of Organizational Research on Job Involvement," *Psychological Bulletin* 120, no. 2 (1996): 235–55.

21. G. M. Spreitzer, "Psychological Empowerment in the Workplace: Construct Definition, Measurement, and Validation," *Academy of Management Journal* 38 (1995): 1442–65; G. M. Spreitzer, "Taking Stock: A Review of More Than Twenty Years of Research on Empowerment at Work," in J. Barling and C. L. Cooper (eds.), *Handbook of Organizational Behavior* (Thousand Oaks, CA: Sage, 2008): 54–72.

22. S. E. Seibert, G. Wang, and S. H. Courtright, "Antecedents and Consequences of Psychological and Team Empowerment in Organizations: A Meta-Analytic Review," *Journal of Applied Psychology* 96, no. 5 (2011): 981–1003.

23. Z. A. Mercurio, "Affective Commitment as a Core Essence of Organizational Commitment: An Integrative Literature Review," *Human Resource Development Review* 14, no. 4 (2015): 389–414; O. N. Solinger, W. van Olffen, and R. A. Roe, "Beyond the Three-Component Model of Organizational Commitment," *Journal of Applied Psychology* 93, no. 1 (2008): 70–83.

24. A. Cooper-Hakim and C. Viswesvaran, "The Construct of Work Commitment: Testing an Integrative Framework," *Psychological Bulletin* 131, no. 2 (2005): 241–59; Solinger, van Olffen, and Roe, "Beyond the Three-Component Model of Organizational Commitment."

25. L. Rhoades, R. Eisenberger, and S. Armeli, "Affective Commitment to the Organization: The Contribution of Perceived Organizational Support," *Journal of Applied Psychology* 86, no. 5 (2001): 825–36.

26. J.-L. Farh, R. D. Hackett, and J. Liang, "Individual-Level Cultural Values as Moderators of Perceived Organizational Support–Employee Outcome Relationships in China: Comparing the Effects of Power Distance and Traditionality," *Academy of Management Journal* 50, no. 3 (2007): 715–29; L. Zhong, S. J. Wayne, and R. C. Liden, "Job Engagement, Perceived Organizational Support, High-Performance Human Resource Practices, and Cultural Value Orientations: A Cross-Level Investigation," *Journal of Organizational Behavior* 37, no. 6 (2016): 823–44.

27. A. O'Byrne, "Nurture Connections to Enhance Expatriate Success," *Training + Development,* May 2018, https://www.td.org/magazines/td-magazine/nurture-connections-to-enhance-expatriate-success

28. D. A. Newman, D. L. Joseph, and C. L. Hulin, "Job Attitudes and Employee Engagement: Considering the Attitude 'A-Factor,'"; D. J. Schleicher, S. D. Hansen, and K. E. Fox, "Job Attitudes and Work Values."

29. Ibid.

30. R. L. Ray, R. Aparicio, P. Hyland, D. A. Dye, J. Simco, and A. Caputo, "DNA of Engagement: How Organizations Can Foster Employee Ownership of Engagement," *The Conference Board,* February 2017, https://www.conference-board .org/dna-engagement2017/

31. M. S. Christian, A. S. Garza, and J. E. Slaughter, "Work Engagement: A Quantitative Review and Test of Its Relations with Task and Contextual Performance," *Personnel Psychology* 64 (2011): 89–136; J. K.

Harter, F. L. Schmidt, and T. L. Hayes, "Business-Unit-Level Relationship between Employee Satisfaction, Employee Engagement, and Business Outcomes: A Meta-Analysis," *Journal of Applied Psychology* 87, no. 2 (2002): 268–79.

32. N. R. Lockwood, *Leveraging Employee Engagement for Competitive Advantage* (Alexandria, VA: Society for Human Resource Management, 2007); R. J. Vance, *Employee Engagement and Commitment* (Alexandria, VA: Society for Human Resource Management, 2006).

33. S. Highhouse and A. S. Becker, "Facet Measures and Global Job Satisfaction," *Journal of Business and Psychology* 8, no. 1 (1993): 117–27; M. S. Nagy, "Using a Single-Item Approach to Measure Facet Job Satisfaction," *Journal of Occupational and Organizational Psychology* 75 (2002): 77–86; M. Roznowski, "Examination of the Measurement Properties of the Job Descriptive Index with Experimental Items," *Journal of Applied Psychology* 74 (1989): 805–14; J. P. Wanous and M. J. Hudy, "Single-Item Reliability: A Replication and Extension," *Organizational Research Methods* 4, no. 4 (2001): 361–75; J. P. Wanous, A. E. Reichers, and M. J. Hudy, "Overall Job Satisfaction: How Good Are Single-Item Measures?" *Journal of Applied Psychology* 82, no. 2 (1997): 247–52.

34. J-E. De Neve and G. Ward, "Happiness at Work," in J. Helliwell, R. Layard, and J. Sachs (Eds.), *World Happiness Report* (World Happiness Report APPENDIX, 2017).

35. N. A. Bowling, M. R. Hoepf, D. M. LaHuis, and L. R. Lepisto, "Mean Job Satisfaction Levels over Time: Are Things Bad and Getting Worse?" *The Industrial-Organizational Psychologist* 50, no. 4 (2013): 57–64.

36. L. Weber, "U.S. Workers Can't Get No (Job) Satisfaction," *The Wall Street Journal: At Work* (blog), June 18, 2014, 12:01 AM, http://blogs.wsj.com/atwork/2014/06/18/u-s-workers-cant-get-no-job-satisfaction/

37. L. Weber, "U.S. Workers Report Highest Job Satisfaction Since 2005," *The Wall Street Journal,* August 29, 2018, 8:00AM, https://www.wsj.com/articles/u-s-workers-report-highest-job-satisfaction-since-2005-1535544000.

38. L. Weber, "U.S. Workers Can't Get No (Job) Satisfaction."

39. C. W. Koh, W. Shen, and T. Lee, "Black-White Mean Differences in Job Satisfaction: A Meta-Analysis," *Journal of Vocational Behavior* 94 (2016): 131–43.

40. S. E. Humphrey, J. D. Nahrgang, and F. P. Morgeson, "Integrating Motivational, Social, and Contextual Work Design Features: A Meta-Analytic Summary and Theoretical Extension of the Work Design Literature," *Journal of Applied Psychology* 92, no. 5 (2007): 1332–56; D. S. Chiaburu and D. A. Harrison, "Do Peers Make the Place? Conceptual Synthesis and Meta-Analysis of Coworker Effect on Perceptions, Attitudes, OCBs, and Performance," *Journal of Applied Psychology* 93, no. 5 (2008): 1082–103; W. J. Shepherd, R. E. Ployhart, and J. Kautz, "The Neglected Role of Collective Customer Perceptions in Shaping Collective Employee Satisfaction, Service Climate, Voluntary Turnover, and Involuntary Turnover: A Cautionary Note," Journal of Applied Psychology (in press).

41. M. D. Triana, M. Jayasinghe, and J. R. Pieper, "Perceived Workplace Racial Discrimination and its Correlates: A Meta-Analysis," *Journal of Organizational Behavior* 36 (2015): 491–513.

42. R. Martin, Y. Guillaume, G. Thomas, A. Lee, and O. Epitropaki, "Leader-Member Exchange (LMX) and Performance: A Meta-Analytic Review," *Personnel Psychology* 69 (2016): 67–121; T. Rockstuhl, J. H. Dulebohn, S. Ang, and L. M. Shore, "Leader-Member Exchange (LMX) and Culture: A Meta-Analysis of Correlates of LMX across 23 Countries," *Journal of Applied Psychology* 97, no. 6 (2012): 1097–130.

43. I-S. Oh, R. P. Guay, K. Kim, C. M. Harold, J-H. Lee, C-G. Heo, and K-H. Shin, "Fit Happens Globally: A Meta-Analytic Comparison of the Relationships of Person-Environment Fit Dimensions with Work Attitudes and Performance Across East Asia, Europe, and North America," *Personnel Psychology* 67 (2014): 99–152.

44. A. L. Rubenstein, Y. Zhang, K. Ma, H. M. Morrison, and D. F. Jorgensen, "Trait Expression Through Perceived Job Characteristics: A Meta-Analytic Path Model Linking Personality and Job Attitudes," *Journal of Vocational Behavior* 112 (2019): 141–57.

45. A. Hess, "The 10 Best Places to Work in 2019, According to Glassdoor," *CNBC: Make It,* December 10, 2018, https://www.cnbc.com/2018/12/04/glassdoor-the-best-places-to-work-in-2019.html

46. See T. A. Judge, D. Heller, and M. K. Mount, "Five-Factor Model of Personality and Job Satisfaction: A Meta-Analysis," *Journal of Applied Psychology* 87, no. 3 (2002): 530–41; P. Steel, J. Schmidt, F. Bosco, and K. Uggerslev, "The Effects of Personality on Job Satisfaction and Life Satisfaction: A Meta-Analytic Investigation Accounting for Bandwidth-Fidelity and Commensurability," Human Relations 72, no. 2 (2019): 217–47.

47. C.-H. Chang, D. L. Ferris, R. E. Johnson, C. C. Rosen, and J. A. Tan, "Core Self-Evaluations: A Review and Evaluation of the Literature," *Journal of Management* 38, no. 1 (2012): 81–128; T. A. Judge and J. E. Bono, "Relationship of Core Self-Evaluations Traits—Self-Esteem, Generalized Self-Efficacy, Locus of Control, and Emotional Stability—with Job Satisfaction and Job Performance: A Meta-Analysis," *Journal of Applied Psychology* 86, no. 1 (2001): 80–92.

48. T. A. Judge, R. F. Piccolo, N. P. Podsakoff, J. C. Shaw, and B. L. Rich, "The Relationship Between Pay and Job Satisfaction: A Meta-Analysis of the Literature," *Journal of Vocational Behavior* 77, no. 2 (2010): 157–67.

49. D. Thorpe, "Why CSR? The Benefits of Corporate Social Responsibility Will Move You to Act," *Forbes,* May 18, 2013, http://www.forbes.com/sites/devinthorpe/2013/05/18/why-csr-the-benefits-of-corporate-social-responsibility-will-move-you-to-act/

50. N. Fallon, "What Is Corporate Responsibility?" *Business News Daily,* December 22, 2014, http://www.businessnews daily.com/4679-corporate-social-responsibility.html

51. R. Feintzeig, "I Don't Have a Job. I Have a Higher Calling," *The Wall Street Journal,* February 25, 2015, B1, B4.

52. See I. Filatotchev and C. Nakajima, "Corporate Governance, Responsible Managerial Behavior, and Corporate Social Responsibility: Organizational Efficiency Versus Organizational Legitimacy?" *Academy of Management Perspectives* 28, no. 3 (2014): 289–306.

53. T. A. Judge, C. J. Thoresen, J. E. Bono, and G. K. Patton, "The Job Satisfaction–Job Performance Relationship: A Qualitative and Quantitative Review," *Psychological Bulletin* 127, no. 3 (2001): 376–407.

54. N. P. Podsakoff, P. M. Podsakoff, and S. B. MacKenzie, "Consequences of Unit-Level Organizational Citizenship Behaviors: A Review and Recommendations for Future Research," *Journal of Organizational Behavior* 35, no. S1 (2014): S87–119.

55. B. J. Hoffman, C. A. Blair, J. P. Meriac, and D. J. Woehr, "Expanding the Criterion Domain? A Quantitative Review of the OCB Literature," *Journal of Applied Psychology* 92, no. 2 (2007): 555–66.

56. B. B. Reiche et al., "Why Do Managers Engage in Trustworthy Behavior? A Multilevel Cross-Cultural Study in 18 Countries," *Personnel Psychology* 67, no. 1 (2014): 61–98.

57. D. S. Chiaburu and D. A. Harrison, "Do Peers Make the Place? Conceptual Synthesis and Meta-Analysis of Coworker Effect on Perceptions, Attitudes, OCBs, and Performance," *Journal of Applied Psychology* 93, no. 5 (2008): 1082–103.

58. R. G. Netemeyer, J. G. Maxham III, and D. R. Lichtenstein, "Store Manager Performance and Satisfaction: Effects on Store Employee Performance and Satisfaction, Store Customer Satisfaction, and Store Customer Spending Growth," *Journal of Applied Psychology* 95, no. 3 (2010): 530–45; E. P. Piening, A. M. Baluch, and T. O. Salge, "The Relationship between Employees' Perceptions of Human Resource Systems and Organizational Performance: Examining Mediating Mechanisms and Temporal Dynamics," *Journal of Applied Psychology* 98, no. 6 (2013): 926–47; M. Schulte, C. Ostroff, S. Shmulyian, and A. Kinicki, "Organizational Climate Configurations: Relationships to Collective Attitudes, Customer Satisfaction, and Financial Performance," *Journal of Applied Psychology* 94 (2009): 618–34.

59. B. Taylor, "Why Amazon Is Copying Zappos and Paying Employees to Quit," *Harvard Business Review,* April 14, 2014, https://hbr.org/2014/04/why-amazon-is-copying-zappos-and-paying-employees-to-quit/.

60. N. A. Bowling, K. J. Eschleman, and Q. Wang, "A Meta-Analytic Examination of the Relationship between Job Satisfaction and Subjective Well-Being," *Journal of Occupational and Organizational Psychology* 83, no. 4 (2010): 915–34; B. Erdogan, T. N. Bauer, D. M. Truxillo, and L. R. Mansfield, "Whistle While You Work: A Review of the Life Satisfaction Literature," *Journal of Management* 38, no. 4 (2012): 1038–83; Steel et al., "The Effects of Personality on Job Satisfaction and Life Satisfaction."

61. O. Stavrova, T. Schlosser, and A. Baumert, "Life Satisfaction and Job-Seeking Behavior of the Unemployed: The Effect of Individual Differences in Justice Sensitivity," *Applied Psychology: An International Review* 64, no. 4 (2014): 643–70.

62. R. Gibney, T. J. Zagenczyk, and M. F. Masters, "The Negative Aspects of Social Exchange: An Introduction to Perceived Organizational Obstruction," *Group & Organization Management* 34, no. 6 (2009): 665–97.

63. A. J. Nyberg and R. E. Ployhart, "Context-Emergent Turnover (CET) Theory: A Theory of Collective Turnover," *Academy of Management Review* 38, no. 1 (2013): 109–31.

64. R. T. Michalak, S. A. Kiffin-Petersen, and N. M. Ashkanasy, "'I Feel Mad So I Be Bad': The Role of Affect, Dissatisfaction and Stress in Determining Responses to Interpersonal Deviance," *British Journal of Management* 30 (2019): 645–67.

65. P. E. Spector, S. Fox, L. M. Penney, K. Bruursema, A. Goh, and S. Kessler, "The Dimensionality of Counterproductivity: Are All Counterproductive Behaviors Created Equal?" *Journal of Vocational Behavior* 68, no. 3 (2006): 446–60; K. Treviño, N. A. den Nieuwenboer, and J. J. Kish-Gephart, "(Un)Ethical Behavior in Organizations," *Annual Review of Psychology* 65 (2014): 635–60.

66. R. S. Dalal, "A Meta-Analysis of the Relationship Between Organizational Citizenship Behavior and Counterproductive Work Behavior," *Journal of Applied Psychology* 90, no. 6 (2005): 1241–55.

67. P. A. O'Keefe, "Liking Work Really Does Matter," *The New York Times,* September 7, 2014, 12.

68. D. Iliescu, D. Ispas, C. Sulea, and A. Ilie, "Vocational Fit and Counterproductive Work Behaviors: A Self-Regulation Perspective," *Journal of Applied Psychology* 100, no. 1 (2015): 21–39.

69. S. Diestel, J. Wegge, and K.-H. Schmidt, "The Impact of Social Context on the Relationship between Individual Job Satisfaction and Absenteeism: The Roles of Different Foci of Job Satisfaction and Work-Unit Absenteeism."

70. R. D. Hackett, "Work Attitudes and Employee Absenteeism: A Synthesis of the Literature," *Journal of Occupational Psychology* 62 (1989): 235–48; J. F. Ybema, P. G. W. Smulders, and P. M. Bongers, "Antecedents and Consequences of Employee Absenteeism: A Longitudinal Perspective on the Role of Job Satisfaction and Burnout," *European Journal of Work and Organizational Psychology* 19, no. 1 (2010): 102–24.

71. J. P. Hausknecht, N. J. Hiller, and R. J. Vance, "Work-Unit Absenteeism: Effects of Satisfaction, Commitment, Labor Market Conditions, and Time," *Academy of Management Journal* 51, no. 6 (2008): 1123–245.

72. G. Chen, R. E. Ployhart, H. C. Thomas, N. Anderson, and P. D. Bliese, "The Power of Momentum: A New Model of Dynamic Relationships Between Job Satisfaction Change and Turnover Intentions," *Academy of Management Journal* 54, no. 1 (2011): 159–81.

73. D. Liu, T. R. Mitchell, T. W. Lee, B. C. Holtom, and T. R. Hinkin, "When Employees Are Out of Step with Coworkers: How Job Satisfaction Trajectory and Dispersion Influence Individual- and Unit-Level Voluntary Turnover," *Academy of Management Journal* 55, no. 6 (2012): 1360–80.

74. T. H. Lee, B. Gerhart, I. Weller, and C. O. Trevor, "Understanding Voluntary Turnover: Path-Specific Job Satisfaction Effects and the Importance of Unsolicited Job Offers," *Academy of Management Journal* 51, no. 4 (2008): 651–71.

75. K. Jiang, D. Liu, P. F. McKay, T. W. Lee, and T. R. Mitchell, "When and How Is Job Embeddedness Predictive of Turnover? A Meta-Analytic Investigation," *Journal of Applied Psychology* 97 (2012): 1077–96; C. M. Porter, R. A. Posthuma, C. P. Maertz Jr., J. R. W. Joplin, J. Rigby, M. Gordon, and K. Graves, "On-the-job and off-the-job embeddedness differentially influence relationships between informal job search and turnover," Journal of Applied Psychology 104, no. 5 (2019): 678–89.

76. M. Schoeff Jr., "Study Seeks Link Between Morale and Stock Price," *Workforce* 85, no. 4, March 6, 2006, https://www .workforce.com/2006/03/06/study-sees-link-between-morale-and-stock-price/

77. A. Edmans, "The Link Between Job Satisfaction and Firm Value, With Implications for Social Responsibility," *Academy of Management Perspectives* 26, no. 4 (2012): 1–19.

78. K. Holland, "Inside the Minds of Your Employees," *The New York Times,* January 28, 2007, B1; P. B. Brown "The Workplace as Solar System," *The New York Times,* October 28, 2006, B5.

79. E. White, "How Surveying Workers Can Pay Off," *The Wall Street Journal,* June 18, 2007, B3.

CHAPTER 4

1. "Police: Angry Fast-Food Worker Beans Supervisor with Burrito," *U.S. News & World Report,* January 23, 2018, https://www.usnews.com/news/offbeat/articles/2018-01-23/police-angry-fast-food-worker-beans-supervisor-with-burrito

2. A. Selyukh, "Amazon Employees Consider Consequences of Company's Minimum Wage Hike," *NPR: All Things Considered,* October 6, 2018, https://www.npr .org/2018/10/06/655246464/amazon-employees-consider-consequences-of-companys-minimum-wage-hike

3. S. G. Barsade and D. E. Gibson, "Why Does Affect Matter in Organizations?" *Academy of Management Perspectives,* 21, no. 1 (2007): 36–59.

4. Ibid.

5. Ibid.

6. A. Ben-Ze'ev, *The Subtlety of Emotions* (Cambridge, MA: MIT Press, 2000), 94.

7. R. Cropanzano, H. M. Weiss, J. M. S. Hale, and J. Reb, "The Structure of Affect: Reconsidering the Relationship Between Negative and Positive Affectivity," *Journal of Management* 29, no. 6 (2003): 831–57.

8. See, for example, G. J. Boyle, E. Helmes, G. Matthews, and C. E. Izard, "Multidimensional Measures of Affects: Emotions and Mood States," in G. J. Boyle, D. H. Saklofske, and G. Matthews (eds.), *Measures of Personality and Social Psychological Constructs* (New York, NY: Elsevier, 2015): 3–15; and M. T. Jarymowicz and K. K. Imbir,

"Toward a Human Emotions Taxonomy (Based on Their Automatic vs. Reflective Origin)," *Emotion Review* 7, no. 2 (2015): 183–88.

9. R. C. Solomon, "Back to Basics: On the Very Idea of 'Basic Emotions,'" *Journal for the Theory of Social Behaviour* 32, no. 2 (2002): 115–44.

10. P. Ekman, *Emotions Revealed: Recognizing Faces and Feelings to Improve Communication and Emotional Life* (New York: Times Books/Henry Holt and Co., 2003); J. L. Tracy and D. Randles, "Four Models of Basic Emotions: A Review of Ekman and Cordaro, Izard, Levenson, and Panksepp and Watt," *Emotion Review* 3, no. 4 (2011): 397–405.

11. P. Ekman, *Emotions Revealed: Recognizing Faces and Feelings to Improve Communication and Emotional Life.*

12. H. A. Elfenbein and N. Ambady, "On the Universality and Cultural Specificity of Emotion Recognition: A Meta-Analysis," *Psychological Bulletin* 128, no. 2 (2002): 203–35.

13. P. Laukka, D. Neiberg, and H. A. Elfenbein, "Evidence for Cultural Dialects in Vocal Emotion Expression: Acoustic Classification Within and Across Five Nations," *Emotion* 14, no. 3 (2014): 445–49.

14. K. Wezowski, "How to get Better at Reading People From Different Cultures," *Harvard Business Review,* September 18, 2018, https://hbr.org/2018/09/how-to-get-better-at-reading-people-from-different-cultures

15. R. Greenbaum, J. Bonner, T. Gray, and M. Mawritz, "Moral Emotions: A Review and Research Agenda for Management Scholarship," Journal of Organizational Behavior 41 (2020): 95–114.

16. P. S. Russell and R. Giner-Sorolla, "Bodily Moral Disgust: What It Is, How It Is Different from Anger, and Why It Is an Unreasoned Emotion," *Psychological Bulletin* 139, no. 2 (2013): 328–51.

17. M. T. Ford, J. P. Agosta, J. Huang, and C. Shannon, "Moral Emotions Toward Others at Work and Implications for Employee Behavior: A Qualitative Analysis Using Critical Incidents," *Journal of Business and Psychology* 33(2018): 155–80; D. Lindebaum, D. Geddes, and Y. Gabriel, "Moral Emotions and Ethics in Organisations," *Journal of Business Ethics* 141 (2017): 645–56.

18. E. Diener, S. Kanazawa, E. M .Suh, and S. Oishi, "Why People Are in a Generally Good Mood," Personality and Social Psychology Review 19, no. 3 (2015): 235–56; T. A. Ito and J. T. Cacioppo, "Variations on a Human Universal: Individual Differences in Positivity Offset and Negativity Bias," Cognition and Emotion 19, no. 1 (2005): 1–26; D. L. Joseph, M. Y. Chan, S. J. Heintzelman, L. Tay, E. Diener, and V. S. Scotney, "The Manipulation of Affect: A Meta-Analysis of Affect Induction Procedures," Psychological Bulletin 146, no. 4 (2020): 355–75.

19. Ibid.

20. S. Lyubomirsky, L. King, and E. Diener, "The Benefits of Frequent Positive Affect: Does Happiness Lead to Success?" *Psychological Bulletin* 131, no. 6 (2005): 803–55; K. M. Shockley, D. Ispas, M. E. Rossi, and E. L. Levine, "A Meta-Analytic Investigation of the Relationship between State Affect, Discrete Emotions, and Job Performance," *Human Performance* 25 (2012): 377–411; C. J. Thoresen, S. A. Kaplan, A. P. Barsky, C. R. Warren, and K. de Chermont, "The Affective Underpinnings of Job Perceptions and Attitudes: A Meta-Analytic Review and Integration," *Psychological Bulletin* 129, no. 6 (2003): 914–45.

21. T. W. H. Ng and K. L. Sorensen, "Dispositional Affectivity and Work-Related Outcomes: A Meta-Analysis," *Journal of Applied Social Psychology* 39, no. 6 (2009): 1255–87.

22. L. M. Poverny and S. Picascia, "There Is No Crying in Business," *Womensmedia.com,* October 20, 2009, http://www .womensmedia.com/new/Crying-at-Work.shtml

23. M.-A. Reinhard and N. Schwartz, "The Influence of Affective States on the Process of Lie Detection," *Journal of Experimental Psychology* 18 (2012): 377–89.

24. D. C. Rubin, R. M. Hoyle, and M. R. Leary, "Differential Predictability of Four Dimensions of Affect Intensity," *Cognition and Emotion* 26, no. 1 (2012): 25–41.

25. H. M. Weiss, J. P. Nicholas, and C. S. Daus, "AN Examination of the Joint Effects of Affective Experiences and Job Beliefs on Job Satisfaction and Variations in Affective Experiences Over Time," Organizational Behavior and Human Decision Processes 78, no. 1 (1999): 1–24; H. R. Young, D. R. Glerum, W. Wang, and D. L. Joseph, "Who Are the Most Engaged at Work? A Meta-Analysis of Personality and Employee Engagement," Journal of Organizational Behavior 39 (2018): 1330–46. J. Anglim, S. Horwood, L. D. Smillie, R. J. Marrero, and J. K. Wood, "Predicting Psychological and Subjective Well-Being from Personality: A Meta-Analysis," Psychological Bulletin 146, no. 4 (2020): 279–323.

26. Ibid.

27. B. P. Hasler, M. S. Mehl, R. R. Bootzin, and S. Vazire, "Preliminary Evidence of Diurnal Rhythms in Everyday Behaviors Associated with Positive Affect," *Journal of Research in Personality* 42 (2008): 1537–46; D. Watson, *Mood and Temperament* (New York: Guilford Press, 2000).

28. Watson, *Mood and Temperament*.

29. A. A. Stone, J. E. Schwartz, D. Schkade, N. Schwarz, A. Krueger, and D. Kahneman, "A Population Approach to the Study of Emotion: Diurnal Rhythms of a Working Day Examined with the Day Reconstruction Method," *Emotion* 6 (2006): 139–49.

30. S. A. Golder and W. M. Macy, "Diurnal and Seasonal Mood Vary with Work, Sleep, and Daylength across Diverse Cultures," *Science* 333, no. 6051, September 30, 2011, 1878–81.

31. Ibid.

32. Ibid.

33. Ibid.

34. T. A. Klimstra et al., "Come Rain or Come Shine: Individual Differences in How Weather Affects Mood," *Emotion* 11, no. 6 (2011): 1495–99.

35. J. J. A. Denissen, L. Butalid, L. Penke, and M. A. G. van Aken, "The Effects of Weather on Daily Mood: A Multilevel Approach," *Emotion* 8, no. 5 (2008): 662–67; M. C. Keller et al., "A Warm Heart and a Clear Head: The Contingent Effects of Weather on Mood and Cognition," *Psychological Science* 16, no. 9 (2005): 724–31.

36. J. J. Lee, F. Gino, and B. R. Staats, "Rainmakers: Why Bad Weather Means Good Productivity," *Journal of Applied Psychology* 99, no. 3 (2014): 504–13.

37. M. T. Ford, R. A. Matthews, J. D. Wooldridge, V. Mishra, U. M. Kakar, and S. R. Strahan, "How Do Occupational Stressor-Strain Effects Vary with Time? A Review and Meta-Analysis of the Relevance of Time Lags in Longitudinal Studies," *Work & Stress* 28, no. 1 (2014): 9–30; J. A. Fuller, J. M. Stanton, G. G. Fisher, C. Spitzmüller, S. S. Russell, and P. C. Smith, "A Lengthy Look at the Daily Grind: Time Series Analysis of Events, Mood, Stress, and Satisfaction," *Journal of Applied Psychology* 88, no. 6 (2003): 1019–33.

38. G. Schaffer, Association for Psychological Science, "What's Good, When, and Why?," *The Observer* 25, no. 9 (2012): 27–29; see also J. D. Nahrgang, F. P. Morgeson, and D. A. Hofmann, "Safety at Work: A Meta-Analytic Investigation of the Link Between Job Demands, Job Resources, Burnout, Engagement, and Safety Outcomes," *Journal of Applied Psychology* 96, no. 1 (2011): 71–94.

39. Sleep Cycle, *Statistics This Week* [Digital Dashboard of Sleep Cycle application users], accessed February 1, 2019, http://www.sleep-cycle.com; and *Sleep in America Poll* (Washington, DC: National Sleep Foundation, 2005), https://sleepfoundation.org/sites/default/files/2005_summary_of_findings.pdf

40. Ibid.

41. H. M. Mullins, J. M. Cortina, C. L. Drake, and R. S. Dalal, "Sleepiness at Work: A Review and Framework of How the Physiology of Sleepiness Impacts the Workplace," *Journal of Applied Psychology* 99, no. 6 (2014): 1096–112.

42. J. D. Minkel et al., "Sleep Deprivation and Stressors: Evidence for Elevated Negative Affect in Response to Mild Stressors When Sleep Deprived," Emotion 12, no. 5 (2012): 1015–20; B. A. Scott and T. A. Judge, "Insomnia, Emotions, and Job Satisfaction: A Multilevel Study," Journal of Management 32, no. 5 (2006): 622–45; L. S. Talbot, E. L. McGlinchey, K. A. Kaplan, R. E. Dahl, and A. G. Harvey, "Sleep Deprivation in Adolescents and Adults: Changes in Affect," Emotion 10, no. 6 (2010): 831–41; M. P. Walker and E. van der Helm, "Overnight Therapy? The Role of Sleep in Emotional Brain Processing," Psychological Bulletin 135, no. 5 (2009): 731–48; D. S. Chester and J. M. Dzierzewski, "Sour Sleep, Sweet Revenge? Aggressive Pleasure as a Potential Mechanism Underlying Poor Sleep Quality's Link to Aggression," Emotion (in press).

43. L. Flueckiger, R. Lieb, A. H. Meyer, C. Witthauer, and J. Mata, "The Importance of Physical Activity and Sleep for Affect on Stressful Days: Two Intensive Longitudinal Studies," *Emotion* 16, no. 4 (2016): 488–97; U. R. Hülsheger, "From Dawn Till Dusk: Shedding Light on the Recovery Process by Investigating Daily Change Patterns in Fatigue," *Journal of Applied Psychology* 101, no. 6 (2016): 905–14.

44. T. W. Puetz, P. J. O'Connor, and R. K. Dishman, "Effects of Chronic Exercise on Feelings of Energy and Fatigue: A Quantitative Synthesis," *Psychological Bulletin* 132, no. 6 (2006): 866–76; A. L. Rebar, R. Stanton, D. Geard, C. Short, M. J. Duncan, and C. Vandelanotte, "A Meta-Meta-Analysis of the Effect of Physical Activity on Depression and Anxiety in Non-Clinical Adult Populations," *Health Psychology Review* 9, no. 3 (2015): 366–78.

45. E. E. Bernstein, J. E. Curtiss, G. W. Y. Wu, P. J. Barreira, and R. J. McNally, "Exercise and Emotion Dynamics: An Experience Sampling Study," Emotion 19, no. 4 (2019): 637-644.

46. See, for example, T. M. Chaplin and A. Aldao, "Gender Differences in Emotion Expression in Children: A Meta-Analytic Review," *Psychological Bulletin* 139, no. 4 (2013): 735–65; and N. M. Else-Quest, A. Higgins, C. Allison, and L. C. Morton, "Gender Differences in Self-Conscious Emotional Experience: A Meta-Analysis," *Psychological Bulletin* 138, no. 5 (2012): 947–81.

47. D. V. Becker, D. T. Kenrick, S. L. Neuberg, K. C. Blackwell, and D. M. Smith, "The Confounded Nature of Angry Men and Happy Women," Journal of Personality and Social Psychology 92 (2007): 179–90; J. S. Hyde, "Gender Differences and Similarities," Annual Review of Psychology 65 (2014): 373–98. A. H. Eagly, C. Nater, D. I. Miller, M. Kaufmann, and S. Sczesny, "Gender Stereotypes Have Changed: A Cross-Temporal Meta-Analysis of U.S. Public Opinion Polls from 1946 to 2018," American Psychologist 75, no. 3 (2020): 301–15.

48. R. Low, "Female Commander Files Gender Discrimination Complaint Against Denver Police: Problem Solvers Investigation," *Fox 31 Denver,* January 28, 2019, https://kdvr.com/2019/01/28/female-commander-files-gender-discrimination-complaint-against-denver-police-problem-solvers-investigation/

49. U. R. Hülsheger and A. F. Schewe, "On the Costs and Benefits of Emotional Labor: A Meta-Analysis of Three Decades of Research," *Journal of Occupational Health Psychology* 16, no. 3 (2011): 361–89; J. D. Kammeyer-Mueller et al. "A Meta-Analytic Structural Model of Dispositional Affectivity and Emotional Labor," *Personnel Psychology* 66, no. 1 (2013): 47–90.

50. A. A. Grandey, "Emotion Regulation in the Workplace: A New Way to Conceptualize Emotional Labor," *Journal of Occupational Health Psychology* 5, no. 1 (2000): 95–110; A. R. Hochschild, *The Managed Heart: Commercialization of Human Feeling* (Berkeley: University of California Press, 1983)

51. J. M. Diefendorff and G. J. Greguras, "Contextualizing Emotional Display Rules: Examining the Roles of Targets and Discrete Emotions in Shaping Display Rule Perceptions," *Journal of Management* 35, no. 4 (2009): 880–98.

52. Kammeyer-Mueller et al. "A Meta-Analytic Structural Model of Dispositional Affectivity and Emotional Labor."

53. H. Nguyen, M. Groth, and A. Johnson, "When the Going Gets Tough, the Tough Keep Working: Impact of Emotional Labor on Absenteeism," *Journal of Management* 42, no. 3 (2016): 615–43; D. T. Wagner, C. M. Barnes, and B. A. Scott, "Driving It Home: How Workplace Emotional Labor Harms Employee Home Life," *Personnel Psychology* 67 (2014): 487–516.

54. U. R. Hülsheger, J. W. B. Lang, A. F. Schewe, and F. R. H. Zijlstra, "When Regulating Emotions at Work Pays Off: A Diary and an Intervention Study on Emotion Regulation and Customer Tips in Service Jobs," *Journal of Applied Psychology* 100, no. 2 (2015): 263–77; J. L. Huang, D. S. Chiaburu, X., Li, N., and Grandey, A. A., "Rising to the Challenge: Deep Acting Is More Beneficial When Tasks Are Appraised as Challenging," *Journal of Applied Psychology* 100, no. 5 (2015): 1398–408; J. D. Kammeyer-Mueller et al., "A Meta-Analytic Structural Model of Dispositional Affectivity and Emotional Labor"; Y. Zhan, M. Wang, and J. Shi, "Interpersonal Process of Emotional Labor: The Role of Negative and Positive Customer Treatment," *Personnel Psychology* 69, no. 3 (2016): 525–57.

55. A. A. Grandey, "When 'The Show Must Go On': Surface Acting and Deep Acting as Determinants of Emotional Exhaustion and Peer-Rated Service Delivery," *Academy of Management Journal* 46, no. 1 (2003): 86–96.

56. S. Diestel, W. Rivkin, and K.-H. Schmidt, "Sleep Quality and Self-Control Capacity as Protective Resources in the Daily Emotional Labor Process: Results from Two Diary Studies," *Journal of Applied Psychology* 100, no. 3 (2015): 809–27; K. L. Wang and M. Groth, "Buffering the Negative Effects of Employee Surface Acting: The Moderating Role of Employee-Customer Relationship Strength and Personalized Services," *Journal of Applied Psychology* 99, no. 2 (2014): 341–50.

57. S. Ohly and A. Schmitt, "What Makes Us Enthusiastic, Angry, Feeling at Rest or Worried? Development and Validation of an Affective Work Events Taxonomy Using Concept Mapping Methodology," *Journal of Business Psychology* 30 (2015): 15–35; H. M. Weiss and R. Cropanzano, "Affective Events Theory: A Theoretical Discussion of the Structure, Causes and Consequences of Affective Experiences at Work," *Research in Organizational Behavior* 18 (1996): 1–74.

58. K. Goldstein, "My Boss Said, 'I Understand What You're Going Through, but you Have a job to Do," *Slate,* January 30, 2019, https://slate.com/human-interest/2019/01/infertility-workplace-pregnancy-challenges-2019.html

59. C. D. Fisher, "Antecedents and Consequences of Real-Time Affective Reactions at Work," *Motivation and Emotion* 26, no. 1 (2002): 3–30; A. A. Grandey, A. P. Tam, and A. L. Brauburger, "Affective States and Traits in the Workplace: Diary and Survey Data from Young Workers," *Motivation and Emotion* 26, no. 1 (2002): 31–55.

60. Grandey, Tam, and Brauburger, "Affective States and Traits in the Workplace."

61. K. L. Wang and M. Groth, "Buffering the Negative Effects of Employee Surface Acting: The Moderating Role of Employee-Customer Relationship Strength and Personalized Services," *Journal of Applied Psychology* 99, no. 2 (2014): 341–50.

62. T. Upshur-Lupberger, "Watch Your Mood: A Leadership Lesson," *The Huffington Post,* April 22, 2015, http://www .huffingtonpost.com/terrie-upshurlupberger/watch-your-mood-a-leaders_b_7108648.html

63. Ibid.

64. CareerBuilder, *"Seventy-One Percent of Employers Say They Value Emotional Intelligence over IQ, According to Career-Builder Survey"* [Press Release], August 18, 2011, https://www.careerbuilder.ca/share/aboutus/pressreleasesdetail .aspx?id=pr652&sd=8%2f18%2f2011&ed=8%2f18%2f2099

65. J. C. Rode, M. Arthaud-Day, A. Ramaswami, and S. Howes, "A Time-Lagged Study of Emotional Intelligence and Salary," *Journal of Vocational Behavior* 101 (2017): 77–89.

66. D. L. Joseph and D. A. Newman, "Emotional Intelligence: An Integrative Meta-Analysis and Cascading Model," *Journal of Applied Psychology* 95, no. 1 (2010): 54–78; P. Salovey and D. Grewal, "The Science of Emotional Intelligence," *Current Directions in Psychological Science* 14, no. 6 (2005): 281–85.

67. CareerBuilder, *Seventy-one Percent of Employers Say They Value Emotional Intelligence Over IQ, According to Career-Builder Survey*; P. Salovey and D. Grewal, "The Science of Emotional Intelligence."

68. D. L. Joseph, J. Jin, D. A. Newman, and E. H. O'Boyle, "Why Does Self-Reported Emotional Intelligence Predict Job Performance? A Meta-Analytic Investigation of Mixed EI," Journal of Applied Psychology 100, no. 2 (2015): 298–342; D. L. Joseph and D. A. Newman, "Emotional Intelligence"; C. Miao, R. H. Humphrey, and S. Qian, "A Meta-Analysis of Emotional Intelligence and Work Attitudes," Journal of Occupational and Organizational Psychology 90, no. 2 (2017): 177–202. C. MacCann, Y. Jiang, L. E. R. Brown, K. S. Double, M. Bucich, and A. Minbashian, "Emotional Intelligence Predicts Academic Performance: A Meta-Analysis," Psychological Bulletin 146, no. 2 (2020): 150–86.

69. C. I. C. Chien Farh, M.-G. Seo, and P. E. Tesluk, "Emotional Intelligence, Teamwork Effectiveness, and Job Performance: The Moderating Role of Job Context," *Journal of Applied Psychology* 97, no. 4 (2012): 890–900; D. Greenidge, D. Devonish, and P. Alleyne, "The Relationship Between Ability-Based Emotional Intelligence and Contextual Performance and Counterproductive Work Behaviors: A Test of the Mediating Effects of Job Satisfaction," *Human Performance* 27 (2014): 225–42; A. Santos, W. Wang, and J. Lewis, "Emotional Intelligence and Career Decision-Making Difficulties: The Mediating Role of Career Decision Self-Efficacy," *Journal of Vocational Behavior* 107 (2018): 295–309.

70. C. P. M. Wilderom, Y. Hur, U. J. Wiersma, P. T. Van Den Berg, and J. Lee, "From Manager's Emotional Intelligence to Objective Store Performance: Through Store Cohesiveness and Sales-Directed Employee Behavior," *Journal of Organizational Behavior* 36 (2015): 825–44.

71. F. I. Greenstein, *The Presidential Difference: Leadership Style from FDR to Clinton* (Princeton, NJ: Princeton University Press, 2001).

72. A. Z. Czarna, P. Leifeld, M. Śmieja, M. Dufner, and P. Salovey, "Do Narcissism and Emotional Intelligence Win Us Friends? Modelling Dynamics of Peer Popularity Using Inferential Network Analysis," *Personality and Social Psychology Bulletin* 42, no. 11 (2016): 1588–99.

73. K. A. Pekaar, A. B. Bakker, M. P. Born, and D. van der Linden, "The Consequences of Self- and Other-Focused Emotional Intelligence: Not all Sunshine and Roses," *Journal of Occupational Health Psychology* 24, no. 4 (2019): 450–66.

74. D. H. M. Pelt, D. van der Linden, and M. P. Born, "How Emotional Intelligence Might Get You a Job: The Relationship Between Trait Emotional Intelligence and Faking on Personality Tests," *Human Performance* 31, no. 1 (2018): 33–54.

75. S. Côté, "Emotional Intelligence in Organizations," *Annual Review of Organizational Psychology and Organizational Behavior* 1 (2014): 59–88.

76. C. MacCann and R. D. Roberts, "New Paradigms for Assessing Emotional Intelligence: Theory and Data," *Emotion* 8, no. 4 (2008):

540–51; and K. Schlegel and M. Mortillaro, "The Geneva Emotional Competence Test (GECo): An Ability Measure of Workplace Emotional Intelligence," *Journal of Applied Psychology* 104, no. 4 (2019): 559–80.

77. S. Hodzic, J. Scharfen, P. Ripoll, H. Holling, and F. Zenasni, "How Efficient Are Emotional Intelligence Trainings: A Meta-Analysis," Emotion Review 10, no. 2 (2018): 138–48; I. Kotsou, D. Nelis, J. Grégoire, and M. Mikolajczak, "Emotional Plasticity: Conditions and Effects of Improving Emotional Competence in Adulthood," Journal of Applied Psychology 96, no. 4 (2011): 827–39; V. Mattingly and K. Kraiger, "Can Emotional Intelligence Be Trained? A Meta-Analytical Investigation," Human Resource Management Review 29 (2019): 140–55; O. J. Sheldon, D. Dunning, and D. R. Ames, "Emotionally Unskilled, Unaware, and Uninterested in Learning More: Reactions to Feedback About Deficits in Emotional Intelligence," Journal of Applied Psychology 99, no. 1 (2014): 125–37.

78. S. L. Koole, "The Psychology of Emotion Regulation: An Integrative Review," *Cognition and Emotion* 23 (2009): 4–41; H. A. Wadlinger and D. M. Isaacowitz, "Fixing Our Focus: Training Attention to Regulate Emotion," *Personality and Social Psychology Review* 15 (2011): 75–102.

79. D. H. Kluemper, T. DeGroot, and S. Choi, "Emotion Management Ability: Predicting Task Performance, Citizenship, and Deviance," *Journal of Management* 39, no. 4 (2013): 878–905.

80. D. J. Hughes, I. K. Kratsiotis, K. Niven, and D. Holman, "Personality Traits and Emotion Regulation: A Targeted Review and Recommendations," Emotion 20, no. 1 (2020): 63–67.

81. J. V. Wood, S. A. Heimpel, L. A. Manwell, and E. J. Whittington, "This Mood Is Familiar and I Don't Deserve to Feel Better Anyway: Mechanisms Underlying Self-Esteem Differences in Motivation to Repair Sad Moods," *Journal of Personality and Social Psychology* 96, no. 2 (2009): 363–80.

82. L. Wang and F. Yan, "Emotion Regulation Strategy Mediates the Relationship Between Goal Orientation and Job Search Behavior Among University Seniors," *Journal of Vocational Behavior* 108 (2018): 1–12.

83. E. Kim, D. P. Bhave, and T. M. Glomb, "Emotion Regulation in Workgroups: The Roles of Demographic Diversity and Relational Work Context," *Personnel Psychology* 66, no. 3 (2013): 613–44.

84. Ibid.

85. S. L. Koole, "The Psychology of Emotion Regulation: An Integrative Review," *Cognition and Emotion* 23, no. 1 (2009): 4–41.

86. L. K. Barber, P. G. Bagsby, and D. C. Munz, "Affect Regulation Strategies for Promoting (or Preventing) Flourishing Emotional Health," *Personality and Individual Differences* 49, no. 6 (2010): 663–66.

87. J. Diefendorff, A. S. Gabriel, M. T. Nolan, and J. Yang, "Emotion Regulation in the Context of Customer Mistreatment and Felt Affect: An Event-based Profile Approach," *Journal of Applied Psychology* 104, no. 7 (2019): 965–83.

88. D. Holman, "How Does Customer Affiliative Behaviour Shape the Outcomes of Employee Emotion Regulation? A Daily Diary Study of Supermarket Checkout Operators," *Human Relations* 69, no. 5 (2016): 1139–62.

89. L. D. Cameron, and N. C. Overall, "Suppression and Expression as Distinct Emotion-Regulation Processes in Daily Interactions: Longitudinal and Meta-Analyses," *Emotion* 18, no. 4 (2018): 465–80; E. Chervonsky and C. Hunt, "Suppression and Expression of Emotion in Social and Interpersonal Outcomes: A Meta-Analysis," *Emotion* 17, no. 4 (2017): 669–83.

90. J. J. Lee and F. Gino, "Poker-Faced Morality: Concealing Emotions Leads to Utilitarian Decision Making," *Organizational Behavior and Human Decision Processes* 126 (2015): 49–64.

91. J. J. Gross, E. Halperin, and R. Porat, "Emotion Regulation in Intractable Conflicts," *Current Directions in Psychological Science* 22, no. 6 (2013): 423–29.

92. A. S. Troy, A. J. Shallcross, and I. B. Mauss, "A Person-by-Person Situation Approach to Emotion Regulation: Cognitive Reappraisal Can Either Help or Hurt, Depending on the Context," *Psychological Science* 24, no. 12 (2013): 2505–14.

93. A. S. McCance, C. D. Nye, L. Wang, K. S. Jones, and C. Chiu, "Alleviating the Burden of Emotional Labor: The Role of Social Sharing," *Journal of Management* 39, no. 2 (2013): 392–415.

94. G. Buruck, D. Dörfel, J. Kugler, and S. S. Brom, "Enhancing Well-Being at Work: The Role of Emotion Regulation Skills as Personal Resources," *Journal of Occupational Health Psychology* 21, no. 4 (2016): 480–93; P. J. Edelman, and D. van Knippenberg, "Training Leader Emotion Regulation and Leadership Effectiveness," *Journal of Business and Psychology* 32, no. 6 (2017): 747–57; K. Hoorelbeke, E. H. W. Koster, I. Demeyer, T. Loeys, and M-A. Vanderhasselt, "Effects of Cognitive Control Training on the Dynamics of (Mal)adaptive Emotion Regulation in Daily Life," *Emotion* 16, no. 7 (2016): 945–56.

95. A. M. Grant, "Rocking the Boat but Keeping It Steady: The Role of Emotion Regulation in Employee Voice," *Academy of Management Journal* 56, no. 6 (2013): 1703–23.

96. E. S. Blanke, A. Brose, E. K. Kalokerinos, Y. Erbas, M. Riediger, and P. Kuppens, "Mix It to Fix It: Emotion Regulation Variability in Daily Life," Emotion 20, no. 3 (2020): 473–485; L. Pruessner, S. Barnow, D. V. Holt, J. Joormann, and K. Schulze, "A cognitive control framework for understanding emotion regulation flexibility," Emotion 20, no. 1 (2020): 21–29.

97. L. Z. Bencharit, Y. Wan Ho, H. H. Fung, D. Y. Yeung, N. M. Stephens, R. Romero-Canyas, and J. L. Tsai, "Should Job Applicants Be Excited or Calm? The Role of Culture and Ideal Affect in Employment Settings," Emotion 19, no. 3 (2019): 377–401.

98. See A. M. Isen, "Positive Affect and Decision Making," in M. Lewis and J. M. Haviland-Jones (eds.), *Handbook of Emotions*, 2nd ed. (New York: Guilford, 2000), 261–77.

99. N. Nunez, K. Schweitzer, C. A. Chai, and B. Myers, "Negative Emotions Felt During Trial: The Effect of Fear, Anger, and Sadness on Juror Decision Making," *Applied Cognitive Psychology* 29, no. 2 (2015): 200–09.

100. S. N. Mohanty and D. Suar, "Decision Making under Uncertainty and Information Processing in Positive and Negative Mood States," *Psychological Reports* 115, no. 1 (2014): 91–105.

101. S.-C. Chuang and H.-M. Lin, "The Effect of Induced Positive and Negative Emotion and Openness-to-Feeling in Student's Consumer Decision Making," *Journal of Business and Psychology* 22, no. 1 (2007): 65–78.

102. D. van Knippenberg, H. J. M. Kooij-De Bode, and W. P. van Ginkel, "The Interactive Effects of Mood and Trait Negative Affect in Group Decision Making," *Organization Science* 21, no. 3 (2010): 731–44.

103. S. Lyubomirsky, L. King, and E. Diener, "The Benefits of Frequent Positive Affect: Does Happiness Lead to Success?" *Psychological Bulletin* 131, no. 6 (2005): 803–55; M. Baas, C. K. W. De Dreu, and B. A. Nijstad, "A Meta-Analysis of 25 Years of Mood-Creativity Research: Hedonic Tone, Activation, or Regulatory Focus," *Psychological Bulletin* 134, no. 6 (2008): 779–806.

104. M. J. Grawitch, D. C. Munz, and E. K. Elliott, "Promoting Creativity in Temporary Problem-Solving Groups: The Effects of Positive Mood and Autonomy in Problem Definition on Idea-Generating Performance," *Group Dynamics* 7, no. 3 (2003): 200–13.

105. S. Lyubomirsky, L. King, and E. Diener, "The Benefits of Frequent Positive Affect: Does Happiness Lead to Success?"

106. J. M. George and J. Zhou, "Understanding When Bad Moods Foster Creativity and Good Ones Don't: The Role of Context and Clarity of Feelings," *Journal of Applied Psychology* 87, no. 4 (August 2002): 687–97; J. P. Forgas and J. M. George, "Affective Influences on Judgments and Behavior in Organizations: An Information Processing Perspective," *Organizational Behavior and Human Decision Processes* 86, no. 1 (2001): 3–34.

107. R. Ilies and T. A. Judge, "Goal Regulation across Time: The Effect of Feedback and Affect," *Journal of Applied Psychology* 90, no. 3 (May 2005): 453–67.

108. J. E. Bono, H. J. Foldes, G. Vinson, and J. P. Muros, "Workplace Emotions: The Role of Supervision and Leadership," *Journal of Applied Psychology* 92, no. 5 (2007): 1357–67.

109. S. G. Liang and S.-C. S. Chi, "Transformational Leadership and Follower Task Performance: The Role of Susceptibility to Positive Emotions and Follower Positive Emotions," *Journal of Business and Psychology* 28, no. 1 (2013): 17–29.

110. V. A. Visser, D. van Knippenberg, G. Van Kleef, and B. Wisse, "How Leader Displays of Happiness and Sadness Influence Follower Performance: Emotional Contagion and Creative versus Analytical Performance," *Leadership Quarterly* 24, no. 1 (2013): 172–88.

111. B. M. Staw, K. A. DeCelles, and P. de Goey, "Leadership in the Locker Room: How the Intensity of Leaders' Unpleasant Affective Displays Shapes Team Performance," Journal of Applied Psychology (in press).

112. P. S. Christoforou and B. E. Ashforth, "Revisiting the Debate on the Relationship Between Display Rules and Performance: Considering the Explicitness of Display Rules," *Journal of Applied Psychology* 100, no. 1 (2015): 249–61; A. Grandey, D. Rupp, and W. N. Brice, "Emotional Labor Threatens Decent Work: A Proposal to Eradicate Emotional Display Rules," *Journal of Organizational Behavior* 36, no. 6 (2015): 770–85; W.-M. Hur, T.-W. Moon, and Y. S. Jung, "Customer Response to Employee Emotional Labor: The Structural Relationship Between Emotional Labor, Job Satisfaction, and Customer Satisfaction," *Journal of Services Marketing* 29, no. 1 (2015): 71–80.

113. P. B. Barker and A. A. Grandey, "Service with a Smile and Encounter Satisfaction: Emotional Contagion and Appraisal Mechanisms," *Academy of Management Journal* 49, no. 6 (2006): 1229–38; E. Y. J. Tee, "The Emotional Link: Leadership and the Role of Implicit and Explicit Emotional Contagion Processes across Multiple Organizational Levels," *Leadership Quarterly* 26, no. 4 (2015): 654–70.

114. D. E. Rupp and S. Spencer, "When Customers Lash Out: The Effects of Customer Interactional Injustice on Emotional Labor and the Mediating Role of Emotions," *Journal of Applied Psychology* 91, no. 4 (2006): 971–78; and W. C. Tsai and Y. M. Huang, "Mechanisms Linking Employee Affective Delivery and Customer Behavioral Intentions," *Journal of Applied Psychology* 87, no. 5 (2002): 1001–08.

115. R. Ilies and T. A. Judge, "Understanding the Dynamic Relationships among Personality, Mood, and Job Satisfaction: A Field Experience Sampling Study," *Organizational Behavior and Human Decision Processes* 89 (2002): 1119–39.

116. T. A. Judge and R. Ilies, "Affect and Job Satisfaction: A Study of Their Relationship at Work and at Home," *Journal of Applied Psychology* 89, no. 4 (2004): 661–73.

117. Z. Song, M. Foo, and M. A. Uy, "Mood Spillover and Crossover among Dual-Earner Couples: A Cell Phone Event Sampling Study," *Journal of Applied Psychology* 93, no. 2 (2008): 443–52.

118. T. J. Zagenczyk, S. L. D. Restubog, C. Kiewitz, K. Kiazad, and R. L. Tang, "Psychological Contracts as a Mediator between Machiavellianism and Employee Citizenship and Deviant Behaviors," *Journal of Management* 40, no. 4 (2014): 1109–22.

119. T. A. Judge, B. A. Scott, and R. Ilies, "Hostility, Job Attitudes, and Workplace Deviance: Test of a Multilevel Mode," *Journal of Applied Psychology* 91, no. 1 (2006): 126–38; S. Kaplan, J. C. Bradley, J. N. Luchman, and D. Haynes, "On the Role of Positive and Negative Affectivity in Job Performance: A Meta-Analytic Investigation," *Journal of Applied Psychology* 94, no. 1 (2009): 152–76.

120. S. C. Douglas, C. Kiewitz, M. Martinko, P. Harvey, Y. Kim, and J. U. Chun, "Cognitions, Emotions, and Evaluations: An Elaboration Likelihood Model for Workplace Aggression," *Academy of Management Review* 33, no. 2 (2008): 425–51.

121. A. K Khan, S. Quratulain, and J. R. Crawshaw, "The Mediating Role of Discrete Emotions in the Relationship between Injustice and Counterproductive Work Behaviors: A Study in Pakistan," *Journal of Business and Psychology* 28, no. 1 (2013): 49–61.

122. S. Kaplan, J. C. Bradley, J. N. Luchman, and D. Haynes, "On the Role of Positive and Negative Affectivity in Job Performance: A Meta-Analytic Investigation;" and J. Maiti, "Design for Worksystem Safety Using Employees' Perception about Safety," *Work—A Journal of Prevention Assessment & Rehabilitation* 41 (2012): 3117–22.

123. J. E. Bono and R. Ilies, "Charisma, Positive Emotions and Mood Contagion," *Leadership Quarterly* 17, no. 4 (2006): 317–34.

CHAPTER 5

1. B. Conerly, "Personality Traits in Your Business: Lessons From Jordan Peterson, Jonathan Haidt and Helen Fisher," *Forbes,* April 8, 2018, https://www.forbes.com/sites/billconerly/2018/04/08/personality-traits-in-your-business-lessons-from-jordan-peterson-jonathan-haidt-and-helen-fisher/#2277eb0266ec

2. D. Leising, J. Scharloth, O. Lohse, and D. Wood, "What Types of Terms Do People Use When Describing an Individual's Personality?" *Psychological Science* 25, no. 9 (2014): 1787–94.

3. L. M. Hough, F. L. Oswald, and J. Ock, "Beyond the Big Five: New Directions for Personality Research and Practice in Organizations," *Annual Review of Organizational Psychology and Organizational Behavior* 2 (2015): 183–209.

4. R. R. McCrae and J. Allik, eds., *The Five-Factor Model of Personality Across Cultures* (New York, NY: Kluwer Academic/Plenum, 2002).

5. A. T. Church, "Personality Traits Across Cultures," *Current Opinion in Psychology* 8 (2016): 22–30.

6. F. M. Cheung, S. F. Chueng, and W. Fan, "From Chinese to Cross-Cultural Personality Inventory: A Combined Emic-Etic Approach to the Study of Personality in Culture," in M. J. Gelfand, C. Y. Chiu, and Y. Y. Hong (eds.), *Advances in Culture and Psychology* (Oxford UP, 2013: vol. 3, 117–80); and Church, "Personality Traits Across Cultures"; M. R. Barrick and L. Parks-Leduc, "Selection for Fit," *Annual Review of Organizational Psychology and Organizational Behavior* 6 (2019): 171–93.

7. H. Baker, "Personality Tests and Why Employers Use Them," *Glassdoor,* July 20, 2016, https://www.glassdoor.co.uk/blog/personality-tests-employers-use/; L. Weber, "To Get a Job, New Hires Are Put to the Test," *The Wall Street Journal,* April 15, 2015, A1, A10.

8. L. Weber and E. Dwoskin, "As Personality Tests Multiply, Employers Are Split," *The Wall Street Journal,* September 30, 2014, A1, A10.

9. D. Belkin, "Colleges Put the Emphasis on Personality," *The Wall Street Journal,* January 9, 2015, A3.

10. M. R. Barrick, M. K. Mount, and T. A. Judge, "Personality and Performance at the Beginning of the New Millennium: What Do We Know and Where Do We Go Next?" *International Journal of Selection and Assessment* 9, nos. 1–2 (2001): 9–30; P. R. Sackett and P. T. Walmsley, "Which Personality Attributes Are Most Important in the Workplace?" *Perspectives on Psychological Science* 9, no. 5 (2014): 538–51.

11. P. R. Sackett, F. Lievens, C. H. Van Iddekinge, and N. R. Kuncel, "Individual Differences and Their Measurement: A Review of 100 Years of Research," *Journal of Applied Psychology* 102, no. 3 (2017): 254–73; N. Schmitt, "Personality and Cognitive Ability as Predictors of Effective Performance at Work," *Annual Review of Organizational Psychology and Organizational Behavior* 1 (2014): 45–65.

12. J. F. Salgado, "A Theoretical Model of Psychometric Effects of Faking on Assessment Procedures: Empirical Findings and Implications for Personality at Work," *International Journal of Selection and Assessment* 24, no. 3 (2016): 209–28.

13. T. D. Letzring, "Observer Judgmental Accuracy of Personality: Benefits Related to Being a Good (Normative) Judge," *Journal of Research in Personality* 54 (2015): 51–60.

14. K. Lee and M. C. Ashton, "Acquaintanceship and Self/Observer Agreement in Personality Judgment," *Journal of Research in Personality* 70 (2017): 1–5.

15. D. H. Kluemper, B. D. McLarty, and M. N. Bing, "Acquaintance Ratings of the Big Five Personality Traits: Incremental Validity beyond and Interactive Effects with Self-Reports in the Prediction of Workplace Deviance," *Journal of Applied Psychology* 100, no. 1 (2015): 237–48; I. Oh, G. Wang, and M. K. Mount, "Validity of Observer Ratings of the Five-Factor Model of Personality Traits: A Meta-Analysis," *Journal of Applied Psychology* 96, no. 4 (2011): 762–73.

16. J. A. Hall, S. D. Gunnery, T. D. Letzring, D. R. Carney, and C. R. Colvin, "Accuracy of Judging Affect and Accuracy of Judging Personality: How and When Are They Related?" *Journal of Personality* 85, no. 5 (2017): 583–92.

17. B. P. Chapman, A. Weiss, and P. R. Duberstein, "Statistical Learning Theory for High Dimensional Prediction: Application to Criterion-Keyed Scale Development," *Psychological Methods* 21, no. 4 (2016): 603–20.

18. P. Harik, P. Baldwin, and B. Clauser, "Comparison of Automated Scoring Methods for a Computerized Performance Assessment of Clinical Judgment," *Applied Psychological Measurement* 37, no. 8 (2013): 587–97.

19. M. C. Campion, M. A. Campion, E. D. Campion, and M. H. Reider, "Initial Investigation into Computer Scoring of Candidate Essays for Personnel Selection," *Journal of Applied Psychology* 101, no. 7 (2016): 958–75.

20 J. Nelson, "Is It Personal or Is It Personality?" *Forbes,* November 13, 2017, https://www.forbes.com/sites/ forbescoachescouncil/2017/11/13/is-it-personal-or-is-it-personality/#aec05126618c

21. M. B. Arthur, "The 'Strange History' Behind the Myers-Briggs Type Indicator—and What That Can Mean for You," *Forbes,* September 16, 2018, https://www.forbes .com/sites/michaelbarthur/2018/09/16/the-strange-history-behind-the-mbti-and-what-that-can-mean-for-career-owners/#2a2fc3ba2fb3

22. A. Grant, "Goodbye to MBTI, the Fad That Won't Die," *Huffington Post,* (September 17, 2013), http://www .huffingtonpost.com/adam-grant/goodbye-to-mbti-the-fad-t_b_3947014.html

23. See, for instance, D. J. Pittenger, "Cautionary Comments Regarding the Myers-Briggs Type Indicator," *Consulting Psychology Journal: Practice and Research* 57, no. 3 (2005): 210–21; L. Bess and R. J. Harvey, "Bimodal Score Distributions and the Myers-Briggs Type Indicator: Fact or Artifact?" *Journal of Personality Assessment* 78, no. 1 (2002): 176–86; R. M. Capraro and M. M. Capraro, "Myers-Briggs Type Indicator Score Reliability across Studies: A Meta-Analytic Reliability Generalization Study," *Educational & Psychological Measurement* 62, no. 4 (2002): 590–602; R. C. Arnau, B. A. Green, D. H. Rosen, D. H. Gleaves, and J. G. Melancon, "Are Jungian Preferences Really Categorical? An Empirical Investigation Using Taxometric Analysis," *Personality & Individual Differences* 34, no. 2 (2003): 233–51.

24. D. Ariely, "When Lame Pick-Up Lines Actually Work," *The Wall Street Journal,* July 19–20, 2014, C12.

25. See, for example, O. P. John, L. P. Naumann, and C. J. Soto, "Paradigm Shift to the Integrative Big Five Trait Taxonomy: History, Measurement, and Conceptual Issues," in O. P. John, R. W. Robins, and L. A. Pervin (eds.), *Handbook of Personality: Theory and Research,* 3rd ed. (New York, NY: Guilford, 2008): 114–58; M. R. Barrick and M. K. Mount, "Yes, Personality Matters: Moving On to More Important Matters," *Human Performance* 18, no. 4 (2005): 359–72.

26. W. Fleeson and P. Gallagher, "The Implications of Big Five Standing for the Distribution of Trait Manifestation in Behavior: Fifteen Experience-Sampling Studies and a Meta-Analysis," *Journal of Personality and Social Psychology* 97, no. 6 (2009): 1097–114.

27. T. A. Judge, L. S. Simon, C. Hurst, and K. Kelley, "What I Experienced Yesterday Is Who I Am Today: Relationship of Work Motivations and Behaviors to Within-Individual Variation in the Five-Factor Model of Personality," *Journal of Applied Psychology* 99, no. 2 (2014): 199–221.

28 See, for instance, Barrick, Mount, and Judge, "Personality and Performance at the Beginning of the New Millennium."

29. P. R. Sackett and P. T. Walmsley, "Which Personality Attributes Are Most Important in the Workplace?" *Perspectives on Psychological Science* 9, no. 5 (2014): 538–51.

30. A. E. Poropat, "A Meta-Analysis of the Five-Factor Model of Personality and Academic Performance," *Psychological Bulletin* 135, no. 2 (2009): 322–38.

31. M. R. Barrick and M. K. Mount, "The Big Five Personality Dimensions and job Performance: A Meta-Analysis," *Personnel Psychology* 44 (1991): 1–26; D. S. Chiaburu, I-S. Oh, C. M. Berry, N. Li, and R. G. Gardner, "The Five-Factor Model of Personality Traits and Organizational Citizenship Behaviors: A Meta-Analysis," *Journal of Applied Psychology* 96, no. 6 (2011): 1140–66; A. Furnham and C. Fudge, "The Five Factor Model of Personality and Sales Performance," *Journal of Individual Differences* 29, no. 1 (2008): 11–16.

32. P. Calanna, M. Lauriola, A. Saggino, M. Tommasi, and S. Furlan, "Using a Supervised Machine Learning Algorithm for Detecting Faking Good in a Personality Self-Report," *Interational Journal of Selection and Assessment* (in press).

33. T. A. Judge, D. Heller, and M. K. Mount, "Five-Factor Model of Personality and Job Satisfaction: A Meta-Analysis," *Journal of Applied Psychology* 87, no. 3 (2002): 530–41; B. W. Swider and R. D. Zimmerman, "Born to Burnout: A Meta-Analytic Path Model of Personality, Job Burnout, and Work Outcomes," *Journal of Vocational Behavior* 76 (2010): 487–506; R. Zimmerman, "Understanding the Impact of Personality Traits on Individuals' Turnover Intentions," *Personnel Psychology* 61 (2008): 309–48.

34. J. L. Huang, A. M. Ryan, K. L. Zabel, and A. Palmer, "Personality and Adaptive Performance at Work: A Meta-Analytic Investigation," *Journal of Applied Psychology* 99, no. 1 (2014): 162–79.

35. Swider and Zimmerman, "Born to Burnout."

36. B. Wille, F. De Fruyt, and M. Feys, "Big Five Traits and Intrinsic Success in the New Career Era: A 15-Year Longitudinal Study on Employability and Work-Family Conflict."

37. Berry, Ones, and Sackett, "Interpersonal Deviance, Organizational Deviance, and Their Common Correlates"; Chiaburu, Oh, Berry, Li, and Gardner, "The Five-Factor Model of Personality Traits and Organizational Citizenship Behaviors"; T. A. Judge and R. Ilies, "Relationship of Personality to Performance Motivation: A Meta-Analytic Review," *Journal of Applied Psychology* 87, no. 4 (2002): 797–807.

38. D. S. DeRue, J. D. Nahrgang, N. Wellman, and S. E. Humphrey, "Trait and Behavioral Theories of Leadership: An Integration and Meta-Analytic Test of Their Relative Validity," *Personnel Psychology*

64 (2011): 7–52; T. A. Judge, J. E. Bono, R. Ilies, and M. W. Gerhardt, "Personality and Leadership: A Qualitative and Quantitative Review," *Journal of Applied Psychology* 87, no. 4 (2002): 765–80.

39. Judge, Heller, and Mount, "Five-Factor Model of Personality and Job Satisfaction"; Swider and R. Zimmerman, "Born to Burnout."

40. M. A. McCord, D. L. Joseph, and E. Grijalva, "Blinded by the Light: The Dark Side of Traditionally Desirable Personality Traits," *Industrial and Organizational Psychology: Perspectives on Science and Practice* 7, no. 1 (2014): 130–37.

41. M. M. Hammond, N. L. Neff, J. L. Farr, A. R. Schwall, and X. Zhao, "Predictors of Individual-Level Innovation at Work: A Meta-Analysis," *Psychology of Aesthetics, Creativity, and the Arts* 5, no. 1 (2011): 90–105.

42. Huang, Ryan, Zabel, and Palmer, "Personality and Adaptive Performance at Work"; Judge, Bono, Ilies, and Gerhardt, "Personality and Leadership."

43. A. Minbashian, J. Earl, and J. E. H. Bright, "Openness to Experience as a Predictor of Job Performance Trajectories," *Applied Psychology: An International Review* 62, no. 1 (2013): 1–12.

44. Allen, Johnson, Saboe, Cho, Dumani, and Evans, "Dispositional Variables and Work-Family Conflict."

45. Allen, Johnson, Saboe, Cho, Dumani, and Evans, "Dispositional Variables and Work-Family Conflict"; Zimmerman, "Understanding the Impact of Personality Traits on Individuals' Turnover Intentions."

46. Berry, Ones, and Sackett, "Interpersonal Deviance, Organizational Deviance, and Their Common Correlates"; Chiaburu, Oh, Berry, Li, and Gardner, "The Five-Factor Model of Personality Traits and Organizational Citizenship Behaviors"; J. Luca Pletzer, M. Bentvelzen, Janneke K. Oostrom, and R. E. de Vries, "A Meta-Analysis of the Relations between Personality and Workplace Deviance: Big Five versus HEXACO," *Journal of Vocational Behavior* 112 (2019): 369–83.

47. R. Fang, B. Landis, Z. Zhang, M. H. Anderson, J. D. Shaw, and M. Kilduff, "Integrating Personality and Social Networks: A Meta-Analysis of Personality, Network Position, and Work Outcomes in Organizations," *Organization Science* 26, no. 4 (2015): 1243–60.

48. D. Choi, I-S. Oh, and A. E. Colbert, "Understanding Organizational Commitment: A Meta-Analytic Examination of the Roles of the Five-Factor Model of Personality and Culture," *Journal of Applied Psychology* 100, no. 5 (2015): 1542–67.

49. M. B. Harari, A. C. Reaves, D. A. Beane, A. J. Laginess, and C. Viswesvaran, "Personality and Expatriate Adjustment: A Meta-Analysis," *Journal of Occupational and Organizational Psychology* 91, no. 3 (2018): 486–517.

50. K. A. Demes and N. Geeraert, "The Highs and Lows of a Cultural Transition: A Longitudinal Analysis of Sojourner Stress and Adaptation Across 50 Countries," *Journal of Personality and Social Psychology* 109, no. 2 (2015): 316–37.

51. J. F. Rauthmann, "The Dark Triad and Interpersonal Perception: Similarities and Differences in the Social Consequences of Narcissism, Machiavellianism, and Psychopathy," *Social Psychological and Personality Science* 3, no. 4 (2012): 487–96.

52. L. ten Brinke, A. Kish, and D. Keltner, "Hedge Fund Managers With Psychopathic Tendencies Make for Worse Investors," *Personality and Social Psychology Bulletin* 44, no. 2 (2018): 214–23.

53. R. D. Hare, *The Predators Among Us* [Keynote Address] (St. John's, Canada: Canadian Police Association Annual General Meeting, August 27, 2002).

54. P. D. Harms and S. M. Spain, "Beyond the Bright Side: Dark Personality at Work," *Applied Psychology: An International Review* 64, no. 1 (2015): 15–24.

55. P. K. Jonason, S. Slomski, and J. Partyka, "The Dark Triad at Work: How Toxic Employees Get Their Way," *Personality and Individual Differences* 52, no. 3 (2012): 449–53.

56. E. H. O'Boyle, D. R. Forsyth, G. C. Banks, and M. A. McDaniel, "A Meta-Analysis of the Dark Triad and Work Behavior: A Social Exchange Perspective," *Journal of Applied Psychology* 97, no. 3 (2012): 557–79.

57. E. Grijalva and P. D. Harms, "Narcissism: An Integrative Synthesis and Dominance Complementarity Model," *Academy of Management Perspectives* 28, no. 2 (2014): 108–27.

58. D. C. Maynard, E. M. Brondolo, C. E. Connelly, and C. E. Sauer, "I'm Too Good for This Job: Narcissism's Role in the Experience of Overqualification," *Applied Psychology: An International Review* 64, no. 1 (2015): 208–32.

59. B. J. Brummel and K. N. Parker, "Obligation and Entitlement in Society and the Workplace," *Applied Psychology: An International Review* 64, no. 1 (2015): 127–60.

60. E. Grijalva and D. A. Newman, "Narcissism and Counterproductive Work Behavior (CWB): Meta-Analysis and Consideration of Collectivist Culture, Big Five Personality, and Narcissism's Facet Structure," *Applied Psychology: An International Review* 64, no. 1 (2015): 93–126; Luca Pletzer et al., "A Meta-Analysis of the Relations between Personality and Workplace Deviance."

61. D. C. Maynard, E. M. Brondolo, C. E. Connelly, and C. E. Sauer, "I'm Too Good for This Job: Narcissism's Role in the Experience of Overqualification."

62 E. Grijalva and P. D. Harms, "Narcissism: An Integrative Synthesis and Dominance Complementarity Model."

63. C. J. Resick, D. S. Whitman, S. M. Weingarden, and N. J. Hiller, "The Bright-Side and Dark-Side of CEO Personality: Examining Core Self-Evaluations, Narcissism, Transformational Leadership, and Strategic Influence," *Journal of Applied Psychology* 94, no. 6 (2009): 1365–81.

64. J. J. Sosik, J. U. Chun, and W. Zhu, "Hang on to Your Ego: The Moderating Role of Leader Narcissism on Relationships between Leader Charisma and Follower Psychological Empowerment and Moral Identity," *Journal of Business Ethics* 120, no. 1 (12, 2013); B. M. Galvin, D. A. Waldman, and P. Balthazard, "Visionary Communication Qualities as Mediators of the Relationship between Narcissism and Attributions of Leader Charisma," *Personnel Psychology* 63, no. 3 (2010): 509–37.

65. D. Meinert, "Narcissistic Bosses Aren't All Bad, Study Finds," *HR Magazine,* March 2014, 18.

66. K. A. Byrne and D. A. Worthy, "Do Narcissists Make Better Decisions? An Investigation of Narcissism and Dynamic Decision-Making Performance," *Personality and Individual Differences* 55, no. 2 (2013): 112–17.

67. O'Boyle, Forsyth, Banks, and McDaniel, "A Meta-Analysis of the Dark Triad and Work Behavior: A Social Exchange Perspective."

68. Ibid.

69. B. Wille, F. De Fruyt, and B. De Clercq, "Expanding and Reconceptualizing Aberrant Personality at Work: Validity of Five-Factor Model Aberrant Personality Tendencies to Predict Career Outcomes," *Personnel Psychology* 66, no. 1 (2013): 173–223.

70. P. K. Jonason, S. Slomski, and J. Partyka, "The Dark Triad at Work: How Toxic Employees Get Their Way," *Personality and Individual Differences*; H. M. Baughman, S. Dearing, E. Giammarco, and P. A. Vernon, "Relationships between Bullying Behaviours and the Dark Triad: A Study with Adults," *Personality and Individual Differences* 52, no. 5 (2012): 571–75.

71. M. C. Ashton, K. Lee, and R. E. de Vries, "The HEXACO Honesty-Humility, Agreeableness, and Emotionality Factors: A Review of Research and Theory," *Personality and Social Psychology Review* 18, no. 2 (2014): 139–52.

72. Ibid.

73. Ashton, Lee, and de Vries, "The HEXACO Honesty-Humility, Agreeableness, and Emotionality Factors"; S. Brocklebank, S. Pauls, D. Rockmore, and T. C. Bates, "A Spectral Clustering Approach to the Structure of Personality: Contrasting the FFM and HEXACO Models," *Journal of Research in Personality* 57 (2015): 100–9; E. P. Kleinlogel, J. Dietz, and J. Antonakis, "Lucky, Competent, or Just a Cheat? Interactive Effects of Honesty-Humility and Moral Cues on Cheating Behavior," *Personality and Social Psychology Bulletin* 44, no. 2 (2018): 158–72.

74. T. A. Judge and J. E. Bono, "A Rose by Any Other Name . . . Are Self-Esteem, Generalized Self-Efficacy, Neuroticism, and Locus of Control Indicators of a Common Construct?," in B. W. Roberts and R. Hogan (eds.), *Personality Psychology in the Workplace* (Washington, DC: American Psychological Association, 2001), 93–118.

75. T. A. Judge, J. E. Bono, A. Erez, and E. A. Locke, "Core Self-Evaluations and Job and Life Satisfaction: The Role of Self-Concordance and Goal Attainment," *Journal of Applied Psychology* 90, no. 2 (2005): 257–68.

76. A. N. Salvaggio, B. Schneider, L. H. Nishi, D. M. Mayer, A. Ramesh, and J. S. Lyon, "Manager Personality, Manager Service Quality Orientation, and Service Climate: Test of a Model," *Journal of Applied Psychology* 92, no. 6 (2007): 1741–50; B. A. Scott and T. A. Judge, "The Popularity Contest at Work: Who Wins, Why, and What Do They Receive?" *Journal of Applied Psychology* 94, no. 1 (2009): 20–33; T. A. Judge and C. Hurst, "How the Rich (and Happy) Get Richer (and Happier): Relationship of Core Self-Evaluations to Trajectories in Attaining Work Success," *Journal of Applied Psychology* 93, no. 4 (2008): 849–63.

77. L. Huang, D. V. Krasikova, and P. D. Harms, "Avoiding or Embracing Social Relationships? A Conservation of Resources Perspective of Leader Narcissism, Leader-Member Exchange Differentiation, and Follower Voice," *Journal of Organizational Behavior* 41 (2020): 77–92.

78. C. W. Rudolph, K. N. Lavigne, and H. Zacher, "Career Adaptability: A Meta-Analysis of Relationships With Measures of Adaptivity, Adapting Responses, and Adaptation Results," *Journal of Vocational Behavior* 98 (2017): 17–34.

79. J. Zhu, C. R. Wanberg, D. A. Harrison, and E. W. Diehn, "Ups and Downs of the Expatriate Experience? Understanding Work Adjustment Trajectories and Career Outcomes," *Journal of Applied Psychology* 101, no. 4 (2016): 549–68.

80. T. A. O'Neill, M. J. McLarnon, L. Xiu, and S. J. Law, "Core Self-Evaluations, Perceptions of Group Potency, and Job Performance: The Moderating Role of Individualism and Collectivism Culture Profiles," *Journal of Occupational and Organizational Psychology* 89, no. 3 (2016): 447–73; B. Wille, J. Hofmans, F. Lievens, M. D. Back, and F. De Fruyt, "Climbing the Corporate Ladder and Within-Person Changes in Narcissism: Reciprocal Relationships over Two Decades," *Journal of Vocational Behavior* (in press).

81. M. Paunova, "Who Gets to Lead the Multinational Team? An Updated Status Characteristics Perspective," *Human Relations* 70, no. 7 (2017): 883–907.

82. D. V. Day and D. J. Schleicher, "Self-Monitoring at Work: A Motive-Based Perspective," *Journal of Personality* 74, no. 3 (2006): 685–714.

83. D. V. Day, D. J. Shleicher, A. L. Unckless, and N. J. Hiller, "Self-Monitoring Personality at Work: A Meta-Analytic Investigation of Construct Validity," *Journal of Applied Psychology* 87, no. 2 (2002): 390–401.

84. H. Oh and M. Kilduff, "The Ripple Effect of Personality on Social Structure: Self-Monitoring Origins of Network Brokerage," *Journal of Applied Psychology* 93, no. 5 (2008): 1155–64; A. Mehra, M. Kilduff, and D. J. Brass, "The Social Networks of High and Low Self-Monitors: Implications for Workplace Performance," *Administrative Science Quarterly* 46, no. 1 (2001): 121–46.

85. T. S. Bateman and J. M. Crant, "The Proactive Component of Organizational Behavior: A Measure and Correlates," *Journal of Organizational Behavior* 14 (1993): 103–18; M. Priesemuth and B. Bigelow, "It Hurts Me too! (or Not?): Exploring the Negative Implications for Abusive Bosses," *Journal of Applied Psychology* 105, no. 4 (2020): 410–421.

86. M. Spitzmuller, H-P. Sin, M. Howe, and S. Fatimah, "Investigating the Uniqueness and Usefulness of Proactive Personality in Organizational Research: A Meta-Analytic Review," *Human Performance* 28 (2015): 351–79; K. Tornau and M. Frese, "Construct Clean-up in Proactivity Research: A Meta-Analysis on the Nomological Net of Work-Related Proactivity Concepts and Their Incremental Values," *Applied Psychology: An International Review* 62, no. 1 (2013): 44–96.

87. W. D. Li, D. Fay, M. Frese, P. D. Harms, and X. Y. Gao, "Reciprocal Relationship between Proactive Personality and Work Characteristics: A Latent Change Score Approach," *Journal of Applied Psychology* 99, no. 5 (2014): 948–65.

88. J. P. Thomas, D. S. Whitman, and C. Viswesvaran, "Employee Proactivity in Organizations: A Comparative Meta-Analysis of Emergent Proactive Constructs," *Journal of Occupational and Organizational Psychology* 83 (2010): 275–300; H. R. Young, D. R. Glerum, W. Wang, and D. L. Joseph, "Who are the Most Engaged at Work? A Meta-Analysis of Personality and Employee Engagement," *Journal of Organizational Behavior* 39 (2018): 1330–46; Y. Lee, C. M. Berry, and E. Gonzalez-Mulé, "The Importance of Being Humble: A Meta-Analysis and Incremental Validity Analysis of the Relationship between Honesty-Humility and Job Performance," Journal of Applied Psychology (in press).

89. Luca Pletzer et al., "A Meta-Analysis of the Relations between Personality and Workplace Deviance."

90. P. D. Converse, P. J. Pathak, A. M. DePaul-Haddock, T. Gotlib, and M. Merbedone, "Controlling Your Environment and Yourself: Implications for Career Success," *Journal of Vocational Behavior* 80, no. 1 (2012): 148–59.

91. S. Parrigon, S. E. Woo, L. Tay, and T. Wang, "CAPTION-ing the Situation: A Lexically-Derived Taxonomy of Psychological Situation Characteristics," *Journal of Personality and Social Psychology* 112, no. 4 (2017): 642–81.

92. R. D. Meyer, R. S. Dalal, and R. Hermida, "A Review and Synthesis of Situational Strength in the Organizational Sciences," *Journal of Management* 36 (2010): 121–40.

93. X. Zheng, B. Wu, C. S. Li, P. Zhang, and N. Tang, "Reversing the Pollyanna Effect: The Curvilinear Relationship between Core Self-Evaluation and Perceived Social Acceptance," *Journal of Business and Psychology* (in press).

94. T. A. Judge and C. P. Zapata, "The Person-Situation Debate Revisited: Effect of Situation Strength and Trait Activation on the Validity of the Big Five Personality Traits in Predicting Job Performance," *Academy of Management Journal* 58, no. 4 (2015): 1149–79.

95. Meyer, Dalal, and Hermida, "A Review and Synthesis of Situational Strength in the Organizational Sciences."

96. R. D. Meyer et al., "Measuring Job-Related Situational Strength and Assessing Its Interactive Effects with Personality on Voluntary Work Behavior," *Journal of Management* 40, no. 4 (2014): 1010–41.

97. A. M. Watson et al., "When Big Brother Is Watching: Goal Orientation Shapes Reactions to Electronic Monitoring during Online Training," *Journal of Applied Psychology* 98, no. 4 (2013): 642–57.

98. H. Chae, J. Park, and J. N. Choi, "Two Facets of Conscientiousness and the Knowledge Sharing Dilemmas in the Workplace: Contrasting the Moderating Functions of Supervisor Support and Coworker Support," *Journal of Organizational Behavior* 40, no. 4 (2019): 387–399; S. Kudret, B. Erdogan, and T. N. Bauer, "Self-Monitoring

Personality Trait at Work: An Integrative Narrative Review and Future Directions," *Journal of Organizational Behavior* 40 (2019): 193–208.

99. Judge and Zapata, "The Person-Situation Debate Revisited."

100. E. Dilan, "Organizational Values: The Most Underutilized Corporate Asset," *Forbes,* April 12, 2018, https://www.forbes.com/sites/forbescoachescouncil/2018/04/12/organizational-values-the-most-underutilized-corporate-asset/#28d6d2c852a3

101. Kudret et al., "Self-Monitoring Personality Trait at Work."

102. "Wells Fargo CEO to Apologize for Betraying Customers' Trust," *CBS NEWS,* September 20, 2016, https://www .cbsnews.com/news/wellsfargo-ceo-to-apologize-for-betraying-customers-trust/

103. A. Bardi, J. A. Lee, N. Hofmann-Towfigh, and G. Soutar, "The Structure of Intraindividual Value Change," *Journal of Personality and Social Psychology* 97, no. 5 (2009): 913–29; G. R. Maio, J. M. Olson, M. M. Bernard, and M. A. Luke, "Ideologies, Values, Attitudes, and Behavior," in *Handbook of Social Psychology,* ed. J. Delamater (New York: Springer, 2003), 283–308.

104. F. Li, T. Chen, N. Y-F. Chen, Y. Bai, and J. M. Crant, "Proactive yet Reflective? Materializing Proactive Personality into Creativity through Job Reflective Learning and Activated Positive Affective States," *Personnel Psychology* (in press); N. Rodrigues and T. Rebelo, "Predicting Innovative Performance through Proactive Personality: Examining Its Criterion Validity and Incremental Validity over the Five-Factor Model," *International Journal of Selection and Assessment* 27 (2019): 1–8.

105. R. Fischer and D. Boer, "Motivational Basis of Personality Traits: A Meta-Analysis of Value-Personality Correlations," *Journal of Personality* 83, no. 5 (2015): 491–510; S. Han, C. M. Harold, and M. Cheong, "Examining Why Employee proactive personality influences empowering leadership: The roles of cognition- and affect-based trust," *Journal of Occupational and Organizational Psychology* 92 (2019): 352–83.

106. Ibid.

107. M. Rokeach, *The Nature of Human Values* (New York: The Free Press, 1973); J. Sun, W-D. Li, Y. Li, R. C. Liden, S. Li, and X. Zhang, "Unintended Consequences of Being Proactive? Linking Proactive Personality to Coworker Envy, Helping, and Undermining, and the Moderating Role of Prosocial Motivation," *Journal of Applied Psychology* (in press).

108. S. H. Schwartz, "Universals in the Content and Structure of Values: Theoretical Advances and Empirical Tests in 20 Countries," *Advances in Experimental Social Psychology* 25 (1992): 1–65.

109. Ibid.

110. See, for example, N. R. Lockwood, F. R. Cepero, and S. Williams, *The Multigenerational Workforce* (Alexandria, VA: Society for Human Resource Management, 2009).

111. E. Parry and P. Urwin, "Generational Differences in Work Values: A Review of Theory and Evidence," *International Journal of Management Reviews* 13, no. 1 (2011): 79–96.

112. J. M. Twenge, S. M. Campbell, B. J. Hoffman, and C. E. Lance, "Generational Differences in Work Values: Leisure and Extrinsic Values Increasing, Social and Intrinsic Values Decreasing," *Journal of Management* 36, no. 5 (2010): 1117–42; K. R. Keeler, W. Kong, R. S. Dalal, and J. M. Cortina, "Situational Strength Interactions: Are Variance Patterns Consistent with Theory?" *Journal of Applied Psychology* (in press).

113. R. S. Dalal, B. Alaybek, Z. Sheng, S. J. Holland, and A. J. Tomassetti, "Extending Situational Strength Theory to Account for Situation-Outcome Mismatch," *Journal of Business and Psychology* (in press).

114. L. Alton, "Millennials and Entitlement in the Workplace: The Good, the Bad, and the Ugly," *Forbes,* November 22, 2017, https://www.

forbes.com/sites/larryalton/2017/11/22/millennials-and-entitlement-in-the-workplace-the-good-the-bad-and-the-ugly/#4dffaec13943

115. S. Stronge, P. Milojev, and C. G. Sibley, "Are People Becoming More Entitled Over Time? Not in New Zealand," *Personality and Social Psychology Bulletin,* 44, no. 2 (2018): 200–13.

116. "Stay Metrics Partners With Twegos to Launch Driver Matching Application" [Press Release], June 29, 2017, https://staymetrics.com/press/stay-metrics-launches-driver-matching/

117. J. L. Holland, *Making Vocational Choices: A Theory of Careers,* 2nd ed. (Englewood Cliffs, NJ: Prentice-Hall, 1985); A. L. Kristof-Brown, R. D. Zimmerman, and E. C. Johnson, "Consequences of Individuals' Fit at Work: A Meta-Analysis of Person-Job, Person-Organization, Person-Group, and Person-Supervisor Fit," *Personnel Psychology* 58 (2005): 281–342; C. Ostroff, "Person-Environment Fit in Organizational Settings," in S. W. J. Kozlowski (ed.), *The Oxford Handbook of Organizational Psychology,* Vol. 1 (Oxford, UK: Oxford University Press, 2012): 373–408.

118. Kristof-Brown, Zimmerman, and Johnson, "Consequences of Individuals' Fit at Work."

119. I-S Oh et al., "Fit Happens Globally: A Meta-Analytic Comparison of the Relationships of Person-Environment fit Dimensions with Work Attitudes and Performance Across East Asia, Europe, and North America," *Personnel Psychology* 67 (2014): 99–152.

120. Y. Lee and J. Antonakis, "When Preference Is Not Satisfied But the Individual Is: How Power Distance Moderates Person-Job Fit," *Journal of Management* 40, no. 3 (2014): 641–57.

121. W. Arthur Jr., S. T. Bell, A. J. Villado, and D. Doverspike, "The Use of Person–Organization Fit in Employment Decision-Making: An Assessment of Its Criterion-Related Validity," *Journal of Applied Psychology* 91, no. 4 (2006): 786–801; J. R. Edwards, D. M. Cable, I. O. Williamson, L. S. Lambert, and A. J. Shipp, "The Phenomenology of Fit: Linking the Person and Environment to the Subjective Experience of Person–Environment Fit," *Journal of Applied Psychology* 91, no. 4 (2006): 802–27.

122. E. E. Kausel and J. E. Slaughter, "Narrow Personality Traits and Organizational Attraction: Evidence for the Complementary Hypothesis," *Organizational Behavior and Human Decision Processes* 114, no. 1 (2011): 3–14; A. Leung and S. Chaturvedi, "Linking the Fits, Fitting the Links: Connecting Different Types of PO Fit to Attitudinal Outcomes," *Journal of Vocational Behavior* 79, no. 2 (2011): 391–402.

123. Kristof-Brown, Zimmerman, and Johnson, "Consequences of Individuals' Fit at Work."

124. M. L. Verquer, T. A. Beehr, and S. E. Wagner, "A Meta-Analysis of Relations between Person–Organization Fit and Work Attitudes," *Journal of Vocational Behavior* 63, no. 3 (2003): 473–89; J. C. Carr, A. W. Pearson, M. J. Vest, and S. L. Boyar, "Prior Occupational Experience, Anticipatory Socialization, and Employee Retention," *Journal of Management* 32, no. 3 (2006): 343–59.

125. D. Wood, G. H. Lowman, P. D. Harms, and B. W. Roberts, "Exploring the Relative Importance of Normative and Distinctive Organizational Preferences as Predictors of Work Attitudes," *Journal of Applied Psychology* 104, no. 2 (2019): 270–92.

126. B. W. Swider, R. D. Zimmerman, and M. R. Barrick, "Searching for the Right fit: Development of Applicant Person-Organization fit Perceptions During the Recruitment Process," *Journal of Applied Psychology* 100, no. 3 (2015): 880–93.

127. K. H. Ehrhart, D. M. Mayer, and J. C. Ziegert, "Web-Based Recruitment in the Millennial Generation: Work-Life Balance, Website Usability, and Organizational Attraction," *European Journal of Work and Organizational Psychology* 21, no. 6 (2012): 850–74.

128. Kristof-Brown, Zimmerman, and Johnson, "Consequences of Individuals' Fit at Work."

129. I. S. Oh et al. "Fit Happens Globally: A Meta-Analytic Comparison of the Relationships of Person-Environment Fit Dimensions with Work Attitudes and Performance across East Asia, Europe, and North America," *Personnel Psychology* 67, no. 1 (2014): 99–152.

130. A. H. D. Van Rossem, "Generations as Social Categories: An Exploratory Cognitive Study of Generational Identity and Generational Stereotypes in a Multigenerational Workforce," *Journal of Organizational Behavior* 40 (2019): 434–55.

131. See The Hofstede Centre, G. Hofstede. *The Hofstede Centre* (website), http://www.geert-hofstede.com

132. L. M. Orr and W. J. Hauser, "A re-inquiry of Hofstede's cultural dimensions: A call for 21st century cross-cultural research," *The Marketing Management Journal* 18, no. 2 (2008): 1-19.

133. Hofstede,G., Hofstede, G. J., and Minkov, M., Cultures and Organizations: Software of the Mind (3rd Ed., New York, NY: 2010): McGraw-Hill

134. G. Hofstede, The Hofstede Centre (website); Hofstede Insights, National Culture, Accessed August 27, 2020, https://hi.hofstede-insights.com/national-culture.

135. C. Erdener, "Hofstede's MAS/FEM dimension," Journal of International Business and Economics 13, no. 2 (2013): 141-146; G. Hofstede, Culture's Consequences: International Differences in Work-related Values (London, UK: 1980): Sage; A. Moulettes, "The absence of women's voices in Hofstede's cultural consequences: A postcolonial reading," *Women in Management Review* 22, no. 6 (2007): 443-455.

136. Ibid.

137. G. Hofstede, G. J. Hofstede, and M. Minkov, *Cultures and Organizations: Software of the Mind* (3rd ed., New York: McGraw-Hill, 2010); Hofstede Insights, *National Culture*. Accessed April 23, 2020, https://hi.hofstede-insights .com/national-culture

138. Q. Guo, Z. Liu, X. Li, and X. Qiao, "Indulgence and Long-Term Orientation Influence Prosocial Behavior at National Level," *Frontiers in Psychology* 9, no. 1798 (2018): 1–10; A. Maleki and M. de Jong, "A Proposal for Clustering the Dimensions of Culture," *Cross-Cultural Research* 48, no. 2 (2014): 107–143.

139. V. Taras, B. L. Kirkman, and P. Steel, "Examining the Impact of Culture's Consequences: A Three-Decade, Multilevel, Meta-Analytic Review of Hofstede's Cultural Value Dimensions," *Journal of Applied Psychology* 95, no. 5 (2010): 405–39.

140. R. J. House, P. J. Hanges, M. Javidan, and P. W. Dorfman, eds., *Leadership, Culture, and Organizations: The GLOBE Study of 62 Societies* (Thousand Oaks, CA: Sage, 2004); O. Schloesser et al., "Human Orientation as a New Cultural Dimension of the GLOBE Project: A Validation Study of the GLOBE Scale and Out-Group Human Orientation in 25 Countries," *Journal of Cross-Cultural Psychology* 44, no. 4 (2012): 535–51.

141. J. P. Meyer et al., "Affective, Normative, and Continuance Commitment Levels Across Cultures: A Meta-Analysis," *Journal of Vocational Behavior* 80, no. 2 (2012): 225–45.

142. K. Harrison, "What's Different About Business Overseas? One Map Says It all," *Forbes,* February 25, 2015, https://www.forbes.com/sites/kateharrison/2015/02/25/whats-different-about-business-overseas-this-map-says-it-all/#4e84496e3937

CHAPTER 6

1. J. Carpenter, "One Type of Diversity We Don't Talk About at Work: Body Size," *CNN,* January 3, 2019, https://www .cnn.com/2019/01/03/success/weight-bias-work/index .html

2. D. Clark, "How to Succeed in a Cross-Cultural Workplace," *Forbes,* June 19, 2014, https://www.forbes.com/sites/dorieclark/2014/06/19/how-to-succeed-in-a-cross-cultural-workplace/#4fd3392ac972

3. R. Rau, E. N. Carlson, M. D. Back, M. Barranti, J. E. Gebauer, L. J. Human, D. Leising, and S. Nestler, "What Is the Structure of Perceiver Effects? On the Importance of Global Positivity and Trait-Specificity Across Personality Domains and Judgment Contexts," *Journal of Personality and Social Psychology* (in press); D. Wood, P. Harms, and S. Vazire, "Perceiver Effects as Projective Tests: What Your Perceptions of Others Say About You," *Journal of Personality and Social Psychology* 99 (2010): 174–90.

4. E. Bernstein, "'Honey, You Never Said. . . ,'" *The Wall Street Journal,* March 24, 2015, D1, D4.

5. K. C. Yam, R. Fehr, and C. M. Barnes, "Morning Employees Are Perceived as Better Employees: Employees' Start Times Influence Supervisor Performance Ratings," *Journal of Applied Psychology* 99, no. 6 (2014): 1288–99.

6. See, for instance, T. Masuda, P. C. Ellsworth, B. Mesquita, J. Leu, S. Tanida, and E. Van de Veerdonk, "Placing the Face in Context: Cultural Differences in the Perception of Facial Emotion," *Journal of Personality and Social Psychology* 94, no. 3 (2008): 365–81.

7. G. Fields and J. R. Emshwiller, "Long After Arrests, Records Live On," *The Wall Street Journal,* December 26, 2014, A1, A10.

8. A. Genevsky and B. Knutson, "Neural Affective Mechanisms Predict Market-Level Microlending," *Psychological Science* 26, no. 9 (2015): 1411–22.

9. Ibid.

10. T. G. Horgan, N. K. Herzog, S. M. Syszlewski, "Does Your Messy Office Make Your Mind Look Cluttered? Office Appearance and Perceivers' Judgments about the Owners' Personality," *Personality and Individual Differences* 138 (2019): 370–79.

11. E. Zell and Z. Krizan, "Do People Have Insight into Their Abilities? A Metasynthesis," *Perspectives on Psychological Science* 9, no. 2 (2014): 111–25.

12. S. P. Perry, M. C. Murphy, and J. F. Dovidio, "Modern Prejudice: Subtle, but Unconscious? The Role of Bias Awareness in Whites' Perceptions of Personal and Others' Biases," *Journal of Experimental Social Psychology* 61 (2015): 64–78.

13. P. Harvey, K. Madison, M. Martinko, T. R. Crook, and T. A. Crook, "Attribution Theory in the Organizational Sciences: The Road Traveled and the Path Ahead," *Academy of Management Perspectives* 28, no. 2 (2014): 128–46; M. J. Martinko, P. Harvey, and M. T. Dasborough, "Attribution Theory in the Organizational Sciences: A Case of Unrealized Potential," *Journal of Organizational Behavior* 32, no. 1 (2011): 144–49.

14. N. Lipkin, "How to Work With Someone You Don't Like," *Forbes,* January 30, 2019, https://www.forbes.com/sites/nicolelipkin/2019/01/30/how-to-work-with-someone-you-dont-like/#425a11105fe4 S. H. Lee and C. M. Barnes, "An Attributional Model of Workplace Gossip," *Journal of Applied Psychology* (in press).

15. J. Y. Kim, T. H. Campbell, S. Shepherd, and A. C. Kay, "Understanding Contemporary Forms of Exploitation: Attributions of Passion Serve to Legitimize the Poor Treatment of Workers," *Journal of Personality and Social Psychology* 118, no. 1 (2020): 121–48.

16. H. H. Kelley, "Attribution Theory in Social Psychology," in D. Levine (ed.), *Nebraska Symposium on Motivation,* Vol. 15 (Lincoln: University of Nebraska, 1967): 129–238; K. Sanders and H. Yang, "The HRM Process Approach: The Influence of Employees' Attribution to Explain the HRM-Performance Relationship," *Human Resource Management* 55, no. 2 (2016): 201–17.

17. M. B. Eberly, E. C. Holley, M. D. Johnson, and T. R. Mitchell, "Beyond Internal and External: A Dyadic Theory of Relational Attributions," *Academy of Management Review* 36, no. 4 (2011): 731–53; M. B. Eberly, E. C. Holley, M. D. Johnson, and T. R. Mitchell, "It's Not Me, It's Not You, It's *Us!* An Empirical Examination of Relational

Attributions," *Journal of Applied Psychology* 102, no. 5 (2017): 711–31; J. Carson, "External Relational Attributions: Attributing Cause to Others' Relationships," *Journal of Organizational Behavior* 40 (2019): 541–53.

18. Kelley, "Attribution Theory in Social Psychology."

19. V. Strauss, "Five Stereotypes About Poor Families and Education," *The Washington Post*, October 28, 2013, https://www.washingtonpost.com/news/answer-sheet/wp/2013/10/28/five-stereotypes-about-poor-families-and-education/?noredirect=on&utm_term=.aed93334f2f8; S. Watts, "Our Brains Trick Us Into Trusting Rich People," *Forbes*, February 14, 2019, https://www.forbes.com/sites/sarahwatts/2019/02/14/our-brains-trick-us-into-trusting-rich-people-heres-how/#6ff334631e7c

20. See, for instance, M. Goerke, J. Moller, S. Schulz-Hardt, U. Napiersky, and D. Frey, "'It's Not My Fault—But Only I Can Change It': Counterfactual and Prefactual Thoughts of Managers," *Journal of Applied Psychology* 89, no. 2 (2004): 279–92; E. G. Hepper, R. H. Gramzow, and C. Sedikides, "Individual Differences in Self-Enhancement and Self-Protection Strategies: An Integrative Analysis," *Journal of Personality* 78, no. 2 (2010): 781–814.

21. J. W. Ridge and A. Ingram, "Modesty in Top Management Team: Investor Reaction and Performance Implications," *Journal of Management* 43, no. 4 (2017): 1283–306; J-Y. Mao, J. T-J. Chiang, L. Chen, Y. Wu., and J. Wang, "Feeling Safe? A Conservation of Resources Perspective Examining the Interactive Effect of Leader Competence and Leader Self-Serving Behaviour on Team Performance," *Journal of Occupational and Organizational Psychology* 92 (2019): 52–73.

22. See, for instance, A. H. Mezulis, L. Y. Abramson, J. S. Hyde, and B. L. Hankin, "Is There a Universal Positivity Bias in Attributions? A Meta-Analytic Review of Individual, Developmental, and Cultural Differences in the Self-Serving Attributional Bias," *Psychological Bulletin* 130, no. 5 (2004): 711–47; C. F. Falk, S. J. Heine, M. Yuki, and K. Takemura, "Why Do Westerners Self-Enhance More Than East Asians?," *European Journal of Personality* 23, no. 3 (2009): 183–203; F. F. T. Chiang and T. A. Birtch, "Examining the Perceived Causes of Successful Employee Performance: An East–West Comparison," *International Journal of Human Resource Management* 18, no. 2 (2007): 232–48; M. Feinberg, R. Fang, S. Liu, and K. Peng, "A World of Blame to Go Around: Cross-Cultural Determinants of Responsibility and Punishment Judgments," *Personality and Social Psychology Bulletin* 45, no. 4 (2019): 634–51.

23. R. Friedman, W. Liu, C. C. Chen, and S.-C. S. Chi, "Causal Attribution for Interfirm Contract Violation: A Comparative Study of Chinese and American Commercial Arbitrators," *Journal of Applied Psychology* 92, no. 3 (2007): 856–64.

24. J. Nguyen, "Meet the Startup That's Pulling Trackable Data From Your Company's Culture," *Forbes*, February 15, 2017, https://www.forbes.com/sites/nguyenjames/2017/02/15/meet-the-startup-thats-pulling-trackable-data-from-your-companys-culture/#5f9daa1a50d8

25. J. M. Beyer, P. Chattopadhyay, E. George, W. H. Glick, D. Ogilvie, and D. Pugliese, "The Selective Perception of Managers Revisited," *Academy of Management Journal* 40, no. 3 (1997): 716–37.

26. See J. P. Forgas and S. M. Laham, "Halo Effects," in R. F. Pohl (ed.), *Cognitive Illusions: Intriguing Phenomena in Thinking, Judgment and Memory*, 2nd ed. (New York: Routledge, 2017): 276–90; P. Rosenzweig, *The Halo Effect* (New York: The Free Press, 2007).

27. P. Agarwal, "Here Is How Bias Can Affect Recruitment in Your Organization," *Forbes*, October 19, 2018, https://www.forbes.com/sites/pragyaagarwaleurope/2018/10/19/how-can-bias-during-interviews-affect-recruitment-in-your-organisation/#506e25921951

28. See, for example, D. Lubbe and A. Nitsche, "Reducing Assimilation and Contrast Effects on Selection Interview Ratings Using Behavior-ally Anchored Rating Scales," *International Journal of Selection and Assessment* 27 (2019): 43–53.

29. J. K. Clark, K. C. Thiem, J. Barden, J. O'Rourke Stuart, and A. T. Evans, "Stereotype Validation: The Effects of Activating Negative Stereotypes after Intellectual Performance," *Journal of Personality and Social Psychology* 108, no. 4 (2015): 531–52.

30. K. L. Milkman, M. Akinola, and D. Chugh, "What Happens Before? A Field Experiment Exploring how pay and Representation Differentially Shape Bias on the Pathway Into Organizations," *Journal of Applied Psychology* 100, no. 6 (2015): 1678–712.

31. A. Cook and C. Glass, "Above the Glass Ceiling: When Are Women and Racial/Ethnic Minorities Promoted to CEO?" *Strategic Management Journal* 35, no. 7 (2014): 1080–89.

32. P. Chakraborty, "How Artificial Intelligence May Eliminate Biases from HR Processes," *Association for Talent Development* [blog], June 28, 2017, https://www.td.org/insights/how-artificial-intelligence-may-eliminate-biases-from-hr-processes

33. N. R. Kuncel, D. M. Klieger, B. S. Connelly, and D. S. Ones, "Mechanical Versus Clinical Data Combination in Selection and Admissions Decisions: A Meta-Analysis," *Journal of Applied Psychology* 98, no. 6 (2013): 1060–72.

34. P. E. Meehl, "Causes and Effects of My Disturbing Little Book," *Journal of Personality Assessment* 50 (1986): 370–75; K. P. Nolan, N. T. Carter, and D. K. Dalal, "Threat of Technological Unemployment: Are Hiring Managers Discounted for Using Standardized Employee Selection Practices," *Personnel Assessment and Decisions* 2, no. 1 (2016): 30–47.

35. B. Fischhoff and S. B. Broomell, "Judgment and Decision Making," *Annual Review of Psychology* 71 (2020): 331–55.

36. D. Proudfoot, A. C. Kay, and H. Mann, "Motivated Employee Blindness: The Impact of Labor Market Instability on Judgment of Organizational Inefficiencies," *Organizational Behavior and Human Decision Processes* 130 (2015): 108–22.

37. See, for example, P. L. Curseu and S. G. L. Schruijer, "Decision Styles and Rationality: An Analysis of the Predictive Validity of the General Decision-Making Style Inventory," *Educational and Psychological Measurement* 72, no. 6 (2012): 1053–62.

38. For a review of the rational decision-making model, see M. Verweij, T. J. Senior, J. F. D. Dominguez, and R. Turner, "Emotion, Rationality, and Decision-Making: How to Link Affective and Social Neuroscience with Social Theory," *Frontiers in Neuroscience* 9, no. 332 (2015).

39. J. G. March, *A Primer on Decision Making* (New York: The Free Press, 2009); D. Hardman and C. Harries, "How Rational Are We?" *The Psychologist* 15, no. 2 (2002): 76–79.

40. J. E. Russo, K. A. Carlson, and M. G. Meloy, "Choosing an Inferior Alternative," *Psychological Science* 17, no. 10 (2006): 899–904.

41. D. Chugh and M. H. Bazerman; "Bounded Awareness: What You Fail to See Can Hurt You," *Mind & Society* 6 (2007): 1–18; N. Halevy and E. Y. Chou, "How Decisions Happen: Focal Points and Blind Spots in Interdependent Decision Making," *Journal of Personality and Social Psychology* 106, no. 3 (2014): 398–417; D. Kahneman, "Maps of Bounded Rationality: Psychology for Behavioral Economics," *The American Economic Review* 93, no. 5 (2003): 1449–75.

42. G. Gigerenzer, "Why Heuristics Work," *Perspectives on Psychological Science* 3, no. 1 (2008): 20–29; A. K. Shah and D. M. Oppenheimer, "Heuristics Made Easy: An Effort-Reduction Framework," *Psychological Bulletin* 134, no. 2 (2008): 207–22.

43. M. C. Kern and D. Chugh, "Bounded Ethicality: The Perils of Loss Framing," *Psychological Science* 20, no. 3 (2009): 378–84.

44. R. Folger, D. B. Ganegoda, D. B. Rice, R. Taylor, and D. X. H. Wo, "Bounded Autonomy and Behavioral Ethics: Deonance and Reactance as Competing Motives," *Human Relations* 66, no. 7 (2013): 905–24; R. Folger and D. R. Glerum, "Justice and Deonance: 'You Ought to be

Fair,'" in M. Ambrose and R. Cropanzano (eds.), *The Oxford Hand-book of Justice in the Workplace* (New York: Oxford, 2015): 331–50.

45. T. Zhang, P. O. Fletcher, F. Gino, and M. H. Bazerman, "Reducing Bounded Ethicality: How to Help Individuals Notice and Avoid Uneth-ical Behavior," *Organizational Dynamics* 44 (2015): 310–17.

46. See A. W. Kruglanski and G. Gigerenzer, "Intuitive and Deliberate Judgments Are Based on Common Principles," *Psychological Review* 118, no. 1 (2011): 97–109.

47. E. Dane and M. G. Pratt, "Exploring Intuition and Its Role in Managerial Decision Making," *Academy of Management Review* 32, no. 1 (2007): 33–54; J. A. Hicks, D. C. Cicero, J. Trent, C. M. Burton, and L. A. King, "Positive Affect, Intuition, and Feelings of Meaning," *Journal of Person-ality and Social Psychology* 98, no. 6 (2010): 967–79.

48. K. Woolley and J. L. Risen, "Closing Your Eyes to Follow Your Heart: Avoiding Information to Protect a Strong Intuitive Preference," *Jour-nal of Personality and Social Psychology* 114, no. 2 (2018): 230–45.

49. W. J. Phillips, J. M. Fletcher, A. D. G. Marks, and D. W. Hine, "Think-ing Styles and Decision Making: A Meta-Analysis," *Psychological Bulletin* 142, no. 3 (2016): 260–90; Y. Wang, S. Highhouse, C. J. Lake, N. L. Petersen, and T. B. Rada, "Meta-Analytic Investigations of the Relation between Intuition and Analysis," *Journal of Behavioral Deci-sion Making* 30 (2017): 15–25.

50. C. Akinci and E. Sadler-Smith, "Intuition in Management Research: A Historical Review," *International Journal of Management Reviews* 14, no. 1 (2012): 104–22.

51. S. P. Robbins, *Decide & Conquer: Making Winning Decisions and Taking Control of Your Life* (Upper Saddle River, NJ: Financial Times/Prentice Hall, 2004), 13.

52. S. Ludwig and J. Nafziger, "Beliefs about Overconfidence," *Theory and Decision* 70, no. 4 (2011): 475–500.

53. E. E. Kausel, S. S. Culbertson, and H. P. Madrid, "Overconfidence in Personnel Selection: When and Why Unstructured Interview Informa-tion Can Hurt Hiring Decisions," *Organizational Behavior and Human Decision Processes* 137 (2016): 27–44.

54. A. Buijsrogge, E. Erous, and W. Duyck, "Often Biased but Rarely in Doubt: How Initial Reactions to Stigmatized Applicants Affect Inter-viewer Confidence," *Human Performance* 29, no. 4 (2016): 275–90.

55. R. Ronay, J. K. Oostrom, N. Lehmann-Willenbrock, S. Mayoral, and H. Rusch, "Playing the Trump Card: Why We Select Overconfident Leaders and Why It Matters," *The Leadership Quarterly* (in press).

56. P. Belmi, M. A. Neale, D. Reiff, and R. Ulfe, "The Social Advantage of Miscalibrated Individuals: The Relationship Between Social Class and Overconfidence and Its Implications for Class-Based Inequality," *Jour-nal of Personality and Social Psychology* 118, no. 2 (2020): 254–282; I. Vitanova, "Nurturing Overconfidence: The Relationship Between Leader Power, Overconfidence, and Firm Performance," *The Leader-ship Quarterly* (in press).

57. E. R. Tenney, N. L. Meikle, D. Hunsaker, D. A. Moore, and C. Ander-son, "Is Overconfidence a Social Liability? The Effect of Verbal Ver-sus Nonverbal Expressions of Confidence," *Journal of Personality and Social Psychology* 116, no. 3 (2019): 396–415.

58. See, for instance, J. P. Simmons, R. A. LeBoeuf, and L. D. Nelson, "The Effect of Accuracy Motivation on Anchoring and Adjustment: Do People Adjust from Their Provided Anchors?" *Journal of Personality and Social Psychology* 99, no. 6 (2010): 917–32.

59. C. Janiszewski and D. Uy, "Precision of the Anchor Influences the Amount of Adjustment," *Psychological Science* 19, no. 2 (2008): 121–27.

60. See, for example, P. Frost, B. Casey, K. Griffin, L. Raymundo, C. Far-rell, and R. Carrigan, "The Influence of Confirmation Bias on Memory and Source Monitoring," *Journal of General Psychology* 142, no. 4 (2015): 238–52; W. Hart, D. Albarracín, A. H. Eagly, I. Brechan, M. Lindberg, and L. Merrill, "Feeling Validated versus Being Correct: A Meta-Analysis of Selective Exposure to Information," *Psychological Bulletin* 135, no. 4 (2009): 555–88.

61. K. A. Costabile and S. Madon, "Downstream Effects of Dispositional Influences on Confirmation Biases," *Personality and Social Psychol-ogy Bulletin* 45, no. 4 (2019): 557–70.

62. M. Marquit, "Don't Let Confirmation Bias Derail Your Startup Plans," *Due* [Blog], October 1, 2018, https://due.com/blog/confirmation-bias-startup-plans/

63. T. Pachur, R. Hertwig, and F. Steinmann, "How Do People Judge Risks: Availability Heuristic, Affect Heuristic, or Both?" *Journal of Experimental Psychology: Applied* 18, no. 3 (2012): 314–30.

64. G. Morgenson, "Debt Watchdogs: Tamed or Caught Napping?" *The New York Times*, December 7, 2009, 1, 32.

65. S. Davidai and T. Gilovich, "The Headwinds/Tailwinds Asymmetry: An Availability Bias in Assessments of Barriers and Blessings," *Jour-nal of Personality and Social Psychology* 111, no. 6 (2016): 835–51.

66. B. M. Staw, "The Escalation of Commitment to a Course of Action," *Academy of Management Review* (October 1981): 577–87.

67. D. J. Sleesman, "Pushing Through the Tension While Stuck in the Mud: Paradox Mindset and Escalation of Commitment," *Organiza-tional Behavior and Human Decision Processes* 155 (2019): 83–96.

68. K. F. E. Wong and J. Y. Y. Kwong, "The Role of Anticipated Regret in Escalation of Commitment," *Journal of Applied Psychology* 92, no. 2 (2007): 545–54.

69. D. J. Sleesman, D. E. Conlon, G. McNamara, and J. E. Miles, "Clean-ing Up the Big Muddy: A Meta-Analytic Review of the Determinants of Escalation of Commitment," *Academy of Management Journal* 55, no. 3 (2012): 541–62.

70. H. Drummond, "Escalation of Commitment: When to Stay the Course?" *Academy of Management Perspectives* 28, no. 4 (2014): 430–46.

71. See, for instance, U. Hahn and P. A. Warren, "Perceptions of Random-ness: Why Three Heads Are Better Than One," *Psychological Review* 116, no. 2 (2009): 454–61.

72. J. Adams, "Tiger Woods Credits Mother for Wearing Red on Sunday," *Heavy* [blog], September 23, 2018, https://heavy.com/sports/2018/09/why-tiger-woods-red-shirt-mother/

73. See, for example, D. J. Keys and B. Schwartz, "Leaky Rationality: How Research on Behavioral Decision Making Challenges Norma-tive Standards of Rationality," *Psychological Science* 2, no. 2 (2007): 162–80; U. Simonsohn, "Direct Risk Aversion: Evidence from Risky Prospects Valued below Their Worst Outcome," *Psychological Science* 20, no. 6 (2009): 686–92.

74. A. Kühberger, "The Influence of Framing on Risky Decisions: A Meta-Analysis," *Organizational Behavior and Human Decision Processes* 75, no. 1 (1998): 23–55; A. Kühberger, M. Schulte-Mecklenbeck, and J. Perner, "The Effects of Framing, Reflection, Probability, and Payoff on Risk Preference in Choice Tasks," *Organizational Behavior and Human Decision Processes* 78, no. 3 (1999): 204–31.

75. A. Chakraborty, S. Sheikh, and N. Subramanian, "Termination Risk and Managerial Risk Taking," *Journal of Corporate Finance* 13, no. 1 (2007): 170–88.

76. D. G. Allen, K. P. Weeks, and K. R. Moffitt, "Turnover Intentions and Voluntary Turnover: The Moderating Roles of Self-Monitoring, Locus of Control, Proactive Personality, and Risk Aversion," *Journal of Applied Psychology* 90, no. 5 (2005): 980–90; C. Vandenberghe, A. Panaccio, and A. K. B. Ayed, "Continuance Commitment and Turnover: Examining the Moderating Role of Negative Affectivity and Risk Aversion," *Journal of Occupational and Organizational Psychology* 84 (2011): 403–24.

77. R. L. Guilbault, F. B. Bryant, J. H. Brockway, and E. J. Posavac, "A Meta-Analysis of Research on Hindsight Bias," *Basic and Applied Social Psychology* 26, nos. 2–3 (2004): 103–17.

78. O. Shani, "Why AI Transformation is Digital Transformation, Fully Realized," *Forbes,* February 11, 2019, https://www.forbes.com/sites/forbestechcouncil/2019/02/11/why-ai-transformation-is-digital-transformation-fully-realized/#1be6caf678fd

79. Ibid.

80. E. Dash and J. Creswell, "Citigroup Pays for a Rush to Risk," *The New York Times,* November 20, 2008, 1, 28; S. Pulliam, S. Ng, and R. Smith, "Merrill Upped Ante as Boom in Mortgage Bonds Fizzled," *The Wall Street Journal,* April 16, 2008, A1, A14.

81. M. Gladwell, "Connecting the Dots," *The New Yorker,* March 10, 2003.

82. S. J. Ward and L. A. King, "Individual Differences in Reliance on Intuition Predict Harsher Moral Judgments," *Journal of Personality and Social Psychology* 114, no. 5 (2018): 825–49; J. A. Yip, D. H. Stein, S. Côté, and D. R. Carney, "Follow Your Gut? Emotional Intelligence Moderates the Association Between Physiologically Measured Somatic Markers and Risk-Taking," *Emotion* 20, no. 3 (2020): 426–472.

83. W. Hart, D. Albarracín, A. H. Eagly, I. Brechan, M. J. Lindberg, and L. Merrill, "Feeling Validated Versus Being Correct: A Meta-Analysis of Selective Exposure to Information," *Psychological Bulletin* 135, no. 4 (2009): 555–88.

84. M. P. Grosz, T. Lösch, and M. D. Back, "The Narcissism-Overclaiming Link Revisited," *Journal of Research in Personality* 70 (2017): 134–38; M. Tamborski, R. P. Brown, and K. Chowning, "Self-Serving Bias or Simply Serving the Self? Evidence for a Dimensional Approach to Narcissism," *Personality and Individual Differences* 52, no. 8 (2012): 942–46.

85. H. Moon, J. R. Hollenbeck, S. E. Humphrey, and B. Maue, "The Tripartite Model of Neuroticism and the Suppression of Depression and Anxiety within an Escalation of Commitment Dilemma," *Journal of Personality* 71, no. 3 (2003): 347–68.

86. J. Musch, "Personality Differences in Hindsight Bias," *Memory* 11, nos. 4–5 (2003): 473–89.

87. T. Huston, "Are Women Better Decision Makers?" *The New York Times,* October 19, 2014, 9.

88. D. Cumming, T. Y. Leung, and O. Rui, "Gender Diversity and Securities Fraud," *Academy of Management Journal* 58, no. 5 (2015): 1572–93.

89. S. Wally and J. R. Baum, "Personal and Structural Determinants of Pace of Strategic Decision Making," *Academy of Management Journal,* 37, no. 4 (1994): 932–56.

90. K. E. Stanovich and R. F. West, "On the Relative Independence of Thinking Biases and Cognitive Ability," *Journal of Personality and Social Psychology* 94, no. 4 (2008): 672–95.

91. N. J. Adler, *International Dimensions of Organizational Behavior*, 4th ed. (Cincinnati, OH: South-Western Publishing, 2002), 182–89; and J. F. Yates and S. de Oliveira, "Culture and Decision Making," *Organizational Behavior and Human Decision Processes* 136 (2016): 106–18.

92. Phillips et al., "Thinking Styles and Decision Making."

93. A. Lai, "For Businesses, Decision-Making During the COVID-19 Crisis Requires a Bias Toward People, Not Profit," *Forbes* (March 19, 2020), https://www.forbes.com/sites/forrester/2020/03/19/decision-making-during-the-covid-19-crisis-requires-a-bias-toward-people-not-profit/#3b3d5e454ddc; B. Lincoln and R. Santorum, "Doctors, Nurses Must Make Hard Decisions in Pandemic. Let's Protect Them from Lawsuits," *USA Today* (April 22, 2020), https://www.usatoday.com/story/opinion/2020/04/22/pandemic-congress-should-protect-doctors-others-lawsuits-column/2995082001/

94. Lai, "For Businesses, Decision-Making During the COVID-19 Crisis Requires a Bias Toward People, Not Profit."

95. P. M. Vaaler and G. McNamara, "Crisis and Competition in Expert Organizational Decision Making: Credit-Rating Agencies and Their Response to Turbulence in Emerging Economies," *Organization Science* 15, no. 6 (2004): 687–703.

96. L. Sayegh, W. P. Anthony, and P. L. Perrewé, "Managerial Decision-Making Under Crisis: The Role of Emotion in an Intuitive Decision Process," *Human Resource Management Review* 14 (2004): 179–99.

97. Santorum, "Doctors, Nurses Must Make Hard Decisions in Pandemic."

98. S. Harvey and V. Y. Haines III, "Employer Treatment of Employees During a Community Crisis: The Role of Procedural and Distributive Justice," *Journal of Business and Psychology* 20, no. 1 (2005): 53–68.

99. Lai, "For Businesses, Decision-Making During the COVID-19 Crisis Requires a Bias Toward People, Not Profit."

100. K. V. Kortenkamp and C. F. Moore, "Ethics under Uncertainty: The Morality and Appropriateness of Utilitarianism When Outcomes Are Uncertain," *American Journal of Psychology* 127, no. 3 (2014): 367–82.

101. See, for example, I. Patil, M. M. Zucchelli, W. Kool, S. Campbell, F. Fornasier, M. Calò, G. Silani, M. Cikara, and F. Cushman, "Reasoning Supports Utilitarian Resolutions to Moral Dilemmas Across Diverse Measures," *Journal of Personality and Social Psychology* (in press).

102. A. Lukits, "Hello and Bonjour to Moral Dilemmas," *The Wall Street Journal,* May 13, 2014, D4.

103. See, for example, Folger and Glerum, "Justice and Deonance."

104. J. Hollings, "Let the Story Go: The Role of Emotion in the Decision-Making Process of the Reluctant, Vulnerable Witness or Whistle-Blower," *Journal of Business Ethics* 114, no. 3 (2013): 501–12.

105. D. E. Rupp, P. M. Wright, S. Aryee, and Y. Luo, "Organizational Justice, Behavioral Ethics, and Corporate Social Responsibility: Finally the Three Shall Merge," *Management and Organization Review* 11, no. 1 (2015): 15–24.

106. R. Folger, "Fairness as Deonance," in S. W. Gilliland, D. D. Steiner, and D. P. Skarlicki (eds.), Research in Social Issues in Management: Theoretical and Cultural Per-spectives on Organizational Justice, Vol. 1 (Charlotte, NC: Information Age, 2001): 3–31; R. Folger, "Deonanace: Behavioral Ethics and Moral Obligation," in D. DeCremer and A. E. Tenbrunsel (eds.), Series in Organization and Management: Behavioral Business Ethics; Shaping an Emerging Field (New York: Routledge, 2011): 123–42; and Folger and Glerum, "Justice and Deonance."

107. M. Hennig and M. Hütter, "Revisiting the Divide Between Deontology and Utilitarianism in Moral Dilemma Judgment: A Multinomial Modeling Approach," *Journal of Personality and Social Psychology* 118, no. 1 (2020): 22–56; M-H. Li and L-L. Rao, "Do People Believe That They Are More Deontological Than Others?" *Personality and Social Psychology Bulletin* 45, no. 8 (2019): 1308–1320; A. Mata, "Social Metacognition in Moral Judgment: Decisional Conflict Promotes Perspective Taking," *Journal of Personality and Social Psychology* (in press).

108. H. Aguinis and A. Glavas, "What We Know and Don't Know About Corporate Social Responsibility: A Review and Research Agenda," *Journal of Management* 38, no. 4 (2012): 932–68.

109. J. B. Cullen, K. P. Parboteeah, and M. Hoegl, "Cross-National Differences in Managers' Willingness to Justify Ethically Suspect Behaviors: A Test of Institutional Anomie Theory," *Academy of Management Journal* 47, no. 3 (2004): 411–21.

110. P. Gerlach, K. Teodorescu, and R. Hertwig, "The Truth About Lies: A Meta-Analysis on Dishonest Behavior," *Psychological Bulletin* 145, no. 1 (2019): 1–44.

111. A. Vrij, M. Hartwig, and P. A. Granhag, "Reading Lies: Nonverbal Communication and Deception," *Annual Review of Psychology* 70 (2019): 295–317.

112. N. Klein and H. Zhou, "Their Pants Aren't on Fire," *The New York Times,* March 25, 2014, D3.

113. Ibid.

114. A. C. Gunia and E. E. Levine, "Deception as Competence: The Effect of Occupational Stereotypes on the Perception and Proliferation of

Deception," *Organizational and Human Decision Processes* 152 (2019): 122–37; J. J. Lee, N. Llewellyn, and A. Whittle, "Lies, Defeasibility and Morality-in-Action: The Interactional Architecture of False Claims in Sales, Telemarketing and Debt Collection Work," *Human Relations* 72, no. 4 (2019): 834–58; M. Ong, B. Parmar, and E. Amit, "Lay Theories of Effortful Honesty: Does the Honesty-Effort Association Justify Making a Dishonest Decision?" *Journal of Applied Psychology* 104, no. 5 (2019): 659–77.

115. S. D. Levitt and S. J. Dubner, "Traponomics," *The Wall Street Journal,* May 10–11, 2014, C1, C2.

116. N. Anderson, K. Potocnik, and J. Zhou, "Innovation and Creativity in Organizations: A State-of-the-Science Review, Prospective Commentary, and Guiding Framework," *Journal of Management* 40, no. 5 (2014): 1297–333.

117. "Is Your Art Killing You?" Investorideas.com, May 13, 2013, www.investorideas.com/news/2013/renewable-energy/05134.asp

118. M. M. Gielnik, A.-C. Kramer, B. Kappel, and M. Frese, "Antecedents of Business Opportunity Identification and Innovation: Investigating the Interplay of Information Processing and Information Acquisition," *Applied Psychology: An International Review* 63, no. 2 (2014): 344–81.

119. G. Anderson, "Three Tips to Foster Creativity at Your Startup," *Arctic-Startup,* May 8, 2013, from http://www .arcticstartup.com/

120. L. Paine Hagtvedt, K. Dossinger, S. H. Harrison, and L. Huang, "Curiosity Made the Cat More Creative: Specific Curiosity as a Driver of Creativity," *Organizational Behavior and Human Decision Processes* 150 (2019): 1–13.

121. M. Karwowski et al., "Is Creativity Without Intelligence Possible? A Necessary Condition Analysis," *Intelligence* 57 (2016): 105–17; K. H. Kim, "Meta-Analyses of the Relationship of Creative Achievement to Both IQ and Divergent Thinking Test Scores," *The Journal of Creative Behavior* 42, no. 2 (2008): 106–30.

122. C. Kandler, R. Riemann, A. Angleitner, F. M. Spinath, P. Borkenau, L. Penke, "The Nature of Creativity: The Roles of Genetic Factors, Personality Traits, Cognitive Abilities, and Environmental Sources," *Journal of Personality and Social Psychology* 111, no. 2 (2016): 230–49.

123. C. K. W. De Dreu, B. A. Nijstad, M. Baas, I. Wolsink, and M. Roskes, "Working Memory Benefits Creative Insight, Musical Improvisation, and Original Ideation through Maintained Task-Focused Attention," *Personality and Social Psychology Bulletin* 38, no. 5 (2012): 656–69.

124. M. Benedek, E. Jauk, M. Sommer, M. Arendasy, and A. C. Neubauer, "Intelligence, Creativity, and Cognitive Control: The Common and Differential Involvement of Executive Functions in Intelligence and Creativity," *Intelligence* 46 (2014): 73–83; C.-H. Wu, S. K. Parker, and J. P. J. de Jong, "Need for Cognition as an Antecedent of Individual Innovation Behavior," *Journal of Management* 40, no. 6 (2014): 1511–34; B. Forthmann, D. Jendryczko, J. Scharfen, R. Kleinkorres, M. Benedek, and H. Holling, "Creative Ideation, Broad Retrieval Ability, and Processing Speed: A Confirmatory Study of Nested Cognitive Abilities," *Intelligence* 75 (2019): 59–72.

125. M. M. Hammond, N. L. Neff, J. L. Farr, A. R. Schwall, and X. Zhao, "Predictors of Individual-Level Innovation at Work: A Meta-analysis," *Psychology of Aesthetics, Creativity, and the Arts* 5, no. 1 (2011): 90–105; M. Zare and C. Flinchbaugh, "Voice, Creativity, and Big Five Personality Traits: A Meta-Analysis," *Human Performance* 32, no. 1 (2019): 30–51.

126. Y. Gong, S. Cheung, M. Wang, and J. Huang, "Unfolding the Proactive Processes for Creativity: Integration of the Employee Proactivity, Information Exchange, and Psychological Safety Perspectives," *Journal of Management* 38, no. 5 (2012): 1611–33.

127. A. Rego, F. Sousa, C. Marques, and M. P. E. Cunha, "Retail Employees' Self-Efficacy and Hope Predicting Their Positive Affect and Creativity," *European Journal of Work and Organizational Psychology* 21, no. 6 (2012): 923–45.

128. M. L. Meyer, H. E. Hershfield, A. G. Waytz, J. N. Mildner, and D. I. Tamir, "Creative Expertise Is Associated with Transcending the Here and Now," *Journal of Personality and Social Psychology* 116, no. 4 (2019): 483–94.

129. C. Wang, S. Rodan, M. Fruin, and X. Xu, "Knowledge Networks, Collaboration Networks, and Exploratory Innovation," *Academy of Management Journal* 57, no. 2 (2014): 484–514.

130. F. Gino and S. S. Wiltermuth, "Evil Genius? Dishonesty Can Lead to Greater Creativity," *Psychological Science* 25, no. 4 (2014): 973–81.

131. S. Keem, C. E. Shalley, E. Kim, and I. Jeong, "Are Creative Individuals Bad Apples? A Dual Pathway Model of Unethical Behavior," *Journal of Applied Psychology* 103, no. 4 (2018): 416–31; L. C. Vincent and M. Kouchaki, "Creative, Rare, Entitled, and Dishonest: How Commonality of Creativity in One's Group Decreases an Individual's Entitlement and Dishonesty," *Academy of Management Journal* 49, no. 4 (2016): 1451–73.

132. D. van Knippenberg and G. Hirst, "A Motivational Lens Model of Person x Situation Interactions in Employee Creativity," *Journal of Applied Psychology* (in press)

133. D. Liu, K. Jiang, C. E. Shalley, S. Keem, and J. Zhou, "Motivational Mechanisms of Employee Creativity: A Meta-Analytic Examination and Theoretical Extension of the Creativity Literature," *Organizational Behavior and Human Decision Processes,* 137 (2016): 236–63.

134. M. Abdur Rahman Malik, J. Nam Choi, and A. Nazir Butt, "Distinct Effects of Intrinsic Motivation and Extrinsic Rewards on Radical and Incremental Creativity: The Moderating Role of Goal Orientations," *Journal of Organizational Behavior* 40 (2019): 1013–26.

135. A.Newman, H. Round, S. Wang, and M. Mount, "Innovation Climate: A Systematic Review of the Literature and Agenda for Future Research," *Journal of Occupational and Organizational Psychology* 92 (2020): 73–109.

136. A. Somech and A. Drach-Zahavy, "Translating Team Creativity to Innovation Implementation: The Role of Team Composition and Climate for Innovation," *Journal of Management* 39, no. 3 (2013): 684–708.

137. L. Sun, Z. Zhang, J. Qi, and Z. X. Chen, "Empowerment and Creativity: A Cross-Level Investigation," *Leadership Quarterly* 23, no. 1 (2012): 55–65.

138. M. Cerne, C. G. L. Nerstad, A. Dysvik, and M. Skerlavaj, "What Goes Around Comes Around: Knowledge Hiding, Perceived Motivational Climate, and Creativity," *Academy of Management Journal* 57, no. 1 (2014): 172–92.

139. Hammond et al., "Predictors of Individual-Level Innovation at Work."

140. S. Sonnenshein, "How Organizations Foster the Creative Use of Resources," *Academy of Management Journal* 57, no. 3 (2014): 814–48.

141. V. Venkataramani, A. W. Richter, and R. Clarke, "Creative Benefits from Well-Connected Leaders: Leader Social Network Ties as Facilitators of Employee Radical Creativity," *Journal of Applied Psychology* 99, no. 5 (2014): 966–75.

142. J. E. Perry-Smith, "Social Network Ties beyond Nonredundancy: An Experimental Investigation of the Effect of Knowledge Content and Tie Strength on Creativity," *Journal of Applied Psychology* 99, no. 5 (2014): 831–46.

143. T. Montag, C. P. Maertz, and M. Baer, "A Critical Analysis of the Workplace Creativity Criterion Space," *Journal of Management* 38, no. 4 (2012): 1362–86.

144. M. Baer, "Putting Creativity to Work: The Implementation of Creative Ideas in Organizations," *Academy of Management Journal* 55, no. 5 (2012): 1102–19.

CHAPTER 7

1. J. LaRosa, *$9.9 Billion Self-Improvement Market Challenged by Younger and More Demanding Millennials, Changing Technology* [press release], August 2, 2017, https://www.webwire.com/ViewPressRel.asp?aId=211649

2. C. C. Pinder, *Work Motivation in Organizational Behavior,* 2nd ed. (New York, NY: Psychology Press, 2008).

3. A. H. Maslow, "A Theory of Human Motivation," *Psychological Review* 50 (1943), 370–96; R. J. Taormina and J. H. Gao, "Maslow and the Motivation Hierarchy: Measuring Satisfaction of the Needs," *American Journal of Psychology* 126, no. 2 (2013): 155–57.

4. H. S. Guest "Maslow's Hierarchy of Needs—The Sixth Level," *Psychologist* 27, no. 12 (2014): 982–83.

5. Guest, "Maslow's Hierarchy of Needs"; J. A. Krems, D. T. Kenrick, and R. Neel, "Individual Perceptions of Self- Actualization: What Functional Motives Are Linked to Fulfilling One's Full Potential?" *Personality and Social Psychology Bulletin* 43, no. 9 (2017): 1337–52.

6. T. R. Mitchell and D. Daniels, "Motivation," in W. Borman, D. Ilgen, and R. Klimoski (eds.), *Handbook of Psychology: Industrial/Organizational Psychology,* Vol. 12 (New York: Wiley, 2002): 225–54.

7. V. M. Bockman, "The Herzberg Controversy," *Personnel Psychology* 24, no. 2 (1971): 155–89; F. Herzberg, "The Motivation-Hygiene Concept and Problems of Manpower," *Personnel Administrator* 27 (1964): 3–7.

8. N. Bassett-Jones and G. C. Lloyd, "Does Herzberg's Motivation Theory Have Staying Power?," *Journal of Management Development* 24, no. 10 (2005): 929–43.

9. See, for instance, V. S. R. Vijayakumar and U. Saxena, "Herzberg Revisited: Dimensionality and Structural Invariance of Herzberg's Two Factor Model," *Journal of the Indian Academy of Applied Psychology* 41, no. 2 (2015): 291–98; R. Worthley, B. MacNab, R. Brislin, K. Ito, and E. L. Rose, "Workforce Motivation in Japan: An Examination of Gender Differences and Management Perceptions," *The International Journal of Human Resource Management* 20, no. 7 (2009): 1503–20.

10. D. C. McClelland, *Human Motivation* (Cambridge, UK: Cambridge University Press, 1987); D. C. McClelland, J. W. Atkinson, R. A. Clark, and E. L. Lowell, *The Achievement Motive* (New York: Appleton-Century-Crofts, 1953).

11. See, for instance, M. G. Koellner and O. C. Schultheiss, "Meta-Analytic Evidence of Low Convergence between Implicit and Explicit Measures of the Needs for Achievement, Affiliation, and Power," *Frontiers in Psychology* 5, no. 826 (2014): 1–20; T. Bipp and K. van Dam, "Extending Hierarchical Achievement Motivation Models: The Role of Motivational Needs for Achievement Goals and Academic Performance," *Personality and Individual Differences* 64 (2014): 157–62.

12. R. Eisenberger, J. R. Jones, F. Stinglhamber, L. Shanock, and A. T. Randall, "Flow Experiences at Work: For High Need Achievers Alone?" *Journal of Organizational Behavior* 26, no. 7 (2005): 755–75.

13. A. K. Kirk and D. F. Brown, "Latent Constructs of Proximal and Distal Motivation Predicting Performance Under Maximum Test Conditions," *Journal of Applied Psychology* 88, no. 1 (2003): 40–49; R. B. Soyer, J. L. Rovenpor, and R. E. Kopelman, "Narcissism and Achievement Motivation As Related to Three Facets of the Sales Role: Attraction, Satisfaction, and Performance," *Journal of Business and Psychology* 14, no. 2 (1999): 285–304.

14. M. G. Koellner and O. C. Schultheiss, "Meta-Analytic Evidence of Low Convergence between Implicit and Explicit Measures of the Needs for Achievement, Affiliation, and Power."

15. J. S. Chun and J. N. Choi, "Members' Needs, Intragroup Conflict, and Group Performance," *Journal of Applied Psychology* 99, no. 3 (2014): 437–50.

16. J. Hofer, H. Busch, and C. Schneider, "The Effect of Motive-Trait Interaction on Satisfaction of the Implicit Need for Affiliation among German and Cameroonian Adults," *Journal of Personality* 83, no. 2 (2015): 167–78.

17. A. Drescher and O. C. Schultheiss, "Meta-Analytic Evidence for Higher Implicit Affiliation and Intimacy Motivation Scores in Women, Compared to Men," *Journal of Research in Personality* 64 (2016): 1–10.

18. J. T. Austin and J. B. Vancouver, "Goal Constructs in Psychology: Structure, Process, and Content," *Psychological Bulletin* 120 (1996): 338–75.

19. E. L. Deci, A. H. Olafsen, and R. M. Ryan, "Self-Determination Theory in Work Organizations: The State of the Science," *Annual Review of Organizational Psychology and Organizational Behavior* 4 (2017): 19–43; R. Ryan and E. Deci, "Self-Determination Theory and the Facilitation of Intrinsic Motivation, Social Development, and Well-Being," *American Psychologist* 55, no. 1 (2000): 68–78.

20. Ibid.

21. C. P. Cerasoli, J. M. Nicklin, and M. T. Ford, "Intrinsic Motivation and Extrinsic Incentives Jointly Predict Performance: A 40-Year Meta-Analysis," *Psychological Bulletin* 140, no. 4 (2014): 980–1008.

22. J. E. Bono and T. A. Judge, "Self-Concordance at Work: Toward Understanding the Motivational Effects of Transformational Leaders," *Academy of Management Journal* 46, no. 5 (2003): 554–71.

23. K. M. Sheldon, A. J. Elliot, and R. M. Ryan, "Self-Concordance and Subjective Well-Being in Four Cultures," *Journal of Cross-Cultural Psychology* 35, no. 2 (2004): 209–23.

24. P. E. Downes, A. L. Kristof-Brown, T. A. Judge, and T. C. Darnold, "Motivational Mechanisms of Self-Concordance Theory: Goal-Specific Efficacy and Person-Organization Fit," *Journal of Business and Psychology* 32, no. 2 (2017): 197–215.

25. Deci et al., "Self-Determination Theory in Work Organizations."

26. A. Van den Broeck, D. L. Ferris, C.-H. Chang, and C. C. Rosen, "A Review of Self-Determination Theory's Basic Psychological Needs at Work," *Journal of Management* 42, no. 5 (2016): 1195–229.

27. C. P. Cerasoli, J. M. Nicklin, and A. S. Nassrelgrgawi, "Performance, Incentives, and Needs for Autonomy, Competence, and Relatedness: A Meta-Analysis," *Motivation & Emotion* 40 (2016): 781–813.

28. M. E. L. Zeijen, P. Petrou, A. B. Bakker, and B. R. van Gelderen, "Dyadic Support Exchange and Work Engagement: An Episodic Test and Expansion of Self-Determination Theory," *Journal of Occupational and Organizational Psychology* (in press).

29. J. Rupp, "Leadership and Mindfulness Secrets for Fortune 100 Companies with Walmart Leadership Coach, Lucy Duncan," *Thrive Global* [interview], February 20, 2019, https://thriveglobal.com/stories/leadership-and-mindfulness-secrets-for-fortune-100-companies-with-walmart-leadership-coach-lucy-duncan/

30. E. A. Locke and G. P. Latham, "New Directions in Goal-Setting Theory," *Current Directions in Psychological Science* 15, no. 5 (2006): 265–68. B. M. Wilkowski, A. Fetterman, S. Lappi, L. Z. Williamson, E. F. Leki, E. Rivera, and B. P. Meier, "Lexical Derivation of the PINT Taxonomy of Goals: Prominence, Inclusiveness, Negativity Prevention, and Tradition," *Journal of Personality and Social Psychology* (in press).

31. Ibid.

32. C. Gabelica, P. Van den Bossche, M. Segers, and W. Gijselaers, "Feedback, a Powerful Lever in Teams: A Review," *Educational Research Review* 7, no. 2 (2012): 123–44.

33. A. Kleingeld, H. van Mierlo, and L. Arends, "The Effect of Goal Setting on Group Performance: A Meta-Analysis," *Journal of Applied Psychology* 96, no. 6 (2011): 1289–304.

34. T. S. Bateman and B. Bruce, "Masters of the Long Haul: Pursuing Long-Term Work Goals," *Journal of Organizational Behavior* 33, no. 7 (2012): 984–1006.

35. Ibid.

36. H. J. Klein, M. J. Wesson, J. R. Hollenbeck, and B. J. Alge, "Goal Commitment and the Goal-Setting Process: Conceptual Clarification and Empirical Synthesis," *Journal of Applied Psychology* 84, no. 6 (1999): 885–96; H. J. Klein, R. B. Lount, H. M. Park, and B. J. Linford, "When Goals Are Known: The Effects of Audience Relative Status on Goal Commitment and Performance," *Journal of Applied Psychology* 105, no. 4 (2020): 372–389.

37. Kleingeld, van Mierlo, and Arends, "The Effect of Goal Setting on Group Performance"; Locke and Latham, "Building a Practically Useful Theory of Goal Setting and Task Motivation."

38. J. W. Beck, A. A. Scholer, and J. Hughes, "Divergent Effects of Distance Versus Velocity Disturbances on Emotional Experiences During Goal Pursuit," *Journal of Applied Psychology* 102, no. 7 (2017): 1109–23.

39. D. F. Crown, "The Use of Group and Groupcentric Individual Goals for Culturally Heterogeneous and Homogeneous Task Groups: An Assessment of European Work Teams," *Small Group Research* 38, no. 4 (2007): 489–508.

40. C. Sue-Chan and M. Ong, "Goal Assignment and Performance: Assessing the Mediating Roles of Goal Commitment and Self-Efficacy and the Moderating Role of Power Distance," *Organizational Behavior and Human Decision Processes* 89, no. 2 (2002): 1140–61.

41. L. D. Ordóñez, M. E. Schweitzer, A. D. Galinsky, and M. H. Bazerman, "Goals Gone Wild: The Systematic Side Effects of Overprescribing Goal Setting," *Academy of Management Perspectives* 23, no. 1 (2009): 6–16; E. A. Locke and G. P. Latham, "Has Goal Setting Gone Wild, or Have Its Attackers Abandoned Good Scholarship?" *Academy of Management Perspectives* 23, no. 1 (2009): 17–23.

42. B. Harkin et al., "Does Monitoring Goal Progress Promote Goal Attainment? A Meta-Analysis of the Experimental Evidence," *Psychological Bulletin* 142, no. 2 (2016): 198–229; C. McChesney, S. Covey, and J. Huling, *The 4 Disciplines of Execution* (New York: Free Press, 2012).

43. E. T. Higgins, "Promotion and Prevention: Regulatory Focus as a Motivational Principle," *Advances in Experimental Social Psychology* 30 (1998): 1–46; E. T. Higgins and J. F. M. Cornwell, "Securing Foundations and Advancing Frontiers: Prevention and Promotion Effects on Judgment & Decision Making," *Organizational Behavior and Human Decision Processes* 136 (2016): 56–67.

44. K. Lanaj, C. D. Chang, and R. E. Johnson, "Regulatory Focus and Work-Related Outcomes: A Review and Meta-Analysis," *Psychological Bulletin* 138, no. 5 (2012): 998–1034; Y. Zhang, Y. Zhang, T. W. H. Ng, and S. S. K. Lam, "Promotion- and Prevention-Focused Coping: A Meta-Analytic Examination of Regulatory Strategies in the Work Stress Process," *Journal of Applied Psychology* 104, no. 10 (2019): 1296–323.

45. M. Roskes, A. J. Elliot, and C. K. W. De Dreu, "Why Is Avoidance Motivation Problematic, and What Can Be Done about It?" *Current Directions in Psychological Science* 23, no. 2 (2014): 133–38; Zhang et al., "Promotion- and Prevention-Focused Coping."

46. R. E. Johnson, S-H. Lin, R. Kark, D. Van Dijk, D. D. King, E. Esformes, "Consequence of Regulatory fit for Leader-Follower Relationship Quality and Commitment," *Journal of Occupational and Organizational Psychology* 90, no. 3 (2017): 379–406.

47. K. R. Thompson, W. A. Hochwater, and N. J. Mathys, "Stretch Targets: What Makes Them Effective?" *Academy of Management Executive* 11, no. 3 (1997): 48–60.

48. M. Juetten, "Failed Startups: Telltale Games," *Forbes,* December 18, 2018, https://www.forbes.com/sites/maryjuetten/2018/12/18/failed-startups-telltale-games/#6bbd67ba6a84; "KEYGroup Survey Finds Nearly Half of All Employees Have No Set Performance Goals," *IPMA-HR Bulletin,* March 10, 2006, 1; J. Schreier, "Video Games Are Destroying the People Who Make Them," *The New York Times,* October 25, 2017 https://www.nytimes.com/2017/10/25/opinion/work-culture-video-games-crunch.html

49. P. Drucker, *The Practice of Management* (New York: Harper, 1954); H. Levinson, "Management by Whose Objectives?," *Harvard Business Review* 81, no. 1 (2003): 107–16.

50. See, for example, E. Lindberg and T. L. Wilson, "Management by Objectives: The Swedish Experience in Upper Secondary Schools," *Journal of Educational Administration* 49, no. 1 (2011): 62–75; R. Rodgers and J. E. Hunter, "Impact of Management by Objectives on Organizational Productivity," *Journal of Applied Psychology* 76, no. 2 (1991): 322–36; A. C. Spaulding, L. D. Gamm, and J. M. Griffith, "Studer Unplugged: Identifying Underlying Managerial Concepts," *Hospital Topics* 88, no. 1 (2010): 1–9.

51. M. B. Kristiansen, "Management by Objectives and Results in the Nordic Countries: Continuity and Change, Differences and Similarities," *Public Performance and Management Review* 38, no. 3 (2015): 542–69.

52. See, for instance, M. Tanikawa, "Fujitsu Decides to Backtrack on Performance-Based Pay," *The New York Times,* March 22, 2001, W1; W. F. Roth, "Is Management by Objectives Obsolete?" *Global Business and Organizational Excellence* 28, no. 4 (2009): 36–43.

53. D. Welsh, J. Bush, C. Thiel, and J. Bonner, "Reconceptualizing Goal setting's Dark Side: The Ethical Consequences of Learning Versus Outcome Goals," *Organizational Behavior and Human Decision Processes,* 150 (2019): 14–27.

54. V. Lopez-Kidwell, T. J. Grosser, B. R. Dineen, and S. P. Borgatti, "What Matters When: A Multistage Model and Empirical Examination of Job Search Effort," *Academy of Management Journal* 56, no. 6 (2012): 1655–78.

55. M. E. Schweitzer, L. Ordóñez, B. Douma, "Goal setting as a motivator of unethical behavior," *Academy of Management Journal* 47, no. 3 (2004): 422–32; D. T. Welsh and L. D. Ordóñez, "The dark side of consecutive high performance goals: Linking goal setting, depletion, and unethical behavior," *Organizational Behavior and Human Decision Processes* 123, no. 2 (2014): 79–89.

56. A. Bandura, *Social Foundations of Thought and Action: A Social Cognitive Theory* (Englewood Cliffs, NJ: Prentice Hall, 1986); A. Bandura, *Self-Efficacy: The Exercise of Control* (New York: W. H. Freeman, 1997); A. Bandura, "Social Cognitive Theory: An Agentic Perspective," *Annual Review of Psychology* 52 (2001): 1–26.

57. A. Bandura, "Cultivate Self-Efficacy for Personal and Organizational Effectiveness," in *Handbook of Principles of Organizational Behavior* (ed.) E. Locke (Malden, MA: Blackwell, 2004), 120–36; S. D. Brown, R. W. Lent, K. Telander, and S. Tramayne, "Social Cognitive Career Theory, Conscientiousness, and Work Performance: A Meta-Analytic Path Analysis," *Journal of Vocational Behavior* 79, no. 1 (2011): 81–90.

58. M. Salanova, S. Llorens, and W. B. Schaufeli, "Yes I Can, I Feel Good, and I Just Do It! On Gain Cycles and Spirals of Efficacy Beliefs, Affect, and Engagement," *Applied Psychology* 60, no. 2 (2011): 255–85. Compare with J. B. Vancouver, C. M. Thompson, and A. A. Williams, "The Changing Signs in the Relationships Among Self-Efficacy, Personal Goals, and Performance," *Journal of Applied Psychology* 86, no. 4 (2001): 605–20; J. B. Vancouver and J. D. Purl, "A Computational Model of Self-Efficacy's Various Effects on Performance: Moving the Debate Forward," *Journal of Applied Psychology* 102, no. 4 (2017): 599–616.

59. T. A. Judge, C. L. Jackson, J. C. Shaw, B. Scott, and B. L. Rich, "Self-Efficacy and Work-Related Performance: The Integral Role of Individual Differences," *Journal of Applied Psychology* 92, no. 1 (2007): 107–27.

60. Ibid.

61. M. Ben-Ami, J. Hornik, D. Eden, and O. Kaplan, "Boosting Consumers' Self-Efficacy by Repositioning the Self," *European Journal of Marketing* 48, no. 11/12 (2014): 1914–38; L. De Grez and D. Van Lindt, "Students' Gains in Entrepreneurial Self-Efficacy: A Comparison of 'Learning-by-Doing' Versus Lecture-Based Courses," *Proceedings of the 8th European Conference on Innovation and Entrepreneurship* (2013): 198–203; K. S. Hendricks, "Changes in Self-Efficacy Beliefs over Time: Contextual Influences of Gender, Rank-Based Placement, and Social Support in a Competitive Orchestra Environment," *Psychology of Music* 42, no. 3 (2014): 347–65.

62. A. M. Paul, "How to Use the 'Pygmalion' Effect," *Time,* April 1, 2013, http://ideas.time.com/2013/04/01/how-to-use-the-pygmalion-effect/

63. R. Kelly, "What 5 Classic Psychological Experiments Can Teach Workplace Leaders," *Entrepreneur,* October 26, 2016, https://www.entrepreneur.com/article/283082

64. D. Frohman and R. Howard, *Leadership the Hard Way: Why Leadership Can't Be Taught—And How You Can Learn It Anyway* (San Francisco: Wiley, 2008).

65. L. Karakowsky, N. DeGama, and K. McBey, "Facilitating the Pygmalion Effect: The Overlooked Role of Subordinate Perceptions of the Leader," *Journal of Occupational and Organizational Psychology* 85, no. 4 (2012): 579–99; P. Whiteley, T. Sy, and S. K. Johnson, "Leaders' Conceptions of Followers: Implications for Naturally Occurring Pygmalion Effects," *Leadership Quarterly* 23, no. 5 (2012): 822–34.

66. G. Chen, B. Thomas, and J. C. Wallace, "A Multilevel Examination of the Relationships among Training Outcomes, Mediating Regulatory Processes, and Adaptive Performance," *Journal of Applied Psychology* 90, no. 5 (2005): 827–41; A. Gegenfurtner, C. Quesada-Pallares, and M. Knogler, "Digital Simulation-Based Training: A Meta-Analysis," *British Journal of Educational Technology* 45, no. 6 (2014): 1097–114; C. L. Holladay and M. A. Quiñones, "Practice Variability and Transfer of Training: The Role of Self-Efficacy Generality," *Journal of Applied Psychology* 88, no. 6 (2003): 1094–103.

67. L. R. Halper, J. B. Vancouver, and K. A. Bayes, "Self-Efficacy Does Not Appear to Mediate Training's Effect on Performance Based on the Moderation-of-Process Design," *Human Performance* 31, no. 4 (2018): 216–37.

68. E. C. Dierdorff, E. A. Surface, and K. G. Brown, "Frame-of-Reference Training Effectiveness: Effects of Goal Orientation and Self-Efficacy on Affective, Cognitive, Skill-Based, and Transfer Outcomes," *Journal of Applied Psychology* 95, no. 6 (2010): 1181–91; R. Grossman and E. Salas, "The Transfer of Training: What Really Matters," *International Journal of Training and Development* 15, no. 2 (2011): 103–20; D. S. Stanhope, S. B. Pond III, and E. A. Surface, "Core Self-Evaluations and Training Effectiveness: Prediction through Motivational Intervening Mechanisms," *Journal of Applied Psychology* 98, no. 5 (2013): 820–31.

69. M. L. Ambrose and C. T. Kulik, "Old Friends, New Faces: Motivation Research in the 1990s," *Journal of Management* 25, no. 3 (1999): 231–92; B. F. Skinner, *Contingencies of Reinforcement* (New York: Appleton-Century-Crofts, 1969).

70. M. J. Goddard, "Critical Psychiatry, Critical Psychology, and the Behaviorism of B. F. Skinner," *Review of General Psychology* 18, no. 3 (2014): 208–15.

71. Y. Rofcanin, M. Las Heras, M. J. Bosch, G. Wood, and F. Mughal, "A Closer Look at the Positive Crossover Between Supervisors and Subordinates: The Role of Home and Work Engagement," *Human*

Relations 72, no. 11 (2019): 1776–804; J. Wu, R. C. Liden, C. Liao, and S. J. Wayne, "Does Manager Servant Leadership Lead to Follower Serving Behaviors? It Depends on Follower Self-Interest.," *Journal of Applied Psychology* (in press).

72. A. Bandura, *Social Learning Theory* (New York: General Learning, 1971); J. R. Brauer and C. R. Tittle, "Social Learning Theory and Human Reinforcement," *Sociological Spectrum* 32, no. 2 (2012): 157–77.

73. W. Van Eerde and H. Thierry, "Vroom's Expectancy Models and Work-Related Criteria," *Journal of Applied Psychology* 81, no. 5 (1996): 575–86; V. H. Vroom, *Work and Motivation* (New York: Wiley, 1964).

74. R. Kanfer, M. Frese, and R. E. Johnson, "Motivation Related to Work: A Century of Progress," *Journal of Applied Psychology* 102, no. 3 (2017): 338–55; J. C. Naylor, R. D. Pritchard, and D. R. Ilgen, *A Theory of Behavior in Organizations* (New York: Academic, 1980); Van Eerde and Thierry, "Vroom's Expectancy Models and Work-Related Criteria."

75. Vroom refers to these three variables as expectancy, instrumentality, and valence, respectively.

76. J. S. Adams, "Inequity in Social Exchange," in L. Berkowitz (ed.), *Advances in Experimental Social Psychology*, Vol. 2 (New York: Academic, 1965), 267–99.

77. See, for example, T-Y. Kim, J. Wang, T. Chen, Y. Zhu, and R. Sun, "Equal or Equitable Pay? Individual Differences in Pay Fairness Perceptions," *Human Resource Management* 58 (2019): 169–86.

78. T. Kollmann, C. Stöckmann, J. M. Kensbock, and A. Peschl, "What Satisfies Younger Versus Older Employees, and Why? An aging Perspective on Equity Theory to Explain Interactive Effects of Employee Age, Monetary Rewards, and Task Contributions on Job Satisfaction," *Human Resource Management* 59 (2020): 101–15.

79. Ibid.

80. M. C. Bolino and W. H. Turnley, "Old Faces, New Places: Equity Theory in Cross-Cultural Contexts," *Journal of Organizational Behavior* 29, no. 1 (2008): 29–50; R. T. Mowday and K. A. Colwell, "Employee Reactions to Unfair Outcomes in the Workplace: The Contributions of Equity Theory to Understanding Work Motivation," in L. W. Porter, G. A. Bigley, and R. M. Steers (eds.), *Motivation and Work Behavior* (Burr Ridge, IL: McGraw-Hill, 2003), 65–113.

81. J. M. Jensen, P. C. Patel, and J. L. Raver, "Is It Better to Be Average? High and Low Performance as Predictors of Employee Victimization," *Journal of Applied Psychology* 99, no. 2 (2014): 296–309; B. K. Miller, "Entitlement and Conscientiousness in the Prediction of Organizational Deviance," *Personality and Individual Differences* 82 (2015): 114–19; H. J. R. Woodley and N. J. Allen, "The Dark Side of Equity Sensitivity," *Personality and Individual Differences* 67 (2014): 103–08.

82. J. A. Colquitt, J. Greenberg, and C. P. Zepata-Phelan, "What Is Organizational Justice? A Historical Overview," in J. Greenberg and J. A. Colquitt (eds.), *Handbook of Organizational Justice* (Mahwah, NJ: Lawrence Erlbaum, 2005): 3–56; J. Greenberg, "Organizational Justice: The Dynamics of Fairness in the Workplace," in S. Zedeck (ed.), *APA Handbook of Industrial and Organizational Psychology: Maintaining, Expanding, and Contracting the Organization*, Vol. 3 (Washington, D.C.: APA, 2011): 271–327.

83. R. Eisenberger, T. Rockstuhl, M. K. Shoss, X. Wen, and J. Dulebohn, "Is the Employee-Organization Relationship Dying or Thriving? A Temporal Meta-Analysis," *Journal of Applied Psychology* 104, no. 8 (2019): 1036–57.

84. Greenberg, "Organizational Justice."

85. K. Gurchiek, "Wages Are Unequal Between White and Black Men Even When Other Factors Are Comparable," *Society for Human*

Resource Management [blog], March 20, 2018, https://www.shrm.org/resourcesandtools/hr-topics/behavioral-competencies/global-and-cultural-effectiveness/pages/wages-are-unequal-between-white-and-black-men-even-when-other-factors-are-comparable.aspx; E. Karageorge, "The Unexplainable, Growing Black-White Wage Gap," *Monthly Labor Review,* November 2017, https://www .bls.gov/opub/mlr/2017/beyond-bls/the-unexplainable-growing-black-white-wage-gap.htm

86. See, for example, R. Cropanzano, J. H. Stein, and T. Nadisic, *Social Justice and the Experience of Emotion* (New York: Routledge/Taylor and Francis Group, 2011); I. SimanTov-Nachlieli and P. Bamberger, "Pay Communication, Justice, and Affect: The Asymmetric Effects of process and Outcome Pay Transparency on Counterproductive Work Behavior," *Journal of Applied Psychology* (in press).

87. N. Robins-Early, "TSA Workers Vent Anger at Shutdown as They Work Without Pay Over Holidays," *Huffington Post,* December 31, 2018, https://www .huffingtonpost.com/entry/tsa-officers-government-shutdown_us_5c2a47aee4b05c88b7029f3c

88. G. S. Leventhal, "What Should Be Done with Equity Theory? New Approaches to the Study of Fairness in Social Relationships," in K. Gergen, M. Greenberg, and R. Willis (eds.), *Social Exchange: Advances in Theory and Research* (New York: Plenum, 1980): 27–55; E. A. Lind and T. R. Tyler, *The Social Psychology of Procedural Justice* (New York: Plenum, 1988); and J. Thibaut and L. Walker, *Procedural Justice: A Psychological Analysis* (Hillsdale, NJ: Erlbaum, 1975); R. Outlaw, J. A. Colquitt, M. D. Baer, and H. Sessions, "How Fair Versus How Long: An Integrative Theory-Based Examination of Procedural Justice and Procedural Timeliness," *Personnel Psychology* 72 (2019): 361–91.

89. Ibid.

90. J. Brockner, B. M. Wiesenfeld, and K. A. Diekmann, "Towards a 'Fairer' Conception of Process Fairness: Why, When, and How May Not Always Be Better Than Less," *Academy of Management Annals* 3 (2009): 183–216; R. Folger, "Distributive and Procedural Justice: Combined Impact of 'Voice' and Improvement on Experienced Inequity," *Journal of Personality and Social Psychology* 35 (1977): 108–19; R. Folger, D. Rosenfield, J. Grove, and L. Corkran, "Effects of 'Voice' and Peer Opinions on Responses to Inequity," *Journal of Personality and Social Psychology*

91. R. J. Bies and J. F. Moag, "Interactional Justice: Communication Criteria on Fairness," in R. J. Lewicki, B. H. Sheppard, and M. H. Bazerman (eds.), *Research on Negotiations in Organizations*, Vol. 1, (Greenwich, CT: JAI, 1986): 43–55.

92. J. C. Shaw, E. Wild, and J. A. Colquitt, "To Justify or Excuse? A Meta-Analytic Review of the Effects of Explanations," *Journal of Applied Psychology* 88, no. 3 (2003): 444–58.

93. R. J. Bies, "Are Procedural and Interactional Justice Conceptually Distinct?" in *Handbook of Organizational Justice*, eds. J. Greenberg and J. A. Colquitt (Mahwah, NJ: Erlbaum, 2005), 85–112; B. A. Scott, J. A. Colquitt, and E. L. Paddock, "An Actor-Focused Model of Justice Rule Adherence and Violation: The Role of Managerial Motives and Discretion," *Journal of Applied Psychology* 94, no. 3 (2009): 756–69.

94. C. P. Zapata, A. M. Carton, and J. T. Liu, "When Justice Promotes Injustice: Why Minority Leaders Experience Bias When They Adhere to Interpersonal Justice Rules," *Academy of Management Journal* 59, no. 4 (2016): 1150–73.

95. J. A. Colquitt, D. E. Conlon, M. J. Wesson, C. O. L. H. Porter, and K. Y. Ng, "Justice at the Millenium: A Meta-Analytic Review of 25 Years of Organizational Justice Research," *Journal of Applied Psychology* 86, no. 3 (2001): 425–45; J. A. Colquitt, B. A. Scott, J. B. Rodell, D. M. Long, C. P. Zapata, D. E. Conlon, and M. J. Wesson, "Justice at the Millennium, A Decade Later: A Meta-Analytic Test of

Social Exchange and Affect-Based Perspectives," *Journal of Applied Psychology* 98, no. 2 (2013): 199–236; N. E. Fassina, D. A. Jones, and K. L. Uggerslev, "Meta-Analytic Tests of Relationships between Organizational Justice and Citizenship Behavior: Testing Agent-System and Shared-Variance Models," *Journal of Organizational Behavior* 29 (2008): 805–28.

96. J. M. Robbins, M. T. Ford, and L. E. Tetrick, "Perceived Unfairness and Employee Health: A Meta-Analytic Integration," *Journal of Applied Psychology* 97, no. 2 (2012): 235–72.

97. D. P. Skarlicki, J. H. Ellard, and B. R. C. Kelln, "Third-Party Perceptions of a Layoff: Procedural, Derogation, and Retributive Aspects of Justice," *Journal of Applied Psychology* 83, no. 1 (1998): 119–27; D. P. Skarlicki and C. T. Kulik, "Third-Party Reactions to Employee (Mis)treatment: A Justice Perspective," *Research in Organizational Behavior* 26 (2005): 183–229; E. E. Umphress, A. L. Simmons, R. Folger, R. Ren, and R. Bobocel, "Observer Reactions to Interpersonal Injustice: The Roles of Perpetrator Intent and Victim Perception," *Journal of Organizational Behavior* 34 (2013): 327–49.

98. S. Caleo, "Are Organizational Justice Rules Gendered? Reactions to Men's and Women's Justice Violations," *Journal of Applied Psychology* 101, no. 10 (2016): 1422–35.

99. K. Leung, K. Tong, and S. S. Ho, "Effects of Interactional Justice on Egocentric Bias in Resource Allocation Decisions," *Journal of Applied Psychology* 89, no. 3 (2004): 405–15; L. Francis-Gladney, N. R. Manger, and R. B. Welker, "Does Outcome Favorability Affect Procedural Fairness as a Result of Self-Serving Attributions," *Journal of Applied Social Psychology* 40, no. 1 (2010): 182–94.

100. F. K. Matta, B. A. Scott, Z. A. Guo, and J. G. Matusik, "Exchanging One Uncertainty for Another: Justice Variability Negates the Benefits of Justice," *Journal of Applied Psychology* 105, no. 1 (2020): 97–110; Y-R. Wang, M. T. Ford, Y. Wang, and J. Jin, "Shifts and Variability in Daily Interpersonal Justice Are Associated with Psychological Detachment and Affect at Home," *Journal of Vocational Behavior* (in press).

101. F. F. T. Chiang and T. Birtch, "The Transferability of Management Practices: Examining Cross-National Differences in Reward Preferences," *Human Relations* 60, no. 9 (2007): 1293–330; M. J. Gelfand, M. Erez, and Z. Aycan, "Cross-Cultural Organizational Behavior," *Annual Review of Psychology* 58 (2007): 479–514.

102. M. C. Bolino and W. H. Turnley, "Old Faces, New Places: Equity Theory in Cross-Cultural Contexts," *Journal of Organizational Behavior* 29, no. 1 (2008): 29–50.

103. R. Shao, D. E. Rupp, D. P. Skarlicki, and K. S. Jones, "Employee Justice across Cultures: A Meta-Analytic Review," *Journal of Management* 39, no. 1 (2013): 263–301.

104. R. M. Vogel et al., "A Cross-Cultural Examination of Subordinates' Perceptions of and Reactions to Abusive Supervision," *Journal of Organizational Behavior* 36, no. 5 (2015): 720–45.

105. B. L. Rich, J. A. LePine, and E. R. Crawford, "Job Engagement: Antecedents and Effects on Job Performance," *Academy of Management Journal* 53, no. 3 (2010): 617–35.

106. R. L. Ray, R. Aparicio, P. Hyland, D. A. Dye, J. Simco, and A. Caputo, "DNA of Engagement: How Organizations Can Foster Employee Ownership of Engagement," https://www .conference–board.org/press/pressdetail.cfm? pressid=6948

107. Christian et al., "Work Engagement."

108. D. A. Newman and D. A. Harrison, "Been There, Bottled That: Are State and Behavioral Work Engagement New and Useful Construct 'Wines'?," *Industrial and Organizational Psychology* 1, no. 1 (2008): 31–35; A. J. Wefald and R. G. Downey, "Job Engagement in Organizations: Fad, Fashion, or Folderol," *Journal of Organizational Behavior* 30, no. 1 (2009): 141–45.

109. H. R. Young, D. R. Glerum, W. Wang, and D. L. Joseph, "Who Are the Most Engaged at Work? A Meta-Analysis of Personality and Employee Engagement," *Journal of Organizational Behavior* 39 (2018): 1330–46.

110. E. R. Crawford, J. A. LePine, and B. L. Rich, "Linking Job Demands and Resources to Employee Engagement and Burnout: A Theoretical Extension and Meta-Analytic Test," *Journal of Applied Psychology* 95, no. 5 (2010): 834–48; Rich et al., "Job Engagement"; W. B. Schaufeli, A. B. Bakker, and W. van Rhenen, "How Changes in Job Demands and Resources Predict Burnout, Work Engagement, and Sickness Absenteeism," *Journal of Organizational Behavior* 30, no. 7 (2009): 893–917; M. Tims, A. B. Bakker, and D. Xanthopoulou, "Do Transformational Leaders Enhance Their Followers' Daily Work Engagement?" *Leadership Quarterly* 22, no. 1 (2011): 121–31; D. Xanthopoulou, A. B. Bakker, E. Demerouti, and W. B. Schaufeli, "Reciprocal Relationships between Job Resources, Personal Resources, and Work Engagement," *Journal of Vocational Behavior* 74, no. 3 (2009): 235–44.

111. J. J. Lawler and R. Elliot, "Artificial Intelligence in HRM: An Experimental Study of an Expert System," *Journal of Management* 22, no. 1 (1996): 85–111; M. C. Sturman, J. M. Hannon, and G. T. Milkovich, "Computerized Decision Aids for Flexible Benefits Decisions: The Effects of Expert System and Decision Support System on Employee Intentions and Satisfaction with Benefits," *Personnel Psychology* 49 (1996): 883–908.

CHAPTER 8

1. L. R. Brown, "Majority of Working Parents Taking On Unpaid Overtime to Keep Up With Workload," *People Management,* February 5, 2019, https://www.peoplemanagement .co.uk/news/articles/majority-working-parents-taking-on-unpaid-overtime-keep-up-workload

2. Ibid.

3. E. Gonzalez-Mulé and B. S. Cockburn, "Job Is (Literally) Killing Me: A Moderated-Mediated Model Linking Work Characteristics to Mortality," *Journal of Applied Psychology* (in press).

4. A. M. Grant, Y. Fried, and T. Juillerat, "Work Matters: Job Design in Classic and Contemporary Perspectives," in S. Zedeck (ed.), *APA Handbook of Industrial and Organizational Psychology: Building and Developing the Organization*, Vol. 1 (Washington DC: APA, 2011): 417–53; S. K. Parker, F. P. Morgeson, and G. Johns, "One Hundred Years of Work Design Research: Looking Back and Looking Forward," *Journal of Applied Psychology* 102, no. 3 (2017): 403–20.

5. J. R. Hackman and G. R. Oldham, "Motivation through the Design of Work: Test of a Theory," *Organizational Behavior and Human Performance* 16 (1976): 250–79; G. R. Oldham and Y. Fried, "Job Design Research and Theory: Past, Present and Future," *Organizational Behavior and Human Decision Processes* 136 (2016): 20–35.

6. S. E. Humphrey, J. D. Nahrgang, and F. P. Morgeson, "Integrating Motivational, Social, and Contextual Work Design Features: A Meta-Analytic Summary and Theoretical Extension of the Work Design Literature," *Journal of Applied Psychology* 92, no. 5 (2007): 1332–56; Oldham and Fried, "Job Design Research and Theory."

7. L. A. Wegman, B. J. Hoffman, N. T. Carter, J. M. Twenge, and N. Guenole, "Placing Job Characteristics in Context: Cross-Temporal Meta-Analysis of Changes in Job Characteristics Since 1975," *Journal of Management* 44, no. 1 (2018): 352–86.

8. W. G. M. Oerlemans and A. B. Bakker, "Motivating Job Characteristics and Happiness at Work: A Multilevel Perspective," *Journal of Applied Psychology* 103, no. 11 (2018): 1230–41.

9. C. B. Gibson, J. L. Gibbs, T. L. Stanko, P. Tesluk, and S. G. Cohen, "Including the 'I' in Virtuality and Modern Job Design: Extending the Job Characteristics Model to Include the Moderating Effect of Individual Experiences of Electronic Dependence and Copresence," *Organization Science* 22, no. 6 (2011): 1481–99.

10. Ibid.

11. See, for instance, D. Holman and C. Axtell, "Can Job Redesign Interventions Influence a Broad Range of Employee Outcomes by Changing Multiple Job Characteristics? A Quasi-Experimental Study," *Journal of Occupational Health Psychology* 21, no. 3 (2016): 284–95.

12. A. Aravindan and F. Ungku, "RPT-Ageing Singapore: City-State Helps Firms Retain Workers Past Retirement Age," *Reuters Asia,* February 4, 2019, https://www.reuters.com/article/asia-ageing-singapore-companies/rpt-ageing-singapore-city-state-helps-firms-retain-workers-past-retirement-age-idUSL3N1ZZ2IN

13. Ibid.

14. M. A. Campion, L. Cheraskin, and M. J. Stevens, "Career-Related Antecedents and Outcomes of Job Rotation," *Academy of Management Journal* 37, no. 6 (1994): 1518–42.

15. Robert Walters, PLC., *Attracting and Retaining Millennial Professionals* [white paper], accessed February 24, 2019, https://www.robertwalters.co.uk/content/dam/robert-walters/country/united-kingdom/files/whitepapers/robert-walters-whitepaper-millennials.pdf

16. A. Christini and D. Pozzoli, "Workplace Practices and Firm Performance in Manufacturing: A Comparative Study of Italy and Britain," *International Journal of Manpower* 31, no. 7 (2010): 818–42; K. Kaymaz, "The Effects of Job Rotation Practices on Motivation: A Research on Managers in the Automotive Organizations," *Business and Economics Research Journal* 1, no. 3 (2010): 69–86.

17. S.-H. Huang and Y.-C. Pan, "Ergonomic Job Rotation Strategy Based on an Automated RGB-D Anthropometric Measuring System," *Journal of Manufacturing Systems* 33, no. 4 (2014): 699–710; P. C. Leider, J. S. Boschman, M. H. W. Frings-Dresen, and H. F. van der Molen, "Effects of Job Rotation on Musculoskeletal Complaints and Related Work Exposures: A Systematic Literature Review," *Ergonomics* 58, no. 1 (2015): 18–32.

18. T. Silver, "Rotate Your Way to Higher Value," *Baseline,* March/April 2010, 12; J. J. Salopek, "Coca-Cola Division Refreshes Its Talent With Diversity Push on Campus," *Workforce Management Online,* March 21, 2011, http://www .workforce.com/2011/03/21/coca-cola-division-refreshes-its-talent-with-diversity-push-on-campus/

19. Singapore Airlines [website], https://www.singaporeair.com/en_UK/us/careers/why-join-us/#, accessed April 12, 2019; Skytrax website review of Singapore Airlines, http://www.airlinequality.com/ratings/singapore-airlines-star-rating/, accessed February 24, 2019.

20. Grant, Fried, and Juillerat, "Work Matters."

21. M. T. Ford and J. D. Wooldridge, "Industry Growth, Work Role Characteristics, and Job Satisfaction: A Cross-Level Mediation Model," *Journal of Occupational Health Psychology* 17, no. 4 (2012): 493–504.

22. G. M. McEvoy and W. F. Cascio, "Strategies for Reducing Employee Turnover: A Meta-Analysis," *Journal of Applied Psychology* 70, no. 2 (1985): 342–53.

23. S. K. Parker, D. M. Andrei, and A. Van den Broeck, "Poor Design Begets Poor Work Design: Capacity and Willingness Antecedents of Individual Work Design Behavior," *Journal of Applied Psychology* 104, no. 7 (2019): 907–928.

24. A. M. Grant, "Leading With Meaning: Beneficiary Contact, Prosocial Impact, and the Performance Effects of Transformational Leadership," *Academy of Management Journal* 55, no. 2 (2012): 458–76; A. M. Grant and S. K. Parker, "Redesigning Work Design Theories: The Rise of Relational and Proactive Perspectives," *Annals of the Academy of Management* 3, no. 1 (2009): 317–75.

25. J. Devaro, "A Theoretical Analysis of Relational Job Design and Compensation," *Journal of Organizational Behavior* 31, no. 2–3 (2010): 279–301. D. P. Bhave, F. Halldórsson, E. Kim, and A. M. Lefter, "The Differential Impact of Interactions Outside the Organization on Employee Well-Being," *Journal of Occupational and Organizational Psychology* 92 (2019): 1–29.

26. A. M. Grant, E. M. Campbell, G. Chen, K. Cottone, D. Lapedis, and K. Lee, "Impact and the Art of Motivation Maintenance: The Effects of Contact With Beneficiaries on Persistence Behavior," *Organizational Behavior and Human Decision Processes* 103, no. 1 (2007): 53–67.

27. M. C. Bolino, T. K. Kelemen, and S. H. Matthews, "Working 9-to-5? A Review of Research on Nonstandard Work Schedules," *Journal of Organizational Behavior* (in press).

28. H. Chung and M. van der Horst, "Women's Employment Patterns After Childbirth and the Perceived Access to and Use of Flextime and Teleworking," *Human Relations* 71, no. 1 (2018): 47–72.

29. B. Croce, "More Firms Seeing Flex Time as Vital to a Productive Office," *Pensions & Investments*, December 10, 2018, https://www.pionline.com/article/20181210/PRINT/181219974/more-firms-seeing-flex-time-as-vital-to-a-productive-office

30. See, for instance, R. J. Thompson, S. C. Payne, and A. B. Taylor, "Applicant Attraction to Flexible Work Arrangements: Separating the Influence of Flextime and Flexplace," *Journal of Occupational and Organizational Psychology* 88, no. 4 (2015): 726–49.

31. Croce, "More Firms Seeing Flex Time as Vital to a Productive Office"; G. M. Spreitzer, L. Cameron, and L. Garrett, "Alternative Work Arrangements: Two Images of the New World of Work," *Annual Review of Organizational Psychology and Organizational Behavior* 4 (2017): 473–99.

32. U. Mead, "Why Employees Say These Companies Have Figured Out Flexible Work," *Fast Company,* July 18, 2018, https://www.fastcompany.com/90202716/why-employees-say-these-companies-have-figured-out-flexible-work

33. Society for Human Resource Management (SHRM), *2018 Employee Benefits: The Evolution of Benefits.* (Alexandria, VA: SHRM, 2018)

34. Society for Human Resource Management (SHRM), *2016 Employee Benefits: Looking Back at 20 Years of Employee Benefits Offerings in the U.S.* (Alexandria, VA: SHRM, 2016); Society for Human Resource Management (SHRM), *2016 Strategic Benefits—Flexible Work Arrangements* (Alexandria, VA: SHRM, 2016).

35. Society for Human Resource Management (SHRM), *Employee Job Satisfaction and Engagement: Revitalizing a Changing Workforce* (Alexandria, VA: SHRM, 2016).

36. R. Waring, "Sunday Dialogue: Flexible Work Hours," *The New York Times,* January 19, 2013, www.nytimes.com

37. B. B. Baltes, T. E. Briggs, J. W. Huff, J. A. Wright, and G. A. Neuman, "Flexible and Compressed Workweek Schedules: A Meta-Analysis of Their Effects on Work-Related Criteria," *Journal of Applied Psychology* 84, no. 4 (1999): 496–513.

38. T. D. Allen, R. C. Johnson, K. M. Kiburz, and K. M. Shockley, "Work-Family Conflict and Flexible Work Arrangements: Deconstructing Flexibility," *Personnel Psychology* 66 (2013): 345–76.

39. I. Spieler, S. Scheibe, C. Stamov-Robnagel, and A. Kappas, "Help or Hindrance? Day-Level Relationships between Flextime Use, Work-Nonwork Boundaries, and Affective Well-Being," *Journal of Applied Psychology* 102, no. 1 (2017): 67–87.

40. C. W. Rudolph and B. B. Baltes, "Age and Health Jointly Moderate the Influence of Flexible Work Arrangements on Work Engagement: Evidence From Two Empirical Studies," *Journal of Occupational Healthy Psychology* 22, no. 1 (2017): 40–58.

41. K. M. Shockley and T. D. Allen, "Investigating the Missing Link in Flexible Work Arrangement Utilization: An Individual Difference Perspective," *Journal of Vocational Behavior* 76, no. 1 (2010): 131–42.

42. C. L. Munsch, C. L. Ridgeway, and J. C. Williams, "Pluralistic Ignorance and the Flexibility Bias: Understanding and Mitigating Flextime and Flexplace Bias at Work," *Work and Occupations* 41, no. 1 (2014): 40–62.

43. "Actors to job-share on touring production," *BBC: Entertainment & Arts,* February 7, 2019, https://www.bbc.com/news/entertainment-arts-47157263

44. Ibid.

45. S. Adams, "Workers Have More Flextime, Less Real Flexibility, Study Shows," *Forbes,* May 2, 2014, http://www .forbes.com/sites/susan-adams/2014/05/02/workers-have-more-flextime-less-real-flexibility-study-shows/

46. K. Guyot and I. V. Sawhill, "Telecommuting Will Likely Continue Long After the Pandemic," *Brookings: Up Front* [blog post], April 6, 2020, https://www.brookings.edu/blog/up-front/2020/04/06/telecommuting-will-likely-continue-long-after-the-pandemic/; T. Knutson, "Telecommuting Surge Likely to Last Past COVID-19 Crisis, Predicts Brookings Report," *Forbes,* April 8, 2020, https://www.forbes.com/sites/tedknutson/2020/04/08/telecommuting-surge-likely-to-last-past-covid-19-crisis-says-brookings-report/#44861f7f74ca

47. R. V. Reeves and J. Rothwell, "Class and COVID: How the Less Affluent Face Double Risks," *Brookings: Up Front* [blog post], March 27, 2020, https://www.brookings.edu/blog/up-front/2020/03/27/class-and-covid-how-the-less-affluent-face-double-risks/

48. Gartner, *Gartner CFO Survey Reveals 74% Intend to Shift Some Employees to Remote Work Permanently* (Press Release, Arlington, VA: April 3, 2020).

49. F. Bélanger and R. W. Collins, "Distributed Work Arrangements: A Research Framework," *Information Society* 14 (1998): 137–52; R. S. Gajendran and D. A. Harrison, "The Good, the Bad, and the Unknown about Telecommuting: Meta-Analysis of Psychological Mediators and Individual Consequences," *Journal of Applied Psychology* 92, no. 6 (2007): 1524–41; B. A. Lautsch and E. E. Kossek, "Managing a Blended Workforce: Telecommuters and Non-Telecommuters," *Organizational Dynamics* 40, no. 1 (2010): 10–17. T. D. Golden and R. S. Gajendran, "Unpacking the Role of a Telecommuter's Job in Their Rerformance: Examining Job Complexity, Problem Solving, Interdependence, and Social Support," *Journal of Business and Psychology* 34 (2019): 55–69.

50. Ibid.

51. Ibid.

52. J. Kotkin, "Marissa Mayer's Misstep and the Unstoppable Rise of Telecommuting," *Forbes,* March 26, 2013.

53. See, for example, Bartel, Wrzesniewski, and Wiesenfeld, "Knowing Where You Stand"; Gajendran and Harrison, "The Good, the Bad, and the Unknown about Telecommuting"; M. Virick, N. DaSilva, and K. Arrington, "Moderators of the Curvilinear Relation between Extent of Telecommuting and Job and Life Satisfaction: The Role of Performance Outcome Orientation and Worker Type," *Human Relations* 63, no. 1 (2010): 137–54.

54. J. B. Windeler, K. M. Chudoba, R. Z. Sundrup, "Getting Away From Them All: Managing Exhaustion From Social Interaction With Telework," *Journal of Organizational Behavior* 38, no. 7 (2017): 977–95.

55. L. M. Lapierre, E. F. Van Steenbergen, M. C. W. Peeters, and E. S. Kluwer, "Juggling Work and Family Responsibilities When Involuntarily Working More From Home: A Multiwave Study of Financial Sales Professionals," *Journal of Organizational Behavior* 37, no. 6 (2016): 804–22; M. C. Noonan and J. L. Glass, "The Hard Truth about Telecommuting," *Monthly Labor Review* (2012): 1459–78. J. Delanoeije, M. Verbruggen, and L. Germeys, "Boundary Role Transitions: A Day-to-Day Approach to Explain the Effects of Home-Based Telework on

Work-to-Home Conflict and Home-to-Work Conflict," *Human Relations* 72, no. 12 (2019): 1843–68.

56. J. Welch and S. Welch, "The Importance of Being There," *BusinessWeek*, April 16, 2007, 92; Z. I. Barsness, K. A. Diekmann, and M. L. Seidel, "Motivation and Opportunity: The Role of Remote Work, Demographic Dissimilarity, and Social Network Centrality in Impression Management," *Academy of Management Journal* 48, no. 3 (2005): 401–19. T. D. Golden and K. A. Eddleston, "Is There a Price Telecommuters Pay? Examining the Relationship Between Telecommuting and Objective Career Success," *Journal of Vocational Behavior* (in press).

57. Bolino et al., "Working 9-to-5?"

58. T. Müller and C. Niessen, "Self-Leadership in the Context of Part-Time Teleworking," *Journal of Organizational Behavior* 40 (2019): 883–898.

59. E. Frauenheim, "COVID-19: Learning to Love Telecommuting," *Great Place to Work* [blog], March 17, 2020, https://www.greatplacetowork.com/resources/blog/covid-19-silver-lining-learning-to-love-telecommuting; M. Tarallo, "How to Create an Effective Teleworking Program," *Society for Human Resource Management* [blog], April 19, 2018, https://www.shrm.org/resourcesandtools/hr-topics/employee-relations/pages/how-to-create-an-effective-teleworking-program.aspx

60. J. Cotton, *Employee Involvement: Methods for Improving Performance and Work Attitudes* (Newbury Park, CA: Sage, 1993); A. Cox, S. Zagelmeyer, and M. Marchington, "Embedding Employee Involvement and Participation at Work," *Human Resource Management Journal* 16, no. 3 (2006): 250–67.

61. See, for example, A. Kim and K. Han, "All for One and One for All: A Mechanism Through Which Broad-Based Employee Stock Ownership and Employee-Perceived Involvement Practice Create a Productive Workforce," *Human Resource Management* 58 (2019): 571–584.

62. See, for example, the literature on empowerment, such as S. E. Seibert, S. R. Silver, and W. A. Randolph, "Taking Empowerment to the Next Level: A Multiple-Level Model of Empowerment, Performance, and Satisfaction," *Academy of Management Journal* 47, no. 3 (2004): 332–49; M. M. Butts, R. J. Vandenberg, D. M. DeJoy, B. S. Schaffer, and M. G. Wilson, "Individual Reactions to High Involvement Work Processes: Investigating the Role of Empowerment and Perceived Organizational Support," *Journal of Occupational Health Psychology* 14, no. 2 (2009): 122–36; M. T. Maynard, L. L. Gilson, and J. E. Mathieu, "Empowerment—Fad or Fab? A Multilevel Review of the Past Two Decades of Research," *Journal of Management* 38, no. 4 (2012): 1231–81.

63. See, for instance, A. Sagie and Z. Aycan, "A Cross-Cultural Analysis of Participative Decision-Making in Organizations," *Human Relations* 56, no. 4 (2003): 453–73; J. Brockner, "Unpacking Country Effects: On the Need to Operationalize the Psychological Determinants of Cross-National Differences," in *Research in Organizational Behavior, vol. 25*, eds. R. M. Kramer and B. M. Staw (Oxford, UK: Elsevier, 2003), 336–40.

64. C. Robert, T. M. Probst, J. J. Martocchio, R. Drasgow, and J. J. Lawler, "Empowerment and Continuous Improvement in the United States, Mexico, Poland, and India: Predicting Fit on the Basis of the Dimensions of Power Distance and Individualism," *Journal of Applied Psychology* 85, no. 5 (2000): 643–58.

65. Z. X. Chen and S. Aryee, "Delegation and Employee Work Outcomes: An Examination of the Cultural Context of Mediating Processes in China," *Academy of Management Journal* 50, no. 1 (2007): 226–38.

66. Z. Cheng, "The Effects of Employee Involvement and Participation on Subjective Wellbeing: Evidence From Urban China," *Social Indicators Research* 118, no. 2 (2014): 457–83.

67. A. Bar-Haim, *Participation Programs in Work Organizations: Past, Present, and Scenarios for the Future* (Westport, CT: Quorum, 2002); J. S. Black and H. B. Gregersen, "Participative Decision-Making:

An Integration of Multiple Dimensions," *Human Relations* 50, no. 7 (1997): 859–78.

68. Ibid.

69. M. Gunderson, "EMS Quality Improvement Through Clinical Specialty Teams," *EMS1* [blog], January 28, 2019, https://www.ems1.com/paramedic-chief/articles/393311048-EMS-quality-improvement-through-clinical-specialty-teams/

70. D. Collins, "The Ethical Superiority and Inevitability of Participatory Management as an Organizational System," *Organization Science* 8, no. 5 (1997): 489–507; T. M. Probst, "Countering the Negative Effects of Job Insecurity through Participative Decision Making: Lessons From the Demand-Control Model," *Journal of Occupational Health Psychology* 10, no. 4 (2005): 320–29.

71. C. M. Linski, "Transitioning to Participative Management," *Organization Development Journal* 32, no. 3 (2014): 17–26.

72. See, for instance, A. Pendleton and A. Robinson, "Employee Stock Ownership, Involvement, and Productivity: An Interaction-Based Approach," *Industrial and Labor Relations Review* 64, no. 1 (2010): 3–29.

73. D. K. Datta, J. P. Guthrie, and P. M. Wright, "Human Resource Management and Labor Productivity: Does Industry Matter?" *Academy of Management Journal* 48, no. 1 (2005): 135–45; D. Gallie, "Direct participation and the quality of work," *Human Relations* 66, no. 5 (2013): 453–73; J. Kim, J. P. MacDuffie, and F. K. Pil, "Employee Voice and Organizational Performance: Team versus Representative Influence," *Human Relations* 63, no. 3 (2010): 371–94.

74. C. J. Travers, *Managing the Team: A Guide to Successful Employee Involvement* (Oxford, UK: Wiley-Blackwell, 1994).

75. A. M. Herman, *Futurework: Trends and Challenges for Work in the 21st Century* (Washington, D.C.: United States Department of Labor, 1999).

76. American Psychological Association and Harris Interactive, *Workforce Retention Survey*, August 2012, http://www.apaexcellence.org/assets/general/2012-retention-survey-final.pdf

77. G. D. Jenkins, A. Mitra, N. Gupta, and J. D. Shaw, "Are Financial Incentives Related to Performance? A Meta-Analytic Review of Empirical Research," *Journal of Applied Psychology* 83, no. 5 (1998): 777–87; C. R. Leana and J. Meuris, "Living to Work and Working to Live: Income as a Driver of Organizational Behavior," *The Academy of Management Annals* 9, no. 1 (2015): 55–95; M. A. R. Malik and A. N. Butt, "Rewards and Creativity: Past, Present, and Future," *Applied Psychology: An International Review* 66, no. 2 (2017): 290–325.

78. M. Sabramony, N. Krause, J. Norton, and G. N. Burns "The Relationship between Human Resource Investments and Organizational Performance: A Firm-Level Examination of Equilibrium Theory," *Journal of Applied Psychology* 93, no. 4 (2008): 778–88.

79. J. M. Beus and D. S. Whitman, "Almighty Dollar or Root of All Evil? Testing the Effects of Money on Workplace Behavior," *Journal of Management* 43, no. 7 (2017): 2147–67.

80. C. Isidore, "Walmart Ups Pay Well above Minimum Wage," *CNN Money*, February 19, 2015, http://money.cnn.com/2015/02/19/news/companies/walmart-wages/

81. See, for example, B. Martinez, "Teacher Bonuses Emerge in Newark," *The Wall Street Journal*, April 21, 2011, A15; K. Taylor, "Differing Results When Teacher Evaluations Are Tied to Test Scores," *The New York Times*, March 23, 2015, A16; D. Weber, "Seminole Teachers to Get Bonuses Instead of Raises," *Orlando Sentinel*, January 19, 2011, www.orlandosentinel.com

82. G. T. Milkovich, J. M. Newman, and B. Gerhart, *Compensation* (11th ed., New York: McGraw-Hill, 2013).

83. See, for example, M. Damiani and A. Ricci, "Managers' Education and the Choice of Different Variable Pay Schemes: Evidence From Italian Firms," *European Management Journal* 32, no. 6 (2014): 891–902.

84. S. Miller, "Bonus Binge: Variable Pay Outpaces Salary," *Society for Human Resource Management*, August 11, 2016, https://www.shrm.org/resourcesandtools/hr-topics/compensation/pages/variable-pay-outpaces-raises.aspx

85. A. M. Paul, "Atlanta Teachers Were Offered Bonuses for High Test Scores. Of Course They Cheated," *The Washington Post*, April 16, 2015, https://www.washingtonpost.com/posteverything/wp/2015/04/16/atlanta-teachers-were-offered-bonuses-for-high-test-scores-of-course-they-cheated/?utm_term=.e4df48aeb80b; N P. von der Embse, A. M. Schoemann, S. P. Kilgus, M. Wicoff, and M. Bowler, "The Influence of Test-Based Accountability Policies on Teacher Stress and Instructional Practices: A Moderated Mediation Model," *Educational Psychology* 37, no. 3 (2017): 312–31; K. Yuan, V.-N. Le, D. F. McCaffrey, J. A. Marsh, L. S. Hamilton, B. M. Stecher, and M. G. Springer, "Incentive Pay Programs Do Not Affect Teacher Motivation or Reported Practices: Results From Three Randomized Studies," *Educational Evaluation and Policy Analysis* 35, no. 1 (2013): 3–22.

86. D. Pohler and J. A. Schmidt, "Does Pay-for-Performance Strain the Employment Relationship? The Effect of Manager Bonus Eligibility on Nonmanagement Employee Turnover," *Personnel Psychology* 69 (2016): 395–429.

87. D. Gläser, S. van Gils, and N. Van Quaquebeke, "Pay-for-Performance and Interpersonal Deviance," *Journal of Personnel Psychology* 16, no. 2 (2017): 77–90.

88. A. Shantz, J. Wang, and A. Malik, "Disability Status, Individual Variable Pay, and Pay Satisfaction: Does Relational and Institutional Trust Make a Difference," *Human Resource Management* 57 (2018): 365–80.

89. H. Kim, K. L. Sutton, and Y. Gong, "Group-Based Pay-for-Performance Plans and Firm Performance: The Moderating Role of Empowerment Practices," *Asia Pacific Journal of Management* 30, no. 1 2013: 31–52; S. Y. Sung, J. N. Choi, and S-C. Kang, "Incentive Pay and Firm Performance: Moderating Roles of Procedural Justice Climate and Environmental Turbulence," *Human Resource Management* 56, no. 2 (2017): 287–305. A.J. Nyberg, M. A. Maltarich, D. D. Abdulsalam, S. M. Essman, and O. Cragun, "Collective Pay for Performance: A Cross-Disciplinary Review and Meta-Analysis," *Journal of Management* 44, no. 6 (2018): 2433–2472.

90. J. Cloutier, D. Morin, and S. Renaud, "How Does Variable Pay Relate to Pay Satisfaction among Canadian Workers?" *International Journal of Manpower* 34, no. 5 (2013): 465–85.

91. Y. Zhang, L. Long, T.-Y. Wu, and X. Huang, "When Is Pay for Performance Related to Employee Creativity in the Chinese Context? The Role of Guanxi HRM Practice, Trust in Management, and Intrinsic Motivation," *Journal of Organizational Behavior* 36, no. 5 (2015): 698–719.

92. E. Belogolovsky and P. A. Bamberger, "Signaling in Secret: Pay for Performance and the Incentive and Sorting Effects of Pay Secrecy," *Academy of Management Journal* 57, no. 6 (2014): 1706–33.

93. Ibid.

94. See, for instance, M. K. Judiesch and F. L. Schmidt, "Between-Worker Variability in Output under Piece-Rate versus Hourly Pay Systems," *Journal of Business and Psychology* 14, no. 4 (2000): 529–52.

95. P. M. Wright, "An Examination of the Relationships among Monetary Incentives, Goal Level, Goal Commitment, and Performance," *Journal of Management* 18, no. 4 (1992): 677–93. K. L. Harper, P. J. Silvia, K. M. Eddington, S. H. Sperry, and T. R. Kwapil, "Conscientiousness and effort-related cardiac activity in response to piece-rate cash incentives," *Motivation and Emotion* 42 (2018): 377–385.

96. J. S. Heywood, X. Wei, and G. Ye, "Piece Rates for Professors," *Economics Letters* 113, no. 3 (2011): 285–87.

97. A. Baker and V. Mertins, "Risk-Sorting and Preference for Team Piece Rates," *Journal of Economic Psychology* 34 (2013): 285–300.

98. E. Della Torre, M. Salimi, and A. Giangreco, "Crowding-out or Crowding-in? Direct Voice, Performance-Related Pay, and Organizational Innovation in European Firms," *Human Resource Management* 59 (2020): 185–99.

99. A. Clemens, "Pace of Work and Piece Rates," *Economics Letters* 115, no. 3 (2012): 477–79.

100. S. L. Rynes, B. Gerhart, and L. Parks, "Personnel Psychology: Performance Evaluation and Pay for Performance," *Annual Review of Psychology* 56, no. 1 (2005): 571–600.

101. Ibid.

102. "Paying Doctors for Performance," *The New York Times*, January 27, 2013, A16.

103. S. Halzack, "Companies Look to Bonuses Instead of Salary Increases in an Uncertain Economy," *The Washington Post*, November 6, 2012, https://www.washingtonpost.com/business/economy/companies-look-to-bonuses-instead-of-salary-increases-in-an-uncertain-economy/2012/11/06/52a7ec12-2751-11e2-9972-71bf64ea091c_story.html

104. A. J. Nyberg, J. R. Pieper, and C. O. Trevor, "Pay-for-Performance's Effect on Future Performance: Integration Psychological and Economic Perspectives Toward a Contingency Perspective," *Journal of Management* 42, no. 7 (2016): 1753–83; S. Park and M. C. Sturman, "The Relative Incentive and Sorting Effects of Merit Pay, Bonuses, and Long-Term Incentives," *Human Resource Management* 55, no. 4 (2015): 697–719.

105. E. J. Castillo, "Gender, Race, and the New (Merit-Based) Employment Relationship," *Industrial Relations* 51, no. S1 (2012): 528–62.

106. Rynes, Gerhart, and Parks, "Personnel Psychology."

107. A-F. Presse, "Goldman Sachs plans to cut bonuses as 1MDB scandal deepens," *The Guardian*, February 8, 2019, https://www.theguardian.com/world/2019/feb/09/goldman-sachs-plans-to-cut-bonuses-as-1mdb-scandal-deepens

108. N. Chun and S. Lee, "Bonus Compensation and Productivity: Evidence From Indian Manufacturing Plant-Level Data," *Journal of Productivity Analysis* 43, no. 1 (2015): 47–58.

109. M. J. Roomkin, *Profit Sharing and Gain Sharing* (Metuchen, NJ: Rutgers University Press, 1990).

110. "Mark Zuckerberg: Executive Compensation," *Salary.com*, accessed February 24, 2019, https://www1.salary.com/Mark-Zuckerberg-Salary-Bonus-Stock-Options-for-FACEBOOK-INC.html

111. E. D. Lawrence, "Fiat Chrysler Workers to get profit sharing of $7,280," *Detroit Free Press*, February 6, 2020, https://www.freep.com/story/money/cars/chrysler/2020/02/06/fiat-chrysler-2019-profit-sharing-checks-earnings/4675843002/

112. D. D'Art and T. Turner, "Profit Sharing, Firm Performance, and Union Influence in Selected European Countries," *Personnel Review* 33, no. 3 (2004): 335–50; D. Kruse, R. Freeman, and J. Blasi, *Shared Capitalism at Work: Employee Ownership, Profit and Gain Sharing, and Broad-Based Stock Options* (Chicago: University of Chicago Press, 2010).

113. A. Bayo-Moriones and M. Larraza-Kintana, "Profit-Sharing Plans and Affective Commitment: Does the Context Matter?" *Human Resource Management* 48, no. 2 (2009): 207–26.

114. N. Chi and T. Han, "Exploring the Linkages between Formal Ownership and Psychological Ownership for the Organization: The Mediating Role of Organizational Justice," *Journal of Occupational and Organizational Psychology* 81, no. 4 (2008): 691–711.

115. J. H. Han, K. M. Barol, and S. Kim, "Tightening Up the Performance-Pay Linkage: Roles of Contingent Reward Leadership and Profit-Sharing in the Cross-Level Influence of Individual Pay-for-Performance," *Journal of Applied Psychology* 100, no. 2 (2015): 417–30.

116. ESOP Association, *ESOP Association's Position on President's Panel on Federal Tax Reform Recommendation on Retirement Savings.*

Washington, DC: Author. F. Mullins, D. Weltmann, D. Kruse, and J. Blasi, "Broad-Based Employee Stock Ownership: What Makes It Effective in the Management of Human Resources," *Human Resource Management* 58 (2019): 567–70.

117. R. P. Garrett, "Does Employee Ownership Increase Innovation?" *New England Journal of Entrepreneurship* 13, no. 2, (2010): 37–46. Mullins et al., "Broad-Based Employee Stock Ownership"; E. H. O'Boyle, P. C. Patel, and E. Gonzalez-Mulé, "Employee Ownership and Firm Performance: A Meta-Analysis," *Human Resource Management Journal* 26, no. 4 (2016): 425–48; T. A. Paterson and T. W. Welbourne, "I Am Therefore I Own: Implications of Organization-Based Identity for Employee Stock Ownership," *Human Resource Management* 59 (2020): 175–83.

118. D. McCarthy, E. Reeves, and T. Turner, "Can Employee Share-Ownership Improve Employee Attitudes and Behaviour?" *Employee Relations* 32, no. 4 (2010): 382–95.

119. A. Pendleton, "Shared Capitalism at Work: Employee Ownership, Profit and Gain Sharing, and Broad-Based Stock Options," *Industrial and Labor Relations Review* 64, no. 3 (2011): 621–22.

120. D. Souder and P. Bromiley, "Timing for Dollars: How Option Exercisability Influences Resource Allocation," *Journal of Management* 43, no. 8 (2017): 2555–79.

121. T. Ren, Y. Xiao, H. Yang, and S. Liiu, "Employee Ownership Heterogeneity and Firm Performance in China," *Human Resource Management* 58 (2019): 621–39.

122. S. Kang and A. Kim, "Employee Stock Ownership and Financial Performance in European Countries: The Moderating Effects of Uncertainty Avoidance and Social Trust," *Human Resource Management* 58 (2019): 641–55.

123. A. Pendleton and A. Robinson, "Employee Stock Ownership, Involvement, and Productivity: An Interaction-Based Approach," *Industrial and Labor Relations Review* 64, no. 1 (2010): 3–29.

124. Z. Lin, J. Kelly, and L. Trenberth, "Antecedents and Consequences of the Introduction of Flexible Benefit Plans in China," *International Journal of Human Resource Management* vol. 22, no. 5 (2011): 1128–45.

125. L. E. Tetrick and C. R. Haimann, "Employee Recognition," in A. Day, E. K. Kelloway, and J. J. Hurrell Jr. (eds.), *Workplace Well-Being: How to Build Psychologically Healthy Workplaces* (Hoboken, NJ: Wiley, 2014), 161–74.

126. L. Shepherd, "Special Report on Rewards and Recognition: Getting Personal," *Workforce Management,* September 2010: 24–29.

127. Globoforce, *Symantec* [Case Study], 2012, http://go.globoforce .com/rs/globoforce/images/Symantec_casestudy.pdf

128. L. Shepherd, "On Recognition, Multinationals Think Globally," *Workforce Management,* September 2010, 26.

129. S. E. Markham, K. D. Scott, and G. H. McKee, "Recognizing Good Attendance: A Longitudinal, Quasi-Experimental Field Study," *Personnel Psychology* 55, no. 3 (2002): 641; S. J. Peterson and F. Luthans, "The Impact of Financial and Nonfinancial Incentives on Business Unit Outcomes over Time," *Journal of Applied Psychology* 91, no. 1 (2006): 156–65.

130. C. Xu and C. Liang, "The Mechanisms Underlying an Employee Recognition Program," in L. Hale and J. Zhang (eds.), *Proceedings of the International Conference on Public Human Resource Management and Innovation* (Marietta, GA: American Scholars Press, 2013), 28–35.

131. See F. Luthans and A. D. Stajkovic, "Provide Recognition for Performance Improvement," in *Handbook of Principles of Organizational Behavior,* ed. E. A. Locke (Malden, MA: Blackwell, 2004): 166–80.

132. X. Zheng, H. H. Zhao, X. Liu, and N. Li, "Network Reconfiguration: The Implications of Recognizing Top Performers in Teams," *Journal of Occupational and Organizational Psychology* 92 (2019): 825–47.

CHAPTER 9

1. G. Curphy, "Important Differences Between Groups and Teams," *Hogan: The Science of Personality* [blog], June 18, 2012, https://www.hoganassessments.com/important-differences-between-groups-and-teams/

2. N. Karelaia and L. Guillen, "Me, a Woman and a Leader: Positive Social Identity and Identity Conflict," *Organizational Behavior and Human Decision Processes* 125, no. 2 (2014): 204–19.

3. B. Bastien, J. Jetten, and L. J. Ferris, "Pain as Social Glue: Shared Pain Increases Cooperation," *Psychological Science* 25, no. 11 (2014): 2079–85; E. J. Boothby, M. S. Clark, and J. A. Bargh, "Shared Experiences Are Amplified," *Psychological Science* 25, no. 12 (2014): 2209–16.

4. B. Cox, "Shavers Celebrate 50 Years," *Journal Review,* February 25, 2019, http://www.journalreview.com/news/article_c9b27c9a-3871-11e9-aec9-bf2e2fdd8562.html

5. See H. Tajfel and J. C. Turner, "The Social Identity Theory of Inter Group Behavior," in S. Worchel & W. G. Austin (eds.), *Psychology of Intergroup Relations* (Chicago, IL: Nelson, 1986); S. V. Bentley, K. H. Greenaway, S. Alexander Haslam, T. Cruwys, N. K. Steffens, C. Haslam, and B. Cull, "Social Identity Mapping Online," *Journal of Personality and Social Psychology* 118, no. 2 (2020): 213–41; H. Tajfel and J. C. Turner, "An Integrative Theory of Intergroup Conflict," in W. G. Austin and S. Worchel (eds.), *The Social Psychology of Intergroup Relations* (Monterey, CA: Brooks/Cole, 1979): 33–47.

6. P. Belmi, R. C. Barragan, M. A. Neale, and G. L. Cohen, "Threats to Social Identity Can Trigger Social Deviance," *Personality and Social Psychological Bulletin* 41, no. 4 (2015): 467–84; C. W. Leach, R. Spears, N. R. Branscombe, and B. Doosje, "Malicious Pleasure: Schadenfreude at the Suffering of Another Group," *Journal of Personality and Social Psychology* 84, no. 5 (2003): 932–43.

7. A. Cheng, "How Wendy's Learned to Stop Worrying and Love its Twitter Roasts of McDonald's," *Forbes,* October 8, 2018, https://www.forbes.com/sites/andriacheng/2018/10/08/wendys-twitter-roasts-have-become-the-envy-of-marketers-heres-how-it-does-it/#3763f504fea4

8. See, for example, T. Cruwys, E. I. South, K. H. Greenaway, and S. A. Haslam, "Social Identity Reduces Depression by Fostering Positive Attributions," *Social Psychological and Personality Science* 6, no. 1 (2015): 65–74.

9. S. Zhang, G. Chen, X.-P. Chen, D. Liu, and M. D. Johnson, "Relational Versus Collective Identification Within Workgroups: Conceptualization, Measurement Development, and Nomological Network Building," *Journal of Management* 40, no. 6 (2014): 1700–31.

10. X. Qin, P. W. Hom, and M. Xu, "Am I a Peasant or a Worker? An Identity Strain Perspective on Turnover Among Developing-World Migrants," *Human Relations* 72, no. 4 (2019): 801–33.

11. M. P. Fladerer, S. Alexander Haslam, N. K. Steffens, and D. Frey, "The Value of Speaking for 'Us': The Relationship Between CEO's Use of I- and We-Referencing Language and Subsequent Organizational Performance," *Journal of Business and Psychology* (in press).

12. M. B. Brewer, "Intergroup Discrimination: Ingroup Love or Outgroup Hate?" in C. Sibley and F. Barlow (eds.), *The Cambridge Handbook of the Psychology of Prejudice* (Cambridge, UK: Cambridge University Press, 2017): 90–110; L. Hamley, C. A. Houkamau, D. Osborne, F. Kate Barlow, and C. G. Sibley, "Ingroup Love or Outgroup Hate (or Both)? Mapping Distinct Bias Profiles in the Population," *Personality and Social Psychology Bulletin* 46, no. 2 (2020): 171–88.

13. D. Armstrong, "Favoritism, not Hostility, Causes Most Discrimination, Says UW Psychology Professor," *University of Washington News* [press release], May 19, 2014, https://www.washington.edu/news/2014/05/19/favoritism-not-hostility-causes-most-discrimination-says-uw-psychology-professor/; A. G. Greenwald and T. F.

Pettigrew, "With Malice Toward None and Charity for Some: Ingroup Favoritism Enables Discrimination," *American Psychologist* 69, no. 7 (2014): 669–84.

14. M. Li, B. Leidner, and S. Fernandez-Campos, "Stepping Into Perpetrators' Shoes: How In-Group Transgressions and Victimization Shape Support for Retributive Justice Through Perspective-Taking With Perpetrators," *Personality and Social Psychology Bulletin* 46, no. 3 (2020): 424–438; Q. McLamore, L. Adelman, and B. Leidner, "Challenges to Traditional Narratives of Intractable Conflict Decrease Ingroup Glorification," *Personality and Social Psychology Bulletin* 45, no. 12 (2019): 1702–16.

15. R. Henderson, "How Modern Life Made Us Angry: Research Reveals Key Factors Underlying Political Tension," *Psychology Today* [blog], January 24, 2019, https://www .psychologytoday.com/us/blog/after-service/201901/how-modern-life-made-us-angry; G. Geher, "Beware the 'All Trump Supporters Are Like That' Trap," *Psychology Today* [blog], November 12, 2016, https://www.psychologytoday .com/us/blog/darwins-subterranean-world/201611/beware-the-all-trump-supporters-are-trap; A.G. Livingstone, L. Fernández Rodríguez, and A. Rothers, "'They Just Don't Understand Us': The Role of Felt Understanding in Intergroup Relations," *Journal of Personality and Social Psychology* (in press).

16. E. Halperin, "Group-Based Hatred in Intractable Conflict in Israel," *Journal of Conflict Resolution* 52 (2008): 713–36; M. Katzir, M. Hoffmann, and N. Liberman, "Disgust as an Essentialist Emotion That Signals Nonviolent Outgrouping With Potentially Low Social Costs," *Emotion* 19, no. 5 (2019): 841–62.

17. S. L. Neuberg et al., "Religion and Intergroup Conflict: Findings From the Global Group Relations Project," *Psychological Science* 25, no. 1 (2014): 198–206.

18. J. Goplen and E. A. Plant, "A Religious Worldview: Protecting One's Meaning System Through Religious Prejudice," *Personality and Social Psychology Bulletin* 41, no. 11 (2015): 1474–87.

19. J. Conrad Jackson, N. Castelo, and K. Gray, "Could a rising robot workforce make humans less prejudiced?" *American Psychologist* (in press).

20. A. Chang, P. Bordia, and J. Duck, "Punctuated Equilibrium and Linear Progression: Toward a New Understanding of Group Development," *Academy of Management Journal* 46, no. 1 (2003): 106–17; M. J. Garfield and A. R. Denis, "Toward an Integrated Model of Group Development: Disruption of Routines by Technology-Induced Change," *Journal of Management Information Systems* 29, no. 3 (2012): 43–86; C. J. Gersick. "Time and Transition in Work Teams: Toward a New Model of Group Development," *Academy of Management Journal* 31, no. 1 (1988): 1–41; M. J. Waller, J. M. Conte, C. B. Gibson, and M. A. Carpenter, "The Effect of Individual Perceptions of Deadlines on Team Performance," *Academy of Management Review* 26, no. 4 (2001): 586–600.

21. M. M. Kazmer, "Disengaging From a Distributed Research Project: Refining a Model of Group Departures," *Journal of the American Society for Information Science and Technology* 61, no. 4 (2010): 758–71.

22. B. B. Morgan, E. Salas, and A. S. Glickman, "An Analysis of Team Evolution and Maturation," *The Journal of General Psychology* 120, no. 3 (1993): 277–91; B. Tuckman, "Some Stages of Development in Groups," *Psychological Bulletin* 63, no. 1 (1965): 384–99.

23. K. Brooks, "What Is the Independent Group and Who Are Its Members?" *BirminghamLive*, February 25, 2019, https://www.birminghammail.co.uk/news/midlands-news/what-independent-group-who-members-15867357; *The Independent Group* [website], accessed February 25, 2019, https://www.theindependent.group/; J. Sharman, "Independent Group For Change Disbands After Losing Every MP at General Election," *The Independent*, December 19, 2019, https://www.independent.co.uk/news/uk/politics/independent-

group-for-change-uk-election-results-mps-anna-soubry-chuka-umunna-a9254166.html

24. T. L. Dumas and T. L. Stanko, "Married With Children: How Family Role Identification Shapes Leadership Behaviors at Work," *Personnel Psychology* 70, no. 3 (2017): 597–633.

25. J. Capitano, M. S. DiRenzo, K. J. Aten, and J. H. Greenhaus, "Role Identity Salience and Boundary Permeability Preferences: An Examination of Enactment and Protection Effects," *Journal of Vocational Behavior* 102 (2017): 99–111.

26. Y. Liu, T. Vriend, and O. Janssen, "To Be (Creative), or Not to Be (Creative)? A Sensemaking Perspective of Creative Role Expectations," *Journal of Business and Psychology* (in press).

27. C-M. Alcover, R. Rico, W. H. Turnley, and M. C. Bolino, "Understanding the Changing Nature of Psychological Contracts in 21st Century Organizations: A Multiple-Foci Exchange Relationships Approach and Proposed Framework," *Organizational Psychology Review* 7, no. 1 (2017): 4–35; D. M. Rousseau, "Psychological and Implied Contracts in Organizations," *Employee Responsibilities and Rights Journal* 2, no. 2 (1989): 121–39; J. A-M. Coyle-Shapiro, S. Pereira Costa, W. Doden, and C. Chang, "Psychological Contracts: Past, Present, and Future," *Annual Review of Organizational Psychology and Organizational Behavior,* 6 (2019): 145–69.

28. N. Wellman, D. M. Mayer, M. Ong, and D. S. DeRue, "When Are Do-Gooders Treated Badly? Legitimate Power, Role Expectations, and Reactions to Moral Objection in Organizations," *Journal of Applied Psychology* 101, no. 6 (2016): 793–814.

29. P. M. Bal, A. H. De Lange, P. G. W. Jansen, and M. E. G. Van Der Velde, "Psychological Contract Breach and Job Attitudes: A Meta-Analysis of Age as a Moderator," *Journal of Vocational Behavior* 72 (2008): 143–58; H. Zhao, S. J. Wayne, B. C. Glibkowski, and J. Bravo, "The Impact of Psychological Contract Breach on Work-Related Outcomes: A Meta-Analysis," *Personnel Psychology* 60 (2007): 647–80; H. Dixon-Fowler, A O'Leary-Kelly, J. Johnson, and M. Waite, "Sustainability and Ideology-Infused Psychological Contracts: An Organizational- and Employee-Level Perspective," *Human Resource Management Review* (in press).

30. P. M. Bal, J. Hofmans, and T. Polat, "Breaking Psychological Contracts With the Burden of Workload: A Weekly Study of Job Resources as Moderators," *Applied Psychology: An International Review* 66, no. 1 (2017): 143–67; P. Bordia, S. L. D. Restubog, S. Bordia, and R. L. Tang, "Effects of Resource Availability on Social Exchange Relationships: The Case of Employee Psychological Contract Explanations," *Journal of Management* 43, no. 5 (2017): 1447–71; M. Priesemuth and R. M. Taylor, "The More I Want, the Less I Have to Give: The Moderating Role of Psychological Entitlement on the Relationship Between Psychological Contract Violation, Depressive Mood States, and Citizenship Behavior," *Journal of Organizational Behavior* 37 (2016): 967–82.

31. K. Kiazad, M. L. Kraimer, and S. E. Seibert, "More Than Grateful: How Employee Embeddedness Explains the Link Between Psychological Contract Fulfillment and Employee Extra-Role Behavior," *Human Relations* 72, no. 8 (2019): 1315–1340.

32. R. L. Kahn, D. M. Wolfe, R. P. Quinn, J. D. Snoek, and R.A. Rosenthal, *Organizational Stress* (Oxford, England: Wiley, 1964).

33. S. Kerr, "On the Folly of Rewarding A, While Hoping for B," *Academy of Management Executive* 9, no. 1 (1995): 7–14; K. S. Wilson and H. M. Baumann, "Capturing a More Complete View of Employees' Lives outside of Work: The Introduction and Development of New Interrole Conflict Constructs," *Personnel Psychology* 68, no. 2 (2015): 235–82.

34. Kahn et al., *Organizational Stress.*

35. B D. Webster and B. D. Edwards, "Does Holding a Second Job Viewed as a Calling Impact One's Work at the Primary Job?" *Journal of Vocational Behavior* 114 (2019): 112–25.

36. C. Collins, "The Real Mommy War Is Against the State," *The New York Times,* February 9, 2019, https://www .nytimes.com/2019/02/09/opinion/sunday/the-real-mommy-war-is-against-the-state.html

37. L. Miller, "Nurses Not Immune to Stress From Disaster," *DailyNurse* [blog], February 16, 2019, https://dailynurse .com/nurses-not-immune-to-stress-from-disaster/

38. See, for example, F. T. Amstad, L. L. Meier, U. Fasel, A. Elfering, and N. K. Semmer, "A Meta-Analysis of Work-Family Conflict and Various Outcomes With a Special Emphasis on Cross-Domain Versus Matching-Domain Relations," *Journal of Occupational Health Psychology* 16, no. 2 (2011): 151–69; E. M. Eatough, C-H. Chang, S. A. Miloslavic, and R. E. Johnson, "Relationships of Role Stressors With Organizational Citizenship Behavior: A Meta-Analysis," *Journal of Applied Psychology* 96, no. 3 (2011): 619–32; S. Gilboa, A. Shirom, Y. Fried, and C. Cooper, "A Meta-Analysis of Work Demand Stressors and Job Performance: Examining Main and Moderating Effects," *Personnel Psychology* 61 (2008): 227–71.

39. D. Vora and T. Kostova. "A Model of Dual Organizational Identification in the Context of the Multinational Enterprise," *Journal of Organizational Behavior* 28 (2007): 327–50.

40. C. Reade, "Dual Identification in Multinational Corporations: Local Managers and Their Psychological Attachment to the Subsidiary versus the Global Organization," *International Journal of Human Resource Management* 12, no. 3 (2001): 405–24.

41. J. Gonzalez, "Shoes Optional: San Francisco Startup Breaks Norms With Shoe-less Office Space," *NBC: Bay Area,* May 28, 2018, https://www.nbcbayarea.com/news/local/Shoes-Optional-San-Francisco-Startup-Breaks-Office-Norms-483883711.html

42. M. S. Hagger, P. Rentzelas, and N. K. D. Chatzisrantis, "Effects of Individualist and Collectivist Group Norms and Choice on Intrinsic Motivation," *Motivation and Emotion* 38, no. 2 (2014): 215–23; M. G. Ehrhart and S. E. Naumann, "Organizational Citizenship Behavior in Work Groups: A Group Norms Approach," *Journal of Applied Psychology* 89, no. 6 (2004): 960–74.

43. A. Lieberman, K. E. Duke, and O. Amir, "How Incentive Framing Can Harness the Power of Social Norms," *Organizational Behavior and Human Decision Processes* 151 (2019): 118–131; D. B. Shank, Y. Kashima, K. Peters, Y. Li, G. Robins, and M. Kirley, "Norm Talk and Human Cooperation: Can We Talk Ourselves Into Cooperation?" *Journal of Personality and Social Psychology* 117, no. 1 (2019): 99–123.

44. Y. Huang, K. M. Kendrick, and R. Yu, "Conformity to the Opinions of Other People Lasts for No More Than 3 Days," *Psychological Science* 25, no. 7 (2014): 1388–93.

45. A. Luksyte, D. R. Avery, and G. Yeo, "It Is Worse When You Do It: Examining the Interactive Effects of Coworker Presenteeism and Demographic Similarity," *Journal of Applied Psychology* 100, no. 4 (2015): 1107–23.

46. E. Delvaux, N. Vanbeselaere, and B. Mesquita, "Dynamic Interplay Between Norms and Experiences of Anger and Gratitude in Groups," *Small Group Research* 46, no. 3 (2015): 300–23.

47. N. Pontus Leander, M. Agostini, W. Stroebe, J. Kreienkamp, R. Spears, T. Kuppens, M. Van Zomeren, S. Otten, and A. W. Kruglanski, "Frustration-Affirmation? Thwarted Goals Motivate Compliance With Social Norms for Violence and Nonviolence," *Journal of Personality and Social Psychology* (in press).

48. R. B. Cialdini and N. J. Goldstein, "Social Influence: Compliance and Conformity," *Annual Review of Psychology* 55 (2004): 591–621.

49. S. E. Asch, "Effects of Group Pressure on the Modification and Distortion of Judgments," in H. Guetzkow (ed.), *Groups, Leadership and Men* (Pittsburgh: Carnegie Press, 1951): 177–90.

50. E. C. Nook, D. C. Ong, S. A. Morelli, J. P. Mitchell, and J. Zaki, "Prosocial Conformity: Prosocial Norms Generalize Across Behavior and Empathy," *Personality and Social Psychology Bulletin* 42, no. 8 (2016): 1045–62.

51. S. Sansfacon and C. E. Amiot, "The Impact of Group Norms and Behavioral Congruence on the Internalization of an Illegal Downloading Behavior," *Group Dynamics: Theory Research and Practice* 18, no. 2 (2014): 174–88; L. Rosh, L. R. Offermann, and R. Van Diest, "Too Close for Comfort? Distinguishing between Team Intimacy and Team Cohesion," *Human Resource Management Review* 22, no. 2 (2012): 116–27.

52. J. S. Hassard, "Rethinking the Hawthorne Studies: The Western Electric Research in Its Social, Political, and Historical Context," *Human Relations* 65, no. 11 (2012): 1431–61.

53. P. Roos, M. Gelfand, D. Nau, and J. Lun, "Societal Threat and Cultural Variation in the Strength of Social Norms: An Evolutionary Basis," *Organizational Behavior and Human Decision Processes* 129 (2015): 14–23.

54. A. B. Carroll, "Corporate Social Responsibility," *Business & Society* 38, no. 1 (1999): 268–95.

55. T. Masson and I. Fritsche, "Adherence to Climate Change-Related Ingroup Norms: Do Dimensions of Group Identification Matter?" *European Journal of Social Psychology* 44, no. 5 (2014): 455–65.

56. A. J. Duff, M. Podolsky, M. Biron, and C. C. A. Chan, "The Interactive Effect of Team and Manager Absence on Employee Absence: A Multilevel Field Study," *Journal of Occupational and Organizational Psychology* 88, no. 1 (2015): 61–79.

57. A. Mandeville, J. Halbesleben, and M. Whitman, "Misalignment and Misperception of Preferences to Utilize Family-friendly Benefits: Implications for Benefit Utilization and Work-Family Conflict," *Personnel Psychology* 69, no. 4 (2016): 895–929.

58. M. M. Duguid and M. C. Thomas-Hunt, "Condoning Stereotyping? How Awareness of Stereotyping Prevalence Impacts Expression of Stereotypes," *Journal of Applied Psychology* 100, no. 2 (2015): 343–59.

59. J. J. Kish-Gephart, D. A. Harrison, and L. K. Treviño, "Bad Apples, Bad Cases, and Bad Barrels: Meta-Analytic Evidence About Sources of Unethical Decisions at Work," *Journal of Applied Psychology* 95, no. 1 (2010): 1–31.

60. N. A. Bowling and T. A. Beehr, "Workplace Harassment From the Victim's Perspective: A Theoretical Model and Meta-Analysis," *Journal of Applied Psychology* 91, no. 5 (2006): 998–1012; J. D. Mackey, R. E. Frieder, J. R. Brees, and M. J. Martinko, "Abusive Supervision: A Meta-Analysis and Empirical Review," *Journal of Management* 43, no. 6 (2017): 1940–65; D. D. van Jaarsveld, S. L. D. Restubog, D. D. Walker, and R. K. Amarnani, "Misbehaving Customers: Understanding and Managing Customer Injustice in Service Organizations," *Organizational Dynamics* 44 (2015): 273–80.

61. See C. Pearson, L. M. Andersson, and C. L. Porath, "Workplace Incivility," in S. Fox and P. E. Spector (eds.), *Counterproductive Work Behavior: Investigations of Actors and Targets* (Washington, DC: American Psychological Association, 2005), 177–200.

62. M. S. Christian and A. P. J. Ellis, "Examining the Effects of Sleep Deprivation on Workplace Deviance: A Self-Regulatory Perspective," *Academy of Management Journal* 54, no. 5 (2011): 913–34.

63. M. Yoshie and D. A. Sauter, "Cultural Norms Influence Nonverbal Emotion Communication: Japanese Vocalizations of Socially Disengaging Emotions," *Emotion* 20, no. 3 (2020): 513–17.

64. M. S. Hagger, P. Rentzelas, and N. K. D. Chatzisrantis, "Effects of Individualist and Collectivist Group Norms and Choice on Intrinsic Motivation."

65. S. Aslani et al., "Dignity, Face, and Honor Cultures: A Study of Negotiation Strategy and Outcomes in Three Cultures," *Journal of Organizational Behavior* 37, no. 8 (2016): 1178–201.

66. E. Stamkou, G. A. van Kleef, A. C. Homan, M. J. Gelfand, F. J. R. van de Vijver, M. C. van Egmond, D. Boer, N. Phiri, N. Ayub, Z. Kinias, K. Cantarero, D. Efrat Treister, A. Figueiredo, H. Hashi-

moto, E. B. Hofmann, R. P. Lima, and I-C. Lee, "Cultural Collectivism and Tightness Moderate Responses to Norm Violators: Effects on Social Perception, Moral Emotions, and Leader Support," *Personality and Social Psychology Bulletin* 45, no. 6 (2019): 947–964.

67. J. Dippong and W. Kalkhoff, "Predicting Performance Expectations From Affective Impressions: Linking Affect Control Theory and Status Characteristics Theory," *Social Science Research* 50 (2015): 1–14; A. E. Randel, L. Chay-Hoon, and P. C. Earley, "It's Not Just About Differences: An Integration of Role Identity Theory and Status Characteristics Theory," in M. C. Thomas-Hunt (ed.), *Research on Managing Groups and Teams* (Bingley, West Yorkshire, UK: Emerald Group Publishing, Ltd., 2005), 23–42.

68. A. E. Randel, L. Chay-Hoon, and P. C. Earley, "It's Not Just About Differences: An Integration of Role Identity Theory and Status Characteristics Theory."

69. P. F. Hewlin, "Wearing the Cloak: Antecedents and Consequences of Creating Facades of Conformity," *Journal of Applied Psychology* 94, no. 3 (2009): 727–41.

70. B. Groysberg, J. T. Polzer, and H. A. Elfenbein, "Too Many Cooks Spoil the Broth: How High-Status Individuals Decrease Group Effectiveness."

71. D. B. Shank, Y. Kashima, S. Peters, Y. Li, G. Robins, and M. Kirley, "Norm Talk and Human Cooperation: Can We Talk Ourselves Into Cooperation," *Journal of Personality and Social Psychology* 117, no. 1 (2019): 99–123.

72. C. Bendersky and N. P. Shah, "The Cost of Status Enhancement: Performance Effects of Individuals' Status Mobility in Task Groups," *Organization Science* 23, no. 2 (2012): 308–22.

73. R. D. Arnett and J. Sidanius, "Sacrificing Status for Social Harmony: Concealing Relatively High Status Identities From One's Peers," *Organizational Behavior and Human Decision Processes* 147 (2018): 108–26.

74. O. Janssen and L. Gao, "Supervisory Responsiveness and Employee Self-Perceived Status and Voice Behavior," *Journal of Management* 41, no. 7 (2015): 1854–72.

75. B. Groysberg, J. T. Polzer, and H. A. Elfenbein, "Too Many Cooks Spoil the Broth: How High-Status Individuals Decrease Group Effectiveness."

76. S. Yu and G. J. Kilduff, "Knowing Where Others Stand: Accuracy and Performance Effects of Individuals' Perceived Status Hierarchies," *Journal of Personality and Social Psychology* (in press).

77. R. Pekrun, K. Murayama, H. W. Marsh, T. Goetz, and A. C. Frenzel, "Happy Fish in Little Ponds: Testing a Reference Group Model of Achievement and Emotion," *Journal of Personality and Social Psychology* 117, no. 1 (2019): 166–85.

78. A. M. Christie and J. Barling, "Beyond Status: Relating Status Inequality to Performance and Health in Teams," *Journal of Applied Psychology* 95, no. 5 (2010): 920–34; G. J. Kilduff, R. Willer, and C. Anderson, "Hierarchy and Its Discontents: Status Disagreement Leads to Withdrawal of Contribution and Lower Group Performance," *Organization Science* 27, no. 2 (2016): 373–90.

79. E. M. Anicich, N. J. Fast, N. Halevy, and A. D. Galinsky, "When the Bases of Social Hierarchy Collide: Power Without Status Drives Interpersonal Conflict," *Organization Science* 27, no. 1 (2016): 123–40; N. A. Hays and C. Bendersky, "Not All Inequality Is Created Equal: Effects of Status Versus Power Hierarchies on Competition for Upward Mobility," *Journal of Personality and Social Psychology* 108, no. 6: 867–82.

80. L. Collins, "How the BBC Women Are Working Toward Equal Pay," *The New Yorker,* July 23, 2018, https://www .newyorker.com/magazine/2018/07/23/how-the-bbc-women-are-working-toward-equal-pay

81. J. B. Pryor, G. D. Reeder, and A. E. Monroe, "The Infection of Bad Company: Stigma by Association," *Journal of Personality and Social Psychology* 102, no. 2 (2012): 224–41; E. Goffman, *Stigma: Notes on the Management of Spoiled Identity* (New York, NY: Touchstone Digital, 2009).

82. J. D. Wellman, C. L. Wilkins, E. E. Newell, and D. Kamiya Stewart, "Conflicting Motivations: Understanding How Low-Status Group Members Respond to Ingroup Discrimination Claimants," *Personality and Social Psychology Bulletin* 45, no. 8 (2019): 1170–83.

83. M. Cikara and J. J. Van Bavel, "The Neuroscience of Intergroup Relations: An Integrative Review," *Perspectives on Psychological Science* 9, no. 3 (2014): 245–74; H. Tajfel, "Social Psychology of Intergroup Relations," *Annual Review of Psychology* 33, no. 1 (1982): 1–39.

84. M. Rubin, C. Badea, and J. Jetten, "Low Status Groups Show In-Group Favoritism to Compensate for Their Low Status and Compete for Higher Status," *Group Processes & Intergroup Relations* 17, no. 5 (2014): 563–76.

85. C. L. Wilkins, J. D. Wellman, L. G. Babbitt, N. R. Toosi, and K. D. Schad, "You Can Win But I Can't Lose: Bias against High-Status Groups Increases Their Zero-Sum Beliefs about Discrimination," *Journal of Experimental Social Psychology* 57 (2014): 1–14.

86. T. J. Bouchard, J. Barsaloux, and G. Drauden, "Brainstorming Procedure, Group Size, and Sex as Determinants of the Problem-Solving Effectiveness of Groups and Individuals," *Journal of Applied Psychology* 59, no. 2 (1974): 135–38.

87. See, for example, R. B. Gallupe, A. R. Dennis, W. H. Cooper, J. S. Valacich, L. M. Bastianutti, and J. Nunamaker, "Electronic Brainstorming and Group Size," *Academy of Management Journal* 35, no. 2 (2012): 350–69.

88. J. S. Valacich, B. C. Wheeler, B. E. Mennecke, and R. Wachter, "The Effects of Numerical and Logical Group Size on Computer-Mediated Idea Generation," *Organizational Behavior and Human Decision Processes* 62, no. 3 (1995): 318–29.

89. R. M. Bray, N. L. Kerr, and R. S. Atkin, "Effects of Group Size, Problem Difficulty, and Sex on Group Performance and Member Reactions," *Journal of Personality and Social Psychology* 36 no. 11 (1978): 1224–40.

90. S. T. La Macchia, W. R. Louis, M. J. Hornsey, and G. J. Leonardelli, "In Small We Trust: Lay Theories About Small and Large Groups," *Personality and Social Psychology Bulletin* 42, no. 10 (2016): 1321–34; M. M. Butts, D. C. Lunt, T. L. Freling, and A. S. Gabriel, "Helping one or helping many? A theoretical integration and meta-analytic review of the compassion fade literature," *Organizational Behavior and Human Decision Processes* 151 (2019): 16–33.

91. R. B. Lount Jr. and S. L. Wilk, "Working Harder or Hardly Working? Posting Performance Eliminates Social Loafing and Promotes Social Laboring in Workgroups," *Management Science* 60, no. 5 (2014): 1098–106; S. M. Murphy, S. J. Wayne, R. C. Liden, and B. Erdogan, "Understanding Social Loafing: The Role of Justice Perceptions and Exchange Relationships," *Human Relations* 56, no. 1 (2003): 61–84; R. C. Liden, S. J. Wayne, R. A. Jaworski, and N. Bennett, "Social Loafing: A Field Investigation," *Journal of Management* 30, no. 2 (2004): 285–304.

92. Karau and Williams, "Social Loafing."

93. D. L. Smrt and S. J. Karau, "Protestant Work Ethic Moderates Social Loafing," *Group Dynamics: Theory Research and Practice* 15, no. 3 (2011): 267–74.

94. M. C. Schippers, "Social Loafing Tendencies and Team Performance: The Compensating Effect of Agreeableness and Conscientiousness," *Academy of Management Learning & Education* 13, no. 1 (2014): 62–81.

95. S. J. Perry, N. M. Lorinkova, E. M. Hunter, A. Hubbard, and J. T. McMahon, "When Does Virtuality Really 'Work'? Examining the Role of Work-Family and Virtuality in Social Loafing," *Journal of Management* 42, no. 2 (2016): 449–79.

96. A. Gunnthorsdottir and A. Rapoport, "Embedding Social Dilemmas in Intergroup Competition Reduces Free-Riding," *Organizational Behavior and Human Decision Processes* 101, no. 2 (2006): 184–99; E. M. Stark, J. D. Shaw, and M. K. Duffy, "Preference for Group Work, Winning Orientation, and Social Loafing Behavior in Groups," *Group & Organization Management* 32, no. 6 (2007): 699–723.

97. M. Casey-Campbell and M. L. Martens, "Sticking It All Together: A Critical Assessment of the Group Cohesion-Performance Literature," *International Journal of Management Reviews* 11 (2009): 223–246; E. Salas, R. Grossman, A. M. Hughes, and C. W. Coultas, "Measuring team cohesion: Observations from the science," *Human Factors* 57, no. 3 (2015): 365–74.

98. D. J. Beal, R. R. Cohen, M. J. Burke, and C. L. McLendon, "Cohesion and Performance in Groups: A Meta-Analytic Clarification of Construct Relations," *Journal of Applied Psychology* 88, no. 6 (2003): 989–1004; J. E. Mathieu, M. R. Kukenberger, L. D'Innocenzo, and G. Reilly, "Modeling Reciprocal Team Cohesion-Performance Relationships, as Impacted by Shared Leadership and Members' Competence," *Journal of Applied Psychology* 100, no. 3 (2015): 713–34.

99. A. Gunnthorsdottir and A. Rapoport, "Embedding Social Dilemmas in Intergroup Competition Reduces Free-Riding;" and E. M. Stark, J. D. Shaw, and M. K. Duffy, "Preference for Group Work, Winning Orientation, and Social Loafing Behavior in Groups."

100. M. J. Keith, G. Anderson, J. E. Gaskin, and D. L. Dean, "Team Video Gaming for Team-Building: Effects on Team Performance," *AIS Transactions on Human-Computer Interaction* 10, no. 4 (2018): 205–31.

101. L. L. Greer, "Group Cohesion: Then and Now," *Small Group Research* 43, no. 6 (2012): 655–61.

102. A. Joshi and H. Roh, "The Role of Context in Work Team Diversity Research: A Meta-Analytic Review," *Academy of Management Journal* 52, no. 3 (2009): 599–627; M. Mayo, M. Kakarika, C. Mainemelis, and N. T. Deuschel, "A Metatheoretical Framework of Diversity in Teams," *Human Relations* 70, no. 8 (2017): 911–39; H. van Dijk, M. L. van Engen, and D. van Knippenberg, "Defying Conventional Wisdom: A Meta-Analytical Examination of the Differences Between Demographic and Job-related Diversity Relationships With Performance," *Organizational Behavior and Human Decision Processes* 119, no. 1 (2012): 38–53; D. van Knippenberg and J. N. Mell, "Past, Present, and Potential Future of Team Diversity Research: From Compositional Diversity to Emergent Diversity," *Organizational Behavior and Human Decision Processes* 136 (2016): 135–45.

103. F. Danbold and M. M. Unzueta, "Drawing the Diversity Line: Numerical Thresholds of Diversity Vary by Group Status," *Journal of Personality and Social Psychology* 118, no. 2 (2020): 283–306.

104. E. H. Chang, K. L. Milkman, D. Chugh, and M. Akinola, "Diversity Thresholds: How Social Norms, Visibility, and Scrutiny Relate to Group Composition," *Academy of Management Journal* 62, no. 1 (2019): 144–71.

105. M. E. Ormiston, "Explaining the Link Between Objective and Perceived Differences in Groups: The Role of the Belonging and Distinctiveness Motives," *Journal of Applied Psychology* 101, no. 2 (2016): 222–36; J. Y. Seong, A. L. Kristof-Brown, W-W. Park, D-S. Hong, and Y. Shin, "Person-Group Fit: Diversity Antecedents, Proximal Outcomes, and Performance at the Group Level," *Journal of Management* 41, no. 4 (2015): 1184–213; M. Shemla, B. Meyer, L. Greer, K. A. Jehn, "A Review of Perceived Diversity in Teams: Does How Members Perceive Their Team's Composition Affect Team Processes and Outcomes?" *Journal of Organizational Behavior* 37 (2016): S89–S106.

106. See, for example, A. K. Bader, L. E. Kemper, and F. J. Froese, "Who Promotes a Value-in-Diversity Perspective? A Fuzzy Set Analysis of Executives' Individual and Organizational Characteristics," *Human Resource Management* 58 (2019): 203–17.

107. M. Mayo, D. van Knippenberg, L. Guillén, and S. Firfiray, "Team Diversity and Categorization Salience: Capturing Diversity-Blind, Intergroup-Biased, and Multicultural Perceptions," *Organizational Research Methods* 19, no. 3 (2016): 433–74.

108. See, for example, J. S. Chun and J. N. Choi, "Members' Needs, Intragroup Conflict, and Group Performance," *Journal of Applied Psychology* 99, no. 3 (2014): 437–50.

109. D. S. Staples and L. Zhao, "The Effects of Cultural Diversity in Virtual Teams Versus Face-to-Face Teams," *Group Decision and Negotiation* 15, no. 4 (2006): 389–406.

110. R. B. Lount, O. J. Sheldon, F. Rink, and K. W. Phillips, "Biased Perceptions of Racially Diverse Teams and Their Consequences for Resource Support," *Organization Science* 26, no. 5 (2015): 1351–64.

111. K. J. Klein, A. P. Knight, J. C. Ziegert, B. C. Lim, and J. L. Saltz, "When Team Members' Values Differ: The Moderating Role of Team Leadership," *Organizational Behavior and Human Decision Processes* 114, no. 1 (2011): 25–36; G. Park and R. P. DeShon, "A Multilevel Model of Minority Opinion Expression and Team Decision-Making Effectiveness," *Journal of Applied Psychology* 95, no. 5 (2010): 824–33.

112. J. S. Chun and J. N. Choi, "Members' Needs, Intragroup Conflict, and Group Performance."

113. A. J. Ferguson and R. S. Peterson, "Sinking Slowly: Diversity in Propensity to Trust Predicts Downward Trust Spirals in Small Groups," *Journal of Applied Psychology* 100, no. 4 (2015): 1012–24.

114. S. T. Bell, A. J. Villado, M. A. Lukasik, L. Belau, and A. L. Briggs, "Getting Specific About Demographic Diversity Variables and Team Performance Relationships: A Meta-Analysis," *Journal of Management* 37, no. 3 (2011): 709–43; S. K. Horwitz and I. B. Horwitz, "The Effects of Team Diversity on Team Outcomes: A Meta-Analytic Review of Team Demography," *Journal of Management* 33, no. 6 (2007): 987–1015; van Dijk et al., "Defying conventional wisdom"; S. S. Webber and L. M. Donahue, "Impact of Highly and Less Job-related Diversity on Work Group Cohesion and Performance: A meta-analysis," *Journal of Management* 27, no. 2 (2001): 141–62.

115. S. Y. Cheung, Y. gong, M. Wang, L. Zhou, and J. Shi, "When and How Does Functional Diversity Influence Team Innovation? The Mediating Role of Knowledge Sharing and the Moderation Role of Affect-based Trust in a Team," *Human Relations* 69, no. 7 (2016): 1507–31.

116. A. C. Homan, S. Gündemir, C. Buengeler, and G. A. van Kleef, "Leading Diversity: Towards a Theory of Functional Leadership in Diverse Teams," *Journal of Applied Psychology* (in press); M. R. Kukenberger and L. D'Innocenzo, "The Building Blocks of Shared Leadership: The Interactive Effects of Diversity Types, Team Climate, and Time," *Personnel Psychology* 73 (2020): 125–150; M. Shemla, E. Kearney, J. Wegge, and S. Stegmann, "Unlocking the Performance Potential of Functionally Diverse Teams: The Paradoxical Role of Leader Mood," *Journal of Occupational and Organizational Psychology* (in press).

117. E. B. Smith and Y. Hou, "Redundant Heterogeneity and Group Performance," *Organization Science* 26, no. 1 (2015): 37–51.

118. H. Huettermann, S. Doering, and S. Boerner, "Understanding the Development of Team Identification: A Qualitative Study in UN Peacebuilding Teams," *Journal of Business and Psychology* 32, no. 2 (2017): 217–34.

119. D. C. Lau and J. K. Murnighan, "Demographic Diversity and Faultlines: The Compositional Dynamics of Organizational Groups," *Academy of Management Review* 23, no. 2 (1998): 325–40; M. Kulkarni, "Language-Based Diversity and Faultlines in Organizations," *Journal of Organizational Behavior* 36, no. 1 (2015): 128–46.

120. L. M. Leslie, "A Status-based Multilevel Model of Ethnic Diversity and Work Unit Performance," *Journal of Management* 43, no. 2 (2017): 426–54.

121. See M. B. Thatcher and P. C. Patel, "Group Faultlines: A Review, Integration, and Guide to Future Research," *Journal of Management* 38, no. 4 (2012): 969–1009.

122. K. Bezrukova, S. M. B. Thatcher, K. A. Jehn, and C. S. Spell, "The Effects of Alignments: Examining Group Faultlines, Organizational Cultures, and Performance," *Journal of Applied Psychology* 97, no. 1 (2012): 77–92.

123. D. Cooper, P. C. Patel, and S. B. Thatcher, "It Depends: Environmental Context and the Effects of Faultlines on Top Management Team Performance," *Organization Science* 25, no. 2 (2014): 633–52; R. Rico, M. Sanchez-Manzanares, M. Antino, and D. Lau, "Bridging Team Faultlines by Combining Task Role Assignment and Goal Structure Strategies," *Journal of Applied Psychology* 97, no. 2 (2012): 407–20; Smith and Hou, "Redundant Heterogeneity and Group Performance."

124. A. C. Homan, C. Buengeler, R. A. Eckhoff, W. P. van Ginkel, and S. C. Voelpel, "The Interplay of Diversity Training and Diversity Beliefs on Team Creativity in Nationally Diverse Teams," *Journal of Applied Psychology* 100, no. 5 (2015): 1456–67.

125. R. Mitchell and B. Boyle, "Professional Diversity, Identity Salience and Team Innovation: The Moderating Role of Open-Mindedness Norms," *Journal of Organizational Behavior* 36, no. 6 (2015): 873–94; and F. Schölmerich, C. C. Schermuly, and J. Deller, "To Believe or Not to Believe? The Joint Impact of Faultlines and Pro-Diversity Beliefs on Diplomats' Performance," *Human Performance* 30, nos. 2–3 (2017): 99–115.

126. A. Hajro, C. B. Gibson, and M. Pudelko, "Knowledge Exchange Processes in Multicultural Teams: Linking Organizational Diversity Climates to Teams' Effectiveness," *Academy of Management Journal* 60, no. 1 (2017): 345–72.

127. J. A. Chatman, L. L. Greer, E. Sherman, and B. Doerr, "Blurred Lines: How the Collectivism Norm Operates Through Perceived Group Diversity to Boost or Harm Group Performance in Himalayan Mountain Climbing," *Organization Science* 30, no. 2 (2019): 235–45.

128. N. Breugst, R. Preller, H. Patzelt, and D. A. Shepherd, "Information Reliability and Team Reflection as Contingencies of the Relationship Between Information Elaboration and Team Decision Quality," *Journal of Organizational Behavior* 39, no. 10 (2018): 1314–1329.

129. G. Park and R. P. DeShon, "Effects of Group-Discussion Integrative Complexity on Intergroup Relations in a Social Dilemma," *Organizational Behavior and Human Decision Processes* 146 (2018): 62–75.

130. M-H. Tsai and C. Bendersky, "The Pursuit of Information Sharing: Expressing Task Conflicts as Debates vs. Disagreements Increases Perceived Receptivity to Dissenting Opinions in Groups," *Organization Science* 27, no. 1 (2016): 141–56.

131. B. B. Baltes, M. W. Dickson, M. P. Sherman, C. C. Bauer, and J. LaGanke, "Computer-mediated Communication and Group Decision Making: A Meta-Analysis," *Organizational Behavior and Human Decision Processes* 87, no. 1 (2002): 156–79.

132. L. Thompson and D. Hrebec, "Lose-lose Agreements in Interdependent Decision Making," *Psychological Bulletin* 120, no. 3 (1996): 396–409.

133. R. I. Swaab, K. W. Phillips, and M. Schaerer, "Secret Conversation Opportunities Facilitate Minority Influence in Virtual Groups: The Influence on Majority Power, Information Processing, and Decision Quality," *Organizational Behavior and Human Decision Processes*," 133 (2016): 17–32.

134. B. Oc, M. R. Bashshur, and C. Moore, "Head Above the Parapet: How Minority Subordinates Influence Group Outcomes and the Consequences They Face for Doing So," *Journal of Applied Psychology* 104, no. 7 (2019): 929–45.

135. P. Satterstrom, J. T. Polzer, L. B. Kwan, O. P. Hauser, W. Wiruchnipawan, and M. Burke, "Thin Slices of Workgroups," *Organizational Behavior and Human Decision Processes* 151 (2019): 104–17.

136. B. L. Bonner, S. D. Sillito, and M. R. Baumann, "Collective Estimation: Accuracy, Expertise, and Extroversion as Sources of Intra-Group Influence," *Organizational Behavior and Human Decision Processes* 103, no. 1 (2007): 121–33.

137. J. E. Kammer, W. Gaissmaier, T. Reimer, and C. C. Schermuly, "The Adaptive Use of Recognition in Group Decision Making," *Cognitive Science* 38, no. 5 (2014): 911–42.

138. G. Stasser and S. Abele, "Collective Choice, Collaboration, and Communication," *Annual Review of Psychology* 71 (2020): 589–612.

139. J. R. Mesmer-Magnus and L. A. DeChurch, "Information Sharing and Team Performance: A Meta-Analysis," *Journal of Applied Psychology* 94, no. 2 (2009): 535–46.

140. I. L. Janis, "Groupthink," *Psychology Today* 5, no. 6 (1971): 43–46.

141. G. Park and R. P. DeShon, "A Multilevel Model of Minority Opinion Expression and Team Decision-Making Effectiveness," *Journal of Applied Psychology* 95, no. 5 (2010): 824–33.

142. R. Benabou, "Groupthink: Collective Delusions in Organizations and Markets," *Review of Economic Studies* 80 (2013): 429–62; J. A. Goncalo, E. Polman, and C. Maslach, "Can Confidence Come Too Soon? Collective Efficacy, Conflict, and Group Performance over Time," *Organizational Behavior and Human Decision Processes* 113, no. 1 (2010): 13–24.

143. See N. Richardson Ahlfinger and J. K. Esser, "Testing the Groupthink Model: Effects of Promotional Leadership and Conformity Predisposition," *Social Behavior & Personality* 29, no. 1 (2001): 31–41; S. Schultz-Hardt, F. C. Brodbeck, A. Mojzisch, R. Kerschreiter, and D. Frey, "Group Decision Making in Hidden Profile Situations: Dissent as a Facilitator for Decision Quality," *Journal of Personality and Social Psychology* 91, no. 6 (2006): 1080–93.

144. E. Burnstein, E. L. Miller, A. Vinokur, S. Katz, and I. Crowley, "Risky Shift Is Eminently Rational," *Journal of Personality and Social Psychology* 20, no. 1 (1971): 462–71.

145. See I. Yaniv, "Group Diversity and Decision Quality: Amplification and Attenuation of the Framing Effect," *International Journal of Forecasting* 27, no. 1 (2011): 41–49.

146. M. P. Brady and S. Y. Wu, "The Aggregation of Preferences in Groups: Identity, Responsibility, and Polarization," *Journal of Economic Psychology* 31, no. 6 (2010): 950–63.

147. Z. Krizan and R. S. Baron, "Group Polarization and Choice-Dilemmas: How Important Is Self-Categorization?" *European Journal of Social Psychology* 37, no. 1 (2007): 191–201; J. Sieber and R. Ziegler, "Group Polarization Revisited: A Processing Effort Account," *Personality and Social Psychology Bulletin* 45, no. 10 (2019): 1482–98.

148. Stasser and Abele, "Collective Choice, Collaboration, and Communication."

149. See R. P. McGlynn, D. McGurk, V. S. Effland, N. L. Johll, and D. J. Harding, "Brainstorming and Task Performance in Groups Constrained by Evidence," *Organizational Behavior and Human Decision Processes* 93, no. 1 (2004): 75–87; R. C. Litchfield, "Brainstorming Reconsidered: A Goal-Based View," *Academy of Management Review* 33, no. 3 (2008): 649–68.

150. N. L. Kerr and R. S. Tindale, "Group Performance and Decision-Making," *Annual Review of Psychology* 55 (2004): 623–55.

151. C. Faure, "Beyond Brainstorming: Effects of Different Group Procedures on Selection of Ideas and Satisfaction With the Process," *Journal of Creative Behavior* 38, no. 1 (2004): 13–34.

152. P. L. Perrewé, K. L. Zellars, G. R. Ferris, A. M. Rossi, C. J. Kacmar, and D. A. Ralston, "Neutralizing Job Stressors: Political Skill as an Antidote to the Dysfunctional Consequences of Role Conflict," *Academy of Management Journal* 47, no. 1 (2004): 141–52.

CHAPTER 10

1. SoaPen [website], accessed March 8, 2019, https://soapen.com/

2. P. R. Nania, "Women-Owned Design Team Builds a Business by Solving a Problem," *WTOP: Health & Fitness News*, March 8, 2019, https://wtop.com/health-fitness/2019/03/women- owned-design-team-builds-a-business-by-solving-a-problem/

3. J. C. Gorman, "Team Coordination and Dynamics: Two Central Issues," *Current Directions in Psychological Science* 23, no. 5 (2014): 355–60.

4. Ibid.

5. J. A. Cannon-Bowers and C. Bowers, "Team Development and Functioning," in S. Zedeck (ed.), *APA Handbook of Industrial and Organizational Psychology: Building and Developing the Organization,* Vol. 1 (Washington, DC: APA, 2011), 597–650; S. W. J. Kozlowski and B. S. Bell, "Work Groups and Teams in Organizations," in N. Schmitt and S. Highhouse (eds.), *Handbook of Psychology: Industrial and Organizational Psychology*, Vol. 12, 2nd ed. (Hoboken, NJ: Wiley, 2013), 412–69.

6. D. Chan, "Team-Level Constructs," *Annual Review of Organiz- ational Psychology and Organizational Behavior* 6 (2019): 325–48; J. E. Mathieu, P. T. Gallagher, M. A. Domingo, and E. A. Klock, "Embracing Complexity: Reviewing the Past Decade of Team Effectiveness Research," *Annual Review of Organizational Psychology and Organizational Behavior* 6 (2019): 17–46.

7. A. C. Edmondson, *Teaming: How Organizations Learn, Innovate, and Compete in the Knowledge Economy* (San Francisco, CA: Wiley, 2012); A. C. Edmondson, "The Three Pillars of a Teaming Culture," *Harvard Business Review,* December 17, 2013, https://hbr.org/2013/12/the-three-pillars-of-a-teaming-culture; K. Einola and M. Alvesson, "The Making and Unmaking of Teams," *Human Relations* 72, no. 12 (2019): 1891–1919; Mathieu et al., "Embracing Complexity."

8. J. Mathieu, M. T. Maynard, T. Rapp, and L. Gilson, "Team Effectiveness 1997–2007: A Review of Recent Advancements and a Glimpse Into the Future," *Journal of Management* 34, no. 3 (2008): 410–76.

9. StackCommerce, "The Direct-to-Consumer Watch Brand Offering Exceptionally Crafted Watches at an Accessible Price," *Entrepreneur,* February 28, 0219, https://www .entrepreneur.com/article/329233

10. M. Larkin, "Kill the Veterinary Practice to Save It," *Journal of the American Veterinary Medical Association News,* March 1, 2019, https://www.avma.org/News/JAVMANews/Pages/190301h.aspx

11. C. C. Manz and H. P. Sims, "Leading Workers to Lead Themselves: The External Leadership of Self-Managing Work Teams," *Administrative Science Quarterly* 32 (1987): 106–28.

12. A. Nederveen Pieterse, J. R. Hollenbeck, D. van Knippenberg, M. Spitzmüller, N. Dimotakis, E. P. Karam, and D. J. Sleesman, "Hierarchical Leadership Versus Self-Management in Teams: Goal Orientation Diversity as Moderator of Their Relative Effectiveness," *The Leadership Quarterly* (in press).

13. Larkin, "Kill the Veterinary Practice to Save It."

14. G. L. Stewart, S. H. Courtright, and M. R. Barrick, "Peer-Based Control in Self-Managing Teams: Linking Rational and Normative Influence With Individual and Group Performance," *Journal of Applied Psychology* 97, no. 2 (2012): 435–47.

15. C. W. Langfred, "The Downside of Self-Management: A Longitudinal Study of the Effects of Conflict on Trust, Autonomy, and Task Interdependence in Self-Managing Teams," *Academy of Management Journal* 50, no. 4 (2007): 885–900.

16. B. H. Bradley, B. E. Postlethwaite, A. C. Klotz, M. R. Hamdani, and K. G. Brown, "Reaping the Benefits of Task Conflict in Teams: The Critical Role of Team Psychological Safety Climate," *Journal of Applied Psychology,* 97, no. 1 (2012): 151–58.

17. J. Devaro, "The Effects of Self-Managed and Closely Managed Teams on Labor Productivity and Product Quality: An Empirical Analysis of a Cross-Section of Establishments," *Industrial Relations* 47, no. 4 (2008): 659–98.

18. K. Lanaj and J. R. Hollenbeck, "Leadership Over-Emergence in Self-Managing Teams: The Role of Gender and Countervailing Biases," *Academy of Management Journal* 58, no. 5 (2015): 1476–94.

19. R. Davis, "IT and Security Need to Start Playing Nice—Here's How," *Forbes,* March 6, 2019, https://www.forbes .com/sites/extra-hop/2019/03/06/it-and-security-need-to-start-playing-niceheres-how/#29f679c92af4

20. F. Aime, S. Humphrey, D. S. DeRue, and J. B. Paul, "The Riddle of Heterarchy: Power Transitions in Cross-Functional Teams," *Academy of Management Journal* 57, no. 2 (2014): 327–52.

21. See, for example, L. L. Gilson, M. T. Maynard, N. C. Young, M. Vartiainen, and M. Hakonen, "Virtual Teams Research: 10 Years, 10 Themes, and 10 Opportunities," *Journal of Management* 41, no. 5 (2015): 1313–37; and L. L. Martins, L. L. Gilson, and M. T. Maynard, "Virtual Teams: What Do We Know and Where Do We Go From Here?" *Journal of Management* 30, no. 6 (2004): 805–35; L. Larson and L. A. DeChurch, "Leading Teams in the Digital Age: Four Perspectives on Technology and What They Mean for Leading Teams," *The Leadership Quarterly* (in press).

22. B. Freyer and T. A. Stewart, "Cisco Sees the Future," *Harvard Business Review* (November 2008): 73–79.

23. J. Eisenberg and N. DiTomaso, "Structural Decisions About Configuration, Assignments, and Geographical Distribution in Teams: Influences on Team Communications and Trust," *Human Resource Management Review* (in press); M. G. Moore, "Theory of Transactional Distance" in D. Keegan (Ed.), *Theoretical Principles of Distance Education* (New York: Routledge, 1993).

24. J. R. Mesmer-Magnus, L. A. DeChurch, M. Jimenez-Rodriguez, J. Wildman, and M. Shuffler, "A Meta-Analytic Investigation of Virtuality and Information Sharing in Teams," *Organizational Behavior and Human Decision Processes* 115 (2011): 214–25; Eisenberg and DiTomaso, "Structural decisions about configuration, assignments, and geographical distribution in teams."

25. C. Breuer, J. Hüffmeier, and G. Hertel, "Does Trust Matter More in Virtual Teams? A Meta-Analysis of Trust and Team Effectiveness Considering Virtuality and Documentation as Moderators," *Journal of Applied Psychology* 101, no. 8 (2016): 1151–77.

26. A. Malhotra, A. Majchrzak, and B. Rosen, "Leading Virtual Teams," *Academy of Management Perspectives* 21, no. 1 (2007): 60–70; J. M. Wilson, S. S. Straus, and B. McEvily, "All in Due Time: The Development of Trust in Computer-Mediated and Face-to-Face Teams," *Organizational Behavior and Human Decision Processes* 19, no. 1 (2006): 16–33.

27. M. M. Luciano, L. A. DeChurch, and J. E. Mathieu, "Multiteam Systems: A Structural Framework and Meso-Theory of System Functioning," *Journal of Management* 44, no. 3 (2018): 1065–96; J. E. Mathieu, M. A. Marks, and S. J. Zaccaro, "Multi-Team Systems," in N. Anderson, D. Ones, H. K. Sinangil, and C. Viswesvaran (eds.), *International Handbook of Work and Organizational Psychology* (London, UK: Sage, 2001): 289–313; M. L. Shuffler and D. R. Carter, "Teamwork Situated in Multiteam Systems: Key Lessons Learned and Future Opportunities," *American Psychologist* 73, no. 4 (2018): 390–406.

28. E. Karter, "Mars Mission Gets Help From Predictive Model, Helps NASA Anticipate Conflicts," *ECN Magazine,* February 21, 2019, https://www.ecnmag.com/news/2019/02/mars-mission-gets-help-predictive-model-helps-nasa-anticipate-conflicts

29. R. B. Davison, J. R. Hollenbeck, C. M. Barnes, D. J. Sleesman, and D. R. Ilgen, "Coordinated Action in Multiteam Systems," *Journal of*

Applied Psychology 97, no. 4 (2012): 808–24.; and L. A. DeChurch and M. A. Marks, "Leadership in Multiteam Systems," *Journal of Applied Psychology* 91, no. 2 (2006): 311–29;.

30. See, for example, J. Wijnmaalen, H. Voordijk, S. Rietjens, and G. Dewulf, "Intergroup Behavior in Military Multiteam Systems," *Human Relations* 72, no. 6 (2019): 1081–1104.

31. B. M. Firth, J. R. Hollenbeck, J. E. Miles, D. R. Ilgen, and C. M. Barnes, "Same Page, Different Books: Extending Representational Gaps Theory to Enhance Performance in Multiteam Systems," *Academy of Management Journal* 58, no. 3 (2015): 813–35.

32. M. Cuijpers, S. Uitdewilligen, and H. Guenter, "Effects of Dual Identification and Interteam Conflict on Multiteam System Performance," *Journal of Occupational and Organizational Psychology* 89 (2016): 141–71.

33. D. R. Carter, K. L. Cullen-Lester, J. M. Jones, A. Gerbasi, D. Chrobot-Mason, and E. Young Nae, "Functional Leadership in Interteam Contexts: Understanding 'What' in the Context of Why? Where? When? and Who?" *The Leadership Quarterly* (in press).

34. M. M. Luciano, J. E. Mathieu, and T. M. Ruddy, "Leading Multiple Teams: Average and Relative External Leadership Influences on Team Empowerment and Effectiveness," *Journal of Applied Psychology* 99, no. 2 (2014): 322–31.

35. S. D. Choudhury, "Noam Wasserman: Not all founders are created equal," *livemint,* May 11, 2014, https://www .livemint.com/Leisure/L8OtTmD3eQIkl9ueMWZ35K/Noam-Wasserman-Not-all-founders-are-equal.html; E. N. Shapiro, "How to Start a Company With Your Best Friend (and Survive to Tell About It)," *Quartz at Work,* March 8, 2019, https://qz.com/work/1567915/how-to-start-a-business-with-a-friend-tips-for-co-founders/; N. Wasserman, *The Founders Dilemmas: Anticipating and Avoiding the Pitfalls That Can Sink a Startup* (Princeton, NJ: Princeton UP, 2012).

36. Ibid.

37. Cannon-Bowers and Bowers, "Team Development and Functioning"; Kozlowski and Bell, "Work Groups and Teams in Organizations"; J. E. Mathieu, J. R. Hollenbeck, D. van Knippenberg, and D. R. Ilgen, "A Century of Work Teams in the *Journal of Applied Psychology*," *Journal of Applied Psychology* 102, no. 3 (2017): 452–67; Mathieu et al., "Embracing complexity."

38. D. E. Hyatt and T. M. Ruddy, "An Examination of the Relationship between Work Group Characteristics and Performance: Once More Into the Breech," *Personnel Psychology* 50, no. 3 (1997): 553–85.

39. G. L. Stewart, "A Meta-Analytic Review of Relationships Between Team Design Features and Team Performance," *Journal of Management* 32, no. 1 (2006): 29–55.

40. G. C. Banks, J. H. Batchelor, A. Seers, E. H. O'Boyle, J. M. Pollack, and K. Gower, "What Does Team-Member Exchange Bring to the Party? A Meta-Analytic Review of Team and Leader Social Exchange," *Journal of Organizational Behavior* 35 (2014): 273–95; Y. Song, Y. Fang, M. Wang, and J. Shi, "A Multiplex View of Leadership Structure in Management Teams," *Personnel Psychology* (in press).

41. J. Y. M. Lai, L. W. Lam, and S. S. K. Lam, "Organizational Citizenship Behavior in Work Groups: A Team Cultural Perspective," *Journal of Organizational Behavior* 34 (2013): 1039–56.

42. N. R. Anderson and M. A. West, "Measuring Climate for Work Group Innovation: Development and Validation of the Team Climate Inventory," *Journal of Organizational Behavior* 19 (1998): 235–58; M. Kivimäki, G. Kuk, M. Elovainio, L. Thomson, T. Kalliomäki-Levanto, and A. Heikkilä, "The Team Climate Inventory (TCI)—Four or Five Factors? Testing the Structure of TCI in Samples of Low and High Complexity Jobs," *Journal of Occupational and Organizational Psychology* 70 (1997): 375–89.

43. V. González-Romá, L. Fortes-Ferreira, and J. M. Peiró, "Team Climate, Climate Strength and Team Performance. A Longitudinal Study," *Journal of Occupational and Organizational Psychology* 82 (2009): 511–36; A. Pirola-Merlo, "Agile Innovation: The Role of Team Climate in Rapid Research and Development," *Journal of Occupational and Organizational Psychology* 83 (2010): 1075–84.

44. A. Li and R. Cropanzano, "Fairness at the Group Level: Justice Climate and Intraunit Justice Climate," *Journal of Management* 35, no. 3 (2009): 564–99.

45. See F. Aime, C. J. Meyer, and S. E. Humphrey, "Legitimacy of Team Rewards: Analyzing Legitimacy as a Condition for the Effectiveness of Team Incentive Designs," *Journal of Business Research* 63, no. 1 (2010): 60–66; P. A. Bamberger and R. Levi, "Team-Based Reward Allocation Structures and the Helping Behaviors of Outcome-Interdependent Team Members," *Journal of Managerial Psychology* 24, no. 4 (2009): 300–27; M. J. Pearsall, M. S. Christian, and A. P. J. Ellis, "Motivating Interdependent Teams: Individual Rewards, Shared Rewards, or Something in Between?" *Journal of Applied Psychology* 95, no. 1 (2010): 183–91.

46. T. Van Thielen, A. Decramer, A. Vanderstraeten, and M. Audenaert, "When Does Performance Management Foster Team Effectiveness? A Mixed-Method Field Study on the Influence of Environmental Extremity," *Journal of Organizational Behavior* 39, no. 6 (2018): 766–82.

47. E. V. Hall, D. R. Avery, P. F. McKay, J. F. Blot, and M. Edwards, "Composition and Compensation: The Moderating Effect of Individual and Team Performance on the Relationship Between Black Team Member Representation and Salary," *Journal of Applied Psychology* 104, no. 3 (2019): 448–63.

48. N. MacLean, *Young Men and Fire* (Chicago, IL: Chicago University Press, 1992); K. E. Weick, "The Collapse of Sensemaking in Organizations: The Mann Gulch Disaster," *Administrative Science Quarterly* 38 (1993): 628–52.

49. Ibid.

50. T. Driskell, E. Salas, and J. E. Driskell, "Teams in Extreme Environments: Alterations in Team Development and Teamwork," *Human Resource Management Review* 28 (2018): 434–49; S. J. Golden, C.H. D. Chang, and S. W. J. Kozlowski, "Teams in Isolated, Confined, and Extreme (ICE) Environments: Review and Integration," *Journal of Organizational Behavior* 39 (2018): 701–15; L. B. Landon, K. J. Slack, and J. D. Barrett, "Teamwork and Collaboration in Long-Duration Space Missions: Going to Extremes," *American Psychologist* 73, no. 4 (2018): 563–75; N. Power, "Extreme Teams: Toward a Greater Understanding of Multiagency Teamwork During Major Emergencies and Disasters," *American Psychologist* 73, no. 4 (2018): 478–90; Red Cross, *Red Cross Disaster Teams Still Serving Communities During COVID-19,* March 26, 2020, https://www .redcross.org/about-us/news-and-events/news/2020/red-cross-disaster-teams-still-serving-communities-during-covid-19.html

51. L. Alison, N. Power, C. van den Heuvel, M. Humann, M. Palasinksi, and J. Crego, "Decision Inertia: Deciding Between Least Worst Outcomes in Emergency Response to Disasters," *Journal of Occupational and Organizational Psychology* 88 (2015): 295–321; S. Waring, J. L. Moran, and R. Page, "Decision-Making in Multiagency Multiteam Systems Operating in Extreme Environments," *Journal of Occupational and Organizational Psychology* (in press).

52. C. Shawn Burke, M. L. Shuffler, and C. W. Wiese, "Examining the Behavioral and Structural Characteristics of Team Leadership in Extreme Environments," *Journal of Organizational Behavior* 39 (2018): 716–30; K. J. Klein, J. C. Ziegert, A. P. Knight, and Y. Xiao, "Dynamic Delegation: Shared, Hierarchical, and Deindividualized Leadership in Extreme Action Teams," *Administrative Science*

Quarterly 51 (2006): 590–621; F. Tschan, N. K. Semmer, D. Gautschi, P. Hunziker, M. Spychiger, and S. U. Marsch, "Leading to Recovery: Group Performance and Coordinative Activities in Medical Emergency Driven Groups," *Human Performance* 19, no. 3 (2006): 277–304.

53. M. A. Valentine and A. C. Edmondson, "Team Scaffolds: How Meso-level Structures Enable Role-Based Coordination in Temporary Groups," *Organization Science* 26, no. 2 (2015): 405–22.

54. A. A. Stachowski, S. A. Kaplan, and M. J. Waller, "The Benefits of Flexible Team Interaction During Crises," *Journal of Applied Pscyhology* 94, no. 6 (2009): 1536–43.

55. S. Kaplan, K. Laport, and M. J. Waller, "The Role of Positive Affectivity in Team Effectiveness During Crisis," *Journal of Organizational Behavior* 34 (2013): 473–91; G. R. Leon, R. Kanfer, R. G. Hoffman, and L. Dupre, "Interrelationships of Personality and Coping in a Challenging Extreme Situation," *Journal of Research in Personality* 25 (1991): 357–71; S. Razinskas and M. Hoegl, "A Multilevel Review of Stressor Research in Teams," *Journal of Organizational Behavior* 41 (2020): 185–209.

56. L. Alison, N. Power, C. van den Heuvel, and S. Waring, "A Taxonomy of Endogenous and Exogenous Uncertainty in High-Risk, High-Impact Contexts," *Journal of Applied Psychology* 100, no. 4 (2015): 1309–18; J. B. Schmutz, Z. Lei, W. J. Eppich, and T. Manser, "Reflection in the Heat of the Moment: The Role of In-Action Team Reflexivity in Health Care Emergency Teams," *Journal of Organizational Behavior* 39 (2018): 749–65; S. Uitdewilligen and M. J. Waller, "Information Sharing and Decision-Making in Multidisciplinary Crisis Management Teams," *Journal of Organizational Behavior* 39 (2018): 731–48.

57. A. Bryant, "Taking Your Skills With You," *The New York Times,* May 31, 2015.

58. Cannon-Bowers and Bowers, "Team Development and Functioning."

59. Ibid.

60. S. T. Bell, "Deep-Level Composition Variables as Predictors of Team Performance: A Meta-Analysis," *Journal of Applied Psychology* 92, no. 3 (2007): 595–615; S. T. Bell, A. J. Villado, M. A. Lukasik, L. Belau, and A. L. Briggs, "Getting Specific about Demographic Diversity Variable and Team Performance Relationships: A Meta-Analysis," *Journal of Management* 37, no. 3 (2011): 709–43; H. van Dijk, M. L. van Engen, and D. van Knippenberg, "Defying Conventional Wisdom: A Meta-Analytical Examination of the Differences Between Demographic and Job-Related Diversity Relationships With Performance," *Organizational Behavior and Human Decision Processes* 119 (2012): 38–53.

61. E. Gonzalez-Mulé, B. S. Cockburn, B. W. McCormick, and P. Zhao, "Team Tenure and Team Performance: A Meta-Analysis and Process Model," *Personnel Psychology* 73 (2020): 151–98.

62. Ibid.

63. Bell, "Deep-Level Composition Variables as Predictors of Team Performance"; M. A. G. Peeters, H. F. J. M. van Tuijl, G. G. Rutte, and I. M. M. J. Reymen, "Personality and Team Performance: A Meta-Analysis," *European Journal of Personality* 20 (2006): 377–96; M. S. Prewett, M. I. Brown, A. Goswami, and N. D. Christiansen, "Effects of Team Personality Composition on Member Performance: A Multilevel Perspective," *Group & Organization Management* 43, no. 2 (2018): 316–48; M. S. Prewett, A. A. G. Walvoord, F. R. B. Stilson, M. E. Rossi, and M. T. Brannick, "The Team Personality-Team Performance Relationship Revisited: The Impact of Criterion Choice, Pattern of Workflow, and Method of Aggregation," *Human Performance* 22 (2009): 273–96.

64. J. R. Mesmer-Magnus, L. A. DeChurch, M. Jimenez-Rodriguez, J. Wildman, and M. Shuffler, "A Meta-Analytic Investigation of Virtuality and Information Sharing in Teams," *Organizational Behavior and Human Decision Processes* 115 (2011): 214–25; B. P. Acton, M. T.

Braun, and R. J. Foti, "Built for Unity: Assessing the Impact of Team Composition on Team Cohesion Trajectories," *Journal of Business and Psychology* (in press).

65. A. P. J. Ellis, J. R. Hollenbeck, and D. R. Ilgen, "Team Learning: Collectively Connecting the Dots." C. O. L. H. Porter, J. R. Hollenbeck, and D. R. Ilgen, "Backing Up Behaviors in Teams: The Role of Personality and Legitimacy of Need," *Journal of Applied Psychology* 88, no. 3 (2003): 391–403; M. C. Schilpzand, D. M. Herold, and C. E. Shalley, "Members' Openness to Experience and Teams' Creative Performance," *Small Group Research* 42, no. 1 (2011): 55–76; Acton et al., "Built for Unity."

66. B. H. Bradley, B. E. Postlewaite, and K. G. Brown, "Ready to Rumble: How Team Personality Composition and Task Conflict Interact to Improve Performance," *Journal of Applied Psychology* 98, no. 2 (2013): 385–92.

67. E. Gonzalez-Mule, D. S. DeGeest, B. W. McCormick, J. Y. Seong, and K. G. Brown, "Can We Get Some Cooperation around Here? The Mediating Role of Group Norms on the Relationship between Team Personality and Individual Helping Behaviors," *Journal of Applied Psychology* 99, no. 5 (2014): 988–99.

68. X. Xu, L. Jiang, and H-J. Wang, "How to Build Your Team for Innovation? A Cross-Level Mediation model of Team Personality, Team Climate for Innovation, Creativity, and Job Crafting," *Journal of Occupational and Organizational Psychology* 92 (2019): 848–72.

69. See, for instance, D. Georgakakis, M. L. M. Heyden, J. D. R. Oehmichen, and U. I. K. Ekanayake, "Four Decades of CEO-TMT Interface Research: A Review Inspired by Role Theory," *The Leadership Quarterly* (in press).

70. Ibid.

71. S. E. Humphrey, F. P. Morgeson, and M. J. Mannor, "Developing a Theory of the Strategic Core of Teams: A Role Composition Model of Team Performance," *Journal of Applied Psychology* 94, no. 1 (2009): 48–61.

72. A. Joshi, "The Influence of Organizational Demography on the External Networking Behavior of Teams," *Academy of Management Review* 31, no. 3 (2006): 583–95.

73. H. van Dijk, M. L. van Engen, and D. van Knippenberg, "Defying Conventional Wisdom: A Meta-Analytical Examination of the Differences Between Demographic and Job-Related Diversity Relationships With Performance," *Organizational Behavior and Human Decision Processes* 119 (2012): 38–53; D. van Knippenberg and J. N. Mell, "Past, Present, and Potential Future of Team Diversity Research: From Compositional Diversity to Emergent Diversity," *Organizational Behavior and Human Decision Processes* 136 (2016): 135–145; J. Wang, G. H-L. Cheng, T. Chen, and K. Leung, "Team Creativity/Innovation in Culturally Diverse Teams: A Meta-Analysis," *Journal of Organizational Behavior* 40 (2019): 693–708.

74. van Dijk et al., "Defying Conventional Wisdom."

75. S. Mohammed and L. C. Angell, "Surface- and Deep-Level Diversity in Workgroups: Examining the Moderating Effects of Team Orientation and Team Process on Relationship Conflict," *Journal of Organizational Behavior* 25, no. 8 (2004): 1015–39.

76. Y. F. Guillaume, D. van Knippenberg, and F. C. Brodebeck, "Nothing Succeeds Like Moderation: A Social Self-Regulation Perspective on Cultural Dissimilarity and Performance," *Academy of Management Journal* 57, no. 5 (2014): 1284–308.

77. D. Coutu, "Why Teams Do not Work," *Harvard Business Review,* May 2009, 99–105. The evidence in this section is described in L. L. Thompson, *Making the Team,* 5th ed. (New York, NY: Pearson, 2013), 65–67. also L. A. Curral, R. H. Forrester, and J. F. Dawson, "It's What You Do and the Way That You Do It: Team Task, Team Size, and Innovation-Related Group Processes," *European Journal of Work*

& *Organizational Psychology* 10, no. 2 (June 2001): 187–204; R. C. Liden, S. J. Wayne, and R. A. Jaworski, "Social Loafing: A Field Investigation," *Journal of Management* 30, no. 2 (2004): 285–304.

78. R. Karlgaard, "Think (Really!) Small," Forbes, April 13, 2015, 32.

79. Karlgaard, "Think (Really!) Small"; and J. S. Mueller, "Why Individuals in Larger Teams Perform Worse," *Organizational Behavior and Human Decision Processes* 117, no. 1 (2012): 111–24.

80. B. R. Staats, K. L. Milkman, and C. R. Fox, "The Team Scaling Fallacy: Underestimating the Declining Efficiency of Larger Teams," *Organizational Behavior and Human Decision Processes* 118, no. 2 (2012): 132–42.

81. See, for example, S. S. Kim and C. Vandenberghe, "The Moderating Roles of Perceived Task Interdependence and Team Size in Transformational Leadership's Relation to Team Identification: A Dimensional Analysis," *Journal of Business and Psychology* 33 (2018): 509–27.

82. "Is Your Team Too Big? Too Small? What's the Right Number? *Knowledge@Wharton,* June 14, 2006, http:// knowledge.wharton.upenn.edu/article/is-your-team-too-big-too-small-whats-the-right-number-2/; see also A. M. Carton and J. N. Cummings, "A Theory of Subgroups in Work Teams," *Academy of Management Review* 37, no. 3 (2012): 441–70.

83. S. A. Kiffin-Peterson and J. L. Cordery, "Trust, Individualism, and Job Characteristics of Employee Preference for Teamwork," *International Journal of Human Resource Management* 14, no. 1 (2003): 93–116.

84. J. A. LePine, R. F. Piccolo, C. L. Jackson, J. E. Mathieu, and J. R. Saul, "A Meta-Analysis of Teamwork Processes: Tests of a Multidimensional Model and Relationships With Team Effectiveness Criteria," *Personnel Psychology* 61, no. 2 (2008): 273–307.

85. J. F. Dovidio, "Bridging Intragroup Processes and Intergroup Relations: Needing the Twain to Meet," *British Journal of Social Psychology* 52, no. 1 (2013): 1–24; J. Zhou, J. Dovidio, and E. Wang, "How Affectively-Based and Cognitively-Based Attitudes Drive Intergroup Behaviours: The Moderating Role of Affective-Cognitive Consistency," *Plos One* 8, no. 11 (2013): article e82150.

86. J. A. LePine, R. F. Piccolo, C. L. Jackson, J. E. Mathieu, and J. R. Saul, "A Meta-Analysis of Teamwork Processes: Tests of a Multidimensional Model and Relationships With Team Effectiveness Criteria;" J. E. Mathieu and T. L. Rapp, "Laying the Foundation for Successful Team Performance Trajectories: The Roles of Team Charters and Performance Strategies," *Journal of Applied Psychology* 94, no. 1 (2009): 90–103.

87. M. A. West, "Reflexivity and Work Group Effectiveness: A Conceptual Integration," in M. A. West (ed.), *The Handbook of Work Group Psychology* (Chichester, NY: Wiley, 1996): 555–79.

88. J. S. Christian, M. S. Christian, M. J. Pearsall, and E. C. Long, "Team Adaptation in Context: An Integrated Conceptual Model and Meta-Analytic Review," *Organizational Behavior and Human Decision Processes* 140 (2017): 62–89.

89. J. Chen, P. A. Bamberger, Y. Song, and D. R. Vashdi, "The Effects of Team Reflexivity on Psychological Well-Being in Manufacturing Teams," *Journal of Applied Psychology* 103, no. 4 (2018): 443–62; S. Rauter, M. Weiss, and M. Hoegl, "Team Learning From Setbacks: A Study in the Context of Start-up Teams," *Journal of Organizational Behavior* 39, no. 6 (2018): 783–95; Schmutz et al., "Reflection in the Heat of the Moment."

90. A. N. Pieterse, D. van Knippenberg, and W. P. van Ginkel, "Diversity in Goal Orientation, Team Reflexivity, and Team Performance," *Organizational Behavior and Human Decision Processes* 114, no. 2 (2011): 153–64.

91. A. Kleingeld, H. van Mierlo, and L. Arends, "The Effect of Goal Setting on Group Performance: A meta-analysis," *Journal of Applied Psychology* 96, no. 6 (2011): 1289–304.

92. See R. P. DeShon, S. W. J. Kozlowski, A. M. Schmidt, K. R. Milner, and D. Wiechmann, "A Multiple-Goal, Multilevel Model of Feedback Effects on the Regulation of Individual and Team Performance," *Journal of Applied Psychology* 89, no. 6 (2004): 1035–56.

93. Kleingeld et al., "The Effect of Goal Setting on Group Performance."

94. Acton et al., "Built for Unity"; N. L. Larson, M. J. W. McLarnnon, and T. A. O'Neill, "Challenging the 'Static' Quo: Trajectories of Engagement in Team Processes Toward a Deadline," *Journal of Applied Psychology* (in press).

95. J. W. Beck, A. M. Schmidt, and M. W. Natali, "Efficient Proximal Resource Allocation Strategies Predict Distal Team Performance: Evidence From the National Hockey League," *Journal of Applied Psychology* 104, no. 11 (2019): 1387–1403.

96. K. Tasa, S. Taggar, and G. H. Seijts, "The Development of Collective Efficacy in Teams: A Multilevel and Longitudinal Perspective," *Journal of Applied Psychology* 92, no. 1 (2007): 17–27; D. I. Jung and J. J. Sosik, "Group Potency and Collective Efficacy: Examining Their Predictive Validity, Level of Analysis, and Effects of Performance Feedback on Future Group Performance," *Group & Organization Management* 28, no. 3 (2003): 366–91; R. R. Hirschfeld and J. B. Bernerth, "Mental Efficacy and Physical Efficacy at the Team Level: Inputs and Outcomes among Newly Formed Action Teams," *Journal of Applied Psychology* 93, no. 6 (2008): 1429–37.

97. S. H. Courtright, G. R. Thurgood, G. L. Stewart, and A. J. Pierotti, "Structural Interdependence in Teams: An Integrative Framework and Meta-Analysis," *Journal of Applied Psychology* 100, no. 6 (2015): 1825–46; S. M. Gully, K. A. Incalcaterra, A. Joshi, and J. M. Beaubien, "A Meta-Analysis of Team Efficacy, Potency, and Performance: Interdependence and Level of Analysis as Moderators of Observed Relationships," *Journal of Applied Psychology* 87, no. 5 (2002): 819–32.

98. A. W. Richter, G. Hirst, D. van Knippenberg, and M. Baer, "Creative Self-Efficacy and Individual Creativity in Team Contexts: Cross-Level Interactions With Team Informational Resources," *Journal of Applied Psychology* 97, no. 6 (2012): 1282–90.

99. T. L. Rapp and J. E. Mathieu, "Team and Individual Influences on Members' Identification and Performance per Membership in Multiple Team Membership Arrangements," *Journal of Applied Psychology* 104, no. 3 (2019): 303–320.

100. N. Ellemers, E. Sleebos, D. Stam, and D. de Gilder, "Feeling Included and Valued: How Perceived Respect Affects Positive Team Identity and Willingness to Invest in the Team," *British Journal of Management* 24, no. 1 (2013): 21–37.

101. M. Riketta and R. van Dick, "Foci of Attachment in Organizations: A Meta-analytic Comparison of Workgroup Versus Organizational Identification and Commitment," *Journal of Vocational Behavior*, 67 (2005): 490–510.

102. Ibid.

103. T. A. De Vries, F. Walter, G. S. Van derr Vegt, and P. J. M. D. Essens, "Antecedents of Individuals' Interteam Coordination: Broad Functional Experiences as a Mixed Blessing," *Academy of Management Journal* 57, no. 5 (2014): 1334–59.

104. J. R. Mesmer-Magnus, R. Asencio, P. W. Seely, and L. A. DeChurch, "How Organizational Identity Affects Team Functioning: The Identity Instrumentality Hypothesis," *Journal of Management* 44, no. 4 (2018): 1530–50.

105. C. Brooks, R. Jensen, and S. Kozlowski, "Research Aids Future NASA Missions to Mars," *MSU Today,* March 4, 2019, https://msutoday.msu.edu/news/2019/research-aids-future-nasa-missions-to-mars/Chang; Kozlowski, "Teams in Isolated, Confined, and Extreme (ICE) Environments."

106. D. J. Beal, R. R. Cohen, M. J. Burke, and C. L. McLendon, "Cohesion and Performance in Groups: A Meta-Analytic Clarification of

Construct Relations," *Journal of Applied Psychology* 88, no. 6 (2003): 989–1004; J. E. Mathieu, M. R. Kukenberger, L. D'Innocenzo, and G. Reilly, "Modeling Reciprocal Team Cohesion–Performance Relationships, as Impacted by Shared Leadership and Members' Competence," *Journal of Applied Psychology* 100, no. 3 (2015): 71–34.

107. Courtright et al., "Structural Interdependence in Teams"; Mathieu et al., "Modeling Reciprocal Team Cohesion–Performance Relationships, as Impacted by Shared Leadership and Members' Competence"; J. R. Mesmer-Magnus and L. A. DeChurch, "Information Sharing and Team Performance," *Journal of Applied Psychology* 94, no. 2 (2009): 535–46.

108. M. M. Maloney, P. Pradhan Shah, M. Zellmer-Bruhn, and S. L. Jones, "The Lasting Benefits of Teams: Tie Vitality After Teams Disband," *Organization Science* 30, no. 2 (2019): 235–245.

109. J. A. Cannon-Bowers and E. Salas, "Reflections on Team Cognition," *Journal of Organizational Behavior* 22 (2001): 195–202; S. Mohammed, L. Ferzandi, and K. Hamilton, "Metaphor No More: A 15-Year Review of the Team Mental Model Construct," *Journal of Management* 36, no. 4 (2010): 876–910.

110. A. P. J. Ellis, "System Breakdown: The Role of Mental Models and Transactive Memory on the Relationships Between Acute Stress and Team Performance," *Academy of Management Journal* 49, no. 3 (2006): 576–89.

111. L. A. DeChurch and J. R. Mesmer-Magnus, "The Cognitive Underpinnings of Effective Teamwork: A Meta-Analysis," *Journal of Applied Psychology* 95, no. 1 (2010): 32–53.

112. S. W. J. Kozlowski and D. R. Ilgen, "Enhancing the Effectiveness of Work Groups and Teams," *Psychological Science in the Public Interest* 7, no. 3 (2006): 77–124; B. D. Edwards, E. A. Day, W. Arthur Jr., and S. T. Bell, "Relationships among Team Ability Composition, Team Mental Models, and Team Performance," *Journal of Applied Psychology* 91, no. 3 (2006): 727–36.

113. D. G. Bachrach, K. Lewis, Y. Kim, P. C. Patel, M. C. Campion, and S. M. B. Thatcher, "Transactive Memory Systems in Context: A Meta-Analytic Examination of Contextual Factors in Transactive Memory Systems Development and Team Performance," *Journal of Applied Psychology* 104, no. 3 (2019): 464–93; K. Lewis and B. Herndon, "Transactive Memory Systems: Current Issues and Future Research Directions," *Organization Science* 22 (2011): 1254–65.

114. Ibid.

115. M. Kolbe, G. Grote, M. J. Waller, J. Wacker, B. Grande, and D. R. Spahn, "Monitoring and Talking to the Room: Autochthonous Coordination Patterns in Team Interaction and Performance," *Journal of Applied Psychology* 99, no. 6 (2014): 1254–67.

116. C. K. W. De Dreu and L. R. Weingart, "Task Versus Relationship Conflict, Team Performance, and Team Member Satisfaction: A Meta-Analysis," *Journal of Applied Psychology* 88, no. 4 (2003): 741–49; F. R. C. de Wit, L. L. Greer, and K. A. Jehn, "The Paradox of Intragroup Conflict: A Meta-Analysis," *Journal of Applied Psychology* 97, no. 2 (2012): 360–90; T. A. O'Neill, N. J. Allen, and S. E. Hastings, "Examining the 'Pros' and 'Cons' of Team *Conf*lict: A Team-Level Meta-Analysis of Task, Relationship, and Process Conflict," *Human Performance* 26 (2013): 236–60.

117. J. Farh, C. Lee, and C. I. C. Farh, "Task Conflict and Team Creativity: A Question of How Much and When," *Journal of Applied Psychology* 95, no. 6 (2010): 1173–80.

118. K. H. Price, D. A. Harrison, and J. H. Gavin, "Withholding Inputs in Team Contexts: Member Composition, Interaction Processes, Evaluation Structure, and Social Loafing," *Journal of Applied Psychology* 91, no. 6 (2006): 1375–84.

119. E. Sherberg, "In Her Own Words: Lindsay Kaplan, Co-Founder of Chief, a Private Network for Powerful Women, Sees Herself as a Stay-at-Home Mom. It's Hard Work." *Bizwomen* (April 21, 2020), https://www.bizjournals.com/bizwomen/news/latest-news/2020/04/in-her-own-words-lindsay-kaplan-co-founder-of.html?page=all

120. A. Cristina Costa, C. Ashley Fulmer, and N. R. Anderson, "Trust in Work Teams: An Integrative Review, Multilevel Model, and Future Research Directions," *Journal of Organizational Behavior* 39 (2018): 169–84.

121. C. Breuer, J. Hüffmeier, and G. Hertel, "Does Trust Matter More in Virtual Teams? A Meta-Analysis of Trust and Team Effectiveness Considering Virtuality and Documentation as Moderators," *Journal of Applied Psychology* 101, no. 8 (2016): 1151–77; B. A. De Jong, K. T. Dirks, and N. Gillespie, "Trust and Team Performance: A Meta-Analysis of Main Effects, Moderators, and Covariates," *Journal of Applied Psychology* 101, no. 8 (2016): 1134–50; J. Feitosa, R. Grossman, W. S. Kramer, and E. Salas, "Measuring Team Trust: A Critical and Meta-Analytical Review," *Journal of Organizational Behavior* (in press).

122. R. Grossman and J. Feitosa, "Team Trust Over Time: Modeling Reciprocal and Contextual Influences in Action Teams," *Human Resource Management Review* 28 (2018): 395–410.

123. P. Daisyme, "Are You Hiring a 'Team' Player—Or Someone Just Looking Out for No. 1," *Entrepreneur,* September 12, 2018, https://www.entrepreneur.com/article/319847

124. "13 Separate Search & Rescue Missions Executed in Lane County During Snow Storm," *NBC 16,* March 5, 2019, https://nbc16.com/news/local/13-separate-search-rescue-missions-executed-in-lane-county-during-snow-storm

125. M. Kesner, "Key Components of a Bonus Plan for Your Dental Team," *Dental Economics,* June 1, 2017, https://www.dentaleconomics.com/articles/print/volume-107/issue-6/practice/key-components-of-a-bonus-plan-for-your-dental-team.html

126. G. Hertel, U. Konradt, and K. Voss, "Competencies for Virtual Teamwork: Development and Validation of a Web-Based Selection Tool for Members of Distributed Teams," *European Journal of Work and Organizational Psychology* 15, no. 4 (2006): 477–504.

127. T. V. Riper, "The NBA's Most Overpaid Players," *Forbes,* April 5, 2013, http://www.forbes.com/sites/tomvanriper/2013/04/05/the-nbas-most-overpaid-players/

128. F. P. Morgeson, S. E. Humphrey, and M. C. Reeder, "Team Selection," in N. Schmitt (ed.), *The Oxford Handbook of Personnel Assessment and Selection* (Oxford, UK: Oxford UP, 2012): 1–30.

129. A. M. Hughes et al., "Saving Lives: A Meta-Analysis of Team Training in Health Care," *Journal of Applied Psychology* 101, no. 9 (2016): 1266–304; and E. Salas et al., "Does Team Training Improve Team Performance? A Meta-Analysis," *Human Factors* 50 (2008): 903–33.

130. H. M. Guttman, "The New High-Performance Player," *The Hollywood Reporter,* October 27, 2008, http://www .hollywoodreporter.com

131. C.-H. Chuang, S. Chen, and C.-W. Chuang, "Human Resource Management Practices and Organizational Social Capital: The Role of Industrial Characteristics," *Journal of Business Research* 66, no. 5 (2013): 678–87.

132. T. Erickson and L. Gratton, "What It Means to Work Here," *BusinessWeek,* January 10, 2008, http://www .businessweek.com

133. Y. Garbers and U. Konradt, "The Effect of Financial Incentives on Performance: A Quantitative Review of Individual and Team-based Financial Incentives," *Journal of Occupational and Organizational Psychology* 87 (2014): 102–37.

134. K. Holcomb, "Ben Affleck and Oscar Isaac Talk Teamwork and New Movie 'Triple Frontier'." *K5 News,* March 4, 2019, https://www.king5.com/article/news/ben-affleck-and-oscar-isaac-talk-teamwork-and-new-movie-triple-frontier/281-5fcb72a0-f6ad-420c-b410-49db6c-c68fea

135. C. E. Naquin and R. O. Tynan, "The Team Halo Effect: Why Teams Are Not Blamed for Their Failures," *Journal of Applied Psychology* 88, no. 2 (2003): 332–40.

136. E. R. Crawford and J. A. Lepine, "A Configural Theory of Team Processes: Accounting for the Structure of Taskwork and Teamwork," *Academy of Management Review* 38, no. 1 (2013): 32–48.

CHAPTER 11

1. S. Zalis, "Power of the Pack: Women Who Support Women Are More Successful," *Forbes,* March 6, 2019, https://www.forbes.com/sites/shelleyzalis/2019/03/06/power-of-the-pack-women-who-support-women-are-more-successful/#109151781771

2. Ibid.

3. J. Keyton, "Communication in Organizations," *Annual Review of Organizational Psychology and Organizational Behavior* 4 (2017): 501–26; M. Scott Poole, "Communication," in S. Zedeck (ed.), *APA Handbook of Industrial and Organizational Psychology* (Washington, DC: APA, 2011): 249–70.

4. Poole, "Communication."

5. S. J. Ashford, N. Wellman, M. S. de Luque, K. E. M. De Stobbeleir, and M. Wollan, "Two Roads to Effectiveness: CEO Feedback Seeking, Vision Articulation, and Firm Performance," *Journal of Organizational Behavior* 39 (2018): 82–95.

6. *Glassdoor* [website], accessed March 2, 2019, http://www .glassdoor.com; H. J. Walker, H. S. Felid, W. F. Giles, A. A. Armenakis, and J. B. Bernerth, "Displaying Employee Testimonials on Recruitment Web Sites: Effects of Communication Media, Employee Race, and Job Seeker Race on Organizational Attraction and Information Credibility," *Journal of Applied Psychology* 94, no. 5 (2009): 1354–64.

7. R. Waldersee and F. Luthans, "The Impact of Positive and Corrective Feedback on Customer Service Performance," *Journal of Organizational Behavior* 15 (1994): 83–95; *Yelp* [website], accessed March 2, 2019, http://www.yelp.com

8. K. DeRosa, "Paramedic's Campaign Collects First Responders' Tales of Trauma," *Times Colonist,* March 7, 2015, https://www.timescolonist.com/news/local/paramedic-s-campaign-collects-first-responders-tales-of-trauma-1.1785572

9. R. Swarns, "After Uneasy First Tries, Coworkers Find a Way to Talk About Race," *The New York Times,* March 23, 2015, A15.

10. D. C. Barnlund, "A Transactional Model of Communication," in C. D. Mortenson (ed.), *Communication Theory* (New Brunswick, NJ: Transaction, 2008), 47–57; see K. Byron, "Carrying Too Heavy a Load? The Communication and Miscommunication of Emotion by E-mail," *Academy of Management Review* 33, no. 2 (2008): 309–27.

11. R. E. Kraut, R. S. Fish, R. W. Root, and B. L. Chalfonte, "Informal Communication in Organizations: Form, Function, and Technology," in S. Oskamp and S. Spacapan (eds.), *People's Reactions to Technology* (Beverly Hills, CA: Sage, 1990): 145–99.

12. E. Salas, D. E. Sims, and C. S. Burke, "Is There a 'Big Five' in Teamwork?" *Small Group Research* 36, no. 5 (2005): 555–99.

13. S. Jhun, Z.-T. Bae, and S.-Y. Rhee, "Performance Change of Managers in Two Different Uses of Upward Feedback: A Longitudinal Study in Korea," *International Journal of Human Resource Management* 23, no. 20 (2012): 4246–64; J. W. Smither and A. G. Walker, "Are the Characteristics of Narrative Comments Related to Improvement in Multirater Feedback Ratings Over Time?" *Journal of Applied Psychology* 89, no. 3 (2004): 575–81.

14. A. Lewis and J. Clark, "Dreams Within a Dream: Multiple Visions and Organizational Structure," *Journal of Organizational Behavior* 41 (2020): 50–76.

15. Z. Witkower, J. L. Tracy, J. T. Cheng, and J. Henrich, "Two Signals of Social Rank: Prestige and Dominance Are Associated with Distinct Nonverbal Displays," *Journal of Personality and Social Psychology* 118, no. 1 (2020): 89–120.

16. S. Hunt, "Shifting Performance Management From Structured Forms to Structured Conversations," *HR Technologist,* March 4, 2019, https://www.hrtechnologist.com/articles/performance-management-hcm/shifting-performance-management-from-structured-forms-to-structured-conversations/; J. S. Lublin, "Managers Need to Make Time for Face Time," *The Wall Street Journal,* March 18, 2015, B6.

17. A. Fisher, "How to Give an Annual Performance Review (If You Must)," *Fortune,* December 19, 2016, http://fortune .com/2016/12/19/annual-performance-review/

18. E. W. Morrison, "Employee Voice and Silence," *Annual Review of Organizational Psychology and Organizational Behavior* 1 (2014): 173–97.

19. Morrison, "Employee Voice and Silence"; A. Starzyk and S. Sonnentag, "When Do Low-Initiative Employees Feel Responsible for Change and Speak Up to Managers," *Journal of Vocational Behavior* (in press).

20. R. D. Lebel, "Overcoming the Fear Factor: How Perceptions of Supervisor Openness Lead Employees to Speak Up When Fearing External Threat," *Organizational Behavior and Human Decision Processes* 135 (2016): 10–21.

21. E. Nichols, "Hyper-Speed Managers," *HR Magazine,* April 2007, 107–10.

22. D. Cray, G. R. Mallory, R. J. Butler, D. Hickson, and D. Wilson, "Sporadic, Fluid, and Constricted Processes: Three Types of Strategic Decision-Making in Organizations," *Journal of Management Studies* 25, no. 1 (1988): 13–39.

23. D. Shadpour, "The Key Elements for Building a Successful Startup Culture," *Forbes,* February 23, 2018, https://www.forbes.com/sites/forbesagencycouncil/2018/02/23/the-key-elements-for-building-a-successful-startup-culture/#d3f28d2368e8

24. S. B. Algoe, P. C. Dwyer, A. Younge, and C. Oveis, "A New Perspective on the Social Functions of Emotions: Gratitude and the Witnessing Effect," *Journal of Personality and Social Psychology* (in press).

25. P. P. Ramos, *Network Models for Organizations* (New York, NY: Palgrave Macmillan, 2012).

26. See, for example, G. Michelson, A. van Iterson, and K. Waddington, "Gossip in Organizations: Contexts, Consequences, and Controversies," *Group & Organization Management* 35, no. 4 (2010): 371–90.

27. J. Baum, M. Rabovsky, S. Benjamin Rose, and R. Abdel Rahman, "Clear Judgments Based on Unclear Evidence: Person Evaluation Is Strongly Influenced by Untrustworthy Gossip," *Emotion* 20, no. 2 (2020): 248–60.

28. N. Tan, K. Chi Yam, P. Zhang, and D. J. Brown, "Are You Gossiping About Me? The Costs and Benefits of High Workplace Gossip Prevalence," *Journal of Business and Psychology* (in press).

29. See, for instance, E. Martinescu, O. Janssen, and B. A. Nijstad, "Gossip as a Resource: How and Why Power Relationships Shape Gossip Behavior," *Organizational Behavior and Human Decision Processes* 153 (2019): 89–102.

30. G. Van Hoye and F. Lievens, "Tapping the Grapevine: A Closer Look at Word-of-Mouth as a Recruitment Source," *Journal of Applied Psychology* 94, no. 2 (2009): 341–52.

31. S. Freeman, "Keys to Hiring (and Keeping) Great People," *Forbes,* March 11, 2019, https://www.forbes.com/sites/theyec/2019/03/11/keys-to-hiring-and-keeping-great-people/#1e30dad45016

32. J. K. Bosson, A. B. Johnson, K. Niederhoffer, and W. B. Swann Jr., "Interpersonal Chemistry Through Negativity: Bonding by Sharing Negative Attitudes About Others," *Personal Relationships* 13, no. 2 (2006): 135–50.

33. T. J. Grosser, V. Lopez-Kidwell, and G. Labianca, "A Social Network Analysis of Positive and Negative Gossip in Organizational Life," *Group & Organization Management* 35, no. 2 (2010): 177–212.

34. R. Feintzeig, "The Boss's Next Demand: Make Lots of Friends," *The Wall Street Journal,* February 12, 2014, B1, B6.

35. R. E. Silverman, "A Victory for Small Office Talkers," *The Wall Street Journal,* October 28, 2014, D2.

36. K. Huang, M. Yeomans, A. W. Brooks, J. Minson, and F. Gino, "It Doesn't Hurt to Ask: Question-Asking Increases Liking," *Journal of Personality and Social Psychology* 113, no. 3 (2017): 430 *Communication Theory* 52.

37. B. Erdogan, T. N. Bauer, and J. Walter, "Deeds That Help and Words That Hurt: Helping and Gossip as Moderators of the Relationship Between Leader-Member Exchange and Advice Network Centrality," *Personnel Psychology* 68 (2015): 185–214.

38. S. Stoyanov, R. Woodward, V. Stoyanova, "Simple Word of Mouth or Complex Resource Orchestration for Overcoming Liabilities of Outsidership," *Journal of Management* 44, no. 8 (2018): 3151–75.

39. R. Raphael, "Doctors Are Using Hospital 'Robots' to Tell Patients They're Dying, Sparking an Outcry," *Fast Company,* March 12, 2019, https://www.fastcompany.com/90318752/doctors-are-using-hospital-robots-to-tell-patients-theyre-dying-sparking-an-outcry

40. E. Bernstein, "How Well Are You Listening?" *The Wall Street Journal,* January 13, 2015, D1.

41. E. Bernstein, "How 'Active Listening' Makes Both Participants in a Conversation Feel Better," *The Wall Street Journal,* January 12, 2015, http://www.wsj.com/articles/how-active-listening-makes-both-sides-of-a-conversation-feel-better-1421082684

42. S. Shellenbarger, "Work & Family Mailbox," *The Wall Street Journal,* July 30, 2014, D2.

43. E. C. Ravlin, A.-K. Ward, and D. C. Thomas, "Exchanging Social Information across Cultural Boundaries," *Journal of Management* 40, no. 5 (2014): 1437–65.

44. D. Pickles, "Why Tom Smykowski Got Fired," *Forbes,* December 28, 2018, https://www.forbes.com/sites/forbestechcouncil/2018/12/26/why-tom-smykowski-got-fired/#6f90bcffebc9

45. M. L. Kern et al., "Gaining Insights From Social Media Language: Methodologies and Challenges," *Psychological Methods* 21, no. 4 (2016): 507–25; O. N. E. Kjell, K. Kjell, D. Garcia, and S. Sikström, "Semantic Measures: Using Natural Language Processing to Measure, Differentiate, and Describe Psychological Constructs," *Psychological Methods* 24, no. 1 (2019): 92–115; J. W. Pennebaker, M. R. Mehl, and K. G. Niederhoffer, "Psychological Aspects of Natural Language Use: Our Words, Our Selves," *Annual Review of Psychology* 54 (2003): 547–77; C. Stanley and M. D. Byrne, "Comparing Vector-based and Bayesian Memory Models Using Large-scale Datasets: User-Generated Hashtag and Tag Prediction on Twitter and Stack Overflow," *Psychological Methods* 21, no. 4 (2016): 542–65.

46. T. Bradley, "New Cybersecurity Company Focuses on Addressing the Weakest Link in the Security Chain," *Forbes,* February 20, 2019, https://www.forbes.com/sites/tonybradley/2019/02/20/new-cybersecurity-company-focuses-on-addressing-the-weakest-link-in-the-security-chain/#6fb58a243745; J. Bresnick, "Medical Artificial Intelligence Market to See 50% CAGR Growth," *Health IT Analytics,* March 11, 2019, https://healthitanalytics.com/news/medical-artificial-intelligence-market-to-see-50-cagr-growth; P. Korzeniowski, "6 AI Applications in Finance Spark Partner Opportunity," *TechTarget,* March 2019, https://searchitchannel.techtarget.com/feature/6-AI-applications-in-finance-spark-partner-opportunity; F. Ohlhorst, "Using AI in Natural Language Processing for B2C, Call Centers," *eWeek,* March 11, 2019, https://www.eweek.com/enterprise-apps/using-ai-in-natural-language-processing-for-b2c-call-centers;

E. Smith, "Machine Learning: Optimize Your Team for Artificial Intelligence," *Associations Now,* March 1, 2019, https://associationsnow.com/2019/03/artificial-intelligence-association-team-planning/; K. Walch, "AI in Accounting Boosts Compliance and Fraud Detection," *TechTarget,* March 2019, https://searchenterpriseai.techtarget.com/feature/AI-in-accounting-boosts-compliance-and-fraud-detection

47. BusinessWire, "The Global Natural Language Processing (NLP) Market Size Is Forecasted to Grow to USD 26.4 Billion by 2024," December 30, 2019, https://www .businesswire.com/news/home/20191230005197/en/Global-Natural-Language-Processing-NLP-Market-Size

48. S. Bonaccio, J. O'Reilly, S. L. O'Sullivan, and F. Chiocchio, "Nonverbal Behavior and Communication in the Workplace: A Review and an Agenda for Research," *Journal of Management* 42, no. 5 (2016): 1044–74; J. A. Hall, T. G. Horgan, and N. A. Murphy, "Nonverbal Communication," *Annual Review of Psychology* 70 (2019): 271–94.

49. N. Dargue, N. Sweller, and M. P. Jones, "When Our Hands Help Us Understand: A Meta-Analysis into the Effects of Gesture on Comprehension," *Psychological Bulletin* 145, no. 8: 765–84.

50. C. K. Goman, "5 Body Language Tips to Increase Your Curb Appeal," *Forbes,* March 4, 2013, www.forbes.com/sites/carolkinseygoman/2013/03/14/5-body-language-tips-to-increase-your-curb-appeal/

51. C. F. Lima, A. Anikin, A. Catarina Monteiro, S. K. Scott, and S. Luís Castro, "Automaticity in the Recognition of Nonverbal Emotional Vocalizations," *Emotion* 19, no. 2 (2019): 219–233; K. R. Scherer, A. Dieckmann, M. Unfried, H. Ellgring, and M. Mortillaro, "Investigating Appraisal-Drive Facial Expression and Inference in Emotion Communication," *Emotion* (in press).

52. G. Willard, K-J. Isaac, and D. R. Carney, "Some Evidence for the Nonverbal Contagion of Racial Bias," *Organizational Behavior and Human Decision Processes,*" 128 (2015): 96–107.

53. A. L. Skinner, K. R. Olson, and A. N. Meltzoff, "Acquiring Group bias: Observing Other People's Nonverbal Signals Can Create Social Group Biases," *Journal of Personality and Social Psychology* (in press).

54. A. R. Feiler and D. M. Powell, "Behavioral Expression of Job Interview Anxiety," *Journal of Business and Psychology* 31 (2016): 155–71; J. Schroeder, J. L. Risen, F. Gino, and M. I. Norton, "Handshaking Promotes Deal-making by Signalling Cooperative Intent," *Journal of Personality and Social Psychology* 116, no. 5 (2019): 743–768; A. Wilhelmy, M. Kleinmann, C. J. König, K. G. Melchers, and D. M. Truxillo, "How and Why Do Interviewers Try to Make Impressions on Applicants? A Qualitative Study," *Journal of Applied Psychology* 101, no. 3 (2016): 313–32.

55. See R. L. Daft and R. H. Lengel, "Organizational Information Requirements, Media Richness and Structural Design," *Management Science* 32, no. 5 (1986): 554–71; N. Kock, "The Psychobiological Model: Towards a New Theory of Computer-Mediated Communication Based on Darwinian Evolution," *Organization Science* 15, no. 3 (2004): 327–48.

56. R. L. Daft and R. H. Lengel, "Information Richness: A New Approach to Managerial Behavior and Organizational Design," *Research in Organizational Behavior* 6 (1984): 191–233; R. L. Daft and R. H. Lengel, "Organizational Information Requirements, Media Richness and Structural Design," *Management Science* 32, no. 5 (1986): 554–71; K. Ishii, M. Madison Lyons, and S. A. Carr, "Revisiting Media Richness Theory for Today and Future," *Human Behavior and Emerging Technologies* 1, no. 2 (2019): 124–31.

57. R. H. Lengel and R. L. Daft, "The Selection of Communication Media as an Executive Skill," *The Academy of Management Executive* 2, no. 3 (1988): 225–232; K. Patterson, J. Grenny, R. McMillan, and A. Switzler, *Crucial Conversations Tools for Talking When Stakes Are High*

(2nd ed., New York, NY: McGraw-Hill, 2012); S. G. Rogelberg, *The Surprising Science of Meetings: How You Can Lead Your Team to Peak Performance* (New York, NY: Oxford University Press, 2019).

58. S. Shellenbarger, "Is This How You Really Talk?" *The Wall Street Journal,* April 24, 2013, D1, D3.

59. G. W. Giumetti, AL. L. Hatfield, J. L. Sciso, A. N. Schroeder, E. R. Muth, and R. M. Kowalski, "What a Rude E-mail! Examining the Differential Effects of Incivility Versus Support on Mood, Energy, Engagement, and Performance in an Online Context," *Journal of Occupational Health Psychology* 18, no. 3 (2013): 297–309; J. Kruger, N. Epley, J. Parker, and Z-W. Ng, "Egocentrism Over E-mail: Can We Communicate as Well as We Think?" *Journal of Personality and Social Psychology* 89, no. 6 (2005): 925–36; Y. Park and V. C. Haun, "The Long Arm of Email Incivility: Transmitted Stress to the Partner and Partner Work Withdrawal," *Journal of Organizational Behavior* 39 (2018): 1268–82; E. M. Richard and M. McFadden, "Saving Face: Reactions to Cultural Norm Violations in Business Request Emails," *Journal of Business and Psychology* 31 (2016): 307–21.

60. B. Giamanco and K. Gregoire, "Tweet Me, Friend Me, Make Me Buy," *Harvard Business Review,* July–August 2012, 88–93.

61. M. J. Tews, K. Stafford, and E. P. Kudler, "The Effects of Negative Content in Social Networking Profiles on Perceptions of Employment Suitability," *International Journal of Selection and Assessment* 28 (2020): 17–30.

62. L. Windscheid, L. Bowes-Sperry, D. L. Kidder, H. K. Cheung, M. Morner, and F. Lievens, "Actions Speak Louder Than Words: Outsiders' Perceptions of Diversity Mixed Messages," *Journal of Applied Psychology* 101, no. 9 (2016): 1329–41.

63. V. Cheung-Blunden, K. Cropper, A. Panis, and K. Davis, "Functional Divergence of Two Threat-Induced Emotions: Fear-Based Versus Anxiety-Based Cybersecurity Preferences," *Emotion* 19, no. 8 (2019): 1353–65.

64. L. A. McNall and S. G. Roch, "A Social Exchange Model of Employee Reactions to Electronic Performance Monitoring," *Human Performance* 22 (2009): 204–24; J. M. Stanton, "Reactions to Employee Performance Monitoring: Framework, Review, and Research Directions," *Human Performance* 13, no. 1 (2000): 85–113; A. Brown Yost, T. S. Behrend, G. Howardson, J. Badger Darrow, and J. M. Jensen, "Reactance to Electronic Surveillance: A Test of Antecedents and Outcomes," *Journal of Business and Psychology* 34 (2019): 71–86.

65. "At Many Companies, Hunt for Leakers Expands Arsenal of Monitoring Tactics," *The Wall Street Journal,* September 11, 2006, B1, B3; B. J. Alge, G. A. Ballinger, S. Tangirala, and J. L. Oakley, "Information Privacy in Organizations: Empowering Creative and Extrarole Performance," *Journal of Applied Psychology* 91, no. 1 (2006): 221–32.

66. R. E. Petty and P. Briñol, "Persuasion: From Single to Multiple to Metacognitive Processes," *Perspectives on Psychological Science* 3, no. 2 (2008): 137–47; F. A. White, M. A. Charles, and J. K. Nelson, "The Role of Persuasive Arguments in Changing Affirmative Action Attitudes and Expressed Behavior in Higher Education," *Journal of Applied Psychology* 93, no. 6 (2008): 1271–86.

67. S. Alhabash, "Facebook Is a Persuasion Platform That is Changing the Advertising Rulebook," *The Media Online,* February 27, 2019, https://themediaonline.co.za/2019/02/facebook-is-a-persuasion-platform-thats-changing-the-advertising-rulebook/; S. Alhabash, N. Almutairi, C. Lou, and W. Kim, "Pathways to Virality: Psychophysiological Responses Preceding Likes, Shares, Comments, and Status Updates on Facebook," *Media Psychology* 22, no. 2 (2019): 196–216.

68. K. L. Blankenship and D. T. Wegener, "Opening the Mind to Close It: Considering a Message in Light of Important Values Increases Message Processing and Later Resistance to Change," *Journal of Personality and Social Psychology* 94, no. 2 (2008): 196–213; Y. H. M. See,

R. E. Petty, and L. R. Fabrigar, "Affective and Cognitive Meta-Bases of Attitudes: Unique Effects of Information Interest and Persuasion," *Journal of Personality and Social Psychology* 94, no. 6 (2008): 938–55.

69. D. C. Zhang, X. S. Zhu, K. J. Ritter, and A. Thiele, "Telling Stories to Communicate the Value of the pre-Employment Structured Job Interview," *International Journal of Selection and Assessment* 27 (2019): 299–314.

70. M. S. Key, J. E. Edlund, B. J. Sagarin, and G. Y. Bizer, "Individual Differences in Susceptibility to Mindlessness," *Personality and Individual Differences* 46, no. 3 (2009): 261–64.

71. M. Reinhard and M. Messner, "The Effects of Source Likeability and Need for Cognition on Advertising Effectiveness under Explicit Persuasion," *Journal of Consumer Behavior* 8, no. 4 (2009): 179–91.

72. S. Sah, P. Malaviya, and D. Thompson, "Conflict of Interest Disclosure as an Expertise Cue: Differential Effects Due to Automatic Versus Deliberative Processing," *Organizational Behavior and Human Decision Processes,* 147 (2018): 127–46.

73. J. J. Guyer, L. R. Fabrigar, and T. I. Vaughan-Johnston, "Speech Rate, Intonation, and Pitch: Investigating the Bias and Cue Effects of Vocal Confidence on Persuasion," *Personality and Social Psychology Bulletin* 45, no. 3 (2019): 389–405; A. B. Van Zant and J. Berger, "How the Voice Persuades," *Journal of Personality and Social Psychology* 118, no. 4 (2020): 661–82.

74. V. S. Ferreira, "A Mechanistic Framework for Explaining Audience Design in Language Production," *Annual Review of Psychology* 70 (2019): 29–51.

75. C. Heath, "Do People Prefer to Pass Along Good or Bad News? Valence and Relevance of News as Predictors of Transmission Propensity," *Organizational Behavior and Human Decision Processes* 68, no. 2 (1996): 79–94.

76. M. T. Wallace, T. G. Woynaroski, and R. A. Stevenson, "Multisensory Integration as a Window into Orderly and Disrupted Cognition and Communication," *Annual Review of Psychology* 71 (2020): 193–219.

77. M. Richtel, "Lost in E-Mail, Tech Firms Face Self-Made Beast," *The New York Times,* June 14, 2008, http://www .nytimes.com/2008/06/14/technology/14email.html

78. S. Norton, "A Post-PC CEO: No Desk, No Desktop," *The Wall Street Journal,* November 20, 2014, B5.

79. H. A. Elfenbein and N. Eisenkraft, "The Relationship Between Displaying and Perceiving Nonverbal Cues of Affect: A Meta-Analysis to Solve an Old Mystery," *Journal of Personality and Social Psychology* 98, no. 2 (2010): 301–18; N. C. Overall, M. S. Clark, G. J. O. Fletcher, B. J. Peters, and V. T. Chang, "Does Expressing Emotions Enhance Perceptual Accuracy of Negative Emotions During Relationship Interactions," *Emotion* 20, no. 3 (2020): 353–67.

80. E. Chervonsky and C. Hunt, "Suppression and Expression of Emotion in Social and Interpersonal Outcomes: A Meta-Analysis," *Emotion* 17, no. 4 (2017): 669–83; Overall et al., "Does Expressing Emotions Enhance Perceptual Accuracy of Negative Emotions During Relationship Interactions."

81. D. S. Lee, A. Orvell, J. Briskin, T. Shrapnell, S. A. Gelman, O. Ayduk, O. Ybarra, and E. Kross, "When Chatting About Negative Experiences Helps—and When It Hurts: Distinguishing Adaptive Versus Maladaptive Social Support in Computer-Mediated Communication," *Emotion* 20, no. 3 (2020): 368–75.

82. P. Briñol, R. E. Petty, and J. Barden, "Happiness Versus Sadness as a Determinant of Thought Confidence in Persuasion: A Self-Validation Analysis," *Journal of Personality and Social Psychology* 93, no. 5 (2007): 711–27.

83. R. C. Sinclair, S. E. Moore, M. M. Mark, A. S. Soldat, and C. A. Lavis, "Incidental Moods, Source Likeability, and Persuasion: Liking Motivates Message Elaboration in Happy People," *Cognition and Emotion*

24, no. 6 (2010): 940–61; V. Griskevicius, M. N. Shiota, and S. L. Neufeld, "Influence of Different Positive Emotions on Persuasion Processing: A Functional Evolutionary Approach," *Emotion* 10, no. 2 (2010): 190–206.

84. See, for instance, J. A. Frimer, M. J. Brandt, Z. Melton, and M. Motyl, "Extremists on the Left and Right Use Angry, Negative Language," *Personality and Social Psychology Bulletin* 45, no. 8 (2019): 1216–31.

85. R. Weisman, "Who Are You Calling Senior? For Older Folks, Some Terms Are Fast Becoming Radioactive," *Boston Globe,* March 7, 2019, https://www.bostonglobe.com/metro/2019/03/07/who-are-you-calling-senior-for-older-folks-some-terms-are-fast-becoming-radioactive/EaCvwK6WJIHbtcoXO63JqO/story.html

86. D. Booher, "5 Communication Skills That Will Identify You as a Leader," *Forbes,* December 18, 2018, https://www.forbes.com/sites/womensmedia/2018/12/18/5-communication-skills-that-will-identify-you-as-a-leader/#61dbce7dc8a5

87. E. Nechanska, E. Hughes, and T. Dundon, "Towards an Integration of Employee Voice and Silence," *Human Resource Management Review* (in press).

88. M. Knoll, R. J. Hall, and O. Weigelt, "A Longitudinal Study of the Relationships Between Four Differentially Motivated Forms of Employee Silence and Burnout," *Journal of Occupational Health Psychology* 24, no. 5 (2019): 572–89; D. Fernando and A. Prasad, "Sex-Based Harassment and Organizational Silencing: How Women Are Led to Reluctant Acquiescence in Academia," *Human Relations* 72, no. 10 (2019): 1565–94.

89. E. Liu and M. E. Roloff, "Exhausting Silence: Emotional Costs of Withholding Complaints," *Negotiation and Conflict Management Research* 8, no. 1 (2015): 25–40; Morrison, "Employee Voice and Silence."

90. M. Kirrane, D. O'Shea, F. Buckley, A. Grazi, and J. Prout, "Investigating the Role of Discrete Emotions in Silence Versus Speaking Up," *Journal of Occupational and Organizational Psychology* 90 (2017): 354–78; H. P. Madrid, M. G. Patterson, and P. I. Leiva, "Negative Core Affect and Employee Silence: How Differences in Activation, Cognitive Rumination, and Problem-Solving Demands Matter," *Journal of Applied Psychology* 100, no. 6 (2015): 1887–98; E. W. Morrison, K. E. See, and C. Pan, "An Approach-Inhibition Model of Employee Silence: The Joint Effects of Personal Sense of Power and Target Openness," *Personnel Psychology* 68, no. 3 (2015): 547–80.

91. L. A. Withers and L. L. Vernon, "To Err Is Human: Embarrassment, Attachment, and Communication Apprehension," *Personality and Individual Differences* 40, no. 1 (2006): 99–110.

92. See, for instance, B. D. Blume, T. T. Baldwin, and K. C. Ryan, "Communication Apprehension: A Barrier to Students' Leadership, Adaptability, and Multicultural Appreciation," *Academy of Management Learning & Education* 12, no. 2 (2013): 158–72; B. D. Blume, G. F. Dreher, and T. T. Baldwin, "Examining the Effects of Communication Apprehension Within Assessment Centres," *Journal of Occupational and Organizational Psychology* 83, no. 3 (2010): 663–71; X. Shi, T. M. Brinthaupt, and M. McCree, "The Relationship of Self-Talk Frequency to Communication Apprehension and Public Speaking Anxiety," *Personality and Individual Differences* 75 (2015): 125–29.

93. See, for example, T. L. Rodebaugh, "I Might Look OK, But I'm Still Doubtful, Anxious, and Avoidant: The Mixed Effects of Enhanced Video Feedback on Social Anxiety Symptoms," *Behaviour Research and Therapy* 42, no. 12 (2004): 1435–51.

94. A. Vrij, M. Hartwig, and P. Anders Granhag, "Reading Lies: Nonverbal Communication and Deception," *Annual Review of Psychology* 70 (2019): 295–317.

95. K. B. Serota, T. R. Levine, and F. J. Boster, "The Prevalence of Lying in America: Three Studies of Self-Reported Lies," *Human Communication Research* 36, no. 1 (2010): 2–25.

96. J. Bundy, M. D. Pfarrer, C. E. Short, and W. Timothy Coombs, "Crises and Crisis Management: Integration, Interpretation, and Research Development," *Journal of Management* 43, no. 6 (2017): 1661–92.

97. T. W. Cole and K. L. Fellows, "Risk Communication Failure: A Case Study of New Orleans and Hurricane Katrina," *Southern Communication Journal* 73, no. 3 (2008): 211–28; A Gheytanchi, L. Joseph, E. Gierlach, S. Kimpara, J. Housley, Z. E. Franco, and L. E. Beutler, "The Dirty Dozen: Twelve Failures of the Hurricane Katrina Response and How Psychology Can Help," *American Psychologist* 62, no. 2 (2007): 118–30.

98. Bundy et al., "Crises and Crisis Management"; D. Y. Liou and C. H. Lin, "Human Resource Planning on Terrorism and Crises in the Asia Pacific Region: Cross-National Challenge, Reconsideration, and Proposition From Western Experiences," *Human Resource Management* 47, no. 1 (2008): 49–72.

99. D. G. Winter, "Power, Affiliation, and War: Three Tests of a Motivational Model," *Journal of Personality and Social Psychology* 65, no. 3 (1993): 532–45; D. G. Winter, "The Role of Motivation, Responsibility, and Integrative Complexity in Crisis Escalation: Comparative Studies of War and Peace Crises," *Journal of Personality and Social Psychology* 92, no. 5 (2007): 920–37.

100. S. Uitdewilligen and M. J. Waller, "Information Sharing and Decision-Making in Multidisciplinary Crisis Management Teams," *Journal of Organizational Behavior* 39 (2018): 731–48.

101. T. Knudsen and K. Srikanth, "Coordinated Exploration: Organizing Joint Search by Multiple Specialists to Overcome Mutual Confusion and Joint Myopia," *Administrative Science Quarterly* 59, no. 3 (2014): 409–41.

102. See, for example, N. Kman, "How Disaster Apps Work—and Don't," *Fast Company,* August 11, 2016, https://www .fastcompany.com/3062786/how-disaster-apps-work-and-dont; L. G. Militello, C. E. Sushereba, M. Branlat, R. Bean, and V. Finomore, "Designing for Military Pararescue: Naturalistic Decision-Making Perspective, Methods, and Frameworks," *Journal of Occupational and Organizational Psychology* 88 (2015): 251–72.

103. N. M. Jones and R. Cohen Silver, "This Is Not a Drill: Anxiety on Twitter Following the 2018 Hawaii False Missile Alert," *American Psychologist* (in press).

104. K. Gurchiek, "Cultural Awareness Is Needed in the U.S. as Well as Overseas," *Society for Human Resource Management: Global and Cultural Effectiveness* [blog], February 8, 2017, https://www.shrm.org/resourcesandtools/hr-topics/behavioral-competencies/global-and-cultural-effectiveness/pages/cultural-awareness-is-needed-in-the-u.s.-as-well-as-overseas.aspx

105. Ibid.

106. Y. P. Chang and S. B. Algoe, "On Thanksgiving: Cultural Variation in Gratitude Demonstrations and Perceptions Between the United States and Taiwan," *Emotion* (in press).

107. See, for instance, M. Yoshie and D. A. Sauter, "Cultural Norms Influence Nonverbal Emotion Communication: Japanese Vocalizations of Socially Disengaging Emotions," *Emotion* 20, no. 3 (2020): 513–17.

108. M. Cioffi, "Navigating Latin American Cultures in Workplace," *Tire Business,* May 29, 2018, https://www .tirebusiness.com/article/20180529/NEWS/180529964/navigating-latin-american-cultures-in-workplace

109. See W. L. Adair, "Integrative Sequences and Negotiation Outcome in Same- and Mixed-Culture Negotiations," *International Journal of Conflict Management* 14, nos. 3–4 (2003): 1359–92; W. L. Adair and J. M. Brett, "The Negotiation Dance: Time, Culture, and Behavioral

Sequences in Negotiation," *Organization Science* 16, no. 1 (2005): 33–51; E. Giebels and P. J. Taylor, "Interaction Patterns in Crisis Negotiations: Persuasive Arguments and Cultural Differences," *Journal of Applied Psychology* 94, no. 1 (2009): 5–19; M. G. Kittler, D. Rygl, and A. Mackinnon, "Beyond Culture or Beyond Control? Reviewing the Use of Hall's High-/Low-Context Concept," *International Journal of Cross-Cultural Management* 11, no. 1 (2011): 63–82.

110. M. C. Hopson, T. Hart, and G. C. Bell, "Meeting in the Middle: Fred L. Casmir's Contributions to the Field of Intercultural Communication," *International Journal of Intercultural Relations* 36, no. 6 (2012): 789–97.

CHAPTER 12

1. D. T. Dingle, "Gloria Boyland, One of the Most Powerful Women in Corporate America, Drives Innovation at FedEx," *Black Enterprise,* March 13, 2019, https://www .blackenterprise.com/most-powerful-women-in-corporate-america-gloria-boyland-fedex/

2. W. Zheng, R. Kark, and A. Meister, "How Women Manage the Gendered Norms of Leadership," *Harvard Business Review,* November 28, 2018, https://hbr.org/2018/11/how-women-manage-the-gendered-norms-of-leadership

3. R. Knight, "How to Increase Your Influence at Work," *Harvard Business Review,* February 16, 2018, https://hbr .org/2018/02/how-to-increase-your-influence-at-work

4. Dingle, "Gloria Boyland, One of the Most Powerful Women in Corporate America, Drives Innovation at FedEx."

5. S. J. Zaccaro, J. P. Green, S. Dubrow, and M. Kolze, "Leader Individual Differences, Situational Parameters, and Leadership Outcomes: A Comprehensive Review and Integration," *The Leadership Quarterly* 29 (2018): 2–43.

6. See, for instance, R. K. Gottfredson and C. S. Reina, "Exploring Why Leaders Do What They Do: An Integrative Review of the Situation-Trait Approach and Situation-Encoding Schemas," *The Leadership Quarterly* (in press); G. Luria, A. Kahana, J. Goldenberg, and Y. Noam, "Contextual Moderators for Leadership Potential Based on Trait Activation Theory," *Journal of Organizational Behavior* 40 (2019): 899–911.

7. B. R. Spisak, P. A. van der Laken, and B. M. Doornenbal, "Finding the Right Fuel for the Analytical Engine: Expanding the Leader Trait Paradigm Through Machine Learning?" *The Leadership Quarterly* 30 (2019): 417–26.

8. N. Ensari, R. E. Riggio, J. Christian, and G. Carslaw, "Who Emerges as a Leader? Meta-Analyses of Individual Differences as Predictors of Leadership Emergence," *Personality and Individual Differences* 51, no. 4 (2011): 532–36.

9. D. S. DeRue, J. D. Nahrgang, N. Wellman, and S. E. Humphrey, "Trait and Behavioural Theories of Leadership: An Integration and Meta-Analytic Test of Their Relative Validity," *Personnel Psychology* 64 (2011): 7–52.

10. DeRue et al., "Trait and Behavioural Theories of Leadership"; M. H. Do and A. Minbashian, "A Meta-Analytic Examination of the Effects of the Agentic and Affiliative Aspects of Extraversion on Leadership Outcomes," *The Leadership Quarterly* 25 (2014): 1040–53.

11. J. Hu, Z. Zhang, K. Jiang, and W. Chen, "Getting Ahead, Getting Along, and Getting Prosocial: Examining Extraversion Facets, Peer Reactions, and Leadership Emergence," *Journal of Applied Psychology* 104, no. 11 (2019): 1369–86.

12. DeRue et al., "Trait and Behavioral Theories of Leadership."

13. Ibid.

14. Ibid.

15. R. B. Kaiser, J. M. LeBreton, and J. Hogan, "The Dark Side of Personality and Extreme Leader Behavior," *Applied Psychology: An International Review* 64, no. 1 (2015): 55–92; K. Landay, P. D. Harms, and M. Credé, "Shall We Serve the Dark Lords? A Meta-Analytic Review of Psychopathy and Leadership," *Journal of Applied Psychology* 104, no. 1 (2019): 1833–96.

16. B. H. Gaddis and J. L. Foster, "Meta-Analysis of Dark Side Personality Characteristics and Critical Work Behaviors among Leaders Across the Globe: Findings and Implications for Leadership Development and Executive Coaching," *Applied Psychology: An International Review* 64, no. 1 (2015): 25–54.

17. E. Grijalva and L. Zhang, "Narcissism and Self-Insight: A Review and Meta-Analysis of Narcissists' Self-Enhancement Tendencies," *Personality and Social Psychology Bulletin* 42, no. 1 (2016): 3–24; L. Huang, D. V. Krasikova, and P. D. Harms, "Avoiding or Embracing Social Relationships? A Conservation of Resources Perspective of Leader Narcissism, Leader-Member Exchange Differentiation, and Follower Voice," *Journal of Organizational Behavior* 41 (2020): 77–92.

18. R. H. Humphrey, J. M. Pollack, and T. H. Hawver, "Leading with Emotional Labor," *Journal of Managerial Psychology* 23, no. 2 (2008): 151–68; M. A. Clark, M. M. Robertson, and S. Young, "'I Feel Your Pain': A Critical Review of Organizational Research on Empathy," *Journal of Organizational Behavior* 40 (2019): 166–92.

19. P. D. Harms and M. Credé, "Emotional Intelligence and Transformational and Transactional Leadership: A Meta-Analysis," *Journal of Leadership & Organizational Studies* 17, no. 1 (2010): 5–17.

20. S. Côté, P. N. Lopes, P. Salovey, and C. T. H. Miners, "Emotional Intelligence and Leadership Emergence in Small Groups," *Leadership Quarterly* 21, no. 3 (2010): 496–508.

21. Ensari et al., "Who Emerges as a Leader?"; A. Tuncdogan, O. A. Acar, and D. Stam, "Individual Differences as Antecedents of Leader Behavior: Towards an Understanding of Multi-Level Outcomes," *The Leadership Quarterly* 28 (2017): 40–64.

22. C. N. Lacerenza, D. L. Reyes, S. L. Marlow, D. L. Joseph, and E. Salas, "Leadership Training Design, Delivery, and Implementation: A Meta-Analysis," *Journal of Applied Psychology* 102, no. 12 (2017): 1686–1718.

23. E. A. Fleishman, "Twenty Years of Consideration and Structure," in E. A. Fleishman and J. G. Hunt (eds.), *Current Developments in the Study of Leadership* (Carbondale, IL: Southern Illinois University Press, 1973): 1–40; T. A. Judge, R. F. Piccolo, and R. Ilies, "The Forgotten Ones? The Validity of Consideration and Initiating Structure in Leadership Research," *Journal of Applied Psychology,* 89 no. 1 (2004): 36–51.

24. Ibid.

25. J. F. Helliwell, M. B. Norton, H. Huang, and S. Wang, "Happiness at Different Ages: The Social Context Matters," *The National Bureau of Economic Research* [Working Paper No. 25121] (Cambridge, MA: NBER, 2018); S. Landrum, "The Importance of Working for a Boss That Supports You," *Forbes,* December 8, 2017, https://www.forbes.com/sites/sarahlandrum/2017/12/08/the-importance-of-working-for-a-boss-that-supports-you/#47e66c40486a; M. Schwantes, "Want Happier Employees? Research Surprisingly Found That You Should Treat Them Like This," *Inc.,* October 22, 2018, https://www.inc.com/marcel-schwantes/want-happier-employees-research-surprisingly-found-that-you-should-treat-them-like-this.html

26. Judge et al., "The Forgotten Ones?"

27. M. Javidan, P. W. Dorfman, M. S. de Luque, and R. J. House, "In the Eye of the Beholder: Cross Cultural Lessons in Leadership from Project GLOBE," *Academy of Management Perspectives* 20, no. 1 (2006): 67–90.

28. H. van Emmerik, H. Wendt, and M. C. Euwema, "Gender Ratio, Societal Culture, and Male and Female Leadership," *Journal of Occupational and Organizational Psychology* 83 (2010): 895–914.

29. J. Gallagher, "Alfred Glancy III, the Detroit Leader Who Helped Save the DSO, Has Died," *Detroit Free Press*, January 11, 2019, https://www.freep.com/story/money/business/john-gallagher/2019/01/11/alfred-glancy-iii-dso/2546584002/

30. F. E. Fiedler, "A Contingency Model of Leadership Effectiveness," *Advances in Experimental Social Psychology* 1 (1964): 149–90; for a more current discussion on the model, see S. Altmae, K. Tuerk, and O.-S. Toomet, "Thomas-Kilmann's Conflict Management Modes and Their Relationship to Fiedler's Leadership Styles (Basing on Estonian Organizations)," *Baltic Journal of Management* 8, no. 1 (2013): 45–65.

31. L. H. Peters, D. D. Hartke, and J. T. Pohlmann, "Fiedler's Contingency Theory of Leadership: An Application of the Meta-Analysis Procedures of Schmidt and Hunter," Psychological Bulletin 97, no. 2 (1985): 274–85; C. A. Schriesheim, B. J. Tepper, and L. A. Tetrault, "Least Preferred Co-Worker Score, Situational Control, and Leadership Effectiveness: A Meta-Analysis of Contingency Model Performance Predictions," *Journal of Applied Psychology* 79, no. 4 (1994): 561–73.

32. R. P. Vecchio, "Situational Leadership Theory: An Examination of a Prescriptive Theory," *Journal of Applied Psychology* 72, no. 3 (1987): 444–51; V. H. Vroom and A. G. Jago, "The Role of the Situation in Leadership," *American Psychologist* 62, no. 1 (2007): 17–24.

33. See, for instance, G. Thompson and R. P. Vecchio, "Situational Leadership Theory: A Test of Three Versions," *Leadership Quarterly* 20, no. 5 (2009): 837–48; R. P. Vecchio, C. R. Bullis, and D. M. Brazil, "The Utility of Situational Leadership Theory—A Replication in a Military Setting," *Small Group Research* 37, no. 5 (2006): 407–24.

34. R. J. House, "A Path-Goal Theory of Leader Effectiveness," *Administrative Science Quarterly* 16 (1971): 321–38; R. J. House and G. Dessler, "The Path-Goal Theory of Leadership: Some Post Hoc and A Priori Tests," in J. G. Hunt and L. L. Larson (eds.), *Contingency Approaches to Leadership* (Carbondale, IL: Southern Illinois University Press, 1974): 29–55.

35. R. R. Vecchio, J. E. Justin, and C. L. Pearce, "The Utility of Transactional and Transformational Leadership for Predicting Performance and Satisfaction within a Path-Goal Theory Framework," *Journal of Occupational and Organizational Psychology* 81 (2008): 71–82.

36. J. C. Wofford and L. Z. Liska, "Path-Goal Theories of Leadership: A Meta-Analysis," *Journal of Management* 19, no. 4 (1993): 857–76.

37. Vroom and Jago, "The Role of the Situation in Leadership."

38. C. Matyszczyk, "In Just a Few Words, Warriors Coach Steve Kerr Gave a Wonderful Lesson in Leadership. The Limits of Leadership, That Is," *Inc.*, September 6, 2018, https://www.inc.com/chris-matyszczyk/in-just-a-few-words-warriors-coach-steve-kerr-gave-a-wonderful-lesson-in-leadership-limits-of-leadership-that-is.html

39. F. Dansereau, G. B. Graen, and W. Haga, "A Vertical Dyad Linkage Approach to Leadership in Formal Organizations," *Organizational Behavior and Human Performance* 13 (1975): 46–78; R. Martin, Y. Guillaume, G. Thomas, A. Lee, and O. Epitropaki, "Leader-Member Exchange (LMX) and Performance: A Meta-Analytic Review," Personnel Psychology 69 (2016): 67–121.

40. J. H. Dulebohn, W. H. Bommer, R. C. Liden, R. L. Brouer, and G. R. Ferris, "A Meta-Analysis of Antecedents and Consequences of Leader-Member Exchange: Integrating the Past With an Eye Toward the Future," *Journal of Management* 38, no. 6 (2012): 1715–59; A. J. Xu, R. Loi, Z. Cai, and R. C. Liden, "Reversing the Lens: How Followers Influence Leader-Member Exchange Quality," *Journal of Occupational and Organizational Psychology* 92 (2019): 475–97.

41. Ibid.

42. Z. Liao, W. Liu, X. Li, and Z. Song, "Give and Take: An Episodic Perspective on Leader-Member Exchange," *Journal of Applied Psychology* 104, no. 1 (2019): 34–51.

43. Ibid.

44. R. Vecchio and D. M. Brazil, "Leadership and Sex-Similarity: A Comparison in a Military Setting," *Personnel Psychology* 60, no. 2 (2007): 303–35.

45. A. Lee, G. Thomas, R. Martin, Y. Guillaume, and A. F. Marstand, "Beyond Relationship Quality: The Role of Leader-Member Exchange Importance in Leader-Follower Dyads," *Journal of Occupational and Organizational Psychology* 92 (2019): 736–63.

46. See, for instance, Martin et al.; for a critique of the LMX literature, see R. K. Gottfredson, S. L. Wright, and E. D. Heaphy, "A Critique of the Leader-Member Exchange Construct: Back to Square One," *The Leadership Quarterly* (in press).

47. A. Lee, A. Gerbasi, G. Schwarz, and A. Newman, "Leader-Member Exchange Social Comparisons and Follower Outcomes: The Roles of Felt Obligation and Psychological Entitlement," *Journal of Occupational and Organizational Psychology* 92 (2019): 593–617.

48. A. Yu, F. K. Matta, and B. Cornfield, "Is Leader-Member Exchange Differentiation Beneficial or Detrimental for Group Effectiveness? A Meta-Analytic Investigation and Theoretical Integration," *Academy of Management Journal* 61, no. 3 (2018): 1158–88.

49. Ibid.

50. L. C. Wang and J. R. Hollenbeck, "LMX in Team-Based Contexts: TMX, Authority Differentiation, and Skill Differentiation as Boundary Conditions for Leader Reciprocation," *Personnel Psychology* 72 (2019): 271–90.

51. T. Rockstuhl, J. H. Dulebohn, S. Ang, and L. M. Shore, "Leader-Member Exchange (LMX) and Culture: A Meta-Analysis of Correlates of LMX Across 23 Countries," *Journal of Applied Psychology* 97, no. 6 (2012): 1097–130.

52. F. K. Matta, B. A. Scott, J. Koopman, and D. E. Conlon, "Does Seeing 'Eye to Eye' Affect Work Engagement and Organizational Citizenship Behavior? A Role Theory Perspective on LMX Agreement," *Academy of Management Journal* 58, no. 6 (2015): 1686–708; A. Chaudhry, P. R. Vidyarthi, R. C. Liden, and S. J. Wayne, "Two to Tango? Implications of Alignment and Misalignment in Leader and Follower Perceptions of LMX," *Journal of Business and Psychology* (in press).

53. S. Patel, "The 5 Characteristics That Make a Charismatic Leader," *Entrepreneur*, August 7, 2017, https://www.entrepreneur.com/article/297710

54. M. Weber, *The Theory of Social and Economic Organization*, trans A. M. Henderson and T. Parsons (Eastford, CT: Martino Fine Books, 2012).

55. R. J. House, "A 1976 Theory of Charismatic Leadership," in J. G. Hunt and L. L. Larson (eds.), *The Cutting Edge* (Carbondale, IL: Southern Illinois University Press, 1977): 189–207; see also J. Antonakis, N. Bastardoz, P. Jacquart, and B. Shamir, "Charisma: An Ill-Defined and Ill-Measured Gift," *Annual Review of Organizational Psychology and Organizational Behavior* 3 (2016): 293–319; L. L. Watts, L. M. Steele, and M. D. Mumford, "Making Sense of Pragmatic and Charismatic Leadership Stories," *The Leadership Quarterly* 30 (2019): 243–59.

56. Ibid.

57. G. C. Banks, K. N. Engemann, C. E. Williams, J. Gooty, K. D. McCauley, and M. R. Medaugh, "A Meta-Analytic Review and Future Research Agenda of Charismatic Leadership," *The Leadership Quarterly* 28 (2017): 508–29.

58. F. Walter and H. Bruch, "An Affective Events Model of Charismatic Leadership Behavior: A Review, Theoretical Integration, and Research Agenda," *Journal of Management* 35, no. 6 (2009): 1428–52.

59. Banks et al., "A Meta-Analytic Review and Future Research Agenda of Charismatic Leadership"; M. A. LePine, Y. Zhang, E. R. Crawford, and B. L. Rich, "Turning Their Pain to Gain: Charismatic Leader Influence on Follower Stress Appraisal and Job Performance," *Academy of Management Journal* 59, no. 3 (2016): 1036–59; E. McClean and C. J. Collins, "Expanding the Concept of Fit in Strategic Human Resource Management: An Examination of the Relationship Between Human Resource Practices and Charismatic Leadership on Organizational Outcomes," *Human Resource Management* 58 (2019): 187–202.

60. T. Maran, M. Furtner, S. Liegl, S. Kraus, and P. Sachse, "In the Eye of a Leader: Eye-Directed Gazing Shapes Perceptions of Leaders' Charisma," *The Leadership Quarterly* (in press).

61. Y. Berson, R. A. Da'as, and D. A. Waldman, "How Do Leaders and Their Teams Bring About Organizational Learning and Outcomes," *Personnel Psychology* 68 (2015): 79–108.

62. A. Erez, V. F. Misangyi, D. E. Johnson, M. A. LePine, and K. C. Halverson, "Stirring the Hearts of Followers: Charismatic Leadership as the Transferal of Affect," *Journal of Applied Psychology* 93, no. 3 (2008): 602–15. On the role of vision in leadership, see M. Hauser and R. J. House, "Lead through Vision and Values," in *Handbook of Principles of Organizational Behavior*, ed. E. A. Locke (Malden, MA: Blackwell, 2004), 257–73.

63. D. N. Den Hartog, A. H. B. De Hoogh, and A. E. Keegan, "The Interactive Effects of Belongingness and Charisma on Helping and Compliance," *Journal of Applied Psychology* 92, no. 4 (2007): 1131–39.

64. J. C. Pastor, M. Mayo, and B. Shamir, "Adding Fuel to Fire: The Impact of Followers' Arousal on Ratings of Charisma," *Journal of Applied Psychology* 92, no. 6 (2007): 1584–96; D. Stam, D. van Knippenberg, B. Wisse, and P. A. Nederveen, "Motivation in Words: Promotion- and Prevention-Oriented Leader Communication in Times of Crisis," *Journal of Management* 44, no. 7 (2018): 2859–87.

65. C. M. Barnes, C. L. Guarana, S. Nauman, and D. T. Kong, "Too Tired to Inspire or Be Inspired: Sleep Deprivation and Charismatic Leadership," *Journal of Applied Psychology* 101, no. 8 (2016): 1191–99.

66. P. Jacquart and J. Antonakis, "When Does Charisma Matter for Top-Level Leaders? Effect of Attributional Ambiguity," *Academy of Management Journal* 58, no. 4 (2015): 1051–74.

67. F. Cohen, S. Solomon, M. Maxfield, T. Pyszczynski, and J. Greenberg, "Fatal Attraction: The Effects of Mortality Salience on Evaluations of Charismatic, Task-Oriented, and Relationship-Oriented Leaders," *Psychological Science* 15, no. 12 (2004), 846–51; J. Griffith, S. Connelly, C. Thiel, and G. Johnson, "How Outstanding Leaders Lead with Affect: An Examination of Charismatic, Ideological, and Pragmatic Leaders," *Leadership Quarterly* 26, no. 4 (2015): 502–17; K. Breevaart and R. E. de Vries, "Followers' HEXACO Personality Traits and Preferences for Charismatic, Relationship-Oriented, and Task-Oriented Leadership," *Journal of Business and Psychology* (in press).

68. See, for instance, J. A. Raelin, "The Myth of Charismatic Leaders," *Training and Development Journal*, March 2003, 47–54; P. A. Vlachos, N. G. Panagopoulos, and A. A. Rapp, "Feeling Good by Doing Good: Employee CSR-Induced Attributions, Job Satisfaction, and the Role of Charismatic Leadership," *Journal of Business Ethics* 118, no. 3 (2013): 577–88.

69. B. M. Galvin, D. A. Waldman, and P. Balthazard, "Visionary Communication Qualities as Mediators of the Relationship between Narcissism and Attributions of Leader Charisma," *Personnel Psychology* 63, no. 3 (2010): 509–37.

70. J. B. Rodell, J. A. Colquitt, and M. D. Baer, "Is Adhering to Justice Rules Enough? The Role of Charismatic Qualities in Perceptions of Supervisors' Overall Fairness," *Organizational Behavior and Human Decision Processes* 140 (2017): 14–28.

71. P. Balkundi, M. Kilduff, and D. A. Harrison, "Centrality and Charisma: Comparing How Leader Networks and Attributions Affect Team Performance," *Journal of Applied Psychology* 96, no. 6 (2012): 1209–22.

72. J. Vergauwe, B. Wille, J. Hofmans, R. B. Kaiser, and F. De Fruyt, "The Double-edged Sword of Leader Charisma: Understanding the Curvilinear Relationship Between Charismatic Personality and Leader Effectiveness," *Journal of Personality and Social Psychology* 114, no. 1 (2018): 110–30.

73. Right Management, "Two-thirds of Managers Need Guidance on How to Coach and Develop Careers," *Thoughtwire* [blog], March 11, 2015, https://www.right.com/wps/wcm/connect/right-us-en/home/thoughtwire/categories/media-center/Two-Thirds-of-Managers-Need-Guidance-on-How-to-Coach-and-Develop-Careers

74. See, for instance, B. M. Bass, *Leadership and Performance Beyond Expectations* (New York, NY: Free Press, 1990); B. M. Bass, "Two Decades of Research and Development in Transformational Leadership," *European Journal of Work and Organizational Psychology* 8 (1999): 9–32; B. M. Bass and R. E. Riggio, *Transformational Leadership*, 2nd ed. (Mahwah, NJ: Lawrence Erlbaum, 2006).

75. T. A. Judge and R. F. Piccolo, "Transformational and Transactional Leadership: A Meta-Analytic Test of Their Relative Validity," *Journal of Applied Psychology* 89, no. 5 (2004): 755–68; H. R. Young, D. R. Glerum, D. L. Joseph, and M. A. McCord, "A Meta-Analysis of Transactional Leadership and Follower Performance: Double-Edged Effects of LMX and Empowerment," *Journal of Management* (in press).

76. S. Willis, S. Clarke, and E. O'Connor, "Contextualizing Leadership: Transformational Leadership and Management-by-Exception-Active in Safety-Critical Contexts," *Journal of Occupational and Organizational Psychology* 90 (2017): 281–305.

77. Bass, *Leadership and Performance Beyond Expectations*; Bass, "Two Decades of Research and Development in Transformational Leadership"; Bass and R. E. Riggio, *Transformational Leadership*.

78. See for a critique, N. Siangchokyoo, R. L. Klinger, and E. D. Campion, "Follower Transformation as the Linchpin of Transformational Leadership Theory: A Systematic Review and Future Research Agenda," *The Leadership Quarterly* (in press).

79. G. C. Altschuler, "Review: 'Leadership in Turbulent Times,' by Doris Kearns Goodwin," *StarTribune*, September 14, 2018, http://www.startribune.com/review-leadership-in-turbulent-times-by-doris-kearns-goodwin/493196541/; D. K. Goodwin, *Leadership in Turbulent Times* (New York, NY: Simon & Schuster, 2018).

80. L. Y. C. Leong and R. Fischer, "Is Transformational Leadership Universal? A Meta-Analytic Investigation of the Multifactor Leadership Questionnaire Across Cultures," *Journal of Leadership & Organizational Studies* 18, no. 2 (2011): 164–74.

81. T. R. Hinkin and C. A. Schriesheim, "An Examination of 'Nonleadership': From Laissez-Faire Leadership to Leader Reward Omission and Punishment Omission," *Journal of Applied Psychology* 93, no. 6 (2008): 1234–48; Judge and Piccolo, "Transformational and transactional leadership."

82. Judge and Piccolo, "Transformational and Transactional Leadership"; Wang et al., "Transformational Leadership and Performance Across Criteria and Levels."

83. Ibid.

84. Ibid.

85. K. A. Arnold, "Transformational Leadership and Employee Psychological Well-being: A Review and Directions for Future Research," *Journal of Occupational Health Psychology* 22, no. 3 (2017): 381–93; Judge and Piccolo, "Transformational and Transactional Leadership"; D. Koh, K. Lee, and K. Joshi, "Transformational Leadership and Creativity: A Meta-Analytic Review and Identification of an Integrated

Model," *Journal of Organizational Behavior* 40, no. 6 (2019): 625–650; Wang et al., "Transformational Leadership and Performance Across Criteria and Levels."

86. A. Deinert, A. Homan, D. Boer, S. C. Voelpel, and D. Gutermann, "Transformational Leadership Sub-Dimensions and Their Link to Leaders' Personality and Performance," *The Leadership Quarterly* 26 (2015): 1095–120.

87. See, for instance, R. K. Gottfredson and H. Aguinis, "Leadership Behaviors and Follower Performance: Deductive and Inductive Examination of Theoretical Rationales and Underlying Mechanisms," *Journal of Organizational Behavior* 38 (2017): 558–91; T. W. H. Ng, "Transformational Leadership and Performance Outcomes: Analyses of Multiple Mediation Pathways," *The Leadership Quarterly* 28 (2017): 385–417.

88. Ng, "Transformational Leadership and Performance Outcomes."

89. Gottfredson and Aguinis, "Leadership Behaviors and Follower Performance"; Ng, "Transformational Leadership and Performance Outcomes."

90. J. A. Shaffer, D. DeGeest, and A. Li, "Tackling the Problem of Construct Proliferation: A Guide to Assessing the Discriminant Validity of Conceptually Related Constructs," *Organizational Research Methods* 19, no. 1 (2016): 80–110.

91. M. A. Robinson and K. Boies, "Different Ways to Get the Job Done: Comparing the Effects of Intellectual Stimulation and Contingent Reward Leadership on Task-Related Outcomes," *Journal of Applied Social Psychology* 46 (2016): 336–53.

92. DeRue et al., "Trait and Behavioural Theories of Leadership"; G. Wang, I-S. Oh, S. H. Courtright, and A. E. Colbert, "Transformational Leadership and Performance Across Criteria and Levels: A Meta-Analytic Review of 25 Years of Research," *Group & Organization Management* 36, no. 2 (2011): 223–70.

93. S. Clarke, "Safety Leadership: A Meta-Analytic Review of Transformational and Transactional Leadership Styles as Antecedents of Safety Behaviors," *Journal of Occupational and Organizational Psychology* 86 (2013): 22–49.

94. Judge and Piccolo, "Transformational and Transactional Leadership."

95. Antonakis et al., "Charisma."

96. See, for example, D. Tourish, *The Dark Side of Transformational Leadership: A Critical Perspective* (New York, NY: Routledge, 2013); Siangchokyoo et al., "Follower Transformation as the Linchpin of Transformational Leadership Theory."

97. D. Van Knippenberg and S. B. Sitkin, "A Critical Assessment of Charismatic–Transformational Leadership Research: Back to the Drawing Board?" *The Academy of Management Annals* 7, no. 1 (2013): 1–60.

98. Ibid; G. Wang, C. H. Van Iddekinge, L. Zhang, and J. Bishoff, "Meta-Analytic and Primary Investigations of the Role of Followers in Ratings of Leadership Behavior in Organizations," *Journal of Applied Psychology* 104, no. 1 (2019): 70–106.

99. F. Luthans and B. J. Avolio, "Authentic Leadership Development," in K. S. Cameron, J. E. Dutton, and R. Quinn (eds.), *Positive Organizational Scholarship: Foundations of a New Discipline* (San Francisco, CA: Barrett-Koehler, 2003): 241–61; F. O. Walumbwa, B. J. Avolio, W. L. Gardner, T. S. Wernsing, and S. J. Peterson, "Authentic Leadership: Development and Validation of a Theory-Based Measure?," *Journal of Management* 34 (2008): 89–126; see for a critique, M. Alvesson and K. Einola, "Warning for Excessive Positivity: Authentic Leadership and Other Traps in Leadership Studies," *The Leadership Quarterly* 30 (2019): 383–95.

100. Bradt, "Practice What You Preach or Pay the Price."

101. S. Braun, C. Peus, and D. Frey, "Connectionism in Action: Exploring the Links Between Leader Prototypes, Leader Gender, and Perceptions of Authentic Leadership," *Organizational Behavior and Human Decision Processes* 149 (2018): 129–44.

102. Ibid.

103. C. Jideonwo, "Practice What You Preach: How to Make the Workplace (and World) a Happier Place," *Forbes*, May 10, 2018, https://www.forbes.com/sites/forbesagencycouncil/2018/05/10/practice-what-you-preach-how-to-make-the-workplace-and-world-a-happier-place/#1a794ccb3af1; D. Remnick, "Hillary Clinton Looks Back in Anger," *The New Yorker*, September 25, 2017, https://www.newyorker.com/magazine/2017/09/25/hillary-clinton-looks-back-in-anger

104. G. C. Banks, K. D. McCauley, W. L. Gardner, and C. E. Guler, "A Meta-Analytic Review of Authentic and Transformational Leadership: A Test for Redundancy," *The Leadership Quarterly* 27 (2016): 634–62.

105. T. Simons, H. Leroy, V. Collewaert, and S. Masschelein, "How Leader Alignment of Words and Deeds Affects Followers: A Meta-Analysis of Behavioral Integrity Research," *Journal of Business Ethics* 132 (2015): 831–44.

106. Q. Mehmood, M. R. W. Hamstra, S. Nawab, and T. Vriend, "Authentic Leadership and Followers' In-Role and Extra-Role Performance: The Mediating Role of Followers' Learning Goal Orientation," *Journal of Occupational and Organizational Psychology* 89 (2016): 877–83.

107. Banks et al., "A Meta-Analytic Review of Authentic and Transformational Leadership,"; G. C. Banks, J. Gooty, R. L. Ross, C. E. Williams, and N. T. Harrington, "Construct Redundancy in Leader Behaviors: A Review and Agenda for the Future," *The Leadership Quarterly* 29 (2018): 236–51; J. E. Hoch, W. H. Bommer, J. H. Dulebohn, and D. Wu, "Do Ethical, Authentic, and Servant Leadership Explain Variance Above and Beyond Transformational Leadership? A Meta-Analysis," *Journal of Management* 44, no. 2 (2018): 501–29.

108. Banks et al., "A Meta-Analytic Review of Authentic and Transformational Leadership."

109. D. N. Den Hartog, "Ethical Leadership," *Annual Review of Organizational Psychology and Organizational Behavior* 2 (2015): 409–34.

110. C. Moore, D. M. Mayer, F. F. T. Chiang, C. Crossley, M. J. Karlesky, and T. A. Birtch, "Leaders Matter Morally: The Role of Ethical Leadership in Shaping Employee Moral Cognition and Misconduct," *Journal of Applied Psychology* 104, no. 1 (2019): 123–45; D. A. Waldman, D. Wang, S. T. Hannah, and P. A. Balthazard, "A Neurological and Ideological Perspective of Ethical Leadership," *Academy of Management Journal* 60, no. 4 (2017): 1285–306; J. T. Bush, D. T. Welsh, M. D. Baer, and D. Waldman, "Discouraging Unethicality Versus Encouraging Ethicality: Unraveling the Differential Effects of Prevention- and Promotion-Focused Ethical Leadership," *Personnel Psychology* (in press); C. Moore, D. M. Mayer, F. F. T. Chiang, C. Crossley, M. J. Karlesky, and T. A. Birtch, "Leaders Matter Morally: The Role of Ethical Leadership in Shaping Employee Moral Cognition and Misconduct," *Journal of Applied Psychology* 104, no. 1 (2019): 123–45.

111. T. W. H. Ng and D. C. Feldman, "Ethical Leadership: Meta-Analytic Evidence of Criterion-Related and Incremental Validity," *Journal of Applied Psychology* 100, no. 3 (2015): 948–65; T. W. H. Ng, Mo Wang, D. Y. Hsu, and C. Su, "Changes in Perceptions of Ethical Leadership: Effects on Associative and Dissociative Outcomes," *Journal of Applied Psychology* (in press).

112. E-R. Lukacik and J. S. Bourdage, "Exploring the Influence of Abusive and Ethical Leadership on Supervisor and Co-Worker-targeted Impression Management," *Journal of Business and Psychology* 34 (2019): 771–789; J. M. Schaubroeck, S. S. K. Lam, and A. C. Peng, "Can Peers' Ethical and Transformational Leadership Improve Coworkers' Service Quality? A Latent Growth Analysis," *Organizational Behavior and Human Decision Processes* 133 (2016): 45–58.

113. Banks et al., "Construct Redundancy in Leader Behaviors"; Hoch et al., "Do Ethical, Authentic, and Servant Leadership Explain Variance Above and Beyond Transformational Leadership?"

114. S.H. Lin, J. Ma, and R. E. Johnson, "When Ethical Leader Behavior Breaks Bad: How Ethical Leader Behavior Can Turn Abusive via Ego Depletion and Moral Licensing," *Journal of Applied Psychology* 101, no. 6 (2016): 815–30.

115. R. Fehr, A. Fulmer, and F. T. Keng-Highberger, "How Do Employees React to Leaders' Unethical Behavior? The Role of Moral Disengagement," *Personnel Psychology* 73 (2020): 73–93.

116. S. A. Eisenbeiss and D. Van Knippenberg, "On Ethical Leadership Impact: The Role of Follower Mindfulness and Moral Emotions," *Journal of Organizational Behavior* 36 (2015): 182–95; X. Qin, M. Huang, Q. Hu, M. Schminke, and D. Ju, "Ethical Leadership, but Toward Whom? How Moral Identity Congruence Shapes the Ethical Treatment of Employees," *Human Relations* 71, no. 8 (2018): 1120–49; C. E. Thiel, J. H. Hardy, D. R. Peterson, D. T. Welsh, and J. M. Bonner, "Too Many Sheep in the Flock? Span of Control Attenuates the Influence of Ethical Leadership," *Journal of Applied Psychology* 103, no. 12 (2018): 1324–34.

117. J. Schindler, "Leading With Ethics," *Forbes*, January 7, 2019, https://www.forbes.com/sites/forbescoachescouncil/2019/01/07/leading-with-ethics/#24f0d254568a

118. J. M. Schaubroeck et al. "Embedding Ethical Leadership within and across Organization Levels," *Academy of Management Journal* 55, no. 5 (2012): 1053–78; M. Kuenzi, D. M. Mayer, and R. L. Greenbaum, "Creating an Ethical Organizational Environment: The Relationship Between Ethical Leadership, Ethical Organizational Climate, and Unethical Behavior," *Personnel Psychology* 73 (2020): 43–71; A. C. Peng and D. Kim, "A Meta-Analytic Test of the Differential Pathways Linking Ethical Leadership to Normative Conduct," *Journal of Organizational Behavior* (in press).

119. J. M. Jensen, M. S. Cole, and R. S. Rubin, "Predicting Retail Shrink From Performance Pressure, Ethical Leader Behaivor, and Store-Level Incivility," *Journal of Organizational Behavior* 40 (2019): 723–39.

120. D. van Dierendonck, "Servant Leadership: A Review and Synthesis," *Journal of Management* 37, no. 4 (2011): 1228–61; J. W. Graham, "Servant-Leadership in Organizations: Inspirational and Moral," *The Leadership Quarterly* 2 (1991): 105–19; N. Eva, M. Robin, S. Sendjaya, D. van Dierendonck, and R. C. Liden, "Servant Leadership: A Systematic Review and Call for Future Research," *The Leadership Quarterly* 30 (2019): 111–32.

121. L.C. Spears, "Character and Servant Leadership: Ten Characteristics of Effective, Caring Leaders," *The Journal of Virtues & Leadership* 1 (2010): 25–30.

122. Banks et al., "Construct Redundancy in Leader Behaviors"; Hoch et al., "Do Ethical, Authentic, and Servant Leadership Explain Variance Above and Beyond Transformational Leadership?"

123. Ibid.

124. A. Panaccio, D. J. Henderson, R. C. Liden, S. J. Wayne, and X. Cao, "Toward an Understanding of When and Why Servant Leadership Accounts for Employee Extra-Role Behaviors," *Journal of Business and Psychology* 30 (2015): 657–76; J. Sun, R. C. Liden, and L. Ouyang, "Are Servant Leaders Appreciated? An Invlestiation of How Relational Attributions Influence Employee Feelings of Gratitude and Prosocial Behaviors," *Journal of Organizational Behavior* 40, no. 5 (2019): 528–40.

125. G. James Lemoine and T. C. Blum, "Servant Leadership, Leader Gender, and Team Gender Role: Testing a Female Advantage in a Cascading Model of Performance," *Personnel Psychology* (in press).

126. Z. Chen, J. Zhu, and M. Zhou, "How Does a Servant Leader Fuel the Service Fire? A Multilevel Model of Servant Leadership, Individual Self-Identity, Group Competition Climate, and Customer Service Performance," *Journal of Applied Psychology* 100, no. 2 (2015): 511–21.

127. Z. Wang, H. Xu, and Y. Liu, "Servant Leadership as a Driver of Employee Service Performance: Test of a Trickle-Down Model and Its Boundary Conditions," *Human Relations* 71, no. 9 (2018): 1179–203; J. Stollberger, M. Las Heras, Y. Rofcanin, and M. José Bosch, "Serving Followers and Family? A Trickle-Down Model of How Servant Leadership Shapes Employee Work Performance," *Journal of Vocational Behavior* 112 (2019): 158–71; J. Wu, R. C. Liden, C. Liao, and S. J. Wayne, "Does Manager Servant Leadership Lead to Followers Serving Behaviors? It Fepends on Follower Self-Interest," *Journal of Applied Psychology* (in press).

128. Banks et al., "Construct Redundancy in Leader Behaviors"; Hoch et al., "Do Ethical, Authentic, and Servant Leadership Explain Variance Above and Beyond Transformational Leadership?"; A. Lee, J. Lyubovnikova, A. Wei Tian, and C. Knight, "Servant Leadership: A Meta-Analytic Examination of Incremental Contribution, Moderation, and Mediation," *Journal of Occupational and Organizational Psychology* 92 (2020): 1–44.

129. F. D. Schoorman, R. C. Mayer, and J. H. Davis, "An Integrative Model of Organizational Trust: Past, Present, and Future," *Academy of Management Review* 32, no. 2 (2007): 344–54; A. Cristina Costa, C. Ashley Fulmer, and N. R. Anderson, "Trust in Work Teams: An Integrative Review, Multilevel Model, and Future Research Directions," *Journal of Organizational Behavior* 39 (2018): 169–84.

130. B. A. Gazdag, M. Haude, M. Hoegl, and M. Muethel, "I Do Not Want to Trust You, but I Do: On the Relationship Between Trust Intent, Trusting Behavior, and Time Pressure," *Journal of Business and Psychology* 34 (2019): 731–743.

131. Schoorman et al., "An Integrative Model of Organizational Trust."

132. B. L. Connelly, T. R. Crook, J. G. Combs, D. J. Ketchen, and H. Aguinis, "Competence- and Integrity-Based Trust in Interorganizational Relationships: Which Matters More?" *Journal of Management* 44, no. 3 (2018): 919–45.

133. See, for instance, K. T. Dirks and D. L. Ferrin, "Trust in Leadership: Meta-Analytic Findings and Implications for Research and Practice," *Journal of Applied Psychology* 87, no. 4 (2002): 611–28.

134. S. Han, C. M. Harold, and M. Cheong, "Examining Why Employee Proactive Personality Influences Empowering Leadership: The Roles of Cognition-and Affect-Based Trust," *Journal of Occupational and Organizational Psychology* 92 (2019): 352–83.

135. R. L. Campagna, K. T. Dirks, A. P. Knight, C. Crossley, and S. L. Robinson, "On the Relation Between Felt Trust and Actual Trust: Examining Pathways to and Implications of Leader Trust Meta-Accuracy," *Journal of Applied Psychology* (in press).

136. J. A. Colquitt, B. A. Scott, and J. A. LePine, "Trust, Trustworthiness, and Trust Propensity: A Meta-Analytic Test of Their Unique Relationships with Risk Taking and Job Performance," *Journal of Applied Psychology* 92, no. 4 (2007): 909–27; S. R. Giessner and D. van Knippenberg, "'License to Fail': Goal Definition, Leader Group Prototypicality, and Perceptions of Leadership Effectiveness After Leader Failure," *Organizational Behavior and Human Decision Processes* 105, no. 1 (2008): 14–35.

137. S. M. Conchie, P. J. Taylor, and I. J. Donald, "Promoting Safety Voice with Safety-Specific Transformational Leadership: The Mediating Role of Two Dimensions of Trust," *Journal of Occupational Health Psychology* 17, no. 1 (2012): 105–15; J. R. Detert and E. R. Burris, "Leadership Behavior and Employee Voice: Is the Door Really Open?," *Academy of Management Journal* 50, no. 4 (2007): 869–84; S. Loretta Kim, "Enticing High Performers to Stay and Share Their Knowledge: The Importance of Trust in Leader," *Human Resource Management* 58 (2019): 341–51.

138. B. A. De Jong, K. T. Dirks, and N. Gillespie, "Trust and Team Performance: A Meta-Analysis of Main Effects, Moderators, and Covariates," *Journal of Applied Psychology* 101, no. 8 (2016): 1134–50.

139. Colquitt, Scott, and LePine, "Trust, Trustworthiness, and Trust Propensity."

140. J. A. Colquitt, B. A. Scott, and J. A. LePine, "Trust, Trustworthiness, and Trust Propensity: A Meta-Analytic Test of Their Unique Relationships with Risk Taking and Job Performance;" M. L. Frazier, C. Tupper, and S. Fainshmidt, "The Path(s) to Employee Trust in Direct Supervisor in Nascent and Established Relationships: A Fuzzy Set Analysis," *Journal of Organizational Behavior* 37 (2016): 1023–43; F. D. Schoorman, R. C. Mayer, and J. H. Davis, "An Integrative Model of Organizational Trust: Past, Present, and Future."

141. Cited in D. Jones, "Do You Trust Your CEO?" *USA Today,* February 12, 2003, 7B.

142. Mayer, Davis, and Schoorman, "An Integrative Model of Organizational Trust."

143. J. A. Simpson, "Foundations of Interpersonal Trust," in *Social Psychology: Handbook of Basic Principles*, 2nd ed., eds. A. W. Kruglanski and E. T. Higgins (New York: Guilford, 2007), 587–607.

144. A. J. Ferguson and R. S. Peterson, "Sinking Slowly: Diversity in Propensity to Trust Predicts Downward Trust Spirals in Small Groups," *Journal of Applied Psychology* 100, no. 4 (2015): 1012–24.

145. X.-P. Chen, M. B. Eberly, T.-J. Chiang, J.-L. Farh, and B.-Shiuan Cheng, "Affective Trust in Chinese Leaders: Linking Paternalistic Leadership to Employee Performance," *Journal of Management* 40, no. 3 (2014): 796–819.

146. J. A. Simpson, "Foundations of Interpersonal Trust"; L. van der Werff and F. Buckley, "Getting to Know You: A Longitudinal Examination of Trust Cues and Trust Development During Socialization," *Journal of Management* 43, no. 3 (2017): 742–70.

147. J. Kaltiainen, J. Kipponen, and B. C. Holtz, "Dynamic Interplay Between Merger Process Justice and Cognitive Trust in Top Management: A Longitudinal Study," *Journal of Applied Psychology* 102, no. 4 (2017): 636–47; J. Lipponen, J. Kaltiainen, L. van der Werff, and N. K. Steffens, "Merger-Specific Trust Cues in the Development of Trust in New Supervisors During an Organizational Merger: A Naturally Occurring Quasi-Experiment," *The Leadership Quarterly* (in press).

148. B. Groysberg and M. Slind, "Leadership Is a Conversation," *Harvard Business Review,* June 2012, 76–84.

149. K. Breevaart and H. Zacher, "Main and Interactive Effects of Weekly Transformational and Laissez-Faire Leadership on Followers' Trust in the Leader and Leader Effectiveness," *Journal of Occupational and Organizational Psychology* 92 (2019): 384–409; B. Shao, "Moral Anger as a Dilemma? An Investigation on How Leader Moral Anger Influences Follower Trust," *The Leadership Quarterly* 30 (2019): 365–82.

150. R. J. Lewicki and C. Brinsfield, "Trust Repair," *Annual Review of Organizational Psychology and Organizational Behavior* 4 (2017): 287–313; H. Zhao, S. J. Wayne, B. C. Glibkowski, and J. Bravo, "The Impact of Psychological Contract Breach on Work-Related Outcomes: A Meta-Analysis," *Personnel Psychology* 60, no. 3 (2007): 647–80.

151. Ibid.

152. D. L. Ferrin, P. H. Kim, C. D. Cooper, and K. T. Dirks, "Silence Speaks Volumes: The Effectiveness of Reticence in Comparison to Apology and Denial for Responding to Integrity- and Competence-Based Trust Violations," *Journal of Applied Psychology* 92, no. 4 (2007): 893–908.

153. K. E. Henderson, E. T. Welsh, and A. M. O'Leary-Kelly, "'Oops, I Did It' or 'It Wasn't Me:' An Examination of Psychological Contract breach Repair Tactics," *Journal of Business and Psychology* (in press).

154. T. Haesevoets, A. Joosten, C. R. Folmer, L. Lerner, D. De Cremer, and A. Van Hiel, "The Impact of Decision Timing on the Effectiveness of Leaders' Apologies to Repair Followers' Trust in the Aftermath of Leader Failure," *Journal of Business and Psychology* 31 (2016): 533–51.

155. M. E. Schweitzer, J. C. Hershey, and E. T. Bradlow, "Promises and Lies: Restoring Violated Trust," *Organizational Behavior and Human Decision Processes* 101, no. 1 (2006): 1–19.

156. K. E. Kram, "Phases of the Mentor Relationship," *Academy of Management Journal* 26 (1983): 608–25; K. E. Kram, *Mentoring at Work: Developmental Relationships in Organizational Life* (Glenview, IL: Foresman, 1985).

157. T. A. Scandura, "Mentorship and Career Mobility: An Empirical Investigation," *Journal of Organizational Behavior* 13 (1992): 169–74.

158. K. Kraiger, L. M. Finkelstein, and L. S. Varghese, "Enacting Effective Mentoring Behaviors: Development and Initial Investigation of the Cuboid of Mentoring," *Journal of Business and Psychology* 34 (2019): 403–424.

159. T. D. Allen, L. T. Eby, M. L. Poteet, E. Lentz, and L. Lima, "Career Benefits Associated With Mentoring for Protégés: A Meta-Analysis," *Journal of Applied Psychology* 89, no. 1 (2004): 127–36; L. T. Eby, T. D. Allen, S. C. Evans, T. Ng, and D. L. DuBois, "Does Mentoring Matter? A Multidisciplinary Meta-Analysis Comparing Mentored and Non-Mentored Individuals," *Journal of Vocational Behavior* 72 (2008): 254–67; R. Ghosh and T. G. Reio, "Career Benefits Associated With Mentoring for Mentors: A Meta-Analysis," *Journal of Vocational Behavior* 83 (2013): 106–16.

160. C. M. Underhill, "The Effectiveness of Mentoring Programs in Corporate Settings: A Meta-Analytical Review of the Literature," *Journal of Vocational Behavior* 68 (2006): 292–307.

161. K. E. O'Brien, A. Biga, S. R. Kessler, and T. D. Allen, "A Meta-Analytic Investigation of Gender Differences in Mentoring," *Journal of Management* 36, no. 2 (2010): 537–54.

162. J. D. Kammeyer-Mueller and T. A. Judge, "A Quantitative Review of Mentoring Research: Test of a Model," *Journal of Vocational Behavior* 72 (2008): 269–83.

163. D. Robson, "COVID-19: What Makes a Good Leader During a Crisis?" *BBC: Worklife* [blog], March 27, 2020, https://www.bbc.com/worklife/article/20200326-covid-19-what-makes-a-good-leader-during-a-crisis

164. Z. Marks, "In a Global Emergency, Women Are Showing How to Lead," *The Washington Post,* April 21, 2020, https://www.washingtonpost.com/opinions/2020/04/21/global-emergency-women-are-showing-how-lead/; S. Miller, "The Secret to Germany's COVID-19 Success: Angela Merkel Is a Scientist," *The Atlantic,* April 20, 2020, https://www .theatlantic.com/international/archive/2020/04/angela-merkel-germany-coronavirus-pandemic/610225/; N. Yancey-Bragg, "Female World Leaders Are Handling Coronavirus Crisis 'in a Really Impressive Manner,' Experts Say," *USA Today,* April 17, 2020, https://www.usatoday.com/story/news/world/2020/04/17/coronavirus-women-world-leaders-praised-handling-crisis/5144421002/

165. S. Alexander Haslam and M. K. Ryan, "The Road to the Glass Cliff: Differences in the Perceived Suitability of Men and Women for Leadership Positions in Succeeding and Failing Organizations," *The Leadership Quarterly* 19 (2008): 530–46; C. Kulich, V. Iacoviello, F. Lorenzi-Cioldi, "Solving the Crisis: When Agency is the Preferred Leadership for Implementing Change," *The Leadership Quarterly* 29 (2018): 295–308; M. K. Ryan, S. Alexander Haslam, T. Morgenroth, F. Rink, J. Stoker, and K. Peters, "Getting on Top of the Glass Cliff: Reviewing a Decade of Evidence, Explanations, and Impact," *The Leadership Quarterly* 27 (2016): 446–55.

166. S. T. Hannah, M. Uhl-Bien, B. J. Avolio, and F. L. Cavaretta, "A Framework for Examining Leadership in Extreme Contexts," *The Leadership Quarterly* 20 (2009): 897–919; E. Hayes James and L. Perry Wooten, *Leading Under Pressure: From Surviving to Thriving Before, During, and After a Crisis* (New York, NY: Routledge, 2010).

167. B. Wansink, C. R. Payne, K. van Ittersum, "Profiling the Heroic Leader: Empirical Lessons From Combat-Decorated Veterans of World War II," *The Leadership Quarterly* 19 (2008): 547–55.

168. L. A. DeChurch, C. Shawn Burke, M. L. Shuffler, R. Lyons, D. Doty, and E. Salas, "A Historiometric Analysis of Leadership in Mission Critical Multiteam Environments," *The Leadership Quarterly* 22 (2011): 152–69; see, also, M. D. Mumford, T. L. Friedrich, J. J. Caughron, and C. L. Byrne, "Leader Cognition in Real-World Settings: How Do Leaders Think About Crises?" *The Leadership Quarterly* 18 (2007): 515–43; J. I. Stoker, H. Garretsen, and D. Soudis, "Tightening the Leash After a Threat: A Multilevel Event Study on Leadership Behavior Following the Financial Crisis," *The Leadership Quarterly* 30 (2019): 199–214.

169. D. J. Carrington, I. A. Combe, and M. D. Mumford, "Cognitive Shifts Within Leader and Follower Teams: Where Consensus Develops in Mental Models During an Organizational Crisis," *The Leadership Quarterly* 30 (2019): 335–50; I. A. Combe and D. J. Carrington, "Leaders' Sensemaking Under Crises: Emerging Cognitive Consensus Over Time Within Management Teams," *The Leadership Quarterly* 26 (2015): 307–22.

170. J. M. Madera and D. B. Smith, "The Effects of Leader Negative Emotions on Evaluations of Leadership in a Crisis Situation: The Role of Anger and Sadness," *The Leadership Quarterly* 20 (2009): 103–14.

171. M. C. Bligh, J. C. Kohles, and J. R. Meindl, "Charisma Under Crisis: Presidential Leadership, Rhetoric, and Media Responses Before and After the September 11th Terrorist Attacks," *The Leadership Quarterly* 15, no. 2 (2004): 211–39; K. M. Davis and W. L. Gardner, "Charisma Under Crisis Revisited: Presidential Leadership, Perceived Leader Effectiveness, and Contextual Influences," *The Leadership Quarterly* 23 (2012): 918–933; J. G. Hunt, K. B. Boal, and G. E. Dodge, "The Effects of Visionary and Crisis-Responsive Charisma on Followers: An Experimental Examination of Two Kinds of Charismatic Leadership," *The Leadership Quarterly* 10, no. 3 (1999): 423–48.

172. Ibid.

173. E. A. Williams, R. Pillai, B. Deptula, and K. B. Lowe, "The Effects of Crisis, Cynicism About Change, and Value Congruence on Perceptions of Authentic Leadership and Attributed Charisma in the 2008 Presidential Election," *The Leadership Quarterly* 23 (2012): 324–41; E. A. Williams, R. Pillai, K. B. Lowe, D. Jung, and D. Herst, "Crisis, Charisma, Values, and Voting Behavior in the 2004 Presidential Election," *The Leadership Quarterly* 20 (2009): 70–86.

174. M. B. Eberly, D. J. Bluhm, C. Guarana, B. J. Avolio, and S. T. Hannah, "Staying After the Storm: How Transformational Leadership Relates to Follower Turnover Intentions in Extreme Contexts," *Journal of Vocational Behavior* 102 (2017): 72–85.

175. Comment by Jim Collins, cited in J. Useem, "Conquering Vertical Limits," *Fortune*, February 19, 2001, 94.

176. See, for instance, S. G. Green and T. R. Mitchell, "Attributional Processes of Leaders in Leader-Member Interactions," *Organizational Behavior & Human Performance* 23, no. 3 (1979): 429–58; B. Schyns, J. Felfe, and H. Blank, "Is Charisma Hyper-Romanticism? Empirical Evidence from New Data and a Meta-Analysis," *Applied Psychology: An International Review* 56, no. 4 (2007): 505–27.

177. J. H. Gray and I. L. Densten, "How Leaders Woo Followers in the Romance of Leadership," *Applied Psychology: An International Review* 56, no. 4 (2007): 558–81; M. J. Martinko, P. Harvey, D. Sikora, and S. C. Douglas, "Perceptions of Abusive Supervision: The Role of Subordinates' Attribution Styles," *Leadership Quarterly* 22, no. 4 (2011): 751–64; J. R. Meindl and S. B. Ehrlich, "The Romance of Leadership and the Evaluation of Organizational Performance," *Academy of Management Journal* 30, no. 1 (1987): 91–109; J. R. Meindl, S. B. Ehrlich, and J. M. Dukerich, "The Romance of Leadership," *Administrative Science Quarterly* 30 (1985): 78–102.

178. W. L. Gardner, E. P. Karam, L. L. Tribble, and C. C. Cogliser, "The Missing Link? Implications of Internal, External, and Relational Attribution Combinations for Leader-Member Exchange, Relationship Work, Self-Work, and Conflict," *Journal of Organizational Behavior* 40, no. 5 (2019): 554–569.

179. M. C. Bligh, J. C. Kohles, C. L. Pearce, J. E. Justin, and J. F. Stovall, "When the Romance Is Over: Follower Perspectives of Aversive Leadership," *Applied Psychology: An International Review* 56, no. 4 (2007): 528–57.

180. B. Schyns, J. Felfe, and H. Blank, "Is Charisma Hyper-Romanticism?"

181. W. Matthew Bowler, J. B. Paul, and J. R. Halbesleben, "LMX and Attributions of Organizational Citizenship Behavior Motives: When Is Citizenship Perceived as Brownnosing?" *Journal of Business and Psychology* 34 (2019): 139–52.

182. F. K. Matta, T. B. Sabey, B. A. Scott, S-H. J. Lin, and J. Koopman, "Not All Fairness Is Created Equal: A Study of Employee Attributions of Supervisor Justice Motives," *Journal of Applied Psychology* 105, no. 3 (2020): 274–93.

183. S. Kerr and J. M. Jermier, "Substitutes for Leadership: Their Meaning and Measurement," *Organizational Behavior & Human Performance* 22, no. 3 (1978): 375–403.

184. R. E. Silverman, "Who's the Boss? There Isn't One," *The Wall Street Journal,* June 20, 2012, B1, B8.

185. J. Koopman, B. A. Scott, F. K. Matta, D. E. Conlon, and T. Dennerlein, "Ethical Leadership as a Substitute for Justice Enactment: An Information Processing Perspective," *Journal of Applied Psychology* 104, no. 9 (2019): 1103–16.

186. S. D. Dionne, F. J. Yammarino, L. E. Atwater, and L. R. James, "Neutralizing Substitutes for Leadership Theory: Leadership Effects and Common-Source Bias," *Journal of Applied Psychology* 87 (2002): 454–64; J. R. Villa, J. P. Howell, P. W. Dorfman, and D. L. Daniel, "Problems with Detecting Moderators in Leadership Research Using Moderated Multiple Regression," *Leadership Quarterly* 14 (2002): 3–23.

CHAPTER 13

1. R. E. Sturm and J. Antonakis, "Interpersonal Power: A Review, Critique, and Research Agenda," *Journal of Management* 41, no. 1 (2015): 136–63; P. Fleming and A. Spicer, "Power in Management and Organization Science," *The Academy of Management Annals* 8, no. 1 (2014): 237–98.

2. C. Anderson and S. Brion, "Perspectives on Power in Organizations," *Annual Review of Organizational Psychology and Organizational Behavior* 1 (2014): 67–97.

3. K. Higginbottom, "The Link Between Power and Sexual Harassment in the Workplace," *Forbes,* June 11, 2018, https://www.forbes.com/sites/karenhigginbottom/2018/06/11/the-link-between-power-and-sexual-harassment-in-the-workplace/#52604e6d190f

4. E. Shaw, A. Hegewisch, and C. Hess, *Sexual Harassment and Assault at Work: Understanding the Costs* [Report No. IWPR#B376] (Washington, DC: Institute for Women's Policy Research, October 15, 2018).

5. J. French and B. Raven, "The Bases of Social Power," in D. Cartwright (ed.), *Studies in Social Power* (Ann Arbor, MI: Institute for Social Research, 1959): 150–67; G. Yukl, "Use Power Effectively," in E. A. Locke (ed.), *Handbook of Principles of Organizational Behavior* (Malden, MA: Blackwell, 2004), 242–47.

6. See, for example, H. Lian, D. J. Brown, D. L. Ferris, L. H. Liang, L. M. Keeping, and R. Morrison, "Abusive Supervision and Retaliation: A Self-Control Framework," *Academy of Management Journal* 57, no. 1 (2014): 116–39.

7. French and Raven, "The Bases of Social Power"; E. A. Ward, "Social Power Bases of Managers: Emergence of a New Factor," *Journal of Social Psychology* (February 2001): 144–47.

8. See, for instance, G. D. Granic and A. K. Wagner, "Where Power Resides in Committees," *The Leadership Quarterly* (in press).

9. S. R. Giessner and T. W. Schubert, "High in the Hierarchy: How Vertical Location and Judgments of Leaders' Power Are Interrelated," *Organizational Behavior and Human Decision Processes* 104, no. 1 (2007): 30–44.

10. N. Wellman, D. M. Mayer, M. Ong, and D. S. DeRue, "When Are Do-Gooders Treated Badly? Legitimate Power, Role Expectations, and Reactions to Moral Objection in Organizations," *Journal of Applied Psychology* 101, no. 6 (2016): 793–814.

11. French and Raven, "The Bases of Social Power"; M. Van Djike and M. Poppe, "Striving for Personal Power as a Basis for Social Power Dynamics," *European Journal of Social Psychology* 27, no. 1 (2006): 537–56.

12. French and Raven, "The Bases of Social Power."

13. Ibid.

14. J. D. Kudisch, M. L. Poteet, G. H. Dobbins, M. C. Rush, and J. A. Russell, "Expert Power, Referent Power, and Charisma: Toward the Resolution of a Theoretical Debate," *Journal of Business and Psychology* 10, no. 1 (1995): 177–95.

15. J. F. Peltz, "Lakers Look to King James' Golden Marketing Touch," *LA Times,* July 3, 2018, https://www.latimes.com/business/la-fi-lebron-lakers-marketing-20180703-story .html

16. T. Schwarzmüller, P. Brosi, M. Spörrle, and I. M. Welpe, "It is the Base: Why Displaying Anger Instead of Sadness Might Increase Leaders' Perceived Power but Worsen Their Leadership Outcomes," *Journal of Business and Psychology* 32 (2017): 691–709.

17. S. Perman, "Translation Advertising: Where Shop Meets Hip Hop," *Time,* August 30, 2010, http://content.time.com/time/magazine/article/0,9171,2011574,00.html

18. Translation, *Beats by Dre—The Shop,* accessed March 19, 2019, https://www.translationllc.com/work/the-shop

19. Sturm and Antonakis, "Interpersonal Power."

20. M. C. J. Caniels and A. Roeleveld, "Power and Dependence Perspectives on Outsourcing Decisions," *European Management Journal* 27, no. 6 (2009): 402–17; R.-J. B. Jean, D. Kim, and R. S. Sinkovics, "Drivers and Performance Outcomes of Supplier Innovation Generation in Customer-Supplier Relationships: The Role of Power-Dependence," *Decision Sciences* 43, no. 6 (2012): 1003–38.

21. D. Acemoglu and P. Restrepo, "Artificial Intelligence, Automation, and Work," in A. Agarwal, A. Goldfarb, and J. Gans (eds.), *Economics of Artificial Intelligence* (forthcoming); L. G. Kletzer, "The Question With AI Isn't Whether We'll Lose Our Jobs—It is How Much We'll Get Paid," *Harvard Business Review,* January 31, 2018, https://hbr.org/2018/01/the-question-with-ai-isnt-whether-well-lose-our-jobs-its-how-much-well-get-paid

22. R.S. Burt, M. Kilduff, and S. Tasselli, "Social Network Analysis: Foundations and Frontiers on Advantage," *Annual Review of Psychology* 64 (2013): 527–47; M. A. Carpenter, M. Li, and H. Jiang, "Social Network Research in Organizational Contexts: A Systematic Review of Methodological Issues and Choices," *Journal of Management* 38, no. 4 (2012): 1328–61; M. Kilduff and D. J. Brass, "Organizational Social Network Research: Core Ideas and Key Debates," *Academy of Management Annals* 4 (2010): 317–57.

23. J. Battilana and T. Casciaro, "Change Agents, Networks, and Institutions: A Contingency Theory of Organizational Change," *Academy of Management Journal* 55, no. 2 (2012): 381–98.

24. B. Landis, M. Kilduff, J. I. Menges, and G. J. Kilduff, "The Paradox of Agency: Feeling Powerful Reduces Brokerage Opportunity

25. Recognition yet Increases Willingness to Broker," *Journal of Applied Psychology* 103, no. 8 (2018): 929–38.

25. C. Cheng, H-Y. Wang, L. Sigerson, and C-L. Chau, "Do the Socially Rich Get Richer? A Nuanced Perspective on Social Network Site Use and Online Social Capital Accrual," *Psychological Bulletin* 145, no. 7 (2019): 734–64; N. David, J. Brennecke, and O. Rank, "Extrinsic Motivation as a Determinant of Knowledge Exchange in Sales Teams: A Social Network Approach," *Human Resource Management* (in press); A. George Nassif, "Heterogeneity and Centrality of 'Dark Personality' Within Teams, Shared Leadership, and Team Performance: A Conceptual Moderated-Mediation Model," *Human Resource Management Review* (in press).

26. R. A. Brands and A. Mehra, "Gender, Brokerage, and Performance: A Construal Approach," *Academy of Management Journal* 62, no. 1 (2019): 196–219.

27. G. Regts, E. Molleman, H. Johan van de Brake, "The Impact of Leader-Member Exchange on Follower Performance in Light of the Larger Social Network," *Human Relations* 72, no. 8 (2019): 1265–1291; V. Yakubovich and R. Burg, "Friendship by Assignment? From Formal Interdependence to Informal Relations in Organizations," *Human Relations* 72, no. 6 (2019): 1013–38.

28. J. E. McCarthy and D. Z. Levin, "Network Residues: The Enduring Impact of Intra-Organizational Dormant Ties," *Journal of Applied Psychology* 104, no. 11 (2019): 1434–45; C. M. Porter, S. Eun Woo, D. G. Allen, and M. G. Keith, "How Do Instrumental and Expressive Network Positions Relate to Turnover? A Meta-Analytic Investigation," *Journal of Applied Psychology* 104, no. 4 (2019): 511–36; C. Tröster, A. Parker, D. van Knippenberg, and B. Sahlmüller, "The Coevolution of Social Networks and Thoughts of Quitting," *Academy of Management Journal* 62, no. 1 (2019): 22–43.

29. R. Kaše, Z. King, and D. Minbaeva, "Using Social Network Research in HRM: Scratching the Surface of a Fundamental Basis of HRM," *Human Resource Management* 52, no. 4 (2013): 473–83; R. Cross and L. Prusak, "The People Who Make Organizations Go—or Stop," *Harvard Business Review,* June 2002, https://hbr.org/2002/06/the-people-who-make-organizations-go-or-stop

30. See, for instance, S. S. De and S. Dehuri, "Machine Learning for Auspicious Social Network Mining," in M. Panda, S. Dehuri, and G-N. Wang (eds.), *Social Networking: Mining, Visualization, and Security* (New York, NY: Springer, 2014); T. Özyer and R. Alhajj (eds.), *Machine Learning Techniques for Online Social Networks* (New York, NY: Springer, 2018).

31. See, for reviews, C. A. Higgins, T. A. Judge, and G. R. Ferris, "Influence Tactics and Work Outcomes: A Meta-Analysis," *Journal of Organizational Behavior* 24 (2003): 89–106; S. Lee, S. Han, M. Cheong, S. L. Kim, and S. Yun, "How Do I Get My Way? A Meta-Analytic Review of Research on Influence Tactics," *The Leadership Quarterly* 28 (2017): 210–28.

32. Ibid.

33. Ibid.

34. Ibid.

35. A. A. Amaral, D. M. Powell, and J. L. Ho, "Why Does Impression Management Positively Influence Interview Ratings? The Mediating Role of Competence and Warmth," *International Journal of Selection and Assessment* 27 (2019): 315–27.

36. Lee et al., "How Do I Get My Way?"; R. E. Petty and P. Briñol, "Persuasion: From Single to Multiple to Metacognitive Processes," *Perspectives on Psychological Science* 3, no. 2 (2008): 137–47.

37. J. Badal, "Getting a Raise from the Boss," *The Wall Street Journal,* July 8, 2006, B1, B5.

38. N. Clarke, N. Alshenalfi, and T. Garavan, "Upward Influence Tactics and Their Effects on Job Performance Ratings and Flexible Work

Arrangements: The Mediating Roles of Mutual Recognition Respect and Mutual Appraisal Respect," *Human Resource Management* 58 (2019): 397–416.

39. Lee et al., "How Do I Get My Way?"

40. Ibid.

41. Ibid.

42. Ibid.

43. Ibid.

44. A. W. Kruglanski, A. Pierro, and E. T. Higgins, "Regulatory Mode and Preferred Leadership Styles: How Fit Increases Job Satisfaction," *Basic and Applied Social Psychology* 29, no. 2 (2007): 137–49; A. Pierro, L. Cicero, and B. H. Raven, "Motivated Compliance with Bases of Social Power," *Journal of Applied Social Psychology* 38, no. 7 (2008): 1921–44.

45. A. N. Smith et al., "Gendered Influence: A Gender Role Perspective on the Use and Effectiveness of Influence Tactics," *Journal of Management* 39, no. 5 (2013): 1156–83.

46 G. Yukl, P. P. Fu, and R. McDonald, "Cross-Cultural Differences in Perceived Effectiveness of Influence Tactics for Initiating or Resisting Change," *Applied Psychology: An International Review* 52, no. 1 (2003): 66–82; P. P. Fu, T. K. Peng, J. C. Kennedy, and G. Yukl, "Examining the Preferences of Influence Tactics in Chinese Societies: A Comparison of Chinese Managers in Hong Kong, Taiwan, and Mainland China," *Organizational Dynamics* 33, no. 1 (2004): 32–46.

47. C. J. Torelli and S. Shavitt, "Culture and Concepts of Power," *Journal of Personality and Social Psychology* 99, no. 4 (2010): 703–23.

48. P. P. Fu, T. K. Peng, J. C. Kennedy, and G. Yukl, "Examining the Preferences of Influence Tactics in Chinese Societies: A Comparison of Chinese Managers in Hong Kong, Taiwan, and Mainland China"; C. Man Zhang and H. R. Greve, "Dominant Coalitions Directing Acquisitions: Different Decision Makers, Different Decisions," *Academy of Management Journal* 62, no. 1 (2019): 44–65.

49. G. R. Ferris, D. C. Treadway, P. L. Perrewé, R. L. Brouer, C. Douglas, and S. Lux, "Political Skill in Organizations," *Journal of Management* 33, no. 3 (2007): 290–320; G. R. Ferris, B. Parker Ellen III, C. P. McAllister, and L. P. Maher, "Reorganizing Organizational Politics Research: A Review of the Literature and Identification of Future Research Directions," *Annual Review of Organizational Psychology and Organizational Behavior* 6 (2019): 299–323; G. R. Ferris, D. C. Treadaway, R. W. Kolodinsky, W. A. Hochwater, C. J. Kacmar, C. Douglas, and D. D. Fink, "Development and Validation of the Political Skill Inventory," *Journal of Management* 31, no. 1 (2005): 126–52.

50. S. Granger, L. Neville, and N. Turner, "Political Knowledge at Work: Conceptualization, Measurement, and Applications to Follower Proactivity," *Journal of Occupational and Organizational Psychology* (in press).

51. M. N. Bing, H. K. Davison, I. Minor, M. M. Novicevic, and D. D. Frink, "The Prediction of Task and Contextual Performance by Political Skill: A Meta-Analysis and Moderator Test," *Journal of Vocational Behavior* 79 (2011): 563–77; R. E. Frieder, G. R. Ferris, P. L. Perrewé, A. Wihler, and C. Darren Brooks, "Extending the Metatheoretical Framework of Social/political Influence to Leadership: Political Skill Effects on Situational Appraisals, Responses, and Evaluations by Others," *Personnel Psychology* 72 (2019): 543–69.

52. G. R. Ferris, D. C. Treadway, P. L. Perrewé, R. L. Brouer, C. Douglas, and S. Lux, "Political Skill in Organizations," *Journal of Management* 33, no. 3 (2007): 290–320; K. J. Harris, K. M. Kacmar, S. Zivnuska, and J. D. Shaw, "The Impact of Political Skill on Impression Management Effectiveness," *Journal of Applied Psychology* 92, no. 1 (2007): 278–85; W. A. Hochwarter, G. R. Ferris, M. B. Gavin, P. L. Perrewé, A. T. Hall, and D. D. Frink, "Political Skill as Neutralizer of Felt Accountability–Job Tension Effects on Job Performance Ratings:

A Longitudinal Investigation," *Organizational Behavior and Human Decision Processes* 102, no. 2 (2007): 226–39; D. C. Treadway, G. R. Ferris, A. B. Duke, G. L. Adams, and J. B. Tatcher, "The Moderating Role of Subordinate Political Skill on Supervisors' Impressions of Subordinate Ingratiation and Ratings of Subordinate Interpersonal Facilitation," *Journal of Applied Psychology* 92, no. 3 (2007): 848–55.

53. C. Anderson, S. E. Spataro, and F. J. Flynn, "Personality and Organizational Culture as Determinants of Influence," *Journal of Applied Psychology* 93, no. 3 (2008): 702–10.

54. T. P. Munyon, J. K. Summers, K. M. Thompson, and G. R. Ferris, "Political Skill and Work Outcomes: A Theoretical Extension, Meta-Analytic Investigation, and Agenda for the Future," *Personnel Psychology* 68 (2015):143–84.

55. G. Blickle, B. P. Kückelhaus, I. Kranefeld, N. Schütte, H. A. Genau, D-N. Gansen-Ammann, and A. Wihler, "Political Skill Camouflages Machiavellianism: Career Role Performance and Organizational Misbehavior at Short and Long Tenure," *Journal of Vocational Behavior* (in press).

56. Munyon et al., "Political Skill and Work Outcomes"; J. K. Summers, T. P. Munyon, R. L. Brouer, P. Pahng, and G. R. Ferris, "Political Skill in the Stressor–Strain Relationship: A Meta-Analytic Update and Extension," *Journal of Vocational Behavior* (in press).

57. Ibid.

58. A. Guinote, "How Power Affects People: Activating, Wanting, and Goal Seeking," *Annual Review of Psychology* 68 (2017): 353–81; L. M. Giurge, M. van Dijke, M. Xue Zheng, and D. De Cremer, "Does Power Corrupt the Mind? The Influence of Power on Moral Reasoning and Self-Interested Behavior," *The Leadership Quarterly* (in press).

59. Ibid.

60 Y. Cho and N. J. Fast, "Power, Defensive Denigration, and the Assuaging Effect of Gratitude Expression," *Journal of Experimental Social Psychology* 48, no. 3 (2012): 778–82.

61. B. Wisse, D. Rus, A. C. Keller, and E. Sleebos, "'Fear of Losing Power Corrupts Those Who Wield It': The Combined Effects of Leader Fear of Losing Power and Competitive Climate on Leader Self-Serving Behavior," *European Journal of Work and Organizational Psychology* 28, no. 6 (2019): 742–55.

62. E. Stamkou, G. A. van Kleef, A. H. Fischer, and M. E. Kret, "Are the Powerful Really Blind to the Feelings of Others? How Hierarchical Concerns Shape Attentions to Emotions," *Personality and Social Psychology Bulletin* 42, no. 6 (2016): 755–68.

63. M. Pitesa and S. Thau, "Masters of the Universe: How Power and Accountability Influence Self-Serving Decisions under Moral Hazard," *Journal of Applied Psychology* 98, no. 3 (2013): 550–58; N. J. Fast, N. Sivanathan, D. D. Mayer, and A. D. Galinsky, "Power and Overconfident Decision-Making," *Organizational Behavior and Human Decision Processes* 117, no. 2 (2012): 249–60; M. J. Williams, "Serving the Self from the Seat of Power: Goals and Threats Predict Leaders' Self-Interested Behavior," *Journal of Management* 40, no. 5 (2014): 1365–95; I. Vitanova, "Nurturing Overconfidence: The Relationship Between Leader Power, Overconfidence and Firm Performance," *The Leadership Quarterly* (in press).

64. D. Orghian, F. de Almeida, S. Jacinto, L. Garcia-Marques, and A. Sofia Santos, "How Your Power Affects My Impression of You," *Personality and Social Psychology Bulletin* 45, no. 4 (2019): 495–509.

65. T. Seppälä, J. Lipponen, A. Bardi, and A. Pirttilä-Backman, "Change-Oriented Organizational Citizenship Behaviour: An Interactive Product of Openness to Change Values, Work Unit Identification, and Sense of Power," *Journal of Occupational and Organizational Psychology* 85, no. 1 (2012): 136–55.

66. Sturm and Antonakis, "Interpersonal Power."

67. Ibid.

68. Ibid.

69. Ibid.

70. J. K. Maner, M. T. Gaillot, A. J. Menzel, and J. W. Kunstman, "Dispositional Anxiety Blocks the Psychological Effects of Power," *Personality and Social Psychology Bulletin* 38, no. 11 (2012): 1383–95.

71. N. J. Fast, N. Halevy, and A. D. Galinsky, "The Destructive Nature of Power Without Status," *Journal of Experimental Social Psychology* 48, no. 1 (2012): 391–94.

72. J. C. Quick and M. Ann McFadyen, "Sexual Harassment: Have We Made Any Progress?" *Journal of Occupational Health Psychology* 22, no. 3 (2017): 286–98; A. E. Tenbrunsel, M. R. Rees, and K. A. Diekmann, "Sexual Harassment in Academia: Ethical Climates and Bounded Ethicality," *Annual Review of Psychology* 70 (2019): 245–70.

73. "Facts About Sexual Harassment," The U.S. Equal Employment Opportunity Commission, accessed June 19, 2015 http:// www.eeoc.gov/facts/fs-sex.html

74. M. Senthilingam, "Sexual Harassment: How It Stands Around the Globe," *CNN,* November 29, 2017, https://www .cnn.com/2017/11/25/health/sexual-harassment-violence-abuse-global-levels/index.html

75. Ibid.

76. F. Ali and R. Kramar, "An Exploratory Study of Sexual Harassment in Pakistani Organizations," *Asia Pacific Journal of Management* 32, no. 1 (2014): 229–49.

77. H. J. Gettman and M. J. Gelfand, "When the Customer Shouldn't Be King: Antecedents and Consequences of Sexual Harassment by Clients and Customers," *Journal of Applied Psychology* 92, no. 3 (2007): 757–70; B. Popken, "Report: 80% of Waitresses Report Being Sexually Harassed," *USA Today,* October 7, 2014, http://www.today.com/money/report-80-waitresses-report-being-sexually-harassed-2D80199724

78. M. S. Hershcovis and J. Barling, "Comparing Victim Attributions and Outcomes for Workplace Aggression and Sexual Harassment," *Journal of Applied Psychology* 95, no. 5 (2010): 874–88; C. R. Willness, P. Steel, and K. Lee, "A Meta-Analysis of the Antecedents and Consequences of Workplace Sexual Harassment," *Personnel Psychology* 60 (2007): 127–62.

79. L. M. Cortina and S. A. Wasti, "Profiles in Coping: Responses to Sexual Harassment Across Persons, Organizations, and Cultures," *Journal of Applied Psychology* (February 2005): 182–92; K. Jiang, Y. Hong, P. F. McKay, D. R. Avery, D. C. Wilson, and S. D. Volpone, "Retaining Employees Through Anti-Sexual Harassment Practices: Exploring the Mediating Role of Psychological Distress and Employee Engagement," *Human Resource Management* 54, no. 1 (2015): 1–21; and J. W. Kunstman, "Sexual Overperception: Power, Mating Motives, and Biases in Social Judgment," *Journal of Personality and Social Psychology* 100, no. 2 (2011): 282–94.

80. M. J. Williams, D. H. Gruenfeld, and L. E. Guillory, "Sexual Aggression When Power Is New: Effects of Acute High Power on Chronically Low-Power Individuals," *Journal of Personality and Social Psychology* 112, no. 2 (2017): 201–23.

81. See, for example, M. E. Bergman, R. Day Langhout, P. A. Palmieri, L. M. Cortina, and L. F. Fitzgerald, "The (Un)reasonableness of Reporting: Antecedents and Consequences of Reporting Sexual Harassment," *Journal of Applied Psychology* 87, no. 2 (2002): 230–42; D. Fernando and A. Prasad, "Sex-Based Harassment and Organizational Silencing: How Women Are Led to Reluctant Acquiescence in Academia," *Human Relations* 72, no. 10 (2019): 1565–94.

82. A. E. Dastagir, "It's Been Two Years Since the #MeToo Movement Exploded. Now What?," *USA Today,* September 30, 2019, https://www.usatoday.com/story/news/nation/2019/09/30/me-too-movement-women-sexual-assault-harvey-weinstein-brett-kavanaugh/1966463001/; A. Langone, "#MeToo and Time's Up Founders Explain the Difference Between the 2 Movements—and How They're Alike," *Time,* March 22, 2018, https://time.com/5189945/whats-the-difference-between-the-metoo-and-times-up-movements/; #MeToo [website], accessed April 30, 2020, https://metoomvmt.org/; Time's Up [website], accessed April 30, 2020, https://timesupnow.org/

83. H. Kwan Cheung, C. B. Goldberg, E. B. King, and V. J. Magley, "Are They True to the Cause? Beliefs About Organizational and Unit commitment to Sexual Harassment Awareness Training," *Group & Organization Management* 43, no. 4 (2018): 531–60; Quick and McFadyen, "Sexual Harassment"; M. V. Roehling and J. Huang, "Sexual Harassment Training Effectiveness: An Interdisciplinary Review and Call for Research," *Journal of Organizational Behavior* 39 (2018): 134–50.

84. Ferris et al., "Development and Validation of the Political Skill Inventory."

85. A. Pullen and C. Rhodes, "Corporeal Ethics and the Politics of Resistance in Organizations," *Organization* 21, no. 6 (2014): 782–96.

86. G. R. Ferris and W. A. Hochwarter, "Organizational Politics," in *APA Handbook of Industrial and Organizational Psychology*, vol. 3, ed. S. Zedeck (Washington, DC: American Psychological Association, 2011), 435–59; Ferris et al., "Reorganizing Organizational Politics Research."

87. Ibid.

88. E. M. Landells and S. L. Albrecht, "The Positives and Negatives of Organizational Politics: A Qualitative Study," *Journal of Business and Psychology* 32 (2017): 41–58.

89. D. A. Buchanan, "You Stab My Back, I'll Stab Yours: Management Experience and Perceptions of Organization Political Behavior," *British Journal of Management* 19, no. 1 (2008): 49–64.

90. P. Belmi and K. Laurin, "Who Wants to Get to the Top? Class and Lay Theories About Power," *Journal of Personality and Social Psychology* 111, no. 4 (2016): 505–29.

91. Ibid.

92. S. M. Rioux and L. A. Penner, "The Causes of Organizational Citizenship Behavior: A Motivational Analysis," *Journal of Applied Psychology* (December 2001): 1306–14; M. A. Finkelstein and L. A. Penner, "Predicting Organizational Citizenship Behavior: Integrating the Functional and Role Identity Approaches," *Social Behavior & Personality* 32, no. 4 (2004): 383–98; J. Schwarzwald, M. Koslowsky, and M. Allouf, "Group Membership, Status, and Social Power Preference," *Journal of Applied Social Psychology* 35, no. 3 (2005): 644–65.

93. See, for example, J. Walter, F. W. Kellermans, and C. Lechner, "Decision Making Within and Between Organizations: Rationality, Politics, and Alliance Performance," *Journal of Management* 38, no. 5 (2012): 1582–610.

94. G. R. Ferris, D. C. Treadway, P. L. Perrewé, R. L. Grouer, C. Douglas, and S. Lux, "Political Skill in Organizations."

95. J. Shi, R. E. Johnson, Y. Liu, and M. Wang, "Linking Subordinate Political Skill to Supervisor Dependence and Reward Recommendations: A Moderated Mediation Model," *Journal of Applied Psychology* 98, no. 2 (2013): 374–84.

96. W. A. Gentry, D. C. Gimore, M. L. Shuffler, and J. B. Leslie, "Political Skill as an Indicator of Promotability among Multiple Rater Sources," *Journal of Organizational Behavior* 33, no. 1 (2012): 89–104; I. Kapoutsis, A. Paplexandris, A. Nikolopoulous, W. A. Hochwarter, and G. R. Ferris, "Politics Perceptions as a Moderator of the Political Skill-Job Performance Relationship: A Two-Study, Cross-National, Constructive Replication," *Journal of Vocational Behavior* 78, no. 1 (2011): 123–35.

97. M. Abbas, U. Raja, W. Darr, and D. Bouckenooghe, "Combined Effects of Perceived Politics and Psychological Capital on Job Satisfaction, Turnover Intentions, and Performance," *Journal of Management* 40,

no. 7 (2014): 1813–30; C. C. Rosen, D. L. Ferris, D. J. Brown, and W.-W. Yen, "Relationships Among Perceptions of Organizational Politics (POPs), Work Motivation, and Salesperson Performance," *Journal of Management and Organization* 21, no. 2 (2015): 203–16.

98. See, for example, M. D. Laird, P. Harvey, and J. Lancaster, "Accountability, Entitlement, Tenure, and Satisfaction in Generation Y," *Journal of Managerial Psychology* 30, no. 1 (2015): 87–100; J. M. L. Poon, "Situational Antecedents and Outcomes of Organizational Politics Perceptions," *Journal of Managerial Psychology* 18, no. 2 (2003): 138–55; K. L. Zellars, W. A. Hochwarter, S. E. Lanivich, P. L. Perrewé, and G. R. Ferris, "Accountability for Others, Perceived Resources, and Well Being: Convergent Restricted Non-Linear Results in Two Samples," *Journal of Occupational and Organizational Psychology* 84, no. 1 (2011): 95–115.

99. T. He, R. Derfler-Rozin, and M. Pitesa, "Financial Vulnerability and the Reproduction of Disadvantage in Economic Exchanges," *Journal of Applied Psychology* 105, no. 1 (2020): 80–96.

100. C-H. Chang, C. C. Rosen, and P. E. Levy, "The Relationship Between Perceptions of Organizational Politics and Employee Attitudes, Strain, and Behavior: A Meta-Analytic Examination," *Academy of Management Journal* 52, no. 4 (2009): 779–801; B. K. Miller, M. A. Rutherford, and R. W. Kolodinsky, "Perceptions of Organizational Politics: A Meta-Analysis of Outcomes," *Journal of Business and Psychology* 22 (2008): 209–22.

101. S. Aryee, Z. Chen, and P. S. Budhwar, "Exchange Fairness and Employee Performance: An Examination of the Relationship between Organizational Politics and Procedural Justice," *Organizational Behavior and Human Decision Processes* 94, no. 1 (2004): 1–14.

102. S. Sun and H. Chen, "Is Political Behavior a Viable Coping Strategy to Perceived Organizational Politics? Unveiling the Underlying Resource Dynamics," *Journal of Applied Psychology* 102, no. 10 (2017): 1471–82.

103. K. M. Kacmar, M. C. Andrews, K. J. Harris, and B. Tepper, "Ethical Leadership and Subordinate Outcomes: The Mediating Role of Organizational Politics and the Moderating Role of Political Skill," *Journal of Business Ethics* 115, no. 1 (2013): 33–44.

104. Ibid.

105. C. Homburg and A. Fuerst, "See No Evil, Hear No Evil, Speak No Evil: A Study of Defensive Organizational Behavior Towards Customer Complaints," *Journal of the Academy of Marketing Science* 35, no. 4 (2007): 523–36.

106. See, for example, S. Yoon, S. Loretta Kim, C. Go, and S. Yun, "Knowledge Sharing, Hypercompetitiveness, and Contextual Factors: Investigating a Three-Way Effect," *Journal of Business and Psychology* (in press).

107. M. C. Bolino, D. Long, and W. Turnley, "Impression Management in Organizations: Critical Questions, Answers, and Areas for Future Research," *Annual Review of Organizational Psychology and Organizational Behavior* 3 (2016): 377–406

108. See, for instance, Bolino et al., "Impression Management in Organizations"; M. C. Bolino, K. M. Kacmar, W. H. Turnley, and J. B. Gilstrap, "A Multi-Level Review of Impression Management Motives and Behaviors," *Journal of Management* 34, no. 6 (2008): 1080–109.

109. H. Deng, F. Walter, and Y. Guan, "Supervisor-Directed Emotional Labor as Upward Influence: An Emotions-as-Social-Information Perspective," *Journal of Organizational Behavior* (in press); F. Gino, O. Sezer, and L. Huang, "To Be or Not Be Your Authentic Self? Catering to Others' Preferences Hinders Performance," *Organizational Behavior and Human Decision Processes* (in press).

110. G. Blickle, C. Diekmann, P. B. Schneider, Y. Kalthöfer, and J. K. Summers, "When Modesty Wins: Impression Management Through Modesty, Political Skill, and Career Success—A Two-Study Investigation,"

European Journal of Work and Organizational Psychology 21, no. 6 (2012): 899–922; T. Bradford Bitterly and M. E. Schweitzer, "The Impression Management Benefits of Humorous Self-Disclosures: How Humor Influences Perceptions of Veracity," *Organizational Behavior and Human Decision Processes* 151 (2019): 73–89.

111. L. A. McFarland, A. M. Ryan, and S. D. Kriska, "Impression Management Use and Effectiveness Across Assessment Methods," *Journal of Management* 29, no. 5 (2003): 641–61; C. A. Higgins and T. A. Judge, "The Effect of Applicant Influence Tactics on Recruiter Perceptions of Fit and Hiring Recommendations: A Field Study," *Journal of Applied Psychology* 89, no. 4 (2004): 622–32; W. C. Tsai, C.-C. Chen, and S. F. Chiu, "Exploring Boundaries of the Effects of Applicant Impression Management Tactics in Job Interviews," *Journal of Management* 31, no. 1 (2005): 108–25; Amaral et al., "Why Does Impression Management Positively Influence Interview Ratings?"; K. Yang Trevor Yu, "Influencing How One Is Seen by Potential Talent: Organizational Impression Management Among Recruiting firms," *Journal of Applied Psychology* 104, no. 7 (2019): 888–906.

112. M. R. Barrick, J. A. Shaffer, and S. W. DeGrassi, "What You See May Not Be What You Get: Relationships Among Self-Presentation Tactics and Ratings of Interview and Job Performance," *Journal of Applied Psychology,* 94, no. 6 (2009): 1394–411.

113. E. Molleman, B. Emans, and N. Turusbekova, "How to Control Self-Promotion Among Performance-Oriented Employees: The Roles of Task Clarity and Personalized Responsibility," *Personnel Review* 41, no. 1 (2012): 88–105.

114. K. J. Harris, K. M. Kacmar, S. Zivnuska, and J. D. Shaw, "The Impact of Political Skill on Impression Management Effectiveness," *Journal of Applied Psychology* 92, no. 1 (2007): 278–85; D. C. Treadway, G. R. Ferris, A. B. Duke, G. L. Adams, and J. B. Thatcher, "The Moderating Role of Subordinate Political Skill on Supervisors' Impressions of Subordinate Ingratiation and Ratings of Subordinate Interpersonal Facilitation," *Journal of Applied Psychology* 92, no. 3 (2007): 848–55.

115. J. D. Westphal and I. Stern, "Flattery Will Get You Everywhere (Especially If You Are a Male Caucasian): How Ingratiation, Boardroom Behavior, and Demographic Minority Status Affect Additional Board Appointments of U.S. Companies," *Academy of Management Journal* 50, no. 2 (2007): 267–88.

116. Y. Liu, G. R. Ferris, J. Xu, B. A. Weitz, and P. L. Perrewé, "When Ingratiation Backfires: The Role of Political Skill in the Ingratiation-Internship Performance Relationship," *Academy of Management Learning & Education* 13, no. 4 (2014): 569–86.

117. See, for instance, G. Blickle, K. Oerder, and J. K. Summers, "The Impact of Political Skill on Career Success of Employees' Representatives," *Journal of Vocational Behavior* 77 (2010): 383–90; G. Blickle, N. Schütte, and A. Wihler, "Political Will, Work Values, and Objective Career Success: A Novel Approach—the Trait-Reputation-Identity Model," *Journal of Vocational Behavior* 107 (2018): 42–56; Y. Liu, J. Liu, and L. Wu, "Are You Willing and Able? Roles of Motivation, Power, and Politics in Career Growth," *Journal of Management* 36, no. 6 (2010): 1432–60.

118. D. Clark, "A Campaign Strategy for Your Career," *Harvard Business Review,* November 2012, 131–34.

CHAPTER 14

1. "The SEC Calls for New Contempt Sanctions for Elon Musk," *BBC News,* March 19, 2019, https://www.bbc.com/news/technology-47626273; L. Gurdus, "Tesla CEO Elon Musk Is Feuding With the SEC Again—Jim Cramer and Other Experts Weigh in on What Could Be Next for the Automaker," *CNBC: Trading Nation,* February

26, 2019, https://www.cnbc.com/2019/02/26/the-sec-targets-tesla-ceo-cramer-and-experts-weigh-in-on-whats-next.html; L. Snapes, "Grimes and Azealia Banks Subpoenaed in Elon Musk Lawsuit," *The Guardian,* January 18, 2019, https://www.theguardian.com/music/2019/jan/18/grimes-and-azealia-banks-subpoenaed-in-elon-musk-lawsuit

2. J. Sonnenfeld, "Asleep at the Wheel: What Tesla's Board Musk Do Now," *Chief Executive,* February 28, 2019, https://chiefexecutive.net/teslas-board-musk/; "Tesla's Board Problem: Too Many Ties to CEO Elon Musk," *CBS News,* August 21, 2018, https://www.cbsnews.com/news/experts-say-tesla-board-may-have-too-many-ties-to-ceo-musk/; R. Ferris, "Elon Musk's Tweets Show That Tesla's Board Either Can't or Won't Try to Keep Him in Check," *CNBC,* February 27, 2019, https://www.cnbc.com/2019/02/27/teslas-directors-seem-to-be-incapable-of-restraining-musk.html

3. "Algorithm Appointed Board Director," *BBC: Technology,* May 16, 2014, https://www.bbc.com/news/technology-27426942; W. Pugh, "Why Not Appoint an Algorithm to Your Corporate Board?" *Slate,* March 24, 2019, https://slate .com/technology/2019/03/artificial-intelligence-corporate-board-algorithm.html

4. See, for instance, A. Avgar, "Integrating Conflict: A Proposed Framework for the Interdisciplinary Study of Workplace Conflict and Its Management," *Industrial and Labor Relations Review* 73, no. 2 (2020): 281–311; M. A. Korsgaard, S. S. Jeong, D. M. Mahony, and A. H. Pitariu, "A Multilevel View of Intragroup Conflict," *Journal of Management* 34, no. 6 (2008): 1222–52; D. Tjosvold, A. S. H. Wong, and N. Y. F. Chen, "Constructively Managing Conflicts in Organizations," *Annual Review of Organizational Psychology and Organizational Behavior* 1 (2014): 545–68.

5. A. Amason, and D. M. Schweiger, "Resolving the Paradox of Conflict, Strategic Decision Making, and Organizational Performance," *International Journal of Conflict Management* 5 (1994): 239–53; K. A. Jehn, "A Multimethod Examination of the Benefits and Detriments of Intragroup Conflict," *Administrative Science Quarterly* 40 (1995): 256–82; K. A. Jehn, "A Qualitative Analysis of Conflict Types and Dimensions in Organizational Groups," *Administrative Science Quarterly* 42 (1997): 530–57.

6. Ibid.

7. F. R. C. de Wit, L. L. Greer, and K. A. Jehn, "The Paradox of Intragroup Conflict: A Meta-Analysis," *Journal of Applied Psychology* 97, no. 2 (2012): 360–90; L. A. DeChurch, J. R. Mesmer-Magnus, and D. Doty, "Moving Beyond Relationship and Task Conflict: Toward a Process-State Perspective," *Journal of Applied Psychology* 98, no. 4 (2013): 559–78; T. A. O'Neill, N. J. Allen, and S. E. Hastings, "Examining the 'Pros' and 'Cons' of Team *Con*flict: A Team-Level Meta-Analysis of Task, Relationship, and Process Conflict," *Human Performance* 26 (2013): 236–60.

8. Ibid.

9. Ibid.

10. Ibid.

11. De Wit et al., "The Paradox of Intragroup Conflict"; O'Neill et al., "Examining the 'Pros' and 'Cons' of Team *Con*flict."

12. DeChurch et al., "Moving Beyond Relationship and Task Conflict."

13. De Wit et al., "The Paradox of Intragroup Conflict."

14. Ibid.

15. J. Farh, C. Lee, and C. I. C. Farh, "Task Conflict and Team Creativity: A Question of How Much and When," *Journal of Applied Psychology* 95, no. 6 (2010): 1173–80; H. Mauersberger, U. Hess, and A. Hoppe, "Measuring Task Conflicts as They Occur: A Real-Time Assessment of Task Conflicts and Their Immediate Affective, Cognitive, and Social Consequences," *Journal of Business and Psychology* (in press); T. A. O'Neill, M. J. W. McLarnon, G. C. Hoffart, H. J. R. Woodley, and N. J. Allen, "The Structure and Function of Team Conflict State Profiles," *Journal of Management* 44, no. 2 (2018): 811–36.

16. S. E. Humphrey, F. Aime, L. Cushenbery, A. D. Hill, and J. Fairchild, "Team Conflict Dynamics: Implications of a Dyadic View of Conflict for Team Performance," *Organizational Behavior and Human Decision Processes* 142 (2017): 58–70.

17. F. R. C. de Wit, K. A. Jehn, and D. Scheepers, "Task Conflict, Information Processing, and Decision-Making: The Damaging Effect of Relationship Conflict," *Organizational Behavior and Human Decision Processes* 122 (2013): 177–89.

18. Farh et al., "Task Conflict and Team Creativity"; P. Petrou, A. B. Bakker, and K. Bezemer, "Creativity Under Task Conflict: The Role of Proactively Increasing Job Resources," *Journal of Occupational and Organizational Psychology* 92 (2019): 305–29.

19. X. Chen, J. Liu, H. Zhang, and H. Kwong Kwan, "Cognitive Diversity and Innovative Work Behavior: The Mediating Roles of Task Reflexivity and Relationship Conflict and the Moderating Role of Perceived Support," *Journal of Occupational and Organizational Psychology* 92 (2019): 671–94; K. A. Graham, M. B. Mawritz, S. B. Dust, R. L. Greenbaum, and J. C. Ziegert, "Too Many Cooks in the Kitchen: The Effects of Dominance Incompatibility on Relationship Conflict and Subsequent Abusive Supervision," *The Leadership Quarterly* 30 (2019): 351–64.

20. R. Sinha, N. S. Janardhanan, L. L. Greer, D. E. Conlon, and J. R. Edwards, "Skewed Task Conflict in Teams: What Happens When a Few Members See More Conflict Than the Rest," *Journal of Applied Psychology* 101, no. 7 (2016): 1045–55.

21. K. A. Jehn and C. Bendersky, "Intragroup Conflict in Organizations: A Contingency Perspective on the Conflict-Outcome Relationship," *Research in Organizational Behavior* 25, no. 1 (2003): 187–242.

22. B. H. Bradley, B. F. Postlethwaite, A. C. Klotz, M. R. Hamdani, and K. G. Brown, "Reaping the Benefits of Task Conflict in Teams: The Critical Role of Team Psychological Safety Climate," *Journal of Applied Psychology* 97, no. 1 (2012), 151–58.

23. G. A. Van Kleef, W. Steinel, and A. C. Homan, "On Being Peripheral and Paying Attention: Prototypicality and Information Processing in Intergroup Conflict," *Journal of Applied Psychology* 98, no. 1 (2013): 63–79.

24. K. W. Thomas, "Conflict and Negotiation Processes in Organizations," in M. D. Dunnette and L. M. Hough (eds.), *Handbook of Industrial and Organizational Psychology* (Palo Alto, CA: Consulting Psychologist's Press, 1992): 651–717.

25. M. A. Korsgaard, S. S. Jeong, D. M. Mahony, and A. H. Pitariu, "A Multilevel View of Intragroup Conflict," *Journal of Management* 34, no. 6 (2008): 1222–52.

26. Ibid.

27. Korsgaard et al., "A Multilevel View of Intragroup Conflict"; R. S. Peterson and K. J. Behfar, "The Dynamic Relationship Between Performance Feedback, Trust, and Conflict in Groups: A Longitudinal Study," *Organizational Behavior and Human Decision Processes* 92, nos. 1–2 (2003): 102–12.

28. M-H. Tsai and C. Bendersky, "The Pursuit of Information Sharing: Expressing Task Conflicts as Debates vs. Disagreements Increases Perceived Receptivity to Dissenting Opinions in Groups," *Organization Science* 27, no. 1 (2016): 141–56.

29. Humphrey et al., "Team Conflict Dynamics."

30. See, for instance, D. R. Rovenpor, T. C. O'Brien, A. Roblain, L. De Guissmé, P. Chekroun, and B. Leidner, "Intergroup Conflict Self-Perpetuates via Meaning: Exposure to Intergroup Conflict Increasing Meaning and Fuels a Desire for Further Conflict," *Journal of Personality and Social Psychology* 116, no. 1 (2019): 119–40.

31. C. Culpepper, "At Ohio State, 'Michigan' Is Pronounced 'That State Up North,'" *The Washington Post,* November 22, 2016, https://www.washingtonpost.com/news/sports/wp/2016/11/22/at-ohio-state-

michigan-is-pronounced-that-state-up-north/; D. Lesmerises, "The Modern Ohio State- Michigan Rivalry: Transfusing Passion From Buckeyes Fans to Coaches and Players New to It," *Cleveland* [blog], November 27, 2019, https://www.cleveland.com/osu/2019/11/the-modern-ohio-state-michigan-rivalry-transfusing-passion-from-buckeyes-fans-to-coaches-and-players-new-to-it.html

32. J. Deventer, J. Wagner, O. Lüdtke, and U. Trautwein, "Are Personality Traits and Relationship Characteristics Reciprocally Related? Longitudinal Analyses of Codevelopment in the Transition out of High School and Beyond," *Journal of Personality and Social Psychology* 116, no. 2 (2019): 331–47; T. M. Glomb and H. Liao, "Interpersonal Aggression in Work Groups: Social Influence, Reciprocal, and Individual Effects," *Academy of Management Journal* 46, no. 4 (2003): 486–96; V. Venkataramani and R. S. Dalal, "Who Helps and Harms Whom? Relational Aspects of Interpersonal Helping and Harming in Organizations," *Journal of Applied Psychology* 92, no. 4 (2007): 952–66.

33. R. Friedman, C. Anderson, J. Brett, M. Olekalns, N. Goates, and C. C. Lisco, "The Positive and Negative Effects of Anger on Dispute Resolution: Evidence From Electronically Mediated Disputes," *Journal of Applied Psychology* 89, no. 2 (2004): 369–76; J. A. Yip and M. E. Schweitzer, "Losing Your Temper and Your Perspective: Anger Reduces Perspective-Taking," *Organizational Behavior and Human Decision Processes* 150 (2019): 28–45.

34. X. Parent-Rocheleau, K. Bentein, G. Simard, and M. Tremblay, "Leader-Follower (Dis)similarity in Optimism: Its Effect on Followers' Role Conflict, Vigor and Performance," *Journal of Business and Psychology* (in press).

35. J. S. Chun and J. N. Choi, "Members' Needs, Intragroup Conflict, and Group Performance," *Journal of Applied Psychology* 99, no. 3 (2014): 437–50.

36. N. Halevy, T. R. Cohen, E. Y. Chou, J. J. Katz, and A. T. Panter, "Mental Models at Work: Cognitive Causes and Consequences of Conflict in Organizations," *Personality and Social Psychology Bulletin,* 40, no. 1 (2014): 92–110.

37. Korsgaard et al., "A Multilevel View of Intragroup Conflict"; A. M. Ness and S. Connelly, "Situational Influences on Ethical Sensemaking: Performance Pressure, Interpersonal Conflict, and the Recipient of Consequences," *Human Performance* 30, nos. 2–3 (2017): 57–78.

38. See, for instance, J. R. Curhan, "What Do People Value When They Negotiate? Mapping the Domain of Subjective Value in Negotiation," *Journal of Personality and Social Psychology* 91, no. 3 (2006): 117–26; N. Halevy, E. Chou, and J. K. Murnighan, "Mind Games: The Mental Representation of Conflict," *Journal of Personality and Social Psychology* 102, no. 1 (2012): 132–48.

39. A. M. Isen, A. A. Labroo, and P. Durlach, "An Influence of Product and Brand Name on Positive Affect: Implicit and Explicit Measures," *Motivation and Emotion* 28, no. 1 (2004): 43–63.

40. Ibid.

41. E. P. Lemay Jr., J. E. Ryan, R. Fehr, and M. J. Gelfand, "Validation of Negativity: Drawbacks of Interpersonal Responsiveness During Conflicts With Outsiders," *Journal of Personality and Social Psychology* (in press).

42. M. Lu, X. Yang, H. H. Fung, and T. Hamamura, "Is Positive Emotion an Amplifier or a Buffer? It Depends: Dialectical Thinking Moderates the Impact of Positive Emotion on Intergroup Conflicts," *Emotion* 20, no. 4 (2020): 700–12; C. Montes, D. Rodriguez, and G. Serrano, "Affective Choice of Conflict Management Styles," *International Journal of Conflict Management* 23, no. 1 (2012): 6–18.

43. K. Brans, P. Koval, P. Verduyn, Y. Lin Lim, and P. Kuppens, "The Regulation of Negative and Positive Affect in Daily Life," *Emotion* 13, no. 5 (2013): 926–39; S. Nolen-Hoeksema, B. E. Wisco, and S. Lyubomirsky, "Rethinking Rumination," *Perspectives of Psychological Science* 3, no. 5 (2008): 400–24.

44. A. A. Kay and D. P. Skarlicki, "Cultivating a Conflict-Positive Workplace: How Mindfulness Facilitates Constructive Conflict Management," *Organizational Behavior and Human Decision Processes* (in press).

45. M. A. Rahim, *Managing Conflict in Organizations*, 4th ed. (New Brunswick, NJ: Transaction Publishers, 2011).

46. Rahim, *Managing Conflict in Organizations*; K. W. Thomas and R. H. Kilmann, *The Thomas-Kilmann Conflict Mode Instrument* (Mountain View, CA: CPP, 1974).

47. R. Gabrielle Swab and P. D. Johnson, "Steel Sharpens Steel: A Review of Multilevel Competition and Competitiveness in Organizations," *Journal of Organizational Behavior* 40 (2019): 147–65.

48. Gabrielle Swab and Johnson, "Steel Sharpens Steel"; S-C. Huang, S. C. Lin, and Y. Zhang, "When Individual Goal Pursuit Turns Competitive: How We Sabotage and Coast," *Journal of Personality and Social Psychology* 117, no. 3 (2019): 605–20.

49. G. Stasser and S. Abele, "Collective Choice, Collaboration, and Communication," *Annual Review of Psychology* 71 (2020): 589–612.

50. M-H. Tsai, N. Velda Melia, and V. B. Hinsz, "The Effects of Perceived Decision-Making Styles on Evaluations of Openness and Competence That Elicit Collaboration," *Personality and Social Psychology Bulletin* 46, no. 1 (2020): 124–139.

51. Rahim, *Managing Conflict in Organizations*.

52. C. K. W. De Dreu, "The Virtue and Vice of Workplace Conflict: Food for (Pessimistic) Thought," *Journal of Organizational Behavior* 29 (2008): 5–18.

53. M-L. Chang, "On the Relationship Between Intragroup Conflict and Social Capital in Teams: A Longitudinal Investigation in Taiwan," *Journal of Organizational Behavior* 38 (2017): 3–27.

54. G. Todorova, J. B. Bear, and L. R. Weingart, "Can Conflict Be Energizing? A Study of Task Conflict, Positive Emotions, and Job Satisfaction," *Journal of Applied Psychology* 99, no. 3 (2014): 451–67.

55. B. A. Nijstad and S. C. Kaps, "Taking the Easy Way Out: Preference Diversity, Decision Strategies, and Decision Refusal in Groups," *Journal of Personality and Social Psychology* 94, no. 5 (2008), pp. 860–70.

56. de Wit et al., "The Paradox of Intragroup Conflict"; DeChurch et al., "Moving Beyond Relationship and Task Conflict"; O'Neill et al., "Examining the 'Pros' and 'Cons' of Team *Con*flict."

57. Ibid.

58. A. M. Carton and B. A. Tewfik, "A New Look at Conflict Management in Work Groups," *Organization Science* 27, no. 5 (2016): 1125–41.

59. Avgar, "Integrating Conflict."

60. B. Mayer, *Staying With Conflict: A Strategic Approach to Ongoing Disputes* (San Francisco, CA: Wiley, 2009).

61. Carton and Tewfik, "A New Look at Conflict Management in Work Groups."

62. Ibid.

63. Ibid.

64. D. Tjosvold, A. S. H. Wong, and N. Y. F. Chen, "Constructively Managing Conflicts in Organizations," *Annual Review of Organizational Psychology and Organizational Behavior* 1 (2014): 545–68.

65. J. Fried, "I Know You Are, but What Am I?" *Inc.,* July/August 2010, 39–40.

66. K. J. Behfar, R. S. Peterson, E. A. Mannix, and W. M. K. Trochim, "The Critical Role of Conflict Resolution in Teams: A Close Look at the Links Between Conflict Type, Conflict Management Strategies, and Team Outcomes," *Journal of Applied Psychology* 93, no. 1 (2008): 170–88; A. G. Tekleab, N. R. Quigley, and P. E. Tesluk, "A Longitudinal Study of Team Conflict, Conflict Management, Cohesion, and Team Effectiveness," *Group & Organization Management* 34, no. 2 (2009): 170–205.

67. A. Somech, H. S. Desivilya, and H. Lidogoster, "Team Conflict Management and Team Effectiveness: The Effects of Task Interdependence and Team Identification," *Journal of Organizational Behavior* 30, no. 3 (2009): 359–78.

68. W. Liu, R. Friedman, and Y. Hong, "Culture and Accountability in Negotiation: Recognizing the Importance of In-Group Relations," *Organizational Behavior and Human Decision Processes* 117, no. 1 (2012): 221–34; B. C. Gunia, J. M. Brett, A. K. Nandkeolyar, and D. Kamdar, "Paying a Price: Culture, Trust, and Negotiation Consequences," *Journal of Applied Psychology* 96, no. 4 (2010): 774–89.

69. M. H. Bazerman, J. R. Curhan, D. A. Moore, and K. L. Valley, "Negotiation," *Annual Review of Psychology* 51 (2000): 279–314; J. Brett and L. Thompson, "Negotiation," *Organizational Behavior and Human Decision Processes* 136 (2016): 68–79.

70. See, for example, D. R. Ames, "Assertiveness Expectancies: How Hard People Push Depends on the Consequences They Predict," *Journal of Personality and Social Psychology* 95, no. 6 (2008): 1541–57; J. R. Curhan, H. A. Elfenbein, and H. Xu, "What Do People Value When They Negotiate? Mapping the Domain of Subjective Value in Negotiation," *Journal of Personality and Social Psychology* 91, no. 3 (2006): 493–512.

71. R. Lewicki, D. Saunders, and B. Barry, *Negotiation,* 6th ed. (New York: McGraw-Hill/Irwin, 2009).

72. See, for example, P. Tipirneni, "How Managers Should Deal With Conflict Between Two Employees," *Ladders,* July 7, 2018, https://www.theladders.com/career-advice/how-managers-should-deal-with-conflict-between-two-employees

73. J. C. Magee, A. D. Galinsky, and D. H. Gruenfeld, "Power, Propensity to Negotiate, and Moving First in Competitive Interactions," *Personality and Social Psychology Bulletin* 33, no. 2 (2007): 200–12.

74. D. D. Loschelder, R. Tröschel, R. I. Swaab, M. Friese, A. D. Galinsky, "The Information-Anchoring Model of First Offers: When Moving First Helps Versus Hurts Negotiators," *Journal of Applied Psychology* 101, no. 7 (2016): 995–1012.

75. J. M. Majer, R. Trötschel, A. D. Galinsky, and D. D. Loschelder, "Open to Offers, but Resisting Requests: How the Framing of Anchors Affects Motivation and Negotiated Outcomes," *Journal of Personality and Social Psychology* (in press).

76. J. Hüffmeier, P. A. Freund, A. Zerres, K. Backhaus, and G. Hertel, "Being Tough or Being Nice? A Meta-Analysis on the Impact of Hard- and Softline Strategies in Distributive Negotiations," *Journal of Management* 40, no. 3 (2014): 866–92.

77. M. Schaerer, D. D. Loschelder, and R. I. Swaab, "Bargaining Zone Distortion in Negotiations: The Elusive Power of Multiple Alternatives," *Organizational Behavior and Human Decision Processes* 137 (2016): 156–71.

78. Hüffmeier et al., "Being Tough or Being Nice?"

79. N. Bhatia and B. C. Gunia, "'I Was Going to Offer $10,000 But...': The Effects of Phantom Anchors in Negotiation," *Organizational Behavior and Human Decision Processes* 148 (2018): 70–86.

80. G. J. Leonardelli, J. Gu, G. McRuer, V. Husted Medvec, and A. D. Galinsky, "Multiple Equivalent Simultaneous Offers (MESOs) Reduce the Negotiator Dilemma: How a Choice of First Offers Increases Economic and Relational Outcomes," *Organizational Behavior and Human Decision Processes* 152 (2019): 64–83.

81. N. Coomber, "Career Coach: The Gender Pay Gap is Real. Here's How to Get Your Fair Share," *The Washington Post,* March 31, 2017, https://www.washingtonpost.com/news/capital-business/wp/2017/03/31/career-coach-the-gender-pay-gap-is-real-heres-how-to-get-your-fair-share/?utm_term=.25147012645c

82. D. Druckman and L. M. Wagner, "Justice and Negotiation," *Annual Review of Psychology* 67 (2016): 387–413.

83. T. He, R. Derfler-Rozin, and M. Pitesa, "Financial Vulnerability and the Reproduction of Disadvantage in Economic Exchanges," *Journal of Applied Psychology* 105, no. 1 (2020): 80–96.

84. This model is based on R. J. Lewicki, D. Saunders, and B. Barry, *Negotiation,* 7th ed. (New York: McGraw-Hill, 2014).

85. R. P. Larrick and G. Wu, "Claiming a Large Slice of a Small Pie: Asymmetric Disconfirmation in Negotiation," *Journal of Personality and Social Psychology* 93, no. 2 (2007): 212–33.

86. L. L. Thompson, J. Wang, and B. C. Gunia, "Negotiation," *Annual Review of Psychology* 61, (2010): 491–515.

87. M. Schaerer, M. Schweinsberg, and R. I. Swaab, "Imaginary Alternatives: The Effects of Mental Simulation on Powerless Negotiators," *Journal of Personality and Social Psychology* 115, no. 1 (2018): 96–117; M. Schaerer, R. I. Swaab, and A. D. Galinsky "Anchors Weigh More Than Power: Why Absolute Powerlessness Liberates Negotiators to Achieve Better Outcomes," *Psychological Science* 26, no. 2 (2014): 170–81:10.1177/0956797614558718.

88. J. A. Hewlin, "The Most Overused Negotiating Tactic Is Threatening to Walk Away," *Harvard Business Review,* September 1, 2017, https://hbr.org/2017/09/the-most-overused-negotiating-tactic-is-threatening-to-walk-away

89. R. L. Pinkley, D. E. Conlon, J. E. Sawyer, D. J. Sleesman, D. Vandewalle, and M. Kuenzi, "The Power of Phantom Alternatives in Negotiation: How *What Could Be* Haunts *What Is*," *Organizational Behavior and Human Decision Processes* 151 (2019): 34–48.

90. R. Trötschel, D. D. Loschelder, B. P. Höhne, and J. M. Majer, "Procedural Frames in Negotiations: How Offering My Resources Versus Requesting Yours Impacts Perception, Behavior, and Outcomes," *Journal of Personality and Social Psychology* 108, no. 3 (2015): 417–35.

91. E. Hart and M. E. Schweitzer, "Getting to Less: When Negotiating Harms Post-Agreement Performance," *Organizational Behavior and Human Decision Processes* 156 (2020): 155–75.

92. J. R. Curhan, H. A. Elfenbein, and G. J. Kilduff, "Getting Off on the Right Foot: Subjective Value Versus Economic Value in Predicting Longitudinal Job Outcomes From Job Offer Negotiations," *Journal of Applied Psychology* 94, no. 2 (2009): 524–34.

93 A. A. Mislin, R. L. Campagna, and W. P. Bottom, "After the Deal: Talk, Trust Building and the Implementation of Negotiated Agreements," *Organizational Behavior and Human Decision Processes* 115 (2011): 55–68.

94. H. A. Elfenbein, N. Eisenkraft, J. R. Curhan, and L. F. DiLalla, "On the Relative Importance of Individual-level Characteristics and Dyadic Interaction Effects in Negotiations: Variance Partitioning Evidence From a Twins Study," *Journal of Applied Psychology* 103, no. 1 (2018): 88–96.

95. C. Amistad, P. D. Dunlop, R. Ng, J. Anglim, and R. Fells, "Personality and Integrative Negotiations: A HEXACO Investigation of Actor, Partner, and Actor-Partner Interaction Effects on Objective and Subjective Outcomes," *European Journal of Personality* 32, no. 4 (2018): 427–42.

96. H. A. Elfenbein, "Individual Difference in Negotiation: A Nearly Abandoned Pursuit Revived," *Current Directions in Psychological Science* 24, no. 2 (2015): 131–36.

97. S. Sharma, H. A. Elfenbein, J. Foster, and W. P. Bottom, "Predicting Negotiation Performance From Personality Traits: A Field Study Across Multiple Occupations," *Human Performance* 31, no. 3 (2018): 145–64.

98. Amistad et al., "Personality and Integrative Negotiations."

99. E. T. Amanatullah, M. W. Morris, and J. R. Curhan, "Negotiators Who Give Too Much: Unmitigated Communion, Relational Anxieties, and Economic Costs in Distributive and Integrative Bargaining," *Journal of Personality and Social Psychology* 95, no. 3 (2008): 723–38.

100. K. S. Wilson, D. S. DeRue, F. K. Matta, M. Howe, and D. E. Conlon, "Personality Similarity in Negotiations: Testing the Dyadic Effects of Similarity in Interpersonal Traits and the Use of Emotional Displays on Negotiation outcomes," *Journal of Applied Psychology* 101, no. 10 (2016): 1405–21.

101. Amanatullah et al., "Negotiators Who Give Too Much."

102. S. Sharma, W. Bottom, and H. A. Elfenbein, "On the Role of Personality, Cognitive Ability, and Emotional Intelligence in Predicting Negotiation Outcomes: A Meta-Analysis," *Organizational Psychology Review* 3, no. 4 (2013): 293–336.

103. A. C. Peng, J. Dunn, and D. E. Conlon, "When Vigilance Prevails: The Effect of Regulatory Focus and Accountability on Integrative Negotiation Outcomes," *Organizational Behavior and Human Decision Processes* 126 (2015): 77–87.

104. K. Schlegel, M. Mehu, J. M. van Peer, and K. R. Scherer, "Sense and Sensibility: The Role of Cognitive and Emotional Intelligence in Negotiation," *Journal of Research in Personality* 74 (2018): 6–15.

105. G. Lelieveld, E. Van Dijk, I. Van Beest, and G. A. Van Kleef, "Why Anger and Disappointment Affect Other's Bargaining Behavior Differently: The Moderating Role of Power and the Mediating Role of Reciprocal Complementary Emotions," *Personality and Social Psychology Bulletin* 38, no. 9 (2012): 1209–21.

106. S. Côté, I. Hideg, and G. A. Van Kleef, "The Consequences of Faking Anger in Negotiations," *Journal of Experimental Social Psychology* 49, no. 3 (2013): 453–63.

107. B. Shao, L. Wang, D. Cheng, and L. Doucet, "Anger Suppression in Negotiations: The Roles of Attentional Focus and Anger Source," *Journal of Business and Psychology* 30 (2015): 747–58.

108. G. A. Van Kleef and C. K. W. De Dreu, "Longer-Term Consequences of Anger Expression in Negotiation: Retaliation or Spillover?" *Journal of Experimental Social Psychology* 46, no. 5 (2010): 753–60.

109. R. L. Campagna, A. A. Mislin, D. T. Kong, and W. P. Bottom, "Strategic Consequences of Emotional Misrepresentation in Negotiation: The Blowback Effect," *Journal of Applied Psychology* 101, no. 5 (2016): 605–24.

110. L. Rees, S.-C. Steve Chi, R. Friedman, and H-L. Shih, "Anger as a Trigger for Information Search in Integrative Negotiations," *Journal of Applied Psychology* (in press).

111. H. Adam and A. Shirako, "Not All Anger Is Created Equal: The Impact of the Expresser's Culture on the Social Effects of Anger in Negotiations," *Journal of Applied Psychology* 98, no. 5 (2013): 785–98.

112. M. Olekalns and P. L Smith, "Mutually Dependent: Power, Trust, Affect, and the Use of Deception in Negotiation," *Journal of Business Ethics* 85, no. 3 (2009): 347–65.

113. A. W. Brooks and M. E. Schweitzer, "Can Nervous Nellie Negotiate? How Anxiety Causes Negotiators to Make Low First Offers, Exit Early, and Earn Less Profit," *Organizational Behavior and Human Decision Processes* 115, no. 1 (2011): 43–54.

114. M. Sinaceur, S. Kopelman, D. Vaslijevic, and C. Haag, "Weep and Get More: When and Why Sadness Expression is Effective in Negotiations," *Journal of Applied Psychology* 100, no. 6 (2015): 1847–71.

115. Druckman and Wagner, "Justice and Negotiation"; A. Shirako, G. J. Kilduff, and L. J. Kray, "Is There a Place for Sympathy in Negotiation? Finding Strength in Weakness," *Organizational Behavior and Human Decision Processes* 131 (2015): 95–109.

116. M. Sinaceur, H. Adam, G. A. Van Kleef, and A. D. Galinsky, "The Advantages of Being Unpredictable: How Emotional Inconsistency Extracts Concessions in Negotiation," *Journal of Experimental Social Psychology* 49, no. 3 (2013): 498–508.

117. K. Leary, J. Pillemer, and M. Wheeler, "Negotiating with Emotion," *Harvard Business Review,* January–February 2013, 96–103.

118. N. B. Rothman and G. B. Northcraft, "Unlocking Integrative Potential: Expressed Emotional Ambivalence and Negotiation Outcomes," *Organizational Behavior and Human Decision Processes* 126 (2015): 65–76.

119. L. A. Liu, R. Friedman, B. Barry, M. J. Gelfand, and Z. Zhang, "The Dynamics of Consensus Building in Intracultural and Intercultural Negotiations," *Administrative Science Quarterly* 57, no. 2 (2012): 269–304.

120. M. Liu, "The Intrapersonal and Interpersonal Effects of Anger on Negotiation Strategies: A Cross-Cultural Investigation," *Human Communication Research* 35, no. 1 (2009): 148–69; H. Adam, A. Shirako, and W. W. Maddux, "Cultural Variance in the Interpersonal Effects of Anger in Negotiations," *Psychological Science* 21, no. 6 (2010): 882–89.

121. M. J. Gelfand et al., "Culture and Getting to Yes: The Linguistic Signature of Creative Agreements in the United States and Egypt," *Journal of Organizational Behavior* 36 (2015): 967–89.

122 J. Schroeder, J. L. Risen, F. Gino, and M. I. Norton, "Handshaking Promotes Deal-making by Signaling Cooperative Intent," *Journal of Personality and Social Psychology* 116, no. 5 (2019): 743–768.

123. M. Hernandez, D. R. Avery, S. D. Volpone, and C. R. Kaiser, "Bargaining While Black: The Role of Race in Salary Negotiations," *Journal of Applied Psychology* 104, no. 4 (2019): 581–592.

124. K. G. Kugler, J. A. M. Reif, T. Kaschner, and F. C. Brodbeck, "Gender Differences in the Initiation of Negotiations: A Meta-Analysis," *Psychological Bulletin* 144, no. 2 (2018): 198–222; J. Mazei, J. Hüffmeier, P. A. Freund, A. F. Stuhlmacher, L. Bilke, and G. Hertel, "A Meta-Analysis on Gender Differences in Negotiation Outcomes and Their Moderators," *Psychological Bulletin* 141, no. 1 (2015): 85–104; A. F. Stuhlmacher and A. E. Walters, "Gender Differences in Negotiation Outcome: A Meta-Analysis," *Personnel Psychology* 52 (1999): 653–77; A. E. Walters, A. F. Stuhlmacher, and L. L. Meyer, "Gender and Negotiator Competitiveness: A Meta-Analysis," *Organizational Behavior and Human Decision Processes* 76, no. 1 (1998): 1–29.

125. W. Shan, J. Keller, and D. Joseph, "Are Men Better Negotiators Everywhere? A Meta-Analysis of How Gender Differences in Negotiation Performance Vary Across Cultures," *Journal of Organizational Behavior* 40 (2019): 651–75.

126. Walters et al., "Gender and Negotiator Competitiveness."

127. Ibid.

128. Kugler et al., "Gender Differences in the Initiation of Negotiations."

129. C. Suddath, "The Art of Haggling," *Bloomberg Businessweek,* November 26, 2012, 98.

130. Stuhlmacher and Walters, "Gender Differences in Negotiation Outcome."

131. Mazei et al, "A Meta-Analysis on Gender Differences in Negotiation Outcomes and Their Moderators."

132. D. T. Kong, K. T. Dirks, and D. L. Ferrin, "Interpersonal Trust Within Negotiations: Meta-Analytic Evidence, Critical Contingencies, and Directions for Future Research," *Academy of Management Journal* 57, no. 5 (2014): 1235–55.

133. A. Hinshaw, P. Reilly, and A. Kupfer Schneider, "Attorneys and Negotiation Ethics: A Material Misunderstanding?" *Negotiation Journal* 29, no. 3 (2013): 265–87; N. A. Welsh, "The Reputational Advantages of Demonstrating Trustworthiness: Using the Reputation Index with Law Students," *Negotiation Journal* 28, no. 1 (2012): 117–45.

134. J. R. Curhan, H. A. Elfenbein, and X. Heng, "What Do People Value When They Negotiate? Mapping the Domain of Subjective Value in Negotiation," *Journal of Personality and Social Psychology* 91, no. 3 (2006): 493–512.

135. W. E. Baker and N. Bulkley, "Paying It Forward vs. Rewarding Reputation: Mechanisms of Generalized Reciprocity," *Organization Science* 25, no. 5 (2014): 1493–510.

136 G. A. Van Kleef, C. K. W. De Dreu, and A. S. R. Manstead, "An Interpersonal Approach to Emotion in Social Decision Making: The Emotions as Social Information Model" in *Advances in Experimental Social Psychology* vol. 42, ed. M. P. Zanna, (2010), 45–96.

137. F. Lumineau and J. E. Henderson, "The Influence of Relational Experience and Contractual Governance on the Negotiation Strategy in Buyer–Supplier Disputes," *Journal of Operations Management* 30, no. 5 (2012): 382–95.

138. U.S. Equal Employment Opportunity Commission, "Questions and Answers About Mediation," accessed June 9, 2015, http://www.eeoc.gov/eeoc/mediation/qanda.cfm

139. N. Halevy, E. Halali, and T. R. Cohen, "Brokering Orientations and Social Capital: Influencing Others' Relationships Shapes Status and Trust," *Journal of Personality and Social Psychology* (in press).

CHAPTER 15

1. N. Smithson, "Google's Organizational Structure & Organizational Culture (An Analysis)," *Panmore Institute,* February 13, 2019, http://panmore.com/google-organizational-structure-organizational-culture

2. S. Kaplan, "Is Organizational Structure the Secret of Innovation," *Inc.,* March 21, 2019, https://www.inc.com/soren-kaplan/is-organizational-structure-secret-to-innovation.html

3. T. J. Giardino, "Is Your Company Struggling? It Might Be a Flaw in the Strategy-Structure Fit," *Forbes,* November 20, 2018, https://www.forbes.com/sites/forbeshumanresources council/2018/11/20/is-your-company-struggling-it-might-be-a-flaw-in-the-strategy-structure-fit/#183e5d0591a0

4. J. Lofgren, "How to Be a Champion for Women in Leadership," *Forbes,* March 11, 2019, https://www.forbes .com/sites/forbescoachescouncil/2019/03/11/how-to-be-a-champion-for-women-in-leadership/#5381093c100d

5. G. P. Huber, "Organizations: Theory, Design, Future," in S. Zedeck (ed.), *APA Handbook of Industrial and Organizational Psychology: Vol. 1, Pt. II: Perspectives on Designing Organizations and Human Resource Systems* (Washington, DC: APA, 2011): 117–60.

6. See, for instance, R. L. Daft, *Organization Theory and Design,* 12th ed. (Boston, MA: Cengage, 2015).

7. T. Hindle, *Guide to Management Ideas and Gurus* (London, UK: Profile Books/The Economist Newspaper, 2008).

8. See, for instance, E. Penrose, *The Theory of the Growth of the Firm,* 4th ed. (Oxford, UK: Oxford, 2009); D. G. Ross, "An Agency Theory of the Division of Managerial Labor," *Organization Science* 25, no. 2 (2013): 494–508.

9. T. W. Malone, R. J. Laubacher, and T. Johns, "The Age of Hyperspecialization," *Harvard Business Review,* July–August 2011, 56–65.

10. For a review, see J. A. Häusser, S. Schulz-Hardt, T. Schultze, A. Tomaschek, and A. Mojzisch, "Experimental Evidence for the Effects of Task Repetitiveness on Mental Strain and Objective Work Performance," *Journal of Organizational Behavior* 35, no. 5 (2014): 705–21.

11. J. R. Hackman and G. R. Oldham, "Motivation Through the Design of Work: Test of a Theory," *Organizational Behavior and Human Performance* 16 (1976): 250–79.

12. J. L. Price, "The Impact of Departmentalization on Interoccupational Cooperation," *Human Organization* 27, no. 4 (1968): 362–8; Y. Maggie Zhou, "Designing for Complexity: Using Divisions and Hierarchy to Manage Complex Tasks," *Organization Science* 24, no. 2 (2013): 339–55.

13. See, for instance, S. Postrel, "Islands of Shared Knowledge: Specialization and Mutual Understanding in Problem- Solving Teams," *Organization Science* 13, no. 3 (2002): 303–20.

14. Ibid.

15. See, for instance, G. M. Kistruck, I. Qureshi, and P. W. Beamish, "Geographic and Product Diversification in Charitable Organizations," *Journal of Management* 39, no. 2 (2013): 496–530.

16. C. Woodyard, "Toyota Brass Shakeup Aims to Give Regions More Control," *USA Today,* March 6, 2013, www.usatoday.com/story/money/cars/2013/03/06/toyota-shakeup/1966489/

17. J. T. Polzer, C. Brad Crisp, S. L. Jarvenpaa, and J. W. Kim, "Extending the Faultline Model to Geographically Dispersed Teams: How Collocated Subgroups Can Impair Group Functioning," *Academy of Management Journal* 49, no. 4 (2006): 679–92; E. Romanelli and O. M. Khessina, "Regional Industry Identity: Cluster Configurations and Economic Development," *Organization Science* 16, no. 4 (2005): 344–58.

18. W. Fong Boh, Y. Ren, S. Kiesler, and R. Bussjaeger, "Expertise and Collaboration in the Geographically Dispersed Organization," *Organization Science* 18, no. 4 (2007): 595–612; K. Laursen, F. Masciarelli, and A Prencipe, "Regions Matter: How Localized Social Capital Affects Innovation and External Knowledge Acquisition," *Organization Science* 23, no. 1 (2012): 177–93; S. Tallman and A. Phene, "Leveraging Knowledge Across Geographic Boundaries," *Organization Science* 18, no. 2 (2007): 252–60.

19. See, for instance, J. Hoffer Gittell, D. Beth Weinberg, A. L. Bennett, and J. A. Miller, "Is the Doctor In? A Relational Approach to Job Design and the Coordination of Work," *Human Resource Management* 47, no. 4 (2008): 729–55.

20. B. Valentine, "The 4x4 Security Program and Organization Structure," *IBM: Security Intelligence,* November 3, 2015, https://securityintelligence.com/the-4x4-security-program-and-organization-structure/

21. S. Ballmer, "One Microsoft: Company Realigns to Enable Innovation at Greater Speed, Efficiency," Microsoft, July 11, 2013, http://blogs.microsoft.com/firehose/2013/07/11/one-microsoft-company-realigns-to-enable-innovation-at-greater-speed-efficiency/

22. J. Lombardo, "Microsoft Corporation's Organizational Structure & Its Characteristics (An Analysis)," *Panmore Institute,* September 8, 2018, http://panmore.com/microsoft-corporation-organizational-structure-characteristics-analysis

23. J. R. Hollenbeck, B. Beersma, and M. E. Schouten, "Beyond Team Types and Taxonomies: A Dimensional Scaling Conceptualization for Team Description," *Academy of Management Review* 37 (2012): 82–106.

24. L. C. Wang and J. R. Hollenbeck, "LMX in Team-Based Contexts: TMX, Authority Differentiation, and Skill Differentiation as Boundary Conditions for Leader Reciprocation," *Personnel Psychology* 72 (2019): 271–90.

25. See, for instance, S. Finkelstein and R. A. D'Aveni, "CEO Duality as a Double-Edged Sword: How Boards of Directors Balance Entrenchment Avoidance and Unity of Command," *Academy of Management Journal* 37, no. 5 (1994): 1079–108; J. Pfeffer, "Management as Symbolic Action: The Creation and Maintenance of Organizational Paradigms," in L. L. Cummings and B. M. Staw (eds.), *Research in Organizational Behavior,* vol. 3 (Greenwich, CT: JAI, 1981): 1–52.

26. "The Multiple Boss Dilemma: Is It Possible to Please More Than One?" *Knowledge@Wharton* [blog], September 2, 2016, https://knowledge.wharton.upenn.edu/article/multiple-boss-dilemma-possible-please-one/; A. Gallo, "Managing Multiple Bosses," *Harvard Business Review,* August 18, 2011, https://hbr.org/2011/08/managing-multiple-bosses.html

27. P. Hinds and S. Kiesler, "Communication Across Boundaries: Work, Structure, and Use of Communication Technologies in a Large Organization," *Organization Science* 6, no. 4 (1995): 373–93.

28. See, for instance, "How Hierarchy Can Hurt Strategy Execution," *Harvard Business Review,* July–August 2010, 74–75.

29. S. Yu, L. L. Greer, N. Halevy, and L. van Bunderen, "Ladders and Pyramids: Hierarchy's Shape Determines Relationships and Performance in Groups," *Personality and Social Psychology Bulletin,* 45, no. 12 (2019): 1717–33.

30. For a review, see D. D. Van Fleet and A. G. Bedeian, "A History of the Span of Management," *Academy of Management Review* 2, no. 3 (1977): 356–72.

31. E. Appelbaum and R. Batt, *The New American Workplace* (Ithaca, NY: ILR, 1994); C. Heckscher and A. Dornellor (eds.), *The Post-Bureaucratic Organization* (Thousand Oaks, CA: Sage, 1994).

32. See, for instance, J. H. Gittell, "Supervisory Span, Relational Coordination, and Flight Departure Performance: A Reassessment of Postbureaucracy Theory," *Organization Science* 12, no. 4: (2001): 468–83.

33. Society for Human Resource Management (SHRM), "Span of Control: What Factors Should Determine How Many Direct Reports a Manager Has?," *SHRM: HR Q&S*, April 25, 2013, https://www.shrm.org/resourcesandtools/tools-and-samples/hr-qa/pages/whatfactorsshoulddeterminehow manydirectreportsamanagerhas.aspx

34. K. C. Bormann, U. Poethke, C. Cohrs, and J. Rowold, "Doing Bad Through Being Selective in Doing Good: The Role of Within-Unit Variability in Ethical Leadership," *European Journal of Work and Organizational Psychology* 27, no. 6 (2018): 683–99; B. Brady, "It Is Time to Stop Trying to Do It All," *Fortune*, May 26, 2016, http://for tune.com/2016/05/26/fortune-500-principal-financial-time-management/; C. E. Thiel, J. H. Hardy III, D. R. Peterson, D. T. Welsh, and J. M. Bonner, "Too Many Sheep in the Flock? Span of Control Attenuates the Influence of Ethical Leadership," *Journal of Applied Psychology* 103, no. 12 (2018): 1324–34.

35. J. Morgan, *The Future of Work: Attract New Talent, Build Better Leaders, and Create a Competitive Organization* (Hoboken, NJ: Wiley, 2014); J. Morgan, "The 5 Types of Organizational Structures: Part 3, Flat Organizations," *Forbes*, July 13, 2015, https://www.forbes.com/sites/jacobmorgan/2015/07/13/the-5-types-of-organizational-structures-part-3-flat-organizations/#5b9001926caa

36. Huber, "Organizations."

37. Ibid.

38. B. Brown and S. D. Anthony, "How P&G Tripled Its Innovation Success Rate," *Harvard Business Review*, June 2011, 64–72.

39. See, for example, E. N. Sherf, R. Sinha, S. Tangirala, and N. Awasty, "Centralization of Member Voice in Teams: Its Effects on Expertise Utilization and Team Performance," *Journal of Applied Psychology* 103, no. 8 (2018): 813–27.

40. Huber, "Organizations"; Society for Human Resource Management (SHRM), "Understanding Organizational Structures," *SHRM: Toolkits*, November 30, 2015, https://www .shrm.org/resourcesandtools/tools-and-samples/toolkits/pages/understandingorganizationalstructures.aspx

41. F. A. Csaszar, "Organizational Structure as a Determinant of Performance: Evidence from Mutual Funds," *Strategic Management Journal* 33, no. 6 (2012): 611–32.

42. A. Leiponen and C. E. Helfat, "Location, Decentralization, and Knowledge Sources for Innovation," *Organization Science* 22, no. 3 (2011): 641–58.

43. K. Parks, "HSBC Unit Charged in Argentine Tax Case," *The Wall Street Journal*, March 19, 2013, C2.

44. K. Lanaj, J. R. Hollenbeck, D. R. Ilgen, C. M. Barnes, and S. J. Harmon, "The Double-Edged Sword of Decentralized Planning in Multiteam Systems," *Academy of Management Journal* 56, no. 3 (2013): 735–57.

45. Huber, "Organizations."

46. P. Hempel, Z.-X. Zhang, and Y. Han, "Team Empowerment and the Organizational Context: Decentralization and the Contrasting Effects of Formalization," *Journal of Management* 38, no. 2 (2012): 475–501.

47. M. Abraham, "Pay Formalization Revisited: Considering the Effects of Manager Gender and Discretion on Closing the Gender Wage Gap," *Academy of Management Journal* 60, no. 1 (2017): 29–54.

48. M. L. Tushman and T. J. Scanlan, "Characteristics and External Orientations of Boundary Spanning Individuals," *Academy of Management Journal* 24 (1981): 83–98.

49. J. E. Perry-Smith and C. E. Shalley, "A Social Composition View of Team Creativity: The Role of Member Nationality-Heterogeneous Ties Outside of the Team," *Organization Science* 25 (2014): 1434–52; J. Han, J. Han, and D. J. Brass, "Human Capital Diversity in the Creation of Social Capital for Team Creativity," *Journal of Organizational Behavior* 35 (2014): 54–71; M. Tortoriello, R. Reagans, and B. McEvily, "Bridging the Knowledge Gap: The Influence of Strong Ties, Network Cohesion, and Network Range on the Transfer of Knowledge Between Organizational Units," *Organization Science* 23, no. 4 (2012): 1024–39; X. Zou and P. Ingram, "Bonds and Boundaries: Network Structure, Organizational Boundaries, and Job Performance," *Organizational Behavior and Human Decision Processes* 120, no. 1 (2013): 98–109.

50. M. Salem, N. Van Quaquebeke, and M. Besiou, "How Field Office Leaders Drive Learning and Creativity in Humanitarian Aid: Exploring the Role of Boundary-Spanning Leadership for Expatriate and Local Aid Worker Collaboration," *Journal of Organizational Behavior* 39 (2018): 594–611.

51. H. Aldrich and D. Herker, "Boundary Spanning Roles and Organization Structure," *Academy of Management Review* 2, no. 2 (1977): 217–30.

52. T. A de Vries, F. Walter, G. S. Van der Vegt, and P. J. M. D. Essens, "Antecedents of Individuals' Interteam Coordination: Broad Functional Experiences as a Mixed Blessing," *Academy of Management Journal* 57, no. 5 (2014): 1334–59.

53. H. Yu, "Uber Hiring a COO: What a Red-Hot Startup Needs to Learn From Boring Old Firms," *Forbes*, March 9, 2017, https://www.forbes.com/sites/howardhyu/2017/03/09/uber-hiring-a-coo-what-a-red-hot-startup-needs-to-learn-from-boring-old-firms/#48e5352e45f2

54. Huber, "Organizations"; H. Mintzberg, *Structure in Fives: Designing Effective Organizations* (Englewood Cliffs, NJ: Prentice Hall, 1983).

55. B. Sugarman, "Stages in the Lives of Organizations," *Administration and Policy in Mental Health* 1, no. 2 (1989): 59–66.

56. See, for instance, M. Myatt, "Businesses Don't Fail—Leaders Do," *Forbes*, January 12, 2012, https://www.forbes .com/sites/mikemyatt/2012/01/12/businesses-dont-fail-leaders-do/#7ad1d7596c97

57. Huber, "Organizations"; and Mintzberg, *Structure in Fives*.

58. J.-F. Harvey, P. Cohendet, L. Simon, and L.-E. Dubois, "Another Cog in the Machine: Designing Communities of Practice in Professional Bureaucracies," *European Management Journal* 31, no. 1 (2013): 27–40.

59. D. Graeber, *The Utopia of Rules: On Technology, Stupidity, and the Secret Joys of Bureaucracy* (New York, NY: Melville House, 2015).

60. V. Gauri, J. C. Jamison, N. Mazar, and O. Ozier, "Motivating Bureaucrats Through Social Recognition: External Validity—a Tale of Two States," *Organizational Behavior and Human Decision Processes* (in press); C. Wolf, "Not Lost in Translation: Managerial Career Narratives and the Construction of Protean Identities," *Human Relations* 72, no. 3 (2019): 505–33.

61. J. R. Galbraith, *Designing Matrix Organizations That Actually Work: How IBM, Procter & Gamble, and Others Design for Success* (San Francisco: Jossey-Bass, 2009); E. Krell, "Managing the Matrix," *HR Magazine*, April 2011, 69–71.

62. V. Ratanjee and N. Dvorak, "Mastering Matrix Management in the Age of Agility," *Gallup: Workplace*, September 18, 2018, https://www.gallup.com/workplace/242192/mastering-matrix-management-age-agility.aspx

63. K. O'Marah, "JFK Snow Disaster and the Question of Centralizing Supply Chain Management," *Forbes*, March 7, 2018, https://www.forbes.com/sites/kevinomarah/2018/03/07/jfk-snow-disaster-and-the-question-of-centralizing-supply-chain-management/#4398e2267f5c

64. R. C. Ford, "Cross-Functional Structures: A Review and Integration of Matrix Organization and Project Management," *Journal of Management* 18, no. 2 (1992): 267–94.

65. O'Marah, "JFK Snow Disaster and the Question of Centralizing Supply Chain Management."

66. See, for instance, M. Bidwell, "Politics and Firm Boundaries: How Organizational Structure, Group Interests, and Resources Affect Outsourcing," *Organization Science* 23, no. 6 (2012): 1622–42.

67. Ford, "Cross-Functional Structures."

68. See, for instance, T. Sy and L. S. D'Annunzio, "Challenges and Strategies of Matrix Organizations: Top-Level and Mid-Level Managers' Perspectives," *Human Resource Planning* 28, no. 1 (2005): 39–48; T. Sy and S. Cotê, "Emotional Intelligence: A Key Ability to Succeed in the Matrix Organization," *Journal of Management Development* 23, no. 5 (2004): 437–55.

69. A-C. Hardy, "Agile Team Organisation: Squads, Chapters, Tribes and Guilds," *Medium,* February 29, 2016, https://medium.com/@achardypm/agile-team-organisation-squads-chapters-tribes-and-guilds-80932ace0fdc; Ratanjee and Dvorak, "Mastering Matrix Management in the Age of Agility."

70. N. Anand and R. L. Daft, "What Is the Right Organization Design?" *Organizational Dynamics* 36, no. 4 (2007): 329–44.

71. Huber, "Organizations."

72. Ibid.

73. D. Kanze, M. A. Conley, and E. Tory Higgins, "The Motivation of Mission Statements: How Regulatory Mode Influneces Workplace Discrimination," *Organizational Behavior and Human Decision Processes* (in press).

74. Huber, "Organizations"; J. B. Quinn and P. Anderson, "Leveraging Intellect," *Academy of Management Executive* 10 (1996): 7–27.

75. E. Steel, "Netflix Refines Its DVD Business, Even as Streaming Unit Booms," *The New York Times*, July 26, 2015, https://www.nytimes.com/2015/07/27/business/while-its-streaming-service-booms-netflix-streamlines-old-business.html?_r=0

76. J. Schramm, "At Work in a Virtual World," *HR Magazine,* June 2010, 152.

77. See, for instance, C. B. Gibson and J. L. Gibbs, "Unpacking the Concept of Virtuality: The Effects of Geographic Dispersion, Electronic Dependence, Dynamic Structure, and National Diversity on Team Innovation," *Administrative Science Quarterly* 51, no. 3 (2006): 451–95; H. M. Latapie and V. N. Tran, "Subculture Formation, Evolution, and Conflict Between Regional Teams in Virtual Organizations," *The Business Review,* Summer 2007, 189–93; S. Davenport and U. Daellenbach, "'Belonging' to a Virtual Research Center: Exploring the Influence of Social Capital Formation Processes on Member Identification in a Virtual Organization," *British Journal of Management* 22, no. 1 (2011): 54–76.

78. O'Marah, "JFK Snow Disaster and the Question of Centralizing Supply Chain Management."

79. See, for instance, M. A. West and L. Markiewicz, *Building Team-Based Working: A Practical Guide to Organizational Transformation* (Malden, MA: Blackwell, 2004).

80. L. L. Greer, B. A. de Jong, M. E. Schouten, and J. E. Dannals, "Why and When Hierarchy Impacts Team Effectiveness: A Meta-Analytic Integration," *Journal of Applied Psychology* 103, no. 6 (2018): 591–613.

81. D. Herath, "Mess Is Good for Business: Some Companies Would Do Better If They Embraced Disorganization," *Newsweek*, February 28, 2017, http://www.newsweek.com/organization-skills-business-efficiency-561985; S. Stevenson, "Who's the Boss? No One." *Slate*, June 2, 2014, http://www.slate.com/articles/business/psychology_of_management/2014/06/the_bossless_office_how_well_do_workplaces_without_managers_function.html; Schumpeter, "The Holes in Holacracy," *The Economist*, July 5, 2014, http://www.economist.com/news/business/21606267-latest-big-idea-management-deserves-some-scepticism-holes-holacracy

82. J. Scheck, L. Moloney, and A. Flynn, "Eni, CNPC Link Up in Mozambique," *The Wall Street Journal,* March 15, 2013, B3.

83. A. G. L. Romme, "Domination, Self-Determination and Circular Organizing," *Organization Studies* 20, no. 5 (1999): 801–31.

84. D. K. Datta, J. P. Guthrie, D. Basuil, and A. Pandey, "Causes and Effects of Employee Downsizing: A Review and Synthesis," *Journal of Management* 36, no. 1 (2010): 281–348.

85. L. Gensler, "American Express to Slash 4,000 Jobs on Heels of Strong Quarter," *Forbes,* January 21, 2015, http://www.forbes.com/sites/laurengensler/2015/01/21/american-express-earnings-rise-11-on-increased-cardholder-spending/

86. T. Borden, "The Coronavirus Outbreak Has Triggered Unprecedented Mass Layoffs and Furloughs. Here Are the Major Companies That Have Announced They Are Downsizing Their Workforces," *Business Insider,* April 29, 2020, https://www.businessinsider.com/coronavirus-layoffs-furloughs-hospitality-service-travel-unemployment-2020; S. Wood, G. Michaelides, and C. Ogbonnaya, "Recessionary Actions and Absence: A Workplace-Level Study," *Human Resource Management* (in press).

87. Datta, Guthrie, Basuil, and Pandey, "Causes and Effects of Employee Downsizing."

88. L. I. Alpert, "Can Imported CEO Fix Russian Cars?," *The Wall Street Journal,* March 20, 2013, http://www.wsj.com/articles/SB10001424127887323639604578370121394214736

89. R. Handfield, "Bo Andersson's Supply Strategy Collides With Vladimir Putin's Russia: The Performance Triangle Collapses," *Supply Chain Resource Cooperative* [NC State Poole College of Management website], April 11, 2016, https://scm.ncsu.edu/blog/2016/04/11/bo-anderssons-supply-strategy-collides-with-vladimir-putins-russia-the-performance-triangle-collapses/

90. G. Stolyarov and C. Lowe, "In Russia's Detroit, Layoffs Are Blamed on Foreign Interlopers," *Reuters: Business News,* April 27, 2016, http://www.reuters.com/article/us-russia-avtovaz-idUSKCN0XO0EE

91. D. Van Dierendonck and G. Jacobs, "Survivors and Victims: A Meta-Analytical Review of Fairness and Organizational Commitment After Downsizing," *British Journal of Management* 23 (2012): 96–109.

92. W. M. Foster, J. S. Hassard, J. Morris, and J. Wolfram Cox, "The Changing Nature of Managerial Work: The Effects of Corporate Restructuring on Management Jobs and Careers," *Human Relations* 72, no. 3 (2019): 473–504.

93. J. R. B. Halbesleben, A. R. Wheeler, and S. C. Paustian-Underdahl, "The Impact of Furloughs on Emotional Exhaustion, Self-Rated Performance, and Recovery Experiences," *Journal of Applied Psychology* 98, no. 3 (2013): 492–503; R. Kalimo, T. W. Taris, and W. B. Schaufeli, "The Effects of Past and Anticipated Future Downsizing on Survivor Well-Being: An Equity Perspective," *Journal of Occupational Health Psychology* 8, no. 2 (2003): 91–109; Van Dierendonck and Jacobs, "Survivors and Victims."

94. G. M. Spreitzer and A. K. Mishra, "To Stay or Go: Voluntary Survivor Turnover Following an Organizational Downsizing," *Journal of Organizational Behavior* 23, no. 6 (2002): 707–29; C. O. Trevor and A. J. Nyberg, "Keeping Your Headcount When All About You Are Losing Theirs: Downsizing, Voluntary Turnover Rates, and the Moderating Role of HR Practices," *Academy of Management Journal* 51, no. 2 (2008): 259–76.

95. T. Burns and G. M. Stalker, *The Management of Innovation* (London, UK: Tavistock, 1961).

96. K. Walker, N. Ni, and B. Dyck, "Recipes for Successful Sustainability: Empirical Organizational Configurations for Strong Corporate Environmental Performance," *Business Strategy and the Environment* 24, no. 1 (2015): 40–57.

97. F. Yang, "Better Understanding the Perceptions of Organizational Politics: Its Impact Under Different Types of Work Unit Structure," *European Journal of Work and Organizational Psychology* 26, no. 2 (2017): 250–62.

98. S. B. Dust, C. J. Resick, and M. B. Mawritz, "Transformational Leadership, Psychological Empowerment, and the Moderating Role of Mechanistic-Organic Contexts," *Journal of Organizational Behavior* 35 (2014): 413–33.

99. See, for instance, A. Drach-Zahavy and A. Freund, "Team Effectiveness Under Stress: A Structural Contingency Approach," *Journal of Organizational Behavior* 28, no. 4 (2007): 423–50.

100. K. Walker, N. Ni, and B. Dyck, "Recipes for Successful Sustainability: Empirical Organizational Configurations for Strong Corporate Environmental Performance," *Business Strategy and the Environment* 24, no. 1 (2015): 40–57.

101. See, for instance, S. M. Toh, F. P. Morgeson, and M. A. Campion, "Human Resource Configurations: Investigating Fit with the Organizational Context," *Journal of Applied Psychology* 93, no. 4 (2008): 864–82.

102. G. P. Pisano, "You Need an Innovation Strategy," *Harvard Business Review*, June 2015, https://hbr.org/2015/06/you-need-an-innovation-strategy

103. "The World's Most Innovative Companies," *Forbes*, accessed March 27, 2019, https://www.forbes.com/innovative-companies/list/

104. K. Aaslaid, "50 Examples of Corporations That Failed to Innovate: Change Is Inevitable and Innovation Is No Different," *Valuer*, November 22, 2018, https://valuer.ai/blog/50-examples-of-corporations-that-failed-to-innovate-and-missed-their-chance/

105. Ibid.

106. Ibid.

107. See, for instance, R. Robinson, "Costs and Cost-Minimisation Analysis," *British Medical Journal* 307 (1993): 726–28.

108. "Jet Airways Plans to Scrap First Class in Its Boeing 777 Planes" [press release], *On Manorama*, November 23, 2017, https://english.manoramaonline.com/business/news/2017/11/23/jet-airways-plans-to-scrap-first-class-in-its-boeing-777-planes.html

109. R. Dooley, "The Paper Towel Test for Customer Experience," *Forbes*, September 27, 2018, https://www.forbes.com/sites/rogerdooley/2018/09/27/paper-towel-test-cx/#5004f0001df7

110. D. Vinjamuri, "Tyson Foods and Piglet Abuse: Is Ethical Behavior Profitable?," *Forbes*, May 11, 2012, https://www.forbes.com/sites/davidvinjamuri/2012/05/11/tyson-foods-and-piglet-abuse-is-ethical-behavior-profitable/#a54a4166f93c

111. "The CFO Imperative: Next-Gen Technology Drives Cost Optimization," *Knowledge@Wharton* [blog], February 13, 2017, http://knowledge.wharton.upenn.edu/article/the-cfo-imperative-next-gen-technology-drives-cost-optimization/

112. See, for instance, J. C. Naranjo-Valencia, D. Jiménez-Jiménez, and R. Sanz-Valle, "Innovation or Imitation? The Role of Organizational Culture," *Management Decision* 49, no. 1 (2011): 55–72.

113. A. Zaleski, "7 Business That Cloned Others and Made Millions," *CNBC*, October 4, 2017, https://www.cnbc.com/2017/10/03/7-businesses-that-cloned-others-and-made-millions.html

114. F. Vermeulen, "Why Copying Successful Firms Can Make You Worse Off," *Forbes*, December 17, 2017, https://www.forbes.com/sites/freekvermeulen/2017/12/12/why-copying-successful-firms-can-make-you-worse-off/#b57d087536e3

115. T. Taylor, "First Oracle, Now MongoDB: Why AWS Keeps Divorcing Its Partners," *TechGenix*, March 11, 2019, http://techgenix.com/mongodb-aws/

116. M. Josefy, S. Kuban, R. D. Ireland, and M. A. Hitt, "All Things Great and Small: Organizational Size, Boundaries of the Firm, and a Changing Environment," *The Academy of Management Annals* 9, no. 1 (2015): 715–802.

117. W. F. Cascio and R. Montealegre, "How Technology Is Changing Work and Organizations," *Annual Review of Organizational Psychology and Organizational Behavior* 3 (2016): 349–75; P. Duran, N.

Kammerlander, M. Van Essen, and T. Zellweger, "Doing More With Less: Innovation Input and Output in Family Firms," *Academy of Management Journal* 59, no. 4 (2016): 1224–64.

118. J. Backaler, "Haier: A Chinese Company That Innovates," *Forbes*, June 17, 2010, http://www.forbes.com/sites/china/2010/06/17/haier-a-chinese-company-that-innovates/

119. T. A. Kochan, C. A. Riordan, A. M. Kowalski, M. Khan, and D. Yang, "The Changing Nature of Employee and Labor-Management Relationships," *Annual Review of Organizational Psychology and Organizational Behavior* 6 (2019): 195–219.

120. A. Mutch, "Technology, Organization, and Structure—a Morphogenetic Approach," *Organization Science* 21, no. 2 (2010): 507–20.

121. Huber, "Organizations."

122. D. Prosperio and G. Zervas, "Study: Replying to Customer Reviews Results in Better Ratings," *Harvard Business Review*, February 14, 2018, https://hbr.org/2018/02/study-replying-to-customer-reviews-results-in-better-ratings

123. See, for instance, J. A. Cogin and I. O. Williamson, "Standardize or Customize: The Interactive Effects of HRM and Environment Uncertainty on MNC Subsidiary Performance," *Human Resource Management* 53, no. 5 (2014): 701–21; G. Kim and M.-G. Huh, "Exploration and Organizational Longevity: The Moderating Role of Strategy and Environment," *Asia Pacific Journal of Management* 32, no. 2 (2015): 389–414.

124. B. Tobin, "Amazon HQ2: Cities Are Trying to Woo Tech Giant After Cancellation of New York Plans," *USA Today*, February 20, 2019, https://www.usatoday.com/story/money/2019/02/20/amazon-hq-2-cities-woo-tech-giant-after-cancellation-queens-plans/2916471002/

125. See, for instance, D. G. Bachrach, K. Lewis, Y. Kim, P. C. Patel, M. C. Campion, and S. M. B. Thatcher, "Transactive Memory Systems in Context: A Meta-Analytic Examination of Contextual Factors in Transactive Memory Systems Development and Team Performance," *Journal of Applied Psychology* 104, no. 3 (2019): 464–93.

126. E. W. M. Au, X. S. Y.-S. Qin, and Z-X. Zhang, "Beyond Personal Control: When and How Executives' Beliefs in Negotiable Fate Foster Entrepreneurial Orientation and Firm Performance," *Organizational Behavior and Human Decision Processes* 143 (2017): 69–84.

127. See, for instance, "VMware Outlines Strategy to Make Security Intrinsic to the Infrastructure" [press release], March 5, 2019, https://www.nasdaq.com/press-release/vmware-outlines-strategy-to-make-security-intrinsic-to-the-infrastructure-20190305-00460

128. D. Chandler and H. Hwang, "Learning From Learning Theory: A Model of Organizational Adoption Strategies at the Microfoundations of Institutional Theory," *Journal of Management* 41, no. 5 (2015): 1446–76; R. Greenwood, C. R. Hinings, and D. Whetten, "Rethinking Institutions and Organizations," *Journal of Management Studies*, 51, no. 7 (2014): 1206–20; A. C. Lewis, R. L. Cardy, and L S. R. Huang, "Institutional Theory and HRM: A New Look," *Human Resource Management Review* 29 (2019): 316–35.

129. S. R. Kessler, A. E. Nixon, and W. R. Nord, "Examining Organic and Mechanistic Structures: Do We Know as Much as We Thought?," *International Journal of Management Reviews* 19 (2017): 531–55.

130. C. S. Spell and T. J. Arnold, "A Multi-Level Analysis of Organizational Justice and Climate, Structure, and Employee Mental Health," *Journal of Management* 33, no. 5 (2007): 724–51; M. L. Ambrose and M. Schminke, "Organization Structure as a Moderator of the Relationship Between Procedural Justice, Interactional Justice, Perceived Organizational Support, and Supervisory Trust," *Journal of Applied Psychology* 88, no. 2 (2003): 295–305.

131. See, for instance, C. S. Spell and T. J. Arnold, "A Multi-Level Analysis of Organizational Justice and Climate, Structure, and Employee Mental Health;" J. D. Shaw and N. Gupta, "Job Complexity, Performance, and Well-Being: When Does Supplies-Value Fit Matter?" *Personnel*

Psychology 57, no. 4 (2004): 847–79; C. Anderson and C. E. Brown, "The Functions and Dysfunctions of Hierarchy," *Research in Organizational Behavior* 30 (2010): 55–89.

132. J. H. Gittell, "Supervisory Span, Relational Coordination, and Flight Departure Performance: A Reassessment of Postbureaucracy Theory," *Organization Science* 12, no. 4 (2001): 468–83; C. A. Wong et al., "Examining the Relationships Between Span of Control and Manager Job and Unit Performance Outcomes," *Journal of Nursing Management* 23, no. 2 (2015): 156–68.

133. R. Hechanova-Alampay and T. A. Beehr, "Empowerment, Span of Control, and Safety Performance in Work Teams after Workforce Reduction," *Journal of Occupational Health Psychology* 6, no. 4 (2001): 275–82.

134. S. Bhargava and A. Kelkar, "Prediction of Job Involvement, Job Satisfaction, and Empowerment from Organizational Structure and Corporate Culture," *Psychological Studies* 45, nos. 1–2 (2000): 43–50; A. P. Kakabadse and R. Worrall, "Job Satisfaction and Organizational Structure: A Comparative Study of Nine Social Service Departments," *The British Journal of Social Work* 8, no. 1 (1978): 51–70; E. G. Lambert, E. A. Paoline III, and N. L. Hogan, "The Impact of Centralization and Formalization on Correctional Staff Job Satisfaction and Organizational Commitment: An Exploratory Study," *Criminal Justice Studies* 19, no. 1 (23–44); G. S. Rai, "Job Satisfaction Among Long-Term Care Staff: Bureaucracy Isn't Always Bad," *Administration in Social Work* 37, no. 1 (2013): 90–9.

135. See, for instance, R. E. Ployhart, J. A. Weekley, and K. Baughman, "The Structure and Function of Human Capital Emergence: A Multilevel Examination of the Attraction-Selection-Attrition Model," *Academy of Management Journal* 49, no. 4 (2006): 661–77.

136. J. B. Stewart, "A Place to Play for Google Staff," *The New York Times,* March 16, 2013, B1.

137. See, for instance, B. K. Park, J. A. Choi, M. Koo, S. Sul, and I. Choi, "Culture, Self, and Preference Structure: Transitivity and Context Independence Are Violated More by Interdependent People," *Social Cognition* 31, no. 1 (2013): 106–18.

CHAPTER 16

1. C. Cancialosi, "How Blending Brand and Culture Can Impact the Customer Experience," *Forbes,* March 21, 2019, https://www.forbes.com/sites/chriscancialosi/2019/03/21/how-blending-brand-and-culture-can-impact-the-customer-experience/#6e4314c41f8c

2. Ibid.

3. B. Rigoni and B. Nelson, "Few Millennials Are Engaged at Work," *Gallup,* August 30, 2016, https://news.gallup.com/businessjournal/195209/few-millennials-engaged-work .aspx

4. See, for example, B. Schneider, M. G. Ehrhart, and W. H. Macey, "Organizational Climate and Culture," *Annual Review of Psychology* 64 (2013): 361–88.

5. E. H. Schein, *Organizational Culture and Leadership* (vol. 2) (New York, NY: John Wiley & Sons, 2010).

6. S. Giorgi, C. Lockwood, and M. A. Glynn, "The Many Faces of Culture: Making Sense of 30 Years of Research on Culture in Organization Studies," *The Academy of Management Annals* 9, no. 1 (2015): 1–54; Schneider et al., "Organizational Climate and Culture."

7. Schneider et al., "Organizational Climate and Culture."

8. Schneider et al., "Organizational Climate and Culture"; B. Schneider, V. González-Romá, C. Ostroff, and M. A. West, "Organizational Climate and Culture: Reflections on the History of the Constructs in the *Journal of Applied Psychology*," *Journal of Applied Psychology* 102, no. 3 (2017): 468–82.

9. C. A. Hartnell, A. Y. Ou, and A. Kinicki, "Organizational Culture and Organizational Effectiveness: A Meta-Analytic Investigation of the Competing Values Framework," *Journal of Applied Psychology* 96 (2011): 677–94; R. E. Quinn and J. Rohrbaugh, "A Special Model of Effectiveness Criteria: Toward a Competing Values Approach to Organizational Analysis," Management Science 29 (1983): 363–77.

10. Schneider et al., "Organizational Climate and Culture."

11. Hartnell et al., "Organizational Culture and Organizational Effectiveness"; C. A. Hartnell, A. Y. Ou, A. J. Kinicki, D. Choi, and E. P. Karam, "A Meta-Analytic Test of Organizational Culture's Association with Elements of an Organization's System and Its Relative Predictive Validity on Organizational Outcomes," Journal of Applied Psychology 104, no. 6 (2019): 832–50.

12. R. A. Cooke and J. C. Lafferty, *Organizational Culture Inventory* (Plymouth, MA: Human Synergistics, 1987); R. A. Cooke and J. L. Szumal, "Measuring Normative Beliefs and Shared Behavioral Expectations in Organizations: The Reliability and Validity of the Organizational Culture Inventory," *Psychology Reports* 72 (1993): 1299–1330; R. A. Cooke and J. L. Szumal, "Using the Organizational Culture Inventory to Understand the Operating Cultures of Organizations," in N. M. Ashkanasy, C. P. M. Wilderom, and M. F. Peterson (Eds.), *Handbook of Organizational Culture & Climate* (Thousand Oaks, CA: Sage, 2000): 147–62.

13. N. M. Ashkanasy, L. E. Broadfoot, and S. Falkus, "Questionnaire Measures of Organizational Culture," in N. M. Ashkanasy, C. P. M. Wilderom, and M. F. Peterson (Eds.), *Handbook of Organizational Culture & Climate* (Thousand Oaks, CA: Sage, 2000): 131–46; C. A. O'Reilly III, J. A. Chatman, and D. F. Caldwell, "People and Organizational Culture: A Profile Comparison Approach to Assessing Person-Organization Fit," *Academy of Management Journal* 34 (1991): 487–516.

14. See, for example, C. Ostroff, A. J. Kinicki, and R. S. Muhammad, "Organizational Culture and Climate," in I. B. Weiner (ed.), *Handbook of Psychology*, 2nd ed. (Hoboken, NJ: Wiley, 2012): 643–76.

15. D. A. Hoffman and L. M. Jones, "Leadership, Collective Personality, and Performance," *Journal of Applied Psychology* 90, no. 3 (2005), 509–22.

16. J. Martin, *Organizational Culture: Mapping the Terrain* (Thousand Oaks, CA: Sage, 2002).

17. P. Lok, R. Westwood, and J. Crawford, "Perceptions of Organisational Subculture and Their Significance for Organisational Commitment," *Applied Psychology: An International Review* 54, no. 4 (2005): 490–514; B. E. Ashforth, K. M. Rogers, and K. G. Corley, "Identity in Organizations: Exploring Cross-Level Dynamics," *Organization Science* 22, no. 5 (2011): 1144–56.

18. J. M. Jermier, J. W. Slocum Jr., L. W. Fry, and J. Gaines, "Organizational Subcultures in a Soft Bureaucracy: Resistance Behind the Myth and Façade of an Official Culture," *Organization Science* 2, no. 2 (1991): 170–94.

19. D. Oyserman, "Culture Three Ways: Culture and Subcultures Within Countries," *Annual Review of Psychology* 68 (2017): 435–63.

20. For discussion of how culture can be evaluated as a shared perception, see D. Chan, "Multilevel and Aggregation Issues in Climate and Culture Research," in B. Schneider and K. M. Barbera (eds.), *The Oxford Handbook of Organizational Climate and Culture* (New York, NY: Oxford University Press, 2014), 484–95; J. B. Sorensen, "The Strength of Corporate Culture and the Reliability of Firm Performance," *Administrative Science Quarterly* (March 2002): 70–91.

21. M. W. Dickson, C. J. Resick, and P. J. Hanges, "When Organizational Climate Is Unambiguous, It Is Also Strong," *Journal of Applied Psychology* 91 (2006): 351–64; L. M. Kotrba, M. A. Gillespie, A. M. Schmidt, R. E. Smerek, S. A. Ritchie, and D. R. Denison, "Do Consistent Corporate Cultures Have Better Business Performance: Exploring the Interaction Effects," *Human Relations* 65, no. 2 (2012): 241–62; B. Schneider, A. N. Salvaggio, and M. Subirats, "Climate Strength: A

New Direction for Climate Research," *Journal of Applied Psychology* 87 (2002): 220–29

22. K. Moody, "Marriott Shares Its 'Secret Sauce' for a People-centric Culture," *HR Dive,* March 27, 2019, https://www.hrdive.com/news/marriott-shares-its-secret-sauce-for-a-people-centric-culture/551369/

23. M. Schulte, C. Ostroff, S. Shmulyian, and A. Kinicki, "Organizational Climate Configurations: Relationships to Collective Attitudes, Customer Satisfaction, and Financial Performance," *Journal of Applied Psychology* 94, no. 3 (2009): 618–34.

24. K. Moody, "Culture Directly Influences Job Performance, Employees Say," *HR Dive,* March 27, 2019, https://www .hrdive.com/news/culture-directly-influences-job-performance-employees-say/551159/; R. O'Donnell, "How Culture Helps Ace Hardware Thrive in a Tough Retail Environment," *HR Dive,* February 11, 2019, https://www.hrdive .com/news/how-culture-helps-ace-hardware-thrive-in-a-tough-retail-environment/547619/

25. E. Ransdell, "The Nike Story? Just Tell It!," *Fast Company* (January–February 2000): 44–46; A. Muccino, "Exclusive Interview with Chuck Eichten," Liquid Brand Summit Blog, February 4, 2011, http://blog.liquidbrandsummit.com/

26. R. Carey, "Passionate About Stories: Nike," *All Good Tales,* October 18, 2018, https://allgoodtales.com/nike-passionate-about-stories/

27. R. Garud, H. A. Schildt, and T. K. Lant, "Entrepreneurial Storytelling, Future Expectations, and the Paradox of Legitimacy," *Organization Science* 25, no. 5 (2014): 1479–92; G. A. Rosile, D. M. Carlon, S. Downs, and R. Saylors, "Storytelling Diamond: An Antenarrative Integration of the Six Facets of Storytelling in Organization Research Design," *Organizational Research Methods* 16, no. 4 (2013): 557–80.

28. S. L. Dailey and L. Browning, "Retelling Stories in Organizations: Understanding the Functions of Narrative Repetition," *Academy of Management Review* 39, no. 1 (2014): 22–43.

29. A. J. Shipp and K. J. Jansen, "Reinterpreting Time in Fit Theory: Crafting and Recrafting Narratives of Fit in Medias Res," *Academy of Management Review* 36, no. 1 (2011): 76–101.

30. See G. Islam and M. J. Zyphur, "Rituals in Organizations: A Review and Expansion of Current Theory," *Group & Organization Management* 34, no. 1 (2009): 114–39; M. J. Rossano, "The Essential Role of Ritual in the Transmission and Reinforcement of Social Norms," *Psychological Bulletin* 138, no. 3 (2012): 529–49.

31. Great Place to Work, "Kimpton Hotels & Restaurants," http://fortune.com/best-companies/kimpton-hotels-restaurants/, accessed April 6, 2019; S. Halzack, "At Kimpton Hotels, Employees Bond Through Housekeeping Olympics," *The Washington Post,* January 6, 2013, https://www .washingtonpost.com/business/capitalbusiness/at-kimpton-hotels-employees-bond-through-housekeeping-olympics/2013/01/04/3a212b2c-535c-11e2-bf3e-76c0a789346f_story .html?utm_term=.c3e004bef157

32. F. G. Massa, W. S. Helms, M. Voronov, and L. Wang, "Emotions Uncorked: Inspiring Evangelism for the Emerging Practice Of Cool-Climate Winemaking in Ontario," *Academy of Management Journal* 60, no. 2 (2017): 461–99.

33. A. W. Brooks et al., "Don't Stop Believing: Rituals Improve Performance by Decreasing Anxiety," *Organizational Behavior and Human Decision Processes* 137 (2016): 71-85; A. D. Tiang, J. Schroeder, G. Häubl, J. L. Risen, M. I. Norton, and F. Gino, "Enacting Rituals to Improve Self-Control," *Journal of Personality and Social Psychology* 114, no. 6 (2018): 851–76.

34. C. Jones, *How Matter Matters: Objects, Artifacts, and Materiality in Organization Studies* (Oxford, UK: Oxford University Press, 2013); and E. H. Schein, *Organizational Culture and Leadership* (4th ed.) (San Francisco, CA: Jossey-Bass, 2010).

35. M. G. Pratt and A. Rafaeli "Artifacts and Organizations: Understanding Our Objective Reality," in A. Rafaeli and M. G. Pratt (eds.) *Artifacts and Organizations: Beyond Mere Symbolism* (Mahwah, NJ: Lawrence Erlbaum, 2006), 279–88.

36. A. Rafaeli and I. Vilnai-Yavetz, "Emotion as a Connection of Physical Artifacts and Organizations," *Organization Science* 15, no. 6 (2004): 671–86.

37. B. Gruley, "Relaxed Fit," *Bloomberg Businessweek,* September 17–23, 2012, 98–99.

38. D. Burkus, "How to Tell If Your Company Has a Creative Culture," *Harvard Business Review,* December 2, 2014, https://hbr.org/2014/12/how-to-tell-if-your-company-has-a-creative-culture

39. Great Place to Work, "Genentech," http://reviews .greatplacetowork.com/genentech, accessed April 18, 2017.

40. Z. Kalou and E. Sadler-Smith, "Using Ethnography of Communication in Organizational Research," *Organizational Research Methods* 18, no. 4 (2015): 629–55; H. M. Trice and J. M. Beyer, *The Cultures of Work Organizations* (Englewood Cliffs, NJ: Prentice Hall, 1993).

41. K. L. Smith, *GovSpeak: A Guide to U.S. Government Acronyms & Abbreviations,* accessed April 6, 2019, https://ucsd .libguides.com/govspeak

42. E. A. Canning, M. C. Murphy, K. T. U. Emerson, J. A. Chatman, C. S. Dweck, and L. J. Kray, "Cultures of Genius at Work: Organizational Mindsets Predict Cultural Norms, Trust, and Commitment," *Personality and Social Psychology Bulletin* 46, no. 4 (2020): 626–42.

43. Schneider et al., "Organizational Climate and Culture."

44. Schein, *Organizational Culture and Leadership.*

45. R. M. Steers, *Made in Korea: Chung Ju Yung and the Rise of Hyundai* (New York, NY: Routledge, 1999).

46. J. Basque and A. Langley, "Invoking Alphonse: The Founder Figure as a Historical Resource for Organizational Identity Work," *Organizational Studies* 39, no. 12 (2018): 1685-1708; S. Oreg and Y. Berson, "The Impact of Top Leaders' Personalities: The Process Through Which Organizations Become Reflections of Their Leaders," *Current Directions in Psychological Science* 27, no. 4 (2018): 241–48; Ostroff et al., "Organizational Culture and Climate."

47. D. Katz and R. L. Kahn, *The Social Psychology of Organizations* (2nd ed., New York, NY: Wiley, 1978).

48. Hartnell et al., "A Meta-Analytic Test of Organizational Culture's Association With Elements of an Organization's System and Its Relative Predictive Validity on Organizational Outcomes."

49. See, for example, D. E. Bowen and C. Ostroff, "The 'Strength' of the HRM System, Organizational Climate Formation, and Firm Performance," *Academy of Management Review* 29, no. 2 (2004): 203–21; Hartnell et al., "A Meta-Analytic Test of Organizational Culture's Association With Elements of an Organization's System and Its Relative Predictive Validity on Organizational Outcomes."

50. D. D. Warrick, J. F. Milliman, and J. M. Ferguson, "Building High Performance Cultures," *Organizational Dynamics* 45 (2016): 64–70.

51. W. Arthur Jr., S. T. Bell, A. J. Villado, and D. Doverspike, "The Use of Person-Organization Fit in Employment Decision Making: An Assessment of Its Criterion-Related Validity," *Journal of Applied Psychology* 91, no. 4 (2006): 786–801; W. Li, Y. Wang, P. Taylor, K. Shi, and D. He, "The Influence of Organizational Culture on Work-Related Personality Requirement Ratings: A Multilevel Analysis," *International Journal of Selection and Assessment* 16, no. 4 (2008): 366–84; A. M. Saks and B. E. Ashforth, "Is Job Search Related to Employment Quality? It All Depends on the Fit," *Journal of Applied Psychology* 87, no. 4 (2002): 646–54.

52. See, for instance, B. R. Dineen, S. R. Ash, and R. A. Noe, "A Web of Applicant Attraction: Person-Organization Fit in the Context of Web-Based Recruitment," *Journal of Applied Psychology* 87, no. 4 (2002): 723–34; N. Roulin and F. Krings, "Faking to Fit in: Applicants' Response Strategies to Match Organizational Culture," *Journal of Applied Psychology* 105, no. 2 (2020): 130–45.

53. G. Hamel, "W. L. Gore: Lessons from a Management Revolutionary," *The Wall Street Journal* [Blog], March 18, 2010, https://blogs.wsj.com/management/2010/03/18/wl-gore-lessons-from-a-management-revolutionary/; J. Kell, "Meet the Culture Warriors: 3 Companies Changing the Game," *Fortune*, March 14, 2017, http://fortune.com/2017/03/14/best-companies-to-work-for-culture/

54. D. C. Hambrick, "Upper Echelons Theory: An Update," *Academy of Management Review* 32, no. 2 (2007): 334–43; M. A. Carpenter, M. A. Geletkanycz, and W. G. Sanders, "Upper Echelons Research Revisited: Antecedents, Elements, and Consequences of Top Management Team Composition," *Journal of Management* 30, no. 6 (2004): 749–78; H. Wang, A. S. Tsui, and K. R. Xin, "CEO Leadership Behaviors, Organizational Performance, and Employees' Attitudes," *Leadership Quarterly* 22, no. 1 (2011): 92–105.

55. C. A. Hartnell, A. J. Kinicki, L. S. Lambert, M. Fugate, and C. P. Doyle, "Do Similarities or differences Between CEO leadership and Organizational Culture Have a More Positive Effect on Firm Performance? A Test of Competing Predictions," *Journal of Applied Psychology* 101, no. 6 (2016): 846-61.

56. T. D. Allen, L. T. Eby, G. T. Chao, and T. N. Bauer, "Taking Stock of Two Relational Aspects of Organizational Life: Tracing the History and Shaping the Future of Socialization and Mentoring Research," *Journal of Applied Psychology* 102, no. 3 (2017): 324–37; T. N. Bauer, T. Bodner, B. Erdogan, D. M. Truxillo, and J. S. Tucker, "Newcomer Adjustment during Organizational Socialization: A Meta-Analytic Review of Antecedents, Outcomes, and Methods," *Journal of Applied Psychology* 92, no. 3 (2007): 707–21.

57. R. E. Silverman, "Companies Try to Make the First Day for New Hires More Fun," *The Wall Street Journal,* May 28, 2013, http://online.wsj.com/article/SB10001424127887323336104578501631475934850.html

58. D. M. Cable, F. Gino, and B. R. Staats, "Breaking Them in or Eliciting Their Best? Reframing Socialization Around Newcomers' Authentic Self-Expression," *Administrative Science Quarterly* 58, no. 1 (2013): 1–36; M. Wang, J. Kammeyer-Mueller, and Y. Liu, "Context, Socialization, and Newcomer Learning," *Organizational Psychology Review* 5, no. 1 (2015): 3–25.

59. C. J. Collins, "The Interactive Effects of Recruitment Practices and Product Awareness on Job Seekers' Employer Knowledge and Application Behaviors," *Journal of Applied Psychology* 92, no. 1 (2007): 180–90.

60. T. N. Bauer, S. Perrot, R. C. Liden, and B. Erdogan, "Understanding the Consequences of Newcomer Proactive Behaviors: The Moderating Contextual Role of Servant Leadership," *Journal of Vocational Behavior* 112 (2019): 356–68; J. D. Kammeyer-Mueller and C. R. Wanberg, "Unwrapping the Organizational Entry Process: Disentangling Multiple Antecedents and Their Pathways to Adjustment," *Journal of Applied Psychology* 88 (2003): 779–94; E. W. Morrison, "Longitudinal Study of the Effects of Information Seeking on Newcomer Socialization," *Journal of Applied Psychology* 78 (2003): 173–83; C. Vandenberghe, A. Panaccio, K. Bentein, K. Mignonac, P. Roussel, and A. Khalil Ben Ayed, "Time-Based Differences in the Effects of Positive and Negative Affectivity on Perceived Supervisor Support and Organizational Commitment Among Newcomers," *Journal of Organizational Behavior* 40 (2019): 264-281; M. Wang, Y. Zhan, E. McCune, and D. Truxillo, "Understanding Newcomers' Adaptability and Work-Related Outcomes: Testing the Mediating Roles of Perceived P-E Fit Variables," *Personnel Psychology* 64, no. 1 (2011): 163–89.

61. See, for instance, C. Woodrow and D. E. Guest, "Pathways Through Organizational Socialization: A Longitudinal Qualitative Study Based on the Psychological Contract," *Journal of Occupational and Organizational Psychology* 93 (2020): 110–33.

62. Bauer, Bodner, Erdogan, Truxillo, and Tucker, "Newcomer Adjustment during Organizational Socialization"; E. W. Morrison, "Newcomers' Relationships: The Role of Social Network Ties During Socialization," *Academy of Management Journal* 45 (2002): 1149–60; A. M. Saks, K. L. Uggerslev, and N. E. Fassina, "Socialization Tactics and Newcomer Adjustment: A Meta-Analytic Review and Test of a Model," *Journal of Vocational Behavior* 70 (2007): 413–46.

63. K. Becker and A. Bish, "A Framework for Understanding the Role of Unlearning in Onboarding," *Human Resource Management Review* (in press); F. Montani, M. Maoret, and L. Dufour, "The Dark Side of Socialization: How and When Divestiture Socialization Undermines Newcomer Outcomes," *Journal of Organizational Behavior* 40 (2019): 506–21.

64. N. Delobbe, H. D. Cooper-Thomas, and R. De Hoe, "A New Look at the Psychological Contract During Organizational Socialization: The Role of Newcomers' Obligations at Entry," *Journal of Organizational Behavior* 37 (2016): 845–67; H. Jia, R. Zhong, and X. Xie, "Helping Others Makes Me Fit better: Effects of Helping Behavior by Newcomers and Coworker-Attributed Motives on Newcomers' Adjustment," *Journal of Business and Psychology* (in press); K. Kim and H. K. Moon, "How Do Socialization Tactics and Supervisor Behaviors Influence Newcomers' Psychological Contract Formation? The Mediating Role of Information Acquisition," *The International Journal of Human Resource Management* (in press); C. Woodrow and D. E. Guest, "Knowledge Acquisition and Effective Socialization: The Role of the Psychological Contract," *Journal of Occupational and Organizational Psychology* 90 (2017): 587–95.

65. S. Liu, P. Bamberger, M. Wang, J. Shi, and S. B. Bacharach, "When Onboarding Becomes Risky: Extending Social Learning Theory to Explain Newcomers' Adoption of Heavy Drinking With Clients," *Human Relations* 73, no. 5 (2020): 682–710.

66. B. Schneider, H. W. Goldstein, and D. B. Smith, "The ASA Framework: An Update," *Personnel Psychology* 48 (1995): 747–73.

67. Saks, Uggerslev, and Fassina, "Socialization Tactics and Newcomer Adjustment"; J. Van Maanen and E. Schein, "Toward a Theory of Organizational Socialization," in B. M. Staw (ed.), *Research in Organizational Behavior* (vol. 1) (Greenwich, CT: JAI, 1979).

68. O. C. Richard, D. R. Avery, A. Luksyte, O. Dorian Boncoeur, and C. Spitzmueller, "Improving Organizational Newcomers' Creative Job Performance Through Creative Process Engagement: The Moderating Role of a Synergy Diversity Climate *Personnel Psychology* 72 (2019): 421–44.

69. Bauer, Bodner, Erdogan, Truxillo, and Tucker, "Newcomer Adjustment During Organizational Socialization"; J. X. Y. Chong, G. Beenen, M. Gagné, and P. D. Dunlop, "Satisfying newcomers' needs: The Role of Socialization Tactics and Supervisor Autonomy Support," *Journal of Business and Psychology* (in press); M. Ikram Nasr, A. El Akremi, and J. A-M. Coyle-Shapiro, "Synergy or Substitution? The Interactive Effects of Insiders' Fairness and Support and Organizational Socialization Tactics on Newcomer Role Clarity and Social Integration," *Journal of Organizational Behavior* 40 (2019): 758–78; Saks, Uggerslev, and Fassina, "Socialization Tactics and Newcomer Adjustment."

70. W. R. Boswell, A. J. Shipp, S. C. Payne, and S. S. Culbertson, "Changes in Newcomer Job Satisfaction Over Time: Examining the Pattern of Honeymoons and Hangovers," *Journal of Applied Psychology* 94, no. 4 (2009): 844–58; W. R. Boswell, J. W. Boudreau, and J. Tichy, "The Relationship Between Employee Job Change and Job Satisfaction: The Honeymoon-Hangover Effect," *Journal of Applied Psychology* 90, no. 5 (2005): 882–92; Y. Zhou, M. Zou, M. Williams, and V. Tabvuma, "Is the Grass Greener on the Other Side? A Longitudinal Study of the Impact of Employer Change and Occupational Change on Job Satisfaction," *Journal of Vocational Behavior* 99 (2017): 66–78.

71. J. D. Kammeyer-Mueller, C. R. Wanberg, A. L. Rubenstein, and Z. Song, "Support, Undermining, and Newcomer Socialization: Fitting in During the First 90 Days," *Academy of Management Journal* 56, no. 4 (2013): 1104–24; M. Jokisaari and J. Nurmi, "Change in Newcomers' Supervisor Support and Socialization Outcomes After Organizational Entry," *Academy of Management Journal* 52, no. 3 (2009): 527–44.

72. C. Vandenberghe, A. Panaccio, K. Bentein, K. Mignonac, and P. Roussel, "Assessing Longitudinal Change of and Dynamic Relationships Among Role Stressors, Job Attitudes, Turnover Intention, and Well-Being in Neophyte Newcomers," *Journal of Organizational Behavior* 32, no. 4 (2011): 652–71.

73. D. Wang, P. W. Hom, and D. G. Allen, "Coping With Newcomer 'Hangover': How Socialization Tactics Affect Declining Job Satisfaction During Early Employment," *Journal of Vocational Behavior* 100 (2017): 196–210.

74. S. Maitlis and M. Christianson, "Sensemaking in Organizations: Taking Stock and Moving Forward," *The Academy of Management Annals* 8, (2014): 57–125; K. Weber and M. T. Dacin, "The Cultural Construction of Organizational Life," *Organization Science* 22, no. 2 (2011): 287–98.

75. C. Kontoghiorghes, "Linking High Performance Organizational Culture and Talent Management: Satisfaction/Motivation and Organizational Commitment as Mediators," *The International Journal of Human Resource Management* 27, no. 16 (2016): 1833–53.

76. S-H. Liao, W.-J. Chang, D-C. Hu, and Y-L. Yueh, "Relationships Among Organizational Culture, Knowledge Acquisition, Organizational Learning, and Organizational Innovation in Taiwan's Banking and Insurance Industries," *The International Journal of Human Resource Management* 23, no. 1 (2012): 52–70.

77. Schneider et al., "Organizational Climate and Culture."

78. E. H. Schein, "Sense and Nonsense About Culture and Climate," in N. M. Ashkanasy, C. P. M. Wilderom, and M. F. Peterson (Eds.), *Handbook of Organizational Culture & Climate* (Thousand Oaks, CA: Sage, 2000): xxxiii–xxx; Schneider et al., "Organizational Climate and Culture."

79. Ostroff et al., "Organizational Culture and Climate"; Schneider, Ehrhart, and Macey, "Organizational Climate and Culture"; D. Zohar and D. A. Hofmann, "Organizational Culture and Climate," in S. W. J. Kozlowski (Ed.), *The Oxford Handbook of Organizational Psychology* (Vol. 1, Oxford, UK: Oxford University Press, 2012): 1-41.

80. See, for instance, K. Fitzgerald, "Safety Culture, Climate and Performance Improvement," *HazardEx,* October 22, 2018, http://www.hazardexonthenet.net/article/162743/Safety-Culture-Climate-and-Performance-Improvement.aspx#; Maritime Knowledge, "Safety Management: Safety Culture vs Safety Climate—What's the Difference?," *Safety4SEA* [blog], March 1, 2019, https://safety4sea.com/cm-safety-management-safety-culture-vs-safety-climate-whats-the-difference/

81. M. Kuenzi and M. Schminke, "Assembling Fragments Into a Lens: A Review, Critique, and Proposed Research Agenda for the Organizational Work Climate Literature," *Journal of Management* 35, no. 3 (2009): 634–717; Schneider, Ehrhart, and Macey, "Organizational Climate and Culture."

82. S. Clarke, "The Relationship Between Safety Climate and Safety Performance: A Meta-Analytic Review," *Journal of Occupational Health Psychology* 11, no. 4 (2006): 315–27; S. Clarke, "An Integrative Model of Safety Climate: Linking Psychological Climate and Work Attitudes to Individual Safety Outcomes Using Meta-Analysis," *Journal of Occupational and Organizational Psychology* 83 (2010): 553–78.

83. J. M. Beus, S. C. Payne, M. E. Bergman, and W. Arthur, "Safety Climate and Injuries: An Examination of Theoretical and Empirical Relationships," *Journal of Applied Psychology* 95, no. 4 (2010): 713–27; See also A. M. Brawley Newlin and C. L. S. Pury, "All of the Above?: An Examination of Overlapping Organizational Climates," *Journal of Business and Psychology* (in press).

84. J. Z. Carr, A. M. Schmidt, J. K. Ford, and R. P. DeShon, "Climate Perceptions Matter: A Meta-Analytic Path Analysis Relating Molar Climate, Cognitive and Affective States, and Individual Level Work Outcomes," *Journal of Applied Psychology* 88, no. 4 (2003): 605–19.

85. M. Schulte, C. Ostroff, S. Shmulyian, and A. Kinicki, "Organizational Climate Configurations: Relationships to Collective Attitudes, Customer Satisfaction, and Financial Performance."

86. M. Kaptein, "Developing and Testing a Measure for the Ethical Culture of Organizations: The Corporate Ethical Virtues Model," *Journal of Business Ethics* 29 (2008): 923–47; L. K. Trevino and G. R. Weaver, *Managing Ethics in Business Organizations: Social Scientific Perspectives* (Stanford, CA: Stanford University Press, 2003).

87. M. Huhtala, M. Kaptein, and T. Feldt, "How Perceived Changes in the Ethical Culture of Organizations Influence the Well-Being of Managers: A Two-year Longitudinal Study," *European Journal of Work and Organizational Psychology* 25, no. 3 (2016): 335–52; M. Huhtala, A. Tolvanen, S. Mauno, and T. Feldt, "The Associations Between Ethical Organizational Culture, Burnout, and Engagement: A Multilevel Study," *Journal of Business and Psychology* 30, no. 2 (2015): 399–414.

88. A. Arnaud and M. Schminke, "The Ethical Climate and Context of Organizations," *Organization Science* 23, no. 6 (2012): 1767–80; A. Simha and J. B. Cullen, "Ethical Climates and Their Effects on Organizational Outcomes: Implications From the Past and Prophecies for the Future," *Academy of Management Perspectives* 26, no. 4 (2012): 20–34; B. Victor and J. B. Cullen, "The Organizational Bases of Ethical Work Climates," *Administrative Science Quarterly* 33, no. 1 (1988): 101–25.

89. M. Kuenzi, D. M. Mayer, and R. L. Greenbaum, "Creating an Ethical Organizational Environment: The Relationship Between Ethical Leadership, Ethical Organizational Climate, and Unethical Behavior," *Personnel Psychology* 73 (2020): 43-71.

90. Kuenzi et al., "Creating an ethical organizational environment"; Simha and Cullen, "Ethical Climates and Their Effects on Organizational Outcomes."

91. Kuenzi et al., "Creating an Ethical Organizational Environment."

92. K. Jiang, J. Hu, Y. Hong, H. Liao, and S. Liu, "Do It Well and Do It Right: The Impact of Service Climate and Ethical Climate on Business Performance and the Boundary Conditions," *Journal of Applied Psychology* 101, no. 11 (2016): 1553–68; A. T. Myer, C. N. Thoroughgood, and S. Mohammed, "Complementary or Competing Climates? Examining the Interactive Effect of Service and Ethical Climates on Company-Level Financial Performance," *Journal of Applied Psychology* 101, no. 8 (2016): 1178–90.

93. J. Howard-Greenville, S. Bertels, and B. Lahneman, "Sustainability: How It Shapes Organizational Culture and Climate," in B. Schneider and K. M. Barbera (eds.), *The Oxford Handbook of Organizational Climate and Culture* (New York, NY: Oxford University Press, 2014), 257–75.

94. E. Cohen, S. Taylor, and M. Muller-Camen, *HRM's Role in Corporate Social and Environmental Sustainability* (Alexandria, VA: Society of Human Resource Management, 2012).

95. J. Pfeffer, "Building Sustainable Organizations: The Human Factor," *Academy of Management Perspectives* 24, no. 1 (2010): 34–45.

96. P. Lacy, T. Cooper, R. Hayward, and L. Neuberger, "A New Era of Sustainability: UN Global Compact-Accenture CEO Study 2010," Joint Report from Accenture and the United Nations: The Global Compact, June 2010, https://www.unglobalcompact .org/docs/news_events/8.1/UNGC_Accenture_CEO_Study_2010.pdf

97. H. R. Dixon-Fowler, D. J. Slater, J. L. Johnson, A. E. Ellstrand, and A. M. Romi, "Beyond 'Does It Pay to Be Green?' A Meta-Analysis of Moderators of the CEP-CFP Relationship," *Journal of Business Ethics* 112 (2013): 353–66; D. S. Siegel, "Green Management Matters Only If It Yields More Green: An Economic/Strategic Perspective," *Academy of Management Perspectives* 23, no. 3 (2009): 5-16.

98. B. Fitzgerald, "Sustainable Farming Will Be Next, 'Revolution in Agriculture,'" *Australian Broadcasting Company: Rural,* May 28, 2015, 10:12PM, http://www.abc.net.au/news/2015-05-29/state-of-tomorrow-sustainable-farming/6504842

99. Siemens, *Sustainability Information 2018* (München, Germany: Siemens, 2018).

100. K. Strauss, "The World's Most Sustainable Companies, 2018," *Forbes,* January 23, 2018, https://www.forbes .com/sites/karsten-strauss/2018/01/23/the-worlds-most-sustainable-companies-2018/#43d5ff7a32b0

101. P. Bansal, "From Issues to Actions: The Importance of Individual Concerns and Organizational Values in Responding to Natural Environmental Issues," *Organization Science* 14, no. 5 (2003): 510–27; P. Bansal, "Evolving Sustainably: A Longitudinal Study of Corporate Sustainable Development," *Strategic Management Journal* 26, no. 3 (2005): 197–218; J. Howard-Grenville and A. J. Hoffman, "The Importance of Cultural Framing to the Success of Social Initiatives in Business," *Academy of Management Executive* 17, no. 2 (2003):70–84.

102. A. R. Carrico and M. Riemer, "Motivating Energy Conservation in the Workplace: An Evaluation of the Use of Group-Level Feedback and Peer Education," *Journal of Environmental Psychology* 31, no. 1 (2011): 1–13.

103. M. Del Giudice, Z. Khan, M. De Silva, V. Scuotto, F. Caputo, and E. Carayannis, "The Microlevel Actions Undertaken by Owner-Managers in Improving the Sustainability Practices of Cultural and Creative Small and Medium Enterprises: A United Kingdom-Italy Comparison," *Journal of Organization Behavior* 38 (2017): 1396–414.

104. J. P. Kotter, "Change Management: Accelerate!" *Harvard Business Review,* November 2012: 44–58.

105. A. Dan, "Droga5's David Droga About Redefining Advertising," *Forbes,* December 13, 2011, https://www.forbes.com/sites/avidan/2011/12/13/the-ad-agency-guru-who-helped-get-obama-elected/#6d1fb4903477

106. J. Beer, "Why Accenture Interactive Buying Ad Agency Droga5 Is Such a Big Deal," *Fast Company,* April 3, 2019, https://www.fastcompany.com/90328733/why-accenture-interactive-buying-ad-agency-droga5-is-such-a-big-deal

107. A. Newman, H. Round, S. Wang, and M. Mount, "Innovation Climate: A Systematic Review of the Literature and Agenda for Future Research," *Journal of Occupational and Organizational Psychology* 93 (2020): 73–109.

108. "How Big Companies Can Innovate Like Small Startups," *Knowledge@Wharton,* January 30, 2019, https://knowledge.wharton.upenn.edu/article/how-big-companies-can-innovate-like-small-startups/

109. J. M. Beus, L. Lucianetti, and W. Arthur Jr., "Clash of the Climates: Examining the Paradoxical Effects of Climates for Promotion and Prevention," *Personnel Psychology* 73 (2020): 241-269; L. Heracleous, C. Wawarta, S. Gonzalez, and S. Paroutis, "How a Group of NASA Renegades Transformed Mission Control," *MIT Sloan Management Review,* April 5, 2019, https://sloanreview.mit.edu/article/how-a-group-of-nasa-renegades-transformed-mission-control/

110. Hartnell et al., "A Meta-Analytic Test of Organizational Culture's Association With Elements of an Organization's System and Its Relative Predictive Validity on Organizational Outcomes."

111. R. Pyrillis, "ChildNet: Optimas Award Winner for General Excellence," *Workforce Management,* November 1, 2012, http://www.workforce.com/2012/11/01/childnet-optimas-award-winner-for-general-excellence/.

112. E. Comen, S. Stebbins, and T. C. Frohlich, "The Worst Companies to Work For," *24/7 Wall ST,* June 10, 2016, http://247wallst.com/special-report/2016/06/10/the-worst-companies-to-work-for-2/3/; C. Hannan, "Dish Network, the Meanest Company in America," *Bloomberg,* January 3, 2013, https://www.bloomberg.com/news/articles/2013-01-02/dish-network-the-meanest-company-in-america

113. A. S. Boyce, L. R. G. Nieminen, M. A. Gillespie, A. M. Ryan, and D. R. Denison, "Which Comes First, Organizational Culture or Performance? A Longitudinal Study of Causal Priority with Automobile Dealerships," *Journal of Organizational Behavior* 36 (2015): 339–59.

114. J. Bandler and D. Burke, "How HP Lost Its Way," *Fortune,* May 21, 2012, 147–64.

115. G. F. Lanzara and G. Patriotta, "The Institutionalization of Knowledge in an Automotive Factory: Templates, Inscriptions, and the Problems of Durability," *Organization Studies* 28, no. 5 (2007): 635–660; T. B. Lawrence, M. K. Mauws, B. Dyck, and R. F. Kleysen, "The Politics of Organizational Learning: Integrating Power Into the 4I Framework," *Academy of Management Review* 30, no. 1 (2005): 180–91.

116. See, for instance, P. Bate, R. Khan, and A. Pye, "Towards a Culturally Sensitive Approach to Organizational Structuring: Where Organizational Design Meets Organizational Development," *Organization Science* 11, no. 2 (2000): 197–211; G. F. Latta, "Modeling the Cultural Dynamics of Resistance and Facilitation: Interaction Effects in the OC3 Model of Organizational Change," *Journal of Organizational Change Management* 28, no. 6 (2015): 1013–37.

117. Y. Kashima, P. G. Bain, and A. Perfors, "The Psychology of Cultural Dynamics: What Is It, What Do We Know, and What Is Yet to Be Known?" *Annual Review of Psychology* 70 (2019): 499-529.

118. D. Markovitz, "The Art of Change," *IndustryWeek,* January 29, 2019, https://www.industryweek.com/leadership/art-change; J. Shook, "How to Change a Culture: Lessons From NUMMI," *MIT Sloan Management Review,* 51, no. 2 (2010): 63-8.

119. See D. L. Stone, E. F. Stone-Romero, and K. M. Lukaszewski, "The Impact of Cultural Values on the Acceptance and Effectiveness of Human Resource Management Policies and Practices," *Human Resource Management Review* 17, no. 2 (2007): 152–165; D. R. Avery, "Support for Diversity in Organizations: A Theoretical Exploration of Its Origins and Offshoots," *Organizational Psychology Review* 1, no. 3 (2011): 239–256; A. Groggins and A. M. Ryan, "Embracing Uniqueness: The Underpinnings of a Positive Climate for Diversity," *Journal of Occupational and Organizational Psychology* 86, no. 2 (2013): 264–282.

120. J. A. Chatman, J. T. Polzer, S. G. Barsade, and M. A. Neale, "Being Different Yet Feeling Similar: The Influence of Demographic Composition and Organizational Culture on Work Processes and Outcomes," *Administrative Science Quarterly* 43 (1998): 749–80.

121. S. D. Pugh, J. Dietz, A. P. Brief, and J. W. Wiley, "Looking Inside and Out: The Impact of Employee and Community Demographic Composition on Organizational Diversity Climate," *Journal of Applied Psychology* 93, no. 6 (2008): 1422–28.

122. Y. Li, S. Perera, C. T. Kulik, and I. Metz, "Inclusion Climate: A Multilevel Investigation of Its Antecedents and Consequences," *Human Resource Management* 58 (2019): 353–69.

123. M. Reinwald, H. Huettermann, and H. Bruch, "Beyond the Mean: Understanding Firm-Level Consequences of Variability in Diversity Climate Perceptions," *Journal of Organizational Behavior* 40 (2019): 472-491.

124. M. J. Gelfand, L. M. Leslie, K. Keller, and C. de Dreu, "Conflict Cultures in Organizations: How Leaders Shape Conflict Cultures and Their Organizational-Level Consequences," *Journal of Applied Psychology* 97, no. 6 (2012): 1131–47.

125. Y. Liu, D. Vrontis, M. Visser, P. Stokes, S. Smith, N. Moore, A. Thrassou, and A. Ashta, "Talent Management and the HR Function in Cross-Cultural Mergers and Acquisitions: The Role and Impact of Bi-Cultural Identity," *Human Resource Management Review* (in press); C. Pike, *Mergers and Acquisitions: Managing Culture and Human Resources* (Stanford, CA: Stanford University Press, 2005).

126. K. Voigt, "Mergers Fail More Often Than Marriages," *CNN,* May 22, 2009, http://edition.cnn.com/2009/BUSINESS/05/21/merger.marriage/.

127. J. Beer, "Why Accenture Interactive Buying Ad Agency Droga5 Is Such a Big Deal."

128. R. M. Sarala, P. Junni, C. L. Cooper, S. Y. Tarba, "A Sociocultural Perspective on Knowledge Transfer in Mergers and Acquisitions," *Journal of Management* 42, no. 5 (2016): 1230–49.

129. A. Ardichvili, J. A. Mitchell, and D. Jondle, "Characteristics of Ethical Business Cultures," *Journal of Business Ethics* 85, no. 4 (2009): 445–51; D. M. Mayer, "A Review of the Literature on Ethical Climate and Culture," in B. Schneider and K. M. Barbera (eds.), *The Oxford Handbook of Organizational Climate and Culture* (New York, NY: Oxford University Press, 2014), 415–40.

130. J. P. Mulki, J. F. Jaramillo, and W. B. Locander, "Critical Role of Leadership on Ethical Climate and Salesperson Behaviors," *Journal of Business Ethics* 86, no. 2 (2009): 125–41; M. Schminke, M. L. Ambrose, and D. O. Neubaum, "The Effect of Leader Moral Development on Ethical Climate and Employee Attitudes," *Organizational Behavior and Human Decision Processes* 97, no. 2 (2005): 135–51; M. E. Brown, L. K. Treviño, and D. A. Harrison, "Ethical Leadership: A Social Learning Perspective for Construct Development and Testing," *Organizational Behavior and Human Decision Processes* 97, no. 2 (2005): 117–34.

131. D. M. Mayer, M. Kuenzi, R. Greenbaum, M. Bardes, and S. Salvador, "How Low Does Ethical Leadership Flow? Test of a Trickle-Down Model," *Organizational Behavior and Human Decision Processes* 108, no. 1 (2009): 1–13; L. J. Christensen, A. Mackey, and D. Whetten, "Taking Responsibility for Corporate Social Responsibility: The Role of Leaders in Creating, Implementing, Sustaining, or Avoiding Socially Responsible Firm Behaviors," *Academy of Management Perspectives* 28, no. 2 (2014): 164–78.

132. B. Sweeney, D. Arnold, and B. Pierce, "The Impact of Perceived Ethical Culture of the Firm and Demographic Variables on Auditors' Ethical Evaluation and Intention to Act Decisions," *Journal of Business Ethics* 93, no. 4 (2010): 531–51.

133. L. Huang and T. A. Paterson, "Group Ethical Voice: Influence of Ethical Leadership and Impact on Ethical Performance," *Journal of Management* 43, no. 4 (2017): 1157–84.

134. M. L. Gruys, S. M. Stewart, J. Goodstein, M. N. Bing, and A. C. Wicks, "Values Enactment in Organizations: A Multi-Level Examination," *Journal of Management* 34, no. 4 (2008): 806–43.

135. D. L. Nelson and C. L. Cooper (eds.) *Positive Organizational Behavior* (London, UK: Sage, 2007); K. S. Cameron, J. E. Dutton, and R. E. Quinn (eds.) *Positive Organizational Scholarship: Foundations of a New Discipline* (San Francisco, CA: Berrett-Koehler, 2003); F. Luthans and C. M. Youssef, "Emerging Positive Organizational Behavior," *Journal of Management* 33, no. 3 (2007): 321–49.

136. Admiral Group, *Our Culture: Ministry of Fun*, Accessed April 6, 2019, https://admiralgroup.co.uk/our-culture/ministry-fun

137. S. Fineman, "On Being Positive: Concerns and Counterpoints," *Academy of Management Review* 31, no. 2 (2006): 270–91.

138. E. Poole, "Organisational Spirituality: A Literature Review," *Journal of Business Ethics* 84, no. 4 (2009): 577–88.

139. L. W. Fry and J. W. Slocum, "Managing the Triple Bottom Line through Spiritual Leadership," *Organizational Dynamics* 37, no. 1 (2008): 86–96.

140. See, for example, C. L. Jurkiewicz and R. A. Giacalone, "A Values Framework for Measuring the Impact of Workplace Spirituality on Organizational Performance," *Journal of Business Ethics* 49, no. 2 (2004): 129–42.

141. See, for example, B. S. Pawar, "Workplace Spirituality Facilitation: A Comprehensive Model," *Journal of Business Ethics* 90, no. 3 (2009): 375–86; L. Lambert, *Spirituality Inc.: Religion in the American Workplace* (New York: University Press, 2009).

142. F. Yang, X. Huang, and L. Wu, "Experiencing Meaningfulness Climate in Teams: How Spiritual Leadership Enhances Team Effectiveness When Facing Uncertain Tasks," *Human Resource Management* 58 (2019): 155-168.

143. M. Oppenheimer, "The Rise of the Corporate Chaplain," *Bloomberg Businessweek*, August 23, 2012, 58–61.

144. See, for instance, S. Chan-Serafin, A. P. Brief, and J. M. George, "How Does Religion Matter and Why? Religion and the Organizational Sciences," *Organization Science* 24, no. 5 (2013): 1585–600.

145. M. Lips-Miersma, K. L. Dean, and C. J. Fornaciari, "Theorizing the Dark Side of the Workplace Spirituality Movement," *Journal of Management Inquiry* 18, no. 4 (2009): 288–300.

146. W-C. Zou and J. Dahling, "Workplace Spirituality Buffers the Effects of Emotional Labour on Employee Well-being," *European Journal of Work and Organizational Psychology* 26, no. 5 (2017): 768–77.

147. J.-C. Garcia-Zamor, "Workplace Spirituality and Organizational Performance," *Public Administration Review* 63, no. 3 (2003): 355–63; L. W. Fry, S. T. Hannah, M. Noel, and F. O. Walumbwa, "Impact of Spiritual Leadership on Unit Performance," *Leadership Quarterly* 22, no. 2 (2011): 259–70.

148. A. Rego and M. Pina e Cunha, "Workplace Spirituality and Organizational Commitment: An Empirical Study," *Journal of Organizational Change Management* 21, no. 1 (2008): 53–75; R. W. Kolodinsky, R. A. Giacalone, and C. L. Jurkiewicz, "Workplace Values and Outcomes: Exploring Personal, Organizational, and Interactive Workplace Spirituality," *Journal of Business Ethics* 81, no. 2 (2008): 465–80; M. Gupta, V. Kumar, and M. Singh, "Creating Satisfied Employees Through Workplace Spirituality: A Study of the Private Insurance Sector in Punjab, India," *Journal of Business Ethics* 122, no. 1 (2014): 79–88.

149. See, for instance, V. Peltokorpi, A. K. Bader, and F. J. Froese, "Foreign and Domestic Company Attractiveness to Host National Employees in Japan: A Person-Organization Fit and Image Theory Perspective," *International Journal of Selection and Assessment* 27 (2019): 392-405.

150. D. J. McCarthy and S. M. Puffer, "Interpreting the Ethicality of Corporate Governance Decision in Russia: Utilizing Integrative Social Contracts Theory to Evaluate the Relevance of Agency Theory Norms," *Academy of Management Review* 33, no. 1 (2008): 11–31.

CHAPTER 17

1. A. Chowdhry, "Apple Surpassed Samsung as Global Phone Market Leader, Says Report," *Forbes*, March 3, 2015, http://www.forbes.com/sites/amitchowdhry/2015/03/04/apple-passes-samsung/; L. Goadsduff and A. A. Forni, "Gartner Says Worldwide Sales of Smartphones Grew 7 Percent in the Fourth Quarter of 2016," *Gartner: Newsroom* [Press Release], February 15, 2017, http://www.gartner.com/newsroom/id/3609817

2. Ibid.

3. Ibid.

4. W. F. Cascio and R. Montealegre, "How Technology Is Changing Work and Organizations," *Annual Review of Organizational Psychology and Organizational Behavior* 3 (2016): 349–75; D. L. Stone, D. L. Deadrick, K. M. Lukaszewski, and R. Johnson, "The Influence of Technology on the Future of Human Resource Management," *Human Resource Management Review* 25 (2015): 216–31.

5. BBC, "How Artificial Intelligence Is Changing the Workplace," January 25, 2018, http://www.bbc.com/story works/specials/how-artificial-intelligence-is-changing-the-workplace/; J. Lindzon, "How AI Is Changing the Way Companies Are Organized," *Fast Company*, February 28, 2017, https://www.fastcompany.com/3068492/how-ai-is-changing-the-way-companies-are-organized

6. *Anywhere Workers* (November 15, 2018, And Co and Remote Year): https://www.and.co/anywhere-workers?utm_source =participantsemail; E. Chickowski, "Ready or Not, the Future of Work Isn't in an Office," *Digirup.IO*, March 25, 2019, https://digirup.io/ready-or-not-the-future-of-work-isnt-in-an-office/; L. Larson and L. A. DeChurch, "Leading Teams in the Digital Age: Four Perspectives on Technology and What They Mean for Leading Teams," *The Leadership Quarterly* (in press).

7. N. Fligstein and A. Goldstein, "The Roots of the Great Recession," in D. B. Grusky, B. Western, and C. Wimer (eds.), *The Great Recession* (New York, NY: Russell Sage Foundation, 2011): 21–56; B. Okay-Somerville and D. Scholarios, "A Multilevel Examination of Skills-Oriented Human Resource Management and Perceived Skill Utilization During Recession: Implications for the Well-Being of All Workers," *Human Resource Management* 58 (2019): 139–154; R. Rich, "The Great Recession," Federal Reserve History, November 22, 2013, https://www .federalreservehistory.org/essays/great_recession_of_200709; H. Smith, "A Year After the Crisis Was Declared Over, Greece Is Still Spiralling Down," *The Guardian*, August 13, 2016, https://www.theguardian.com/business/; S. Wood, G. Michaelides, and C. Ogbonnaya, "Recessionary Actions and Absence: A Workplace-Level Study," *Human Resource Management* (in press).

8. European Commission Joint Research Centre, "The Number of People Affected by Food Crises Remains at Alarming Levels," *ScienceDaily*, April 2, 2019, https://www .sciencedaily.com/releases/2019/04/190402113217.htm

9. C. Schnure, "A Recession May Be Coming, but Not for Commercial Real Estate Investors," *Barron's*, March 25, 2019.

10. S. Ping Chan, "Coronavirus: 'World Faces Worst Recession Since Great Depression,'" *BBC*, April 14, 2020, https://www .bbc.com/news/business-52273988; Schnure, "A Recession May Be Coming, but Not for Commercial Real Estate Investors"; N. Smith, "How Bad Might It Get? Think the Great Depression: The Coronavirus Collapse Has the Ingredients to Surpass the Disaster of the 1930s," *Bloomberg*, April 22, 2020, https://www.bloomberg.com/opinion/articles/2020-04-22/the-coronavirus-recession-will-rival-the-great-depression

11. J. Bourke, *Which Two Heads Are Better Than One? How Diverse Teams Create Breakthrough Ideas and Make Smarter Decisions* (Sydney, Australia: Australian Institute of Company Directors, December 11, 2017); K. Casey, "Why Diverse IT Teams Have a Competitive Edge," *The Enterprisers Project,* January 15, 2019, https://enterprisersproject.com/article/2019/1/why-diverse-it-teams-have-competitive-edge

12. R. Dixon, "5 Business Trends That Will Continue to Rise in 2019," *Entrepreneur,* December 26, 2018, https://www .entrepreneur.com/article/323660

13. Epsilon, *New Epsilon Research Indicates 80% of Consumers Are More Likely to Make a purchase When Brands Offer Personalized Experiences* [press release], January 9, 2018, https://us.epsilon.com/pressroom/new-epsilon-research-indicates-80-of-consumers-are-more-likely-to-make-a-purchase-when-brands-offer-personalized-experiences

14. C. Tode, "Dunkin' Donuts' Winning Mobile Triple Play: Geofencing, Behavioral Targeting and Coupons," *Retail Dive*, August 4, 2014, https://www.retaildive.com/ex/mobile-commercedaily/dunkin-donuts-winning-mobile-triple-play-geofencing-behavioral-targeting-and-coupons

15. P. Bansal and H.-C. Song, "Similar but Not the Same: Differentiating Corporate Sustainability From Corporate Responsibility," *Academy of Management Annals* 11, no. 1 (2017): 106–49.

16. B. Casselman, P. Cohen, S. Cowley, C. Dougherty, N. Kulish, D. McCabe, and K. Weise, "Coronavirus Cost to Businesses and Workers: 'It Has All Gone to Hell,'" *The New York Times,* March 15, 2020, https://www.nytimes.com/2020/03/15/business/economy/coronavirus-economy-impact.html

17. "Brexit: All you need to know about the UK leaving the EU," *BBC*, February 17, 2020, https://www.bbc.com/news/uk-politics-32810887; J. Campbell, "Brexit Uncertainty 'Major Feature' of Private Sector Dip," *BBC News,* April 8, 2019, https://www.bbc.com/news/uk-northern-ireland-47851368; W. Schomberg, "Factbox: No-deal Brexit — What It Might Mean for UK Economy," *Reuters,* April 2, 2019, https://www.reuters.com/article/us-britain-eu-deal-factbox/factbox-no-deal-brexit-what-it-might-mean-for-uk-economy-idUSKCN1RE1FV

18. D. L. Bradford and W. W. Burke (eds.), Reinventing Organization Development: New Approaches to Change in Organizations (San Francisco, CA: Pfeiffer, 2005).

19. See, for instance, J. Birkinshaw, G. Hamel, and M. J. Mol, "Management Innovation," *Academy of Management Review* 33, no. 4 (2008): 825–45; J. Welch and S. Welch, "What Change Agents Are Made Of," *BusinessWeek*, October 20, 2008, 96.

20. See, for instance, S. Konlechner, M. Latzke, W. H. Güttel, E. Höfferer, "Prospective Sensemaking, Frames and Planned Change Interventions: A Comparison of Change Trajectories in Two Hospital Units," *Human Relations* 72, no. 4 (2019): 706–32.

21. M. Helft, "How the Tech Elite Plans to Reinvent Senior Care," *Forbes*, April 2, 2015, http://www.forbes.com/sites/miguelhelft/2015/04/02/how-the-tech-elite-plans-to-reinvent-senior-care

22. P. G. Audia and S. Brion, "Reluctant to Change: Self-Enhancing Responses to Diverging Performance Measures," *Organizational Behavior and Human Decision Processes* 102, no. 2 (2007): 255–69.

23. M. Fugate, A. J. Kinicki, and G. E. Prussia, "Employee Coping With Organizational Change: An Examination of Alternative Theoretical Perspectives and Models," *Personnel Psychology* 61, no. 1 (2008): 1–36.

24. S. Turgut, A. Michel, L. M. Rothenhöfer, and K. Sonntag, "Dispositional Resistance to Change and Emotional Exhaustion: Moderating Effects at the Work-Unit Level," *European Journal of Work and Organizational Psychology* 25, no. 5 (2016): 735–50.

25. R. B. L. Sijbom, O. Janssen, and N. W. Van Yperen, "How to Get Radical Creative Ideas Into a Leader's Mind? Leader's Achievement Goals and Subordinates' Voice of Creative Ideas," European Journal of Work and Organizational Psychology 24, no. 2 (2015): 279–96.

26. D. R. King, D. Bauer, Q. D. Weng, S. Schriber, and S. Tarba, "What, When, and Who: Manager Involvement in Predicting Employee Resistance to Acquisition Integration," *Human Resource Management* 59 (2020): 63–81.

27. J. D. Ford, L. W. Ford, and A. D'Amelio, "Resistance to Change: The Rest of the Story," *Academy of Management Review* 33, no. 2 (2008): 362–77.

28. Q. N. Huy, K. G. Corley, and M. S. Kraatz, "From Support to Mutiny: Shifting Legitimacy Judgments and Emotional Reactions Impacting the Implementation of Radical Change," *Academy of Management Journal* 57, no. 6 (2014): 165–80.

29. R. K. Smollan, "The Multi-Dimensional Nature of Resistance to Change," *Journal of Management & Organization* 17, no. 6 (2011): 828–49.

30. P. C. Fiss and E. J. Zajac, "The Symbolic Management of Strategic Change: Sensegiving via Framing and Decoupling," *Academy of Management Journal* 49, no. 6 (2006): 1173–93.

31. A. E. Rafferty and S. L. D. Restubog, "The Impact of Change Process and Context on Change Reactions and Turnover During a Merger," *Journal of Management* 36, no. 5 (2010): 1309–38.

32. M. Fugate and G. Soenen, "Predictors and Processes Related to Employees' Change-Related Compliance and Championing," *Personnel Psychology* 71 (2018): 109–32; J. Kaltiainen, J. Lipponen, M. Fugate, and M. Vakola, "Spiraling Work Engagement and Change Appraisals: A Three-Wave Longitudinal Study During Organizational Change," *Journal of Occupational Health Psychology* (in press).

33. A. Vaccaro and G. Palazzo, "Values Against Violence: Institutional Change in Societies Dominated by Organized Crime," *Academy of Management Journal* 58, no. 4 (2015): 1075–101.

34. Q. N. Huy, "Emotional Balancing of Organizational Continuity and Radical Change: The Contribution of Middle Managers," *Administrative Science Quarterly* (March 2002): 31–69; D. M. Herold, D. B. Fedor, and S. D. Caldwell, "Beyond Change Management: A Multilevel Investigation of Contextual and Personal Influences on Employees' Commitment to Change," *Journal of Applied Psychology* 92, no. 4 (2007): 942–51; G. B. Cunningham, "The Relationships Among Commitment to Change, Coping With Change, and Turnover Intentions," *European Journal of Work and Organizational Psychology* 15, no. 1 (2006): 29–45.

35. R. Peccei, A. Giangreco, and A. Sebastiano, "The Role of Organizational Commitment in the Analysis of Resistance to Change: Co-Predictor and Moderator Effects," *Personnel Review* 40, no. 2 (2011): 185–204.

36. K. Alfes, A. D. Shantz, C. Bailey, E. Conway, K. Monks, and N. Fu, "Perceived Human Resource System Strength and Employee Reactions Toward Change: Revisiting Human Resource's Remit as Change Agent," *Human Resource Management* 58 (2019): 239–52; Turgut et al., "Dispositional Resistance to Change and Emotional Exhaustion."

37. Huy, Corley, and Kraatz, "From Support to Mutiny"; J. P. Kotter, "Leading Change: Why Transformational Efforts Fail," *Harvard Business Review* 85 (January 2007): 96–103.

38. K. van Dam, S. Oreg, and B. Schyns, "Daily Work Contexts and Resistance to Organisational Change: The Role of Leader–Member Exchange, Development Climate, and Change Process Characteristics," *Applied Psychology: An International Review* 57, no. 2 (2008): 313–34.

39. H. H. Zhao, S. E. Seibert, M. S. Taylor, C. Lee, and W. Lam, "Not Even the Past: The Joint Influence of Former Leader and New Leader During Leader Succession in the Midst Of Organizational Change," *Journal of Applied Psychology* 101, no. 12 (2016): 1730–38.

40. A. H. Y. Hon, M. Bloom, and J. M. Crant, "Overcoming Resistance to Change and Enhancing Creative Performance," *Journal of Management* 40, no. 3 (2014): 919–41.

41. G. Jacobs and A. Keegan, "Ethical Considerations and Change Recipients' Reactions: 'It's Not All About Me,'" *Journal of Business Ethics* 152, no. 1 (2018): 73–90.

42. D. B. Fedor, S. Caldwell, and D. M. Herold, "The Effects of Organizational Changes on Employee Commitment: A Multilevel Investigation," *Personnel Psychology* 59, no. 1 (2006): 1–29; R. D. Foster, "Resistance, Justice, and Commitment to Change," *Human Resource Development Quarterly* 21, no. 1 (2010): 3–39.

43. See, for instance, D. E. Krause, "Consequences of Manipulation in Organizations: Two Studies on Its Effects on Emotions and Relationships," Psychological Reports 111, no. 1 (2012): 199–218.

44. J. Kelly, "Netflix's Fyre Festival Documentary Is a Cautionary Tale of Bad Leadership," *Forbes,* January 29, 2019, https://www.forbes.com/sites/jackkelly/2019/01/29/netflixs-fyre-festival-documentary-is-a-cautionary-tale-of-bad-leadership/#2bad92ea2826; M. Torres, "Work Is Not Your Family, as the Fyre Festival Doc Reminds Us," *The Huffington Post,* January 28, 2019, https://www.huffpost .com/entry/work-is-not-your-family-fyre-festival_1_5c4f20cfe4b06ba6d3bf6654

45. S. Oreg, "Personality, Context, and Resistance to Organizational Change," *European Journal of Work and Organizational Psychology* 15, no. 1 (2006): 73–101.

46. S.-H. Chung, Y.-F. Su, and S.-W. Su, "The Impact of Cognitive Flexibility on Resistance to Organizational Change," *Social Behavior and Personality* 40, no. 5 (2012): 735–46; I. B. Saksvik and H. Hetland, "Exploring Dispositional Resistance to Change," *Journal of Leader-*

ship & Organizational Studies 16, no. 2 (2009): 175–83; H. Toch and J. D. Grant, *Reforming Human Services Change Through Participation* (Beverly Hills, CA: Sage, 1982); C. R. Wanberg and J. T. Banas, "Predictors and Outcomes of Openness to Changes in a Reorganizing Workplace," *Journal of Applied Psychology* 85, no. 1 (2000): 132–42.

47. J. W. B. Lang and P. D. Bliese, "General Mental Ability and Two Types of Adaptation to Unforeseen Change: Applying Discontinuous Growth Models to the Task-Change Paradigm," *Journal of Applied Psychology* 94, no. 2 (2009): 411–28.

48. K. J. McClanahan, "Viva la Evolution: Using Dual-Strategies Theory to Explain Leadership in Modern Organizations," *The Leadership Quarterly* (in press).

49. See, for instance, A. Karaevli, "Performance Consequences for New CEO 'Outsiderness': Moderating Effects of Pre- and Post-Succession Contexts," *Strategic Management Journal* 28, no. 7 (2007): 681–706.

50. K. Lewin, "Frontiers in Group Dynamics: Concept, Method and Reality in Social Science: Equilibrium and Social Change," *Human Relations* 1, no. 1 (1947): 5–41. Compare with S. Cummings, T. Bridgman, and K. G. Brown, "Unfreezing Change as Three Steps: Rethinking Kurt Lewin's Legacy for Change Management," *Human Relations* 69, no. 1 (2016): 33–60.

51. P. G. Audia, E. A. Locke, and K. G. Smith, "The Paradox of Success: An Archival and a Laboratory Study of Strategic Persistence Following Radical Environmental Change," *Academy of Management Journal* 43, no. 5 (2000): 837–53; P. G. Audia and S. Brion, "Reluctant to Change: Self-Enhancing Responses to Diverging Performance Measures," *Organizational Behavior and Human Decision Processes* 102, no. 2 (2007): 255–69.

52. J. M. Bartunek and R. W. Woodman, "Beyond Lewin: Toward a Temporal Approximation of Organization Development and Change," *Annual Review of Organizational Psychology and Organizational Behavior* 2 (2015): 157–82.

53. Ibid.

54. J. Kotter, *Leading Change* (Boston, MA: Harvard Business School, 1996); J. Kotter, *Our Iceberg Is Melting* (New York, NY: St. Martin's, 2005); J. Kotter, *A Sense of Urgency* (Boston, MA: Harvard Business School, 2008); J. Pollack and R. Pollack, "Using Kotter's Eight Stage Process to Manage an Organisational Change Pro-gram: Presentation and Practice," *Systemic Practice and Action Research* 28, no. 1 (2015): 41–66.

55. For reviews, see I. Bleijenbergh, J. van Mierlo, and T. Bondarouk, "Closing the Gap Between Scholarly Knowledge and Practice: Guidelines for HRM Action Research," *Human Resource Management Review* (in press); C. Cassell and P. Johnson, "Action Research: Explaining the Diversity," *Human Relations* 59, no. 6 (2006): 783–814.

56. C. Knight, M. Patterson, J. Dawson, and J. Brown, "Building and Sustaining Work Engagement—A Participatory Action Intervention to Increase Work Engagement in Nursing Staff," *European Journal of Work and Organizational Psychology* 26, no. 5 (2017): 634–49.

57. A. Touboulic and H. Walker, "A Relational, Transformative and Engaged Approach to Sustainable Supply Chain Management: The Potential of Action Research," *Human Relations* 69, no. 2 (2016): 301–43.

58. A. Malhotra, A. Majchrzak, W. Bonfield, and S. Myers, "Engaging Customer Care Employees in Internal Collaborative Crowdsourcing: Managing the Inherent Tensions and Associated Challenges," *Human Resource Management* 59 (2020): 121–34.

59. V. M. Desai, "Collaborative Stakeholder Engagement: An Integration Between Theories of Organizational Legitimacy and Learning," *Academy of Management Journal* 61, no. 1 (2018): 220–44.

60. Bradford and Burke (eds.), *Reinventing Organization Development*; M.-Y. Cheung-Judge and L. Holbeche, *Organization Development: A*

Practitioner's Guide for OD and HR (London, UK: Kogan, 2011); B. Burnes and B. Cooke, "The Past, Present and Future of Organization Development: Taking the Long View," *Human Relations* 65, no. 11 (2012): 1395–429.

61. See, for instance, Burnes and Cooke, "The Past, Present and Future of Organization Development."

62. S. Highhouse, "A History of the T-Group and Its Early Application in Management Development," *Group Dynamics: Theory, Research, & Practice* 6, no. 4 (2002): 277–90.

63. See, for instance, R. J. Solomon, "An Examination of the Relationship Between a Survey Feedback O.D. Technique and the Work Environment," *Personnel Psychology* 29 (1976): 583–94.

64. F. Lambrechts, S. Grieten, R. Bouwen, and F. Corthouts, "Process Consultation Revisited: Taking a Relational Practice Perspective," *Journal of Applied Behavioral Science* 45, no. 1 (2009): 39–58; E. H. Schein, *Process Consultation—Volume 1: Its Role in Organization Development* (2nd ed.) (Reading, MA: Addison Wesley, 1988); E. H. Schein, *Process Consultation Revisited: Building the Helping Relationship* (Reading, MA: Addison Wesley, 1999).

65. W. W. G. Dyer, W. G. Dyer, and J. H. Dyer, *Team Building: Proven Strategies for Improving Team Performance* (Hoboken, NJ: Jossey-Bass, 2007); M. L. Shuffler, D. DiazGranados, and E. Salas, "There's a Science for That: Team Development Interventions in Organizations," *Current Directions in Psychological Science* 20, no. 6 (2011): 365–72.

66. A. Bonire, "4 Ways Escape Room Games Enhances Employees Team Spirit," *Thrive Global,* March 11, 2019, https://thriveglobal.com/stories/4-ways-escape-room-games-enhances-employees-team-spirit/

67. N. Coffin, "Mystery Industry: Breakout Games' Escape Rooms Foster Team-Building, Problem-Solving in Lutherville Timonium," *Baltimore Sun,* April 2, 2019, https://www .baltimoresun.com/news/maryland/baltimore-county/towson/ph-tt-escape-rooms-20190320-story.html

68. See, for instance, W. A. Randolph and B. Z. Posner, "The Effects of an Intergroup Development OD Intervention as Conditioned by the Life Cycle State of Organizations: A Laboratory Experiment," Group & Organization Studies 7, no. 3 (1982): 335–52.

69. U. Wagner, L. Tropp, G. Finchilescu, and C. Tredoux, eds., *Improving Intergroup Relations* (New York, NY: Wiley-Blackwell, 2008).

70. R. Fry, F. Barrett, J. Seiling, and D. Whitney (eds.), *Appreciative Inquiry and Organizational Transformation: Reports from the Field* (Westport, CT: Quorum, 2002); R. J. Ridley-Duff and G. Duncan, "What Is Critical Appreciation? Insights from Studying the Critical Turn in an Appreciative Inquiry," *Human Relations* 68, no. 10 (2015): 1579–99; D. van der Haar and D. M. Hosking, "Evaluating Appreciative Inquiry: A Relational Constructivist Perspective," *Human Relations* 57, no. 8 (2004): 1017–36.

71. Case Western Reserve University, *Appreciative Inquiry Commons,* https://appreciativeinquiry.case.edu/, accessed April 20, 2017.

72. L. Godwin, "Appreciative Inquiry Accelerates What's Working," *HR Dive,* August 28, 2018, https://www.hrdive.com/news/appreciative-inquiry-accelerates-whats-working/530916/

73. J. Schad, M. W. Lewis, S. Raisch, and W. K. Smith, "Paradox Research in Management Science: Looking Back to Move Forward," *The Academy of Management Annals* 10, no. 1 (2016): 5–64; D. A. Waldman, L. L. Putnam, E. Miron-Spektor, and D. Siegel, "The Role of Paradox Theory in Decision Making and Management Research," *Organizational Behavior and Human Decision Processes* 155 (2019): 1–9.

74. J. Jay, "Navigating Paradox as a Mechanism of Change and Innovation in Hybrid Organizations," *Academy of Management Journal* 56, no. 1 (2013): 137–59.

75. E. Miron-Spektor, A. Ingram, J. Keller, W. K. Smith, and M. W. Lewis, "Microfoundations of Organizational Paradox: The Problem Is How We Think About the Problem," *Academy of Management Journal* 61, no. 1 (2018): 26–45.

76. See, for instance, G. T. Fairhurst, W. K. Smith, S. G. Banghart, M. W. Lewis, L. L. Putnam, S. Raisch, and J. Schad, "Diverging and Converging: Integrative Insights on a Paradox Meta-Perspective," *The Academy of Management Annals* 10, no. 1 (2016): 173–82.

77. M. Pina e Cunha, E. Gomes, K. Mellahi, A. S. Miner, and A. Rego, "Strategic Agility Through Improvisational Capabilities: Implications for a Paradox-Sensitive HRM," *Human Resource Management Review* (in press); D. A. Waldman and D. E. Bowen, "Learning to Be a Paradox-Savvy Leader," *Academy of Management Perspectives* 30, no. 3 (2016): 316–27; Y. Zhang and Y.-L. Han, "Paradoxical Leader Behavior in Long-Term Corporate Development: Antecedents and Consequences," *Organizational Behavior and Human Decision Processes* 155 (2019): 42–54; Y. Zhang, D. A. Waldman, Y. Han, and X. Li, "Paradoxical Leader Behaviors in People Management: Antecedents and Consequences," *Academy of Management Journal* 58, no. 2 (2015): 538–66.

78. D. J. Sleesman, "Pushing Through the Tension While Stuck in the Mud: Paradox Mindset and Escalation of Commitment," *Organizational Behavior and Human Decision Processes* 155 (2019): 83–96.

79. N. Anderson, K. Potočnik, and J. Zhou, "Innovation and Creativity in Organizations: A State-of-the-Science Review, Prospective Commentary, and Guiding Framework," *Journal of Management* 40, no. 5 (2014): 1297–333; G. P. Pisano, "You Need an Innovation Strategy," *Harvard Business Review* (June 2015): 44–54; and J. Zhou and I. J. Hoever, "Research on Workplace Creativity: A Review and Redirection," *Annual Review of Organizational Psychology and Organizational Behavior* 1 (2014): 333–59.

80. Anderson, Potočnik, and Zhou, "Innovation and Creativity in Organizations"; H. W. Volberda, F. A. J. Van den Bosch, and C. V. Heij, "Management Innovation: Management as Fertile Ground for Innovation," *European Management Review* (2013): 1–15.

81. Anderson, Potočnik, and Zhou, "Innovation and Creativity in Organizations."

82. K. Byron and S. Khazanchi, "Rewards and Creative Performance: A Meta-Analytic Test of Theoretically Derived Hypotheses," *Psychological Bulletin* 138, no. 4 (2012): 809–30; A. Lee, A. Legood, D. Hughes, A. Wei Tian, A. Newman, and C. Knight, "Leadership, Creativity, and Innovation: A Meta-Analytic Review," *European Journal of Work and Organizational Psychology* 29, no. 1 (2020): 1–35.

83. See, for instance, V. Mueller, N. Rosenbusch, and A. Bausch, "Success Patterns of Exploratory and Exploitative Innovation: A Meta-Analysis of the Influence of Institutional Factors," *Journal of Management* 39, no. 6 (2013): 1606–36.

84. U. R. Hülsheger, N. Anderson, and J. F. Salgado, "Team-Level Predictors of Innovation at Work: A Comprehensive Meta-Analysis Spanning Three Decades of Research," *Journal of Applied Psychology* 94, no. 5 (2009): 1128–45; P. Schepers and P. T. van den Berg, "Social Factors of Work-Environment Creativity," *Journal of Business and Psychology* 21, no. 3 (2007): 407–28.

85. M. Erez, A. H. van de Ven, and C. Lee, "Contextualizing Creativity and Innovation Across Cultures," *Journal of Organizational Behavior* 36 (2015): 895–98.

86. R. Y. J. Chua, Y. Roth, and J-F. Lemoine, "The Impact of Culture on Creativity: How Cultural Tightness and Cultural Distance Affect Global Innovation Crowdsourcing Work," *Administrative Science Quarterly* 60, no. 2 (2015): 189–227.

87. J. G. Lu, A. C. Hafenbrack, P. W. Eastwick, D. J. Wang, W. W. Maddux, and A. D. Galinsky, "Going Out of the Box: Close Intercultural Friendships and Romantic Relationships Spark Creativity, Workplace Innovation, and Entrepreneurship," *Journal of Applied Psychology* 102, no. 7 (2017): 1091–108.

88. See, for instance, M. Frese and N. Keith, "Action Errors, Error Management, and Learning in Organizations," *Annual Review of Psychology* 66 (2015): 661–87.

89. R. S. Friedman and J. Förster, "The Effects of Promotion and Prevention Cues on Creativity," *Journal of Personality and Social Psychology* 81, no. 6 (2001): 1001–13.

90. Hülsheger, Anderson, and Salgado, "Team-Level Predictors of Innovation at Work."

91. Ibid.

92. Anderson, Potočnik, and Zhou, "Innovation and Creativity in Organizations."

93. S. Chang, L. Jia, R. Takeuchi, and Y. Cai, "Do High-Commitment Work Systems Affect Creativity? A Multilevel Combinational Approach to Employee Creativity," *Journal of Applied Psychology* 99, no. 4 (2014): 665–80.

94. E. García-Buades, V. Martínez-Tur, S. Ortiz-Bonnín, and J. M. Peiró, "Engaged teams Deliver Better Service Performance in Innovation Climates," *European Journal of Work and Organizational Psychology* 25, no. 4 (2016): 597–612.

95. M. E. Mullins, S. W. J. Kozlowski, N. Schmitt, and A. W. Howell, "The Role of the Idea Champion in Innovation: The Case of the Internet in the Mid-1990s," *Computers in Human Behavior* 24, no. 2 (2008): 451–67.

96. J. M. Howell and C. A. Higgins, "Champions of Technological Innovation," *Administrative Science Quarterly* 35 (1990): 317–41.

97. K. J. Jansen, A. J. Shipp, and J. H. Michael, "Champions, Converters, Doubters, and Defectors: The Impact of Shifting Perceptions on Momentum for Change," *Personnel Psychology* 69 (2016): 673–707.

98. C. Y. Murnieks, E. Mosakowski, and M. S. Cardon, "Pathways of Passion: Identity Centrality, Passion, and Behavior among Entrepreneurs," *Journal of Management* 40, no. 6 (2014): 1583–1606.

99. S. C. Parker, "Intrapreneurship or Entrepreneurship?" *Journal of Business Venturing* 26, no. 1 (2011): 19–34.

100. M. Č, M. Jaklič, and M. Škerlavaj, "Decoupling Management and Technological Innovations: Resolving the Individualism-Collectivism Controversy," *Journal of International Management* 19, no. 2 (2013): 103–117.

101. P. M. Senge, *The Fifth Discipline: The Art & Practice of the Learning Organization* (2nd ed.) (New York, NY: Random House, 2006); V. I. Sessa and M. London, *Continuous Learning in Organizations: Individual, Group, and Organizational Perspectives* (Mahwah, NJ: Lawrence Erlbaum, 2006); and J. H. Song and T. J. Chermack, "A Theoretical Approach to the Organizational Knowledge Formation Process: Integrating Concepts of Individual Learning and Learning Organization Culture," *Human Resource Development Review* 7, no. 4 (2008): 424–42.

102. J. Kim, T. Egan, and H. Tolson, "Examining the Dimensions of the Learning Organization Questionnaire: A Review and Critique of Research Utilizing the DLOQ," *Human Resource Development Review* 14, no. 1 (2015): 91–112.

103. Senge, *The Fifth Discipline.*

104. A. Michel and M. G. González-Morales, "Reactions to Organizational Change: An Integrated Model of Health Predictors, Intervening Variables, and Outcomes," in S. Oreg, A. Michel, and R. T. By (eds.), *The Psychology of Organizational Change: Viewing Change From the Employee's Perspective* (New York, NY: Cambridge University Press, 2013).

105. D. Meinert, "Wings of Change," HR Magazine (November 2012): 30–36; Michel and González-Morales, "Reactions to Organizational Change."

106. M. Healy, "America's Psychologists Want You to Understand How Racism Holds Our Country Back," *Los Angeles Times,* December 21, 2018, https://www.latimes.com/science/sciencenow/la-sci-sn-race-america-psychologists-20181221-story.html

107. E. Gonzalez-Mulé and B. S. Cockburn, "This Job Is (Literally) Killing Me: A Moderated-Mediated Model Linking Work Characteristics to Mortality," *Journal of Applied Psychology* (in press).

108. J. Reynolds, "11 Shocking Stats About Stress at Work and How to Remedy Them," *TINYpulse,* June 28, 2016, https://www.tinypulse.com/blog/stats-stress-in-the-workplace-how-to-remedy-them

109. B. Mirza, "Workplace Stress Hits Three-Year High," *HR Magazine,* April 2012, 15.

110. "Stress in America 2019," *American Psychological Association,* November 2019, https://www.apa.org/news/press/releases/stress/2019/stress-america-2019.pdf

111. P. D. Bliese, J. R. Edwards, and S. Sonnentag, "Stress and Well-being at Work: A Century of Empirical Trends Reflecting Theoretical and Societal Influences," *Journal of Applied Psychology* 102, no. 3 (2017): 389–402; C. L. Cooper, P. J. Dewe, and M. P. O'Driscoll, *Organizational Stress: A Review and Critique of Theory, Research, and Applications* (Thousand Oaks, CA: Sage, 2002); S. Razinskas and M. Hoegl, "A Multilevel Review of Stressor Research in Teams," *Journal of Organizational Behavior* 41 (2020): 185–209; K. M. Richardson, "Managing Employee Stress and Wellness in the New Millennium," *Journal of Occupational Health Psychology* 22, no. 3 (2017): 423–28.

112. Ibid.

113. J. A. LePine, M. A. LePine, and C. L. Jackson, "Challenge and Hindrance Stress: Relationships with Exhaustion, Motivation to Learn, and Learning Performance," *Journal of Applied Psychology* 89, no. 5 (2004): 883–91; K. E. O'Brien and T. A. Beehr, "So Far, So Good: Up to Now, the Challenge-Hindrance Framework Describes a Practical and Accurate Distinction," *Journal of Organizational Behavior* 40 (2019): 962–972; P. E. Spector, "Introduction: The Challenge-Hindrance Stressor Model," *Journal of Organizational Behavior* 40 (2019): 947–948.

114. J. J. Mazzola and R. Disselhorst, "Should We Be 'Challenging' Employees?: A Critical Review and Meta-Analysis of the Challenge- Hindrance Model of Stress," *Journal of Organizational Behavior* 40 (2019): 949–961; N. P. Podsakoff, J. A. LePine, and M. A. LePine, "Differential Challenge-Hindrance Stressor Relationships with Job Attitudes, Turnover Intentions, Turnover, and Withdrawal Behavior: A Meta-Analysis," *Journal of Applied Psychology* 92, no. 2 (2007): 438–54.

115. E. R. Crawford, J. A. LePine, and B. L. Rich, "Linking Job Demands and Resources to Employee Engagement and Burnout: A Theoretical Extension and Meta-Analytic Test," *Journal of Applied Psychology* 95, no. 5 (2010): 834–48; J. A. LePine, N. P. Podsakoff, and M. A. LePine, "A Meta-Analytic Test of the Challenge Stressor-Hindrance Stressor Framework: An Explanation for Inconsistent Relationships Among Stressors and Performance," *Academy of Management Journal* 48, no. 5 (2005): 764–75; C. C. Rosen, N. Dimotakis, M. S. Cole, S. G. Taylor, L. S. Simon, T. A. Smith, and C. S. Reina, "When Challenges Hinder: An Investigation of When and How Challenge Stressors Impact Employee Outcomes," *Journal of Applied Psychology* (in press).

116. S. Clarke, "The Effect of Challenge and Hindrance Stressors on Safety Behavior and Safety Outcomes: A Meta-Analysis," *Journal of Occupational Health Psychology* 17, no. 4 (2012): 387–97; LePine, Podsakoff, and LePine, "A Meta-Analytic Test of the Challenge Stressor-Hindrance Stressor Framework"; Podsakoff, LePine, and LePine, "Differential Challenge-Hindrance Stressor Relationships with Job Attitudes, Turnover Intentions, Turnover, and Withdrawal Behavior."

117. R. Prem, S. Ohly, B. Kubicek, and C. Korunka, "Thriving on Challenge Stressors? Exploring Time Pressure and Learning Demands as Antecedents of Thriving at Work," *Journal of Organizational Behavior* 38, no. 1 (2017): 108–23.

118. M. Kronenwett and T. Rigotti, "When Do You Face a Challenge? How Unnecessary Tasks Block the Challenging Potential of Time Pressure and Emotional Demands," *Journal of Occupational Health Psychology* 24, no. 5 (2019): 512–26.

119. M. R. Tuckey, B. J. Searle, C. M. Boyd, A. H. Winefield, and H. R. Winefield, "Hindrances Are Not Threats: Advancing the Multidimensionality of Work Stress," *Journal of Occupational Health Psychology* 20, no. 2 (2015): 131–47.

120. K. A. French, T. D. Allen, and T. G. Henderson, "Challenge and Hindrance Stressors and Metabolic Risk Factors," *Journal of Occupational Health Psychology* 24, no. 3 (2019): 307–21.

121. See, for instance, A. B. Bakker and E. Demerouti, "Job Demands–Resources Theory: Taking Stock and Looking Forward," *Journal of Occupational Health Psychology* 22, no. 3 (2017): 273–85; A. B. Bakker, E. Demerouti, and A. I. Sanz-Vergel, "Burnout and Work Engagement: The JD–R Approach," *Annual Review of Organizational Psychology and Organizational Behavior* 1 (2014): 389–411.

122. See, for instance, M. Mathieu, K. J. Eschleman, and D. Cheng, "Meta-Analytic and Multiwave Comparison of Emotional Support and Instrumental Support in the Workplace," *Journal of Occupational Health Psychology* 24, no. 3 (2019): 387–409.

123. G. M. Alarcon, "A Meta-Analysis of Burnout With Job Demands, Resources, and Attitudes," *Journal of Vocational Behavior* 79, no. 2 (2011): 549–62; Bakker and Demerouti, "Job Demands-Resources Theory"; Crawford, LePine, and Rich, "Linking Job Demands and Resources to Employee Engagement and Burnout."

124. D. C. Ganster and C. C. Rosen, "Work Stress and Employee Health: A Multidisciplinary Review," *Journal of Management* 39, no. 5 (2013): 1085–122.

125. P. Sterling, "Allostasis: A Model of Predictive Regulation," *Physiology & Behavior* 106, no. 1 (2012): 5–15.

126. A. E. Rafferty and M. A. Griffin, "Perceptions of Organizational Change: A Stress and Coping Perspective," *Journal of Applied Psychology* 71, no. 5 (2007): 1154–62; K. Starcke and M. Brand, "Effects of Stress on Decisions Under Uncertainty: A Meta-Analysis," *Psychological Bulletin* 142, no. 9 (2016): 909–33.

127. A. Waytz and M. I. Norton, "Botsourcing and Outsourcing: Robot, British, Chinese, and German Workers Are for Thinking—Not Feeling—Jobs," *Emotion* 14, no. 2 (2014): 434–44.

128. Ibid.

129. R. Ilies, N. Dimotakis, and I. E. De Pater, "Psychological and Physiological Reactions to High Workloads: Implications for Well-Being," *Personnel Psychology* 63, no. 2 (2010): 407–36; A. B. Bakker, E. Demerouti, and A. I. Sanz-Vergel, "Burnout and Work Engagement: The JD–R Approach," *Annual Review of Organizational Psychology and Organizational Behavior* 1 (2014): 389–411.

130. T. L. Smith-Jackson and K. W. Klein, "Open-Plan Offices: Task Performance and Mental Workload," *Journal of Environmental Psychology* 29, no. 2 (2009): 279–89.

131. M. A. Griffin and S. Clarke, "Stress and Well-Being at Work," in S. Zedeck (ed.), *APA Handbook of Industrial and Organizational Psychology: Maintaining, Expanding, and Contracting the Organization* (vol. 3) (Washington, DC: American Psychological Association, 2011): 359–97.

132. C. Fritz and S. Sonnentag, "Antecedents of Day-Level Proactive Behavior: A Look at Job Stressors and Positive Affect during the Workday," *Journal of Management* 35, no. 1 (2009): 94–111.

133. N. A. Bowling and T. A. Beehr, "Workplace Harassment From the Victim's Perspective: A Theoretical Model and Meta-Analysis," *Journal of Applied Psychology* 91, no. 5 (2006): 998–1012; P. Priscilla Lui and L. Quezada, "Associations Between Microaggression and Adjustment Outcomes: A Meta-Analytic and Narrative Review," *Psychological Bulletin* 145, no. 1 (2019): 45–78; M. B. Nielsen and S. Einarsen, "Outcomes of Exposure to Workplace Bullying: A Meta-Analytic Review," *Work & Stress* 26, no. 4 (2012): 309–32; and C. R. Willness, P. Steel, and K. Lee, "A Meta-Analysis of the Antecedents and Consequences of Workplace Sexual Harassment," *Personnel Psychology* 60, no. 1 (2007): 127–62.

134. L. Yang, J. Bauer, R. E. Johnson, M. W. Groer, and K. Salomon, "Physiological Mechanisms That Underlie the Effects of Interactional Unfairness on Deviant Behavior: The Role of Cortisol Activity," *Journal of Applied Psychology* 99, no. 2 (2014): 310–21.

135. M. T. Schmitt, N. R. Branscombe, T. Postmes, and A. Garcia, "The Consequences of Perceived Discrimination for Psychological Well-Being: A Meta-Analytic Review," *Psychological Bulletin* 140, no. 4 (2014): 921–948.

136. C. Nohe, L. L. Meier, K. Sonntag, and A. Michel, "The Chicken or the Egg? A Meta-Analysis of Panel Studies of the Relationship Between Work-Family Conflict and Strain." *Journal of Applied Psychology* 100, no. 2 (2015): 522–36.

137. B. Litwiller, L. A. Snyder, W. D. Taylor, and L. M. Steele, "The Relationship Between Sleep and Work: A Meta-Analysis," *Journal of Applied Psychology* 102, no. 4 (2017): 682–99.

138. "Stress in America: Paying With Our Health," *American Psychological Association*, February 4, 2015, http://www.apa .org/news/press/releases/stress/2014/stress-report.pdf.

139. F. T. Amstad, L. L. Meier, U. Fasel, A. Elfering, and N. K. Semmer, "A Meta-Analysis of Work-Family Conflict and Various Outcomes With a Special Emphasis on Cross-Domain Versus Matching-Domain Relations," *Journal of Occupational Health Psychology* 16, no. 2 (2011): 151–69.

140. Nohe et al., "The Chicken or the Egg?"

141. "Stress in America."

142. M. T. Ford, R. A. Matthews, J. D. Wooldridge, V. Mishra, U. M. Kakar, and S. R. Strahan, "How Do Occupational Stressor-Strain Effects Vary With Time? A Review and Meta-Analysis of the Relevance of Time Lags in Longitudinal Studies," *Work & Stress* 28, no. 1 (2014): 9–30; and Q. Hu, W. B. Schaufeli, and T. W. Taris, "The Job Demands–Resources Model: An Analysis of Additive and Joint Effects of Demands and Resources," *Journal of Vocational Behavior* 79, no. 1 (2011): 181–90.

143. C. A. Demsky, C. Fritz, L. B. Hammer, and A. E. Black, "Workplace Incivility and Employee Sleep: The Role of Rumination and Recovery Experiences," *Journal of Occupational Health Psychology* 24, no.2 (2019): 228–40; Y. Park and S. Kim, "Customer Mistreatment Harms Nightly Sleep and Next-Morning Recovery: Job Control and Recovery Self-Efficacy as Cross-Level Moderators," *Journal of Occupational Health Psychology* 24, no.2 (2019): 256–69.

144. E. Bruehlman-Senecal and O. Ayduk, "This Too Shall Pass: Temporal Distance and the Regulation of Emotional Distress," *Journal of Personality and Social Psychology* 108, no. 2 (2015): 354–75.

145. Crawford, LePine, and Rich, "Linking Job Demands and Resources to Employee Engagement and Burnout."

146. See J. B. Halbesleben, "Sources of Social Support and Burnout: A Meta-Analytic Test of the Conservation of Resources Model," *Journal of Applied Psychology* 91, no. 5 (2006): 1134–45; N. Bolger and D. Amarel, "Effects of Social Support Visibility on Adjustment to Stress: Experimental Evidence," *Journal of Applied Psychology* 92, no. 3 (2007): 458–75; C. Fernet, M. Gagné, and S. Austin, "When Does Quality of Relationships with Coworkers Predict Burnout Over Time? The Moderating Role of Work Motivation," *Journal of Organizational Behavior* 31, no. 8 (2010): 1163–80.

147. Mathieu et al., "Meta-Analytic and Multiwave Comparison of Emotional Support and Instrumental Support in the Workplace."

148. See, for instance, B. W. Swider and R. D. Zimmerman, "Born to Burn-out: A Meta-Analytic Path Model of Personality, Job Burnout, and Work Outcomes," *Journal of Vocational Behavior* 76, no. 3 (2010): 487–506; Q. Wang, N. A. Bowling, and K. J. Eschleman, "A Meta-Analytic Examination of Work and General Locus of Control," *Journal of Applied Psychology* 95, no. 4 (2010): 761–68.

149. See, for example, C. M. Middeldorp, D. C. Cath, A. L. Beem, G. Willemsen, and D. I. Boomsma, "Life Events, Anxious Depression, and Personality: A Prospective and Genetic Study," *Psychological Medicine* 38, no. 11 (2008): 1557–65; A. A. Uliaszek et al. "The Role of Neuroticism and Extraversion in the Stress-Anxiety and Stress-Depression Relationships," *Anxiety, Stress, and Coping* 23, no. 4 (2010): 363–81.

150. J. D. Kammeyer-Mueller, T. A. Judge, and B. A. Scott, "The Role of Core Self-Evaluations in the Coping Process," *Journal of Applied Psychology* 94, no. 1 (2009): 177–95.

151. For a review, see M. A. Clark, J. S. Michel, L. Zhdanova, S. Y Pui, and B. B. Baltes, "All Work and No Play? A Meta-Analytic Examination of the Correlates and Outcomes of Workaholism," *Journal of Management* 42, no. 7 (2016): 1836–73.

152. C. Liu, P. E. Spector, and L. Shi, "Cross-National Job Stress: A Quantitative and Qualitative Study," *Journal of Organizational Behavior* 28, no. 2 (2007): 209–39.

153. P. E. Spector et al., "Cross National Differences in Relationships of Work Demands, Job Satisfaction, and Turnover Intention With Work-Family Conflict," *Personnel Psychology* 60, no. 4 (2007): 805–35.

154. P. J. Gianaros and T. D. Wager, "Brain-Body Pathways Linking Psychological Stress and Physical Health," *Current Directions in Psychological Science* 24, no. 4 (2015): 313–21.

155. A. E. Nixon, J. J. Mazzola, J. Bauer, J. R. Krueger, and P. E. Spector, "Can Work Make You Sick? A Meta-Analysis of the Relationships Between Job Stressors and Physical Symptoms," *Work & Stress* 25, no. 1 (2011): 1–22.

156. G. S. Shields, M. A. Sazma, A. M. McCullough, and A. P. Yonelinas, "The Effects of Acute Stress on Episodic Memory: A Meta-Analysis and Integrative Review," *Psychological Bulletin* 143, no. 6 (2017): 636–75.

157. R. Ilies, N. Dimotakis, and I. E. DePater, "Psychological and Physiological Reactions to High Workloads: Implications for Well-Being," *Personnel Psychology* 63, no. 2 (2010): 407–63.

158. D. Örtqvist and J. Wincent, "Prominent Consequences of Role Stress: A Meta-Analytic Review," *International Journal of Stress Management* 13, no. 4 (2006): 399–422.

159. J. J. Hakanen, A. B. Bakker, and M. Jokisaari, "A 35-Year Follow-Up Study on Burnout Among Finnish Employees," *Journal of Occupational Health Psychology* 16 no. 3 (2011): 345–60; E. R. Crawford, J. A. LePine, and B. L. Rich, "Linking Job Demands and Resources to Employee Engagement and Burnout: A Theoretical Extension and Meta-Analytic Test," *Journal of Applied Psychology* 95, no. 5 (2010): 834–48; G. A. Chung-Yan, "The Nonlinear Effects of Job Complexity and Autonomy on Job Satisfaction, Turnover, and Psychological Well-Being," *Journal of Occupational Health Psychology* 15, no. 3 (2010): 237–51.

160. L. L. Meier, N. K. Semmer, A. Elfering, and N. Jacobshagen, "The Double Meaning of Control: Three-Way Interactions between Internal Resources, Job Control, and Stressors at Work," *Journal of Occupational Health Psychology* 13, no. 3 (2008): 244–58.

161. E. M. de Croon, J. K. Sluiter, R. W. B. Blonk, J. P. J. Broersen, and M. H. W. Frings-Dresen, "Stressful Work, Psychological Job Strain, and Turnover: A 2-Year Prospective Cohort Study of Truck Drivers," *Journal of Applied Psychology* 89, no. 3 (2004): 442–54; R. Cropanzano, D. E. Rupp, and Z. S. Byrne, "The Relationship of Emotional Exhaus-

tion to Work Attitudes, Job Performance, and Organizational Citizenship Behaviors," *Journal of Applied Psychology* 88, no. 1 (2003): 160–69; S. Diestel and K. Schmidt, "Costs of Simultaneous Coping With Emotional Dissonance and Self-Control Demands at Work: Results From Two German Samples," *Journal of Applied Psychology* 96, no. 3 (2011): 643–53.

162. S. Gilboa, A. Shirom, Y. Fried, and C. L. Cooper, "A Meta-Analysis of Work Demand Stressors and Job Performance: Examining Main and Moderating Effects," *Personnel Psychology* 61, no. 2 (2008): 227–71.

163. J. C. Wallace, B. D. Edwards, T. Arnold, M. L. Frazier, and D. M. Finch, "Work Stressors, Role-Based Performance, and the Moderating Influence of Organizational Support," *Journal of Applied Psychology* 94, no. 1 (2009): 254–62.

164. K. M. Richardson and H. R. Rothstein, "Effects of Occupational Stress Management Intervention Programs: A Meta-Analysis," *Journal of Occupational Health Psychology* 13, no. 1 (2008): 69–93.

165. Y. Zhang, Y. Zhang, T. W. H. Ng, and S. S. K. Lam, "Promotion- and Prevention-Focused Coping: A Meta-Analytic Examination of Regulatory Strategies in the Work Stress Process," *Journal of Applied Psychology* 104, no. 10 (2019): 1296–1323.

166. A. J. Vanhove, M. N. Herian, A. L. U. Perez, P. D. Harms, and P. B. Lester, "Can Resilience Be Developed at Work? A Meta-Analytic Review of Resilience-Building Programme Effectiveness," *Journal of Occupational and Organizational Psychology* 89 (2016): 278–307.

167. L. T. Eby, T. D. Allen, K. M. Conley, R. L. Williamson, T. G. Henderson, and V. S. Mancini, "Mindfulness-Based Training Interventions for Employees: A Qualitative Review of the Literature," *Human Resource Management Review* 29 (2019): 156-178; C. Kröll, P. Doebler, and S. Nüesch, "Meta-Analytic Evidence of the Effectiveness of Stress Management at Work," *European Journal of Work and Organizational Psychology* 26, no. 5 (2017): 677–93; S. Sonnentag, L. Venz, and A. Casper, "Advances in Recovery Research: What Have We Learned? What Should be Done Next?," *Journal of Occupational Health Psychology* 22, no. 3 (2017): 365–80; M. Virgili, "Mindfulness-Based Interventions Reduce Psychological Distress in Working Adults: A Meta-Analysis of Intervention Studies," *Mindfulness* 6, no. 2 (2015): 326–37.

168. Y. Zhang, Y. Zhang, T. W. H. Ng, and S. S. K. Lam, "Promotion- and Prevention-focused Coping: A Meta-Analytic Examination of Regulatory Strategies in the Work Stress Process," *Journal of Applied Psychology* 104, no. 10 (2019): 1296–1323.

169. R. W. Renn, D. G. Allen, and T. M. Huning, "Empirical Examination of Individual-Level Personality-Based Theory of Self-Management Failure," *Journal of Organizational Behavior* 32, no. 1 (2011): 25–43; P. Gröpel and P. Steel, "A Mega-Trial Investigation of Goal Setting, Interest Enhancement, and Energy on Procrastination," *Personality and Individual Differences* 45, no. 5 (2008): 406–11.

170. J. H. Riskind and E. Calvete, "Anxiety and the Dynamic Self as Defined by the Prospection and Mental Simulation of Looming Future Threats," *Journal of Personality* 88 (2020): 31–44; R. E. White, M. M. Kuehn, A. L. Duckworth, E. Kross, and Ö. Ayduk, "Focusing on the Future Self From Afar: Self-Distancing From Future Stressors Facilitates Adaptive Coping," *Emotion* 19, no. 5 (2019): 903–16.

171. E. E. Bernstein, J. E. Curtiss, G. W. Y. Wu, P. J. Barreira, and R. J. McNally, "Exercise and Emotion Dynamics: An Experience Sampling Study," *Emotion* 19, no. 4 (2019): 637–44; Sonnentag, Venz, and Casper, "Advances in Recovery Research"; M. L. M. van Hooff, R. M. Benthem de Grave, and S. A. E. Geurts, "No Pain, No Gain? Recovery and Strenuousness of Physical Activity," *Journal of Occupational Health Psychology* 24, no. 5 (2019): 499–511.

172. Eby et al., "Mindfulness-Based Training Interventions for Employees"; U. R. Hülsheger, J. W. B. Lang, F. Depenbrock, C. Fehrmann, F.

R. H. Zijlstra, and H. J. E. M. Alberts, "The Power of Presence: The Role of Mindfulness at Work for Daily Levels and Change Trajectories of Psychological Detachment and Sleep Quality," *Journal of Applied Psychology* 99, no. 6 (2014): 1113–28; V. Perciavalle, M. Blandini, P. Fecarotta, A. Buscemi, D. Di Corrado, L. Bertolo . . . and M. Coco, "The Role of Deep Breathing on Stress," *Neurological Sciences* 38, no. 3 (2017): 451–58; R. Q. Wolever, K. J. Bobinet, K. McCabe, E. R. Mackenzie, E. Fekete, C. A. Kusnick, and M. Baime, "Effective and Viable Mind-Body Stress Reduction in the Workplace: A Randomized Controlled Trial," *Journal of Occupational Health Psychology* 17, no. 2 (2012): 246–58.

173. K. M. Richardson and H. R. Rothstein, "Effects of Occupational Stress Management Intervention Programs: A Meta-Analysis," *Journal of Occupational Health Psychology* 13, no. 1 (2008): 69–93.

174. L. S. Sharman, G. A. Dingle, A. J. J. M. Vingerhoets, and E. J. Vanman, "Using Crying to Cope: Physiological Responses to Stress Following Tears of Sadness," *Emotion* (in press).

175. S. Reddy, "Doctor's Orders: 20 Minutes of Meditation Twice a Day," *The Wall Street Journal*, April 15, 2013, https://www .wsj.com/articles/SB10001424127887324345804578424863782143682

176. V. C. Hahn, C. Binnewies, S. Sonnentag, and E. J. Mojza, "Learning How to Recover from Job Stress: Effects of a Recovery Training Program on Recovery, Recovery-Related Self-Efficacy, and Well-Being," *Journal of Occupational Health Psychology* 16, no. 2 (2011): 202–16; J. Krajewski, R. Wieland, and M. Sauerland, "Regulating Strain States by Using the Recovery Potential of Lunch Breaks," *Journal of Occupational Health Psychology* 15, no. 2 (2010): 131–39; and M. Sianoja, C. J. Syrek, J. de Bloom, K. Korpela, and U. Kinnunen, "Enhancing Daily Well-Being at Work Through Lunchtime Park Walks and Relaxation Exercises: Recovery Experiences as Mediators," *Journal of Occupational Health Psychology* 23, no. 3 (2018): 428–42.

177. L. Bartlett, A. Martin, A. L. Neil, K. Memish, P. Otahal, M. Kilpatrick, K. Sanderson, "A Systematic Review and Meta-Analysis of Workplace Mindfulness Training Randomized Control Trials," *Journal of Occupational Health Psychology* 24, no.1 (2019): 108-126; Kröll et al., "Meta-Analytic Evidence of the Effectiveness of Stress Management at Work;" L. P. Maricuțoiu, F. A. Sava, and O. Butta, "The Effectiveness of Controlled Interventions on Employees' Burnout: A Meta-Analysis," *Journal of Occupational and Organizational Psychology* 89 (2016): 1–27.

178. S. L. Parker, S. Sonnentag, N. L. Jimmieson, and C. J. Newton, "Relaxation During the Evening and Next-Morning Energy: The Role of hassles, Uplifts, and Heart Rate Variability During Work," *Journal of Occupational Health Psychology* 25, no. 2 (2020): 83–98.

179. I. Brissette, M. F. Scheier, and C. S. Carver, "The Role of Optimism in Social Network Development, Coping, and Psychological Adjustment During a Life Transition," *Journal of Personality and Social Psychology* 82, no. 1 (2002): 102–11.

180. Y. Kalish, G. Luria, S. Toker, and M. Westman, "Till Stress Do Us Part: On the Interplay Between Perceived Stress and Communication Network Dynamics," *Journal of Applied Psychology* 100, no. 6 (2015): 1737–51.

181. L. K. Kammrath, B. F. Armstrong III, S. P. Lane, M. K. Francis, M. Clifton, K. M. McNab, and O. M. Baumgarten, "What Predicts Who We Approach for Social Support? Tests of the Attachment Figure and Strong Ties Hypotheses," *Journal of Personality and Social Psychol-*

ogy 118, no. 3 (2020): 481–500; Y. Park and C. Fritz, "Spousal Recovery Support, Recovery Experiences, and Life Satisfaction Crossover Among Dual-Earner Couples," *Journal of Applied Psychology* 100, no. 2 (2015): 557–66.

182. Vanhove et al., "Can Resilience Be Developed at Work?

183. P. Miquelon and R. J. Vallerand, "Goal Motives, Well-Being, and Physical Health: Happiness and Self-Realization as Psychological Resources Under Challenge," *Motivation and Emotion* 30, no. 4 (2006): 259–72.

184. A. M. Cianci, H. J. Klein, and G. H. Seijts, "The Effect of Negative Feedback on Tension and Subsequent Performance: The Main and Interactive Effects of Goal Content and Conscientiousness," *Journal of Applied Psychology* 95, no. 4 (2010): 618–30.

185. Cianci, Klein, and Seijts, "The Effect of Negative Feedback on Tension and Subsequent Performance"; S. J. Perry, L. A. Witt, L. M. Penney, and L. Atwater, "The Downside of Goal-Focused Leadership: The Role of Personality in Subordinate Exhaustion," *Journal of Applied Psychology* 95, no. 6 (2010): 1145–53.

186. P. W. Lichtenthaler and A. Fischbach, "A Meta-Analysis of Promotion- and Prevention-Focused Job Crafting," *European Journal of Work and Organizational Psychology* 28, no. 1 (2019): 30–50.

187. M. M. Butts, R. J. Vandenberg, D. M. DeJoy, B. S. Schaffer, and M. G. Wilson, "Individual Reactions to High Involvement Work Processes: Investigating the Role of Empowerment and Perceived Organizational Support," *Journal of Occupational Health Psychology* 14, no. 2 (2009): 122–36.

188. Griffin and Clarke, "Stress and Well-Being at Work."

189. L. Shen, "These 19 Great Employers Offer Paid Sabbaticals," *Fortune*, March 7, 2016, http://fortune.com/2016/03/07/best-companies-to-work-for-sabbaticals/

190. O. B. Davidson, D. Eden, M. Westman, Y. Cohen-Charash, L. B. Hammer, A. N. Kluger, . . . and P. E. Spector, "Sabbatical Leave: Who Gains and How Much?," *Journal of Applied Psychology* 95, no. 5 (2010): 953–64.

191. H. De La Torre and R. Goetzel, "How to Design a Corporate Wellness Plan That Actually Works," *Harvard Business Review*, March 31, 2016, https://hbr.org/2016/03/how-to-design-a-corporate-wellness-plan-that-actually-works; M. R. Frone, *Alcohol and Illicit Drug Use in the Workforce and Workplace* (Washington, DC: American Psychological Association, 2013); A. Kohll, "8 Things You Need to Know About Employee Wellness Programs," *Forbes*, April 21, 2016, https://www.forbes.com/sites/alankohll/2016/04/21/8-things-you-need-to-know-about-employee-wellness-programs/#38054a8840a3; C. J. Ott-Holland, W. J. Shepherd, and A. Marie Ryan, "Examining Wellness Programs Over Time: Predicting Participation and Workplace Outcomes," *Journal of Occupational Health Psychology* 24, no. 1 (2019): 163-179.

192. K. M. Richardson and H. R. Rothstein, "Effects of Occupational Stress Management Intervention Programs: A Meta-Analysis."

193. L. L. Berry, A. M. Mirabito, and W. B. Baun, "What's the Hard Return on Employee Wellness Programs?" *Harvard Business Review,* December 2010, https://hbr.org/2010/12/whats-the-hard-return-on-employee-wellness-programs

194. ITA Group, "Workplace Wellness Program Statistics You Need to Know," November 16, 2018, https://www.itagroup .com/insights/workplace-wellness-programs

195. Ott-Holland et al., "Examining Wellness Programs Over Time."

GLOSSARY

ability An individual's capacity to perform the various tasks in a job.

accommodating The willingness of one party in a conflict to place the negotiation partner's interests above their own.

action research A change process based on the systematic collection of data and the selection of a change action based on what the analyzed data indicate.

affect A term used to describe a broad range of feelings that people experience.

affect intensity Individual differences in the strength with which individuals experience their emotions.

affective component The emotional or feeling segment of an attitude.

affective events theory (AET) A model that suggests that workplace events cause emotional reactions on the part of employees, which then influence workplace attitudes and behaviors.

agreeableness A personality dimension that describes someone who is good natured, cooperative, and trusting.

allostasis Working to change behavior and attitudes to find stability.

anchoring bias A tendency to fixate on initial information, from which one then fails to adequately adjust for subsequent information.

anthropology The study of societies to learn about human beings and their activities.

appreciative inquiry An approach that seeks to identify the unique qualities and special strengths of an organization, which can then be built on to improve performance.

arbitrator A third party to a negotiation who has the authority to dictate an agreement.

attitudes Evaluative statements or judgments concerning objects, people, or events.

attribution theory An attempt to explain the ways we judge people differently depending on the meaning we attribute to a behavior, such as determining whether an individual's behavior is internally or externally caused.

attribution theory of leadership A leadership theory that states that leadership is merely an attribution that people make about other individuals.

authentic leaders Leaders who are self-aware and are anchored by their mission, consider others' opinions and all relevant information before acting, and display their true selves when interacting with employees.

authority The rights inherent in a managerial position to give orders and to expect the orders to be obeyed.

automatic processing A relatively superficial consideration of evidence and information that takes little time or effort and makes use of heuristics.

autonomy The degree to which a job provides substantial freedom and discretion to the individual in scheduling the work and in determining the procedures to be used in carrying it out.

availability bias The tendency for people to base their judgments on information that is readily available to them.

avoiding The desire to withdraw from or suppress a conflict.

BATNA The best alternative to a negotiated agreement; the least the individual should accept.

behavioral component An intention to behave in a certain way toward someone or something.

behavioral ethics Analyzing how people behave when confronted with ethical dilemmas.

behavioral theories of leadership Theories proposing that specific behaviors differentiate leaders from nonleaders.

behaviorism A theory that behavior follows stimuli in a relatively unthinking manner.

big five model A personality model that proposes five basic dimensions encompass most of the differences in human personality.

biographical characteristics Personal characteristics—such as age, gender, race, and length of tenure—that are objective and easily obtained from personnel records. These characteristics are representative of surface-level diversity.

bonus A pay plan that rewards employees for recent performance rather than historical performance.

boundary spanning When individuals form relationships outside their formally assigned groups.

bounded rationality A simplified process of making decisions by perceiving and interpreting the essential features of problems without capturing their complexity.

brainstorming An idea-generation process that specifically encourages any and all alternatives while withholding any criticism of those alternatives.

bureaucracy An organization structure with highly routine operating tasks achieved through specialization, very formalized rules and regulations, departmentalization, centralized authority, narrow spans of control, and decision making that follows the chain of command.

centralization The degree to which decision making is concentrated at a single point in an organization.

chain of command The unbroken line of authority that extends from the top of the organization to the lowest echelon and clarifies who reports to whom.

challenge stressors Stressors associated with workload, pressure to complete tasks, and time urgency.

change When things become different from the way they were.

change agents People who act as catalysts and assume the responsibility for managing change activities.

channel richness The amount of information that can be transmitted during a communication episode.

charismatic leadership theory A leadership theory that states that followers make attributions of heroic or extraordinary leadership abilities when they observe certain behaviors.

circular structure An organization structure in which executives are at the center, spreading their vision outward in rings grouped by function (managers, then specialists, then workers).

coercive power A power base that is dependent on fear of the negative results from failing to comply.

cognitive component The opinion or belief segment of an attitude.

cognitive dissonance Any incompatibility between two or more attitudes or between behavior and attitudes.

cognitive evaluation theory A sub-theory of self-determination theory in which extrinsic rewards for behavior tend to decrease the overall level of motivation, if the rewards are seen as controlling or reduce their sense of competence.

cohesiveness The shared bond driving group members to work together and to stay in the group.

collaborating A situation in which the parties in a conflict each desires to satisfy fully the concerns of all parties.

collectivism A national culture attribute that describes a tight social framework in which people expect others in groups of which they are a part to look after them and protect them. Collectivistic countries/cultures are those in which people see themselves as interdependent and seek community and group goals. Collectivistic values are found in Asia, Africa, and South America, for example.

communication The transfer and the understanding of meaning.

communication apprehension Undue tension and anxiety about oral communication, written communication, or both.

communication process The steps between a source and a receiver that result in the transfer and understanding of meaning.

competing A desire to satisfy one's interests, regardless of the impact on the other party to the conflict.

compromising A situation in which each party to a conflict is willing to give up something.

conciliator A trusted third party who provides an informal communication link between the negotiator and the negotiation partner.

confirmation bias The tendency to seek out information that reaffirms past choices and current views, and to discount information that challenges them.

conflict A process that begins when one party perceives that another party has negatively affected, or is about to negatively affect, something that the first party cares about.

conflict management The use of resolution and stimulation techniques to achieve the desired level of conflict.

conformity The adjustment of one's behavior to align with the norms of the group.

conscientiousness A personality dimension that describes someone who is responsible, dependable, persistent, and organized.

consideration The extent to which a leader is likely to have job relationships characterized by mutual trust, respect for subordinates' ideas, and regard for their feelings.

contingency variables Situational factors or variables that moderate the relationship between two or more variables.

contrast effect Evaluation of a person's characteristics that is affected by comparisons with other people recently encountered who rank higher or lower on the same characteristics.

controlled processing A detailed consideration of evidence and information relying on facts, figures, and logic.

core self-evaluation (CSE) Believing in one's inner worth and basic competence.

core values The primary or dominant values that are accepted throughout the organization.

corporate social responsibility (CSR) An organization's self-regulated actions to benefit society or the environment beyond what is required by law.

cost-minimization strategy A strategy that emphasizes tight cost controls, avoidance of unnecessary innovation or marketing expenses, and price cutting.

counterproductive work behavior (CWB) Actions that actively damage the organization, including stealing, behaving aggressively toward coworkers, or being late or absent.

creativity The ability to produce novel and useful ideas.

cross-functional teams Employees from about the same hierarchical level, but from different work areas, who come together to accomplish a task.

dark triad A constellation of negative personality traits consisting of Machiavellianism, narcissism, and psychopathy.

decisions Choices made from among two or more alternatives.

deep acting Trying to modify one's true inner feelings based on display rules.

deep-level diversity Differences in values, personality, and work preferences that become progressively more important for determining similarity as people get to know one another better.

defensive behaviors Reactive and protective behaviors to avoid action, blame, or change.

demands Responsibilities, pressures, obligations, and even uncertainties that individuals face in the workplace.

demography The degree to which members of a work unit share a common demographic attribute, such as age, sex, race, educational level, or length of service in an organization.

deonance A perspective in which ethical decisions are made because you "ought to" in order to be consistent with moral norms, principles, standards, rules, or laws.

departmentalization The basis by which jobs in an organization are grouped together.

dependence The extent to which people depend or rely upon a powerful person.

deviant workplace behavior Voluntary behavior that violates significant organizational norms and, in so doing, threatens the well-being of the organization or its members. Also called antisocial behavior or workplace incivility.

discrimination Noting a difference between things; often we refer to unfair discrimination, which means making judgments about individuals based on stereotypes regarding their demographic group.

displayed emotions Emotions that are organizationally required and considered appropriate in a given job.

distributive bargaining Negotiation that seeks to divide up a fixed amount of resources; a win–lose situation.

distributive justice Perceived fairness of the amount and allocation of rewards among individuals.

diversity The extent to which members of a group are similar to, or different from, one another.

diversity management The process and programs by which managers make everyone more aware of and sensitive to the needs and differences of others.

dominant culture A culture that expresses the core values that are shared by most of the organization's members.

downsizing A systematic effort to make an organization leaner by closing locations, reducing staff, or selling off business units that do not add value.

driving forces Forces that direct behavior away from the status quo.

dyadic conflict Conflict that occurs between two people.

dysfunctional conflict Conflict that hinders group performance.

effectiveness The degree to which an organization meets the needs of its clientele or customers.

efficiency The degree to which an organization can achieve its ends at a low cost.

emotion regulation The process of identifying and modifying felt emotions.

emotional contagion The process by which people's emotions are caused by the emotions of others.

emotional dissonance Inconsistencies between the emotions people feel and the emotions they project.

emotional intelligence (EI) The ability to detect and to manage emotional cues and information.

emotional labor An employee's organizationally desired emotions during interpersonal transactions at work.

emotional stability A personality dimension that characterizes someone as calm, self-confident, and secure (positive) versus nervous, anxious, and insecure (negative).

emotions Intense, discrete, and short-lived feeling experiences that are often caused by a specific event.

employee engagement The degree of enthusiasm an employee feels for the job.

employee involvement and participation (EIP) A participative process that uses the input of employees to increase employee commitment to organizational success.

employee recognition program A plan to encourage specific employee behaviors by formally appreciating specific employee contributions.

employee stock ownership plan (ESOP) A company-established benefits plan in which employees acquire stock, often at below-market prices, as part of their benefits.

encounter stage The stage in the socialization process in which a new employee sees what the organization is really like and confronts the possibility that expectations and reality may diverge.

environment Forces outside an organization that potentially affect the organization's structure.

equity theory A theory stating that individuals compare their job inputs and outcomes with those of others and then respond to eliminate any inequities.

escalation of commitment An increased commitment to a previous decision, despite negative information.

ethical culture The shared concept of right and wrong behavior in the workplace that reflects the true values of the organization and shapes the ethical decision making of its members.

ethical dilemmas and ethical choices Situations in which individuals are required to define right and wrong conduct.

evidence-based management (EBM) The basing of managerial decisions on the best available scientific evidence.

exit Dissatisfaction expressed through behavior directed toward leaving the organization.

expectancy The probability perceived by the individual that exerting a given amount of effort will lead to performance.

expectancy theory A theory that the strength of a tendency to act in a certain way depends on the strength of an expectation that the act will be followed by a given outcome and on the attractiveness of that outcome to the individual.

expert power Power based in influence through possessing expertise, special skills, or knowledge.

extraversion A personality dimension describing someone who is sociable, gregarious, and assertive.

faultlines The perceived divisions that split groups into two or more subgroups based on individual differences such as sex, race, age, work experience, language, and education.

feedback The degree to which carrying out the work activities required by a job results in the individual obtaining direct and clear information about the effectiveness of their performance.

felt conflict Emotional involvement in a conflict that creates anxiety, tension, frustration, or hostility.

felt emotions An individual's actual emotions.

femininity A national culture attribute that indicates little differentiation between male and female roles; a high rating indicates that women are treated as the equals of men in all aspects of the society.

Fiedler contingency model The theory that effective groups depend on a proper match between a leader's style of interacting with subordinates and the degree to which the situation gives control and influence to the leader.

filtering The manipulation of information so that it will be seen more favorably by the receiver.

fixed pie The belief that there is only a set amount of goods or services to be divvied up between the parties.

flexible benefits A benefits plan that allows each employee to put together a benefits package individually tailored to their own needs and situation.

flextime Flexible work hours.

formal channels Communication channels established by an organization to transmit messages related to the professional activities of members.

formal group A designated workgroup defined by an organization's structure.

formalization The degree to which a job is standardized.

full range of leadership model A model that depicts seven leadership styles on a continuum: laissez-faire, management by exception, contingent reward leadership, individualized consideration, intellectual stimulation, inspirational motivation, and idealized influence.

functional conflict Conflict that supports the goals of the group and improves its performance.

fundamental attribution error The tendency to underestimate the influence of external factors and overestimate the influence of internal factors when making judgments about the behavior of others.

general mental ability (GMA) An overall factor of intelligence, as suggested by the positive correlations among specific intellectual ability dimensions.

globalization The process in which worldwide integration and interdependence is promoted across national borders.

goal-setting theory A theory that specific and difficult goals, with feedback, lead to higher performance.

grapevine An organization's informal communication network.

group Two or more individuals, interacting and interdependent, who have come together to achieve certain objectives.

group cohesion The extent to which members of a group support and validate one another while at work.

group functioning The quantity and quality of a group's work output.

groupshift A change between a group's decision and an individual decision that a member within the group would make; the shift can be toward either conservatism or greater risk, but it generally is toward a more extreme version of the group's original position.

groupthink A phenomenon in which the norm for consensus overrides the realistic appraisal of alternative courses of action.

halo effect The tendency to draw a general impression about an individual based on a single characteristic.

hierarchy of needs Abraham Maslow's hierarchy of five needs—physiological, safety, social, esteem, and self-actualization—in which, as each need is well-satisfied, the next need becomes dominant.

high-context cultures Cultures that rely heavily on nonverbal and subtle situational cues in communication.

hindrance stressors Stressors that keep you from reaching your goals (for example, red tape, office politics, confusion over job responsibilities).

hindsight bias The tendency to believe falsely, after an outcome of an event is known, that one would have accurately predicted that outcome.

horns effect The tendency to draw a negative general impression about an individual based on a single characteristic.

hygiene factors Factors—such as company policy and administration, supervision, and salary—that, when adequate in a job, placate workers and limit job dissatisfaction.

idea champions Individuals who take an innovation and actively and enthusiastically promote the idea, build support, overcome resistance, and ensure that the idea is implemented.

idea evaluation The process of creative behavior involving the evaluation of potential solutions to problems to identify the best one.

idea generation The process of creative behavior that involves developing possible solutions to a problem from relevant information and knowledge.

illusory correlation The tendency of people to associate two events when in reality there is no connection.

imitation strategy A strategy that seeks to move into new products or new markets only after their viability has already been proven.

impression management (IM) The process by which individuals attempt to control the impression others form of them.

individualism A national culture attribute that describes the degree to which people prefer to act as individuals rather than as members of groups.

influence tactics Ways in which individuals translate power bases into specific actions.

informal channels Communication channels that are created spontaneously and that emerge as responses to individual choices.

informal group A group that is not defined by an organization's structure; such a group appears in response to other needs, such as social clubs or interest groups.

information gathering The stage of creative behavior when possible solutions to a problem incubate in an individual's mind.

information overload A condition in which information inflow exceeds an individual's processing capacity.

informational justice The degree to which employees are provided truthful explanations for decisions.

ingroup The members of a group we belong to. We tend to play favorites with our ingroup.

initiating structure The extent to which leaders define and structure their roles and those of their subordinates in pursuit of goal attainment.

innovation A new idea applied to initiating or improving a product, process, or service.

innovation strategy A strategy that emphasizes the introduction of major new products and services.

inputs Variables like personality, group structure, and organizational culture that lead to processes.

institutionalization A condition that occurs when an organization takes on a life of its own, apart from any of its members, and acquires immortality.

institutions Cultural factors, especially those factors that might not lead to adaptive consequences, that lead many organizations to have similar structures.

instrumentality The degree to which the individual believes performing at a certain level will lead to the attainment of a desired outcome.

instrumental values Preferable modes of behavior or means of achieving one's terminal values.

integrative bargaining Negotiation that seeks one or more settlements that can create a win–win solution.

intellectual abilities The capacity to do mental activities—thinking, reasoning, and problem solving.

intentions Decisions to act in a particular way.

interacting groups Typical groups in which members interact with each other, relying on both verbal and nonverbal communication.

interactional justice Sensitivity to the quality of interpersonal treatment.

intergroup conflict Conflict between different groups or teams.

intergroup development Organizational development efforts to change the attitudes, stereotypes, and perceptions that groups have of each other.

interpersonal justice The degree to which employees are treated with dignity and respect.

interrole conflict A situation in which the expectations of an individual's different, separate groups are in opposition.

intragroup conflict Conflict that occurs within a group or team.

intuition An instinctive feeling not necessarily supported by research.

intuitive decision making An unconscious process created out of distilled experience.

job characteristics model (JCM) A model that proposes that any job can be described in terms of five core job dimensions: skill variety, task identity, task significance, autonomy, and feedback.

job design The way the elements in a job are organized.

job engagement The investment of an employee's physical, cognitive, and emotional energies into job performance.

job enrichment Adding high-level responsibilities to a job to increase intrinsic motivation.

job involvement The degree to which a person identifies with a job, actively participates in it, and considers performance important to their self-worth.

job rotation The periodic shifting of an employee from one task to another.

job satisfaction A positive feeling about one's job resulting from an evaluation of its characteristics.

job sharing An arrangement that allows two or more individuals to split a traditional full-time job.

leader–member exchange (LMX) theory A theory that suggests (1) leaders and followers have unique relationships that vary in quality and (2) these followers comprise ingroups and outgroups; subordinates with ingroup status will likely have higher performance ratings, less turnover, and greater job satisfaction.

leader–member relations The degree of confidence, trust, and respect subordinates have in their leader.

leader-participation model A leadership theory that provides a set of rules to determine the form and amount of participative decision making in different situations.

leadership The ability to influence a group toward the achievement of a vision or set of goals.

learning organization An organization that has developed the continuous capacity to adapt and change.

least preferred coworker (LPC) questionnaire An instrument that measures whether a person is task or relationship oriented.

legitimate power Power based on a person's position in the formal hierarchy of an organization.

long-term orientation A national culture attribute that emphasizes the future, thrift, and persistence.

low-context cultures Cultures that rely heavily on words to convey meaning in communication.

loyalty Dissatisfaction expressed by passively waiting for conditions to improve.

Machiavellianism The degree to which an individual is pragmatic, maintains emotional distance, and believes that ends can justify means.

management by objectives (MBO) A program that encompasses specific goals, participatively set, for an explicit time period and including feedback on goal progress.

masculinity A national culture attribute that describes the extent to which the culture favors traditional masculine work roles of achievement, power, and control. Societal values are characterized by assertiveness and materialism.

material symbols Physical objects, or artifacts, that symbolize values, beliefs, or assumptions inherent in the organization's culture.

matrix structure An organization structure that creates dual lines of authority and combines functional and product departmentalization.

mechanistic model A structure characterized by extensive departmentalization, high formalization, a limited information network, and centralization.

mediator A neutral third party who facilitates a negotiated solution by using reasoning, persuasion, and suggestions for alternatives.

mental models Team members' knowledge and beliefs about how the work gets done by the team.

mentor A senior employee who sponsors and supports a less-experienced employee, called a protégé.

merit-based pay plan A pay plan based on performance appraisal ratings.

metamorphosis stage The stage in the socialization process in which a new employee changes and adjusts to the job, workgroup, and organization.

model An abstraction of reality, a simplified representation of some real-world phenomenon.

moods Feelings that tend to be longer lived and less intense than emotions and that lack a contextual stimulus.

moral emotions Emotions that have moral implications because of our instant judgment of the situation that evokes them.

motivating potential score (MPS) A predictive index that suggests the motivating potential in a job.

motivation The processes that account for an individual's intensity, direction, and persistence of effort toward attaining a goal.

multiteam system A collection of two or more interdependent teams that share a superordinate goal; a team of teams.

Myers–Briggs Type Indicator (MBTI) A personality test that taps four characteristics and classifies people into one of sixteen personality types.

narcissism The tendency to be arrogant, have a grandiose sense of self-importance, require excessive admiration, and have a sense of entitlement.

need for achievement (nAch) The need to excel or achieve to a set of standards.

need for affiliation (nAff) The need to establish friendly and close interpersonal relationships.

need for autonomy The need to feel in control and autonomous at work.

need for cognition A personality trait of individuals depicting the ongoing desire to think and learn.

need for competence The need to feel like we are good at what we do and proud of it.

need for power (nPow) The need to make others behave in a way in which they would not have behaved otherwise.

negative affect A mood dimension that consists of emotions such as nervousness, stress, and anxiety at the high end and relaxation and calmness at the low end.

neglect Dissatisfaction expressed through allowing conditions to worsen.

negotiation A process in which two or more parties exchange goods or services and attempt to agree on the exchange rate for them.

neutralizers Attributes that make it impossible for leader behavior to make any difference to follower outcomes.

nominal group technique A group decision-making method in which individual members meet face to face to pool their judgments in a systematic but independent fashion.

norms Acceptable standards of behavior within a group that are shared by the group's members.

openness to experience A personality dimension that characterizes someone in terms of imagination, artistic sensitivity, and curiosity.

organic model A structure that is flat, uses cross-hierarchical and cross-functional teams, has low formalization, possesses a comprehensive information network, and relies on participative decision making.

organizational behavior A field of study that investigates the impact individuals, groups, and structure have on behavior within organizations, for the purpose of applying such knowledge toward improving an organization's effectiveness.

organizational citizenship behavior (OCB) Discretionary behavior that contributes to the psychological and social environment of the workplace.

organizational climate The shared perceptions organizational members have about their organization and work environment; particularly, the policies, practices, and procedures that are in place.

organizational commitment The degree to which an employee identifies with a particular organization and its goals and wishes to maintain membership in the organization.

organizational culture A system of shared meaning held by members that distinguishes the organization from other organizations. This system is characterized by values, beliefs, and underlying assumptions that serve several purposes.

organizational development (OD) A collection of planned change interventions, built on humanistic–democratic values, that seeks to improve organizational effectiveness and employee well-being.

organizational identification The extent to which employees define themselves by the same characteristics that define one's organization, forming the basis for which attitudes are engendered.

organizational justice An overall perception of what is fair in the workplace, composed of distributive, procedural, informational, and interpersonal justice.

organizational structure The way in which job tasks are formally divided, grouped, and coordinated.

organizational survival   The degree to which an organization is able to exist and grow over the long term.

outcomes   Key factors that are affected by some other variables.

outgroup   The inverse of an ingroup; an outgoup can mean anyone outside the group, but more usually it is an identified other group.

overconfidence bias   A tendency to be overconfident about our own abilities or the abilities of others.

paradox theory   The theory that the key paradox in management is that there is no final optimal status for an organization.

participative management   A process in which subordinates share a significant degree of decision-making power with their immediate superiors.

path–goal theory   A theory that states that it is the leader's job to assist followers by providing the necessary resources to achieve their goals, to ensure that the path to accomplishing these goals is understandable or clear, and to reduce any roadblocks that may be making goal achievement difficult.

perceived conflict   Awareness by one or more parties of the existence of conditions that create opportunities for conflict to arise.

perceived organizational support (POS)   The degree to which employees believe an organization values their contribution and cares about their well-being.

perception   A process by which individuals organize and interpret their sensory impressions in order to give meaning to their environment.

personality   The sum total of ways in which an individual reacts to and interacts with others.

personality traits   Enduring characteristics that describe an individual's behavior.

personality–job fit theory   A theory that identifies six personality types and proposes that the fit between personality type and occupational environment determines satisfaction and turnover.

person–organization fit   A theory that people are attracted to and selected by organizations that match their values and leave when there is no compatibility.

physical abilities   The capacity to do tasks that demand stamina, dexterity, strength, and similar characteristics.

piece-rate pay plan   A pay plan in which workers are paid a fixed sum for each unit of production completed.

planned change   Change activities that are proactive, intentional, and goal oriented.

political behavior   Activities that are not required as part of a person's formal role in the organization but that influence, or attempt to influence, the distribution of advantages and disadvantages within the organization.

political skill   The ability to influence others in such a way as to enhance one's objectives.

position power   Influence derived from one's formal structural position in the organization; includes power to hire, fire, discipline, promote, and give salary increases.

positive affect   A mood dimension that consists of specific positive emotions such as excitement, enthusiasm, and elation at the high end and boredom, sluggishness, and tiredness at the low end.

positive organizational culture   A culture that values building on employee strengths, rewards more than it punishes, and encourages individual vitality and growth.

positive organizational scholarship   An area of OB research that concerns how organizations develop human strengths, foster vitality and resilience, and unlock potential.

positivity offset   The tendency of most individuals to experience a mildly positive mood at zero input (when nothing in particular is going on).

power   The capacity, discretion, and means to enforce one's will over others.

power distance   A national culture attribute that describes the extent to which a society accepts that power in institutions and organizations is distributed unequally.

prearrival stage   The period of learning in the socialization process that occurs before a new employee joins the organization.

prevention focus   A self-regulation strategy that involves striving for goals by fulfilling duties and obligations.

proactive personality   People who identify opportunities, show initiative, take action, and persevere until meaningful change occurs.

problem   A discrepancy between the current state and some desired state.

problem formulation   The stage of creative behavior that involves identifying a problem or opportunity requiring a solution that is as yet unknown.

problem-solving teams   Groups of five to twelve employees from the same department who meet for a few hours each week to discuss ways of improving quality, efficiency, and the work environment.

procedural justice   The perceived fairness of the process used to determine the distribution of rewards.

process conflict   Conflict over how work gets done.

process consultation (PC)   A meeting in which a consultant assists a client in understanding process events with which they must deal and identifying processes that need improvement.

processes   Actions that individuals, groups, and organizations engage in as a result of inputs and that lead to certain outcomes.

productivity   The combination of the effectiveness and efficiency of an organization.

profit-sharing plan   An organization-wide program that distributes compensation based on some established formula designed around a company's profitability.

promotion focus   A self-regulation strategy that involves striving for goals through advancement and accomplishment.

psychological contract   An unwritten agreement between employees and employers that establishes mutual expectations.

psychological empowerment   Employees' belief in the degree to which they affect their work environment, their competence, the meaningfulness of their job, and their perceived autonomy in their work.

psychology   The science that seeks to measure, explain, and sometimes change the behavior of humans and other animals.

psychopathy   The tendency for a lack of concern for others and a lack of guilt or remorse when actions cause harm.

punctuated equilibrium model   A set of phases that temporary groups go through that involve transitions between inertia and activity.

randomness error   The tendency of individuals to believe that they can predict the outcome of random events.

rational   A style of decision making characterized by making consistent, value-maximizing choices within specified constraints.

rational decision-making model   A decision-making model that describes how individuals should behave in order to maximize some outcome.

reference groups   Important groups to which individuals belong or hope to belong, and which adopt norms with which individuals are likely to conform.

referent power Power based on identification with a person who has desirable resources or personal traits.

reflexivity A team characteristic of reflecting on and adjusting their purpose or plan when necessary.

reinforcement theory A theory that behavior is a function of its consequences.

relational job design Constructing jobs so employees see the positive difference they can make in the lives of others directly through their work.

relationship conflict Conflict based on interpersonal relationships.

representative participation A system in which workers participate in organizational decision making through a small group of representative employees.

resources Things within an individual's control that can be used to resolve demands.

restraining forces Forces that hinder movement from the existing equilibrium.

reward power Power based on the ability to distribute rewards that others view as valuable.

risk aversion The tendency to prefer a sure gain of a moderate amount over a riskier outcome, even if the riskier outcome might have a higher expected payoff.

rituals Repetitive sequences of activities that express and reinforce the key values of the organization, which goals are most important, which people are important, and which are expendable.

role A function assumed by someone occupying a given position in a group.

role conflict A situation in which an individual is confronted by divergent role expectations.

role expectations How others believe a person should act in a given situation.

role perception An individual's view of how they are supposed to act in a given situation.

selective perception The tendency to selectively interpret what one sees based on one's interests, background, experience, and attitudes.

self-concordance The degree to which people's reasons for pursuing goals are consistent with their interests and core values.

self-determination theory A meta-theory of motivation at work that is concerned with autonomy, intrinsic motivation, extrinsic motivation, and the satisfaction of psychological work needs.

self-efficacy theory An individual's belief that they are capable of performing a task.

self-managed work teams Groups of ten to fifteen people who autonomously implement solutions and take responsibility for the outcomes (responsibilities normally given to supervisors).

self-monitoring A personality trait that measures an individual's ability to adjust their behavior to external, situational factors.

self-serving bias The tendency for individuals to attribute their own successes to internal factors and put the blame for failures on external factors.

sensitivity training Training that seeks to change behavior through unstructured group interaction.

servant leadership A leadership style marked by going beyond the leader's own self-interest and instead focusing on opportunities to help followers grow and develop.

sexual harassment Any unwanted activity of a sexual nature that affects an individual's employment and creates a hostile work environment.

short-term orientation A national culture attribute that emphasizes the present and accepts change.

simple structure An organization structure characterized by a low degree of departmentalization, wide spans of control, authority centralized in a single person, and little formalization.

situation strength theory A theory indicating that the way personality translates into behavior depends on the strength of the situation.

situational leadership theory (SLT) A contingency theory that focuses on followers' readiness, or the extent to which they are willing and able to accomplish a specific task.

skill variety The degree to which a job requires a variety of activities using different skills or talents.

social identity theory A perspective that considers when and why individuals consider themselves members of groups.

social loafing The tendency for individuals to expend less effort when working collectively than when working individually.

social psychology An area of psychology that blends concepts from psychology and sociology to focus on the influence of people on one another.

socialization A process that enables new employees to acquire the social knowledge and necessary skills in order to adapt to the organization's culture.

social-learning theory The view that we can learn through both observation and direct experience.

sociology The study of people in relation to their social environment or culture.

span of control The number of subordinates a manager can efficiently and effectively direct.

status A socially defined position or rank given to groups or group members by others.

status characteristics theory A theory that states that differences in status characteristics create status hierarchies within groups.

stereotype threat The degree to which we are concerned with being judged by or treated negatively based on a certain stereotype.

stereotyping Judging someone based on one's perception of the group to which that person belongs.

strain A psychological and physical unpleasant response due to an appraisal of the stressor.

stress A psychological process in which an individual is confronted with an opportunity, demand, or resource related to what the individual desires and for which the outcome is perceived to be both uncertain and important (e.g., stressors).

strong culture A culture in which the core values are intensely held and widely shared.

subcultures Minicultures within an organization, typically defined by department designations or geographical separation.

substitutes Attributes, such as experience and training, that can replace the need for a leader's support or ability to create structure.

surface acting Hiding one's inner feelings and forgoing emotional expressions in response to display rules.

surface-level diversity Differences in easily perceived characteristics such as gender, race, ethnicity, age, or disability, that do not necessarily reflect the ways people think or feel but that may activate certain stereotypes.

survey feedback technique The use of questionnaires to listen to members and identify discrepancies among member perceptions; discussion follows and remedies are suggested.

sustainability Organization practices that can be sustained over a long period of time because the tools or structures that support them are not damaged by the processes.

systematic study Looking at relationships, attempting to attribute causes and effects, and drawing conclusions based on scientific evidence.

task conflict Conflict over content and goals of the work.

task identity The degree to which a job requires completion of a whole and identifiable piece of work.

task performance The combination of effectiveness and efficiency at doing core job tasks.

task significance The degree to which a job has a substantial impact on the lives or work of other people.

task structure The degree to which job assignments follow a specific procedure.

team building High interaction among team members to increase trust and openness.

team cohesion A situation when team members are emotionally attached and bonded to one another and committed toward the team.

team efficacy A team's collective belief among team members that they can succeed at their tasks.

team identity A team member's affinity for and sense of belongingness to their team.

team structure An organization structure that replaces departments with empowered teams, and that eliminates horizontal boundaries and external barriers between customers and suppliers.

technology The way in which an organization transfers its inputs into outputs.

telecommuting Working from home at least two days a week through virtual devices that are linked to the employer's office.

terminal values Desirable end-states of existence; the goals a person would like to achieve during their lifetime.

threat of technological unemployment A situation in which professional decision makers resist certain decision-making improvements (e.g., AI and structured approaches alike), because they reduce the extent the decision makers are relied on for expert judgment, lessening the value they provide the organization.

trait activation theory (TAT) A theory that predicts that some situations, events, or interventions "activate" a trait more than others.

trait theories of leadership Theories that consider personal qualities and characteristics that differentiate leaders from nonleaders.

transactional leaders Leaders who guide or motivate their followers in the direction of established goals by clarifying role and task requirements, allocating rewards and punishment where needed, and (passively or actively) intervening when the situation calls for it.

transformational leaders Leaders who inspire followers to transcend their own self-interests for the good of the organization.

trust A psychological state of mutual positive expectations between people—both depend on each other and are genuinely concerned for each other's welfare.

trust propensity How likely an employee is to trust a leader.

two-factor theory A theory that relates intrinsic factors to job satisfaction and associates extrinsic factors with dissatisfaction. Also called motivation–hygiene theory.

uncertainty avoidance A national culture attribute that describes the extent to which a society feels threatened by uncertain and ambiguous situations and tries to avoid them.

(un)ethical leadership The idea that leaders serve as ethical role models to followers, and thus demonstrate appropriate (or inappropriate) behavior by using their power in (un)ethical ways and/or by treating others fairly (or unfairly).

unity of command The idea that a subordinate should have only one superior to whom they are directly responsible.

utilitarianism An ethical perspective in which decisions are made to provide the greatest good for all.

valence The degree to which organizational rewards satisfy an individual's personal goals or needs and the attractiveness of those potential rewards for the individual.

value system A hierarchy based on a ranking of an individual's values in terms of their intensity.

values Basic convictions that a specific mode of conduct or end-state of existence is personally or socially preferable to an opposite or converse mode of conduct or end-state of existence.

variable-pay program A pay plan that bases a portion of an employee's pay on some individual and/or organizational measure of performance.

virtual structure A small, core organization that outsources major business functions.

virtual teams Teams that use technology to tie together physically dispersed members in order to achieve a common goal.

vision A long-term strategy for attaining a goal or goals.

vision statement A formal articulation of an organization's vision or mission.

voice Dissatisfaction expressed through active and constructive attempts to improve conditions.

wellness programs Organizationally supported programs that focus on the employee's total physical and mental condition.

whistleblowers Individuals who report unethical practices by their employer to outsiders.

withdrawal behavior The set of actions employees take to separate themselves from the organization.

work specialization The degree to which tasks in an organization are subdivided into separate jobs.

work team A group whose individual efforts result in performance that is greater than the sum of the individual inputs.

workforce diversity The concept that organizations are becoming more heterogeneous in terms of gender, age, race, ethnicity, sexual orientation, and other characteristics.

workgroup A group that interacts primarily to share information and make decisions to help all members perform within their respective areas of responsibility.

workplace spirituality The recognition that people have an inner life that nourishes and is nourished by meaningful work that takes place in the context of community.

zero-sum approach An approach to reward allocation that treats the reward "pie" as fixed, so any gain one person or group achieves comes at the expense of another person or group.

INDEX